A History of the Old South

Thomas Jefferson, by Rembrandt Peale (1778–1860). (Courtesy of the New York Historical Society)

A History of the Old South

The Emergence of a Reluctant Nation

Third Edition

Clement Eaton

Emeritus, University of Kentucky
Pitt Professor of American History, Cambridge University, 1968–1969

Macmillan Publishing Co., Inc.
NEW YORK

Collier Macmillan Publishers
LONDON

Macmillan Publishing Co., Inc.
866 Third Avenue, New York, New York 10022

Collier-Macmillan Canada, Ltd.

Library of Congress Cataloging in Publication Data

Eaton, Clement, (date)
  A history of the Old South.
  Bibliography: p.

  1. Southern States—History—1775–1865.
2. Southern States—History—Colonial period,
ca. 1600–1775. I. Title.
F213.E2   1975   917.5'03'3   74-5718
ISBN: 0-02-331310-2

Printing: 3 4 5 6 7 8   Year: 8 9 0

To the memory of my father
in gratitude for the ambition
and high ideals he gave to me.

Preface

Within the last ten years Southern history has been modified more profoundly, I believe, than any other aspect of American history. There is good reason for this, aside from the great economic strides that have been made by the Southern states. The civil rights struggle, the new status of the Negro, the advance of women, and the recent concern for the poor and disadvantaged have given a new orientation to the history of the region. I have been strongly affected by these new currents of thought in my revision of *A History of the Old South*. One of the advantages of the new edition is that I have dealt more fully, and I hope, more perceptively, with these subjects. Indeed, I have changed my mind on some aspects of slavery, particularly on the issue of the profitability of slavery but not on the effects of slavery on Southern economy and society. I have modified my opinions on the extent of the internal slave trade and its cruelty in separating families. I have examined more carefully some of the testimony of ex-slaves. I have also upgraded my view of the efficiency of Southern slaves and have removed, I hope, traces of racism that may have lingered from my Southern upbringing. The belief, expressed in *The Mind of the Old South* (the enlarged edition of 1967) that there was much more opportunity for slaves to develop their abilities and personalities within the framework of slavery than had previously been thought, has been strengthened by further research and reflection.

My views on other subjects have been liberalized by the influence of my time or enlightened by recent scholarship. My rather romantic view of women, I am sorry to say, has been impaired by the new spirit of realism that permeates modern society. Accordingly, I have devoted more space to antebellum women than I did in the earlier volume, including the addition of other portraits of Southern women to the single one among the twenty illustrations of the older, male-oriented volume. I have presented, I believe, a more realistic picture of the Southern aristocracy, noting, for example, the large proportion of planters who dispensed with the overseer system and supervised their plantations themselves with the aid of Negro foremen and drivers. I have always had a sympathy for the underdog in any society, and I have, therefore, established a new chapter entitled "The Middle Class and the Disadvantaged," in which I examine more closely the unprivileged classes in antebellum Southern society. Perhaps influenced by the recent antiwar feeling of the academic community and the student uprisings, I have expressed a higher opinion of the agitators of another age, the abolitionists. Yet I have tried to preserve historical objectivity and have refused to surrender to the present liberal orthodoxy in academic circles.

I have not revised very drastically the chapters on the colonial period although I have benefited from reading the journal of Landon Carter, which was published after the last revision. Rather, the major revisions come in the later chapters where I deal with the changes produced by modern scholarship

and a new way of looking at the antebellum period. Because of space limitations I have had to reduce or omit some material of the earlier volume. It has
been a hard decision to make as to what to omit or reduce and what to retain.
I have, on the other hand, enlarged my discussions, added new material, or
changed my former interpretations in regard to the South's identity, slavery,
women, the antebellum poor, colonial society, the causes of the Revolution,
Kentucky constitution-making, Jefferson, the Federalist party, Jackson, the
development of Southern industry, particularly the manufacture of whiskey,
lumbering, and gold and coal mining, the nullification controversy and Calhoun, the changing attitudes of Southern people to slavery, the previously
forbidden subject of miscegenation, Southern oratory, the theater, town life
and urbanization, and the forces that led the Southern states to found a new
nation, the Confederate States of America. The earlier edition ended with the
Montgomery Convention of February, 1861, but the present one includes
the secession of the states of the upper South. Fresh personalities appear in the
revised pages, such as the Negro overseers, "Jem" Sykes and Andrew; outstanding women such as Dolly Madison; Mrs. Charles Colcock Jones; Gertrude Thomas of Georgia; Calhoun's daughter, Anna; Mary Boykin Chesnut
of South Carolina; the Kentucky belle, Sally Ward; the Mississippi yeoman
Ferdinand Steel, who kept a vivid diary; and the aristocratic planters Robert
Barnwell, Dr. Richard Eppes, Dr. J. L. M. Ramsey, and the preacher-planter
Charles Colcock Jones. This volume has new and more illustrations and a
great many more footnotes than the older volume. Indeed, the extensive
bibliography of the volume is to be found in the footnotes, where they will
be of most value to scholars and students.

Finally, I think it is pertinent at the beginning of a broad, general history
such as this volume to state forthrightly my philosophy of history and ideas
of style. As a young man I was influenced by reading Emerson, Thoreau, and
Carlyle, as well as by my Southern environment, which emphasized the
importance of personality, in believing that great men often determined the
course of history. But at Harvard University, swayed by the teachings of that
great realist, Professor Arthur M. Schlesinger, Sr., I changed my uncritical
philosophy of history. I was converted to the belief that impersonal forces,
especially economic currents, determine history, and that only in details do
individual leaders or thinkers modify the course of history. In this volume,
however, I present my mature point of view, namely, that the role of individuals, such as Jefferson, Jackson, and Polk, as well as impersonal forces are
decisive, thereby refusing to downgrade either. Indeed, I have gone through
somewhat the same cycle of changing my views on the importance of individual leaders as has Secretary of State Kissinger, who commented to a *Time
Magazine* representative, February 4, 1974:

> [As a professor at Harvard University] "I tended to think of history as run
> by impersonal forces. But when you see it in practice you see the difference
> that the personalities make. The overtures to China would not have worked
> without Chou En-lai. There would have been no settlement in the Middle
> East without Sadat and Golda Meir and Dayan."

Did the South go to war in 1861 to maintain a new nation because of impersonal forces? I should say, yes, principally. Did the North go to war because of impersonal forces driving it? It is hard to tell, but undoubtedly, the diplomacy of a shrewd, masterful statesman, President Lincoln, in guiding public opinion and in making the fateful Fort Sumter decision, played a tremendous role in the coming of the Civil War.

As to historical style, I have been warned by my son, "Dad, don't write like John Fiske!" [the Harvard professor of the nineteenth century]. Forced in a history course to read Fiske's *The Critical Period in American History* my son compared the experience to wading through a bog of mud. But there is for the historian today another bog to avoid that might well be compared to the dolorous "Slough of Despond" in *Pilgrim's Progress*. It is the pitfall of following what one hopes is the transient fashion of writing in sociological and psychological jargon and clichés, which serve mainly to impress other scholars but at the same time to dehumanize history and deprive it of color and drama.

I am grateful to the following persons for reading and criticizing certain chapters and assisting in securing illustrations: Dr. Edmund Berkeley, Jr., of the Alderman Library of the University of Virginia; J. Winston Coleman, Jr., of Lexington, Kentucky; Professor Charles B. Dew of the University of Missouri; Professor Ernest Lander, Jr., of Clemson University; Professor Russell B. Nye of Michigan State University; Dr. Edward Reilly of Colonial Williamsburg Foundation; Professor Charles P. Roland of the University of Kentucky; Professor William K. Scarborough of Southern Mississippi University; my artist sister, Margaret Eaton Smithdeal of High Point, N. C.; Professor Bertram Wyatt-Brown of Case Western Reserve University; and the able and considerate Macmillan editor, Bertrand Lummus. I am under especial obligation to Professor William F. Willingham of the University of Kentucky, a specialist in the history of seventeenth and eighteenth century America, who read the first ten chapters; Professor Eugene Genovese of the University of Rochester for allowing me to read his manuscript on slavery, which he is preparing for publication; and Professor Robert W. Fogel of the University of Chicago and Stanley L. Engerman of the University of Rochester whose volumes, *Time on the Cross, the Economics of American Negro Slavery,* I had the privilege of reading in manuscript. To Dorothy Leathers, who typed part of the manuscript, and to Natalie Schick, the almost perfect secretary of the history department of the University of Kentucky, who typed the major portion of the manuscript and corrected many errors, I owe much. And last, I should like to thank my wife, Mary Elizabeth, for her forbearance and sacrifice during the period when I was obsessed with research, writing, and revision. Nor should I neglect to say that her wit and humor relaxed me on many occasions and contributed, I hope, to a lighter and more human tone to the volume.

University of Kentucky   C. E.

Contents

Illustrations

Maps

The Southerners—
Their Colonial Origins

DR. RICHARD EPPES, a Tidewater planter in Virginia in 1860, left a very revealing diary that shows how different the Southerner was from the Northerner in 1860.[1] Above all, his diary shows the influence of slavery and the plantation upon the Southerner that made him a distinctive species of the American. Dr. Eppes was well educated for his day at the University of Virginia, where he studied medicine. But after he had inherited two plantations, he drifted away from practicing medicine and became an enthusiastic planter. He was a paternal slaveholder, who rewarded his slaves for good work but personally whipped some of them with fifteen lashes when he thought they needed correction. His paternalism might be questioned today, for when his slaves had a chance to escape during the Civil War, all but 13 of the 127 left. Dr. Eppes was a devout low church Episcopalian, whose active life of supervising his plantation and slaves left him little time to read. His chief amusements, typical of the Southern planters, were unsophisticated —hunting, smoking "segars," entertaining visitors, and going to church. In politics Dr. Eppes was a moderate who did not approve of the fireaters, but he was loyal to his section and became a good Confederate citizen. He was a type of the Southern gentleman who would be inconceivable in a Northern setting.

But there were many types of the Southern gentleman, and the South Carolina type, of whom Robert Barnwell of Beaufort was a prime example, was a special breed. Tall, slim, fair-haired, meticulously dressed, with beautiful courtly manners, Barnwell impressed the Greenville Unionist Benjamin F. Perry as being like "a young English nobleman." Supported by a wealthy planter family of high social rank, Barnwell went to Harvard for his education, graduating with Ralph Waldo Emerson with the class of 1821. There he was ambitious, popular, a member of the exclusive Porcellian Club. Emerson wrote to him after the Civil War urging him to attend the Harvard commencement, referring to "the high, affectionate, exceptional regard in which I, in common I believe with all of your contemporaries of 1817–21, have firmly held you as our avowed chief, in days when boys, as we then were,

[1] The manuscript diary of Dr. Eppes, 1851–1854 and 1858–1861, is in the Alderman Library of the University of Virginia.

1

give a tender and romantic value to that distinction which they cannot later give.[2] But when he returned to South Carolina he was assailed for the rest of his life by a mysterious self-doubt. After being elected to Congress for two terms without opposition, he became president of South Carolina College for several years, but resigned because he thought he was a failure, although Mrs. Chesnut observed in her diary that he was loved and revered by his former students. He was appointed Senator to fulfill John C. Calhoun's unexpired term, but he resigned that position too; he was chosen temporary president of the Montgomery Convention that established the Confederate government, but rejected an offer of the Secretaryship of State of the Confederacy. He desired to be an Episcopal clergyman but eventually abandoned this ambition.[3] With everything in his favor in South Carolina society, what was the source of his self-doubt? Barnwell confessed that he was indolent and timid, and that he always had the easy life of a wealthy planter to fall back upon. But probably the main cause of his numerous renunciations was that he never resolved what Erik Erikson has called an "identity crisis," such as Martin Luther and Gandhi had resolved and then went on to lives of affirmation and passionate struggle. Barnwell remained too much a conventional South Carolina gentleman who never questioned the rightness of slavery and went along with his state in accepting nullification, voting against the Compromise of 1850, and supporting the cause of the Confederacy. His end was pitiable. His slaves freed, his plantations confiscated, his world fallen in, he tried to support himself by teaching at a girls' school and serving for a paltry sum as librarian of the University of South Carolina—this man who once was called "the Chevalier Bayard of the South."

Planters such as Barnwell and Eppes were distinctive of the Southern upper class, but they represented only a tiny fraction of the whole of Southern society. There was, for example, a vastly larger middle class of yeoman farmers and villagers, whom Richard Malcolm Johnston in his *Dukesboro Tales* (1870) has so realistically portrayed. Johnston emphasized the lack of consciousness of social distinctions and class divisions among the population of middle Georgia. Although the great mass of Southerners could not live like the privileged planters, they absorbed something of the spirit and sense of values of the Southern gentry. William Thomson, a Scottish weaver, who traveled and worked in the South as well as in the North in the 1840's, observed: "The character of the southern states for hospitality is not overrated. They are quite a distinct race from the 'Yankees'." He was impressed with the high sense of honor of the Southerners—not merely of the gentry but of plain farmers and tradesmen as well, who treated every white man as an equal. "All over the country," he wrote, "men of business and mechanics consider themselves men of honour; but more especially in the south, where

[2] Clement Eaton, *The Mind of the Old South* (Baton Rouge, Enlarged Ed., 1967), 65.
[3] Jack Barnwell, "Robert W. Barnwell and South Carolina Politics, 1850–1852," M.A. thesis, University of North Carolina, 1972.

they more frequently resent any indignity shown them, even at the expense of their life, or of that of those who venture to insult them." [4] Thomson also admired the sociability and friendliness of the Southerners, their great politeness, especially toward women, and their kindness to children and to their slaves (which he contrasted with the cruel treatment of factory children and other employees in England and Scotland). He disapproved, on the other hand, of Southerners' habits of chewing tobacco and swearing, which were so common below the Mason and Dixon line, and he commented on the lack of labor-saving machines in the South, except for steamboats and railroads.

Most of the differences between the North and the South noticed by outsiders, however, were a matter of degree rather than of absolutes. Southerners were more military-minded, for example, than Northerners. Henry S. Commager has observed that the members of the upper class in the South went into the army but not in the North.[5] They placed a higher value on family and personal relationships and they had a deeper love for the land, partly because they were a less urbanized society. This difference Edmund Ruffin, the Virginia agricultural reformer and ardent secessionist, illustrated by comments in his manuscript diary. On June 30, 1862, he rode out to *Beechwood* and found the plantation deserted save for a few aged and infirm Negroes who had not fled to the Yankees. Ruminating on the good life that had been lived there, he wrote, "I walked or rode through the lovely grounds near and below the house—the garden, the thinned and open woods and the Wilderness. It was a melancholy gratification. I do not expect to see them again while existing circumstances continue and the residents are exiles from their dearly beloved and beautiful home." He wandered into the family cemetery—an important reason for the love of the home-place among Southerners. "And here," he continued, "I addressed to God my customary daily prayers and added others for the welfare of my family and country . . ." [6] This elegy on the passing of the Old South was, in truth, a *Sic transit gloria mundi*.

Southern women, also probably because of their command of servants and because of the cult of virility among Southern men, were more feminine and less educated than their Northern counterparts. Perhaps another explanation of greater femininity was that Southerners of this period seem to have been more susceptible to certain elements of the Romantic movement, as evidenced by the craze for Scott's novels and Byron's poetry and the staging of medieval tournaments. The Southerners' reputation for greater hospitality and courtesy than was displayed by Yankees seems to have been deserved, although one important Northern visitor, the fastidious Frederick Law Olmsted, believed that the presumed hospitality of the Southerners was a myth, citing as evi-

[4] William Thomson, *A Tradesman's Travels in the United States and Canada in the Years 1840, 41 and 42* (Edinburgh, 1842), 20–25.
[5] J. A. Garraty, *Interpreting American History: Conversations with Historians* (New York, 1970), I, 109.
[6] Diary of Edmund Ruffin, June 30, 1862. MS in Library of Congress. Courtesy of William K. Scarborough, editor of the Ruffin diary.

dence the fact that during his extensive travels in the region between 1852 and 1854 he had to pay for meals and lodging in private homes.[7] But it was not a myth that Southerners were distinguished by a remarkable sense of pride that led them to fight duels and uphold a code of gentlemanly conduct. *Honor,* both personal and regional, was a talismanic word in the Southern vocabulary and was an important cause of secession.

One could "spot" a Southerner easily by his speech, "the Southern accent," and the old-fashioned words that he used. Modern students believe that the most important cause for the peculiarities of Southern speech was the survival in the South of a large part of the English language as was spoken in the seventeenth and eighteenth centuries, which was brought over by the colonists.[8] The pronunciations of *get* as "git," *ask* as "ax," *boil* as "bile," *oblige* as "obleege," and *master* as "marster" or "marse" were common usage in the southern part of England during the seventeenth century. Even the dropping of the final *g,* as in "darlin" for *darling,* or the elision of *r*—supposedly common Southern failings—were practices of old English speech during the period of emigration. Likewise, the pronunciation of *e* as *i* in such words as *tennis* ("tinnis"), *men* ("min"), and *pen* ("pin") is an archaic form of English pronunciation. Furthermore, the Southern colonists brought over with them pronunciations peculiar to the numerous dialects of the mother country, especially those of southern and southwestern England. Expressions such as "gwine" for *going* and "ain't" for *isn't* antedate the coming of the Negroes to the South. Many of the pronunciations and even the drawl that are regarded today as peculiarly "Southern" were also current in New England in the seventeenth and eighteenth centuries.

The variation of Southern speech from the New England and also the General American or Western type should not be attributed primarily to the linguistic laziness of the people, induced by a languorous climate, but to the greater conservatism of the South in not changing its speech. In the late eighteenth century there was a change of speech in the London district when the broad *a* became fashionable and standard British pronunciation. In general, Southern speech continued to retain the older pronunciation of *a.* There were exceptions, however, in Tidewater Virginia and in the Charleston district, which had close connections with England and tended to imitate more readily the fashions current in the mother country. New England was also similarly affected and, moreover, the influence of New England schoolmarms and the printed page tended to eradicate some of the elisions of *r*'s and final *g*'s that continued in Southern speech.

The influence of the Negroes may have tended to make Southern speech more conservative and archaic. The Negroes imitated the phonetics of the

---

[7] Frederick Law Olmsted, *The Cotton Kingdom,* ed. by A. M. Schlesinger, Sr., (New York, 1953), 368, 550.
[8] See N. E. Eliason, *Tarheel Talk: An Historical Study of the English Language in North Carolina* (Chapel Hill, 1956).

master class, and they were unaffected by the influence of spelling and the printed page. Consequently, they tended to perpetuate the older type of speech of the English colonists. The slaves imported a few words from Africa into Southern speech, in such as "goober" for *peanuts,* "yam" for *sweet potato,* "cooter" for *terrapin,* and "voodoo" for *magic,* and probably some African inflections and grammar survived in Negro speech. The word *boss,* which the Negroes often used in addressing white men, was of Dutch origin, probably introduced through the slave trade. In general, the Negro imitated the phonetics of the overseers, indentured servants, and persons of the lower economic strata with whom he came in contact and forgot his old African tongue.[9]

Southerners, then, were different from Northerners, but why? The eminent Southern historian U. B. Phillips in his superb *Life and Labor in the Old South* (1929) attempted to explain the Southerner. "Let us begin," he wrote, "by discussing the weather, for that has been the chief agency in making the South distinctive." [10] Phillips, however advanced another, more controversial thesis in an essay entitled, "The Central Theme of Southern History," namely, that the decisive element in Southernism was the determination to keep the South "a white man's country," in other words, to control the Negro and, unfortunately, to exploit him.[11] That thesis is clearly outmoded today, but has merit as applied to the South in the nineteenth century.

A modern historian, C. Vann Woodward, in a provocative essay, entitled "The Search for Southern Identity," has found this thread in a different history from the North—a history of defeat, of guilt, and of poverty, in contrast to the uninterrupted story of victory, success in every undertaking, material abundance, and a tradition of innocence (this before the Vietnam War and Watergate) of the North.[12] But this explanation of Southern difference hardly applies to the antebellum South, for the South at that time shared in the history of the nation and in the American dream of innocence (for the proslavery argument seems to have convinced the vast majority of Southerners that they were doing no wrong in holding slaves). Furthermore, the South had developed a curious case of insularity in believing, as Charles S. Snydor maintained in his chapter entitled "The Affirmation of Southern Perfection" in *The Development of Southern Sectionalism, 1819–1848* that it had created a society that was superior to that of the North.[13]

---

[9] For a modern study of Negro speech, see J. L. Dillard, *Black English: Its History and Usage in the United States* (New York, 1972), Lorenzo Turner, *Africanisms in the Gullah Dialect* (Chicago, 1947), and Mason Crum, *Gullah: Negro Life in the Carolina Sea Islands* (Durham, 1940).

[10] U. B. Phillips, *Life and Labor in the Old South* (Boston, 1929), 3.

[11] U. B. Phillips, "The Central Theme of Southern History," *American Historical Review, XXXIV* (October, 1928), 30–43.

[12] C. V. Woodward, *The Burden of Southern History* (Baton Rouge, 1960), chap. I.

[13] C. S. Sydnor, *The Development of Southern Sectionalism, 1819–1848* (Baton Rouge, 1948), chap. XV.

Other seekers to discover "the enigma of the South" have found the key in the folk culture of the region, in the overwhelming rural nature of the South as contrasted with the Northern thrust toward industry and urbanization, in the relatively homogeneous population after the end of the period of immigration in the eighteenth century, in the prevalent ideal of the English country gentleman, in the violence that marred Southern society, owing in part to its longer exposure to frontier conditions, and in its fervent religious conservatism. Still another important differentiator was the greater importance of the family and of kin in the South. The novelists William Faulkner, Eudora Welty, and Harper Lee have realized this fact more perceptively than the historians. Faulkner, for example, in "An Odor of Verbena" has vividly described some of the archaic virtues of the Old South, notably a deep sense of obligation to the family and a willingness to put one's life in jeopardy, for the honor of the family. The myths of the South, particularly the Cavalier myth and the plantation legend, were an ingredient of no small importance in nurturing the feeling of Southernism. Such a quest, however, for a *single* explanation of the South's uniqueness is contrary to common sense—very much like the Scholastics of the Middle Age squabbling over an abstraction.

The boundaries of "the South" are a matter of controversy, because sentiment, the feeling of Southernism, was an important criterion in determining them. For example, a much larger number of Kentucky's soldiers fought for the Union than for the Confederacy during the Civil War; yet the state was economically and psychologically a part of the Old South. It is a significant and surprising fact that in 1860 Kentucky had a greater number of slaveholders than any other Southern state except Virginia and Georgia, although South Carolina, Mississippi, and Alabama contained far more slaves than did the Bluegrass State. The curving frontier line of the Old South included eastern Maryland, a land of tobacco plantations and of slaves, as well as the western part of Virginia (with the exception of the Panhandle), which, in the course of the Civil War, separated from the mother state. Although Delaware remained a slave state until 1865, her ties were with Pennsylvania and the Middle states, which made her loyal to the Union during the Civil War. Missouri, a border slave state, was more definitely Southern, tempered, however, by the influence of the West and of a large German population in the St. Louis area. In 1850 the persons of Southern birth in Missouri outnumbered those of Northern birth by considerably more than three to one. Of the fifteen states that sanctioned slavery, only eleven joined the Southern Confederacy, although its flag carried thirteen stars, claiming Kentucky and Missouri, states that did not secede but had governments-in-exile that were loyal to the Confederate cause.

The states of the Old South were grouped naturally into the upper South, consisting of Maryland, Virginia (which then included West Virginia), North Carolina, Tennessee, and Kentucky, with Missouri occupying an ambiguous position; and the lower South, which included South Carolina, Georgia,

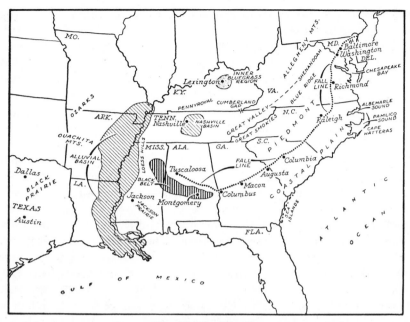

The Physical South

Florida, Alabama, Mississippi, Louisiana, Texas, and Arkansas. There were marked differences between the two tiers of states; the climate was different, the staple crops were not the same, there was a disparity in the concentration of slaves, and the attitude of the people of the upper South to sectional issues was cooler and a greater liberality of mind prevailed. Nonetheless, the upper South had a feeling of unity with the lower South and acted with it in a crisis.

Physically, the Old South was far from being a homogeneous land. Within it were regions that varied in topography, climate, and economic interests. As Frederick Jackson Turner observed, there was not *one* South but *many* Souths. The main geographic regions were the sandy low-lying coastal plain, covered to a large extent with pine forests, which ended with the fall line, where there were falls or shoals in the rivers. Here the hilly Piedmont region began, then came the Appalachian highlands, the Mississippi Valley, the Ozark Mountain region, and the Texas plains to the one hundredth parallel of longitude, where the area of insufficient rainfall for agriculture (less than sixteen to twenty inches) stopped temporarily the march of the farmer. Within these great divisions there were subregions, such as the Shenandoah Valley of Virginia, lying between the Blue Ridge and the Allegheny mountains, the Bluegrass region of Kentucky, with Lexington at its center, the Nashville basin, the delta country of the lower Mississippi Valley, the black belt of Alabama and Mississippi, and the black waxy lands around Dallas, Texas. Although the Southern states as a whole were not unusually rich in fertile lands, wherever rich soil appeared and where water navigation gave an outlet to market, the plantation system arose.

When did the concept of "the South" emerge, or in other words, when did the inhabitants of the Southern region begin to develop a sectional consciousness? If one considers only the political history of the region, one is likely to conclude that "the South" did not begin until 1820, the time of the Missouri Compromise debates. It was not until then that Southerners began to be seriously alarmed over the danger to their way of life posed by the growing antislavery feeling in the North. During the acrimonious debates John Randolph of Roanoke popularized the phrase the *Mason-Dixon line*, a surveyor's line drawn in 1767 by Jeremiah Dixon and Charles Mason ending a long-standing dispute between Pennsylvania and Maryland over the intercolonial boundary, as the symbolic boundary between the North and the South. Long before 1820, however, there had developed a realization of a community of interest among the slave states as opposed to that of the Northern states. This was the germ, or embryo, of a consciousness of a "South," which appeared as early as the eighteenth century, when William Byrd II sarcastically referred to "the Saints of England," those sharp-trading sea captains and crews who brought goods to exchange with the inhabitants of North Carolina for their tobacco "without troubling themselves with paying that impertinent Duty of a Penny a Pound." [14] This slowly emerging sense of difference, the concept of "the first South," as an able historian has termed it, did not appear strongly until the Revolutionary and Constitution-making periods when the representatives of the Southern area feared that in the organization of a central government their section would become a minority within the Union, oppressed by the Northeastern states.[15]

The beginnings of Southern civilization lie in the Elizabethan Age, when Sir Walter Raleigh, influenced by the writings of the elder and the younger Richard Hakluyt and by the spirit of Elizabethan exuberance and lust for gold, sent an exploring expedition to America in 1584 under Philip Amadas and Arthur Barlowe that landed on Roanoke Island behind the sandbars of the North Carolina coast. Here, on a third expedition the English founded an ill-fated colony, called "the lost colony" because of its mysterious disappearance. But it was not until April, 1607, that a permanent English settlement was made on the American continent at Jamestown on an unhealthy island thirty miles from the mouth of the James River. The colony was named Virginia, after Elizabeth, the Virgin Queen. It was financed through the organization of a joint stock company, the London Company (subsequently called the Virginia Company, which eventually had 659 stockholders). The unfitness of the first settlers for a frontier adventure was pathetic, for a large proportion of the 144 settlers were gentlemen unused to

[14] W. K. Boyd (ed.), *William Byrd's Histories of the Dividing Line Betwixt Virginia and North Carolina* (Raleigh, 1929), 42.
[15] See John Alden, *The First South* (Baton Rouge, 1961).

manual labor. They were accompanied by a barber and a perfumer, and were handicapped from the start by an illusion that they would find in Virginia another Peru, rich in gold and silver.[16]

The colony was saved from extinction by the exertions of Captain John Smith, who made the first British attempt at adapting to the ways of the American wilderness. This soldier of fortune, twenty-seven years old, equipped with bristling moustachios and iron armor, was a natural leader, hardy and resourceful. He rendered indispensable service to the colony by trading with the Indians for food, defending it from the unfriendly savages, and forcing the "gentlemen" to plant corn instead of searching for gold. After he returned to England in 1609 because of an injury from an explosion of gunpowder, the colony suffered "a starving time." Emaciated and dis-spirited, the settlers abandoned Jamestown in 1610 and were returning to England when they met an advance boat of Lord De La Warr's expedition bringing supplies and new colonists, and so they returned.

In the early years of Virginia a lack of proper food, disease, the hardships of the wilderness, and the Indian massacres took a frightful toll of human life. During the process of becoming acclimated many settlers died from malaria, "the Virginia sickness," which was described by Ebenezer Cook in the satirical poem "The Sot-Weed Factor: or, a Voyage to Maryland" (1708):

> With Cockerouse [a man of quality] as I was sitting,
> I felt a Feaver Intermitting;
> A fiery pulse beat in my Veins,
> From Cold I felt resembling Pains
> This cursed seasoning I remember
> Lasted from *March* to Cold *December*.[17]

During the first few years the Virginia colony operated under a communal regime, in which the men lived in barracks and worked in gangs under over-seers, and the land was held entirely by the company. Under this system the colony languished. In 1614, Governor Thomas Dale gave some of the more responsible settlers three-acre plots of land to cultivate, and two years later the colonist-adventurers received farms of one hundred acres each.[18] In 1619, a cargo of ninety virtuous maidens was sent from England to be mar-ried to the planters, who paid their passage. And in the same year the seeds of both democracy and the race problem were planted in Virginia. By the order of the treasurer of the Virginia Company in London, the liberal

[16] See W. F. Craven, *The Southern Colonies in the Seventeenth Century, 1607–1689* (Baton Rouge, 1949).
[17] Ebenezer Cook, *The Sot-Weed Factor, or A Voyage to Maryland* (London, 1708).
[18] R. L. Morton gives an excellent account in *Colonial Virginia* (Chapel Hill, 1960), I, chap. 1. Those who arrived after 1616 and paid their passage received fifty acres of land free.

Sir Edwin Sandys, rather than because of the demand of the settlers, a representative legislature of twenty-four men met in Jamestown. Thus one of the provisions of the original charter of the company, namely, that the colonists who emigrated to Virginia should retain the liberties and rights of Englishmen, "as if they had been abiding and born within this our Realm of England," was fulfilled.[19] In this year too, a Dutch ship landed in Jamestown carrying the first African "Negars" who were sold either as slaves or long-term indentured servants.

The great tragedy that, together with other misfortunes, led to the dissolution of the Virginia Company was the Indian Massacre of 1622. Over 350 persons were killed, nearly a third of the colonists. Moreover, factionalism weakened the council of the company in London; its efforts to stimulate the raising of crops other than tobacco, such as grapes for wine-making and mulberry trees for raising silkworms, were failures; the company after eighteen years of operation had only losses to show for its huge investments of £1,200,000. At the trial of the company in 1624 by the king's court, it was disclosed that since the granting of its charter in 1606, the company had sent out a total of 6,000 colonists, but that in February of that year only 1,275 persons were left in the colony. Accordingly, because of mismanagement, the court annulled the charter of the company, and Virginia became a royal colony.[20]

In contrast to the unhappy early history of the Virginia colony, the settlements of Maryland, the Carolinas, and Georgia were on the whole peaceful and relatively free from hardship and disease. Immigration into these colonies was promoted by several noble proprietors and by a humanitarian board of trustees. The first settlement of Maryland, at St. Mary's, on the Chesapeake Bay, in 1634, was directed by Lord Baltimore, a Catholic nobleman to whom the land between the Potomac River and the fortieth degree of latitude had been granted as a proprietary province. Lord Baltimore not only wished to make his colony an asylum for persecuted Catholics but also to gain profits from its settlement. Actually, relatively few Catholics emigrated to Maryland, and it became necessary for the legislature to protect the Catholic minority from persecution by passing the Maryland Toleration Act of 1649, which granted religious toleration only to Catholics and Protestants. Although Lord Baltimore granted over sixty patents for the establishment of manors, not many Americans were willing to become tenants when ownership of land could be easily acquired, and consequently in the course of years the manors were subdivided into tobacco plantations. Puritans from Virginia founded Annapolis in 1648 and led a movement in 1655 that for a few years overthrew the proprietary rule.[21]

[19] H. S. Commager (ed.), *Documents of American History* (New York, 1963), 10.
[20] See W. F. Craven, *The Dissolution of the Virginia Company: The Failure of a Colonial Experiment* (New York, 1932).
[21] See C. C. Hall (ed.), *Narratives of Early Maryland 1633–1684* (New York, 1910, reprinted 1952), and C. M. Andrews, *The Colonial Period of American History* (New Haven, 1934), I.

The colonization of the Carolinas was undertaken by the eight Lord Proprietors to whom in 1663 the imperial domain between Virginia and Spanish Florida had been granted by Charles II. Efforts to establish feudal institutions in Carolina failed in the presence of frontier conditions. Although John Locke's fantastic frame of government for Carolina, based on a feudal landholding nobility, was not put into operation, it had the virtue of providing for religious toleration. The northern part of the huge colony, around Albemarle Sound, was settled as early as 1654 by people from Virginia, mostly indentured servants who had served their time, bankrupts, persons fleeing from the sheriff, and poor but respectable farmers. In 1670 Charles Towne (Charleston) was founded by colonists from England and the West Indian island of Barbados. The northern part of the colony, called North Carolina after 1691, was given a separate governor by the Lord Proprietors in 1712. A Swiss nobleman, De Graffenried, led a colony of Swiss and Germans in 1710 to found New Bern on the coast of North Carolina, which became the colonial capital of North Carolina. The Proprietors failed to provide efficient government for their distant colony, and after two bloody Indian wars with the Yamassee in South Carolina and the Tuscaroras in North Carolina, the colonists petitioned the royal government to take them over from the Proprietors. Consequently, in 1721 South Carolina, and eight years later North Carolina, became royal colonies.[22]

A valuable admixture to the English blood in the Southern colonies was brought, especially into South Carolina, by the coming of French settlers. The impulse that originally drove these Gallic colonists across the Atlantic Ocean to Southern shores was religious intolerance. During the latter part of the seventeenth century the French government severely persecuted its Protestant inhabitants, the Huguenots, who were located chiefly in western and northern France. After the revocation of the Edict of Nantes (1685), which had granted toleration to Protestants, many of them fled to other parts of the continent or to America. Some of them, such as the Clement family, first settled in Germany, where they lived for several generations and became Germanized before they emigrated to America. The Huguenot emigration scattered Frenchmen throughout the American colonies, but the largest concentration of them occurred in South Carolina. The Huguenots began to enter this colony as early as 1680, but after the revocation of the Edict of Nantes they came in increasing numbers. Although a few of these immigrants were from aristocratic lineage, the majority of them were of the middle class; skilled workers, petty tradesmen, and farmers. The French settlers became plantation owners and merchants in Charleston and intermarried with the English, and most of them eventually joined the Church of England. At the close of the colonial period, the French element constituted about 3 per cent of the population of South Carolina. Despite its small numbers, the French

---

[22] See A. S. Salley (ed.), *Narratives of Early Carolina, 1650–1708* (New York, 1911), and W. L. Saunders (ed.), *Colonial Records of North Carolina, 1662–1776* (Raleigh, 1886–1890), 10 vols.

element has in the course of history made a notable contribution to the leadership of the South, producing Francis Marion, William Moultrie, Hugh Swinton Legaré, Joel Poinsett, the Le Conte brothers, Sidney Lanier, John Sevier, and Matthew Fontaine Maury.[23]

The last of the thirteen English colonies in America to be settled was Georgia. Seventy years after the issuing of the Carolina charter, the king granted the territory between South Carolina and Spanish Florida to a board of twenty-one trustees, headed by the Irish Earl of Egmont and General James Oglethorpe, to found and administer for a period of twenty years a colony for the relief of imprisoned debtors.[24] Since the colony was also planned to be a buffer against Spanish attacks, Parliament made an annual appropriation of £8,000 for its maintenance. Oglethorpe led the first group of colonists and in 1733 established the settlement of Savannah. These original colonists seemed strangely unfitted for pioneer life since there were only three agriculturists. Despite its original design, modern studies have disclosed that "only a handful of debtors [released from prison] ever came to Georgia—a dozen would be a fair estimate." [25] Germans from Salzburg settled Ebenezer, a short distance up the river from Savannah, and New Englanders founded the town of Midway and the port of Sunbury.

The attempt to establish a paternalistic government in Georgia was of short duration. In the early years of the colony the settlers had no legislature and were ruled by a trusteeship, of which Oglethorpe was the chief administrator. The colonists were required to plant mulberry trees for the raising of silk-worms and were prohibited from holding slaves, importing rum, or owning more than five hundred acres of land, and only males could inherit land. This regime caused many settlers to abandon Georgia for colonies with a freer government and larger economic opportunities. The trustees accordingly were forced gradually to relax their restrictions and in 1751 gave up their charter. Georgians thus attained the freedom of other colonists, the freedom to get drunk, to rest in the shade while their black slaves were working, to hold as much land as they could win by honesty or unscrupulousness, and to wrangle with the royal governor in their legislature.

The most important cause for emigration to the Southern colonies was economic considerations. Some of the stronger stimulants to emigration were the Inclosure Movement in England by which agricultural lands were converted into sheep pastures, releasing many cultivators of the soil from their

---

[23] A. H. Hirsch, *The Huguenots of Colonial South Carolina* (Durham, 1929) and J. Fontaine, *Memoirs of a Huguenot Family, 1715–1716*, ed. by A. Maury (New York, 1972).

[24] See A. A. Ettinger, *James Edward Oglethorpe, Imperial Idealist* (Oxford, 1936).

[25] A. B. Saye, *New Viewpoints in Georgia History* (Athens, Ga., 1943), preface v, also p. 31; K. Coleman, "Life in Oglethorpe's Georgia," *Georgia Review XVII* (Fall, 1963), 293–305; and D. Boorstin, *The Americans: The Colonial Experience* (New York, 1958); and R. A. Hudnut and H. Baker-Crothers, "Acadian Transients in South Carolina," *American Historical Review, XLIII* (April 1938), 500–513.

traditional occupation, the high land rents resulting from monetary inflation, and the exhaustion and erosion of the soil. The political troubles in England, particularly the struggle between the king and Parliament, sent immigrants across the Atlantic. Also, the class structure of English society, which made it difficult to improve one's station in life, drove sons of the gentry to seek larger economic opportunities.[26] Although the population of England in the early part of the seventeenth century was hardly larger than 3 million people, the central and southeastern sections of England, from which many of the immigrants came, were regarded as overpopulated. Indeed, economic forces provided the mainspring of emigration to the American colonies; love of adventure, the missionary impulse, and flight from religious persecutions played only minor roles. Among the important agents promoting emigration were the suppliers of indentured servants, who persuaded naïve country lads to emigrate by painting rosy pictures of America. The headright system, which granted fifty acres of land to the *importer* of each head, whether that of freeman, indentured servant, relative, or slave into the colony, also stimulated immigration.

Moreover, the promotional literature of the seventeenth century affected the literate members of society who felt maladjusted in England and it seeped down into the lower strata of ignorant country folk. One of the early boosters of Virginia was Captain John Smith, who in 1624 published his *Generall Historie of Virginia, New England, and the Summer Isles,* which portrayed the richness and opportunity of this virgin land. Possibly he had his eye on a big sale of his volume when he wrote such passages as the following, describing a Virginia mask that he witnessed:

> Then presently they were presented with this anticke; thirtie young women came naked out of the woods, onely covered behind and before with a few greene leaves, their bodies all painted . . . singing and dauncing with most excellent ill varietie, oft falling into their infernall passions, and solemnly againe to sing and daunce . . . they solemnly invited him to their lodgings, where he was no sooner within the house, but all these Nymphes more tormented him than ever, with crowding, pressing, and hanging about him, most tediously crying, Love you not me? Love you not me? [27]

The basic stock of the settlers of the Southern colonies was English. Census officials have estimated from a study of the personal names in the first

---

[26] See W. Notestein, *The English People on the Eve of Colonization, 1603–1630* (New York, 1954).

[27] Older historians doubted the veracity of John Smith, especially his account of being saved from death by the Indian princess Pocahontas, but more recent scholarship accepts his accounts as "the fabulous truth." See P. L. Barbour, *The Three Worlds of Captain John Smith* (Boston, 1964), and Edward Arber and A. G. Bradley (eds.), *Travels and Works of Captain John Smith* (Edinburgh, 1910), 2 vols.; for the promotional literature of the era, see H. T. Lefler, "Promotional Literature of the Southern Colonies," *Journal of Southern History, XXXIII* (November 1967), 3–25.

census that 82.1 per cent of the American people in 1790 were of English ancestry, but these estimates undoubtedly exaggerated the importance of the English element, for many foreign immigrants anglicized their names. Indeed, more recent studies indicate that the English element in the American colonies in 1775 constituted only 60 per cent of the white population. In the Southern colonies, the soundest estimates indicate that less than two thirds of the white population was of English blood, the next largest national group being the Scots, approximately 11 per cent. Scottish merchants, factors, and tutors came in great numbers after the Act of Union of 1708 opened the trade opportunities of the empire to them. The Germans constituted over 8 per cent, the Scotch-Irish 7.8 per cent, the Celtic Irish approximately 5 per cent, and the French less than 2 per cent of the white population.[28] The difficulty of distinguishing between the Presbyterian "Irishman" and the Catholic Celtic "Irishman" is so great that the estimate of 5 per cent for the latter may be too large. Marcus L. Hansen, a respected author on American immigration before 1860, has declared that in the first half of the eighteenth century, the Catholic Irishman was a comparative rarity in the American colonies.[29] The colonial period was preeminently the time of the mixing bowl or of the melting pot in the South. After 1800 foreign immigration flowed into the North and, with the exception of large seaports and a few river towns, avoided the land of Dixie. Consequently, this region has remained the most "American" part of the United States, with its population derived predominantly from colonial lineage.

The American environment wrought a revolution in the habits of the European colonists. The Englishman was a heavy beef and mutton eater. In America his descendants became primarily pork eaters but supplemented their "hog and hominy" fare with venison, bear meat, and turkey. In the rank, virgin soil of the South, wheat tended to grow up in tall stalks without much grain, whereas corn flourished. As a result the Southerner was nourished on corn bread and hominy, or "grits," in contrast to wheat bread, which was universally consumed both in England and in the North. Why the colonists did not continue the English practice of drinking huge quantities of ale and beer is a mystery. Ultimately they developed into rum drinkers on account of the West India trade and in the South distilled a potent alcoholic beverage from Indian corn. In England the half-timbered cottage with thatch roof was the home of the laboring man; in the Southern colonies, the abundance of wood led to the construction of the log cabin, with a roof of shingles instead of thatch. In the mother country the high, stiff-backed chair was the seat of repose; in America, where the restless frontier spirit prevailed,

[28] "Report of the Committee on Linguistic and National Stocks in the United States," *Annual Report of the American Historical Association, 1930* (Washington, 1932), **I,** 124, 307.

[29] Marcus L. Hansen, *The Atlantic Migration, 1607–1860* (New York, 1961), 50. The great period of Irish migration was in the 1840's and 1850's after the catastrophic failures of the potato crop.

the rocking chair became the emblem of the dynamic energy of the people, who even in their leisure, must always be "on the move." As many of these restless Americans rocked, they exercised their jaws chewing tobacco and spitting, a habit that gave way in the twentieth century to gum chewing.

Although environment has been a potent factor in its evolution, the civilization of the Old South did not arise entirely as the result of a passive people yielding to the all-powerful determination of physical geography. After all allowance is made for the modifying effect of the environment. The fact remains that American culture was largely a continuation of European civilization in a new land. Furthermore, the conditions of nature—a warm climate and the diversity of Southern topography—would not alone have created the virulent sectionalism that led to the Civil War. Regionalism is partly man-made, a human or artificial creation. Indeed, so different are some of the regions within the land of Dixie that until the slavery issue became emotionalized it was difficult to get the Southern states to act as a unit.

The Evolution of the Plantation

THE PRIME REQUISITE for founding a permanent English colony in the Chesapeake Bay country was the discovery of the profitable export commodity. In 1612 John Rolfe, who married the Indian princess Pocahontas, led the way to prosperity by experimenting with the growing of new varieties of tobacco from the West Indies that were free from the bitter taste of the native variety and enabled Virginia tobacco to supplant Spanish tobacco in the English market. Sir Walter Raleigh had popularized the smoking of the American weed among the gentry of England, but conservatives strongly condemned the use of tobacco for hedonistic purposes. In 1604 King James wrote a violent pamphlet against the use of tobacco, entitled "Counter-Blaste to Tobacco," in which he declared that smokers were "guilty of sinful and shameful lust." But his condemnation could not prevent a steady demand for the delightful plant, and soon the Jamestown planters were growing tobacco in the streets. Charles I, who succeeded James in 1625, was also hostile to the growth of a crop that produced only unsubstantial smoke. He tried to establish a royal monopoly by a contract to buy and sell the entire Virginia output, but his action was vigorously resisted by the planters. Nevertheless, he aided the colonists by prohibiting the cultivation of tobacco in England and by excluding the more desirable Spanish tobacco from the English market or admitting only a very small quantity.[1]

The Virginia Company and the British government made strenuous efforts to divert the colonists from growing tobacco and turn their energies into more productive channels. They encouraged silk culture, wine-making, the cultivation of olives, almonds, ginger, citrus fruits, indigo, and cotton; the establishment of iron works; and the manufacture of glass beads. The colonial legislature, by means of bounties, and the British government, by the Trade Acts, sought to encourage a diversification of agriculture in the Southern colonies. These endeavors to establish a planned economy in the Southern colonies failed, owing partly to the fact that the king was unwilling to assume any of the financial burdents of colonization. Moreover, tobacco flourished perversely in the soil of the Chesapeake Bay country, whereas the more useful plants for a self-sufficing British Empire withered or were killed by nipping frosts. Accordingly, tobacco, the bane of the moralists, but the poor man's luxury, triumphed as the money crop of Virginia, Maryland, and North Carolina, and the economic pattern of that region was fixed for years to come.

[1] See J. C. Robert, *The Story of Tobacco in America* (New York, 1949).

Indeed, tobacco was an ideal crop to ship across the Atlantic, for it had small bulk and high value, and so it could bear the expense of the high freight rates. Consequently, it became the dominant economic interest, the money crop, of the Chesapeake Bay country. It was also grown in the Albemarle Sound region of North Carolina. The competition of this tobacco caused the Virginia Assembly in 1679 to pass an act forbidding the importation of Carolina tobacco into Virginia or its shipment through Virginia ports. This selfish policy of the Old Dominion struck a serious blow at North Carolina, for the province lacked good harbors and was dependent upon Norfolk for the shipment of its tobacco. For fifty years the province was held back in its economic development by Virginia's embargo. Finally, in 1731, shortly after North Carolina became a royal colony, the Albemarle planters secured the disallowance of the Virginia discriminatory law.

The tobacco plant was cultivated on rich virgin soil beneath the tall trees of the forest, which had been killed by the process of girdling.[2] The Indians had taught the colonists this easy way of clearing the land by cutting a band of bark from the tree, causing it to die. The wind tore the branches from these dead monarchs of the forests and later the colonists built fires around the trunks and burned them. During the colonial period plows were not practical in cultivating the plants beneath the girdled trees; hoes had to be used.

Tobacco at first brought a high price, five shillings a pound, but overproduction caused the price to fall rapidly, so that as early as 1630 it had declined to 2 pence a pound. To remedy the situation the Virginia government turned to the expedient of crop control (a forerunner of the Roosevelt policies of the AAA), and in 1629 limited each planter by law to the cultivation of only three thousand plants and in the following year, to two thousand. Such restrictions, however, proved to be ineffective, for the neighboring colony of Maryland refused to cooperate and expanded its crop when Virginia limited its production. In 1682, after prices fell to a disastrous level, some of the small planters staged a tobacco riot, during which they went through the fields, cutting down the plants in order to curtail overproduction.

Tobacco became a legal medium of exchange in Virginia, Maryland, and North Carolina. Very few gold and silver coins circulated in the colonies, partly as a result of the mercantilistic policy of England, and therefore tobacco filled a dominant position in the currency. Salaries of ministers were paid in tobacco, usally sixteen thousand pounds. Since there were two important varieties of the plant grown in Virginia, the Sweet-Scented, which was the more valuable, and the Oronoko, which was the common variety, the clerical salaries were unequal. Fortunate was the parson whose lot fell in a Sweet-Scented parish. In order to keep up the quality of Virginia tobacco, the colony provided for a rigid system of inspection by officials. The Inspection Law of 1730 required that bonded inspectors should be appointed at public

---

[2] William Tatham, *An Historical and Practical Essay on the Culture and Commerce of Tobacco* (London, 1800), 5–27, 107–129.

Getting Tobacco to Market in the Colonial period and early nineteenth century. (Edward King, *The Great South* (1875), p. 634)

warehouses to examine all tobacco for export and burn all inferior tobacco. For good tobacco stored in warehouses the inspectors gave receipts that were legal tender for debts and taxes.

The tobacco trade had a profound influence on the development of society in the Chesapeake Bay country. It was a lifesaver in providing the colonists with a valuable money crop to pay for imports from England and the continent. The tobacco ships arrived from England late in the fall or the early winter, bringing with them luxuries and necessities from the mother country. Sailing up the rivers, they stopped leisurely at the individual wharves of the planters, unloading their goods, and engaging tobacco for the return trip. They did not return to England with their freight of tobacco until the spring. Throughout the colonial period there was a dearth of ships to carry staple exports to Europe, a condition that placed the planter in an unfavorable position in bargaining for cheap freight rates. Indeed, the cost of transporting tobacco to England was excessive, partly on this account, but also because of the uneconomical method of loading the ships. Instead of loading and unloading at central towns, the sea captains spent many days going from plantation to plantation, thus piling up the expense of sailors' wages, storage, loss of interest on the capital invested in ships, and so on. The prevalent freight rate of £7 a ton was equal to approximately 18 per cent of the gross sale price of tobacco. Efforts were made by the Virginia Assembly to force the trade into ports of entry through the creation of towns by legislation, but since the large planters found the old system more convenient and profitable to them such laws were repealed.

The tobacco trade was carried on through London factors. These business-men were commission merchants who received the assignment of tobacco and sold it on commission. They credited the planter with the balance after various charges, commissions, tariff duties, and freight rates had been paid. The total of these charges was so great that the planters usually received only about 35 per cent of the gross sale price. The captains of the tobacco ships brought orders from the planters for English goods. The factors obtained these goods from various ships and warehouses in London and dispatched them to the planter in the fall and winter trips. The planters bitterly complained at times that shop-worn and unfashionable goods were sent to them—the refuse of the London shops. Also often the amount of articles ordered was greater than the profits from the sale of the tobacco assignment and thus many planters were thrown into chronic debt.[3]

During the period of the Commonwealth in England, the decade 1650–1660, the Southern planters enjoyed practically free trade with the world. They exported a large amount of their tobacco to the continent, especially to Holland, and secured cheap freight rates in the Dutch ships. But after the restoration of the Stuarts in 1660, the tobacco trade was severely regulated to secure a revenue for the king. Tobacco from the American colonies was thus channeled into English ports, where it paid a tariff duty ranging from 200 per cent of the value in 1660 to 600 per cent in 1705. Although the incidence of this excessive tax fell chiefly on the British consumer, the high retail price of tobacco that resulted must have restricted the market for South-ern tobacco and thus adversely affected the interests of the tobacco planters.

While the Chesapeake Bay colonies were exploiting tobacco, the younger colonies to the south were developing rice, indigo, and naval stores as valu-able commodities of export. The fur trade and the sale of Indian slaves to the West Indies had formed an unsubstantial and transitory foundation upon which to build a Carolina aristocracy. The introduction of rice culture, how-ever, provided an economic substratum for plantation life. Rice had been unsuccessfully tried in Virginia before the middle of the seventeenth century, but the swampy lands of coastal South Carolina, with its warmer climate, proved a favorable location for rice plantations. There is a tradition, which may be true, that the cultivation of rice in South Carolina resulted from the introduction in 1694 of seed from Madagascar.[4] At first this cereal was culti-vated on small streams and swamp land by impounding rain and swamp

---

[3] J. S. Bassett, "The Relation between the Virginia Planter and the London Factor," *Annual Report of the American Historical Association for the Year 1901* (Washing-ton, 1902), I, 551–575.

[4] D. C. Heyward, *Seed from Madagascar* (Chapel Hill, 1937).

water to be used in the periodic flowings of the rice fields. In 1758 a planter of the Georgetown district, McKewn Johnstone, developed the tidal flow method. By this means the rice fields adjacent to the rivers and streams flowing into the ocean were flooded with fresh water by the flow of the tide pushing the river water upstream. Dikes, sluices, "trunks," or water gates, and canals made it possible to flood the rice fields with fresh water at the proper intervals. If salt water got into the fields, however, they were ruined for several years.

Rice culture was extended to include the sea islands and the coastal region of South Carolina, the southeastern corner of North Carolina, and the coast of Georgia. Negro slavery was admirably suited to rice growing. The slaves were given fixed tasks in the fields, and when their tasks had been completed, they were allowed to enjoy any leisure time they had earned. A slave could tend about four acres of this cereal, as well as raise provisions for himself. A good hand usually raised at least four barrels of rice, weighing five hundred pounds each, which brought fifty shillings per hundred weight in a favorable market. The cultivation of rice was subject to many hazards, such as hurricanes, which might drive salt water into the fields and thus temporarily ruin them, floods that would break levees and dikes, the activity of alligators and muskrats that might start disastrous breaks in the embankments, or the depredation of the yellow and black "rice birds" (bobolinks). After the cereal had ripened in September, it was cut with a sickle, threshed with flails, or by the treading of animals, and then taken to a mill, which removed the husks by the pounding of pestles in mortars and finally polished the grains.

The British trade acts required rice to be shipped to English ports for distribution, despite the fact that Great Britain and the British West Indies together consumed less than one fifteenth of the colonial exports of rice. In 1730, however, the British government permitted the export of Carolina rice directly to ports on the continent of Europe south of Cape Finisterre (the northwestern tip of Spain). Although the Southern colonies monopolized the rice trade with Portugal, only about 22.6 per cent of their total exports of rice was absorbed by countries south of Cape Finisterre. More than 74 per cent of the Carolina rice was sold to Holland, Germany, Denmark, and Sweden, and thus had to detour by England.

The dry land crop of colonial South Carolina and Georgia was indigo. The successful growing of this crop was begun in 1742 by a remarkable woman, Eliza Lucas, on her plantation *Wappoo,* near Charleston, from seed sent by her father, the governor of the West Indian Island of Antigua. In 1748 the British government offered a bounty of 6 pence a pound, which greatly stimulated production. Eight years later Moses Lindo, a West Indian Jew, came to Charleston and taught the planters his skill in grading indigo. There were three kinds of indigo produced: (1) the copper-colored variety, used in dyeing woolens, which brought the highest price, (2) the purple, used in the dyeing of linens, and (3) the blue variety, used by the silk industry. In addition to its use in the dyeing industry, indigo was employed by domestic householders in the laundering of clothes. The South Carolina planters could raise only two crops of indigo annually as contrasted with three of four crops in the French West Indies, and also their indigo tended to be hard on the surface without being fully cured in the center.

Indigo was obtained from the leaves of a plant that looks somewhat like asparagus. After it was cut during full bloom, the plant was placed in a vat of water and beaten while it was fermenting. At a certain stage limewater was added, which precipitated the indigo material and caused it to sink to the bottom of the vat. The water was then drained and the indigo pressed into cubes. A slave could tend about four acres, which usually yielded less than one hundred pounds an acre. With the addition of the British bounty, the indigo grower made large profits in the colonial period, so that some planters doubled their capital every three or four years. The American Revolution, resulting in the discontinuance of the bounty and the loss of a favorable market, struck a serious blow to the Carolina indigo industry. Then a plague of caterpillars and the competition of East India indigo and of cotton completed the ruin of indigo growing in the South. In modern times a coal-tar product has been substituted for vegetable indigo.[5]

In North Carolina the chief export became naval stores, consisting of turpentine, tar, and pitch. The vast forests of longleaf pine in the coastal region were ideally suited for supplying the British navy and shipping industry with these indispensable products. So distinctive of North Carolina was this forest industry that the inhabitants were nicknamed "Tar Heels." Turpentine was obtained by cutting gashes in the pine trees, from which the sap flowed into small boxes attached beneath the gashes.[6] Tar was made by burning pine logs in kilns covered with sand and clay. The supremacy of North Carolina in the production of naval stores did not decline until after the Civil War.

It was the raising of staple crops for a European market that provided the major force in creating the Southern plantation. The two basic elements in this institution were the acquisition of large estates and the use of a considerable labor force, consisting at first of white indentured servants and later of black slaves. The main incentive for the rise of such large units of agricultural production was the profits to be obtained from the cultivation of tobacco and rice on an extensive scale for the European market. In the seventeenth and eighteenth centuries the planter had the advantage over the small farmer in marketing the staple crops, in obtaining credit from the London factors, in purchasing supplies in bulk, and in having his own wharf.

The practice of using only relatively virgin soils for the cultivation of tobacco also contributed to the development of large plantations. Tobacco was planted for four or five years in succession in the same field, a practice

---

[5] See U. B. Phillips, *Life and Labor in the Old South* (Boston, 1929), chap. 7.
[6] For a description of the pine forests and the making of naval stores, see Frederick Law Olmsted, *A Journey in the Seaboard Slave States* (New York, 1856), chap. 5.

that exhausted the fertility of the soil, but brought quick returns. Such rapid exploitation of the land, as well as the ravages of erosion, led to the constant abandonment of old fields and the clearing of new fields. This wasteful, frontier method of agriculture was followed primarily because of the high cost of labor and the illimitable reserves of land in America rather than because of ignorance or carelessness. Nevertheless, it had bad results. Every planter realized the necessity of acquiring extensive reserves of land, and this need led to the growth of lonely plantations and the dispersion of population. Consequently, the tobacco planters marched slowly to the West, leaving behind them abandoned tobacco fields that in the course of years became covered with pine trees and broom sedge. By the time of the Revolution much of Tidewater Virginia and Maryland had been left in a state of desolation.

The accumulation of large estates in the South was facilitated by the headright system. This practice led to great frauds. Some unscrupulous planters magnified the number of servants they had imported or the number of acres patented by adding zeros to the documents. A collusion between landgrabbing squires and colonial officials often made possible the accumulation of broad estates.[7] Also, aspiring planters consolidated their landholdings by marrying widows possessed of goodly acres. The breakup or subdivision of these semifeudal landholdings was prevented to some extent by the laws of primogeniture and entail. According to the rule of primogeniture, the lands of an estate were inherited intact by the oldest son if the father died without a will, but as a matter of fact, many planters divided their plantations among their children by their wills. The aristocratic law of entail permitted the descent of estates and of slaves to be fixed, so that they could not be sold, but must be inherited by the family from generation to generation. By the time of the Revolution, however, many estates were not entailed, and the law had become so burdensome that the legislature frequently docked entails on plantations.[8]

Measures could have been taken to give free land to poor farmers and to prevent or retard the growth of huge estates. The strict enforcement of the payment of quitrents would have discouraged the holding of vast tracts of unused lands, but the payment of this tax on the land, usually two shillings per one hundred acres, was often evaded.[9] When some of the royal governors, notably Francis Nicholson and Alexander Spotswood of Virginia, tried to prevent the rise of land monopoly, to expose frauds, and to sue the great planters for arrears in quitrents, they were defeated by the influential men who profited from landgrabbing and who dominated the colonial government. Spotswood, finding that it was fruitless to buck the powerful planters and champion the cause of a more democratic distribution of the land, reversed his policy and

[7] T. J. Wertenbaker, *The Old South: the Founding of American Civilization* (New York, 1942).

[8] Lawrence H. Gipson, *The British Empire before the American Revolution; the Southern Plantations* (Caldwell, Idaho, 1936), II, chap. 1.

[9] B. W. Bond, *The Quit-Rent System in the American Colonies* (New Haven, 1919).

joined the scramble to obtain huge land grants. Although the quitrent system was a relic of feudalism, the efficient collection of these taxes on large preserves of unused land would have forced a fairer distribution of the land. These dues were thoroughly hated in the South and the Middle colonies, where they were collected with difficulty. New England was free from this burden. In Pennsylvania on the eve of the Revolution, only one third of the amount due was collected, in Virginia less than one half, in South Carolina between £ 2,000 and £ 3,000, but in Maryland nearly the entire rent roll of £ 8,000 was exacted.

The growth of extensive estates in the South formed the economic substratum for a dominant aristocracy. "King" Robert Carter, noted for his haughty demeanor, died in 1732, possessing three hundred thirty-three thousand acres of land and seven hundred slaves. Other examples of regal estates were Beverley's Manor at Staunton, the immense landholdings of the Byrd family of *Westover,* the estates of the Carroll and Dulany families in Maryland, the Granville tract and the McCulloh "principality" in North Carolina, and the plantations of Sir James Wright in Georgia. A huge domain between the Potomac and Rappahannock rivers was granted in 1673 by Charles II to the Earl of Arlington and Lord Culpeper.[10] This area, known as the "Northern Neck of Virginia," contained approximately 1 million acres of land from which the family collected the hated quitrents. This immense grant was eventually inherited by Thomas, Lord Fairfax, who in 1747 settled at *Greenway Court,* near Winchester, the only British peer who made his permanent residence in the colonies. These great estates of the eighteenth century were made possible by the introduction of the institution of Negro slavery. The only landholdings comparable to them in the northern colonies were those of the Narragansett (Rhode Island) planters and the spacious estates of the Hudson Valley, which had been initiated by the patroon system.

The principal source of labor for the plantations during the seventeenth century were the white indentured servants brought from England. In the mother country the farm hands and laboring class received miserably low wages. For example, a plowman in the first half of the seventeenth century received fifty shillings a year. The Inclosure movement had produced a number of unemployed agricultural laborers, and the Elizabethan poor laws prevented the free migration of laborers from one parish to another by making each parish responsible for its own poor. Such poor people found it almost impossible to save £ 6, the average cost of passage to America. The only method by which they could transfer their labor from a cheap market in England to a dear market in America was the indenture system, really a credit, or installment, system to pay the passage money of crossing the At-

---

[10] It is a complicated story, which Douglas S. Freeman has skillfully told in *George Washington, a Biography* (New York, 1948), I, 4–14, and Appendix, 447–513. In 1649 Charles I granted the Northern Neck to seven favorites. In 1688 Lord Culpeper, who had previously become proprietor, secured a renewal of the grant in perpetuity with greatly expanded boundaries.

Robert ("King") Carter of Corotoman, 1663–1732. One of the wealthiest and most influential men in Virginia. As President of Council, he served as Acting Governor of the Colony, 1726–1727. (Courtesy of the Reverend Dabney Wellford and the Colonial Williamsburg Foundation)

lantic. The servant signed a contract by which he sold his labor to a master for a period usually of four or five years.

Immigration into the colonies was vastly stimulated by the profitable business of securing servants for the American market. Some sea captains made a practice of transporting redemptioners, those servants who were given the privilege of selecting their masters within a period of two weeks after arrival, or whose bond for performance of services was redeemed by relatives or friends upon arrival in the colonies. John Harrower, an indentured servant in Virginia, described in his diary, which he kept from 1773 to 1776, a class of merchants called Soul Drivers, who met immigrant and convict ships at the docks to buy servants, whom they then drove through the colonies "like a parcell of Sheep" to sell to the highest bidder.[11] Such servants were sold for prices ranging from £20 for the highest type, Scottish soldiers captured after the Jacobite revolt, to £4 for Irish vagrants.

Most of the indentured servants were young men and women under twenty-five years of age. Hugh Jones reported that these young servants were commonly called "kids" (an early derivation of the term now applied in the United States to young children).[12] They could look upon their four years of service in the new world as an apprenticeship in the art of growing tobacco. According to the testimony of George Alsop, an indentured servant who wrote a description of Maryland in 1666, their lot was not hard in comparison with working conditions in England. They worked only five and a half days a week; in the winter they did very little work; and during the hot summer days they were allowed a three-hour rest period in the middle of the day. They were fed much better food than was available to the English laboring class, enjoying turkey, oysters, and venison so often that it became a "tiresome meat." [13] After a servant had fulfilled his contract he was given "freedom dues." These rewards varied in the different colonies, but usually consisted of an outfit of clothing, a certain number of barrels of corn, and agricultural tools or a musket, or a money payment. In Maryland he was given fifty acres of land until 1683, in North Carolina a similar amount of land during the Proprietary period, and in South Carolina fifty acres of land in the eighteenth century; but in Virginia he was not given land.

Under some masters indentured servitude approximated the conditions of slavery. The master had the right to punish his white servant by whipping, and the servant could not leave the plantation without permission. If a servant married without consent or if a maidservant had an illegitimate baby, the term of service was extended for one year. If a servant ran away and was arrested, he or she was punished by extending the term of service two days extra in Virginia and ten days in Maryland for every day of absence. Cruel treatment led to strikes and revolts on the part of white servants, caused particularly by the failure of masters to observe the custom of the country in providing their white servants with meat at least three times a week. The servants were protected from abuse to a considerable extent by custom and by their right to appeal to the courts.

[11] John Harrower, *The Journal of John Harrower, an Indentured Servant in the Colony of Virginia, 1773–1776*, ed. by Edward M. Riley (New York, 1963), 39.

[12] Hugh Jones, *The Present State of Virginia*, ed. by Richard L. Morton (Chapel Hill, 1956), 87.

[13] C. C. Hall (ed.), *Narratives of Early Maryland, 1633–1684* (New York, 1910), 354–360.

The labor shortage in America was so great that it led to the dark crime of kidnapping. There were professional agents in England known as "spirits" who kidnapped "drunks" in taverns and young persons on the streets to ship them to America for sale as servants. The illegal abduction of servants became so serious that in 1664 the British government created a Registry, which recorded the name, age, birthplace, and the terms of contract of each servant going to America, as well as an acknowledgment that the servant left the shores of England without coercion. Perhaps more cruel than kidnapping in its total effect was the deception of thousands of naive country lads and girls by agents called "crimps" in England and "newlanders" in Germany who portrayed America in a rosy and fallacious light.

The British government used the Southern colonies as well as the islands of Jamaica and Barbados as a dumping ground for convicts. In addition to genuine criminals there was a class of political prisoners (much smaller in number than the jailbirds) who were transported to America to be sold as bond servants. In seventeenth-century England there were over two hundred crimes listed as felonies punishable by death, but many petty criminals, especially thieves, were pardoned on condition of being transported to America. These jailbirds from the great prisons of Newgate and Old Bailey were undesirable citizens, and both Virginia and Maryland passed laws prohibiting their entrance into the colony. Such laws protecting the colonies from the immigration of convicts, however, were disallowed by the English government.

A careful student of this subject has found that during the last half of the seventeenth century a total of 4,431 persons were pardoned in England for transportation to America, but most of these were sent to Jamaica and other islands in the West Indies.[14] The merchant or captain who transported these criminals had to give bond to land them in America and had to pay various fees, equal to £3, but the services of the criminal could be sold in the colony and the importer could receive a headright of fifty acres for each convict. In 1717 the British Parliament passed a law facilitating the transportation of felons to America and setting the terms of exile at seven years for minor offenders and fourteen years for more serious criminals. Furthermore, the government paid merchant contractors to transport these undesirable citizens to America. Most of the convicts sent to the mainland colonies were taken to Virginia and Maryland, where their sale to the tobacco planters was very profitable. One student of white bondage in the American colonies has estimated from reliable data that during the eighteenth century over twenty thousand convicts were received by Virginia and Maryland, the principal colonies to which criminals were sent.[15]

Although the convict was exiled for seven years from England, his period of service as an indentured servant in the colonies was usually less than that

[14] A. E. Smith, "The Transportation of Convicts to the American Colonies in the Seventeenth Century," *American Historical Review*, XXXIX (October 1933), 238.
[15] A. E. Smith, *Colonists in Bondage, White Servitude and Convict Labor in America, 1607–1776* (Chapel Hill, 1947), 119.

term. Defoe in his novel of the famous whore and thief, *Moll Flanders,* who was transported to Virginia, has given a graphic account of the hardened criminals sent to the Southern colonies. "Many a Newgate-bird became a great man," one of his characters in Virginia says, "and we have several justices of the peace, officers of the trained bands, and magistrates of the towns they live in that have been burnt in the hand." Yet he shows how in this young society they could rehabilitate their lives and acquire tobacco land, tools, and supplies from the merchants "upon the credit of their crop before it is grown" (a forerunner of the crop lien after the Civil War).[16]

Throughout the seventeenth century white servants, rather than slaves, performed most of the labor of clearing the land and cultivating the tobacco fields. Between fifteen hundred and two thousand indentured servants came into Virginia annually, and considerable numbers into Maryland. In 1671 Governor Berkeley estimated that in Virginia there were six thousand white indentured servants and two thousand slaves in a total population of forty-five thousand people. The by-product of this form of labor was the development of a large class of yeoman farmers. Until 1660 it was easy for ex-indentured servants to acquire land and rise in world, because tobacco brought good prices.[17] A number of former indentured servants became members of the House of Burgesses. In 1632 six of the forty-four burgesses had been servants, and the legislature of 1663 contained thirteen ex-servants. Chief Justice Roger B. Taney of Maryland and General Thomas Sumter of South Carolina, "the Game Cock of the Revolution," were descended from indentured servants.

The golden age for the indentured servant in the Southern colonies ended with the restoration of the Stuarts, when Charles II ascended the throne. The passage of the Navigation Acts shortly thereafter deprived Virginia and Maryland of a free world market for their tobacco and of cheap freight rates in Dutch ships. This adverse blow caused the profits from the cultivation of tobacco to fall and made it difficult for the freedman to acquire land. The raising of tobacco for a small profit was more efficiently conducted on large estates tilled by slave labor, and the planters often supplemented their income by the fur trade and by selling merchandise to the farmers. The stream of white indentured servants that had invigorated the middle class of Virginia for a century dwindled by 1718 to a trickle of only 101 servants, and after that time until 1768, it was chiefly skilled artisans who were imported as indenture servants.

Accordingly, the yeoman class in Virginia and Maryland declined, and the society of the tobacco colonies became decidedly more aristocratic. Contemporaneous with this great social revolution, the character of immigrants

[16] Daniel Defoe, *The Fortunes and Misfortunes of the Famous Moll Flanders* (The Bibliophilist Society, 1931), 71.
[17] T. J. Wertenbaker has made a basic study of indentured servants in *Planters of Colonial Virginia* (Princeton, 1922); see also R. B. Morris, *Government and Labor in Colonial America* (New York, 1941).

into the Southern colonies also changed from English settlers of the seventeenth century to Germans and the Scotch-Irish of the eighteenth century. During the five years preceding the Revolution, however, immigration from England, which had fallen off so greatly since 1700, was strongly revived; the port of Annapolis, Maryland, for example, showed a striking rise in the arrivals of indentured servants and convicts from England.

The nature of this later immigration can be ascertained from the reports of the British port officials on emigrants leaving Great Britain during the years 1773–1776. A recent study has shown that only 34 per cent of them paid their passage to America; 55 per cent went as indentured servants, and 6 per cent went as redemptioners; 5 per cent were convicts. It is surprising to find that only 16 per cent were farmers and 11 per cent laborers; the great majority of immigrants, 63 percent, were craftsmen or tradespeople. The emigrants came from every county in England, but the largest number were from the London area and the North of England, particularly Yorkshire. Few of them emigrated to New England, the most popular destinations being, first, Maryland, second, Pennsylvania, an excellent market for craftsmen, and third, Virginia. Perhaps one of the reasons that Southern colonies received such a large proportion of immigrants was that the tobacco ships leaving for the Southern ports were only slightly laden with cargo. The English clergyman Hugh Jones, who taught in William and Mary College, noted in *The Present State of Virginia* (1724) that many of these ships stopped at Irish ports for provisions, where they also took on indentured servants and other emigrants. In answer to the questionnaire of the customs officials in England as to why they were leaving their homes, the usual answer was "to improve my condition" or "to seek a better livelihood." [18] In the 1760's economic conditions in England were bad for the poorer class of people, and many left Yorkshire because the Inclosure Movement had led to a prodigious increase in the rents of farming land.

Maryland and Virginia represented the Promised Land to many poor and landless men in Great Britain. Undoubtedly, emigration to these Southern colonies marked a step upward for the majority of the emigrants. Nevertheless, the hardships and disillusionments of the early years of planting the colonies established a bad tradition concerning the New World for some time. In order to refute such a reputation John Hammond wrote in 1656 his glowing promotional pamphlet entitled *Leah and Rachel, or, the Two Fruitfull Sisters Virginia and Mary-land.* "The Country is reported to be an unhealthy place," he wrote, "a nest of Rogues, whores, desolute [sic] and rooking persons; a place of intolerable labour, bad usage and hard Diet, etc.," but Hammond proclaimed Virginia and Maryland to be superior to England as homes for poor people.[19] He was undoubtedly right, for labor was much

---

[18] Mildred Campbell, "English Emigration on the Eve of the American Revolution," *American Historical Review*, LXI (October 1955), 1–20.
[19] Hall (ed.), *Narratives of Early Maryland*, 284.

more valuable in the Southern colonies, perhaps four or five times more so, than in England. The indentured servants had to go through a seasoning process, in which many of them died from malaria, "the Virginia sickness," but after 1671 the planters learned the use of Peruvian bark, or quinine, as a remedy, which greatly decreased mortality from the disease.

A vivid, human document of the indentured servants in America is a journal kept by one of them, John Harrower, 1773–1776, the only diary extant of this lowly class. Harrower was a bankrupt merchant in the Shetland Islands who, unable to find employment in Great Britain to support his family, in desperation indentured himself for four years of service in Virginia. On February 6, 1773, his ship, the *Planter,* set sail from London for Fredericksburg, Virginia, with seventy indentured servants on board. Most of them were young men of the artisan class, with only eight farmers among them. Harrower, forty years old at the time, was one of the oldest of the group. On May 24, he left the ship to become indentured as a schoolmaster to Colonel William Daingerfield, whose plantation *Belvidera* lay on the river seven miles below Fredericksburg. By this time the colonel had abandoned the cultivation of tobacco on his thirteen hundred-acre plantation and with his thirty field slaves raised wheat and corn for export.

Harrower taught the three children of the master and was also permitted to teach about ten other children of neighboring planters, whom he charged a fee. He was well treated by his master, sat at the dining table with the family and the white housekeeper, went on fishing parties with the colonel, rode into Fredericksburg to see the races, visited with other tutors on nearby plantations, danced to the fiddle, and occasionally got drunk on rum. He wrote his wife that he lived in a genteel fashion, and his wardrobe indicated this fact, for he had six ruffled shirts, a claret-colored waistcoat, buckled shoes, and a wig. Harrower hoped to bring his wife to Virginia to make of her "a Virginia Lady among the woods of America" and to enjoy "more wheat Bread in your old age than what you have done in your Youth," but before he could do so he died of disease, and his master, Colonel Daingerfield, discouraged by his losses as a planter, ended his struggle against the frustrations of the New World by cutting his own throat.[20]

What happened to the servant after his indenture had been completed? In some cases he went to the frontier and became a yeoman farmer. But the pleasant generalization that the majority of the freed servants became sturdy yeoman farmers has been questioned by a modern student. He takes the view that many of these servants were riffraff, poor human material for colonists, who lacked the ambition to become independent farmers. He concludes that only 7 per cent of the five thousand indentured servants who came to Maryland in the decade 1670–1680 seized the opportunity to acquire the free grant of fifty acres of land and settle as farmers. Some sold their rights immediately, only a small fraction even went to the trouble of proving their

[20] Harrower, *Journal of John Harrower,* 76.

rights to the fifty-acre grant, and the majority either became artisans, laborers, overseers, or "poor whites" or returned to England.[21]

In the last quarter of the seventeenth century the black tide of Negro slavery overwhelmed the white workers in the Virginia and Maryland tobacco fields. Africa contained great reservoirs of black slaves who could be used as a cheaper and more stable labor force than white indentured servants to cultivate the staple crops of the Southern colonies. Mungo Park, who made his famous exploration of Africa in 1795, estimated that three fourths of the native Africans (probably an exaggeration) were held in slavery, in most cases in a brutal and relentless type of bondage. The kindhearted Bishop Las Casas is credited with introducing African slavery into the West Indies to save the Indians who were dying rapidly under Spanish exploitation. Captain John Hawkins, a devout man, was the pioneer Englishman in the slave-trading business to the New World (1562), and it is an ironic commentary on the divorce of religion from humanitarianism that his slave ship was named *Jesus*.

The Negro servants introduced in Virginia in 1619 by a Dutch ship seem to have been sold to the planters as long-term indentured servants, but this is a matter of dispute. Slavery was afterward gradually established by custom, and in 1660 by law in Virginia, when it was enacted that the status of a person was determined by whether his mother was free or a slave—that rule was to remain in force until slavery ended. For a long time there was considerable doubt whether Christian baptism freed a slave, but in 1667 the Virginia legislature settled the question by enacting a law that declared that baptism did not affect the legal status of a slave. When slavery supplanted white servitude in the Southern colonies, the laws governing the slaves greatly resembled the laws regulating the white indentured servants.

Did prejudice against Negroes in the Southern colonists develop because they were enslaved, or did prejudice of color play an important role in fastening slavery upon the Negroes who were originally indentured servants? One school of thought maintains that prejudice of color arose after the Negro was enslaved and because of his enslavement; another maintains that prejudice, brought by the colonists from England, was partly responsible, along with economic reasons, for the gradual transformation of indentured servitude of the Negro into slavery. Certainly prejudice was exhibited early in Virginia and Maryland against the dark-skinned Negro servants. In 1630, a Virginian court ordered a white man whipped for "defiling his body in lying with a Negro"; in 1664, Maryland prohibited interracial marriages, which were stigmatized as "shameful matches," and "the disgrace of our nation"; Virginia prohibited such marriages in 1691. These laws against miscegenation remained in force in many states until only recently when they were found unconstitutional by the Supreme Court. In the seventeenth century, Negro women servants were employed in field work, but white indentured female

21 Smith, *Colonists in Bondage,* 299.

servants were usually not sent to the hard labor of the fields. A recent student of this important subject of the emergence of prejudice against the Negro concludes that prejudice was both a cause and a result of enslaving the Negro in the Southern colonies, and thus it seems to the writer.[22]

The English did not participate extensively in slave trading until the reorganization of the Royal African Company in 1672 (founded in 1662, with the king's brother, the Duke of York, as president). This company was given a monopoly of the African slave trade until 1697 when private traders were admitted for a period of fourteen years to this traffic in human flesh upon the payment of 10 per cent duty. The slave trade was carried on by means of "factories," or trading establishments, defended by forts on the west coast of Africa. In 1750 the Royal African Company had nine factories, the chief of which was Cape Coast Castle, with a strong fort built on a huge rock that projected into the sea. It was an expensive enterprise to maintain these forts and trading posts. In fact, the company was prevented from going into bankruptcy by an annual grant from Parliament of £10,000. The competition of French slave traders, who paid more for their human merchandise than the English company, was especially formidable since the French African Company was heavily subsidized by its government. In 1750 the African trade was again thrown open to private traders, who were incorporated as "The Company of Merchants Trading to Africa." Two years later the old corporation came to an end, the British government paying to the company £112,142 for its assets.[23]

During the first half of the eighteenth century Bristol and Liverpool were the great slave-trading ports of the British Empire. In 1750 a total of 155 British and colonial ships were engaged in the slave trade, of which 20 came from the American colonies, principally from Rhode Island. Toward the close of the colonial period, however, there were 150 Rhode Island ships employed in this traffic as compared with 192 English ships, a record to which Southerners pointed during the antislavery controversy.

These ships often were engaged in a triangular trade with England or the American colonies, the west coast of Africa, and the West Indies. To Africa the slave ships carried trading goods, bars of iron, rum—"well-watered"—firearms, lead, beads, and cloth, which they exchanged for slaves. The latter were transported to the sugar islands of the West Indies and exchanged for molasses, rum, and gold coins. In New England the molasses was manufactured into rum to exchange for more slaves. The "middle passage" was the leg of the journey between Africa and the West Indies. During the passage

---

[22] Winthrop D. Jordan, "Modern Tensions and the Origin of American Slavery," *Journal of Southern History,* XXVIII (February 1962), 18–30; and Oscar and Mary Handlin, "Origin of the Southern Labor System," *William and Mary Quarterly,* S. 3, *VII* (April 1950), 119–122; Jordan observes in *White over Black: American Attitudes Toward the Negro, 1550–1812* (Chapel Hill, 1968) that in the Europe from which the settlers emigrated, the color of black was associated with evil.

[23] Gipson, *British Empire* [The Southern Plantations], II, chap. 10.

Africans on the deck of the bark, *Wildfire,* brought into Key West, Florida in April, 1860. (*Harper's Weekly*)

across the Atlantic the slaves were confined in close quarters, the space between some decks being only three feet high, and they were manacled except when taken upon the top deck in small numbers for exercise and while their quarters were being cleaned with vinegar.[24] The middle passage was at times a journey of horror, with slaves dying from dysentery, smallpox, and the yaws. Some slaves committed suicide by the strange African method of swallowing the tongue. There was a strong human stench that was wafted from a

[24] See D. P. Mannix and Malcolm Cowley, *Black Cargoes: A History of the Atlantic Slave Trade, 1518–1865* (New York, 1962).

slave ship. The average mortality of the slaves on the middle passage has been estimated by the best authorities at from 8 to 13 per cent.[25] The captains of slave ships tried to preserve the health of their valuable cargo. Nevertheless, this trade was a brutal process of eliminating the weak and sickly—of those who remained after the large number of slaves who died on the trek from the interior to the "factories" on the seacoast.

The slaves of the Southern colonies came from many different tribes of Africa with various characteristics, but the major source was Angola. Some of the slaves were Mohammedans, such as the Foulah Negroes, who could read and write and who performed ablutions and rites of prayer and refrained from the drinking of liquor. Those who brought the best prices were the Gold Coast, or Whydah Negroes, and the Cormantees (Koromantyns).[26] These people were strong, tall, coal-black, and warlike. They were regarded as dangerous because they were not as docile as other Negroes and more liable to insurrection. There were also Paw Paws, or Popows, noted for their thieving propensities; Senegalese, unusually intelligent; and Angolas, who were more submissive. The Eboes, prognathous in facial angle, were particularly emotional and prone to commit suicide. Mandingos were a more delicate type of Negro, with thinner lips and less kinky hair. The Gaboons were noted for their garrulity, and the natives of the Congo were regarded as exceptionally stupid. All these immigrants from Africa had to go through a seasoning process, often fatal, in America and the West Indies, where they grew accustomed to the strange food and the climate and were trained to work by distribution among the older slaves. A far greater number of slaves were imported into the British West Indies, where the mortality was very high and the natural increase very low, than into the Southern colonies. Indeed, the Southern colonies received their slaves largely from the West Indies instead of directly from Africa. One authority, Philip D. Curtin, has estimated that less than 5 per cent of the slaves imported into the Western hemisphere were brought directly to the area of the present United States.[27]

---

[25] U. B. Phillips, *American Negro Slavery* (New York, 1940), 38; Elizabeth Donnan (ed.), *Documents Illustrative of the History of the Slave Trade to America* (Washington, 1935), LV, 35, 97, 175–8; Gunnar Myrdal, *An American Dilemma* (New York, 1944), I, 121, II, 1202. For a good survey of the development of slavery in the South, by an outstanding Negro historian, see John Hope Franklin *From Slavery to Freedom, A History of American Negroes* (New York, 1973).

[26] The recently published papers of the great Charleston merchant Henry Laurens, who retired from business to a plantation, indicate that the South Carolina planters selected, whenever they could, slaves from the Gold Coast and from Gambia and avoided purchasing "The Slaves of Calabar" (the Eboes), suggesting, as Jack Greene has observed, that this selectivity may explain characteristics of the rice coast slaves. *The Papers of Henry Laurens*, ed. by P. M. Hamer and G. C. Rogers, Jr. (Columbia, 1970–73), 3 vols.: review, *Journal of Southern History*, XXXIX (May 1973), 281.

[27] P. D. Curtin, *The Atlantic Slave Trade: A Census* (Madison, 1969), and C. V. Woodward, *American Counterpoint: Slavery and Racism in the North-South Dialogue* (Boston, 1971), chap. 3.

Negro workers were well suited to the hot climate of the South. They perspired freely and were less subject to malaria and hookworm than the whites; they were also less expensive than white servants because they required hardly any clothes. The gang system was evolved to direct their reluctant labor. Usually a plantation employed about thirty slaves and an overseer, the work was routinized, and the staple crops of rice, cotton, and tobacco did not permit the slave to hide from the observation of the overseer. Slaves multiplied in the Southern colonies until at the end of the colonial period they constituted two thirds of the population of South Carolina, approximately one half of the population of Virginia, and one third of the population of North Carolina, Maryland, and Georgia. The largest slaveholdings were in South Carolina, an average of thirty-three slaves to a master, but in the other Southern colonies the ratio was much lower. There were some colonial "millionaires," such as Ralph Izard of South Carolina, who owned 594 slaves, Charles Carroll of Maryland with 316, George Mason of *Gunston Hall* with 300, and George Washington with 188, but these men were rare exceptions to the generality of planters.[28]

The Negroes lived in whitewashed log or frame huts that were usually congregated in a "quarter" that satisfied their gregarious propensities. Each week the slaves were given an allowance of cornmeal, bacon, and molasses, or rice. The women worked in the fields as well as the men, but were given leisure during the childbearing period. In America, the Negroes were probably healthier than in Africa, lived in superior houses, had medical attention, and came into contact with the Christian religion. Although the South Carolina slave code, affected by the code of Barbados, was harsh, it was tempered in practice.[29] The slaves of Virginia and Maryland seem to have been more humanely treated. Nevertheless, the diary of William Byrd II indicates that even the most educated Virginia planters turned sadistic at times and inflicted severe punishment on their slaves. Mrs. Byrd would fly into a rage and beat the maid with tongs or brand her servants. Byrd himself tortured his slaves occasionally by putting a bit with a screw on the tongue of the offending slave. Philip Fithian, a tutor in the household of Robert Carter of Virginia, saw a Negro coachman chained to the coach and was told by a Virginian that his particular method of punishing a Negro was curry him with a curry comb and then after salting him to rub him with dry chaff.

It has been assumed by many students of American history that slavery was from the very beginning a serious handicap to Southern development. But in the colonial period slavery was probably an economic benefit to the Southern colonies, and it was not regarded as a moral stigma to own slaves. Slavery gave the planters a stable labor supply that had many advantages

---

[28] U. S. Bureau of the Census, *Heads of Families at the First Census of the United States in the Year 1790* (Washington, 1907–1908), 11 vols.
[29] See P. W. Wood, *Black Majority: Negroes in Colonial South Carolina From 1670 Through the Stono Rebellion* (New York, 1974).

over white indentured servitude. Its establishment in the South was the natural outgrowth of economic "laws," especially Wakefield's law, which laid down the premise that the presence of plentiful and cheap land suitable for agriculture and the lack of labor bred slavery, for free men seldom will work for wages when they can become independent farmers.

The evils of slavery were very great and cannot be morally justified; nevertheless, on the basis of black slavery the golden age of colonial aristocracy and culture in the South arose. Slaves were necessary to the large-scale production of tobacco and rice, the export of which had the effect on the Southern colonies of strengthening the social and cultural ties with England. Slavery also was an important element in the development of leadership, in producing such qualities as the habit of command, poise in the presence of dependents, a feeling of responsibility for a large family of blacks and whites, and the military virtues. This economic institution gave the privileged classes the concentration of wealth and the leisure that enabled them to build beautiful Georgian homes, cultivate the social graces, and import luxuries and books from Europe. If Virginia, Maryland, and the Carolinas had remained free labor colonies, it is doubtful that the South would have produced the culture of a William Byrd II, the plantation life of *Mount Vernon* or *Monticello,* or the galaxy of able leaders who led in the Revolutionary movement. Like feudalism or serfdom, Southern colonial slavery was a mixture of good and bad. The evils implicit in slavery, especially its pernicious effects on the whites and blacks and its economic drawbacks, became more apparent in the nineteenth century.

The Piedmont Society

THE FIRST FRONTIER of the South was the pristine wilderness that confronted the colonists from England. In making the early settlements, they were naïve and had to learn by painful experience to adapt themselves to the strange new life. The Indians, though often hostile, were their first teachers. From the aboriginal inhabitants in America the colonists learned many ways of adapting themselves to the environment of the New World. Contrary to a prevalent stereotype, most of the Southern Indians were engaged in a primitive agriculture, raising maize, sweet potatoes, squash, melons, pumpkins, gourds, and tobacco, to which they introduced their white conquerers. The white man learned from this primitive people how to make canoes, how to girdle trees, how to hunt game, how to make moccasins, how to cultivate tobacco and smoke it, and how to adapt himself to forest warfare. Perhaps the Indian eloquence heard at councils and on treaty-making occasions, affected early Southern oratory, giving to it a more florid tone. Certainly college boys are indebted to the Cherokee Indians for the game of lacrosse, which they played with a deerskin ball and racquets about two feet in length, accompanied by furious betting on the part of the spectators. Today the main physical survivals of Indian culture in the South are the mounds that they built, especially the remarkable group at Moundville, Alabama, containing one mound fifty-eight feet high, and those at Etowah and Macon, Georgia. These strange relics of a vanished people were principally truncated pyramids of earth forming platforms for the council and ceremonial houses rather than mounds for burial purposes.

Advancing from the seacoast along the river valleys, the English settlers in Virginia had reached the fall line by 1676, the time of Bacon's Rebellion. Beyond this line of demarcation lay the Piedmont, a region of hills and forests, which had been deplored as early as 1671 by Thomas Batts and Robert Fallam, sent out by Captain Abraham Wood, who had a trading post at modern Petersburg on the falls of the Appomattox. Their explorations extended as far as the New River, one of the branches of the Kanawha, and they were perhaps the first English to reach the headwaters of streams flowing into the Mississippi River. The settlement of the region between the fall line and the eastern rim of the Appalachian Mountains, which Frederick Jackson Turner called "the Old West," created a new type of society. Here first developed many of the characteristics that were to distinguish Americans from Europeans.[1]

[1] See Arthur M. Schlesinger, Sr., "What then is the American, this New Man?", *American Historical Review, XLVIII* (January 1943), 225–244.

As the Virginia frontier approached the fall line, aggressive frontiersmen violated the rights of the Indian inhabitants, provoking Indian hostilities. Out of this trouble arose Bacon's Rebellion. The champion of the ruthless group of frontiersmen and speculators was Nathaniel Bacon, a young, well-educated Englishman, who had come to Virginia only the year before the outbreak of the Rebellion that bears his name. When the overseer of his outer plantation at the falls of the James River was murdered by Indians, he demanded a commission from Governor William Berkeley to lead an expedition against them. The governor refused this demand, partly because his policy was to defend the frontier by forts and a small force of mounted infantry. Although Berkeley's policy may have been the humane and sensible one, the frontiersmen opposed it as ineffective and as necessitating increased taxation.

Moreover, his refusal of a military commission to Bacon came at a time when there was a growing resentment throughout the colony against the governor's arbitrary rule. Berkeley had been sent to Virginia as governor in 1642, when he was a young man of fashion in London, the author of a play called *The Lost Lady*. For ten years his rule was popular except for his persecution of the dissenters from the Church of England. In 1644 he defeated the Indians, under the leadership of the aged Opechancanough, after they had killed many settlers. Thus a vast area of western land was opened for settlement. Also he had advanced the economic interests of the colony, particularly by his liberal policy in regard to foreign trade. With a munificent salary and a fine estate at *Greenspring,* four miles from Jamestown, this bachelor governor entertained lavishly. A staunch royalist, he succeeded in having the Virginia Assembly recognize Charles II as king after the regicide of Charles I. For such loyalty to the crown Virginia was later given the title of a dominion within the British realm and was called the Old Dominion. In 1652 Berkeley was deposed from his governorship by the Puritan Commonwealth, but after the overthrow of the Puritan regime in England he resumed his old position in 1660.

In this second period of administration he became exceedingly reactionary and autocratic. By giving special favors to members of the Council and of the House of Burgesses and by allowing them to acquire land unlawfully, he reduced these branches of the colonial government to pliant tools of his will. He refused to hold any elections for new members of the legislature but continued to adjourn the so-called Long Assembly from year to year, because its members, elected in the first flush of enthusiasm for the royal cause after the restoration of Charles II, were favorable to him. Moreover, he had grown avaricious and arbitrary with the passing of the years, especially after his marriage to an heiress.

When the young upstart defied the old governor and attacked the Indians on the frontier. Berkeley proclaimed him an outlaw. Upon his return from the expedition, however, the rebel made peace with the governor, asked forgiveness, and was pardoned. In the meanwhile the rise of discontent with the colonial government forced the governor to order a new election. In this election Bacon, together with a large number of his followers, were elected members of the House of Burgesses. This assembly passed a number of liberal acts, called "Bacon's Laws." Bacon became the champion of the grievances of the people, who were stirred to opposition not only by Indian troubles but by the low price of tobacco, high taxation, and Berkeley's high-handed administration. The civil war that now broke out was complex in nature, and aristocrats as well as yeomen supported both sides. In the course of the conflict, Bacon captured Jamestown, very unchivalrously using the captured wives and daughters of some of the governor's supporters as a shield for his advancing troops. The governor fled to the Eastern Shore in Maryland, and Bacon burned the town. Led step by step into more radical courses, he appealed to the people of Maryland to unite with his forces to resist the misrule of the king's officers. But this early American revolt collapsed, in the autumn of 1676, when the popular leader suddenly died.

How shall the historian evaluate this complex and confusing movement known as Bacon's Rebellion? To Thomas Jefferson Wartenbaker, who made a careful study, Bacon was the leader of a liberal reform movement, "the torchbearer of the American Revolution." A recent student, Wilcombe Washburne, rejects this interpretation and calls it "the rise of a democratic myth." He sides with Berkeley, portraying him as one of the greatest of colonial governors and Bacon as a spoiled and ungovernable young man who had no genuine interest in political reform except to attract recruits, and whose Indian campaign killed only friendly Indians on the frontier while the real marauders came from outside the colony.[2] The truth is difficult to obtain and probably lies between these extreme interpretations. Washburne's glorification of Berkeley does not agree with the fact that the governor had bought two Indian slaves and that he wrote of an earlier campaign against the Indians as attracting recruits becuse it offered an opportunity of winning booty by capturing Indian women and children for slaves.[3]

In the early eighteenth century the western hinterland attracted the eye of Lieutenant Governor Alexander Spotswood, who developed ambitious plans of expanding the Virginia colony and of preventing the French from hemming the English into the narrow region of the coastal plain. At the same time he was eager to increase his personal fortune by land speculation and Indian trade. When he found that expansion along the James River, the best avenue into the Piedmont, was blocked by the Byrd family, who had obtained the land around the falls at which Richmond is located, he began to advance up the Rappahannock River. In 1714 he imported some Germans whom he located in the back country on the Rapidan River at a colony he named

[2] The conflicting interpretations are presented by T. J. Wertenbaker, *Torchbearer of the Revolution: The Story of Bacon's Rebellion and Its Leader* (Princeton, 1940), and W. E. Washburne, *The Governor and the Rebel, a History of Bacon's Rebellion in Virginia* (Chapel Hill, 1957); and Bernard Bailyn, in J. M. Smith (ed.), *Seventeenth Century America* (Chapel Hill, 1959).

[3] Carl Bridenbaugh's review, *American Historical Review*, LXIII (July 1954), 1002–3.

Germanna. These immigrants, brought over to work the iron deposits discovered near the falls of the Rappanhannock, were given no land but were tenants on the governor's land. In the same year Spotswood established Fort Christiana on the Meherrin River, a tributary of the Roanoke, for the purpose of Indian trade.

In 1716 the governor led a part of gentlemen, provided with a liberal supply of wine and liquor, to the top of the Blue Ridge, where they drank copious toasts in champagne, claret, and Burgundy. In preparation for the journey the horses of the company had been equipped with horseshoes, a practice that was not usually followed in the Tidewater, where the soils were sandy and free from stones. To commemorate this trip of exploration and assertion of England's claims Spotswood created the order of the Knights of the Golden Horseshoe and gave to each of the adventurers a gold pin in the shape of a horseshoe.[4]

The leaders of the movement into the Virginia Piedmont were the wealthy planters of the Tidewater. Because tobacco growing as practiced in the colonial period quickly exhausted the soil, large reserves of virgin soil were needed. Consequently, when lands in the Tidewater began to wear out, the farsighted planters began to plan for the future by acquiring fertile lands in the Piedmont. Furthermore, money was to be made by speculating in western lands. The advance into the Piedmont along the James was led by the aristocratic Randolph family, their friends, and their relatives. Frequently the Tidewater planter would send his overseer and a gang of slaves into the western wilderness to clear the ground, build a house, and prepare for the later removal of the planter's household. The Beverley family, for example, obtained a district of more than one hundred thousand acres in the Valley of Virginia at the site of the present town of Staunton. William Byrd II patented an enormous number of acres along the Roanoke River, including the famous Indian trading island of Occaneechee, where the Dan and the Staunton rivers unite to form the Roanoke, and here he built a hunting lodge, *Bluestone Castle*. Many of these large grants of land were held by speculators who had secured them on the condition of settling one family on the land for every 1,000 acres patented. To facilitate the settlement of the back country of Virginia two huge, relatively empty counties were created in 1720, Spotsylvania in northern Virginia and Brunswick in the southern Piedmont.

The advance of the frontier in the colonial period was not always the simple process described by some historians, in which the vanguard of settlement was led by small pioneer farmers followed after a time interval by substantial farmers and planters. Frequently, the movement of acquiring western lands in the South was initiated by wealthy planters seeking reserves for tobacco lands.[5] However, many small tobacco farmers also left the Tide-

[4] Leonidas Dodson, *Alexander Spotswood, Governor of Colonial Virginia* (Philadelphia, 1932).

[5] T. P. Abernethy, *Three Virginia Frontiers* (University, La., 1940), has made a significant modification of Frederick Jackson Turner's theories.

water and moved into the Piedmont in quest of virgin soils. Here they continued the culture of tobacco, which they transported to market by floating the hogsheads in canoes and double canoes (the latter originated in 1749 by the Reverend Robert Rose of Virginia) down the rivers or by rolling them along the ground. In this picturesque method of transportation the hogshead was drawn by a horse hitched by means of a pair of shafts to a pole that pierced the cylinder heads. Numerous yeomen who settled in the Valley of Virginia became wheat farmers, engaged in subsistence farming, for the problem of transportation to the seacoast was so difficult as to discourage the extensive cultivation of tobacco. Still other small farmers occupied the wild lands of southwest Virginia, including the Roanoke Valley region.

In the back country of North Carolina ex-indentured servants and yeoman farmers from Virginia settled on the land as squatters without a legal title. William Byrd II maligned the inhabitants of this region by insinuating that the chief colonizing agents of the rude Carolina frontier were the sheriffs of Virginia who stimulated the emigration of undesirable citizens into the wilderness to the south.[6] The best lands of the Carolina back country were monopolized by rich speculators. Furthermore, the oldest and most populous part of the colony, the Granville Tract, was controlled by the noble Granville family of England. Their agent, located at Edenton, granted land patents and collected quitrents, but he found his job of collecting quitrents from squatters a perilous enterprise. A huge tract of land, "a principality," in western North Carolina was granted in 1736 by the Crown to Henry McCulloh and associates on condition of settling on the land 600 European Protestants within ten years. When the son of the proprietor, Henry Eustace, attempted to survey this domain, on which squatters had located, his agents were beaten by mobs, and eventually he was frustrated in his dream of obtaining a princely revenue from his wild lands in Carolina. Despite the undemocratic system of granting large areas of land to individuals, the North Carolina back country was populated by poor people. Between 1733 and 1754 the population of the colony more than doubled, chiefly by the settlement of the back country, and by the middle of the eighteenth century it contained a white population twice the size of South Carolina's white inhabitants.

The occupation of the back country of South Carolina was artificially stimulated by the provincial government. In 1730 the royal governor, Robert Johnson, secured the adoption of a scheme for the settlement of poor Protestant immigrants in eleven townships on the frontier. The motives for this colonization scheme were to guard the colony from the peril of Indian and Spanish attacks and by increasing the white population to diminish the danger from servile insurrection. So many slaves had been imported into the colony that they formed two thirds of the population and were a constant

6 See William K. Boyd (ed.), *William Byrd's Histories of the Dividing Line Betwixt Virginia and North Carolina* (Raleigh, 1929).

danger to security, which was demonstrated by the Stono insurrection of 1739. Under Governor Johnson's scheme each white immigrant who settled in one of these outlying townships was given fifty acres of land for each member of his household, agricultural tools, a cow and calf for each five persons, provisions for a year, and freedom from payment of quitrents for ten years. Also either the Crown or the colony paid the passage of many of these settlers who located on the exposed frontier. The colony set aside the customs receipts from the duty on slaves as a fund to pay these charges. Attracted by these terms a group of largely French-speaking Swiss in 1735 founded Purrysburg on the Savannah River where they produced silk. Other settlements of Swiss and Germans were made during the decade of the 1730's at Amelia, Saxe Gotha, and Orangeburg. Also Scotch-Irish came directly from Belfast to found Williamsburg township, and Welsh Baptists arrived from Delaware to settle at Queensboro in the Pee Dee Valley. All of these settlements were in the coastal plain below the fall line, where the colonists cultivated wheat, corn, hemp, flax, and indigo. These settlers of this period came through the port of Charleston or from the older settlements of the colony. No other English colony gave such liberal inducements to stimulate immigration.[7]

The hilly region between the fall line and the Blue Ridge was the cradle of the typical American pioneer. It was settled largely by German and Scotch-Irish immigrants, who entered the South from Pennsylvania through the corridor of the Great Valley. The first settler to locate in the northern end of the Shenandoah Valley was Adam Miller, or Müller, from Lancaster, Pennsylvania, who brought a group of German families in 1726 or 1727 to this rich agricultural region. In 1732 Jost Hite led a migration of sixteen families from Pennsylvania to the Valley of Virginia. Most of these Pennsylvania "Dutchmen" had come to the great immigrant port of Philadelphia from the Rhine Valley and from southern Germany. In the old country they had been peasants, badly exploited by their landlords, the remains of whose romantic castles one sees today on a trip down the Rhine. The Germans were driven from their homeland partly because of religious persecution (after the Elector of the Palatinate, John William, had tried to force his people early in the eighteenth century to accept Catholicism) but predominantly by a desire to escape from the low standard of living in the Rhone Valley caused by avaricious landlords and the devastation of invading armies.

When the desirable lands of the Pennsylvania back country had been absorbed, they pushed southward into the Great Valley and spilled over the Blue Ridge into the Piedmont of Virginia and the Carolinas. Entering Maryland, they settled around Hagerstown and Frederick.[8] In the Shenandoah Valley, the towns of Winchester, Stephensburg, Strasburg, and Woodstock

---

[7] R. L. Meriwether, *The Expansion of South Carolina, 1729–1765* (Kingsport, Tenn., 1940).

[8] See Dieter Cunz, *The Maryland Germans, a History* (Princeton, 1948).

became disinctly Germanic in atmosphere.[9] In North Carolina the Pennsylvania Germans settled especially in the Piedmont counties of Rowan, Guilford, Forsyth, and Davidson, with Salisbury as the principal town. Thus a "new Germany of the South" was created, based on a Pennsylvania-German culture rather than the unmodified civilization of the old country.

Only recently have scholars recognized the many valuable contributions to the society of the Southern back country made by non-English stocks.[10] The Germans, for example, brought with them the art of building superior log cabins, constructed of squared rather than round logs and mortised at the ends by a peculiar notch. The German craftsmen of Pennsylvania had developed an effective rifle with a long barrel, later known as the "Kentucky long rifle." In the Conestoga Valley of Pennsylvania they had invented the Conestoga wagon, a durable, covered wagon, which, with some adaptations, became the prairie schooner of the Far West. The skill of the German craftsmen did much to make the back country economically independent of the Tidewater and of the shipment of manufactured goods from Europe. The German immigrants into America brought with them the art of making glazed pottery, and they produced superior tinsmiths, cabinetmakers, wagon makers, tanners, coopers, and ironworkers.

Into the back country of the Southern colonies they imported their churches and German pietism. Many an old father gave his young son emigrating to America a large Gothic Bible inscribed with his blessing. Such an inscription was written on the flyleaf of the Bible of John Conrad Clement, who left Hesse-Darmstadt in 1765 for Pennsylvania and whose children trekked down the Great Valley to the neighborhood of the village of Mocksville in Piedmont, North Carolina, carrying the sacred book with them. The old German father wrote in the Bible given to his son about to depart for America, "if I am no more with thee in body, yet am I with thee in spirit and with my prayers, for prayer is a strong tower against crafty attacks of Satan and of the world and of our corrupt flesh and blood. . . . Be this the end and good night forever. . . . The Spirit of God lead and direct thee and me and us all in his time out of this wearisome and troubled life into the eternal blessed life through Jesus Christ our Lord to whom be praise and honor from eternity to eternity, Amen." [11]

The most interesting group of Germans in the back country were the Moravians, a religious sect officially known as the *Unitas Fratrum,* founded early in the eighteenth century by religious refugees living on the estate of Count Zinzendorf in Moravia. In 1753 they purchased a large tract of land

---

[9] J. W. Wayland, *The German Element of the Shenandoah Valley* (Charlottesville, 1907).

[10] Notably, T. J. Wertenbaker, *The Old South: The Founding of American Civilization* (New York, 1942), chap. V., and Louis Wright, *Cultural Life of the American Colonies* (New York, 1957), chap. 3.

[11] MS in possession of the late Miss Mary Jane Heitman, Mocksville, North Carolina, translated by Adelaide L. Fries.

in the Piedmont region of North Carolina that had been selected by the Moravian Bishop Spangenberg. From their center in America at Bethlehem, Pennsylvania, they sent a group of brothers ahead to build houses and prepare for the migration of families to their new home in the wilderness. Three little German villages, Bethabara, Bethania, and Salem were founded (the last in 1776), destined to become a part of the modern city of Winston-Salem. They erected communal houses, such as the Brothers' House, in which the single men lived, and the virginal Sisters' House, still surviving at Salem, as well as dignified brick churches. Their architecture was sober and Germanic in style, with red tile roofs, arched hoods over the doors, and vaulted cellars. The religion of the Moravians was based on brotherly love and peace, and their graveyards were characterized by uniform, horizontal grave stones, a symbol of the democarcy of the dead. Among their unique ceremonies were a beautiful Easter service at dawn and the Love Feast, in which lighted candles were held by the congregation and Moravian sugar bread was served. Furthermore, they established missions among the Indians and the Negro slaves.[12]

These Pennsylvanian Dutchmen brought with them a deep love for music. The Moravians had trombone choirs that played the fervent, emotional, religious music of the German folk. Also they had a talented organ maker, Joseph Bullitschek, who in 1773 made the organ for the Bethania church, an instrument which is still capable of producing exquisite tones. In the vicinity of the Blue Ridge Mountains of Virginia lived the Germans, Joseph Funk and his sons, who for nearly fifty years made their home, called Singer's Glen, a center not only for teaching music but for publishing music books.

The German settlers were regarded as "odd-looking" people by their English neighbors. They wore wide-brimmed hats with low crowns and peculiarly cut coats without lapels. The Amish and Mennonites among them abstained from the sinful device of buttons, and both the young and the old men grew patriarchal beards. From Pennsylvania they hauled their iron stove plates, decorated with Bible scenes, their dower chests on which were painted birds and tulips (the Persian flower of love), and their quaint Bibles. They continued to eat sauerkraut and doughnuts, to drink clabber milk, and to sleep under feather mattresses. Their weddings were picturesque affairs, somewhat reminiscent of Pieter Brueghel's paintings, in which a prodigious dinner was served and the groomsmen wore white embroidered aprons. Much hilarity was evoked on these occasions by the attempts of the guests to steal the bride's slipper.

Gradually, the German inhabitants gave up their folk art and their, to the other Americans, peculiar customs. At the end of the eighteenth century they began to abandon speaking their original tongue. The churches, Lutheran, German Reformed, Mennonite, Dunker, and Moravian, were the last strong-

---

[12] Adelaide L. Fries (ed.), *Records of the Moravians in North Carolina* (Raleigh, 1922–1947), 7 vols.; *The Road to Salem* (Chapel Hill, 1944).

holds of the German dialects. In 1855 the Moravian Church at Salem stopped keeping the church records in the language of their forefathers. In a number of cases, even the trace of German origin was eradicated by the anglicizing of surnames—Müller becoming Miller; Schmidt, Smith; Klein, Short, Small, or Little; and Hoenes, Hanes.

Although the Germans of the South surrendered in many respects to their environment, they continued their type of agriculture, perhaps their greatest contribution to their adopted land. The English settlers of the Tidewater had pursued a type of agriculture that stripped the soil of its fertility, sacrificing the soil in order to conserve labor and produce a money crop for export. The Germans, on the other hand, practiced a careful and farsighted agriculture. They were skilled in choosing good land for their farms, especially the rich limestone soils. Their lands were conserved by crop rotation, by developing meadows, by preserving their woodlands, and by a careful husbandry of deep plowing and of the use of animal maures. Instead of concentrating on a single exhaustive crop, such as tobacco, they engaged in a diversified subsistence agriculture. It is true that the location of their settlements, distant from markets, contributed to saving them from the absorption in tobacco culture, but their Germanic traditions were also important in their continuance of a thrifty agriculture.[13] Whereas the English farmer exhausted the fertility of his soil and abandoned his farm, the Germans saved the soil and transmitted their farms, undepleted, to their children. Wherever the Germans tilled the land, there stood the large Swiss-style barns, more commodious than their houses. In contrast to these thrifty farmers the English of the Tidewater, according to a French traveler of 1788, "know not the use of barns," providing neither shelter nor hay for their cattle during the winter and thus depriving their families of milk.[14]

Through the Great Valley from Pennsylvania the Scotch-Irish followed the Germans into the back country of the South. The home of these hardy immigrants had been northern Ireland, the Ulster district, to which their forefathers had been transported from lowland Scotland by James I to hold the wild Irish down and make Ireland Protestant. The immigrants who left Belfast for Philadelphia were principally Presbyterian Scotsmen, but they also included an admixture of Celtic Irish and of English who had originally crossed over into the Scottish lowlands, from whence they had gone to northern Ireland. In Ireland these transplanted Scotsmen tilled small farms, which they leased from landlords for one hundred years, and developed a thriving industry of weaving linen and woolen cloth. In the first half of the eighteenth century their leases began to expire and their absentee landlords demanded higher rents—rack rent. Furthermore, the British mercantilists

[13] R. H. Shryock, "Cultural Factors in the History of the South," *Journal of Southern History*, V (August 1939), 341–342.
[14] J. P. Brissot De Warville, *New Travels in the United States of America Performed in 1788* (New York, 1792), 234.

secured the passage of legislation excluding the export of Irish woolens to England, although the linen industry was encouraged. Added to these economic grievances was a religious injustice, the establishment of the Anglican church in this Presbyterian district, which forced the Scotch-Irish to pay taxes to support Anglican clergymen whom they did not desire. Consequently, the Scotch-Irish began to leave Ireland in droves to find new homes in America.[15]

They came in such numbers to the United States during the eighteenth century that they far exceeded the great Puritan immigration into New England of the preceding century. Finding the good lands near the Atlantic seaboard occupied or pre-empted, they were forced to push on to the frontier. In Pennsylvania they founded such towns in the hinterland as Carlisle and Pittsburgh. Then, during the three decades preceding the Revolution, they settled in great numbers in the lower Great Valley and the Southern Piedmont. The route they followed was the Great Philadelphia Wagon Road, 435 miles in length from the Quaker City to its terminus on the Yadkin River in North Carolina, passing through Lancaster and Harrisburg in Pennsylvania, through the Shenandoah Valley, crossing the James River at Looney's Ferry (Buchanan), passing the site of Roanoke to the German settlements in Wachovia, and after 1760 extending to Camden, South Carolina.[16] The migration of John C. Calhoun's ancestors illustrates this epic movement of the Scotch-Irish into the South. The Calhoun family first settled in western Pennsylvania in 1733, then moved to the New River Valley in Wythe County, Virginia, and made a final remove to the frontier region near Abbeville, South Carolina, during the French and Indian War. Calhoun's grandmother was killed by the Cherokee in the course of that war.

The Scotch-Irish had strongly marked characteristics that made them admirably suited to being the cutting edge of the frontier. Tall, angular, with jutting chins and forceful countenances, they were noted for their fighting qualities, their tenacity of will, and their practicality. They were self-reliant and devoted to principle—these serious Presbyterian folk, who often lacked humor, demonstrativeness, and an appreciation for esthetic qualities. Accustomed to turbulent border fighting in Ireland, they made excellent frontiersmen and Indian fighters. They were distinguished from their German neighbors by their zest and capacity in politics. Many Southern statesmen, including several Presidents, were descended from this virile stock—Andrew Jackson, John C. Calhoun, George McDuffie, James K. Polk, the Breckinridges, Andrew Johnson, and Woodrow Wilson.

The Scotch-Irish have been called the blue blood of the South and have perhaps been glorified in Southern tradition. Nevertheless, some of them were described by travelers as shiftless, given to drunkenness and sexual

---

[15] H. J. Ford, *The Scotch-Irish in America* (Princeton, 1915).
[16] Carl Bridenbaugh, *Myths and Realities: Societies of the Colonial South* (Baton Rouge, 1952), 129.

immorality, and unclean in their persons and houses.[17] Coming later than the Germans, they did not have the choice of good lands accessible to market that their predecessors enjoyed, and those among them who exhibited such unattractive qualities may have suffered from a hard struggle to sustain themselves. The majority of the Scotch-Irish settlers brought an element of vigorous industry into the South. Although they readily accepted slavery, they were nevertheless hard working and thrifty farmers, intent on improving their condition in life. They had a tradition of opposition to landlordism that caused them to become a thorn in the flesh of proprietors and quitrent collectors, often squatting on the unoccupied lands and proclaiming that the soil should be free to actual settlers. The Scotch-Irish women brought their spinning wheels and looms from the old country, and one of the important tasks of the Scotch-Irish maidens in the Piedmont was spinning flax and making linen and woolen cloth for the household. The men frequently were distillers of corn liquor and of apple and peach brandy, occupations that apparently did not conflict with their stern Presbyterianism.

Closely related to the Scotch-Irish were the Highland Scot and Welsh settlers. The latter have been ignored by social historians, but some of the South's eminent men, Thomas Jefferson, John Marshall, General George H. Thomas, William L. Yancey ("the orator of secession"), and Jefferson Davis were descendants of Welshmen. The Welsh were usually strong Baptists in religion, and one of the most interesting settlements of the Welsh Baptists was Society Hill (Welsh Neck) in South Carolina, whose St. David's Society established a celebrated academy.

The first of the Highland Scots came over in 1735, in the *Prince of Wales,* which sailed from the port of Inverness to Georgia, bringing one hundred and thirty Highland men and fifty women and children. Their lands in Scotland had been confiscated as a result of participating in Jacobite uprisings. Consequently, they were glad to accept land in America even if it was located on the exposed frontier of the Altamaha River in Georgia. Here they founded the town of New Inverness (later called Darien) near the mouth of the river. They are noted for their opposition to the introduction of slavery in the colony, which was especially urged by the inhabitants around Savannah. The Highland Scots of New Inverness, under the leadership of John Mohr McIntosh, joined with the German settlers at Ebenezer in 1738 to petition the trustees to continue the prohibition of slavery. They produced many valuable citizens of Georgia, notably the great planter Thomas Spalding of Sapelo Island.

The North Carolina contingent of the Highland Scottish immigration came at a later date, following the defeat of "Bonnie Prince Charlie" at the battle of Culloden Moor in 1746 and the cruel suppression of the Scottish rebellion by the Duke of Cumberland. The Highland emigration was also stimulated by the expansion of sheep grazing, which deprived many small farmers of

17 See James G. Leyburn, *The Scotch-Irish, a Social History* (Chapel Hill, 1962).

their livelihood, and by the breakup of the clan system in the eighteenth century, that produced crime and disorder. Then the tacksmen system, by which the tacksman, or chief tenant, would sublet to lesser tenants, resulted in oppression and rack rents, thus increasing unrest in Scotland and emigration to America. The Highland Scots who came to North Carolina settled at Fayetteville (called Cross Creek before the Revolution) on the Cape Fear River. They retained their Gaelic speech and their Presbyterian faith, as well as a fierce loyalty to an oath. At the beginning of the American Revolution, having sworn loyalty to the King, they became Tories and fought valiantly for the royal cause in the battle of Moore's Creek Bridge near Wilmington (February 27, 1776).[18]

This immigrant stock—both Highland Scots and Scotch-Irish—made two extremely valuable contributions to the spiritual life of the South by the introduction of the Presbyterian church and by the impulse they gave to the education of the youth. They remained staunch followers of John Knox, with his fatalistic and gloomy interpretation of the Christian faith. Wherever they went, they established their Presbyterian Church, which emphasized the importance of honesty and truthfulness, the sacredness of a contract or the covenant. Because their church required educated ministers and a laity well-read in the Bible, they were also a great force in establishing academies, and later such colleges as Hampden-Sydney, Washington and Lee, Davidson, and Oglethorpe University in the South and Princeton in New Jersey.

The inhabitants of the back country developed a bitter grievance against the people of the Tidewater, because the latter did not give them a fair share in the control of the government. It was natural that Tidewater planters were not disposed to allow the reins of government to pass into the hands of the newcomers, who arrived in waves of immigration from Pennsylvania. Consequently, the colonial legislatures apportioned representation so that the yeomen of the back country, who owned few slaves, were either not represented at all in the legislature or underrepresented. In Virginia the counties, regardless of size or population, sent two representatives each to the House of Burgesses. The back country counties were much larger than the Tidewater ones, and when they filled up with population, a great inequality of representation resulted. In South Carolina the up-country was practically unrepresented in the legislature and the 25 lowland parishes sent delegates of varying numbers without much correlation to population. Furthermore, the influence of the back country in the making of laws was greatly curtailed in the Southern colonies by the high property qualifications for officeholding and voting. In South Carolina on the eve of the Revolution the members of the General Assembly were required to own five hundred acres in a "settled" plantation and *ten slaves*. The colonial legislatures, thus constituted, ignored pretty much the needs and petitions of the back country. The Tidewater

[18] See Ian C. Graham, *Colonists from Scotland: Emigration to North America, 1707–1783* (Ithaca, 1956).

region was not very responsive to voting taxes for frontier defense, building roads, and improving internal navigation or to freeing the dissenters of the back country from the necessity of paying taxes to support the Anglican Church.

The settlement of the back country (called the upcountry in South Carolina) introduced a vigorous and independent group of yeoman farmers into Southern society, who became the main force in fighting the battles of the common man. It has been estimated that the back country population in 1776 constituted approximately a fourth of the people of Virginia, two fifths of the inhabitants of North Carolina, nearly half of the inhabitants of South Carolina (79 per cent of its white population), and approximately 15 per cent of the population of Georgia.[19] The struggle that arose between the back country inhabitants and the Tidewater squirearchy was really a conflict between two different ways of life, produced in part by geographic differences. The Tidewater was a more mature region than the hinterland, possessing greater wealth and education, closer contacts with Europe, and a greater refinement of life. The back country, on the other hand, was handicapped by difficulties of transportation and consequently was forced to rely upon a subsistence type of agriculture. Except in certain favored river valleys, it was the home of the yeoman and the small farmer.

The most palpable difference between the two sections was the dominance of slave labor in the Tidewater and the prevalence of free labor in the interior. The Germans of the back country, especially, were opposed to the introduction of slavery into their communities. Exceedingly thrifty, these immigrants from Pennsylvania had a contempt for the shiftless slave labor they had observed in the South. Slavery was not adapted to their style of self-sufficient farming, based on wheat, potatoes, barley, oats, hay, and orchard products. Their large families of sturdy sons and buxom, hustling girls afforded an abundance of intelligent and careful labor. Moreover, they were unaccustomed to slave labor when they entered the South, and their churches were opposed to slaveholding on moral grounds. Consequently, in areas with a large German population, such as Shenandoah County, Virginia, and the Salisbury district in North Carolina, only a small percentge of the families held slaves.

Social differences between the back country and the Tidewater were very pronounced. The people of the Tidewater were overwhelmingly English in stock; the inhabitants of the back country, in contrast, had a strong infusion of German and Scotch-Irish blood. The Tidewater gentry tried to imitate the manner of living of the English squirearchy; the inhabitants of the back country, on the other hand, hated snobbery and the pretensions to aristocracy. In the Tidewater the Anglican church was dominant; in the back country, dissenting sects, such as Presbyterians, Lutherans, and Baptists prevailed. The people of the back country felt a sort of inferiority complex in the presence of the more polished Tidewater aristocrats.

[19] Bridenbaugh, *Myths and Realities*, 121.

In Virginia the Piedmont society had by the time of the Revolution become a somewhat diluted extension of the Tidewater society. The great difference in mode of living was between that of the inhabitants of the Valley and the rest of the colony. The inhabitants of the Great Valley and the more primitive regions of the Piedmont were called "Cohees," probably from the uncouth phrase used by them, *Quo(th) he*, and the eastern planters were called "Tuckahoes," from an edible swamp root grown in eastern Virginia. The Tuckahoes were inclined to be hedonistic, loving good wine and companionship; the Cohees, having a different set of values, were too busy tilling their fields to waste time on social pursuits.

A curious light is thrown upon social conditions in the back country of the Carolinas on the eve of the Revolution by the journal of Reverend Charles Woodmason of the Anglican church. This obstreperous individual had emigrated from England to Charleston in 1752. During the first thirteen years of his residence in the colony he devoted himself to material pursuits, acquiring large tracts of land, operating a store in the back country, and holding various small public offices. Suddenly and inexplicably he abandoned his worldly life in Charleston and in 1765 went to England to be ordained as an Anglican missionary to carry religion to the back country. Belonging to the gentry and being well educated, he was shocked by the crudeness and sinful practices of the back country; he found the people largely without the benefit of churches and clergymen, rude in their manners, neglectful of their children (who were usually extremely dirty), and possessing low morals. He estimated that 94 per cent of the women that he married in the back country were pregnant and that nine tenths of the inhabitants had a venereal disease. Woodmason seems, however, to have been prone to exaggeration and hyperbole; his nature was censorious and unhappy, possibly because shortly after his arrival in the colony he was kicked by a horse in a place that rendered him unfitted, as he lamented, "for Nuptial Rites," and his wife in England refused to join him. Perhaps the most significant contribution of his journal is the information that it gives on the un-Christian warfare of the different religious sects and on the conditions that led to the Regulator Movement of 1769.[20]

Woodmason portrays this movement as an uprising of the better citizens of the back country to put down the lawless element by extralegal means. Their primary grievance was that the legislature neglected to establish courts in the back country, so that the inhabitants had to travel long distances to attend court in Charleston. Because this circumstance was profitable to the merchants and tavern keepers of that city, the people of the low country resisted reform of the courts. Nevertheless, the Regulators won their main contention, and judicial districts were created in the back country.[21]

---

[20] Charles Woodmason, *The Carolina Backcountry on the Eve of the Revolution: The Journal and other Writings of Charles Woodmason, Anglican Itinerant*, ed. by Richard J. Hooker (Chapel Hill, 1953).
[21] See Richard M. Brown, *The South Carolina Regulators* (Cambridge, Mass., 1963).

In North Carolina at approximately the same time, the inhabitants of the back country, calling themselves "Regulators" arose to fight the ruling oligarchy.[22] The inhabitants of the Piedmont in this colony had many grievances: their underrepresentation in the legislature, the excessive legal fees charged by corrupt officials, the collection of quitrents, the absorption of the best lands by speculators in the huge Granville tract, the requirement that dissenters pay taxes to support the Anglican Church, and the erection of a magnificent palace at New Bern by Governor William Tryon with the taxes taken from the people. Incited by two popular agitators, Hermon Husband and Rednap Howell, the latter a writer of doggerel satires, the outraged farmers of the back country formed mobs, who interfered with the operation of the courts and attacked hated county officials.[23] The back country lawyer Waightstill Avery recorded in his diary, April 12, 1769: "A Set of Banditti who stiled themselves Regulators had on the evening before brought a large quantity of hickory Switches to menace the Clerk of the court (or Col. Spencer) whom they threatened and flogged his writer." [24]

In May, 1771, Governor Tryon marched westward with an army of a 1,068 men, commanded by an enormous number of commissioned officers, and attacked the Regulators in the battle of Alamance Court House. The Regulator army, an unwieldy mob of about two thousand men, was defeated, and the ringleaders were executed. Some of the defeated Regulators, embittered by the failure of the popular cause, emigrated to the pioneer settlements of east Tennessee.

Thus, during the eighteenth century arose a sectionalism within the Southern colonies that has left enduring traces. An interesting hangover of the pervasive force of such sectionalism was displayed well into the twentieth century at the University of North Carolina, where boys from the western part of the state joined the Dialectic Literary Society, and those from the eastern section, the Philanthropic Society. Political alignments were often determined by the bitter resentments generated by sectionalism. Patrick Henry led the back country patriots in Virginia in the Revolutionary movement against the conservatism of the Tidewater aristocrats. In some communities, the Tories were motivated in siding with the British government by their hatred of the lowland gentry, who joined the patriot cause. Hostile feelings between the East and the West were allayed somewhat by the expansion of slavery and of tobacco and cotton plantations into the Piedmont. But intrastate sectionalism was kept alive until the very end of the antebellum period by quarrels over internal improvements, slave taxation,

---

[22] John Spencer Bassett, "The Regulators of North Carolina (1765–1771), *"Annual Report of American Historical Association for the Year, 1894* (Washington, 1895), 140–212.

[23] William K. Boyd (ed.), *Some Eighteenth Century Tracts Concerning North Carolina* (Raleigh, 1927).

[24] Diary of Col. Waightstill Avery, 1769, North Carolina MSS Draper Collection, Wisconsin Historical Society Library.

public education, and apportionment of representation.[25] Even in the Civil War one of the most important reasons for the existence of Unionism in the Appalachian Highlands was the influence of the deep scars of sectionalism rather than any devotion to the cause of preserving the Union or hatred of slavery.

[25] See Charles H. Ambler, *Sectionalism in Virginia from 1776 to 1861* (Chicago, 1910).

4

The Rise of a Native Aristocracy

ACCORDING to the romantic tradition, the Southern colonies were settled by Cavaliers, or aristocrats. New England, in contrast, was so unfortunate as to be populated by humble folk, particularly the plebeian Round Heads, who fought for Parliament during the Civil War that rent England. In 1649, after King Charles I had been beheaded, Governor Berkeley invited the royalists to seek asylum in Virginia. The historian John Fiske has popularized the idea of an exodus of Cavaliers from England to Virginia, pointing out that the population of Virginia increased from fifteen thousand in 1649, the date of the regicide of Charles I, to thirty-eight thousand in 1660, when the Stuarts were restored to the throne.[1] It seems reasonable to conclude that a larger number of royalists came to Virginia than to Puritan New England, for in Virginia the Anglican church was established and country estates could be acquired. Some of these immigrants were of gentle blood, but the term *Cavalier* was a political designation, including common foot soldiers and tradesmen who supported the king in the Puritan Revolution.

Modern research has discredited the old idea that Southerners were descended principally from Cavalier, or aristocratic, origins, whereas New Englanders came from Round Head, or plebeian, immigrants. Actually, the great majority of immigrants to both areas during the colonial period belonged to the middle or lower classes of Englishmen. Titled persons who made their permanent residence in America were extremely rare. Those who were in a fortunate position in the mother country were unlikely to emigrate to a raw country, which was the haven for the poor, the discontented, and the socially maladjusted. It has been estimated that at least one half of all the white immigrants to the colonies south of New England arrived as indentured servants. An eminent authority on the colonial South, Thomas Jefferson Wertenbaker, has dispelled many illusions concerning the aristocratic origins of the great majority of Virginians, who above all Southerners have prided themselves on descent from gentle blood. The continuous immigration of white indentured servants, who became freemen at the expiration of their terms of indenture, was constantly refreshing the class of yeomen. A study of the quitrent roll of Governor Francis Nicholson of 1704 indicates that 90

[1] John Fiske, *Old Virginia and Her Neighbors* (Boston, 1900), II, 16; T. J. Wertenbaker notes that population in Virginia expanded from fifteen thousand in 1649 to forty thousand in 1662, but attributes this immigration, not to a "Cavalier exodus" from England, but to "the prosperity which attended the economic freedom of the Commonwealth period." *The First Americans* (New York, 1929), 313.

percent of the people of Virginia at that time were small farmers and that 65 per cent of them owned neither slaves nor indentured servants. Indeed, a realistic picture of Virginia in the seventeenth century shows it to be a land of small yeoman farmers, with a sprinkling of large planters.

The Wertenbaker thesis maintains that most of the prominent families of Virginia, the F.F.V.'s, or First Families of Virginia, who attained wealth and prestige in the colonial period were derived from middle-class or bourgeois origins, particularly the merchant class, in England and Scotland.[2] The Byrd family, who developed an elegant style of life at *Westover,* were descended from a London goldsmith, the Blands from a skinner, and the founder of the great Carter family was an immigrant of nameless background. The Lees, the Washingtons, and the Randolphs, however, came from the English squire-archy.[3] The tone of society in Virginia of the seventeenth century was bourgeois rather than Cavalier. In the Southern colonies, as well as in New England, this century has been described as the age of pewter and of small cottages rather than of silver and of Georgian mansions. The aristocratic code of honor and the practice of dueling were absent from the mores of Southerners of the seventeenth century, attaining a vogue only late in the colonial period.

It is probable that modern scholarship has swung to the extreme left in discarding the older Cavalier tradition. Philip Alexander Bruce, in *Social Life of Virginia in the Seventeenth Century,* has brought forward an impressive amount of evidence to show the gentle birth of many Virginia families. Although very few titled persons came to the colony to reside, some younger sons of the gentry and of the nobility emigrated to the tobacco colonies. The laws of primogeniture and entail, which reserved the ancestral estate for the eldest son, necessitated the younger sons' entering trade or the professions or emigrating to the colonies. Consequently, many of the merchants and members of the guilds had the same blood and rearing as the country gentry. Some of the Virginia families were descended from ship captains and from officers of the royalist troops during the Puritan Revolution. Bruce observed that the rent-roll of Governor Nicholson did not apply to the Northern Neck of Virginia, between the Rappahannock and Potomac rivers, where many of the powerful aristocracy were settled. Even in the narrow limits of the settled part of Virginia in the seventeenth century there were at least four hundred and fifty families who owned from one thousand to ten thousand or more acres. Indeed, he concluded, in conflict with the Wertenbaker thesis, that "one in every four families in Virginia at the end of the seventeenth century owned from five hundred acres to twenty thousand acres," a proportion of large landed proprietors comparable to the distribution of the gentry in aristocratic England.[4]

[2] T. J. Wertenbaker, *Patrician and Plebeian in Virginia* (Charlottesville, 1910).
[3] See Burton J. Hendrick, *The Lees of Virginia: Biography of a Family* (Boston, 1935).
[4] P. A. Bruce, *Social Life of Virginia in the Seventeenth Century* (Richmond, 1927), 99.

It is much more to the credit of the Southern aristocracy of the eighteenth century, however, that most of its members arose by their own efforts from virile middle-class stock than that they were transplanted from a decadent aristocracy of the Old World. The development of a native aristocracy in the Southern colonies was aided by the continuous operation of certain powerful forces, the most important of which was the acquisition of large plantations tilled by slaves and protected until the middle of the eighteenth century from disintegration by the laws of primogeniture and entail. In addition, the immigrants from England brought with them a traditional conception of a social stratification. Consequently, it was natural for them to continue in the New World social distinctions, expressed in the titles of address, the yeoman being called "goodman," the gentleman, "Mister," a member of the governor's council, "Esquire," and high civil officials, "Honorable." Military titles also flourished in this truncated society that was devoid of a nobility. Around the royal governor clustered a group known as "the governor's set," composed of the great planters, the Anglican clergy, and the lawyers, who formed the nucleus of the colonial aristocracy. Also merchants who had acquired wealth frequently purchased plantations, married planters' daughters, and thus entered this upper group of colonial society. Indeed, the social position of merchants in the colonial South was very honorable, but in the antebellum period trade and mercantile pursuits were disparaged.

During the decade before the Revolution a new class of lawyers arose in the colonies who became leaders in public affairs. In Maryland, particularly, legal skill was in constant demand by the large planters to protect their vested interests, and accordingly the lawyers in that province became a powerful and affluent group. The lawyers of colonial days learned their law by apprenticeship to an established lawyer, using a textbook the *Institutes of the Laws of England* by "Old Coke," whom Jefferson praised highly as preserving traditions of liberty, whereas Blackstone's text, published 1765–1769, on the other hand, made Tories of later generations of lawyers. The legal profession in the colonial South is admirably mirrored in the manuscript diary of Waightstill Avery, a Connecticut Yankee educated at Princeton, who settled in Mecklenburg County, North Carolina, in 1769. In the practice of his profession he rode from one courthouse to another, often spending the night in "nasty" log cabins, at times losing his way among the woods, the few people he saw too ignorant to direct him, nearly drowning in crossing fords, and suffering from ague and fever. Indeed, his diary pictures a society of strong contrasts on the one side, containing "Gentlemen Merchants," "Gentlemen Attorneys," some of whom were deists, and cultivated planters, and on the other side, rude farmers, who entertained themselves on court days by getting drunk and by fights of "bruising, Goughing, Biting, and balloching." [5]

When Avery arrived in North Carolina, at the time of the Regulator

[5] Diary of Colonel Waightstill Avery, 1769, Draper Collection, North Carolina MSS (Wisconsin Historical Society Library).

troubles, lawyers were bitterly hated, because they were accused of charging excessive fees, despite the law regulating fees. However, the fee book of Avery, which is preserved in the Draper Collection at the University of Wisconsin, indicates that his profits were not exorbitant according to relative standards today—15 shillings for small cases and 1 Pound, 5 shillings, for larger cases. During six months in 1775 he recorded fees totaling £ 164 from 146 cases, which compares favorably with the earnings of Jefferson as a lawyer during this period—£ 147 cash and £ 223 uncollected, from 198 cases in the year 1769.[6]

Aristocratic distinctions were reflected by the marked difference between the dress of the upper class and of the common people. The aristocrats dressed in a lavish and colorful fashion, wearing scarlet, pearl, or yellow vests, waistcoats, knee breeches, and long coats of various colors, silk stockings, ruffles on their shirts, shoes with silver buckles. Toward the close of the seventeenth century the long locks of the Cavaliers were cut off and periwigs, which were very expensive, were donned. They were oiled or greased, and powder was dusted upon them. In the wigwearing days the gentleman put on a linen or worsted nightcap when he laid aside his heavy wig, for otherwise a shorn head would have been a comical sight in my lady's boudoir. By the time of the American Revolution wigs had been abandoned, and aristocrats wore their hair in a queue, powdered, beneath three-cornered cocked hats. "Ladies" wore large hoop skirts, made of rich silks and satins, stays or corsets, high-heeled shoes, and elaborate coiffeurs. Children were dressed very much like grownups.

Members of the poorer class were clad in homespun, or "Osnibrick," a coarse cloth made in Osnabrück, Germany. The men often wore buckskin breeches or leggings, and the women spun and wove out of flax and wool linsey-woolsey cloth, from which they made shapeless dresses. If a common man or woman dared to dress above his class, he was fined, as in New England, for such impudence and extravagance. A tradesman was even fined for participating in the aristocratic sport of horse racing. Democracy in clothes did not arrive until the early part of the nineteenth century, after the French Revolution had popularized the pantaloons of the peasants, and the sansculottes, and stigmatized the breeches of the aristocrats. James Monroe was the last president to wear the knee breeches of the colonial aristocrats.

Although the attractive life of the aristocracy has been extensively portrayed by historians, the history of the poor in the colonial South, as well as in the antebellum period, has been shamefully neglected. This neglect is explained primarily by the lack of easily accessible records and the absence of outstanding leaders. Yet the poor constituted the great majority of the people as Aubrey C. Land has shown by his studies of the amount of tobacco pro-

[6] Clement Eaton, "A Mirror of the Southern Colonial Lawyer: The Fee Books of Patrick Henry, Thomas Jefferson, and Waightstill Avery," *William and Mary Quarterly*, VIII (October 1951), 520–534.

duced on individual farms and by the appraisal of estates in the settlement of wills in the Chesapeake Bay areas in the colonial period. Land found that in the decade of the 1750's, 40 per cent of the tobacco raisers in southern Maryland marketed crops of less than four hogsheads of tobacco (virtually the only money crop they raised) while an additional 40 per cent raised less than ten hogsheads; the large planters constituted only 2 per cent of the growers. This latter group had become "the rich," by commercial activities as well as by planting, operating stores, speculating in land, manufacturing, especially pig iron, and lending money. The whole society was one based on debt to each other and ultimately to British businessmen.[7] Yet little class antagonism surfaced.

The often violent life of the submerged poor came out in records of the county court, whose sessions, which ranked as "among the most prized of colonial entertainments," were attended by half of the population of the county. Here the dramas connected with murders, bastardy, slander, assaults, indentured servants seeking freedom, witchcraft, and cases involving blacks were enacted. The latter received harsh sentences, whereas "the rich," as so often happens in this world, received light sentences or escaped punishment entirely, especially by pleading benefit of clergy in murder cases by the simple expedient of proving that they could read—a vivid testimony to the widespread illiteracy of the colonial South and lingering tradition. The concentration of wealth, the illiteracy of the masses, and the idea of social stratification brought from England made the leadership of the aristocracy prevail.

So dominant was the aristocracy in the Southern colonies during the eighteenth century that travelers hardly deigned to notice the lower classes. Thomas Anburey, a lieutenant in Burgoyne's army, who after the surrender at Saratoga was quartered near Charlottesville, declared that the lower class in Virginia was smaller in proportion to the whole population than perhaps in any country in the world. They dwelt in log cabins that had oiled paper or wooden shutters instead of glass in the windows, wooden or leather hinges on the doors, and chimneys made frequently of wooden sticks held together by clay. Although the journal of Benjamin H. Latrobe, later to become architect of the national Capitol, was written thirteen years after the colonial period had ended, his description of the poor whites of Virginia is probably an accurate picture of the lower class throughout the eighteenth century. He described "the hundreds of half-starved, miserably lodged, idle, besotted and fever-smitten families that inhabit the country on the Potomac, and indeed all the back country of the slave States . . ."[8] They fished and hunted, owned a few pigs and a cow, which were kept at hardly any expense in the woods, cultivated a few acres of land, chiefly raising corn and cabbage. The women

[7] A. C. Land, "Economic Behavior in a Planting Society: The Eighteenth Century Chesapeake," *Journal of Southern History*, XXXIII (November 1967), 469–485.
[8] B. H. Latrobe, *The Journal of Latrobe* (New York, 1905), 34.

were prolific breeders of children and, like Indian squaws, were beasts of burden. The barefooted men did very little labor, but their great source of bliss was whiskey. Some of these poor whites were tenants to great land-owners, particularly in Maryland, or possessed small farms, as did the Germans of the Shenandoah Valley, or hired themselves occasionally as agricultural laborers.

The crudeness of life in the back country is portrayed, perhaps exaggerated, in the journal of the Anglican missionary Charles Woodmason. He has described his congregations in the back country of South Carolina on the eve of the Revolution as follows: "The men with only a thin Shirt and pair of Breeches or Trousers on—barelegged and barefooted—the Women bare-headed, barelegged and barefoot with only a thin Shift and under Petticoat—Yet I cannot break [them] of this—for the heat of the weather admits not of any [but] thin clothing—I can hardly bear the weight of my Whig and Gown, during service. The Young Women have a most uncommon Practise, which I cannot break them of. They draw their Shift as tight as possible to the Body, and pin it close, to shew the roundness of their Breasts, and slender Waists (for they are generally finely shaped) and draw their Petticoats close to their Hips to shew the fineness of their Limbs—so that they might as well be in Puri Naturalibus." [9]

Social stratification was very discernible in the amusements of gentlemen and the ruder diversions of the common people. The aristocrats of the Tide-water were passionately fond of stately dances, such as the minuet and the Virginia reel, of following the latest styles of dress in England, and of travel-ing in their coaches, decorated with coats of arms. They were heavy drinkers and gamblers. One of these aristocrats, George Washington, kept a careful record over a period of four years of his losses and gains at cards, computing a gain of £72 and a loss of £78. They attended cockfights, played billiards, bowled on the green, and were enthusiasts over racing and breeding fine horses. Fox hunting was par excellence the sport of the aristocrats. The red fox was imported, it is believed, about 1680 from England, so that the country gentlemen of Virginia could imitate a distinctive diversion of the English squires.

The lower classes, particularly in the backwoods, found amusement in shooting matches to test their marksmanship and in wrestling and boxing con-tests in which there were no rules of fair play. Biting, scratching, "Abelard-ing," and especially gouging out the eye of an opponent were practiced. Anburey described some ruffians as keeping the nails of their thumbs and second fingers long and pointed, hardening them over a candle flame, in order to be ready to "gouge" more effectively.[10] According to William

[9] Woodmason, *The Carolina Backcountry,* 61.
[10] Thomas Anburey, *Travels through the Interior Parts of America* (London, 1789), II, 349, 375; see also William Tatham, *An Historical and Practical Essay on the Culture and Commerce of Tobacco* (London, 1800).

Tatham, however, the farmers kept their nails long in order more easily to "sucker" tobacco or pinch off the superfluous sprouts. The common people delighted in betting on quarter races, which were different from the longer races over oval tracks patronized by the aristocrats. The quarter races were held on straight courses of one fourth of a mile, usually near "ordinaries," the colonial name for taverns. The common people also enjoyed corn shuckings and logrollings, at which liquor was served; group singing was participated in, and practical jokes were played.

One of the most riotous holidays of the plebeians, as well as of the aristocrats, was muster day. Several times a year the militia was drilled and reviewed by its officers at the various county seats. Every able-bodied freeman between the ages of eighteen and forty-five was enrolled in the militia and required to attend muster or be fined. It was his duty to keep a rifle or a musket and a supply of powder and lead. The colonial militia system encouraged the growth of an aristocratic spirit, for the officers were appointed by the governor from the prominent families. Travelers in the South were impressed by the many captains, majors, colonels, and generals whom they met—a substitute for European titles of nobility. After the Revolution, however, the militia system tended to the growth of a more democratic spirit, for the officers, including even major-generals, were elected. Consequently, there arose a feeling of equality between the privates and the officers and a lack of proper discipline. On muster day the American freemen appeared on the parade grounds in various quaint and ridiculous uniforms, and the musters were accompanied by much drinking, fighting, and electioneering.[11]

The customs of both the upper and the lower classes were powerfully affected by the American environment, which hastened marriages and encouraged large families. John Lawson, who wrote a natural history of North Carolina before he was burned at the stake by the Tuscarora Indians in 1711, observed concerning the Carolina girls: "They marry very young; some at Thirteen or Fourteen; and She that stays till Twenty is reckoned a Stale maid. . . ."[12] Widows with property were snapped up quickly by ambitious suitors in this day of the "belleship of widows."[13] Divorces were not sanctioned by the Anglican church and were therefore rare in the colonial South. A large family of children was an asset in a huge, empty country. The upper class as well as the common people were very prolific, but there was an appalling amount of infant mortality among both the whites and the blacks. Mrs. Robert Carter, the gracious mistress of *Nomini Hall,* had seventeen children; Patrick Henry was a member of a family of nineteen; Henry Clay's mother had sixteen children; and John Marshall was one of fifteen children.

[11] For a humorous, yet realistic, description of the muster, see Augustus B. Longstreet, *Georgia Scenes* (Augusta, Ga., 1835).

[12] John Lawson, *The History of Carolina, Containing Exact Description and Natural History of that Country* [1718] (Raleigh, 1860), 143.

[13] The pragmatic view of marriage in the colonial South is reflected in E. Pinckney (ed.), *The Letterbook of Eliza Lucas Pinckney* (Chapel Hill, 1972).

Women in the American colonies either willingly or perforce accepted male dominance. Nevertheless, there was many a spirited lady, such as William Byrd's first wife, who put up a stiff fight to live her own life. Byrd quarreled furiously with her when, in a fit of temper, she beat one of her slaves with a pair of tongs, and again when she extravagantly ordered a long list of luxurious goods from England, and on another occasion when she differed with him in regard to the new method of singing psalms. He reveals his childish desire to be the cock of the walk in his account of an altercation with Mrs. Byrd because she wished to pluck her eyebrows before going to the governor's ball: "My wife and I quarreled about her pulling her brows. She threatened she would not go to Williamsburg if she might not pull them; I refused, however, and got the better of her, and maintained my authority." [14] Occasionally, a Southern woman, such as Eliza Lucas in South Carolina or Margaret Brent in Maryland, overcame great obstacles and participated in the world of affairs, which was dominated by the lordly males.

The legal position of women in the colonial South, as in New England, reflected attitudes that went back through the Middle Ages to Biblical times. The English common law, which prevailed in the colonies, recognized male supremacy, so that a husband could legally administer reasonable chastisement to his wife by whipping her. The married woman could not make a will or a contract or sue in court, and in case of divorce the husband was entitled to the custody of all the children. The husband acquired all the property that his wife owned or inherited and also any wages she might earn. The single woman, however, had the right to sue, make contracts and wills, and control her property. A widow was entitled to a dower in her husband's estate of one third of his personal property and the use for life of one third of his lands and slaves. The independence of women today would have shocked our ancestors, who held with *The Spectator* that "separate purses between man and wife" were "as unnatural as separate beds." [15]

The household routine of our colonial forefathers seems remote from modern habits. Cooking was done in the large open-hearth fireplace of the kitchen, which on the Southern plantations was detached from the house. Dinner was served at three o'clock in the afternoon. The numerous flies were brushed away by little Negro boys with peacock-tail fans. In the evening after supper the planter might, as William Byrd II reported, "prattle with the ladies and drink whipped syllabub." At nine o'clock he usually retired to his high canopied bed, but his rest was likely to be disturbed by bedbugs, for the slovenly servants, even in the homes of the most elegant aristocrats, did not keep the houses very clean. Baths were not taken often, although William Byrd (and later Thomas Jefferson) made it a rule to wash his feet daily.

[14] Louis B. Wright and Marion Tinling (eds.), *The Secret Diary of William Byrd of Westover, 1709–1712* (Richmond, 1941), 296.
[15] Julia C. Spruill, *Women's Life and Work in the Southern Colonies* (Chapel Hill, 1938), 366.

In the stately homes of the Virginia and Carolina Tidewater, there was a juxtaposition of inherited British culture and the crude frontier. The legend of the aristocratic colonial South has suppressed the crudities and played up the elegancies, presenting a stage version, lit dimly by romantic candlelight. On the other hand, the diary of William Byrd reveals the colonial aristocrat to have been more of the hard-working, ambitious, and self-seeking type of man than the gay Cavalier. This bewigged planter on occasion played the stock role of the polished eighteenth-century British gentleman, but he also could be so undignified as to kick the slave cook out of the dining room at *Westover* because she brought in the bacon half cooked. Moreover, the frank sensuality of Byrd's diary reminds one of the *London Journal* of James Boswell, particularly in its references to sexual adventures with Negro slaves and chambermaids in taverns (Dr. Louis Wright, editor of the diary, has commented that it was surprising how many chambermaids turned the Virginia aristocrat down).

The folkways of the American people—both of the aristocrats and the commoners—were illustrated in the medical practice of colonial days. Great faith was placed in concoctions, brews, and elixirs, consisting of such revolting ingredients as toads, snails, snakes, urine, and cow and hen dung, mixed with various herbs like rosemary and lavender. The sovereign herb was ginseng, whose root was dug in the wilds of the Southern colonies. William Byrd II, an amateur scientist and a member of the Royal Society, praised it extravagantly as a panacea for practically all ailments except declining virility. It was exported in large quantities from Southern ports and was much desired by Chinese physicians. Actually, the ginseng root had little medical value except for its psychic effects on believers in its efficacy. As for obstetrics, it was practiced largely by midwives, contributing to a very high mortality rate among infants and mothers. Physicians in the colonial South had to learn their craft as a rule by an apprenticeship to an established physician. The German physician Johann David Schoepf in 1783 described a typical country doctor who lived in Edenton, North Carolina, a town of one hundred frame houses. The doctor had an apothecary shop in which he sold little besides tartar emetic, flowers of antimony, saltpetre, and Peruvian bark.

Practitioners of the eighteenth century resorted to heroic measures of empiricism, relying mainly on bleeding, purging, and blisters. George Washington had a strong and hearty constitution, but in his last illness in 1799 he could not survive the ignorant medical practice of his age. On a snowy December day he came from a tour of his plantation and sat down to dinner without changing his wet clothes. As a consequence, he developed a sore throat and a bad cold. To combat his sickness he was bled four times, losing at the first bleeding a half pint of blood. His power of resistance was further weakened by doses of calomel and by blisters. It is not strange that the great man died under such treatment. Remarkable is the contrast between the age when people were bled during illness and our own time when patients are strengthened by blood plasma and extra blood from blood banks.

Gout was almost a class disease of the colonial aristocracy. Colonel Robert Carter described its ravages in a letter to his London factor of March, 1720, in which he wrote that he had been confined to his chamber for a "sennight" after the disease had made him lame with a swollen ankle and instep that were very painful.[16] Another self-made Virginia aristocrat, Colonel William Fitzhugh, explained why he was exempt from the ailment: "I never much frequented Bacchus Orgyes & always avoided Adoration to Ceres shrine, & never was one of Venus Votarys: To speak plainly to you, I never courted unlawfull pleasures with women, avoided hard drinking as much as lay in my power, & avoided feasting & consequently the surfeits occasioned thereby. . . ." [17]

The two most useful medical discoveries made during the colonial period (by accident) were the introduction of cinchona, or Peruvian bark, as a specific for malaria, and the adoption of the practice of inoculation to prevent or lessen the ravages of smallpox. The Peruvian Indians had discovered a remedy for malaria by using a native bark, which was named cinchona after the wife of the Viceroy of Peru, who brought this medicine in 1640 to Spain, whence fourteen years later it was carried to England. The method of inoculating persons to prevent smallpox was imported by Lady Mary Wortley Montagu from Constantinople into England, from whence it was introduced into Boston about 1720 by Cotton Mather and Dr. Zabdiel Boylston. This innovation provoked bitter opposition from the conservative clergy, who regarded this Turkish practice as an interference with the inscrutable ways of Providence.

The Southern colonies had the crudeness and shortcomings, as well as the virtues, of a new country. The observations of Durand of Dauphiné, a Huguenot gentleman who landed in Tidewater Virginia in 1686, point to this condition. He crossed the ocean with a group of immigrants who were to be sold as indentured servants, including "twelve prostitutes & fifteen of the boldest & most insolent young scoundrels in England." He found a distinct difference between the lower class and the gentry, as did Janet Schaw almost a century later when she visited North Carolina and wrote her delightful *Journal of a Lady of Quality*.[18] The former were rude and uncivil, disposed to fleece the foreigner, while the latter were very hospitable. All classes were heavy drinkers of rum, brandy, punch, and wine, and "every body smokes, men, women, girls, and boys from the age of seven years." Durand was impressed by the laziness of the people and the vast amount of time they consumed in visiting each other. He observed the harshness of the legal code: "Robbery is punished so severely that if a man is convicted of having stolen

[16] Louis B. Wright (ed.), *Letters of Robert Carter, 1720–1727, The Commercial Interests of a Virginia Gentleman* (San Marino, Calif., 1940), 86.

[17] Richard Beale Davis (ed.), *William Fitzhugh and His Chesapeake World, 1676–1701; The Fitzhugh Letters and Other Documents* (Chapel Hill, 1963), 366.

[18] Charles M. Andrews and Evangeline W. Andrews (eds.), *Journal of a Lady of Quality* (New Haven, 1934).

a chicken, he is hanged." [19] This new land had execrable roads, zigzag rail fences, the signs of a thriftless agriculture, and swarms of mosquitos and prevalent malaria, and in contrast to Europe, lack of towns. At the same time the French traveler was impressed by the beauty and fertility of the country, its cheap or free land, its freedom from beggars, and its religious toleration.

Dr. Alexander Hamilton's *Itinerarium,* perhaps the best travel account of the colonial period, makes some comparisons between the societies of the Southern and Northern colonies which give a valuable perspective. Hamilton was a well-educated Scotch physician who practiced medicine at Annapolis. In 1744 he made a leisurely trip for the sake of his health from Annapolis to Boston, which he described with humor and with a penetrating insight into the character and manners of the American colonists. He discovered that medical science in the Northern colonies was as primitive as in the Southern colonies. "The doctors here [at Albany] are all barbers," he wrote in disdain of their empiric trade of dosing and of shaving. He noted wretchedly poor people on his route, families who ate out of a dish without fork, spoon, or knife, ignorant and relentlessly inquisitive rustics of New England, comparable to the poor farmers below the Potomac, and the prevalence of hard drinking, tobacco chewing, and immoderate swearing. At the conclusion of his *Itinerarium,* he summarized his observations by noting that he had found little difference between the various provinces in the manners and character of the people, especially as to politeness and humanity, but that the Northern colonies were better settled than Maryland, healthier, and more civilized in the large towns.[20]

A truthful picture of Southern society in the eighteenth century cannot omit the prevalence of idleness and laziness among many of the people. Harry Toulmin, a traveling English minister, observed in Tidewater Virginia in 1793 the ennui of little villages abounding with "indolent young men, who have no religion and no business, and who kill their time no more than perhaps six days in the week at a public billiard table." [21] He explained this phenomenon as produced by slavery and a warm climate. But this curse of the South continued long after the end of slavery, until the spread of education, the improvement of transportation, better health, and wider industrial opportunities lessened the stagnation of ruralness.

The most striking social fact about the Southern colonies in the eighteenth century was that from the plantations was emerging a remarkable class of gentlemen, who were to become leaders of the American Revolution. Durand had drawn charming vignettes of some of the planters of the late seventeenth century, such as Ralph Wormeley of *Rosegill* and Colonel William Fitzhugh

---

[19] Durand of Dauphiné, *A Frenchman in Virginia* (Privately Printed, 1923), 114.

[20] Alexander Hamilton, *Hamilton's Itinerarium* (St. Louis, 1907), 199–200; a more modern edition edited by Carl Bridenbaugh is entitled *Gentleman's Progress, The Itinerarium of Dr. Alexander Hamilton, 1744* (Chapel Hill, 1948).

[21] Harry Toulmin, *The Western Country in 1793* (San Marino, Calif., 1948), 30.

of *Eagle's Nest*. Wormeley had studied at Oxford and was a hospitable and cultivated gentleman. When Durand approached *Rosegill* he thought he was entering a large village, for the house of the planter was surrounded by so many outbuildings. Wormeley owned a vast amount of land in scattered plantations, but his labor force consisted of only twenty-six slaves and twenty indentured servants. Colonel Fitzhugh illustrated the lavish hospitality of the planters when he entertained a group of twenty unexpected guests, furnishing them with beds, as well as quantities of alcoholic beverages, and sending for three fiddlers, a jester, a tightrope dancer, and an acrobat who tumbled around.

Fitzhugh was a typical example of the progenitor of an aristocratic family in Virginia. The son of a woolen draper, he emigrated to Virginia in approximately 1673. Here he shrewdly practiced his profession of the law, married a girl eleven years old, who brought him a dowry of land and slaves, and before his death in 1701, at the age of fifty, had laid a firm economic foundation for prestige and advancement of his family. His progress upward into the gentry was marked by appointment to the office of justice of peace, election to the House of Burgesses, and appointment as land agent of Lord Culpeper, the proprietor of the Northern Neck of Virginia. Ambitious to attain high status in the Chesapeake Bay society, he purchased a coach and instructed his tobacco factor in England to invest his surplus funds in silver marked with a coat of arms. "I esteem it as well politic as reputable," he wrote, "to furnish myself with an handsome Cupboard of plate, which gives myself the present use & Credit, is a sure friend at a dead lift, without much loss, or is a certain portion for a Child after my decease. . . ." [22]

The diary of Landon Carter of *Sabine Hall,* born in 1710, died in 1778, reveals some surprising aspects of planter life in the eighteenth century that are at variance with the stereotype. Carter studied for five years in England and his father, "King Carter," at first thought of apprenticing his bright son of "agreeable obliging behaviour" to a London business house "to breed him up a Virginia merchant," a fact that indicates that the aristocracy at this time did not denigrate trade. Instead, Landon Carter became a hard-working planter, the inheritor of eight plantations equipped with slaves. Through the rest of his life he carefully supervised his plantations and practiced intelligent agriculture with the exception of his prejudice against using plows and his insistence until the latter part of his life that his slaves cultivate the tobacco fields with hoes. The myth of the Virginia aristocracy has the planters living a carefree, hedonistic life of gaiety. The reverse was true of Carter and doubtless of many other planters, for there was a strong strain of puritanism in him. He believed in the Puritan ethic of work; he was introspective ,and thought that men in general were evil; his diary is full of condemnation of gambling, hard drinking, the concern for fashionable clothes, extravagance, permissive parents, and the pursuit of pleasure. Although he was very reli-

[22] Davis (ed.), *William Fitzhugh,* 246.

gious, he was a severe master who often whipped the slaves and considered them "devils." He would entertain the Lees and Randolphs at *Sabine Hall* but would serve no wine (imagine their disappointment!). He tortured himself in grieving over the delinquencies of his children, especially "Wild Bob," a playboy who spent his nights gambling and drinking and his days sleeping, seldom ever reading a book, while his daughters were constantly "figiting" from one Virginia home to another and attending the horse races.

Carter's virtues were his strong sense of public duty as a justice of the peace and member of the House of Burgesses, his industry and thrift, which kept him largely out of debt while many of his fellow planters were burdened with debt to their English factors, and his indomitable sense of independence. It was perhaps this latter quality that made him one of the foremost planters in opposing the English Parliament's taxation of the colonies and in writing pamphlets in support of their constitutional position. Nevertheless, he denounced Tom Paine's *Common Sense* as too rash, preferring instead to give the British government an opportunity to redress the colonial grievances. Carter was opposed both to an aristocratic government and to a government controlled by men who sought popularity. His son Bob displeased him when he, as well as Francis Lightfoot Lee, in seeking election to the Convention of 1776 "kissed the arses" of the people, who nevertheless defeated them.[23] The fact that Carter himself was defeated three times before he was elected to the House of Burgesses and was later "thrown out" of the legislature because he refused to cultivate the people, throws some light on whether colonial Virginia was an aristocracy of a democracy. At the end of his life Carter was a disappointed and bitter man who felt that he had not been properly recognized for his abilities; he was constantly plagued by unreliable overseers, exasperating slaves, the ravages of his crops by piss ants, grasshoppers, rust, and bad weather, the callous behavior of his children toward him, the ills of advancing age (his left arm became so incapacitated that he could not raise it to pick his nose). He was constantly practicing an empiric medicine on himself, his familly, his slaves, and neighbors. Indeed, his diary raises the question of how serene was the life of a majority of the planters.

The most honorable position a planter in the colonial period could attain, was to become a member of the colonial council. This governing board was composed of twelve or more men, recommended by the governor but appointed by the king, usually for life. Chosen from the leading planters, the members exercised great control over the administration by virtue of their wealth, prestige, and knowledge of local conditions. According to Leonard Labaree, in *Conservatism in Early American History,* twenty-three families contributed nearly two thirds of the membership of the Virginia Council between 1680 and the beginning of the Revolution.[24] Furthermore, these fami-

---

[23] J. P. Greene (ed.), *The Diary of Colonel Landon Carter of Sabine Hall* (Charlottesville, 1965), II, 108–109.
[24] Leonard Labaree, *Conservatism in Early American History* (New York, 1948).

lies were bound into close relationship by marriages. The Council formed the upper house of the legislature, served as the advisory body for the governor, and acted as the supreme court of the colony. The only appeal from its decisions in civil cases was to the King—in cases involving over £300. This clique of wealthy colonials usually sided with the governor in the struggle with the lower house of the legislature, but occasionally they supported the popular cause, as in 1635, when the Virginia Council deposed Governor Sir John Harvey and sent him back to England. One of the coveted advantages of belonging to the Council was that, with the governor, it exercised the authority of making large land grants, and the powerful gentry on the Council were not at all backward in logrolling to help each other acquire vast land-holdings.[25]

Another highly regarded and coveted position in the colonies was membership in the lower house of the legislature, in Virginia called the House of Burgesses, and in South Carolina, North Carolina, and Georgia, the House of Commons. It was composed in Virginia of two representatives from each of the counties and from the towns of Jamestown, Williamsburg, and Norfolk and one representative from the College of William and Mary. The privilege of voting for members of the legislature was usually confined to freeholders or owners of fifty acres of unsettled land, or twenty-five acres upon which a house was built, and to townsmen who owned a house and lot. In Maryland the qualification for voting was a fifty-acre freehold or ownership of £40 sterling of personal estate; but in 1718 Catholics were disfranchised. Although land was cheap, such property requirements undoubtedly excluded a large proportion of the adult white males from voting. In Virginia, it has been estimated, only half of them could qualify, and of this number not more than half actually exercised the right of suffrage.[26] Thus in this colony there was only a slight check by the people as a whole upon the colonial government especially because the election for members of the legislature was the only election held. Consequently, the gentry controlled the lower house of the legislature as well as the Council.

A Virginia election in the eighteenth century has been vividly described by Colonel Robert Munford in *The Candidates; or the Humors of a Virginia Election* (1770), the first American comedy.[27] The elections were held at the county seat, to which the voters often had to ride twenty-five miles or more.

[25] See Carl Bridenbaugh, *Seat of Empire, the Political Role of Eighteenth Century Williamsburg* (Charlottesville, 1958).

[26] On the other hand, Chilton Williamson's study, *American Suffrage from Property to Democracy, 1760–1860* (Princeton, 1960), chap. 2, reveals a considerably larger colonial electorate than had been previously thought. He shows that in North Carolina at the close of the colonial period in some counties as high as 83 per cent of the adult white males held as much as fifty acres of land and were qualified to vote and in Virginia, in the Northern Neck, one fourth of the adult males were leaseholders and tenants who should be included in the electorate.

[27] Edited by J. B. Hubbell and Douglas Adair, *William and Mary Quarterly,* Third Series, *V* (April 1948), 217–257.

The sheriff presided while the candidates sat at the ends of a long table. Each voter would approach the table and announce his choice by voice, which was then recorded by the county clerk. Thereupon the favored candidate would arise, doff his hat, and thank the voter personally. This custom gave the voter a sense of consequence as well as enhanced the influence of the gentry over the votes of poor and ignorant men. Seldom did the candidates of this era make political speeches to win votes, and it was against the custom for candidates to vote for themselves. They did, however, treat the voters with liquor and at times with public balls and dinners. When Washington was a candidate for the House of Burgesses, for example, he provided both liquor and a supper and ball for the voters. Douglas Southall Freeman, in his biography of Washington, notes the astounding fact that Washington's agent, in treating the voters, dispensed 160 gallons of alcoholic beverages to 391 voters and some hangers-on, or more than a quart and a half per voter. This practice of treating the voters with rum punch was called "swilling the planters with Bumbo." A candidate for the House of Burgesses was not confined to offering himself to the voters of his own county; Washington, for example, a resident of Westmoreland County, was elected to represent Frederick County in the West, and Patrick Henry was elected to the legislature from Louisa County rather than from his home county of Hanover.

Charles S. Sydnor has shown in his study *Gentlemen Freeholders: Political Practices in Washington's Virginia* that the members of the Virginia legislature came almost exclusively from the gentry or the influential families. The gentry exercised decisive influence in choosing members of the House of Burgesses by the use of various devices: (1) *viva voce* voting; (2) plural voting—a man could vote in any county where he held property; (3) the custom of treating the voters, a practice usually beyond the means of the poor man; and (4) the discriminating power of the sheriff in conducting the elections.[28]

One of the strongest props of the Southern aristocracy was their control over local government. This began with their dominance over the parishes, the smallest unit of local government. The county of the Tidewater was subdivided into two or three parishes, which were both religious and governmental divisions. In the thinly settled western districts, however, there was frequently only one parish to a county. The executive body of the parish was the vestry, consisting of twelve of the leading members of the Church of England or the Episcopal Church. Originally elected by the people, the vestry was converted into a closed corporation that filled vacancies in its membership by co-option. The vestrymen selected the clergyman, administered the parish glebe, or church land, looked after the poor, decided various church matters, apportioned the parish taxes, and presented lawbreakers to the county court.[29]

[28] Charles S. Sydnor, *Gentlemen Freeholders: Political Practices in Washington's Virginia* (Chapel Hill, 1952).
[29] Philip A. Bruce, *Institutional History of Virginia in the Seventeenth Century* (New York, 1910).

In this basic unit of local government, modeled after the English shire, the aristocracy was strongly entrenched. In South Carolina the normal functions of the counties were performed by the parishes, of which there were twenty-five during the colonial period. The county governments that operated in the colonial and antebellum periods were remarkable instances of the union of executive, legislative, and judicial functions in the hands of one political body. Later the idea of the separation of governmental powers became a cardinal principle of American political theory, but actually the organization of the county governments continued to ignore this theory. In each county there were between ten and fifteen justices of the peace, appointed by the governor for an indefinite period, usually for life. These amateur judges tried petty cases individually, but once a month they met at the county seat and constituted a court to try the more serious cases, and every three months they came together as the Court of Quarterly Sessions. The law that they recognized was the common law of England as modified and expanded by the colonial statutes. Not only did this group form a judicial body but it also exercised administration functions, such as apportioning local taxes, supervising the roads, and issuing certificates for land grants.

The county courts have been aptly described as little "county oligarchies." They enlarged their powers by precedent and custom; for example, the governor theoretically appointed the justices of the peace, but actually by virtue of custom he followed the recommendation of the county courts in appointing new justices, so that in effect the county courts became self-perpetuating bodies. Moreover, they obtained control of the actual appointment of all the county officers, the sheriff, county clerk, coroner, militia officers, and so on, for the governor commissioned only those who were recommended by the court. The sheriff, appointed technically by the governor annually, collected the taxes levied by the county court, for which he received a fee of 10 per cent, arrested criminals, had charge of the jail, executed orders of the county court, summoned jurors, and supervised the election of the burgesses.

The composition of the county courts reflected clearly the aristocratic structure of Virginia society and government in the eighteenth century. The justices of the peace were chosen almost exclusively from the county gentry. Sydnor's researches have established the fact that of the sixteen hundred justices appointed in Virginia during the twenty years preceding the Revolution four hundred and twenty came from fifty-five prominent families. Although the justices and their families constituted approximately only 2 per cent of the white population, they owned 22.3 per cent of the coaches (with coats of arms painted on them), the emblem of aristocracy, a costly luxury partly because of the carriage tax.[30]

The aristocratic nature of local government in the South should be viewed

---

[30] This view of the dominance of the aristocracy in Virginia has been challenged by R. E. and B. K. Brown in *Virginia, 1705–1786: Democracy or Aristocracy?* (East Lansing, Mich., 1964), but I think the correct view of the structure of government and society in the Southern colonies recognizes the existence of both democratic and aristocratic elements, the latter predominating.

in the light of English tradition and the lack of education of the masses. It was not an ideal system; indeed, Jefferson criticized it and believed that the New England town meeting system was much superior.[31] A weakness in aristocratic control of government in Virginia was glaringly revealed at the death of Speaker of the House of Burgesses, John Robinson, in 1766. He was one of the wealthiest men in the colonies and had held the positions of Speaker and Treasurer for a period of twenty-eight years. The speaker had become so powerful and secure in office that there was virtually no check on him by the legislature. When his financial affairs were investigated after his death, it was discovered that he had loaned large sums of money of the colony that were in his keeping, totaling £100,761, to members of the House of Burgesses and the Council, largely residents of the Tidewater. The largest individual sum loaned was £14,291 to William Byrd III, whom David J. Mays, the biographer of Edmund Pendleton, the executor of the Robinson estate, has described as lacking the ability of the earlier Byrds and moreover as being "unlucky at cards." [32] Robinson rescued many of the ruling class from financial distress by his cavalier treatment of the public treasury. Despite this notable case of laxity (in which the kind and affable Robinson had not personally profited from his loans of public money to friends), the aristocratic system of government worked well in the Southern colonies. It had a large role in developing a spirit of public service in the ruling class and in training a remarkable group of leaders who came to the forefront during the Revolution and in the making of the Constitution of 1787.

[31] Jefferson might well have been surprised at the findings of a recent article by W. F. Willingham, entitled "Deference Democracy and Town Government in Windham, Connecticut, 1755 to 1786," *William and Mary Quarterly*, XXX, No. 3, July 1973, which shows by quantification methods that although the people could vote, they chose their "betters," the prominent citizens, to office; and accordingly the actual practice with respect to aristocratic leadership in Connecticut towns closely paralleled the situation in the colonial South.

[32] David J. Mays, *Edmund Pendleton, 1721–1803, A Biography* (Cambridge, Mass., 1952), 2 vols.

5

The Embellishment of Life

ALTHOUGH THE SOUTHERNERS of the colonial period were in the main provincials, the upper class developed an appealing culture that owed much to English influence. The wealthy Southerners refined and embellished their lives by the importation of books from England in the returning tobacco ships; they sought to give their sons a Renaissance type of education; they aspired to live like English country gentlemen—a formative ideal; they built beautiful homes, furnished with engraved silver, candelabras, and elegant mahogany furniture; they had their portraits painted; they sought through the church, especially the Church of England, to improve their spiritual life; and they developed a peculiarly Southern emphasis on the art of conversation, hospitality, and polished manners. All of this elegance did exist, but only among a very small class of privileged persons who also displayed great contrasts of crudities and incongruities, as the diaries of William Byrd II and Landon Carter reveal.

The Marquis de Chastellux, who visited Thomas Jefferson at Monticello in 1782, wrote that Jefferson was "the first American who has consulted the Fine Arts to know how he should shelter himself from the weather." [1] This sprightly bon mot was far from the truth, for it ignored the numerous elegant homes built by the Tidewater aristocracy before the Revolution. While the Tidewater planters were evolving an aristocratic type of society and government they were also adapting English architecture to the American environment. The first settlers built cabins of vertical logs, instead of the familiar cabins of the American frontier with horizontal logs daubed with clay, or they constructed half-timbered cottages with thatch roofs reminiscent of the English countryside. Later they built unpainted frame houses with roofs of clapboard shingles and chimneys at the ends instead of the middle of the house, as were common in the colder climate of New England. These comparatively small houses represented a survival of mediaeval or Gothic architecture, which lingered for a surprisingly long period in the Tidewater South, even beyond the eighteenth century. Characteristic of this style were thick walls, the cross design of the homes of the squires, the overhang, casement windows with diamond-shaped panes, and gable roofs. The churches, such as St. Luke's at Smithfield, Virginia, probably the oldest Protestant church building in the New World, were also Gothic in architecture, adorned with

[1] Francois Jean, Marquis de Chastellux, *Travels in North America in the Years 1780, 1781, and 1782,* ed. by Howard C. Rice, Jr. (Chapel Hill, 1963), II 391.

Carter's Grove, near Williamsburg, Virginia, built by an architect brought from England by Carter Burwell. In a room in this mansion Rebecca Burwell rejected the suit of Thomas Jefferson. (Courtesy of Library of Congress)

massive square towers and Gothic arches. Relatively few buildings in the seventeenth-century Southern colonies were constructed of brick, partly because of the difficulty of procuring lime for mortar. Two of the rare brick edifices of this century that have survived are the Adam Thoroughgood cottage in Princess Anne County and the so-called Bacon's Castle, south of the James River, near Williamsburg, a medieval-looking manor house with steep roof, chimney containing three stacks, and Flemish curved gable ends.[2]

In the eighteenth century a new style of architecture arose in the colonies that expressed the wealth and stately elegance of the aristocracy. This new style was imported from England and was called Georgian after the name of the three Georges who ruled England from 1714 to 1820. The planters selected their designs from the English architectural books, such as those written by James Gibbs and Batty Langley. The work of the great English architects, Indigo Jones and Sir Christopher Wren, profoundly influenced American colonial architecture. Indeed, the first important Georgian building

[2] See T. T. Waterman and J. A. Barrows, *Domestic Colonial Architecture of Tidewater Virginia* (Chapel Hill, 1947); and H. C. Forman, *The Architecture of the Old South: The Medieval Style, 1585–1850* (Cambridge, Mass., 1948).

Brafferton Hall, College of William and Mary, completed in 1723. (Courtesy of Colonial Williamsburg)

in the South, Brafferton Hall at William and Mary College, was designed by Sir Christopher Wren or a disciple, and completed in 1723.

In contrast to the Gothic houses of the seventeenth century, the Georgian houses were symmetrical, usually rectangular in shape, and more commodious. On the exterior the Georgian house was adorned with classic details, beautiful classic doorways, large symmetrical sash instead of casement windows, dormer windows, cornices, balustrades on the roofs, pilasters, and so on. Some of these mansions, such as the Brewton House in Charleston and *Shirley* in the James River Valley, had exquisite double-decker porticoes supported by white classic pillars. The Southern mansions were built for coolness, containing a large central hallway, high ceilings, chimneys on the end walls, and detached kitchens. The interiors of these Georgian homes were characterized by elegant simplicity, expressed in the white paneling, classic mantels, and beautiful stairways. Although this architecture of the Georgian period was an imitation of the current English style and had little originality, it nevertheless produced beautiful and dignified homes, an ideal setting for the well-poised aristocrats of the eighteenth century.[3]

The lover of colonial architecture can find two notable shrines of Georgian

[3] S. F. Kimball, *Domestic Architecture of the American Colonies and of the Early Republic* (New York, 1927); and Oliver W. Larkin, *Art and Life in America* (New York, 1960).

architecture at Williamsburg and at Annapolis, Maryland. Williamsburg has been restored, not to say glorified, as a colonial village by the wealth of John D. Rockefeller, Jr. One of the most appealing buildings of Old Williamsburg was the Governor's Palace, similar to Eaton Hall in England, of seventeenth-century Renaissance style. Other notable edifices were the Capitol, which was designed in 1699, the so-called Christopher Wren building on the campus of William and Mary College, and the Raleigh Tavern, built in 1735, where young Tom Jefferson danced with the entrancing Rebecca Burwell, who rejected his suit, and where many of the Revolutionary meetings took place. In Annapolis the Georgian style flowered in such homes as the Hammond House, one of the most exquisite houses in America, designed and built by an indentured artisan, William Buckland, the Chase House, and the Paca House. No account of Georgian architecture in America should neglect *Gunston Hall* on the Potomac, the home of George Mason (completed in 1759), with its Chinese Chippendale interior, or the lovely *Westover,* residence of the Byrds on the James River. In North Carolina at New Bern, the colonial capital, Governor William Tryon erected a magnificent palace in the Georgian style. He brought over from England a master builder, John Hawks, who completed it in 1770. (Partially destroyed by fire in 1798, the palace has been lavishly reconstructed.) Outside of these homes were charming gardens of the formal English type, with boxwood borders, neatly clipped and pruned, growing herbs for the medicine chest, and sweet-smelling flowers, such as the gardenia, the honeysuckle, and the cape jessamine.

The furniture of these Georgian homes was often imported from England or made by native cabinetmakers who followed dominant English styles. The earliest of the grand styles of colonial furniture was the Chippendale (named after Thomas Chippendale, a London cabinetmaker), which flourished from 1740 to 1780. The Chippendale chair was characterized by the cabriole, or bowed leg, with claw and ball foot, and the back was carved into graceful designs, such as the tracery of Gothic rose windows, the Chinese Chippendale design, and the "ladder back." The Hepplewhite style, which flourished from 1775 to 1795, was distinguished by lightness and delicacy. The chair, the card table, the highboy, all had straight, tapering legs, fragile in appearance, precarious furniture for a lusty beefeater, or a gouty old gentleman. Hepplewhite carved the backs of his chairs into the shapes of a heart, or an oval, or a shield, and he was fond of using satinwood inlay and painting festoons and decorations on his handiwork. The Sheraton style, which was fashionable at the close of the eighteenth century, resembled the Hepplewhite in its delicacy and use of inlays of exotic woods, but it was more strongly built. The chairs, having square or rectangular backs with a cross rail a little above the seat, were supported by fluted legs. In all these styles mahogany wood was the principal material, and the chairs, sofas, and love seats were covered with sumptuous damask and brocades.[4]

[4] See Joseph Downs, *American Furniture: Queen Anne and Chippendale Periods in the Henry Francis du Pont Winterthur Museum* (New York, 1952).

The elegant aristocrats who lived in these Georgian homes on the eve of the Revolution had achieved a happy adaptation of English culture to the American environment. In the Southern colonies they had begun to evolve a way of life different from the pattern of the English squires or from the communal life of New England. During the seventeenth century there had been a much higher degree of similarity between the cultures of the Northern and Southern colonies than was apparent in the eighteenth century. In this last century the Southern colonies became differentiated from New England by the shaping forces of environment, the substitution of Negro slavery for white indentured servitude, the development of staple crops, the dominance of the Anglican Church, and the emergence of a powerful plantation aristocracy. In the middle of the eighteenth century the South was more cosmopolitan in its mental outlook than ever in its history. Not only had immigration added variety to the pattern of the Southern population, but the tobacco and rice aristocrats were kept in continuous contact with European culture through the intercourse of a flourishing trade. Furthermore, the intellectual horizon of the colonists was broadened by the connection with the British Empire and its officials and by the practice of wealthy planters of sending their sons to Europe to be educated.

But the culture of the colonial South was narrowly confined to an upper class. Philip A. Bruce, the able Virginia historian, in examining over eighteen thousand county records of Virginia of the seventeenth century found that nearly half of the male citizens and three fourths of the women could not write their names and had to sign with a mark.[5] Governor William Berkeley in 1671 thanked God that there were no free schools or newspapers in Virginia, for the former bred disobedience and heresy, and the latter spread libels against the government. Actually, there were at least two free schools in Virginia at that time, the Syms School and the Eaton School, endowed by the wills of two enlightened and benevolent men. Also in the eighteenth century there were free schools in Charleston, New Bern, and other Southern towns, founded by the Society for the Propagation of the Gospel in Foreign Parts, and the Winyah Indigo Society's school at Georgetown. In Annapolis was King William's School, which developed after the Revolution into St. John's College. Nevertheless, the education of the youth was regarded in the colonial South as a private responsibility, which was assumed by the planter, who either taught his children himself or employed a tutor or sent them to schools in England.[6]

The delightful journal of Philip Fithian, tutor in the home of "Councillor" Robert Carter of *Nomini Hall* in the years 1773–1774, gives an insight into the method of educating children by a tutor on the plantation. Fithian, a graduate of Princeton, who was preparing to become a Presbyterian minister,

[5] Cited in Daniel Boorstin, *The Americans: The Colonial Experience* (New York, 1958), 302–303.
[6] See Louis B. Wright, *The Cultural Life of the American Colonies, 1607–1690* (New York, 1929), chap. 5; and Wertenbaker, *The First Americans*, chap. 10.

accepted the job of a tutor in Virginia with some trepidation, for he had heard that Virginia was a worldly place, where he might be corrupted. He was paid a salary of £40 a year to teach the seven Carter children and a nephew English, Latin, Greek, mathematics, and the history of England. In addition to this education in books, the Carter children were instructed in music and formal dancing by masters who traveled on regular routes from plantation to plantation. The Southern gentry were genuinely concerned in giving their children a Renaissance type of education. In addition to a knowledge of the classics, they were taught to ride, to dance, to play on some musical instrument, to speak English correctly, to acquire an amateur knowledge of English law, to keep accounts, and to manage a plantation. Yet the realization of this ideal of versatility was often defeated by the laziness of Southern youth, as Fithian found, by their passionate love of horses and out-of-door life and by their delight in dancing, fine clothes, and gay parties.[7]

To supply educated ministers for the colony and to provide an Indian school, William and Mary College was founded at Williamsburg in 1693, the second oldest college in the country. The founder of this notable institution was Reverend James Blair, Commissary of the Church of England in Virginia, a masterful figure who sat on the governor's council. The student at this pioneer college first entered the grammar school, where he was taught Latin and Greek, and then he put on the cap and gown of a student in the college proper, where he studied rhetoric, logic, ethics, and mathematics as well as the classic authors. William Byrd II noted in his diary in 1712 that there were only twenty-two students at the college and that the head master was dismissed for being a sot. Fithian observed on the eve of the Revolution that some of the professors were seen drunk in the streets and that they gambled with cards all night in the public tavern. Nevertheless, there were other eminent professors at the college, such as George Wythe, who became the first professor of law in America, and Professor William Small, who inspired Thomas Jefferson when he was a student at Williamsburg. Also the Phi Beta Kappa Society was founded at William and Mary in 1776 to encourage scholarship and debating. Some of the most distinguished statesmen produced by the South, such as Jefferson, Marshall, Monroe, Edmund Randolph, and John Tyler, were educated at William and Mary College. Many Southerners, however, especially from South Carolina, went to England to be educated as gentlemen; despite the culture of the upper class in South Carolina there was no college in the colony. A study of Americans who were admitted as students to the Inns of Court in England prior to 1860 reveals that two thirds of them came from the Southern colonies and states.[8]

The culture of the Southern planters was indicated to some extent by their

[7] H. D. Farish (ed.), *Journal and Letters of Philip Vickers Fithian, 1773–1774: A Plantation Tutor of the Old Dominion* (Williamsburg, 1943).
[8] J. G. de R. Hamilton, "Southern Members of the Inns of Court," *North Carolina Historical Review*, X (October 1933), 274.

libraries. The library of Ralph Wormeley of *Rosegill* in Virginia was one of the best seventeenth-century colonial collections of books, 385 volumes, of which 26 were medical books and 80 were religious works. Over one third of the library of "King" Carter at *Corotoman,* or approximately 100 titles, were law books. George Washington, although he was not a voracious reader, had a library of 903 volumes at *Mount Vernon.* The finest library in the American colonies was at *Westover,* on the James River, where William Byrd II had gathered 3,600 volumes. Another superb library was the collection of "Councillor" Carter at *Nomini Hall,* which contained a wide variety of books by such authors as Locke, Grotius, Puffendorf, Sidney, Blackstone, Palladio, Voltaire, Molière, Donne, Chaucer, Dryden, and Congreve. At the close of the eighteenth century the greatest book connoisseur in the South was Thomas Jefferson, who gathered a library that he estimated at between 9,- and 10,000 volumes. A large proportion of these libraries of the more cultivated planters consisted of Greek and Roman classics, but there were many works on their shelves dealing with such practical subjects as agriculture, law, medicine, architecture, gardening, and military science. Scholarly studies have shown that the planters did much "purposeful reading," and that religious books, such as Richard Alstree's *The Whole Duty of Man,* occupied a large space in their libraries.[9] In addition to these private collections, Dr. Thomas Bray, Commissary of the Church of England to Maryland, established libraries in each of the thirty parishes of that colony, with the stipulation that any inhabitant could borrow books by promising to return them within one to four months. The Society for the Propagation of the Gospel in Foreign Parts, which he also founded in 1701, started libraries for public use in other Southern colonies.

The great majority of planters were not collectors or readers of books but practical men too busy and too extroverted for intellectual pursuits. Hugh Jones, the author of *The Present State of Virginia* (1724), wrote of the planters: "They are more inclinable to read men by business and conversation, than to dive into books, and are for the most part only desirous of learning what is aboslutely necessary, in the shortest and best method." Nevertheless, he found the colonial gentry to be a refined and attractive social class. "At the Capitol [at Williamsburg]," he wrote, "at publick times, may be seen a great number of handsom, well-dressed, compleat gentlemen. And at the Governor's House upon birth-nights, and at balls and assemblies, I have seen as fine an appearance, as good diversion, and as splendid entertainment in Governor Spotswood's time as I have seen any where else." [10]

The outstanding literary figure in the Southern colonies was William Byrd II, whose major works were not published until long after his death in 1744.

[9] Louis B. Wright, *The First Gentlemen of Virginia: Intellectual Qualities of the Early Ruling Class* (San Marino, 1940), chap. 5.
[10] Hugh Jones, *The Present State of Virginia* [1724], ed. by Richard L. Morton (Chapel Hill, 1956), 70.

Portrait of William Byrd II (1674–1744). (Courtesy of Colonial Williamsburg)

Byrd was trained as a man of fashion in London, where he enjoyed the life of the coffeehouses, the companionship of wanton women and pleasure-loving nobles, and the drama of the English stage.[11] In fact, he never cured himself of his nostalgia for England, which he regarded as "home." On his

[11] Louis B. Wright and Marion Tinling (eds.), *William Byrd of Virginia: The London Diary and Other Writings, 1717–1721* (New York, 1958).

James River estate of *Westover* he arose at five o'clock in the morning and regularly read before breakfast a portion of Homer, Terence, Petronius, or the Greek version of Josephus, or a passage from the Hebrew. He also read Italian, Dutch, and French works in the original, as well as kept up with current English literature.[12] In 1728 he wrote his most important work, *History of the Dividing Line,* which described his experiences as one of the commissioners who surveyed the boundary line between Virginia and North Carolina. Although it was written partly to gain adequate remuneration for his arduous labor in surveying the boundary, it gives a vivacious, if prejudiced, picture of social conditions in North Carolina at the time. It has also real literary merit, because it is permeated with the comic spirit, an aristocratic type of wit, that contrasts pleasurably with the dull religious literature produced in contemporary New England, the land of "the saints." [13]

A colorful and able historian of the colonial South was the sarcastic and forthright Robert Beverley. A member of the Virginia aristocracy, Beverley suffered various misfortunes that caused him to retire to his huge estate of *Beverley Park,* where he lived a solitary and Spartan life until his death in 1722. His *History and Present State of Virginia,* published in London in 1705, describes the early settlement of the colony, its natural history, its laws and government, as well as the customs and manners of the Indians. Possessing an ardent love of his land, he tried to encourage his fellow Virginians to become economically independent of England. Accordingly, he set them an example by using native manufactures and by making wine from his own vineyards. The first edition of his history is filled with ironic references to the colonial officials, but in a second edition (1722) he deleted most of his pungent criticism of his contemporaries.[14]

The most cultivated community and the only "city" of the Southern colonies was Charleston. Its population of approximately twelve thousand inhabitants was far below that of Philadelphia, the largest city of the American colonies in 1776, which boasted thirty-five thousand people. Moreover, at least half of the population of Charleston was composed of Negroes. During the colonial period it did not have local autonomy but was ruled by the provincial legislature that the planters controlled. The inhabitants of this semi-West Indian city were threatened by dangers of slave insurrections, disastrous fires and epidemics, such as yellow fever and smallpox. The great fire of 1740, which destroyed a large part of the city, caused the enactment of a law that all houses within the limits must be built of stone or brick. Charleston was the second city in America to have a fire engine. Despite its

---

[12] Louis B. Wright and Marion Tinling (eds.), *The Secret Diary of William Byrd, 1709–1712* (Richmond, 1941).

[13] For an interesting life of Byrd, see Richard C. Beatty, *William Byrd of Westover* (Boston, 1932).

[14] Robert Beverley, *The History and Present State of Virginia* [1705], ed. by Louis B. Wright (Chapel Hill, 1947); Vernon L. Parrington, *The Colonial Mind, 1620–1800:* vol. I of *Main Currents of American Thought* (New York, 1929).

delightful location, it was one of the most unhealthful spots on the continent, although it was much freer from malarial mosquitoes than the surrounding rice plantations. This fortunate exemption partly explains why the rice grandees lived in the city during the hot seasons. Thus Charleston virtually became a city-state, the focus of plantation culture.[15]

Travelers who visited Charleston and the homes of the rice planters were surprised at the high state of culture of the upper class of society. Johann David Schoepf, a physician to German troops during the Revolution, wrote, "throughout, there prevails here a finer manner of life, and on the whole there are more evidences of courtesy than in the northern cities." [16] The architecture of colonial Charleston was influenced partly by the West Indies —many of the brick houses were stuccoed and colored with soft pink, green, yellow, and blue tints. Iron balconies and tile roofs also suggested French Huguenot ancestry. In addition to these styles of architecture there were numerous symmetrical Georgian houses ornamented with classical details. The classical influence was also expressed in St. Philip's church and the aristocratic St. Michael's, built in 1752, patterned after the London church, St. Martins-in-the-Felds. Although South Carolina failed to establish a colonial college, it had a remarkable Charleston Library Society, founded in 1748, which accumulated a large circulating library. In 1732 an apprentice of Benjamin Franklin founded the *South Carolina Gazette* at Charleston, four years before the *Virginia Gazette* was started at Williamsburg.

Charleston had a remarkably rich cultural life for a remote colonial town.[17] This city had the first scientific museum in America, and scientific studies were carried on by Dr. John Lining and Dr. Alexander Garden, the last an amateur botanist after whom the gardenia is named. Charleston was the home of the first colonial to hold a genuine degree of Doctor of Medicine, William Bull, who in 1734 received a medical degree from the University of Leyden. In 1762 one of the earliest musical societies in the colonies was organized, the St. Cecilia Society, at which distinguished concerts were given. In the Charleston theater, founded in 1735, traveling troupes of English actors, particularly the Hallams, performed the plays of Shakespeare and the latest London successes. At the same time social life was stimulated by twenty different clubs in the city, such as the Hell-Fire Club. Indeed, the club movement was widespread throughout the colonies, producing such various organizations as political clubs, Masonic lodges, smoking societies,

---

[15] See Carl Bridenbaugh, *Cities of the Wilderness, the First Century of Urban Life in America, 1625–1742* (New York, 1938); and *Cities in Revolt, Urban Life in America, 1743–1776* (New York, 1955).

[16] Johann David Schoepf, *Travels in the Confederation* [1783–1784] (Philadelphia, 1911), II, 167.

[17] See Frederick P. Bowes, *The Culture of Early Charleston* (Chapel Hill, 1942); T. J. Wertenbaker, *The Golden Age of Colonial Culture* (New York, 1942); G. C. Rogers, Jr., *Charleston in the Age of the Pinckneys* (Norman, Oklahoma, 1969); and Edmund Berkeley, Jr., *Dr. Alexander Garden of Charleston* (Chapel Hill, 1969).

the Maryland Jockey Club, and even golf clubs, introduced by Scotsmen at Savannah and Augusta.

The colonial planters were appreciative of the fine arts, especially portrait painting, but were not creative in this field. Between 1708 and 1729, Henrietta Johnson, an Englishwoman who had settled in Charleston, was doing charming portraits of the rice planters in pastel. She has been called the first woman painter in America as well as the first Southern artist. A little later Jeremiah Theus, a Swiss, was painting coats of arms and crests for coaches and chaises, as well as portraits of the Charleston grandees. The Boston painter, John Singleton Copley, also painted the portraits of some of the colonial dignitaries of the South in their colorful costumes of silks and satins, such as the portraits of Mr. and Mrs. Izard of South Carolina, and of the North Carolina merchant, John Burgwin. In Maryland the Swedish-born painter, Gustavus Hesselius (d. 1775), and his son, John, worked at their profession, Gustavus painted a "Last Supper" for St. Barnabas Church, Queen Anne's County, which is the earliest religious painting produced in the United States that has survived. John Hesselius is noted chiefly for being the first teacher of Charles Willson Peale.

Charles Willson Peale, a native of Queen Anne's County, Maryland (d. 1827), will occupy a permanent place in the history of American art as the painter of portraits of George Washington in his prime. He was an amazingly versatile and dynamic person. His youth was spent as an apprentice to a saddler, but during his long life he worked as a silversmith, made coaches and clocks, and lectured as a popular scientist. His most curious skill was the making of false teeth, notably a set for President Washington that were held in place by creaking springs. After he had acquired the skeleton of a mastodon, he learned taxidermy and started a famous museum of natural history and a portrait gallery in Philadelphia. Peale studied art under Benjamin West in England and returned to America to become a portrait painter. He fought as a soldier in the Revolution, and he has preserved for posterity the appearance of Washington as a colonel of Virginia militia (1772) and as commander of the Revolutionary Army. His portraits of the national hero lack the subtlety and penetration of character that Gilbert Stuart's portraits of the aged Washington have, but Peale's likenesses are realistic and show Washington's countenance before its expression was altered by his false teeth. Peale was a prolific father, who named his sons Raphael, Rubens, Titian, and Rembrandt, the latter attaining fame as a portrait painter.[18]

Culture is much deeper than a taste for the fine arts or the accretion of knowledge; it is also concerned with the spirit, the province of religion. In all of the Southern colonies the Church of England became the established, or the official, church. The clergyman, chosen by the parish vestry, was given

[18] See C. C. Sellers, *Charles Willson Peale* (New York, 1969); Larkin, *Art and Life in America;* James T. Flexner, *First Flowers of Our Wilderness* (New York, 1947), and *The Light of Distant Skies, 1760–1835* (New York, 1954).

Charles Willson Peale of Maryland (1741–1827). Self-portrait. Painter of portraits of eminent men of the Revolutionary and of the early republic. (Courtesy of the Pennsylvania Academy of the Fine Arts)

a glebe (a house and several acres of land) and was paid a salary from the taxation of the freemen regardless of their creed. Supervision over the American churches was exercised by the Bishop of London, who sent over commissaries to represent him. On account of the scattered population, it was often necessary for the colonial parishes to depart from the practices of the Church in England. The dead were buried in family graveyards instead of the consecrated churchyards. Various violations of the liturgy occurred, such as the failure of the ministers to wear the proper vestments and the performing of marriages in private houses. The clergymen were unable to perform the sacraments or conduct religious services at the right intervals, because they had to travel by horseback to distant churches in their parishes. Consequently "chapels of ease" were established in remote places, where prayers and printed sermons were read by laymen. A further difficulty that hampered the growth of the Anglican church in America was that ministers had to cross the Atlantic to be ordained.[19]

In the seventeenth century the Southern colonies were far more puritanical in laws and mores than the Cavalier tradition represents them. Compulsory attendance at church on Sundays was a rigidly enforced law, and profane swearing or Sabbath-breaking were severely punished by the magistrates. In the eighteenth century, however, a more hedonistic atmosphere prevailed and greater laxity in religious performances occurred. There was slight supervision over the clergy, and some ministers were a disgrace to their profession. The Reverend Andrew Burnaby, who traveled in Virginia, 1759–1760, described the clergy, about sixty-five in number, as in general men of "sober and exemplary lives." On the other hand, Fithian's journal portrays a certain Parson Giberne, one of the most popular and admired preachers in Virginia, who stayed up late three nights in succession drinking and playing cards, a bout that sent him reeling to bed. Fithian also noted that the minister in his parish preached only fifteen minutes, contrasting with the long two-hour sermons of New England. His description of a Sunday in Virginia just before the Revolution suggests that the people were far less puritanical than their predecessors of the seventeenth century. The men assembled at the church early in order to talk over business and politics. The lower classes used Sunday for rude diversions, and the Negroes spent the holy day fishing, working in their gardens, or patching their quarters. Indeed, Virginia had a reputation for having no "heart religion" but for being a land of tippling, gambling with cards or dice, dancing, and swearing. The young tutor in the Carter family wrote in praise of Priscilla, a girl in her teens, she "never swears, which is here a distinguished virtue." [20]

The religion of the planters seems to have been predominantly formal, practical, and decorous. William Byrd II, for example, went to church regularly and took the sacrament, but it was difficult for this wordly gentleman to stay awake during the sermons. At night he invariably said his prayers, recording in his secret diary, written in a shorthand that has only in this century been decoded, "I said my prayers and had good health, good thoughts, and good humor, thank God Almighty." He also read many sermons and other religious works along with his daily stint of reading in the classics. Nevertheless, his religion did not prevent him from quarreling with

[19] Wertenbaker, *The First Americans,* chap. 5, A Transplanted Church; and Louis Wright, *Cultural Life of the American Colonies,* chap. 4, Diversity of Religion, and D. M. Brydon, *Virginia's Mother Church* . . . (Richmond and Philadelphia, 1947–1952), 2 vols.
[20] Farish (ed.), *Journal and Letters of Philip Vickers Fithian,* 62, 65, 180–181.

his wife, cheating her at cards in order to establish male ascendancy, avariciously seeking to monopolize land, or violating the sexual moral code. At sixty-five years of age he confessed in his secret diary, "played the fool with Sally, God forgive me." [21] Nor did his religion place a taboo on his enjoyment of the hedonistic pleasures of the fashionable set, gay parties, drinking heavily, dancing, gambling with dice, and attending horse races and cockfights. He had the comfortable belief that his sins would be forgiven.

The record of religion in the Southern colonies is very much the eternal story of religion—representing a dichotomy, often unconscious, between belief and practice. "King" Carter, for example, was ruthless in his land-grabbing; he imported slaves for sale; he was proud and demanding of respect; so that when he built a church, the parishioners did not dare enter until the proud planter preceded them; yet at the same time he wrote that he was resolved his sons at school in England should have religion instilled into them, "as I am of the Church of England way [the low church], so I desire they should be. But the high-flown-up top notions and the great stress that is laid upon ceremonies, any farther than decency and conformity, are what I cannot come into the reason of. Practical goodliness is the substance—these are but the shell." [22] And Fitzhugh, in buying slaves, often sought very young boys, callous of their suffering in separating them from their families; nevertheless, he wrote in a devout fashion consoling a friend for the death of his young children by observing that they had changed "a troublesome & uncertain terrestrial being, for a certain & happy Celestial habitation, & you have this happiness continually to joy you, that you have of your Offspring in Heaven, continually singing Halleujah's to the most highest, their Regeneration in Baptism washing off all Original Sin. . . ." [23]

The Anglican church was the church of the colonial aristocracy and did not meet the emotional needs and the democratic striving of the common people. These needs were satisfied by the rise of dissenting sects, such as the Quakers, the Baptists, and the Presbyterians. The Quakers were the first dissenters to invade the South. When they began to arrive in the colonies during the decade of the 1650's, they were severely persecuted in New England, where some of them were hanged, but in Virginia they were merely fined or expelled. The Quakers found a refuge in the back country of North Carolina, which George Fox, the founder of the sect, visited in the decade of the 1670's. The violent persecution of this devoted group of Christians, who refused to take oaths, or show respect for authority, or fight in the militia, was stopped after the passage of the Toleration Act by Parliament in 1689. The Baptists spread from Rhode Island and Philadelphia into the Southern

[21] Maude H. Woodfin and M. Tinling (eds.), *Another Secret Diary of William Byrd of Westover, for the Years 1739–1741* (Richmond, 1942), 70.

[22] Louis Wright (ed.), *Letters of Robert Carter, 1720–1727, the Commercial Interests of a Virginia Gentleman* (San Marino, Calif., 1940), 25.

[23] Davis (ed.), *William Fitzhugh and His Chesapeake World*, 198.

colonies by means of itinerant preachers, who were often arrested as vagrants or disturbers of the peace. The Methodist church was introduced into America in Georgia by John Wesley, the founder, and George Whitefield, the great evangelist, in the decade of the 1730's. During the colonial period the Methodists did not organize a separate church but remained affiliated with the Anglican church. The immigration of the Scotch-Irish into the back country of the South spread the Presbyterian faith, based on Calvinism.

Around 1740 the Southern colonies were deeply agitated by the Great Awakening, a religious movement that was a reaction from the formalism of the Episcopal church. The Great Awakening was accomplished by a series of revivals that swept through the thirteen colonies, perhaps the first social movement in which all the colonies shared prior to the political movement of opposition to British mercantilism.[24] The ministers of the Great Awakening preached the necessity of a religious experience—first, a conviction of sinfulness, and then the great emotional catharsis of being pardoned. They discounted education and wealth, and preached in barns and open-air gatherings as well as in churches. There were economic reasons also for the Great Awakening in the South, since the dissenting sects were bitterly resentful against the compulsion of paying taxes to support the Anglican clergy and against the monopoly that the latter enjoyed of performing marriages, thus reserving to themselves the profits of the marriage fees. The two leaders of this far-reaching religious movement in the South were the traveling evangelist George Whitefield, one of the most eloquent orators of his age, an arresting figure with cross eyes, and Samuel Davies, who engaged in a heroic crusade to spread the Presbyterian faith in the Virginia back country. The Great Awakening appealed to the common people and stimulated the growth of the Baptist, Methodist, and Presbyterian churches. The Presbyterians split into two factions over the question of accepting the new methods of evangelism, the "New Lights" and the "Old Side." The conservative and aristocratic Church of England frowned upon the unconventional and emotional methods of saving souls adopted by the apostles of the Great Awakening.

The most significant intellectual difference between the Southern and Northern colonies was reflected in their attitudes toward religion. Dr. Hamilton observed that disputation about religion was more in vogue in New England, and the Sabbath day was kept more fanatically in this land of white steeples than in the tobacco plantation region. Indeed, he declared that to talk in the dialect of New England about theology—original sin, reprobation, regeneration, justification, and so on—would in "our part of the world" be like speaking in Greek or Arabic.[25]

[24] See Wesley M. Gewehr, *The Great Awakening in Virginia, 1740–1790* (Durham, 1930).
[25] Carl Bridenbaugh (ed.), *Gentleman's Progress: The Itinerarium of Dr. Alexander Hamilton* (Chapel Hill, 1948), 65–66, 163.

In contrast with Dr. Hamilton's observation of the relative religious tolerance practised in the Tidewater, the Anglican missionary Charles Woodmason encountered bitter opposition when he tried to carry the decorous religion of the Church of England into the back country of the Carolinas on the eve of the Revolution. The Presbyterians were especially intolerant and sought by various means to break up his religious services. While he was preaching near Granny's Quarter, he reported, they gave away two barrels of whiskey to make the people who had gathered drunk in order to disturb the service, "for this being the 1st time that the Communion [of the Church of England] was ever celebrated in this Wild remote part of the World, it gave Great Alarm, and caus'd them much Pain and Vexation. The Company got drunk by 10 o'th Clock and we could hear them firing, hooping, and hallowing like Indians." On another occasion the passionate adherents of the Kirk "hir'd a Band of rude fellows to come to service who brought with them 57 dogs (for I counted them) which in time of Service they set fighting, and I was obliged to stop." [26]

Woodmason's experience indicates that there existed great extremes of culture and crudeness in the Southern colonies. Notwithstanding his stark picture of backwoods society, the Tidewater section of the Southern colonies in the eighteenth century was richly provided with refined and aristocratic gentlemen and ladies. Lieutenant Anburey described a specimen of the latter class at the time of the Revolution in the person of Colonel Randolph and his appealing way of life on his plantation *Tuckahoe,* located on the upper James River. The house at *Tuckahoe* was built for hospitality and pleasure as well as for a living place, containing many guest rooms and a commodious ballroom equipped with four "sophas" for lounging. A lover of fine horses, the colonel had imported from England the magnificent dappled-gray "Shakespeare" to head his stud. When a popular clamor arose against the hospitality shown to the paroled officers of Burgoyne's troops at Charlottesville, Colonel Randolph and other planters of breeding resisted such illiberality, for being gentlemen of affluence and authority, they disdained the popular clamor. Nevertheless, the Revolution introduced a spirit of equality, the "leveling principle," into the caste system of colonial days. Anburey saw three countrymen enter the mansion of *Tuckahoe* and sit down with the colonel, pulling off their muddy boots and spitting on the floor, as they discussed the terms for grinding their grain at the colonel's mill. [27]

Although "the first gentlemen of Virginia" have been elaborately delineated by historians, the gentry of Carolina have been neglected. A typical gentleman of this class has been described by John Davis, a tutor on *Ocean Plantation,* near Coosohatchie, South Carolina, at the close of the eighteenth century. The master, a member of the powerful Drayton family, treated the

[26] Hooker (ed.), *The Carolina Backcountry,* 30.
[27] Thomas Anburey, *Travels Through the Interior Parts of America* (Boston, 1923), II, 215.

Drayton Hall, 1738, the peak of Georgian architecture in low-country South Carolina, home of an aristocratic family from Barbados, saved from destruction by Sherman's army for its owner turned it into a hospital for Negroes sick with smallpox. (Courtesy of the Library of Congress)

young tutor with the utmost consideration, providing him with a horse, a library, and an abundant supply of "segars." When the family moved in May to another estate on the Ashley River, near magnificent *Drayton Hall,* the home of an elder brother, Davis wrote, "I was now breathing the politest atmosphere in America." [28] Indeed, a society that produced the Pinckneys, the Rutledges, the Middletons, the Manigaults, the Izards, and the Draytons contained much culture. Some of the homes and gardens of Tidewater South Carolina, such as *Drayton Hall, Middleton Place, Magnolia, Mulberry,* and *The Elms,* vied in elegance with the famous Virginia mansions of *Mt. Airy, Blenheim, Marmion, Shirley* and *Carter's Grove.*

The proprietors of these ancestral estates were not as a rule playboys, enervated by slavery and luxury, but industrious, masterful leaders. They tried to imitate the style of life of the English country gentry, but conditions in America were different. In England, a mark of gentility was the ownership

[28] John Davis, *Travels of John Davis in the United States of America, 1798 to 1802* (Boston, 1910), II, 130.

of a deer park, and poaching by the yeomen was a rather common crime; but in America deer were plentiful and the common man could easily hunt them in the woods with his rifle.[29] The gentry of Virginia, Maryland and the Carolinas, in spite of rather primitive conditions, developed the stately, formal manners with the courtly bow and the curtsey of the English upper class, and some of them read books on manners, such as Richard Braithwait's *The English Gentleman* (1630) and later Lord Chesterfield's *Letters to His* [natural] *Son* (1774). To a much greater degree than our own generation, they regarded letter writing as a fine art, and conversation too. Frequent visits to each other's plantations kept up the amenities of life. Even Jefferson, who liked the life of the mind, was impressed by the refining influence of this social intercourse of the planters, noting that when he himself retired from society he tended to become boorish.

[29] Boorstin, *The Americans: The Colonial Experience,* chap. 4.

The Movement for Independence
from the British Empire

A WEB OF COMMERCE based on reciprocal exchange of goods, in contrast to the one-way commerce of the antebellum period, connected the Southern colonies with England. In 1769, the exports from the Southern colonies to Great Britain were four times more valuable than the products sent there from the colonies north of Maryland. At the same time Southerners imported goods from the mother country that were twice as valuable as those imported by the Northern colonists. The Northern colonies, on the other hand, had a much larger commerce with Southern Europe and the West Indies than the Southern colonies enjoyed. Not only did this commerce bind the colonists, the Southern colonists particularly, to Europe, but it contributed to making them less provincial-minded. Moreover, it was the very basis for the growth of the Southern towns. Principal among these towns were Williamsburg, the colonial capital of Virginia for one hundred years until 1799 when it was superseded by Richmond; Raleigh, which succeeded New Bern in 1792 as the capital of North Carolina; Columbia, which supplanted Charleston as the capital of South Carolina in 1790; and Milledgeville, which took the place of Savannah as the capital of Georgia in 1804.

Charles Town (Charleston) was the most thriving port of the colonial South, having an important export trade in deerskins, rice, indigo, beef, pork, corn, lumber, and naval stores.[1] Also among the exports from this city in 1748 were two hundred and ninety-six thousand oranges. In that year two hundred vessels carried the exports of Charles Town to distant markets —sixty-eight to Europe, eighty-seven to the West Indies, and thirty-seven to Northern ports. In return, extensive invoices of luxuries were imported for the rich merchants and the grandees of the rice plantations. In the middle of the eighteenth century Governor James Glen lamented the fact that the South Carolinians imported so many luxuries, which he listed as Flanders laces, Dutch linens, French cambrics and chintzes, silks, gold and silver lace, Hyson tea and other East Indian products, and great quantities of Madeira

---

[1] For a study of the Indian trade in deerskins and for the sale of Indian slaves, centering in Charleston, see Verner W. Crane, *The Southern Frontier,* 1670–1732 (Philadelphia, 1929).

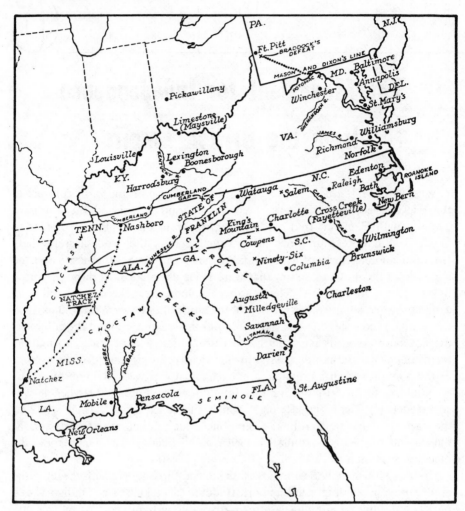

The South in the Eighteenth Century

wine.[2] The ledgers of John Norton and Sons, Scottish merchants at Yorktown, Virginia, reveal the similar fashionable and luxurious tastes of the
tobacco planters, their love of gay clothes, and their taste for books.[3]

The commerce of the Southern colonies was harassed at times by pirates,
especially from 1650 to 1720, a period that has been called "the golden age
of piracy." The haunts of these gangsters of the ocean were the Bahama
Islands, particularly Nassau, then called New Providence, and the hideouts

[2] James Glen, *A Description of South Carolina* (London, 1761); see also Leila Sellers,
Charleston Business on the Eve of the American Revolution (Chapel Hill, 1934).
[3] F. N. Mason (ed.), *John Norton and Sons, Merchants of London and Virginia*
(Richmond, 1937).

behind the sandbars of the Carolina coast. Indeed, Ocracoke Inlet, south of Cape Hatteras, became the capital of the Southern pirates. The most notorious pirates who operated along the Carolina coast were Edward Teach, known as "Blackbeard," and Captain Stede Bonnet. Teach was a melodramatic villain who curled his long black beard and moustachios, burned brimstone on his ship to overawe his men, and was reputed to have had fourteen wives. His boldest deed was to intercept a ship sailing from Charleston in 1718 with some prominent Charlestonians on board. He held these citizens as hostages until the town authorities sent the medical and other supplies that he demanded. Teach openly appeared at Bath and Edenton, North Carolina, where Governor Charles Eden and Tobias Knight, secretary of the colony, were suspected of sharing his booty. Stede Bonnet also frequented the Carolina coasts. A former major in the British army, he had become a wealthy and respected citizen of Barbados until 1717, when he turned to the trade of a buccaneer. Although he knew nothing of navigation, nevertheless, by the sheer force of his personality, he was able to command the crew of his ship, the *Royal James,* in a brief but amazing career of piracy.

In 1718 a campaign was undertaken to eliminate the nuisance of these gangsters of the ocean. In that year a British fleet under Woodes Rogers drove the pirates from their great base at New Providence Island. At the same time Governor Alexander Spotswood of Virginia sent out an expedition to capture "Blackbeard," who was killed in battle near Ocracoke Inlet. Finally, the governor of South Carolina dispatched Colonel William Rhett to the Cape Fear region. His ship pursued the *Royal James* until both the pirate vessel and Rhett's ship were stranded within pistol shot of each other. Victory depended on which ship was first freed by the tide. Colonel Rhett's ship was the lucky one, and he captured Stede Bonnet and his crew, whom he took to Charleston for trial. The pirate leader, so brave in battle, was terrified as he faced the gibbet and begged piteously for his life. But stern justice was administered by the hanging of Bonnet and twenty-two of his crew. The significance of these early buccaneers is that they brought into the colonies much needed gold and silver, sold goods cheaply, and paid high prices for provisions. When they began, however, to interfere with the rice and tobacco trade, the Southern colonies were stirred to action to eliminate these highwaymen of the sea.[4]

The British government attempted by a piecemeal process to force the trade of the colonies to conform to the prevailing theory of economics, known as mercantilism. The goal of this policy of economic nationalism was the development of a self-sufficient empire. The principal means for accomplishing this goal were the establishment of a favorable balance of trade and the regulation of commerce between the mother country and the colonies so that there was a specialization of labor, the colonies to provide the raw

[4] See J. F. Jameson (ed.), *Privateering and Piracy in the Colonial Period* (New York, 1923), and H. F. Rankin, *The Golden Age of Piracy* (Williamsburg, 1969).

materials, the mother country the manufactured articles.[5] The first important act of Parliament to carry out the principles of mercantilism was the Navigation Act of 1651. This law was really a measure to strike a blow against the Dutch, who were rapidly absorbing much of the carrying trade of the world, including the freightage of tobacco from the Southern colonies. The Navigation Act required that all goods shipped from the colonies to England, or in the coastal trade, must be transported in English or colonial ships, the captain and the majority of the crew of which must be English or colonials. Furthermore, all commodities imported into England or the colonies must be carried in English or colonial bottoms or by vessels belonging to the European countries in which the goods were produced. After 1654, the year in which the war between England and Holland ended, this law was largely disregarded by the colonies.

With the restoration of Charles II to the throne of England, there began an intensification of the regulation of colonial trade in accordance with mercantilistic ideas. The dominance of the British merchants and shipowners over Parliament was demonstrated by the passage of trade acts designed to benefit their interests. In 1660, Parliament passed a more stringent Navigation Act at the urgent solicitation of George Downing, a Harvard College graduate and ardent imperialist. This law required that the crews of English and colonial ships should be three fourths Englishmen or colonials, and British monopoly was extended by the stipulation that these ships engaged in the carrying trade must be built in British or colonial shipyards. The effect of these laws was to protect the New England shipbuilding industry and merchant marine, but at the same time to injure the tobacco planters of Maryland and Virginia, who had to pay higher freight rates after the exclusion of Dutch competition. The navigation acts, nevertheless, contributed to the creation of a powerful British navy.

The Restoration policy of strict regulation of colonial trade was carried a step farther by the act of 1660 establishing a list of "enumerated goods" that must be shipped to English ports, even if such goods were destined for continental ports. This list included sugar, tobacco, cotton, indigo, ginger, and dye woods, none of which were produced in the Southern colonies at this time in any appreciable quantity, except tobacco. From time to time additions were made to this list: rice in 1704, naval stores in 1705, copper and furs in 1722, and lumber in 1764. Colonial commerce was further restricted by the Staple Act of 1663, which required that all commodities imported from Europe to America, except salt for the New England fisheries and wine from the Azores and Madeira Islands, had to go through British ports. The Southern colonies throughout the colonial period did not have the privilege that New England and the Middle colonies enjoyed of importing their salt directly from the Cape Verde Islands, Portugal, or Spain. Although

[5] The classic study of mercantilism is E. F. Heckscher, *Mercantilism* (London, 1935), 2 vols.

they could obtain a strong, corrosive salt from Turk's Island or Tortuga in the West Indies, they were forced to import most of their salt for beef and pork from the Northern colonies at an increased price and higher freight charges. Another instance of discrimination between different parts of the empire was that Ireland, and Scotland until the Act of Union of 1707, were considered foreign countries as far as the trade laws were concerned.[6]

There were strong inducements for Southern planters to evade the trade laws, because the main markets for rice and tobacco were in continental Europe. In order to suppress evasions of these acts, Parliament passed a law in 1673 that required a bond that enumerated goods would be shipped only to England, or, as an alternative, that the exporter must pay a high "plantation duty" at the shipping port if he carried his cargo to another colonial harbor. In 1696 Parliament enacted a drastic law requiring colonial governors to take an oath to enforce the trade laws and establishing vice-admiralty courts in the colonies to try smugglers. These courts dispensed with local juries, who were prone to be lenient with evaders of the trade acts. In 1733 a lobby of absentee West Indian planters put pressure on Parliament to pass an obnoxious bill, known as the Molasses Act, which favored their special interest. This law placed a prohibitive duty of sixpence a gallon on all molasses shipped from the French and Spanish West Indies into British possessions. The enforcement of this act would have adversely affected the West India trade of the Southern colonies, but fortunately for the American colonies as a whole it became a dead letter law until it was revived in 1764 by George Grenville. The New Englanders were the chief offenders in the smuggling business. On the other hand, according to Governor Glen of South Carolina (1750), "No Country in this Part of the World hath less illegal Trade than *South Carolina;* at least, so far as I can learn." [7]

As to the effect of the trade laws on the Southern colonies, there is a considerable divergence of opinion among American scholars. The imperial school of historians has discarded the view held by Bancroft and older historians that the trade laws were acts of tyranny that produced the American Revolution.[8] They maintain that the Trade Acts did not seriously affect the economic prosperity of the colonies, for it was to the advantage of the colonies to buy and sell in England. They point out that these laws, especially those affecting the Northern colonies and the West Indian trade, were not enforced until 1764 and that there were no great protests against them until the decade preceding the Revolution.

They observe that the colonists did not appreciate the value of a self-

[6] For the trade acts, see G. L. Beer, *Origins of the Brtiish Colonial System, 1578–1660* (New York, 1908), and *The Old Colonial System, 1660–1754* (New York, 1912); Lawrence A. Harper, *The Navigation Laws* (New York, 1939).

[7] Glen, *A Description of South Carolina,* 48.

[8] Notably Charles M. Andrews, Herbert Osgood, and Lawrence Gipson; see especially Oliver M. Dickerson, *The Navjgation Acts and the American Revolution* (Philadelphia, 1951).

sufficing empire or the economic benefits they received from the imperial connection. The tobacco planters, for example, were given a monopoly of the British market by tariffs that practically excluded the superior Spanish tobacco. English farmers were forbidden to grow tobacco, and royal dragoons were sent to trample the fields of violators of this law. Moreover, the Southern colonies received a high bounty for the export of indigo, naval stores, and pig iron. Also the colonists did not appreciate the protection of the British navy and army. The lightness of imperial taxation was another example of the liberality of the British Empire before 1763. Indeed, the chief taxes the colonists had to pay were a poll tax to the local government and a tithe for the support of the Anglican church. In the Southern colonies, they were required to pay a quitrent of two shillings per one hundred acres, but this charge on the land was frequently uncollected. Governor Arthur Dobbs reminded the assembly of North Carolina in 1754 that although the British government was loaded with debts it "hath not only protected these colonies but indulged them in . . . the easiest taxes (spent for their support) of any Civilized nation of the Globe." [9]

Unlike New England, the Southern colonies fitted well into the scheme of a self-sufficing empire. New England and the Middle colonies had a climate much like that of the British Isles, producing raw materials and products that were not greatly needed in the mother country. Consequently, they had to obtain money to pay for the unfavorable balance of trade with England by trade with the West Indies and Africa. The Southern colonies, on the other hand, produced semitropical products, such as rice, tobacco, indigo, and naval stores, the staples that England needed. Furthermore, the British laws that prohibited the colonies from manufacturing for intercolonial export, the Hat Act, the Woolens Act, and the Iron Act, scarcely affected the Southern colonies, except possibly impeding the growth of an incipient iron industry in Virginia and Maryland.

The British trade laws, however, bore unequally upon different economic interests in the colonies. They favored the West Indian sugar planters, who were given a monopoly of the British market. The rice planters also persuaded Parliament in 1730 to permit them to export rice directly to markets south of Cape Finisterre, but their main market was in Germany and Holland, and Carolina rice going there had to pass through British ports. From 1767 to the Revolution however, rice, which had paid a duty of approximately 6 shillings, 4 pence a hundredweight, was admitted free of customs into England, but an export duty of 8 pence per hundredweight was imposed. A large portion of the rice sent to England on the eve of the Revolution, amounting to 79 per cent, was re-exported, and also 40 per cent of the indigo was re-exported. The production of indigo was aided by a bounty of 6 pence a pound and, furthermore, it paid no duty in England.

[9] L. H. Gipson, *British Empire before the American Revolution* (New York, 1946), VI, 9.

So profitable was the bounty on naval stores that North Carolina had little complaint to make of the working of the mercantilist system. This bounty was inaugurated in 1705 as a result of the difficulty in England of obtaining tar and pitch from Sweden. After the Stockholm Tar Company had been granted a monopoly on these forest products by the Swedish government the price to English customers had been doubled. Furthermore, the Great Northern War, between Sweden and Russia, 1699–1721, seriously threatened England's supply from the Baltic countries. To encourage colonial production Parliament granted bounties of £4 a ton on tar and pitch and £3 a ton on turpentine imported from the colonies, thus equalizing the costs of production in America with the costs in the Baltic countries. As a result of these subsidies a new industry was practically created in the Carolinas to produce tar after the Swedish model from green trees rather than from fallen trees and pine knots. But the Carolinians resisted changing to this technique, and accordingly the bounty was discontinued for four years, 1725–1729. As a consequence, the importation of tar and pitch from the colonies into England dropped from 81,033 barrels to 34,277 barrels, and the importation of naval stores from the Baltic countries was resumed. In 1729 the bounties were restored, owing to the clamor of the colonial naval stores producers, the merchant marine interests, which had suffered from the decline of this trade, and the advocates of mercantilistic policies. Thus Carolina tar, although often mixed with chips and sand and less desirable than Swedish tar, captured the English market and cost the British taxpayers an annual sum of approximately £34,000 for bounties during the decade prior to the American Revolution.[10]

The yoke of the trade and navigation laws was most galling to the tobacco planters of the Chesapeake Bay country. In respect to freight rates, the tobacco planters of the seventeenth century found that the use of Dutch vessels was the cheapest method of getting their crops to market. A realistic student of the effect of the Navigation Acts on the thirteen colonies has observed that the Dutch paid most for American goods, carried freight most economically, and granted the most liberal terms of credit, so that in a free market the American colonies would have been drawn irresistibly into the economic orbit of the Netherlands.[11] Such an extreme view, however, discounts the tastes of the colonists, who were habituated to English goods and who were affected by strong emotional bonds with the motherland. All this Dutch trade, except smuggling, was stopped by the Navigation Acts of the Stuarts.

An ironic fact about the tobacco trade was that a very large proportion of the American tobacco was re-exported from England to the continent of

[10] J. Williams, "English Mercantilism and Carolina Naval Stores, 1705–1776," *Journal of Southern History*, I (May 1935), 169–185.

[11] Lawrence A. Harper, "The Effect of the Navigation Acts on the Thirteen Colonies," in Richard B. Morris (ed.), *The Era of the American Revolution* (New York, 1939), 5.

Europe. In 1773 Great Britain used less than 4 million pounds of the golden leaf, and 100,482,007 pounds were re-exported, mostly to Holland and Germany. The shippers of re-exported tobacco received a refund, or drawback, of nearly the whole of the tariff duty, but the tobacco planter was forced to pay additional freight, insurance, commissions, and handling charges, which went into the pockets of British businessmen. Such indirect routing of tobacco was clearly unjust and a violation of the natural laws of economics.

The tobacco planters suffered heavy burdens, indeed, from the application of mercantilism. England was not the natural entry port for Southern tobacco, and the customs duty on this luxury was exceedingly great. In 1732 the tobacco planters presented a petition to the British government, *The Case of the Planters of Tobacco in Virginia,* in which they asked that the tariff duty be reduced from 6½ pence to 4 pence, that the government provide warehouses to store the tobacco until the duty was paid, and that no duty be charged on re-exported tobacco.

There is good reason to believe that the indirect routing of tobacco and rice through England cost the planters a considerable share of the profits of their crops. After the American Revolution had broken the restraints of the Trade Acts, the tobacco planters, who had sent 99.8 per cent of their exports for the foreign market to England in 1773, sent only 62.2 per cent of their exports to England in 1790 and 31.7 per cent in 1821. The shipment of rice to England in 1790 also dropped to less than half the amount sent during the later colonial period. Because of the low price received for tobacco and the increased costs of production in the eighteenth century as well as their extravagance, the Southern planters were in a state of chronic debt to the British merchants.

The money policy of the imperial government in regard to the American colonies, some historians believe, was far more injurious to the economic development of the colonies than were the Trade Acts.[12] Not only did England prohibit the export of English coins to the American colonies but also even forbade them to mint a supply of money from foreign bullion. A slight concession was granted in 1722 when the colonies were allowed to issue copper currency in values of farthings, half pennies, and pennies. This illiberal policy was based partly on a mistaken notion of mercantilism that the amount of gold and silver a nation retained was the measure of its wealth.

Throughout the colonial period the American colonies were constantly being drained of specie. This condition was caused by the unfavorable balance of trade with England, the interest charges on debts, especially those of the Southern planters, and the paper money issues, which depreciated and drove coins from circulation. The colonists were therefore forced to devise expedients such as tobacco warehouse certificates in Virginia, Maryland, and

---

[12] Curtis P. Nettles, *The Money Supply of the Colonies before 1720* (Madison, Wis., 1934).

North Carolina and buckskins in less developed regions to serve for money. They also obtained the specie needed to compensate for the unfavorable balance of trade with the mother country by importing foreign coin, especially through the trade with the West Indies and with pirates. Consequently, the colonists were accustomed to use such foreign coins as gold Portuguese "Joes," French livres, Dutch guilders, and Spanish gold pistoles, doubloons, and silver pieces of eight. Although foreign coins circulated almost exclusively in the colonies, the nomenclature of English currency as a rule was employed in business transactions.

Since the colonists lacked specie, they resorted to paper money. Bills of exchange, or drafts of a planter or colonial merchant on a London factor, were also used to supply in part the deficiency of coin, particularly to pay for imports. During Queen Anne's War the Southern colonies began to issue paper money, at first public promissory notes authorized by the colonial legislatures. Such paper money was frowned upon by the British government, which was very solicitous of the interests of British merchants. Royal governors were instructed to veto paper money acts, or they were disallowed in England. In 1764, Parliament passed an act forbidding the colonial legislatures to issue paper money as legal tender, although they could issue it for local purposes with provision for redemption. Accordingly, a severe money shortage existed in the colonies during the decade preceding the Revolution. This policy of drastically regulating the money supply of the colonies was only part of the larger system of mercantilism that bred a deep sense of grievance in the minds of the colonists and was the prelude to the American Revolution.[13]

Another source of friction between the American colonies and the mother country was the imperial land policy adopted after the French and Indian War.[14] Land was the great source of wealth, speculation, and trade in the Southern colonies. Speculation in Western lands offered a lucrative opportunity at this time to Southern planters, for immigration and the great growth of population had put pressure on the acquisition of lands. Accordingly, the Loyal Land Company, the Greenbriar Company, and the Ohio Company were formed to exploit the Western country. Among their stockholders were such persons as George Mason, the Washington brothers, Dr. Thomas Walker, Peter Jefferson, father of the future president, and Lieutenant Governor Robert Dinwiddie of Virginia. The most important of these enterprises was the Ohio Company, which in 1749 received a grant of two hundred thousand acres in the Ohio Valley on condition of settling two hundred families in that region within seven years. During the next year the company sent out Christopher Gist, a famous frontiersman of Maryland, to explore the Ohio River and report on the location of good lands. As a base for the fur trade,

[13] See Edward Channing, *A History of the United States* (New York, 1932), 6 vols.
[14] See Thomas P. Abernethy, *Western Lands and the American Revolution* (New York, 1937).

the company established a trading post at Will's Creek (now Cumberland, Maryland) near the great bend of the Potomac River. In 1752 the treaty of Logstown, an Indian village eighteen miles below the forks of the Ohio, was concluded with the Indians, giving permission for the Ohio Company to erect two fortified trading houses on the Ohio River and to plant settlements south of the river.

It was unfortunate for the welfare of the British Empire in America that colonial rivalries hampered this penetration of the Ohio Valley. The Ohio Company planned to build a fort below the forks of the Ohio River at McKee's Rocks, but they were opposed by the Pennsylvania fur traders with the backing of their provincial government. The Pennsylvania authorities believed that the forks of the Ohio lay within the limits of their colony, whose western boundary had been fixed at five degrees west of the Delaware River. This line had not been surveyed at that time. They attempted to thwart the expansion of the Virginia company toward the northwest, especially by turning the Indians of the region against the Virginia traders. Furthermore, the Ohio Company itself was hindered from a vigorous prosecution of its designs by powerful rivals within the Virginia colony, particularly the Blair and the Greenbriar companies, which dominated the colonial council.[15]

Meanwhile, the French governor of Canada, Marquis Duquesne, began to build a chain of forts from Lake Erie down the Allegheny River to the forks of the Ohio. Alarmed by the French advance, Governor Dinwiddie of Virginia sent George Washington, then twenty-one years old, to warn the French that they were trespassing on English territory (1753). Washington was guided through the wilderness by Christopher Gist, who on one occasion during the journey saved the life of the young Virginian. The French at Fort Le Boeuf laughed at Washington's demand that they retire from their forts along the Allegheny River. The Ohio Company had failed to realize the significance of the forks of the Ohio River, but Washington's report pointed out its strategic value, and the company now hastened to send an expedition that began to build a rude fort at this point.[16] The French also sent a detachment of soldiers to the forks of the Ohio, who drove away the Virginians before they had completed their fort, and erected Fort Duquesne on the coveted location. Shortly afterward, in April, 1754, Washington precipitated the French and Indian War by a petty clash with a French scouting party he met at Great Meadows in southwestern Pennsylvania.[17]

This great struggle for empire between France and England, called in Europe the Seven Years' War, was caused by clashes over colonial expansion and by power politics. Because the war was fought largely by British regulars,

[15] See John R. Alden, *John Stuart and the Southern Colonial Frontier, 1754–1775* (Ann Arbor, 1944).
[16] *The Journal of Major George Washington* (Charlottesville, 1963).
[17] See L. K. Koontz, *Robert Dinwiddie; His Career in American Colonial Government and Westward Expansion* (Glendale, Calif., 1941), and John R. Alden, *Robert Dinwiddie; Servant of the Crown* (Charlottesville, 1973).

and on the Canadian border, the Southern colonies were affected only slightly by its military activities—principally by Indian attacks on their frontiers that allowed the defeat of Braddock near Fort Duquesne in 1755. Nevertheless, the Southern colonies were affected profoundly by the war in the economic and political realms. The Peace of Paris in 1763, by ceding Canada to Great Britain, removed the ever-standing danger of French attack upon the colonial borders, and, therefore, made the colonies less dependent upon the mother country. Another provision of the peace was the cession by Spain of Florida to Great Britain, which ruled it as a British province from 1763 to 1783.

The war led to a sharp break in British colonial policy, indeed to such a divergence of treatment of the colonists that the period after 1763 is called the New Colonial Empire whereas the earlier period is called the Old Colonial Empire. In the earlier period the dominant political figure had been Prime Minister Sir Robert Walpole, who pursued a policy of "salutary neglect." After the war, owing partly to the illegal and unpatriotic trade between the lines with the French, and partly to a tremendous war debt, Parliament and the king determined to rationalize and more strictly regulate their colonial administration. Although the war stimulated temporarily a stronger sense of British patriotism in the colonies, the period of euphoria passed away in the next few years. One reason for disenchantment with British rule was the great corruption of which the Americans were convinced existed in the British government. Sir Robert Walpole's administration had also been corrupt, but it had only slightly affected colonial welfare; the corruptions of King George's government, on the other hand, the Americans believed, seriously threatened American political liberty, and was an important reason for the American Revolution.

The older interpretation of the causes of the American Revolution emphasized the resentment over the Trade Acts and other economic grievances. The most recent interpretations have rejected this simple explanation and have focused on the growing maturity of the colonies and their fears of losing the political liberty that they had enjoyed under the Old Empire before a change occurred in 1763. The imperial school of historians, Beer, Osgood, Andrews, and Gipson, had pointed out the mildness of the British rule of the colonies and the benefits of the imperial connection; the new school emphasizes the blunders that the British Parliament and ministry made after 1763 in dealing with the colonies and the ideological background of the American Revolution.[18] Bernard Bailyn of Harvard University, who has studied deeply the numerous political pamphlets issued in America prior to the Revolution, has concluded that the great majority of the pamphlets were informed with

---

[18] Jack P. Greene, "The Flight from Determinism: A Review of Recent Literature on the Coming of the American Revolution," *South Atlantic Quarterly,* LXI (Spring 1962), 235–259; Bernard Bailyn (ed.), *Pamphlets of the American Revolution 1750–1776* (Cambridge, Mass., 1965) and *Ideological Origins of the American Revolution* (Cambridge, Mass., 1967).

a very radical spirit. Their political philosophy went beyond the works of John Locke to the ferment of the Puritan Commonwealth, to the political thought of James Harrington and Algernon Sidney.

The situation within the British government after 1763 explains to a considerable degree the mishandling of the American problem. The studies of British politics and administration at this time by Sir Lewis Namier, Richard Pares, and John Brooke show the short-sightedness of British politicians. There was a lack of planning and of clear-cut issues in Parliament, because it was divided into factions and family groups struggling for office and not for principle. George III did not have tyrannical designs, as the Americans thought; rather he was a good Whig defending the power of Parliament, which he could manipulate.[19] Three thousand miles of ocean and the insularity of the eighteenth-century British mind prevented Parliament and the ministers from understanding the changed American attitude that arose after the Stamp Act episode, an attitude of suspicion of the British government. The British held the conception of a static constitution of the empire, while the Americans had evolved a new view of their relation with the mother country as based on the idea of equality.

The spirit of independence had evolved in the colonies especially as a result of the continuing struggle between the colonial legislatures and the royal governors. The royal governor stood at the apex of colonial administration and was both the symbol and reality of imperial rule. He arrived in the colony with a set of instructions drawn up in England, and his function was to represent the royal authority.[20] His powers were very extensive, including the appointing power; the authority to summon and dissolve the assembly, to veto laws, and to pardon; the control over the military forces of the colony; the power to grant land patents with the consent of the council; and the authority to issue proclamations. Many of the royal governors were unfit appointees, favorites of the king, placemen, or bankrupt nobles who came to America to recoup their fortunes. Nevertheless, the Southern colonies had a few superior royal governors, such as the Scotsmen, Spotswood and Dinwiddie in Virginia, Glen in South Carolina, and Wright in Georgia, who identified themselves with colonial interests and made excellent administrators.[21] The royal type of government gradually superseded the corporate and proprietary types, so that at the outbreak of the Revolution all the Southern colonies, with the exception of Maryland, were royal colonies.

During the seventeenth century the legislatures had made little headway in the South in their struggles with the governors. In the eighteenth century,

[19] See Sir Lewis Namier, *Structure of Politics at the Accession of George III* (London, 1929), 2 vols.; Richard Pares, *George III and the Politicians* (Oxford, England, 1953); and John Brooke, *King George III* (New York, 1972), which maintains that George III tried faithfully to observe the English Constitution.

[20] Leonard W. Labaree, *Royal Government in America* (New Haven, 1930).

[21] William W. Abbott, *The Royal Governors of Georgia, 1754–1775* (Chapel Hill, 1959).

however, they succeeded remarkably in whittling away the arbitrary powers of the royal governors and establishing precedents of independence. They took the position that the royal instructions to the governors did not bind them; they so increased the power of the Speaker, whom they elected, that he became a formidable antagonist to the governor; and they extended their financial authority to the auditing of the accounts of all public officials. Their control over appropriations—the purse—was a lever of great power, for in some colonies the governor was dependent on the legislature for his salary. Thus in a pragmatic and piecemeal fashion, they continually encroached on the royal prerogative. Using the time-honored argument of possessing the "rights of Englishmen," which had not been forfeited by emigration to America, they ultimately claimed for their legislatures complete equality with Parliament under the crown. In this evolution of the spirit of independence, the emergence of a group of able and articulate leaders, such as Speaker Robinson in Virginia, and Daniel Dulany, the younger, in Maryland, was especially important.[22]

The colonial assemblies regarded themselves as similar to Parliament in England and entitled to Parliamentary privileges. A noteworthy difference between the two bodies, however, was that the members of the colonial legislatures, except in South Carolina, were paid for attendance. Their independence was curtailed by the fact that the governor had the authority to summon, to prorogue, and to dissolve the assembly. Many memorable conflicts occurred between the legislature, representing the interests of the colonists, and the royal governor, upholding the prerogative of the king. The greatest power of the assembly was its control over the purse, through which it could bring pressure to bear on the governor to accede to its will by refusing to appropriate money for his salary. But the Virginia, Maryland, and Georgia assemblies, lost this valuable power of protecting their interests before the colonial period had ended. In Virginia the imperial government was granted as early as 1680 a permanent tax of 2 shillings on the export of each hogshead of tobacco, the receipts of which were set aside to pay the governor's salary.

The colonial legislatures were given liberal discretion in making laws, for seldom did the British government after 1713 exercise its right of disallowing the laws passed by the North Carolina legislature were disallowed in England, and nearly nine tenths of the Virginia colonial laws were confirmed. Of the eighty-five hundred laws passed by colonial legislatures and submitted to the Privy Council, only 5 per cent, approximately, were disallowed. Nevertheless, the British government possessed a double check over colonial legislation, in the first instance, by the veto of the royal governor, and then by the disallowance of the Privy Council. The practice of annulling colonial laws was exercised to protect the royal prerogative and the interests of British mer-

---

[22] Jack P. Greene, *The Quest for Power; the Lower Houses of Assembly in the Southern Royal Colonies, 1689–1776* (Chapel Hill, 1964).

chants as well as to prevent the passage of colonial laws that conflicted with the common law or the statutes of Parliament. Colonial laws went into force after their passage by the assembly. Laws objectionable to the British government, therefore, might operate for years in the colonies, owing to the delay of disallowing them caused by the difficulty of communication across the Atlantic and by the procrastination of officials in England. Indeed, the average length of time that elapsed between the passage of a law by the colonial legislature and its disallowance in England was three years and five months.[23]

Until 1763 the Southern colonies were reasonably content with their position within the British Empire. But this amicable relationship was disturbed as a result of the French and Indian War, which led to a reorganization of the British Empire unfavorable to American liberty. In the so-called New Empire, Parliament took a more decisive control over American affairs. The expenses of a long war had resulted in the accumulation of an enormous imperial debt. The British government after the conclusion of the Peace of Paris in 1763 determined to raise more revenue in the colonies in order to lighten the burdens of the taxpayers at home. The ministry under the lead of George Grenville began vigorously to enforce the Trade Acts, which had in some cases become dead-letter laws. In 1764 the enactment of the Sugar Act seriously threatened the illegal trade of the colonies with the West Indies. Thus a new policy of regulation was adopted that in effect reorganized the previous loose and tolerant colonial system.[24]

Probably more irritating to the Southern colonists than the new trade regulations was the adoption of a land policy that severely limited western expansion and injured the land speculators. In October, 1763, the British government promulgated the Proclamation of 1763, drafted by the Earl of Shelburne, president of the Board of Trade. It prohibited settlement in the territory west of a line drawn through the sources of the rivers flowing into the Atlantic Ocean, or in other words, the country beyond the Appalachian Mountains—prohibiting colonial governors and councils to issue patents for Western land. The Proclamation Line of 1763 was intended as a temporary expedient to prevent Indian warfare, but this measure was retained as part of British policy and enforced by the Earl of Hillsborough and Lord Dartmouth, secretaries of state for the colonies, who were hostile to westward expansion. In 1768 the British government adopted the policy of a boundary line between the settled area and the Indian country which would be changed periodically as a result of negotiations with the Indians.

The Virginia expansionists feared that the British government would yield to the pressure of groups of speculators in England and in the Northern

[23] See E. B. Russell, *The Review of American Colonial Legislation by the King in Council* (New York, 1915); and Lawrence H. Gipson, *The Coming of the Revolution, 1763–1775* (New York, 1954), 41.
[24] See Robert L. Schuyler, *The Fall of the Old Colonial System* (Oxford, England, 1945).

colonies and grant huge areas of land in the West to their rivals. A group of Pennsylvania merchants and fur traders, headed by Samuel Wharton and William Trent, was urging the British authorities to make a large grant for a colony in the present state of West Virginia to be called Vandalia, when the Revolution stopped their designs. In 1774 the Crown issued stringent new regulations for the sale of Western land, doubling quitrents, requiring the sale of all tracts at auction to the highest bidder, and forbidding the practice of an irregular survey to include only choice fertile lands within a tract. Also in this year the Quebec Act attached all the territory north of the Ohio River and west of Pennsylvania to the Catholic province of Quebec, reserving it as an Indian country and fur-trading preserve. "British land policy as finally formulated in 1774," observes one modern authority, "declared a virtual embargo on colonial expansion in the West." [25] Thus the British government on the eve of the Revolution frustrated one of the strongest urges in American history, westward expansion.

One aspect of the changed colonial policy was the passage on March 22, 1765, of a Stamp Act, ostensibly to pay a part of the expense of maintaining a British army in the colonies. It placed a graduated stamp duty on all legal documents, playing cards, newspapers, pamphlets, almanacs, and even college diplomas. This tax was an innovation. Previously Parliament had enacted trade and customs laws, taxing the colonists indirectly at the seaports, but the Stamp Act levied a direct, internal tax.

The promulgation of the Stamp Act produced a tremendous repercussion in the American colonies.[26] The first great protest against this revenue act was made in the Virginia legislature by Patrick Henry. At this time Henry was twenty-nine years old and had already acquired a reputation as a radical. Born on the Virginia frontier in Hanover County, he had developed a love of freedom and "an itch for popularity." He had not made a success in private life, for he was too lazy to study or work at a business. Failing as a country storekeeper, he acquired a smattering of law and became a lawyer, a member of "a talking profession," and a representative in the House of Burgesses. He delighted in playing the fiddle, in joking with his neighbors, and in hunting and fishing. According to Thomas Jefferson, he would hunt for weeks without changing his shirt or taking a bath, and it bored him to read a book. Nevertheless, this tall, redheaded, young man was a natural orator, who seemed to young Jefferson "to speak as Homer wrote." [27] Patrick Henry became a powerful figure in the Revolutionary movement because he devoted his talents as an agitator to arousing the fears of Americans that their political liberty was endangered by Parliamentary taxation of the colonies. Not an intellectual himself, he reached with his emotional oratory and slogans the

---

[25] Curtis P. Nettels, *The Roots of American Civilization* (New York, 1963), 610.
[26] Edmund S. Morgan, *The Stamp Act Crisis: Prologue to the Revolution* (Chapel Hill, 1953).
[27] Lipscomb and Bergh (eds.), *Writings of Thomas Jefferson*, I, 5, 12; XIV, 341.

Patrick Henry (1736–1799), Orator of the Revolution, and so popular that he was elected governor of Virginia six times. Portrait by Thomas Sully. (Courtesy of Colonial Williamsburg)

great mass of Americans who did not read the newspapers or pamphlets containing the constitutional arguments of the intellectuals.[28]

[28] For more favorable views of Henry, see Robert D. Meade, *Patrick Henry: Patriot in the Making* (Philadelphia, 1957); and Bernard Mayo's essay "The Enigma of Patrick Henry," in *Myths and Men* (New York, 1963). Mayo points out that Henry was less conservative in his old age than he has been represented and that the responsible voters elected him governor of Virginia six times.

Henry was a volcanic radical in his youth and a conservative in his old age. He had gained fame as a radical in the Parson's Case of 1763, in which he maintained that the king and his Privy Council had no constitutional right to veto a law of the colonial legislature. In the Virginia legislature of 1765 he made one of the most effective speeches in the history of American oratory. Carried away by his own extemporaneous oratory he declaimed against the usurpations of the British monarch, comparing him to Caesar, Charles I, and Cromwell, although the real culprit in the attempt to tax the colonies was Parliament, which had passed the Stamp Act. A French spy who witnessed the occasion recorded that after the Speaker had called Henry to order for treasonable utterance, he made an apology for his flaming words and declared his loyalty to the Crown.[29] Later in the evening this backwoods radical was seen walking down the streets of Williamsburg clad in buckskin breeches leading a lame horse.

In addition to his bold speech, Henry introduced seven resolutions in regard to the Stamp Act. They maintained that the colonists possessed all the rights of Englishmen, that taxation without representation was a violation of the British constitution, and that the Virginia assembly alone had the right to tax the colony. His sixth and seventh resolutions declared that the colony was not bound to obey an act of Parliament taxing the colonies, and that anyone who should assert the contrary was an enemy of the colony. When these resolutions were presented to the Virginia assembly most of the members had gone home, leaving only 39 of the 116 members present. Five of Henry's resolves were passed by narrow majorities in the rump legislature, but the radical sixth and seventh resolutions were rejected. The vote was along sectional lines, the Piedmont representatives favoring, while the aristocratic Tidewater representatives voted in the negative.

Opposition to the Stamp Act was expressed by mobs and by a Stamp Act Congress, which met in October, 1765, in New York and asserted the doctrine of no taxation without representation. The colonies of North Carolina, Georgia, and Virginia were unrepresented in this Congress. Petitions were sent to the king, the House of Lords, and the House of Commons, asking for the repeal of the Stamp Act. The colonists found a more efficacious means of bringing about the repeal of the obnoxious measure than petition, namely, a boycott against the importation of British goods.[30] The English merchants then forced Parliament to repeal the act, but at the same time it passed the Declaratory Act, asserting the right of Parliament to legislate for the colonies "in all cases whatsoever."

The Southern participation in initiating the American Revolution may have been influenced, although certainly to a minor degree, by the desire of planters to free themselves from the incubus of debts owed to British mer-

[29] "Journal of a French Traveller in the Colonies, 1765," *American Historical Review,* XXVI (July 1921), 745.
[30] Arthur M. Schlesinger, Sr., *The Colonial Merchants and the American Revolution, 1763–1776* (New York, 1918); and Richard Walsh, *Charleston's Sons of Liberty: A Study of Artisans 1763–1789* (Columbia, S.C., 1959).

chants. The planters had the usual psychology of debtors toward creditors, which was intensified by their belief that the British merchants habitually fleeced them. By the time of the American Revolution the indebtedness of the colonists to their English creditors amounted to £4,000,000, of which approximately one half was owed by Southern planters. The imperial land policy, its money policy, and the Trade Acts, especially as related to the tobacco trade, produced discontent with British rule after 1763 but the main grievance of the Southern colonists, as well as of their Northern neighbors, seems to have been political.[31] The great authority on the American colonies, Charles M. Andrews, has called attention to the significant fact that of the twenty-seven indictments made in the Declaration of Independence only one was concerned with an economic grievance.[32] Although the revived mercantilistic system of regulating trade was a source of irritation, the issue of taxation by Parliament appears to have been of more vital concern to the American colonists as a whole. The colonists were resolved not to submit to the new imperial policy of Great Britain after the French and Indian War that threatened their political liberty.

As early as 1760 the inhabitants of the tobacco colonies had evolved a bold and independent spirit that was the forerunner of the American Revolution. This fact was noted by the Reverend Andrew Burnaby who was traveling in Virginia and Maryland at that time. "The public or political character of the Virginians," this Englishment wrote, "corresponds with their private one; they are haughty and jealous of their liberties, impatient of restraint, and can scarcely bear the thought of being controlled by any superior power. Many of them consider the colonies as independent states, not connected with Great Britain, otherwise than by having the same common king, being bound to her by natural affection." [33] Thus the inhabitants of the English colonies in America had imperceptibly become Americans. During the next ten years the American colonies developed more vigorously this rudimentary idea of a federal empire, in which each component had the right to pass laws and levy taxes for itself through its own legislature. Their concept of the federal, rather than the unitary, empire was belatedly adopted by the British government in 1931 by the Statute of Westminster.

The American Revolution cannot be adequately explained without considering the growth of the colonial mind. Two profound influences had changed the mental outlook of the colonists of 1775 from the temper and point of view of their seventeenth-century forefathers. They had been affected by the American environment, particularly the plantation and the

[31] For a discussion of the causes of the American Revolution, see C. H. Van Tyne, *The Causes of the War of Independence* (Boston, 1922); and John C. Miller, *Origins of the American Revolution* (Boston, 1943); and Bernard Bailyn, *Ideological Origins of the American Revolution* (Cambridge, Mass., 1967).

[32] C. M. Andrews, *The Colonial Period of American History* (New Haven, 1938), IV, 427.

[33] Andrew Burnaby, *Travels through the Middle Settlements in North America in the Years 1759–1760* (London, 1775), 24.

American frontier, and by the European Enlightenment. The principal effect both of the frontier and of the plantation life was to intensify the natural tendency of men to resist the imposition of outside authority or intermeddling with their affairs. Southern planters were little kings on their planations, and they resented the intrusion of distant British authority, which had become more efficient and meddlesome, upon the liberties that they had previously enjoyed. The European Enlightenment liberated their minds from excessive reverence for authority of all kinds, particularly religious and governmental. The old patterns of thought that had upheld authority were breaking down under the impact of the growing scientific spirit, following the epochal discoveries of Isaac Newton. This spirit was manifest in the growth of rationalism in religion, in the emergence of new economic doctrines of laissez faire, which found classic expression in Adam Smith's *The Wealth of Nations,* and in the spread of the natural rights philosophy elaborated by John Locke and Rousseau. The natural rights philosophy taught the dignity of man, that he has certain natural rights that must be respected by government.

The masses would probably have remained inert if they had not been stirred to action by a well-organized and determined minority of radicals.[34] In Charleston, South Carolina, the most effective agitator was Christopher Gadsden, who led the mechanic and lower classes in the "Liberty Tree Party," later called "Sons of Liberty," although he himself belonged to the aristocracy. Public opinion was inflamed by such dramatic episodes as the burning of the tea ship *Peggy Stewart,* at Annapolis, Maryland, and the Edenton (North Carolina) Tea Party, in which a group of ladies burned their household supplies of tea to protest against Parliamentary taxation. A powerful weapon in arousing the colonists was the boycott of British goods, which was enforced in the local communities by committees of safety, dominated in the Southern colonies by planters and lawyers. Also cooperation with the Northern radicals was advanced by committees of correspondence.

The drastic punishment of Boston after the Tea Party of December 16, 1773, crystallized the spirit of resistance in the colonies. Virginia generously sent food to the New England city, whose harbor had been closed until the destroyed tea had been paid for. The indentured servant John Harrower noted in his diary that his master, owner of a plantation near Fredericksburg, had donated one hundred bushels of wheat and 50 bushels of corn to the inhabitants of Boston on this occasion. The Virginia assembly set aside June 1, 1774, as a solemn day of fasting and prayer to protest against the punishment of Boston by the "Intolerable Acts"—a dramatic piece of propaganda to arouse the people. Lord Dunmore, the governor, dissolved the legislature for this disloyal act, but the burgesses assembled in the Apollo Room of the Raleigh Tavern at Williamsburg and summoned the first Continental Congress to meet in Philadelphia.[35]

---

[34] See Arthur M. Schlesinger, Sr., *Prelude to Independence: The Newspaper War On Britain, 1764–1776* (New York, 1958).

[35] See E. C. Burnett, *The Continental Congress* (New York, 1941) and *Letters of Members of the Continental Congress* (Washington, 1921).

A clash at arms between the colonial patriots and royal troops occurred at Lexington, Massachusetts, on April 19, 1775. Two months later the Second Continental Congress appointed George Washington commander-in-chief of the Continental army. He was, in reality, an amateur, but less so than his suborbinate generals, his chief of artillery, Henry Knox, for example, being a Boston bookseller, and his greatest general, Nathanael Greene, being a Rhode Island blacksmith. For over a year after the Battle of Lexington the colonists fought for redress of grievances rather than for independence. On June 7, 1776, Richard Henry Lee of Virginia introduced a resolution proposing a declaration of independence. This resolution was adopted July 2, and two days later a formal Declaration of Independence, written by Thomas Jefferson, was accepted by a unanimous vote.[36]

Public opinion in the Southern as well as the Northern colonies, however, was seriously divided in regard to the support of the Revolution. In Virginia there were perhaps fewer Loyalists or Tories than in any other colony, and in Maryland also they were very weak. In North Carolina the Tories and the Patriots (often called Whigs) were about evenly matched, whereas in South Carolina and Georgia perhaps a majority of the population were hostile to the independence movement. It is a significant fact that Massachusetts contributed more soldiers to the Continental army than did the five combined Southern states.[37]

Various motives explain the loyalty of Southern Tories to the British Empire. The Scottish merchants as a rule were opposed to the Revolution, because it would destroy their trade connections with England. Probably a majority of the Anglican clergy was disposed to remain loyal, because of the establishment of the Church of England in the Southern colonies and its close connection with the mother country. The "governor's set" was naturally loyal to the royal government. The *Letters from America,* written by William Eddis, secretary of Governor Robert Eden of Maryland, reflect the point of view of this group, who were hostile to the revolutionary movement. Although the great planters and lawyers of the Southern colonies as a whole supported the patriotic cause, there were some who became Tories or pursued a noncommittal or inactive course during the Revolution. In Maryland the most prominent Loyalist was Daniel Dulany, a brilliant lawyer, who wrote an influential pamphlet in 1765 against the Stamp Act, in which he maintained that taxation without representation was a violation of the English common law. After hostilities began, nevertheless, he became a Loyalist, and most of his property was confiscated by the Maryland Assembly.[38] In Virginia Wil-

[36] See Carl Becker, *The Declaration of Independence* (New York, 1922); and Julian Boyd, *The Declaration of Independence; the Evolution of the Text* (Washington, 1943).
[37] See R. O. DeMond, *The Loyalists in North Carolina during the Revolution* (Durham, 1940), 60–61; J. S. Harrell, *Loyalism in Virginia* (Philadelphia, 1926); Lorenzo Sabine, *The American Loyalists* (Boston, 1847), 31; and William H. Nelson, *The American Tory* (New York, 1961).
[38] A. C. Land, *The Dulanys of Maryland* (Baltimore, 1955).

liam Byrd III, Lord Fairfax, and John Randolph, the Attorney General, were Loyalists, and Robert Carter of *Nomini Hall* took no part in the Revolution. In South Carolina some of the large planters and lawyers, such as Rawlins Lowndes, were opposed to radical measures that would lead to independence, yet they favored resistance to Parliamentary taxation. Ultimately they joined the revolutionary movement, hoping that England would make concessions and that a reconciliation would take place.

In each of the colonies there were local and special influences that operated to turn men to the Tory or the Patriot cause. Many of the inhabitants of the back country, particularly former Regulators, were disposed to remain loyal because of their hatred of the Tidewater aristocracy, who had denied them equality in the colonial assemblies. The Scotch Highlanders of North Carolina remained true to their oath of allegiance to the king and fought for the British. The German Moravians of North Carolina adopted a neutral attitude in the contest. In Virginia the odious conduct of the last royal governor, Lord Dunmore, who tried to foment a servile insurrection in 1775 and who ordered the seaport of Norfolk to be burned, tended to consolidate wavering opinion behind the Patriot cause. Also, the Virginia government allowed the numerous debtors of British merchants to settle their debts by paying sums due into the state treasury in depreciated paper money. In Maryland the Catholics were led by Father John Carroll, who aided the Continental Congress in trying to enlist the support of the French Canadians, and the very wealthy planter, Charles Carroll, espoused the Whig cause, setting an example to other Catholic landowners. On the other hand, in Georgia there were several factors favoring the Loyalist side, the generosity of Parliament in giving the colony an annual subsidy of £8,000, the presence of hostile Indian tribes on the frontier, the popularity of the royal governor, Sir James Wright, and the proximity of the British province of East Florida, which could be used as a base for attack on the Georgia frontier.

The South was relatively free from the devastation of British armies until near the end of the war.[39] Failing in the North, the British military command undertook a campaign in the South that at first was successful, resulting in the capture of the seaport of Savannah (December 29, 1778) and of Charleston (May 12, 1780). An attempt by General Horatio Gates to retrieve the American cause in the South ended in ignominious disgrace when his green troops fled from the battlefield of Camden, South Carolina. The fighting in the South often assumed the character of a civil war, Tories against Patriots, and of a guerilla warfare, waged notably in South Carolina by Francis Marion, "the Swamp Fox," and Thomas Sumter, the "Gamecock." In the battle of King's Mountain, on the border between North and South

---

[39] For military events in the South, see W. M. Wallace, *Appeal to Arms, a Military History of the Revolution* (New York, 1951); Christopher Ward, *The War of the Revolution* (New York, 1952), 2 vols.; and William B. Willcox, *Portrait of a General* [Sir Henry Clinton] (New York, 1964).

George Washington at Yorktown, by Charles Willson Peale. (Courtesy of Kirby Collection, Lafayette College)

Carolina (October 7, 1780), a band of backwoodsmen led by Isaac Shelby, John Sevier, and William Campbell administered a decisive defeat to the Tories commanded by Colonel Patrick Ferguson and checked the British use of the Tories. A few months later American troops under General Daniel Morgan defeated the hated General Banastre Tarleton at the battle of Cowpens in western South Carolina. General Cornwallis, who had succeeded General Clinton in command in the South, now invaded North Carolina.

After an indecisive battle at Guilford Court House in which the American troops were led by Nathanael Greene, Cornwallis retired to the Yorktown peninsula in Virginia. Here the British commander was surrounded by American forces under Washington and Lafayette, as well as by a French fleet, under De Grasse and a French army under Rochambeau. Thus trapped, the British army was forced to surrender, October 19, 1781, but the war did not end formally until the signing of the Treaty of Paris two years later, which recognized the independence of the American states with a western boundary extending to the Mississippi River. Great Britain also returned Florida to Spain.

The impact of the Revolution on the Southern colonies seems to have been greater on their social and political life than on their economy. The confiscation of Tory estates did result in the elimination of certain huge concentrations of land, notably the Lord Baltimore estate, the Fairfax estate, the Granville Tract in North Carolina, and the extensive holdings of Sir James Wright in Georgia, which were divided into small farms and plantations.[40] But the market for Southern staples was not seriously disturbed by the breaking of the political connection with Great Britain. Furthermore, the loss of the monopoly of the British market was more than compensated for by freeing the planters from British trade restrictions. Theoretically, commerce with the British West Indies was prohibited to American ships after the Revolution, not to be opened until Jackson's treaty in 1830, but actually Southern trade with the Caribbean ports flourished.[41] The Revolution resulted in the withdrawal of the bounty on indigo, and subsequently the cultivation of the plant declined, but not primarily because of the loss of the bounty. On the other hand, the removal of the burden of quitrents and the abolition of the remnants of primogeniture and entail represented an economic gain, though primogeniture did not disappear in South Carolina until 1791.

The Southern states shared in the postwar economic depression that affected the whole nation. In order to relieve the debtor class, the states issued large quantities of paper money, especially in 1785 and 1786. In South Carolina the paper money issues were conservatively managed and they did not depreciate badly, owing partly to the Hint Club, which sent ropes as reminders to persons who would not accept the paper currency of the state. In North Carolina and Georgia the radicals triumphed over the conservatives and secured the passage of inflationary paper money bills. In North Carolina the paper currency declined to one half the value of specie. Virginia, however, escaped the evil consequences of the paper money rage. She had paid her Revolutionary soldiers with land warrants for wild land in Kentucky, and the conservatives controlled the state.

The American Revolution stimulated a movement to eradicate slavery from the South. Not only did the natural rights philosophy of the Revolu-

---

[40] See J. F. Jameson, *The American Revolution Considered as a Social Movement* (Princeton, 1926).
[41] See John R. Alden, *The South in the Revolution, 1763–1789* (Baton Rouge, 1957).

tionary period predispose men's minds to unshackling the fetters of the slaves but the unprofitableness of slavery in the tobacco region following the Revolution created economic conditions favorable to an emancipation movement. The Southern states abolished the African slave trade during this period, Virginia in 1778, Georgia being the last, in 1798. Jefferson was the leader in his native state in urging the adoption of a plan for the gradual emancipation of the slaves. Although his advice was not followed, Virginia did pass a law in 1782 making the process of emancipating slaves by individual masters much easier. In 1784 Jefferson drew up an ordinance for the government of the unsettled Federal territory, which he presented to the Congress of the Confederation. It contained a provision abolishing slavery after the year 1800 in all the vast region of the Mississippi Valley then owned by the United States. When this measure was defeated by one vote, Jefferson lamented: "Thus we see the fate of millions unborn hanging on the tongue of one man, and Heaven was silent in that awful moment!" [42] The Negro historian W. E. B. DuBois has pointed out that the most favorable opportunity to effect the emancipation of the slaves came in the period following the Revolution, before the invention of the cotton gin (1793). Nevertheless, the great opportunity of peaceful emancipation was allowed to slip by, and it never came again, for the expansion of cotton culture resuscitated the languishing institution and men's economic interests became more deeply involved in perpetuating slavery.

Social life in the Southern states was affected indirectly by the Revolution in many ways. The officers of the American army established the Society of the Cincinnati to perpetuate patriotic memories, but it was regarded by stern republicans as an aristocratic organization that should not be countenanced. Anglophobia, generated by the Revolution, continued for many years to affect American politics, and the precedent of elevating military heroes into political positions was established. The Revolutionary struggle also contributed to the spread of dueling, especially in the Southern colonies. The example of the French officers who aided the American cause was contagious in the adoption of this artificial code of honor that required men to fight duels when they thought themselves insulted or their honor impugned. After Alexander Hamilton was killed by Aaron Burr in a duel in 1804, the pernicious practice was strongly condemned by public opinion in the North and fell into disuse in that region, but in the Southern states dueling flourished until the Civil War. A humanitarian movement arose during and after the American Revolution that led to the revision of the harsh criminal codes of the colonial period. In Virginia, Jefferson, who was a student of the Italian legal reformer Beccaria, succeeded in revising the criminal code in 1779 so that only two crimes, treason and murder, were made punishable by death. [43]

[42] Bernard Mayo (ed.), *Jefferson Himself* (Boston, 1942), 109.
[43] See Marie Kimball, *Jefferson, War and Peace, 1776 to 1784* (New York, 1947); and William E. Dodd, *Statesmen of the Old South* (New York, 1911). Dodd exaggerated Jefferson's achievements in reform.

The American Revolution had a liberating influence on the religious life of the South. The Church of England was disestablished in the Southern states, and the principle of the separation of the church and state was gradually accepted. In Virginia, Jefferson drafted a noble Statute for Religious Freedom, which was introduced into the legislature in 1779. This bill declared that "all men shall be free to profess, and by argument to maintain, their opinions in matter of religion, and that the same shall in no wise diminish, enlarge, or affect their civil capacities." It was not adopted at that time, but while Jefferson was absent as minister in France, the question was revived in 1784, when a bill was introduced to pay the teachers of the Christian religion by a general assessment on taxpayers. This proposal was supported by a combination of Episcopalians and Presbyterians as well as by the Revolutionary leaders, George Washington, Patrick Henry, and Richard Henry Lee. The fight in the legislature for the principle of religious toleration and the complete separation of church and state was led by James Madison, who in 1786 secured the passage by the legislature of Jefferson's famous statute. In contrast to the liberal action of the Southern states in disestablishing the Anglican church, the Congregational church in Connecticut was not disestablished until 1818 and in Massachusetts not until 1833.

The Revolution contributed to the nationalizing of the American churches. John Wesley, the English founder of Methodism, had opposed the American Revolution, but at the conclusion of the war he advised a separate organization of the American church. This step was taken at the Baltimore Conference, Christmas, 1784, when a set of doctrines and a constitution were adopted for the new church, which was named the Methodist Episcopal church. Francis Asbury, the first American bishop of the church, spread its influence over the back country and among the poorer classes by the establishment of the typical American institution of the Methodist circuit rider.[44] Despite a frail body and frequent sickness he traveled incessantly on horseback to preach to touchingly ignorant and naïve people in the South and West, who gathered to hear him in barns, in the forests, and in humble log cabins, as well as in the more formal church buildings. His journal shows that he was imbued with the booster spirit. When he died in 1816 he had traveled approximately three hundred thousand miles during his religious crusade, had preached more than sixteen thousand sermons, and had ordained at least four thousand ministers.

In contrast to English practice, but following the precedent of the colonial charters, all the colonies adopted written constitutions during the Revolution. South Carolina was the first Southern state to draw up a constitution, in March, 1776, and Georgia was the last, in February, 1777. In framing these fundamental laws, Maryland, Virginia, and South Carolina were firmly controlled by the conservatives. The new constitutions were hastily drawn up by

---

[44] Elmer T. Clark (ed.), *The Journal and Letters of John Wesley* (London, 1958), 3 vols.

a few dominant personalities, such as George Mason in Virginia; Samuel Chase, Charles Carroll, and William Paca in Maryland; Willie Jones and Richard Caswell in North Carolina; and John Rutledge in South Carolina. Furthermore, they were not submitted to the people for ratification.

The Revolution did not disturb seriously the power of the colonial aristocracy.[45] In no case was free manhood suffrage granted by the new constitutions of the Southern states. In Maryland and South Carolina a property qualification of fifty acres of land, in Virginia twenty-five acres of settled land or five hundred unsettled, was required of all voters; in North Carolina and Georgia all taxpayers were permitted to vote. Relatively high property qualifications were imposed on members of the legislature and state officials. Even in one of the most radical of the Southern states, North Carolina, a state senator had to own three hundred acres of land, and the conservative constitution of Maryland prescribed a property qualification for senators of £2,000. Members of the lower house of the legislature had to be substantial citizens, owning £500 of property in Maryland, £250 in Georgia, and one hundred acres in North Carolina. The governor of South Carolina had to be a patrician worth £10,000 or more, but in North Carolina the qualification was only £1,000. In addition to these property qualifications on voting and officeholding, the colonial aristocracy perpetuated its power by arranging representation in the legislature so that the wealthy slaveowning Tidewater outvoted the Piedmont with its larger population of poorer freemen.[46]

The Revolutionary constitutions reflected the experience of the colonists in their struggle with the royal governors. The powers of the governors were severely curbed by depriving them of the veto power, the authority to summon or dissolve the legislature, and most of the appointive power. In South Carolina the chief executive was called president until 1779, when the title governor was substituted. Although the principle of separation of the executive, legislative, and judicial powers was universally held in the states, the legislature was given excessive authority over the government. Not only did it exercise many of the executive functions, such as the appointive power, but it also elected the governor and the judges. The lower house of the legislature was chosen by a minority of the people in annual elections, and the upper house was elected by popular vote only in Virginia and North Carolina. In Maryland the senators were chosen by an electoral college, in South Carolina by the lower house; and in Georgia there was no upper house. Georgia and South Carolina represented the extremes of government in the Southern states, South Carolina having the most aristocratic frame of government, and Georgia the most democratic form. Only in Georgia were

---

[45] See Elisha P. Douglass, *Rebels and Democrats: The Struggle for Equal Political Rights and Majority Rule during the American Revolution* (Chapel Hill, 1955).
[46] Fletcher M. Green, *Constitutional Development in the South Atlantic States, 1776–1860* (Chapel Hill, 1930), is a pioneer work in the realistic study of Southern constitutional history.

the judges selected by popular vote, and its radical unicameral legislature had no parallel in the United States, save the eccentric constitution of Pennsylvania. The early state constitutions revealed a distrust of democracy and of executive authority, a tender regard for the rights of property, and were in many respects at variance with the philosophy of the Declaration of Independence.

Nevertheless, the Revolutionary constitutions made a long step toward the ideal of human liberty in the incorporation of bills of rights. The first and most important of these statements of personal liberties was the Declaration of Rights drafted by George Mason of *Gunston Hall* and adopted June 12, 1776, as a part of the Virginia constitution. It served as a model for other states, and some of its doctrines were incoporated three weeks later in Jefferson's Declaration of Independence. These bills of rights were based on the concept of the limited state, derived from a social compact. The Virginia Declaration of Rights declared that men are "by nature equally free and independent" and that they have certain natural and inalienable rights that governments should respect. These bills of rights preserved both the ancient and recently acquired liberties of Englishmen, such as the rights of jury trial, indictment by a grand jury, freedom from excessive bail or from cruel and unusual punishments or arbitrary arrests, the right of petition, freedom of speech and of the press, and religious toleration. Included in these documents were the principles of the separation of church and state and the subordination of the military to the civil government. The preservation of civil liberties by a written constitution is one of the most enduring achievements of the Revolutionary period. Although the natural rights theory that underlay the bills of rights has been discredited, the doctrine of the free individual, the assertion of the dignity of American citizens, found in these documents, remains as a precious heritage of our Revolutionary past.

Through the Cumberland Gap

Lay down, boys, an' take a little nap,
Fourteen miles to the Cum-ber-land Gap.

The first white man in Cumberland Gap
Was Doctor Walker, an English chap.

Daniel Boone on Pinnacle Rock,
He killed Indians with an old flintlock.

I've got a woman in Cumberland Gap
She's got a boy that calls me "pap."

Lay down, boys, an' take a little nap,
They're all raisin' Hell in Cumberland Gap.

CUMBERLAND GAP has the romantic interest in the history of the American frontier that the pass of Thermopylae had in ancient Greece. It was the scene of conflicts between Indians and frontiersmen, and it was the funnel through which the westward movement passed. Located at the point where the three states of Virginia, Kentucky, and Tennessee meet, it was discovered in 1674 by an illiterate frontiersman, Gabriel Arthur, who had been sent to the Cherokee country by Abraham Wood, the Indian trader located at the falls of the Appomattox (present-day Petersburg). In 1750 the pass was rediscovered and named by Dr. Thomas Walker of Virginia, agent of the Loyal Land Company, who built a cabin near Barbourville, Kentucky. Through this famous rift in the mountains ran the Great Warrior Path, which was used by the Shawnee and Iroquois Indians to attack the southern tribes. "Stand at Cumberland Gap," wrote Frederick Jackson Turner in his epochal essay on the significance of the frontier in American history, "and watch the procession of civilization, marching single file—the buffalo following the trail to the salt springs, the Indian, the fur-trader and hunter, the cattle-raiser, the pioneer farmer—and the frontier has passed by." [1]

Thus, Turner stated his great generalization that has had such a fruitful influence on the interpretation of American history. He conceived of the frontier not only as a region of thin population, the edge of settlement, a line moving westward, but also as a sociological process whereby society in America was continually evolving from more primitive stages into higher and more complex forms. The first frontier of the explorer and hunter was followed by the second stage of evolution, the frontier of the fur trader; then

[1] F. J. Turner, *The Frontier in American History* (New York, 1921), 12.

came the frontier of the cattle pens, at times supplemented by the mining frontier; agricultural advance into the lonely wilderness was led by the pioneer farmer with his ax on his shoulder; and finally the substantial farmer firmly established civilization with his school and church. Turner believed that the frontier left a strong imprint on American society as it moved westward, like the terminal moraines of a retreating glacier. The American frontier converted the European settler into an American and developed distinctive American qualities, such as individualism, a love of democracy, resourcefulness and versatility, optimism, a feeling of nationalism, and a curious blend of materialism and idealism. The frontier, he believed, offered an escape for disappointment or underprivileged persons in the East, a safety valve for labor in the older part of the country.

The Turner frontier thesis has been attacked as presenting too great a simplification of American history.[2] The revisionists have pointed out that Turner's theory was primarily geographic determinism, leaving little freedom to the individual personality, and that it failed to take account sufficiently of cultural ideas and institutions brought from Europe. The safety valve thesis particularly has been severely attacked, because few laborers in the eastern cities had either the skill needed to cope with the wilderness or the money to escape from bad laboring conditions to the frontier. Furthermore, the fact that emigration to the West was greatest during boom periods and declined during periods of depression throws serious doubts on the validity of the safety valve theory. In his analysis of the various stages of the frontier the Wisconsin and Harvard historian failed to appreciate the significant role of the land speculator and the overlapping of frontiers. Even Turner's originality has been denied by some scholars, who observe that his basic ideas were derived from census officials, especially Francis A. Walker, superintendent of the Census of 1870, and Henry Gannett, and from his teachers at the University of Wisconsin. Despite these criticisms, Turner's frontier thesis has great value in explaining social evolution in the South, where the frontier process was modified and colored by the presence of Negro slavery. Turner's ideas are especially fruitful in pointing the way to the study of regionalism, or sectionalism, in American history, which underlies so much of American politics. He believed that the history of the nation could be understood only by studying the emergence of sections and the way they acted, illustrating their behavior by various maps. Thus he has furnished an invaluable tool for the historian of the South.[3]

---

[2] G. W. Pierson, "The Frontier and American Institutions: A Criticism of the Turner Theory," *New England Quarterly,* XV (June 1942), 224–255; M. Kane, "Some Considerations of the Frontier Concept of Frederick Jackson Turner," *Mississippi Valley Historical Review,* XXVII (December 1940), 379–400; and F. A. Shannon, "A Post-Mortem on the Labor-Safety-Valve Theory," *Agricultural History* (January, 1945), 31–37.

[3] The author recalls vividly that when he was a graduate student at Harvard University in one of Turner's last classes, his interest had shifted to sectionalism, which he

The South experienced an especially glamorous phase of its frontier history just before and during the Revolution when hunters and explorers crossed the mountains into Kentucky and Tennessee and the first settlements there were made. At the time of the Revolution, Kentucky, though teeming with wild game, was unoccupied by any Indian tribe. The Shawnee, an Algonquin tribe, had a famous trading village, Eskippakithiki, in central Kentucky near Winchester, but they had abandoned it in 1754. The Iroquois, with the aid of the white man's guns, prevented this beautiful country from being appropriated by any tribe. When the Long Hunters and Daniel Boone entered Kentucky it was indeed a debatable land between the northern and southern tribes, "the dark and bloody ground."

Around the name of Daniel Boone has grown a mighty legend, which has magnified the exploits and the importance of this worthy pioneer. The myth-making process began with the publication in 1784 of John Filson's *Discovery, Settlement, and Present State of Kentucke*. Filson was a schoolmaster and Kentucky's first historian, who claimed to have preserved in this volume Boone's autobiography, but who used such stilted language and embroidered the plain narrative of the old frontiersman to such an extent that his work is unreliable.[4] John James Audubon also contributed to the Boone myth by his anecdotes and his description of the hero as gigantic in size. Actually, Boone was of medium height, although extraordinarily agile and muscular. The only authentic picture of him was painted by Chester Harding in 1819, the year before Boone died, when he was a hale old man of eighty-five years. He had mild blue eyes, and in young manhood light hair and yellow eyebrows, a fine forehead, and a Roman nose. He had a passion for the untrammeled life of the wilderness, and in association with "civilized" men, he was unworldly. Pleasant, quiet-spoken, and free from the frontier vices, he was distinguished by a remarkable serenity of mind.

The great frontiersman Daniel Boone was born in 1734 near Reading, Pennsylvana, into a Quaker family who engaged in weaving, the trade of blacksmith, and farming. In 1751 they emigrated to the Yadkin Valley in the back country of North Carolina, where at Joppa graveyard in Davie County is the grave of Squire Boone, Daniel's father. The young "Nimrod of the Yadkin" took part in the Braddock expedition during the French and Indian War, not as a fighter, but as a teamster and blacksmith. In 1765 he visited Pensacola, Florida, and thought of settling there, but his wife refused to move. In the backwoods of North Carolina he became highly skilled in the ways of the woods and in the use of his flintlock rifle. Although his spelling and grammar were semiliterate, he acquired such an accurate knowledge of Indian character and warfare that he could "think Indian."

---

illustrated by maps and charts of voting patterns—a forerunner of modern quantification. See R. A. Billington *Frederick Jackson Turner: Historian, Scholar, Teacher* (New York, 1973).

[4] John Walton, *John Filson of Kentucke* (Lexington, 1956).

Daniel Boone in Missouri in 1819, the year before he died. By Chester Harding (1792–1866). (Courtesy of Filson Club of Louisville, Kentucky)

The Boone myth represents its hero as the first explorer of Kentucky, and also as the first white man to plant a settlement in Kentucky. Neither of these claims is true. Boone was only one of a considerable number of explorers and hunters who visited Kentucky and Tennessee before the region was settled. In the decade of the 1760's the Long Hunters, or groups of men who hunted for considerable periods of time in the western wilderness, had traversed a large part of Kentucky and Tennessee and had named many of the natural features of the country. Indeed, Boone was told of "Kaintuck," a paradise for hunters, by John Finley, a Pennsylvania fur trader who had hunted in that region. He first met Finley in the Braddock campaign, but in the winter of 1768–1769 Finley wandered into the Yadkin Valley as a peddler and fired Boone's imagination by his narrative of Kentucky. Boone was desperately poor at this time, and he welcomed an opportunity to recruit his fortunes by a trip into this fabulous hunting ground for peltry and deerskins, which sold for a dollar a skin. Piloted by Finley, he and several associates in the spring of 1769 passed through the Cumberland Gap into Kentucky, where they collected many deerskins and beaver furs. In the winter of 1770 Boone spent three months living alone in the wilderness of Kentucky, but he found this dangerous life exhilarating. Although he and his brother Squire, who had joined him, gathered a valuable supply of furs, they were robbed by a band of Cherokee as they were returning home.[5]

In September, 1773, Boone led a party of frontiersmen and their families to plant a settlement in this fabulous land. The expedition was attacked by Indians in Powell's Valley, near Cumberland Gap, during which Boone's eldest son was killed, and the group became so discouraged that they returned home. As a result of this disaster, the first white man to accomplish a settlement in Kentucky was not Boone but James Harrod of Pennsylvania, who in 1774 founded Harrodsburg in central Kentucky. The outbreak of Lord Dunmore's War caused the temporary abandonment of the little settlement, but it was reoccupied the next year.

The Boone myth also neglects the important role of Judge Richard Henderson in the settlement of Kentucky. Henderson was a wealthy aristocrat, member of a law firm of Salisbury, North Carolina, who was an insatiable land speculator. In 1774 he formed the Transylvania Company to buy the Indian claims to the rich lands of Kentucky between the Cumberland and Kentucky rivers. In the following year he assembled more than a thousand Cherokee at Sycamore Shoals on the Watauga River (in northeastern Tennessee) and purchased from them by treaty their shadowy claim to Kentucky as well as a path from Long Island in the Holston River to the Cumberland Gap. Although they were given £10,000 worth of trading goods, the sale was vehemently opposed by a faction led by Dragging Canoe and Groundhog-Sausage. Finally, the white men won over the fickle savages with the aid of the friendly chief Little Carpenter. It is doubtful whether the Cherokee could have given a valid title to this area of wild land, which they did not occupy. Furthermore, the right of the Transylvania Company to purchase this huge tract of land between the Kentucky and Cumberland rivers from the Indians without a Crown grant was highly dubious.

In the spring of 1775, Boone, as an employee of the Transylvania Company, with thirty axmen blazed Boone's Trace, which became a part of the

---

[5] See Reuben G. Thwaites, *Daniel Boone* (New York, 1902); and John Bakeless, *Daniel Boone, Master of the Wilderness* (New York, 1939).

Wilderness Road through the Cumberland Gap to the Bluegrass region of Kentucky. On the Kentucky River he founded the pioneer settlement of Boonesborough. A few weeks later Judge Richard Henderson led another contingent of settlers to this capital of Transylvania. In May, 1775, Henderson summoned a legislature to meet under a gigantic elm at Boonesborough, which drew up a bill of rights guaranteeing religious liberty and a democratic form of government. Henderson and his associates conceived of the Transylvania colony as a proprietary colony like Maryland. They hoped to make lucrative profits from the sale of land and from charging an annual quitrent of 2 shillings for each one hundred acres.[6]

The grandiose plans of the Transylvania proprietors were thwarted by the independent spirit of the frontiersmen who had settled at various stations in Kentucky. The resistance movement to the proprietorship was initiated by the men of Harrodsburg, who were urged to bold action by George Rogers Clark. This tall redheaded adventurer, who was born near Charlottesville, Virginia, the son of a planter, was engaged in surveying in Kentucky at the time. In 1776 he and another delegate were selected by the people of Harrodsburg to carry a petition to the Virginia government, protesting against the claims of Henderson and his partners and asking to be incorporated into Virginia. After a journey of incredible hardships and peril along the Wilderness Road, Clark arrived at Williamsburg. His mission was eminently successful, for the Virginia authorities sent a large supply of powder to Kentucky and in December, 1776, created the county of Kentucky, embracing all the scattered settlements in this vast area. Thus the ambitious project of the state of Transylvania collapsed, but Henderson was compensated by a grant of two hundred thousand acres of land at the mouth of the Green River, where the town of Henderson stands today.[7]

Daniel Boone's later career in Kentucky demonstrated that shrewdness in woodcraft and Indian warfare did not fit a man for coping with the complexities of a more civilized society. Shortly after his founding of Boonesborough he graduated from hunter and explorer to frontier surveyor. The Kentucky land system became a mass of conflicting and overlapping claims, because of the loose and unsystematic surveys that were often based on the location of trees or other temporary landmarks. Boone took out patents for numerous tracts of land ranging from four hundred acres to ten thousand. Unfortunately, he failed to follow the proper legal procedure in recording his titles, so that his land was taken away from him by a series of ejection suits. For a while he became a tavern keeper and merchant at Limestone (Maysville), the chief gateway to Kentucky from the north. He was also appointed a justice of the peace and represented Fayette County in the Virginia legislature. This master of woodcraft was robbed of $20,000 as he slept in a

[6] Archibald Henderson, *The Conquest of the Old Southwest* (New York, 1920); Theodore Roosevelt, *The Winning of the West* (New York, 1889–1896), 4 vols.; and W. S. Lester, *The Transylvania Colony* (Spencer, Ind., 1935).

[7] Robert L. Kincaid, *The Wilderness Road* (Indianapolis, 1947).

tavern during a journey to Richmond in 1780 to purchase land warrants for himself and neighbors. Disgusted with his failures, the loss of land, and the disappearance of the old freedom of the frontier as a result of the growth of population, he abandoned Kentucky in 1788 and lived in the valley of the Great Kanawha River. Ten years later he removed to the Femme Osage Creek in eastern Missouri. Here he was granted one thousand arpents of land by the Spanish authorities, became a syndic, or official, and went on long hunts for bear and deer. He enjoyed a serene old age, dying in 1820, but not before he had made a last visit to Kentucky to pay his old debts. His body was later brought back to the scene of his early exploits and interred at Frankfort on the banks of the Kentucky River.

During the course of the American Revolution the Kentucky settlements were forced to defend themselves from formidable Indian attacks. In addition to Boonesborough, there had developed a number of isolated little settlements, such as Harrodsburg, Logan's Fort, Bryan's Station, Limestone on the Ohio River, and Lexington, which was named by the frontiersmen after they had received news of the battle of Lexington in far-off Massachusetts.[8] These settlements were protected from Indian attacks by palisades built around the clusters of cabins, with blockhouses at the four corners of the enclosure. Brave Indian fighters and land seekers, such as George Rogers Clark, Simon Kenton, the Todds, the Calloways, and Benjamin Logan kept Kentucky from being abandoned as a result of the Indian menace.

Indian attacks on the Kentucky frontier during the Revolution were instigated by the commandant at Detroit, Governor Henry Hamilton, called the "Hair Buyer" by his savage allies. In January, 1778, Boone and a party of frontiersmen were engaged in boiling salt water from the springs of the Lower Blue Licks in huge kettles when they were surprised by a band of Indians, and Boone was captured. The captives were taken to the Shawnee village of Little Chillicothe in Ohio, where Boone was adopted as a member of the family of the chief, Black Fish. However, the skilled frontiersman managed to escape from his captivity and reach Boonesborough in time to warn settlers to strengthen the fortifications and prepare for an attack. Early in September, 1778, Black Fish appeared before Boonesborough with four hundred warriors, including some forty French-Canadians. Finding the inhabitants alert, they laid seige unsuccessfully to the palisaded village for nine days, a record for Indian constancy in continuing a siege.

In August, 1782, occurred the darkest hour in Kentucky's struggle to survive Indian warfare. A band of braves, led by British officers and including the famous renegade Simon Girty, attacked Bryan's Station, five miles from Lexington, but were repulsed. The frontiersmen were so elated over this success that force of 182 men under Colonel John Todd set out in pursuit of the retiring enemy. When they reached the Licking River, in northern Kentucky, Boone and other experienced frontiersmen advised caution and

8 See Kathryn H. Mason, *James Harrod of Kentucky* (Baton Rouge, 1951).

waiting for reinforcements, but a daredevil spirit led to an impetuous charge across the river. Here near the Blue Lick Springs the main body of the Indians were lying in ambush. The Kentuckians fought bravely but were badly defeated and left seventy of their number dead on the field of battle.

The most effective method of protecting the Kentucky frontier was to capture the Illinois country and its chief military post, Detroit, the source of instigation and of supply to hostile Indians. Such a plan was carried out by George Rogers Clark in a bold campaign during 1778–1779. Commissioned by Governor Patrick Henry and given £1,200 of depreciated paper money, he gathered a little army of 175 men at his rendezvous and base of operations on Corn Island, near the present site of Louisville. He was accompanied from Fort Pitt down the Ohio River by thirteen families in flatboats who founded at the falls of the river the future city of Louisville. In a thrilling campaign of surprise and bold initiative he captured the Creole towns of Kaskasia, Cahokia, and Vincennes. He took as prisoner the British lieutenant governor of the Northwest, Lord Henry Hamilton, who has left a fascinating journal of his experiences as he was conducted by an armed guard, in imminent peril of being mobbed, along the Wilderness Road to the jail at Williamsburg, Virginia.[9] This conquest of the Northwest country strengthened the claim of the United States during the negotiation of the Treaty of Paris to this region and to the Mississippi River as our western boundary. The apogee of Clark's life was attained in the Revolutionary War, when he was less than thirty years old, but his later career was a sad anticlimax. Virginia voted him two swords but failed to pay him for his services and expenditures in the conquest of the Northwest. Finally settling at Louisville, he drank to excess and died in 1818, a morose and frustrated hero of the frontier.[10]

Throughout the Revolution population continued to flow into Kentucky along the Wilderness Road from Cumberland Gap to Louisville on the Ohio River, passing through the little frontier settlements of Logan's Station (Stanford), Danville, and Harrodsburg. The Wilderness Road was fed by the Great Valley Road, which followed the Indian warpath down the Shenandoah and Holston valleys to Cumberland Gap. Hundreds of pioneers entering Kentucky were scalped by the Indians, and this pathway through the Cumberland Gap was bloody and dangerous indeed until Colonel William Whitley of *Sportsman Hill* in 1794 led a punitive expedition against the Chickamauga Indians.[11] Two years before this smashing blow against the Indians the old pack trail had been widened into a wagon road as a result of the effort of Kentucky's first governor, Isaac Shelby.

Along the Wilderness Road in 1796 came Moses Austin, famous in con-

[9] This manuscript is in the Harvard University Widener Library, extracts from which are published in Kincaid, *The Wilderness Road,* 139–145.

[10] J. A. James, *The Life of George Rogers Clark* (Chicago, 1928).

[11] See Charles G. Talbert, *Benjamin Logan, Kentucky Frontiersman* (Lexington, Ky., 1962).

nection with the colonization of Texas, who described the poverty-stricken procession of humanity he passed, some of them barefoot and ragged, seeking the Promised Land:

> Ask these Pilgrims what they expect when they git to Kentuckey the Answer is Land. have you any. No, but I expect I can git it. have you any thing to pay for land, No. did you Ever see the Country. No but Every Body says its good land. can any thing be more Absurd than the Conduct of man, here is hundreds Travelling hundreds of Miles, they Know not for what Nor Whither, except its to Kentuckey, passing land almost as good and easy obtaind, the Proprietors of which would gladly give on any terms, but it will not do its not Kentuckey its not the Promised land its not the goodly inheratence the Land of Milk and Honey. and when arrived at this Heaven in Idea what do they find? a goodly land I will allow but to them forbiden Land. exhausted and worn down with distress and disappointment they are at last Obliged to become hewers of wood and Drawers of water.[12]

This seeking of the Promised Land was the essence of the restless spirit of the American pioneer. Elizabeth Madox Roberts, in one of the finest of American historical novels, *The Great Meadow,* has portrayed this magnification in the minds of the home-seekers of "Caintuck," the lush land, with "soil as rich as cream," the wild plum in bloom, the game at the salt licks, and the green, velvety meadows.[13]

The frontiersmen who settled the trans-Appalachian region were not a homogeneous group. The majority came from the Piedmont and Great Valley region and were humble farmers, "cabin and corn patch men." There were some pioneers, such as Daniel Boone, who left the old settlements in imminent danger of being imprisoned for debt, or Simon Kenton, the famous scout, who fled from Virginia to escape the law after he had brutally beaten a rival suitor. Others were speculators, or foreign immigrants, or aristocrats such as Colonel David Meade, who sent his slaves ahead from Old Virginia to prepare a plantation for the removal of his family. Near Lexington in the Bluegrass he developed one of the most famous plantations in Kentucky, *Chaumiere du Prairie.* In Kentucky and Tennessee the frontiersmen encountered tremendous canebrakes, particularly in the river bottoms, whose leaves prevented their cattle from starving and nourished the bears that furnished meat for the family. Contrary to the common misconception, the frontiersmen frequently suffered from ill health, particularly from diseases that have practically disappeared or have greatly diminished in our era, such as malaria or ague, milk sickness, smallpox, scalded feet, and rheumatism. Milk sickness, caused by drinking the milk of cows that had eaten of the

[12] "A Memorandum of M. Austin's Journey to the Lead Mines," *American Historical Review,* V (April 1900), 525–526.
[13] For a careful delineation of Southern frontier life, see Harriette S. Arnow, *Seed-Time on the Cumberland* and *Flowering of the Cumberland* (New York, 1960 and 1963).

A pioneer home of the better sort in Kentucky near Barboursville. (Courtesy of J. Winston Coleman, Jr.)

white snakeroot, killed Nancy Hanks, the mother of Lincoln. The speech of the frontiersmen was picturesque and earthy, redolent of their life in the wilderness, containing such phrases as *playing possum, I'm stumped, the latchstring hangs out, logrolling,* and *he won't do to tie to,* which have survived in the American idiom.[14]

In the conquest of the Southern frontier, the American ax played a decisive role that has hardly been noticed by historians. The settlers of the Tidewater had brought with them an ax of ancient Roman design, weighing about three pounds, with wide flaring blade, lacking a pounding head, and held by a long straight handle. By 1740, however, the "American ax" had been evolved, having a blunt head, weighing up to seven pounds, and perfectly balanced. The "Kentucky Long Eye," with a blade 4¾ inches wide was popular in the coastal plain in the 1830's, and in the Piedmont the "Kentucky Small Eye" was the "very pattern wanted." Country blacksmiths in the interior and Negro artisans on the plantations fashioned rough axes, but after the frontier had passed, many small farmers purchased their axes from merchants in the towns as the fall line, who secured them during a yearly trip to New York or from seaport towns such as Charleston. An

---

[14] See Everett Dick, *The Dixie Frontier, A Social History* (New York, 1948) chap. 30; and Thomas D. Clark, *The Rampaging Frontier* (Indianapolis, 1939).

enterprising agent of a Yankee ax company wrote to his employer that in the back country, where the population was chiefly white, superior axes were appreciated, but in the slaveholding districts "the Slave holders accustom themselves to considering any tool good enough for a Negro to use and spoil." [15]

The symbol of advancing civilization in the forested lands east of the Mississippi River was the frontiersman's log cabin. It was different from the Indian cabin or the log structures erected by the first English settlers, which were made with pointed logs driven upright in the ground. The typical log cabin of the Piedmont and Appalachian frontier was introduced into this country by the Finns and Swedes of the Delaware settlement and was spread by the Germans during their migration in the eighteenth century into the back country of the South.[16] The logs were laid parallel to the ground and mortised by a notch at the corners. The logs, stripped of their bark, were then plastered in the crevices to keep the rain out, and the rude structure was roofed with rough-hewn shingles; a chimney of rocks or sticks plastered with mud was placed at the narrow end of the cabin. Later more substantial and comfortable structures were built, in which the logs were squared and fitted neatly together. The log cabin became a political symbol of democratic antecedents during the presidential campaign of 1840. Thereafter politicians such as Robert La Follette found it to be a political asset to boast of being born in a log cabin.

In 1769 the spearhead of the westward movement had penetrated the rugged mountains in the extreme northeastern corner of Tennessee, where land seekers from Virginia had founded a settlement in the Watauga Valley. The pioneers of this new frontier had come largely from the Piedmont, an area called by Professor Turner "the Old West," where they had learned much of frontier skill. To this remote corner of the Southern frontier also had emigrated some of the Regulators after their defeat at the Battle of Alamance. When North Carolina ignored the petition of the settlers of the Watauga Valley to establish a local government for them, they formed the Watauga Association (in 1772 or 1773) creating a frontier democracy. This frame of government established a legislature of thirteen members, one from each little fort or palisaded settlement. Belatedly, in 1776, North Carolina incorporated the Watauga settlement, including the whole future state of Tennessee, into Washington County.

The two most forceful leaders in the rude settlements of Tennessee were James Robertson and John Sevier. Robertson, a close-mouthed, uneducated, but fearless frontiersman of Scotch-Irish descent, arrived in 1770 from Wake County, North Carolina. Sevier was born and reared in the Shenandoah Valley of Virginia, where he matured rapidly and married at the age of seventeen. Tall, handsome, debonair, he was the Cavalier type in this rough

[15] A. R. Moen, Petersburg, Va., August 22, 1831 to Messrs. Collins & Co., of Hartford, Conn. MS owned by Thomas D. Clark, University of Kentucky.
[16] H. R. Shurtleff, *The Log Cabin Myth* (Cambridge, Mass., 1939).

wilderness environment. Indeed, he was one of the few cultivated men on the frontier. He combined a gift for making friends and for diplomacy with the virile fighting qualities which made "Nolichucky Jack" a terror to the Cherokee on the warpath.[17]

After Sevier had superseded the quiet Robertson as the leader of the Watauga settlement, Robertson moved to a new frontier, the Nashville limestone basin. In the winter of 1779–1780 he led a group of pioneers overland to the French Lick in the Cumberland Valley, where he founded Nashborough (Nashville). In this undertaking he was the agent of Richard Henderson, the ambitious land speculator. Another party, led by Colonel John Donelson, including his daughter Rachel, the future wife of Andrew Jackson, went down the Tennessee River by flatboats, up the Ohio, and then up the Cumberland River to Nashville. They arrived at this frontier settlement in the winter of 1780, after an Odyssey of nearly a thousand miles of peril from Indian ambuscades and water hazards.

The early history of Tennessee was strongly colored by the activity of powerful land speculators. A group of landgrabbers, headed by William Blount, persuaded North Carolina's legislature in 1784 to cede her western lands to the Congress of the Confederation in order to secure protection from the Indians for prospective settlers on their vast holdings. Later in the same year, this act of cession was repealed by a new legislature. In the interval, the people of east Tennessee met in a convention at Jonesborough and set up the precocious state of Franklin. The Blount group of speculators was opposed to this independence movement, but finally joined it to control it and protect their land titles. Indeed, one of their men, John Sevier, was elected the first governor. The formation of the state of Franklin was not the purely spontaneous assertion of frontier democracy that the older historians portrayed but was at least partly motivated by land speculation.

The government of North Carolina proclaimed the formation of the state of Franklin null and void. Also Congress refused to act favorably on a petition of the inhabitants of Tennessee to recognize the new state. Nonetheless, despite Indian warfare and the efforts of North Carolina to restore control over the rebellious inhabitants, this little frontier republic precariously survived for four years. A faction opposed to Sevier, led by John Tipton, tried to subvert the de facto state and to reduce it to subordination to North Carolina. At times two governmens were functioning in the region; rival sheriffs and competing courts clashed; and blood was shed in internal strife. Finally Sevier was captured and taken to prison at Morganton, North Carolina, but melodramatically escaped. Not until the Federal Constitution was adopted did this *opéra bouffe* war come to an end and the state of Franklin succumb. Then Sevier was pardoned from the charge of being a traitor, and in 1790 North Carolina retroceded her western lands to the national government.[18]

---

[17] See C. S. Driver, *John Sevier* (Chapel Hill, 1932).
[18] See S. C. Williams, *History of the Lost State of Franklin* (New York, 1933).

The Tennessee and Kentucky communities needed outlets to the ocean for the marketing of their crops. Unfortunately, Spain controlled the two best outlets, the mouth of the Mississippi and the route by the Tombigbee River to Mobile. Spain used her strategic position as a lever to try to detach the western settlements from the United States and to persuade them to join her empire. Thus arose the so-called Spanish Conspiracy, most active in 1786–1787, when the West was incensed by the proposed Jay-Gardoqui Treaty, which would have surrendered the right of Americans to navigate the Mississippi River for a period of twenty-five years. In Tennessee a group of land speculators, John Sevier, William Blount, and others, flirted with Spain in the hope of securing an outlet along the Tombigbee River for a colony they planned at Muscle Shoals.

In Kentucky the leader of the Spanish Party was the adventurer James Wilkinson, who later intrigued with Aaron Burr. In 1787 Wilkinson, who had established himself as a merchant and speculator at Frankfort, which he founded, made a trip to New Orleans to confer with Spanish authorities. He advised Spain that the best method of protecting Louisiana from an attack by the Westerners, aided by a fleet of Great Britain, was to foment an independence movement in Kentucky. He accepted the role of Spanish agent in return for a pension and the right to ship Kentucky produce to New Orleans. Wilkinson's motive seems to have been purely mercenary, to extract money from Spain.[19] The great majority of Kentuckians, however, remained loyal to the confederation of states, and only a few prominent leaders, such as Judge Benjamin Sebastian, negotiated with Spain to secure bribes. Any chance for the success of a separatist movement was destroyed by the Pinckney Treaty of 1795, which granted the right of deposit in New Orleans, and by the purchase of Louisiana in 1803. Consequently, when Aaron Burr initiated his conspiracy in 1806, he found the Western states loyal to the United States, but willing perhaps to countenance a filibustering expedition against Spain.

During its formative years Kentucky was a battleground between the radical and the conservative forces for the control of the government. The settlement of Kentucky was accelerated by the practice of Virginia of paying its Revolutionary soldiers in land warrants entitling the holder to locate his grant in western lands. Many of these warrants were purchased cheaply by speculators. The advance of the frontier into the Bluegrass region was financed by speculators, and most of the good land was acquired by masterful men with money. "The Bluegrass country," a modern scholar has observed, "was never a poor man's frontier." [20] The poor people settled principally below the Green River, where they later followed the leadership of the demagogue Felix Grundy.

[19] See J. R. Jacobs, *Tarnished Warrior: Major General James Wilkinson* (New York, 1938).

[20] T. P. Abernethy, *Three Virginia Fontiers* (Baton Rouge, La., 1940), 65.

The efforts of Kentucky to separate from Virginia and form a new state led to the holding of the incredible number of nine conventions at Danville between 1784 and 1792. The delegates were divided into three parties, the aristocratic "court" party of Virginian-born lawyers and officials, the "country party" of surveyors and some large landowners, headed by the Marshall family, and "the partisans" of the poor and landless people.[21] The most important quarrel dividing these groups was over the distribution of land and land titles, but the delegates were also torn in dissension over the terms of Virginia's Enablement Act, the use of the Mississippi as a trade outlet, the Spanish conspiracy, and the political form of the Constitution. The poor people demanded manhood suffrage, election of all local and state officials by the people, the ballot instead of the viva voce method practised in Virginia, a legislature of one chamber, and strangely, the omission of a bill of rights. The reason for this last demand was the fear of the radical party that a bill of rights would protect vested interests, including slavery, which they wished to abolish. In the constitutional convention of 1792, the leader of the antislavery group was the Presbyterian minister of Danville, David Rice, but he was defeated in the attempt to make Kentucky free soil. The conservatives, led by George Nicholas, wished to make the new state a replica of Virginia, with the institution of slavery as the basis of aristocratic control.

The constitution that emerged from this conflict was a compromise. Although it contained provisions for manhood suffrage, the second in the nation to do so, the ballot, and the apportionment of representation in the legislature according to population, slavery was preserved, ministers were disqualified from serving in the legislature, and both the governor and the Senate were to be chosen by an electoral college. With such a frame of government, influenced both by Virginia and by the democratic constitution of Pennsylvania, Kentucky was admitted into the Union in 1792 as the first state beyond the Appalachians. Seven years later a new constitutional convention was convened, in which the radicals succeeded in abolishing the electoral college. However, the Virginia practices of the viva voce method of voting and of the appointment of sheriffs and justices of the peace by the governor were adopted. An attempt by reformers and idealists in the convention of 1799 led by the Lexington editor John Bradford and the youthful Henry Clay, to incorporate in the constitution a provision for the gradual abolition of slavery was defeated by the conservatives.

Tennessee was the second state in the West to be admitted into the Union (in 1796). Although its constitution granted manhood suffrage, it contained a number of aristocratic features. Land speculators had a powerful influence in its politics. One of the most aggressive of these men was Andrew Jackson, who joined in a partnership with John Overton to found the city of Memphis

---

[21] Patricia Watlington, *The Partisan Spirit: Kentucky Politics, 1779–1792* (New York, 1972).

in 1819. Overton became perhaps the richest citizen of Tennessee and a member of the "Nashville Junto" that promoted the presidential candidacy of Jackson. Political democracy, however, was not achieved in Tennessee until the reforms of the constitutional convention of 1834.[22]

In the economic development of Kentucky and Tennessee, the introduction of the steamboat played a major role. The first steamboat to make the voyage upstream from New Orleans to Louisville, Kentucky, was the *Enterprise,* in the year 1815. The epochal nature of this event was registered in the decline of Lexington as the metropolis of the West, following the introduction of the new mode of transportation. Lexington was an inland town fifteen miles from the Kentucky River, but it was on the main road from the Ohio River at Limestone (the modern Maysville) to the interior of Kentucky, and it was the capital of the Bluegrass. In 1810 it was a thriving center of trade, with a population of 4,326, and was rapidly developing manufactures—ropewalks, bagging and cordage factories, textile mills, powder mills, and so on, which made its citizens ardent for protective tariffs. The coming of the steamboat caused a sharp decline in its economic supremacy, for in the decade of the 1820's Louisville, at the falls of the Ohio, surpassed it. But Lexington remained the cultural and political center of Kentucky. It boasted the pioneer newspaper of the West, the *Kentucke Gazette,* founded by the surveyor John Bradford in 1787 during the agitation for statehood. Moreover, it contained Transylvania University, the home of Henry Clay, and many cultivated and aristocratic citizens, that entitled it to be called the "Athens of the West." [23]

From Nashville, Tennessee, a famous frontier path, nearly six hundred miles long, ran through Indian territory to Natchez on the Mississippi River. In 1801 treaties with the Indians permitted the Natchez Trace to be widened into a wagon road, and two years later a mail service was established. Along this road came pioneers from Kentucky and Tennessee to settle the Southwest, for it was a shortcut to the longer route down the Mississippi River. Flatboatmen and the crews of arks that had drifted down the Mississippi often returned by the Natchez Trace, especially before the days of steamboats. Unfortunately, this lonely road was infested with robbers and murderers, such as the homicidal maniac "Little Harpe," Samuel Mason, a Revolutionary soldier and justice of the peace in Kentucky who turned to the trade of highwayman, Joseph Hare, the dandy, and John A. Murrell and his gang.

Natchez at the end of the journey was the extreme western point of the frontier in 1800. Originally a French town, which was destroyed by the Natchez Indians in 1729, Natchez became once more a center of settlement when the English acquired this territory in 1763 and built Fort Panmure.

[22] T. P. Abernethy, *From Frontier to Plantation in Tennessee* (Chapel Hill, 1932).
[23] Bernard Mayo, "Lexington: Frontier Metropolis," in Eric F. Goldman (ed.), *Historiography and Urbanization* (Baltimore, 1941); and Richard Wade, *The Urban Frontier; The Rise of Western Cities, 1790–1830* (Cambridge, Mass., 1959).

After the conquest of the town by Galvez during the American Revolution it remained under Spanish rule until 1798. In that year Natchez was surrendered to the United States in fulfillment of the Pinckney Treaty (also called San Lorenzo) of 1795, which had fixed the boundary between Florida and the United States at the thirty-first degree of latitude. The chief relic of Spanish rule was the palace of the Governor Gayoso, *Concord,* which survived well into the nineteenth century. At first the main crops were tobacco and indigo, especially the "pigeon neck" variety, so called because of its prismatic colors. After the introduction in 1795 of the Whitney gin, cotton became the great money crop.

Following the Louisiana Purchase in 1803, the Natchez region rapidly advanced in prosperity and culture. A considerable number of educated men settled there, so that probably the earlier generation of settlers was more cultivated than their sons. The surprising luxury enjoyed by this remote frontier town is indicated by a manifest of goods imported into Natchez in 1801 by the merchant John McDonogh in the ship *Carlisle* from Baltimore, Maryland. From the cargo there were landed 720 casks of claret, 2,400 bottles of Medoc wine, 15 pipes of brandy, 70 dozen of men's white stockings, 312 dozen kid gloves, 18 gross white playing cards, 96 reams of "faint blue" paper, wall paper of various kinds, including "9 muses dark grounded," as well as such articles of luxuries as sweet oil, almonds, soap, cambrics, and linen. As early as 1790, Andrew Marschalk, an army officer, had introduced a printing press, and nine years later a newspaper was started. Many rich planters and professional people built beautiful homes in and around Natchez-on-the-Bluff, but below, on the river bank, flourished wicked and rowdy Natchez-under-the-Hill, where hundreds of flatboats and steamboats floated at the docks.

Contrary to a common misconception, this rapidly maturing town on the frontier did not favor laissez-faire methods of government, but strictly regulated many business activities.[24] The surrounding region of farmers and planters revolted from the domination of the town after Jefferson appointed the young Republican W. C. C. Claiborne as governor of Mississippi Territory. The farmers and planters obtained control of the legislature and deprived the aristocrats of Natchez of the advantage of having the capital located in their city. They transferred the seat of government to the brand-new village of Washington, six miles to the east, and here also they located the pioneer Jefferson College, chartered in 1802 but not opened until 1811. In 1808, Christian Schultz, Jr., in his *Travels on an Inland Voyage* described the worldly, hedonistic atmosphere of this river town of three thousand inhabitants as follows: "all make love; most of them play [gamble]; and a few make money. With Religion they have nothing to do." [25] In truth, Natchez at

---

[24] Charles S. Sydnor, *A Gentleman of the Old Natchez Region: Benjamin L. C. Wailes* (Durham, 1938), chap. 1.
[25] Christian Schultz, Jr., *Travels on an Inland Voyage* (New York, 1810), II, 134.

this time was a prismatic blend of the frontier, evidenced by skins of the "spotted tiger" killed in the surrounding wilderness hanging in the stores, the river trade with its boastful half-horse, half-alligator boatmen and their copper-colored prostitutes, and of the slave-tilled cotton economy, which was destined to make Natchez one of the wealthiest and most cultured communities in the United States.

Ascendancy of the Southern
Federalists

WHILE THE REVOLUTION was in progress the thirteen colonies formed a loose central government under the Continental Congress. In November, 1777, the Continental Congress adopted a constitution entitled "The Articles of Confederation," but it was not ratified by all the states until four years later. The reason for this delay was that Maryland refused to sign the document until the states had agreed to surrender their claims of Western land to the central government. The claims of Virginia, under a sea-to-sea charter and by Clark's conquest of the Ohio region, where especially obnoxious to a small state like Maryland, which had a narrowly limited western boundary. After Virginia surrendered her claims and it became evident that the various titles of the states to Western territory would be given to the central government, Maryland ratified the Articles of Confederation. Not until 1802, however, did Georgia surrender her claim to Western lands, the last of the states to do so.

The adoption of Articles of Confederation represented a victory of the radicals over the conservatives in the struggle between conflicting interests, or "parties," of the Revolutionary period. The Articles of Confederation were permeated by the spirit of the Declaration of Independence, based on the idea that liberty could best be preserved by decentralization. But the conservatives were hostile to a constitution which permitted the thirteen sovereign states to give a free rein to the radicals within the states. In contrast to the big business leaders of the New Deal period, who advocated States rights, the property interests of the 1770's and 1780's sought a more centralized government to curb rampant democracy.[1]

The older historians, influenced by Federalist propaganda, have exaggerated the weaknesses and centrifugal tendencies of the government during the Confederation, which was called by John Fiske "the critical period" of American history.[2] They have, for example, continued the myth that the states erected tariff barriers against each other, when, in reality, the discriminations were directed against Great Britain. The new central government, like the Weimar Republic, was discredited by an economic depression, which

[1] Merrill Jensen, *The Articles of Confederation* (2d ed., Madison, Wis. 1948), VII–XV, 239–245.
[2] John Fiske, *The Critical Period in American History, 1783–1789* (Boston, 1916).

has been exaggerated by historians.[3] After the crisis of the Revolution had passed, the radicals lost their organization, and the conservatives finally won the upper hand by calling the Constitutional Convention of 1787. The property interests were aided in this victory by the alarm produced by Shay's Rebellion of the veterans and small farmers of Massachusetts in 1786 and by the menace of paper money inflation.[4]

The immediate steps that led to the calling of a Constitutional Convention in Philadelphia in 1787 were taken by Southern men. In 1785 a conference was held at *Mount Vernon,* Washington's estate on the Potomac, to secure cooperation between Maryland and Virginia over the navigation of the Potomac River. At this meeting a decision was made to invite all the thirteen states to a convention at Annapolis, Maryland, the following year for the purpose of adopting uniform trade regulations. Only five states attended, but one of the delegates, Alexander Hamilton from New York, proposed the summoning of another convention with a much larger scope than the consideration of commercial measures, namely to revise the old Articles of Confederation. The Congress of the Confederation finally called such a convention to meet at Philadelphia on May 14, 1787, to which all the states, except Rhode Island, sent delegates.

The ace in this reform movement was securing the attendance at the convention of Washington, who was finally persuaded to go and was elected president of the convention. The fifty-five delegates were chosen not by popular vote but by the legislatures, which in turn were elected by a small minority of the adult white males—the property holders. In the Convention, voting was by states. By far the most brilliant and useful of the various groups was the Virginia delegation. In addition to Washington, it included James Madison, George Mason, the author of the Virginia Declaration of Rights, George Wythe, one of the great liberals of America, and the youthful Governor Edmund Randolph, a polished orator, the spokesman for the delegation. Patrick Henry, although chosen a delegate, refused to attend, because he was hostile to a strong central government and "smelt a rat." Thomas Jefferson was also absent, for he was serving as minister to France. All the Virginia delegates, except Madison, lived in the Tidewater area.

Of the fifty-five delegates to the Constitutional Convention, James Madison was the most valuable member. He was better prepared than any other delegate by his study of the history of the various leagues and confederations of the past. Although he was only thirty-six years old at the time, he had a profound grasp of the problems of government, especially in relation to economic interests. He prepared "the Virginia plan," which represented the views of the larger states about the basis of representation. The sessions of the Convention were secret; the newspapers could not report its proceedings.

---

[3] Merrill Jensen, *The New Nation; A History of the United States during the Confederation, 1781–1789* (New York, 1950).
[4] Allan Nevins, *The American States during and after the Revolution, 1775–1789* (New York, 1924).

However, Madison took a front seat in the Convention and kept an accurate set of notes on the debates, which constitute our only complete account of the great debates on the framing of the Constitution. Strangely, these notes were not published until 1840, probably because he later changed his strong Federalist views in favor of Jeffersonian ideas. He has rightly been singled out as "the father of the constitution," although the completed document was the work of many minds and a number of compromises.[5]

The other Southern states sent, in general, their conservative leaders. From South Carolina came John Rutledge, called "Dictator"; Charles Cotesworth Pinckney, Revolutionary leader; the brilliant Charles Pinckney, only twenty-nine years old, next-to-the-youngest member of the Convention, who claimed erroneously in his old age to have presented the blueprint upon which the Constitution was based; and Pierce Butler, proud of his descent from the Duke of Ormond, a great planter devoted to the preservation of slavery. Of Maryland's five delegates three were wealthy conservatives, but Luther Martin, a Princeton graduate, was an able and strenuous advocate of the point of view of the small farmers and the debtors. The delegation from North Carolina contained the land speculator William Blount; William R. Davie, later instrumental in founding the University of North Carolina; Richard Dobbs Spaight, an owner of seventy-one slaves; and Hugh Williamson, the intellectual leader of the group. Williamson was born in Pennsylvania and was graduated from the University of Edinburgh, and afterward settled in Edenton, North Carolina as a merchant and physician. Georgia sent Abraham Baldwin, the son of a Connecticut blacksmith, educated at Yale College, who later became one of the founders of the University of Georgia, and William Few, a representative of the small farmer group as well as a bankrupt merchant and a scion of the planter aristocracy. The delegates of Delaware included Richard Bassett, owner of the six thousand acres of *Bohemia Manor,* and John Dickinson, famed as a pre-Revolutionary pamphleteer.

The Constitutional Convention had been called for the purpose of revising the old Articles of Confederation. Nevertheless, the delegates resolved to create a new government instead of trying to revamp the old decentralized government of the Confederation. In so doing, they accomplished a peaceful revolution. The revolutionary nature of their proceedings is clearly seen in their decision on ratification: when nine of the thirteen states accepted the new Constitution, it should go into effect in those states. The old Articles of Confederation had prescribed a unanimous consent of the states for any alteration of the frame of government. In drawing up the Constitution, the delegates were guided primarily by English models of government and by their practical experience with the colonial governments and with the weaknesses and inefficiency of the Confederation.

On May 29, four days after the Convention opened, Edmund Randolph

[5] See Irving Brant, *James Madison, the Nationalist, 1780–1787* (Indianapolis, 1948); for his early career, see W. T. Hutchinson and W. M. E. Rachal (eds.), *The Papers of James Madison* (Chicago, 1962—), 8 vols., to March 1786.

presented the Virginia Plan in a series of resolutions for a new frame of government for the thirteen states. This blueprint became the basis of discussion and the matrix of the completed document. The essential point to note about the Virginia plan was that it proposed a legislature of two houses, in which representation should be proportional to population, rather than the equal votes of states, big and little, which was the rule in the unicameral legislature of the Congress of the Confederation. The upper house, according to this plan, was to be chosen by the lower house from candidates nominated by the state legislatures. The Madison draft of a constitution encountered violent opposition from the small states, whose counterproposal for equal representation of the states was presented by William Paterson, and is known as the New Jersey Plan.[6]

A compromise offered by Oliver Ellsworth of Connecticut, called the Grand Compromise, was finally adopted. According to this decision the states were given equal representation in the upper house, or Senate, selected by the state legislatures, but representation in the lower house was apportioned according to population. Two qualifications to this solution were added, namely, that all money bills must originate in the lower house and that no amendment should ever be made that would deprive any state without its consent of its equal vote in the Senate.

Apart from the struggle between the large and small states over the basis of representation, the real cleavage in the Convention was between the Northern and Southern States, which had conflicting economic interests.[7] One of the questions in which Northern and Southern interests were opposed was the status of the slaves in apportioning representation in Congress. The Southern delegates wished slaves to be counted as population in determining the numbers of representatives each state should have in the House of Representatives. The Northern delegates opposed this formula, pointing out that slaves were considered as property in the South. They argued that slaves should not be counted at all as persons in apportioning representation, but should be taxed as persons in assessing direct taxes on the states, a proposition highly repugnant to the Southerners. The latter demanded slave representation in Congress to protect slavery from any attempt to abolish it that might later be made by the Northern states. They threatened to leave the Convention unless such security was given them. Finally, a compromise was adopted by which slaves were to be counted as three fifths their actual number in apportioning both representation and direct taxes. This three-fifths compromise (called the Federal ratio) was suggested by the fact that under

[6] See Max Farrand (ed.), *Records of the Federal Convention of 1787* (New York, 1911), 3 vols.
[7] Good modern accounts of the making of the federal Constitution are to be found in Fred Rodell, *Fifty-Five Men* (Harrisburg, 1936); and Broadus and Louise Mitchell, *A Biography of the Constitution of the United States* (New York, 1964), and Richard Hofstadter, *The Amercan Political Tradition and the Men Who Made It* (New York, 1948).

the Articles of Confederation such a ratio had been proposed in assessing requisitions for taxes on the states. It was a genuine victory for the South, because direct taxes were levied by the Federal government only three times during the existence of slavery, whereas the Federal ratio gave to a Southerner residing in a state with a large preponderance of slaves, such as South Carolina or Mississippi, political power in the House of Representatives almost equal to the vote of two Northerners.

The adoption of the three-fifths ratio made the South more willing to accept the Constitution and especially to agree to another compromise favorable to the North. This adjustment was in regard to the power of enacting tariff laws. The Southern delegates demanded that all tariff laws should require the vote of a two-thirds majority, for they feared that the power of levying duties on imports or exports would be used to exploit the staple-producing states. Ultimately, a compromise was worked out that granted to Congress the authority to pass tariff bills by a simple majority vote, but prohibited that body from levying an export duty, which would have fallen heavily on the agricultural class of the South.

Another compromise that primarily affected the Southern states related to the prohibition of the slave trade. The upper South, which had a superfluity of Negro field hands, wished to close the African slave trade, but Georgia and South Carolina demanded that it remain open. These two states of the lower South secured allies in the New England shipping states, which were gaining profits from importing slaves into the South. This pressure group was able to force the adoption of a compromise leaving the African slave trade open for a period of twenty years, during which Congress was prohibited from laying duty on slaves greater than $10 a head.

A great majority of the members of the Convention seem to have been ashamed of the existence of slavery in this country, and when a committee under the leadership of Gouverneur Morris phrased the Constitution in final form, it carefully avoided including the words slave or slavery in the famous document. The fugitive slave clause of the Constitution, for example, used a euphemism in referring to slaves as follows: "No person held to service or labor in one state, under the laws thereof, escaping into another, shall in consequence of any law or regulation therein be discharged from such service or labor, but shall be delivered up on claim of the party to whom such service or labor may be due."

The Southern delegates shared the aversion to radical democracy that dominated the Convention. A reaction of the pendulum from the enthusiasm for human rights of the Revolutionary period had swung in the direction of protecting property rights from the depredations of a numerical majority, but it cannot correctly be described as a counterrevolution. Shays' Rebellion, the Stay Laws, and the paper money panaceas had frightened the property classes, evoking the specter of social revolution. Consequently, most of the fifty-five members of the Convention wished to curb rabid democracy by a system of checks and balances and indirect elections in order to make property safe. The Virginia Plan presented by Randolph had provided for representation in Congress to be based both on population and on the wealth of the citizens of a state as measured by the amount of taxes paid. Baldwin of Georgia declared in the Convention that the Senate "ought to be the representation of property." The wealthy Pierce Butler of South Carolina, "contended strenuously," according to Madison's notes, "that property was the only just measure of representation," [8] a theory of government that was supported by William R. Davie of North Carolina and by John Rutledge and Charles Cotesworth Pinckney of South Carolina.

The Constitution was completed by September 17, 1787, and was then signed by twenty of the thirty Southern delegates. Four of the Virginia delegates, George Mason, James McClurg, George Wythe, and Edmund Randolph, failed to sign the document. William R. Davie and Alexander Martin of North Carolina, Luther Martin and John Francis Mercer of Maryland, and William Pierce and William Houston of Georgia were the other Southern delegates who did not sign, either because of opposition to the document or because they had left the Convention. The objections of Mason to the Constitution are an important critique on that frame of government by one of the ablest and wealthiest of Southern planters.[9] He deplored the absence of a bill of rights protecting civil liberties, the compromise on the slave trade, which he believed should be closed entirely, and the absence of a cabinet for the president. His objections also reflected the fear that the agricultural class held that the North would control the government and exploit the South. Consequently, Mason demanded that commercial and navigation acts should be passed only by a two-thirds vote of Congress. He declared that the Constitution gave excessive power to the Senate and that the judiciary would become so powerful that it would destroy the state courts, and finally he saw great danger in the so-called elastic clause of the Constitution that gives Congress the authority "To make all Laws which shall be necessary and proper for carrying into Execution the foregoing Powers . . ." [10]

An instructive parallel exists between the debate over the adoption of the federal Constitution and the debate over the strengthening of the United Nations government. In 1787–1788 it was difficult to get Americans to think nationally; today it is almost equally difficult to persuade people to think internationally. As an able writer has suggested, the debate over the ratification of the Constitution was "the Great Rehearsal" for the acceptance of a world federation. Most of the arguments pro and con in the debate of 1787–1788 are applicable today in regard to entrusting stronger powers to a world government. There was the fear of small states that they would be dominated

[8] Gaillard Hunt and J. B. Scott (eds.), *The Debates in the Federal Convention of 1787 . . . Reported by James Madison* (New York, 1920), 190.

[9] See R. A. Rutland (ed.), *The Papers of George Mason* (Chapel Hill, 1970), vol. III.

[10] P. L. Ford (ed.), *Pamphlets on the Constitution of the United States* (Brooklyn, 1888), 327–332; see also Robert A. Rutland, *George Mason, Reluctant Statesman* (New York, 1961).

by the large states; there was the apprehension on the part of provincial people of oppression by a distant centralized government; and there was the belief among many Southerners that the economic interests of their region would be sacrificed in a more closely knit union, where the Congress would be controlled by the numerically stronger North. Indeed, the strong consciousness of sectional interests was clearly exhibited in these debates, antedating by many years the famous clash between the Northern and Southern states in 1820 over the admission of Missouri to the Union. There were men both in the South and in New England who agreed with Benjamin Randall of Sharon, Massachusetts, that "our manners are widely different from the southern states" and that in any close union the two sections would continually be at variance.[11] Thus early, serious differences between the Northern and Southern states, as well as a struggle between the planting and the commercial classes, were foreshadowed.

The Constitution was not submitted to popular vote but to specially summoned conventions. The delegates to these conventions, however, seem to have followed, with few exceptions, instructions from the electorate.[12] In all the Southern states, and in most of the Northern states, there were property qualifications for voting for the members of these conventions. It is surprising to find that only a small fraction, certainly less than one fourth, of the white males voted in this election, which was to determine under what type of government they and their descendants should live. Nonvoting of the qualified voters in truth has had a long continuity in the United States. Although many of the nonvoters in 1788 were kept away from the polls by lack of property, a large number of those qualified failed to exercise their sovereign privilege of voting in this critical election on account of indifference, travel difficulties, and so on.

Delaware, elated over the victory of the small states in obtaining the Grand Compromise, was the first state to ratify the Constitution, December 7, 1787 —by a unanimous vote. Georgia quickly followed, January 2, 1788, also by a unanimous vote, partly motivated by a desire to secure the protection of a strong central government against the Indians and the Spaniards on her frontier. In Maryland Luther Martin and Samuel Chase, later to be a Justice of the Supreme Court whom the Jeffersonians impeached, fought vigorously against ratification, but they were defeated by a vote of sixty-three in favor to eleven against accepting the Constitution. South Carolina likewise overwhelmingly ratified the new document. Rawlins Lowndes, an aristocrat of the low country, was the leader of the up-country opposition. He objected to the Constitution because of its prohibition of the slave trade after twenty years, because of the excessive power of the Senate, and because he believed that it

[11] Carl Van Doren, *The Great Rehearsal, the Story of the Making and Ratifying of the Constitution of the United States,* (New York, 1948), 203–204.
[12] See Johnathan Elliott (ed.), *The Debates in the Several State Conventions on the Adoption of the Federal Constitution* (Philadelphia, 1891), 5 vols.

inadequately protected minority rights. He wishes his epitaph to contain the words "Here lies the man that opposed the Constitution because it was ruinous to the liberty of America." [13]

In Virginia occurred the ablest debate in the nation on the merits of the Constitution. The Anti-Federalists, the opponents of adopting the Constitution, or at least without strong modificaions, had as their spokesmen some of the most prominent men of the state, Patrick Henry, George Mason, Richard Henry Lee, James Monroe, and John Tyler. On the other side were Madison, George Wythe, Edmund Pendleton, "Light Horse Harry" Lee, and John Marshall. Although Washington was not a member of the ratifying convention, his support of the Constitution had great weight in forming public opinion, particularly in influencing the Revolutionary soldiers. Patrick Henry took a leading part in opposing the ratification of the Constitution and was greatly feared by the Federalists. At this time he was fifty-three years of age, but was prematurely old. Having lost his hair early in life, he wore a brown wig, which he would twist awry on his bald head in a comical manner during his excitement in orating on the dangers of establishing a strongly centralized government. He pointed out the expense of the new government, the dangerous power of the Supreme Court, and the failure to safeguard personal liberty by a bill of rights, and he strenuously objected to its national character, based on the people rather than the states. He gained the support of most of the Kentucky delegates in the convention by arousing their fear that the congress of the proposed government, dominated by the North, would surrender the right to navigate the Mississippi.

The Federalists won a great triumph when Governor Edmund Randolph, who had refused to sign the Constitution in Philadelphia, changed his attitude and spoke in favor of Virginia's accepting the new instrument of government. He had favored a stronger central government, but had refused to sign the Constitution because he believed that it should be amended by another convention. Now he had concluded that it was wise for his state to ratify in order to prevent a dissolution of the Union, and later to secure amendments. This method of promising amendments was the strategy of victory. The Virginia Convention, after a violent struggle, ratified the Constitution, June 25, 1788, by a narrow margin of ten votes. Hugh Blair Grigsby, who made a thorough study of Virginia's ratification of the Constitution, reached the conclusion that two thirds of the people of that state were opposed to this new frame of government.[14]

Shortly before Virginia's decision New Hampshire had ratified the Constitution, becoming the ninth state to do so, thus furnishing enough acceptances to establish the new government. Victory for the adoption of the Constitution

[13] Allan Johnson and Dumas Malone (eds.), *Dictionary of American Biography,* XI, 473.
[14] Hugh B. Grigsby, *The History of the Virginia Federal Convention of 1788* (Richmond, 1891), I, 41.

was attained partly because of the underrepresentation of the back country in the ratifying conventions. Fortunately, too, the Federalists were better organized, more aggressive, and better informed on the nature of the proposed central government than the Anti-Federalists. Furthermore, they had the advantage of using the arguments of a very able series of essays called "The Federalist Papers," written by James Madison, John Jay, and Alexander Hamilton.[15] Finally, the advocates of the adoption of the Constitution promised the addition of a bill of rights to the instrument, the omission of which had alarmed some of the Southerners.[16]

In the backward state of North Carolina a convention met at Hillsborough, in the Piedmont section, July 21, 1788 to decide the question of ratifying the Constitution. The convention was dominated by Willie Jones, a wealthy aristocrat who held democratic views. Jones advocated a procedure proposed by his friend Thomas Jefferson that North Carolina should refrain from joining the new government until the Constitution had been amended and a bill of rights had been added. This argument as well as the influence of the paper money crowd swayed the convention to adjourn without ratifying the Constitution. The Anti-Federalists in the convention included some of the old Regulators, such as Thomas Person of Granville County and the Presbyterian leader, Reverend David Caldwell of Guilford County. In the eastern part of the state the Anti-Federalist leader was Timothy Bloodworth, of Wilmington, a versatile man whose career combined farming, preaching, and the trade of blacksmith with his political activities as the organizer of the mechanics and small farmers against the merchants and wealthy planters who were, in general, Federalists. North Carolina remained outside of the Union until November 22, 1789, when a second convention met at Fayetteville and ratified the Constitution. Thus, North Carolina was next to the last state in the Union in joining the Federal government, Rhode Island being the last.[17]

Until recently the interpretation of the Constitutional Convention and of the ratification of the Constitution has been dominated by the point of view of Charles A. Beard, whose *Economic Interpretation of the Constitution* (1913) was written during the Progressive movement and was much influenced by that movement. The Columbia University historian adopted a new technique in studying the making of the Constitution by minutely examining the economic interests of the delegates to the Constitutional Convention. From this study Beard concluded that they were primarily concerned with protecting or advancing their own economic interests. The delegates were a group of conservative wealthy men with not a single representative of the laboring class (how different would the situation be today, with our powerful labor unions, should a Constitutional Convention be called) and only one

[15] Jacob E. Cooke (ed.), *The Federalist* (Middletown, Conn., 1961); and John C. Miller, *The Federalist Era, 1789–1801* (New York, 1960).
[16] Robert A. Rutland, *The Birth of the Bill of Rights* (Chapel Hill, 1955).
[17] L. I. Trenholme, *Ratification of the Federal Constitution in North Carolina* (New York, 1932).

representative of the small farming class. The holding of public securities and bonds (forty of the delegates did), Beard emphasized, constituted the dynamic element in bringing about the adoption of the Constitution.[18]

Beard found many evidences in the completed document that the delegates were intent on protecting property from the assaults of the radicals and the debtor interests, particularly the paper money crowd. Fearful of democracy, they included in the new Constitution such devices as checks and balances, an electoral college to choose the president, a Senate elected by the legislatures instead of by the people, judicial review, which, although not explicitly stated, was intended to operate, and clauses prohibiting the states from issuing paper money or impairing the obligation of a contract, and providing for the passage of tariff acts by a majority vote, and other benefits to industrial and creditor interests.

In his interpretation of the ratification of the Constitution, Beard held that the wealthier Tidewater areas and the cities were in favor of its adoption and the back country was against it. Some of the studies made by O. G. Libby of the geographic distribution of votes on the ratification tended to support this view, but other of his statistics do not fit this neat pattern of behavior. In Virginia, for example, 80 per cent of the Tidewater voted for and 20 per cent against the adoption of the Constitution; the Piedmont, 26 per cent for and 74 percent against ratification; the Shenandoah Valley, 97 per cent for and 3 per cent against ratification; and the relatively undeveloped part of the state now included in West Virginia voted sixteen to one for the ratification of the Constitution.[19] In North Carolina all the six towns represented in the convention of 1788, except Hillsborough in the Piedmont, favored the ratification of the Constitution. The wealthy planters, the merchants, and the business people of the South were usually Federalists, as those who favored the Constitution were called. The Anti-Federalists were frequently debtors or small farmers and yeomen. The debtor class objected to restrictions placed by the Constitution on the issuing of paper money or impairing the obligation of a contract by the states. Some of the agitators of the Revolution, such as Patrick Henry and Samuel Adams, were hostile to the ratification of the Constitution because they believed that the new semifederal, seminational government would crush personal liberty.

Such strong stuff as the Beardian interpretation with its bias against the wealthy was very appealing to the reformers of the Progressive Era and to the disillusioned generations that followed World War I and II. But a reaction

---

[18] Charles A. Beard, *An Economic Interpretation of the Constitution of the United States* (New York, 1st ed., 1913, 2d ed., 1935). He also found (though the accuracy of his statistics has been challenged) that fourteen of the delegates held Western land for speculation; twenty-four had money at interest; eleven represented mercantile, manufacturing, and shipping interests; and fifteen owned slaves; all of whom would be benefitted economically by the establishment of a strong central government.

[19] O. G. Libby, *The Geographic Distribution of the Vote of the Thirteen States on the Federal Constitution, 1787–88* (Madison, Wis., 1894), 34–35.

has occurred against Beard's extreme economic interpretation and it has been recently replaced by a more balanced one. The Philadelphia Convention was not merely a conclave of rich men, but appears to have represented a cross section of the country's economic interests and political factions. Recent investigation has shown that although some of the delegates owned large landholdings, they were also heavily in debt and that one fourth of the members of the convention had voted in the state legislatures for paper money and debtor-relief laws.[20] In other words, Beard's interpretation is too mechanical and simplistic, ignoring the complex motivation of the delegates. The legislatures chose their most prominent and most intelligent men to send to the Constitutional Convention, and it was highly probable that such forceful personalities would have accumulated considerable property. Most of the delegates seem to have been motivated by a desire to give their country a government strong enough to preserve the republican experiment of government in America, which appeared to be in danger of disintegrating. Conservative men had been frightened by the menace of debtors' securing the passage of laws favorable to their interest, such as paper money and stay laws. Consequently, they believed that one of the most fundamental functions of government was to protect property.

The revisionists also take issue with Beard in his interpretation of the ratification of the Constitution. The ratification by the state conventions, they hold, reflected to a considerable degree the varying abilities of the different states to solve their problems as semi-independent unities under the Confederation's loose organization. Virginia and North Carolina, where the opposition to ratification was powerful, felt strong enough to go it alone, whereas Delaware, Georgia, and Maryland, the weaker states, felt the need of a strong central government to aid them in coping with their difficulties. South Carolina occupied an intermediate position between the two extremes, and accordingly the state was rather even divided on the issue of ratification. The revisionists maintain, moreover, that contrary to Beard's contention, the members of the conventions who held no public securities supported the adoption of the Constitution as strongly as did the holders of such securities (although they admit that the majority of the large holders of securities voted for ratification). It appears that in the Southern states there was no strong economic interest dividing the delegates in the ratifying conventions, the overwhelming majority being small farmers and planters (many of the latter debtors), and the holding of public securities seems to have had little to do with the voting on ratification. More important considerations were ignorance and provincialism among the opponents and a higher degree of intelligence and education among the supporters.

---

[20] See Robert E. Brown, *Charles Beard and the Constitution, a Critical Analysis* (Princeton, 1956); Forrest McDonald, *We the People, the Economic Origins of the Constitution* (Chicago, 1958); and Howard K. Beale, *Charles A. Beard, an Appraisal* (Lexington, 1954).

Fortunately for the secure establishment of the central government, Washington was elected the first president and the friends of the Constitution were elected to Congress, both from the Southern and Northern states. An exception to this rule was Virginia, which sent Richard Henry Lee and William Grayson, staunch Anti-Federalists, to the Senate. After the Constitution went into effect in 1789 and the first ten amendments were added two years later (1791), new issues arose that led to the emergence of our first national parties, the Federalist and Republican parties. The three most important issues that caused this political alignment were the financial proposals of Alexander Hamilton, the interpretation of the Constitution, and conflicting sympathies in foreign affairs. The Federalists supported Hamilton's financial measures, advocated a liberal interpretation of the Constitution, and were sympathetic to England. The party struggle, according to Charles A. Beard's economic interpretation, was a contest of "fluid capital versus agrarianism" —a prodigious oversimplification.[21] It is true that the Southern Federalists, in general, represented the old aristocratic, agrarian families who held a conservative viewpoint. Interested in protecting property from the assaults of radicalism, they looked upon universal manhood suffrage with strong disapproval. The Republicans under the leadership of Jefferson opposed the efforts of Hamilton to favor the commercial classes, advocated a strict interpretation of the Constitution, and were ardent supporters of the French Revolution. Moreover, those who had opposed the ratification of the Constitution, the Anti-Federalists, formed the bulk of the Republican party, whereas the supporters of the adoption of the Constitution remained Federalists, although there occurred desertions to the Republican party.

But the political experience of Virginia in the 1790's should warn against accepting uncritically the stereotypes of political parties, which often ignore the contradictions and anomalies in politics. One would expect, for example, the center of Federalist strength to be in the area of large slave plantations, but, on the contrary, it was in the "Northern Neck," those counties bordering on the Potomac River with Alexandria as its port, the Shenandoah Valley, and northwestern Virginia. One reason for the anomaly was that the grain farmers of these areas had shifted from growing tobacco to cultivating wheat, a process that had begun before the Revolution, and now believed that a strong central government would be able to open markets for their crops, particularly in the West Indies.

The wealthy tobacco planters of the Piedmont, on the other hand, possessing secure and established markets, did not feel this need and were attracted to the Republican party because of their distrust of a strong central government, which they could not control. Moreover, the publication in 1795 of the Jay Treaty, which provided for a commission to settle debts owed by the tobacco planters before the Revolution to British merchants, aroused such opposition in the state that it generally strengthened the

[21] See Charles A. Beard, *The Economic Origins of Jeffersonian Democracy* (New York, 1915).

Republican party and "dealt a heavy blow to Federalism in Virginia." [22] The Federalist party appealed to large numbers of voters in the western part of the state because it supported reapportionment of the legislature, internal improvements, and public education. In these respects it was more liberal and progressive than the Republican party, despite its national image of conservatism. The Federalist party reached its height in the congressional election of 1799 when it won eight out of the state's nineteen representatives, but thereafter declined.

The greatest of the Southern Federalists was George Washington. This Virginia planter disclaimed any connection with a political party and, in fact, strongly advised his countrymen in his farewell address (September 17, 1796), which was revised by Hamilton, to avoid the formation of parties on a geographical basis or to give encouragement to the party spirit. More than any other Southern statesman, Washington had a national outlook. In his cabinet, Jefferson, secretary of state, and Hamilton, secretary of the treasury, represented opposing points of view and were constantly seeking to determine the policy of the administration. Although Washington did not have the brilliant, creative intellect of Hamilton or the culture and philosophic mind of Jefferson, he had finer judgment than either of his subordinates. Gradually he decided more frequently for the Hamiltonian measures against the Jeffersonian point of view, until Jefferson resigned in 1793.[23] Later, Edmund Randolph, the attorney general, and the other Southerner in the cabinet, also resigned, so that the president's advisers became entirely Northern Federalists. Washington leaned to the Federalist side because he saw the wisdom of strengthening the central government. His nationalism was displayed in his will, in which he directed that part of his estate be devoted to the foundation of a national university. One of his greatest services as president to the nation was the wise precedents he set, which became a part of the unwritten Constitution.

When Washington retired from office in 1797, he had lost his popularity in the South and Federalism was on the wane. He was not the genial type of Southerner who could win friends by cordial and democratic manners. Fond of ceremony and form, Washington drove in a coach pulled by four or six horses with outriders and lackeys in livery. He held stately levees or receptions on Tuesdays at which the guests were not invited to sit down and the president formally bowed instead of shaking hands. Indeed, this dignified and reserved man encouraged no familiarity from his visitors or associates. He was a poor speechmaker and consequently lacked that resource of appealing to the people.[24]

[22] N. K. Risjord, "The Virginia Federalists," *Journal of Southern History*, XXXIII (November 1967), 502.

[23] The most recent biographer of Washington, J. T. Flexner, maintains that Washington was not unduly influenced by Hamilton and that actually he sided more often with Jefferson than with Hamilton. *George Washington* (Boston, 1972), vol. IV.

[24] See Douglas S. Freeman, *George Washington, a Biography* (New York, 1948–54), 7 vols., and Bernard Mayo, *Myths and Men* (New York, 1963), chap. 2.

Moreover, there were a number of specific reasons why Washington's second administration was bitterly criticized in the South. When France executed her king and established the French Republic in 1792, she was attacked by a coalition of monarchies, including England. The French cause was very popular in the South, but Washington was determined to preserve the neutrality of the United States and refused aid to our former ally. He also firmly repressed the Whiskey Rebellion of 1794 by calling out fifteen thousand militia against the poor farmers of Pennsylvania who were distilling corn whiskey and refusing to pay the inequitable excise tax. Finally, Washington was severely condemned for his support of the Jay Treaty of 1795, which ended a threat of war with England by truckling, Southerners thought, to the hated Britishers. Also he was regarded as the tool of Hamilton.

The Federalist party stood for policies and principles that were growing in disfavor in the South. This party was aristocratic in tone and showed a distrust of political democracy, whereas the South under the lead of Thomas Jefferson was moving toward a more democratic type of government. Hamilton's financial schemes of funding the national debt at par, which benefited speculators, his policy of a tariff that would aid manufactures, and his advocacy of a National Bank and of a liberal interpretation of the Constitution were unpopular in the South, a predominantly agricultural region that feared the control of the central government by the Northern business interests. Although Jefferson aided in the passage of the Assumption Bill, by which the debts of the states were assumed by the national government, the legislature of his native state protested vehemently against this measure. In a memorial to Congress the Virginia legislature declared that the Federal government had no authority delegated to it by the Constitution to assume the state debts. It asserted "the doctrine of sentinelship," that the state legislatures should be the sentinels to prevent the encroachment of the Federal government on the rights and powers of the states.

Bucking this trend of the South away from Federalism was Patrick Henry, who had become a land speculator and who had strangely been converted from Anti-Federalism to a support of the Federalist party. At this time the old Revolutionary leader was living at *Red Hill,* his plantation on the Staunton River in the back country, broken in health and fortune. President Washington offered him the post in his Cabinet of secretary of state (1795) and later chief justice of the Supreme Court, which he declined, although he was greatly flattered by these offers. Consequently when Washington asked him to be a candidate for the Virginia House of Delegates to fight in behalf on the Federalist cause, he consented and won the election after a brilliant speech against the youthful John Randolph, a candidate for Congress, at Charlotte Courthouse in 1799. He died in this year, an example of a flaming radical in his youth who had grown conservative in his old age.

The swing of the South to State rights was seen especially in the refusal of Georgia to appear as a defendant before the Supreme Court in *Chisholm* v.

Georgia (1792).[25] Georgia maintained that it could not be sued by a private citizen of another state without its consent, because it was a sovereign state. A resolution introduced into the legislature declared that acquiescence in this suit "would effectually destroy the retained sovereignty of the States, and would actually tend in its operation to annihilate the very shadow of State government, and to render them but tributary corporations to the government of the United States." [26] Accordingly, Georgia refused to appear before the federal court, and a decision by default was given in favor of Chisholm. The protest of Georgia and of other states led to the ratification in 1798 of the Eleventh Amendment, which exempts states from suits by citizens of another state or of a foreign state in the Federal courts.

Federalist principles and the Federalist party were more strongly entrenched in South Carolina than elsewhere in the South. This allegiance may be partially explained by the presence in that state of a powerful aristocracy of rice planters and merchants, to whom the Federalist doctrine of government by the well-born was appealing. The South Carolina Federalists had some very able leaders, Charles Cotesworth Pinckney and Thomas Pinckney, John Rutledge, and Robert Goodloe Harper. The last was a very aggressive and insolent spokesman of the aristocratic point of view, a Princeton graduate, who changed from a zealous Anti-Federalist to an overzealous Federalist, but in 1801 he married a daughter of the wealthy Carrols of Maryland and moved to Baltimore. In 1796 Thomas Pinckney was the Federalist candidate for vice-president, and in 1804 and 1808 his brother Charles Cotesworth was the Federalist nominee for president.

The leader of the Republican party in the state, on the other hand, was an ambitious young lawyer, Charles Pinckney, a cousin of the Federalist Pinckneys, who had made a contrary switch of political principles from that of Robert Goodloe Harper. He was called "Blackguard Charlie," or apostate, by the aristocratic clique of Charleston, who looked upon him as a demagogue. Under his lead the state was redeemed from Federalism, casting its electoral vote in 1800 for Thomas Jefferson.[27] The Alien and Sedition laws, which are discussed in the next chapter, contributed greatly to the ruin of the Federalist party in the South. The dissensions in the party, especially the rivalry between Hamilton and Adams, and the unpatriotic conduct of New England Federalists during the War of 1812 also did much to weaken the party. By 1815 the party of Washington and John Marshall was dead. Its traditions and fundamental principles were carried on by the National Republicans and later by the Whig party, the parties of conservatism.[28]

---

25 See U. B. Phillips, *Georgia and State Rights* (Washington, 1902).

26 Homer C. Hockett, *The Constitutional History of the United States, 1776–1826* (New York, 1939), I, 284–285.

27 U. B. Phillips, "The South Carolina Federalists," *American Historical Review*, XIV, (April and July 1909), 529–542, 731–743, and G. C. Rogers, Jr., *Evolution of a Federalist: William Loughton Smith of Charleston, 1758–1812* (Columbia, S.C., 1962).

28 Shaw Livermore, in *The Twilight of Federalism* (Princeton, 1962), maintains that the Federalist party did not die suddenly after 1815 but continued to be active in

After the death of Washington in 1799 the outstanding Southern Federalist was John Marshall. Born in a log cabin in the Piedmont region of Virginia, he spent his youth on the frontier without the advantage of much schooling. Nevertheless, the "blue blood" of the Randolphs flowed through his veins, and he was a cousin of Thomas Jefferson. Perhaps the greatest factor in molding his views and making him such a strong nationalist was his four years of experience in the Revolutionary army. Here he conceived a deep admiration for Washington and a realization of the weakness and inefficiency of the state governments. After the victory at Yorktown, Marshall studied law at William and Mary College for two months, taking notes on the lectures of the famous George Wythe, but his mind must have been far away from the dry rules of law, for the name of his sweetheart, Mary Ambler, was scribbled over the pages of his notebook. With a guinea in his pocket, he married Mary Ambler, then only seventeen years of age, and began to practice law in Richmond.

He became the leading Federalist of Virginia, whose ability was recognized by John Adams in appointing him an envoy to France during the X.Y.Z. affair, then briefly secretary of state, and finally chief justice of the Supreme Court. This last appointment was made by Adams in 1801, after the Federalists had been defeated at the polls, but before Thomas Jefferson was inaugurated as president. Thus Jefferson was deprived of the opportunity of appointing his choice, the eminent Virginia jurist, Spencer Roane, a strong believed in states' rights, to this position. Although the Federalist party was retired from power in 1801, its principles survived in the judicial decisions of John Marshall, who served as chief justice until his death in 1835.

This remarkable man was very Southern in his personality, manners, and tastes, but his political and economic philosophy belonged to the North, to the moneyed interests and industrial society of that region. Six feet tall, with raven black hair, shaggy eyebrows, and rough-hewn features, he possessed a virile and forceful personality combined with great geniality and kindliness. He dressed in the negligent fashion of the Southern planters and had very democratic manners. Indeed, after he became chief justice, he continued to buy the fish and meat for the family and bring them home in a market basket. He enjoyed pitching horseshoes with the citizens of Richmond, gambling with cards, drinking Madeira wine, attending balls and barbecues, and forgetting his judicial dignity in the companionship of convivial clubs. One of the most attractive of his traits was his devotion to his invalid wife. During her illness he would take off his shoes and enter the house in his stocking feet in order not to disturb her.[29]

---

state elections in the North, although it did not contest presidential eelctions after 1816. Livermore does not consider the Southern Federalists. See George C. Rogers, *Evolution of a Federalist: William Loughton Smith of Charleston, 1758–1812* (Columbia, S.C., 1962).

[29] Albert Beveridge, *The Life of John Marshall* (Boston, 1929), 4 vols. in 2 vols.

As a Supreme Court judge, Marshall was dominated by his Federalist principles. He was never learned in the law, he knew little concerning the principles of economics, and he was very indolent. His five-volume biography of Washington was lifeless and full of plagiarisms. Nevertheless, he was a man of powerful intelligence and of reasoning ability. His judicial decisions were based largely on his splendid common sense and his strong Federalist bias. Many of his opinions ranged far outside of the strict limits of the case and would be regarded as *obiter dicta* from the standpoint of a narrow definition of the judicial function. His Federalist prejudices, however, happened to correspond with the need of the times to strengthen the central government.

These prejudices, or principles, if you will, were a decided leaning in favor of property rights and an equally strong feeling of nationalism. During the long period when he was chief justice, his decisions were usually at variance with the prevailing views and the economic interests of his native section, the South. Indeed, he bitterly disliked and distrusted his cousin Thomas Jefferson, and the latter's political principles, which became the faith of the Southern states. Democratic in manners, Marshall showed a deep distrust of the extension of political democracy. In this prejudice, he represented the Hamiltonian view of government.

Marshall wrote 519 of the 1,106 opinions delivered by the Court during his long occupancy of the position of chief justice. One of his most enduring achievements was establishing the doctrine of judicial review, which the Constitution did not explicitly establish. Although Justice Iredell of North Carolina, in the case of *Bayard* v. *Singleton,* had adopted the doctrine of judicial review prior to the Constitution, it is debatable whether the framers of the Constitution intended to incorporate judicial review in our Federal system, and it is certain that they would have been shocked to see the doctrine used as a tool of social reform legislation as it is today. Marshall first established the doctrine in the case of *Marbury* v. *Madison* (1803), in which he upheld the power of the Supreme Court to declare a *law of Congress* unconstitutional.[30] Then, in *Fletcher* v. *Peck* (1810) he set a precedent of the Supreme Court declaring a *state law* unconstitutional. This decision also reflected Marshall's concern to protect property rights against human rights. *Fletcher* v. *Peck* was a Southern case that dealt with the Yazoo Land Fraud. The legislature of Georgia had been corrupted by several land companies, to which a huge area of 35 million acres of land in the present states of Alabama and Mississippi had been sold in 1795 for approximately 1½ cents an acre. The people of the state were so outraged by this fraudulent transaction, in which every member of the legislature except one had been bribed, that in the next election in 1796 they chose a new group of legislators, who

---

[30] It is interesting to note that never afterward in his long career as chief justice did he and his court declare a law of Congress unconstitutional, although they exercised the doctrine of judicial review in a number of state cases.

repealed the dishonest grant. Marshall declared this act of the Georgia legislature unconstitutional and, therefore, null and void, because it impaired the obligation of a contract.[31]

In one of his most notable decisions, *McCulloch* v. *Maryland* (1819), Marshall definitely rejected the interpretation of the Constitution that was popular in the South, the strict interpretation of that document. Rather, he put the imprint of judicial authority upon the implied powers doctrine of Hamilton and thus tremendously expanded the federal power. The case arose as the result of Maryland attempting to tax out of existence a branch of the United States Bank at Baltimore. The cashier, McCulloch, appealed to the Supreme Court for protection. Maryland was represented by the famous Luther Martin, whose drunkenness caused the court obligingly to adjourn until he became sober. Marshall decided in this case that Congress had a constitutional right to charter the United States Bank and that a state could not tax an agency of the Federal government, for the power to tax was the power to destroy.

The decision that aroused most resentment in his native Virginia was *Cohens* v. *Virginia* (1821). The Cohen brothers had violated a law of Virginia in selling lottery tickets in that state. These lottery tickets were authorized in the District of Columbia by a law of Congress. The Cohen brothers appealed from an adverse decision of the State Supreme Court to John Marshall's court. Marshall ruled that the Supreme Court could review and reverse decisions of the highest state courts and that, despite the Eleventh Amendment, the Supreme Court could hear cases on appeal from individuals against states if the latter had originally instituted the suit. The decision aroused the wrath of Spencer Roane, the chief justice of the Supreme Court of Virginia, and of Thomas Jefferson, in retirement at Monticello. These Virginians expressed Southern opinion in criticizing Marshall's decision as overthrowing the rightful balance between the Federal and the state governments.[32]

Marshall dominated the Supreme Court almost as an autocrat. Not only did he write nearly half of the opinions delivered during his tenure but only eight times did he dissent from the majority opinion. When Madison appointed a Republican, Joseph Story, as associate justice, Story was converted by Marshall to his nationalist views. Marshall was a judicial lawmaker rather than a learned and objective judge. It was correctly said prior to the 1950's that this country had been governed since 1787 by three constitu-

[31] See Charles Warren, *The Supreme Court in United States History* (Boston, 1960), 2 vols.; and Edward S. Corwin, *The Constitution and What It Means Today* (Princeton, 1954).

[32] The history of the constitutional development of the United States has been written almost entirely from the Federalist point of view. A brilliant exception, however, is Charles Grove Haines, *The Role of the Supreme Court in American Government and Politics, 1789–1835* (Berkeley, 1934). See especially his discussion of Marshall's opposition to democratic ideals and principles, chap. 17.

tions, the limited one drawn up at Philadelphia by the framers, the expanded one formulated by the judicial decisions of John Marshall, and the Constitution as modified by the Reconstruction Amendments.[33] Although the views of Marshall and Washington in favor of strengthening the national government were rejected by the agrarian South, the course of history has vindicated them. Indeed, the federal government has become far more centralized and powerful than even John Marshall ever dreamed.

[33] A fourth Constitution should be added to this list, namely, the Constitution as modified by the Warren Court during the 1950's and 1960's in respect to civil liberties, protection of the rights of accused persons, a just apportionment of congressional representation, and racial integration of public schools.

The Great Generation

HEROIC AND NOBLE QUALITIES are likely to lie dormant in men until a great occasion arises. It is this historic occasion that shakes them out of preoccupation with their private concerns and forces them to think and act in the interest of the nation. Ordinary individuals are like the plant that has been thwarted in its growth by being shaded but blossoms luxuriantly when strong sunlight pours upon it. The generation that fought in the Revolution, founded the federal Constitution and the early republic, and then passed away with the death of Jefferson in 1826 was a remarkable generation. Yet the sage of *Monticello* (as Jefferson was called in his old age) has warned us against idealizing this unique generation. In 1816 he wrote to the Virginia historian Samuel Kercheval:

> Some men look at constitutions with sanctimonious reverence and deem them like the ark of the covenant, too sacred to be touched. They ascribe to the men of the preceding age a wisdom more than human, and suppose what they did to be beyond amendment. I knew that age well; I belonged to it, and labored with it. It deserved well of the country. It was very like the present, but without the experience of the present. . . .[1]

Since the great Virginia liberal was the most distinguished and versatile leader of that generation and moreover has left a prodigious correspondence,[2] a study of his life should afford a clue to the question "Why did the Southerners of the Revolutionary and early republican periods constitute the great generation in the entire history of the South?" The generation of Southerners that followed produced no great men, with the possible exception of Lee, and it blundered into the catastrophe of the Civil War.

An answer to this question may be found in examining the backgrounds of some of the political leaders, especially Jefferson and Madison. The Virginia background of Jefferson gave him an excellent preparation to become the leader of a democratic movement. His boyhood was spent on a plantation in the Piedmont region of the colony near Charlottesville, which in the eighteenth century was one of the newer settled areas, although it was

---

[1] A. A. Lipscomb and A. L. Bergh (eds.), *Writings of Thomas Jefferson* (Washington, D.C., 1903) XV, 32–34.

[2] Jefferson carefully kept copies of his letters, and his preserved correspondence (much of it in the Library of Congress) is enormous. Julian Boyd is editing the *Jefferson Papers* (Princeton, 1950—). The last published volume carries the correspondence to March 31, 1791. Vol. 19.

not the crude frontier of Boone and Crockett. Influenced to some extent by this semifrontier region, he was principally the product of the culture of the colonial aristocracy. Although his father was a self-made man, modern researchers show that he came from good stock and was associated with the gentry.[3] Jefferson's mother, Jane Randolph, was a member of one of the first families of Virginia. When he was seventeen, he entered to College of William and Mary, where he displayed a passion for learning comparable to the zest for knowledge manifested by Goethe, the great European exponent of self-culture. Fully as important in educating the young Virginian as his college courses were his friendships with three cultivated men in Williamsburg, William Small, who stimulated his interest in science, George Wythe, his law instructor, who influenced him in the direction of liberalism, and Governor Francis Fauquier, a charming man of the world and a freethinker, who often invited the young student to dinner. Jefferson was a violin player, and one of his great pleasures was to join Governor Fauquier and others in a quartette of chamber music.

In his early youth he developed an enduring passion for the study of the antique world. He mastered Greek and Latin so that he could read the classics in the original. In his notebooks (the so-called *Literary Bible*) he copied passages from the wisdom of Euripides, Cicero, Horace, Tacitus, and other classical writers. But his attitude toward the past was far from being uncritical and sentimental. Indeed, his study of the ancient world, as a modern scholar has observed, revealed to him "the dark side of humanity" and liberated him from a reverence for tradition. From his classical studies Jefferson derived many fruitful ideas of architecture, a lifelong interest in the growth of language, particularly through neologisms, and a passionate love of political and intellectual freedom. Jefferson's remarkable serenity, although partly the result of temperament and good health, was undoubtedly strengthened by his unceasing conversation with classical authors who taught the individual to become "impassible and unassailable by the evils of life, and for preserving his mind in a state of constant serenity." [4] Jefferson mingled his knowledge of antiquity with his daily experience in government, agriculture, and observation of people, each illuminating the other. His education in the classics did not stop with his college days at Williamsburg, but was continuously enriched by constant reading of the great literary works of Greece and Rome.

After completing seven years of study at the College of William and Mary and in the law office of Wythe, Jefferson began to practice law at Charlottesville. Although he obtained a good income from his profession, he disliked controversy and the necessity of making public speeches. His aversion to the legal profession was expressed in his statement that the lawyer's trade is "to question everything, yield nothing, and talk by the hour." Fortunately, Jeffer-

---

[3] Marie Kimball, *Jefferson, the Road to Glory, 1743–1776* (New York, 1947), 138.
[4] Karl Lehmann, *Jefferson, American Humanist* (New York, 1947), 138.

George Wythe (1726–1806), signer of the Declaration of Independence, delegate
to the Continental Congress and the Constitutional Convention, first law professor
in America at William and Mary College, 1779–90, teacher of Thomas Jefferson,
John Marshall and Henry Clay. (Courtesy of Colonial Williamsburg)

son did not have to depend upon his profession for a living. He became a
wealthy young man through inheritance from his father and by his marriage
to a widow who owned considerable property. One of the large landed
proprietors of the South, he owned ten thousand acres of land, divided into
nine plantations, which were cultivated by two hundred and four slaves. His

income enabled him to satisfy his tastes in buying books, in acquiring musical instruments, and in enjoying the delights of a gentleman farmer without the sweat and toil of physical labor in the sun.

Returning from Philadelphia after he had composed the Declaration of Independence, he entered upon one of the most fruitful periods of his life when, as a member of the Virginia legislature, he worked for "the great reforms." He succeeded almost immediately in having the law of entails abolished, which he regarded as equivalent to cutting the roots of the tree of aristocracy in his native state. The repeal of the law of primogeniture came later, as well as his famous statute for religious freedom, which was not adopted until 1786. He made an important contribution in revising the legal code of Virginia with "a single eye to reason" and the public welfare.[5] He proposed abolition of capital punishment for all crimes execpt murder and treason, but this humanitarian measure was not adopted until nearly twenty years later. The legislature abolished the slave trade in 1778, a reform that he had urged, but the successful bill was introduced by another man. The two most basic reforms that he advocated, which would have revolutionized the state and probably have prevented the Civil War, the gradual emancipation and colonization of the slaves and a liberal system of free public education, were rejected. It is a significant commentary on the evolution of his democratic thought that he proposed to retain the property qualification on voting in Virginia's first constitution but to give gratis to each adult male citizen fifty acres of land, which would enable him to qualify for the suffrage.

From June, 1779, to June, 1781, he was war governor of Virginia. In striving to furnish supplies and soldiers for the Continental army he neglected local defense, and the state was ravaged by invading armies. Accordingly, he was severely criticized for his administration of state affairs. So keenly was he hurt by these attacks that he resolved never again to hold public office. This period of bitterness was accentuated by grief over his wife's death, marking the nadir of his life. Despite his resolution of the renunciation of public office, we find him serving for six months in the Congress of the Confederation and in 1784 going to Paris as the American minister. Thus, for five years he was absent from the United States at a period when the Federal Constitution was being drafted and ratified. Nevertheless, he had a significant influence in securing the addition of the first ten amendments to the Constitution, known as the Bill of Rights. He advised his followers in America that he favored the ratification of the Constitution by nine states, insuring its acceptance, but that four states should withhold ratification until a bill of rights had been added. It is indicative of Jefferson's economic liberalism that he advocated the incorporation in this bill of rights of a provision outlawing monopolies, which was not adopted.

American politics has been characterized by an ebb and flow of conserva-

---

[5] The best biography of Jefferson is by Dumas Malone, *Jefferson and His Time.* vol. I, *Jefferson the Virginian* (Boston, 1948), covers the early period of his life to 1784, when he sailed as the American minister to France, chaps. 17–20.

tism and liberalism.[6] A flowing tide of liberalism reached a high point in the adoption of the Declaration of Independence and of such social reforms as the abolition of primogeniture and entail and the disestablishment of the Anglican church. Following the Revolution, a conservative reaction led to the framing and ratification of the Federal Constitution, in which many checks were placed on rabid democracy. For ten years after the new government went into operation the aristocratic and conservative class of society controlled the administration. During this period, however, a new party, the Republican, was gathering strength to overthrow the dominant Federalist faction.

Jefferson and Madison were the main organizers. Madison's role in the formulation of democratic theory and in the organization of the Republican party until recently has been greatly subordinated to Jefferson's role, but actually the work of the two men should be described as "the great collaboration." [7] Despite his idealistic theories and philosophic outlook, Jefferson was a practical politician. One of the first important examples of his willingness to engage in the art of practical politics to attain his objectives was his deal with Hamilton in the summer of 1791 over the assumption of the state debts. Hamilton proposed that the national government take over about $18 million of state debts and pay them at par. The Virginia legislature strongly opposed this proposal in a resolution drafted by Patrick Henry, pointing out the danger to liberty and "the prostration of agriculture at the feet of commerce" by the adoption of such an unconstitutional measure perpetuating an enormous debt upon the nation. Nevertheless, Jefferson agreed to secure enough votes to pass this measure if Hamilton would use his influence to locate the national capital on the banks of the Potomac after a ten-year period in Philadelphia. The deal went through, and the South thus obtained the seat of the nation's capital. The District of Columbia was created out of adjoining parts of Maryland and Virginia, but in 1846 the Virginia portion containing the town of Alexandria, was retroceded to the Old Dominion.

In this same summer of 1791 Jefferson's skill as an adroit politician was demonstrated by his "botanizing trip" up the Hudson River. At that time he and James Madison went ostensibly on a botanical excursion, but actually for the purpose of forming political alliances in New York, where Governor George Clinton, the Livingston clan, and Aaron Burr, the manipulator of St. Tammany Society of New York City, were opposed to the Federalist administration. In 1792 Virginia, North Carolina, Georgia, and New York voted for George Clinton for vice-president instead of for John Adams. Thus began the Virginia–New York Alliance, which has played such a significant role in the rise of the Republican and Democratic parties.[8]

[6] Arthur M. Schlesinger, Sr., "The Tides of National Politics," Paths to the Present (New York, 1949), 77–92.
[7] Adrienne Koch, Jefferson and Madison, the Great Collaboration (New York, 1964).
[8] See Dumas Malone, Jefferson and His Time. III. Jefferson and the Ordeal of Liberty (Boston, 1962).

After Jefferson resigned from Washington's cabinet in 1793, he devoted himself to organizing a political party of opposition. By a variety of means he built up the early Republican party. He gathered around him some of the most brilliant of the Southern leaders, particularly James Madison, who was converted from his strong Federalist allegiance. Realizing the need of propaganda and the fact that the newspapers were controlled by the Federalists, he gave Philip Freneau, the poet, a clerkship in the State Department, which enabled the latter partly to support himself while he was editing the *National Gazette,* the journal of the Republican party. Also Benjamin Franklin Bache, a grandson of Benjamin Franklin, edited the *Aurora* in Philadelphia, which violently attacked the Federalist policies. Jefferson hated to make public speeches, but he accomplished much in mobilizing his party by writing letters to key men in the states and by conversation. He and his cohorts continually attacked the Federalist party as having "monarchical" designs. In 1796 the Virginia leader was the candidate of the Republicans for president against John Adams, who won the election by the narrow margin of three electoral votes. Jefferson became vice-president, which made him presiding officer of the Senate and gave him further opportunities quietly to organize his party.

A splendid opportunity to agitate for the advancement of the Republicans occurred in the autumn of 1798, when the Federalists in Congress secured the passage of the Alien and Sedition Acts. The Sedition Act was rightly regarded as a violation of the First Amendment of the Constitution, protecting the freedom of speech and of the press.[9] Moreover, these laws were harshly enforced by partisan Federalist judges, and most of the persons prosecuted were Republican editors. Jefferson determined to arouse the people to protest against these arbitrary acts and at the same time to formulate a platform for his party. Since he was vice-president, however, he felt that he should not take an open part in the attack. Consequently, his authorship of a strong protest against the arbitrary acts of the Federalists, called the Kentucky Resolutions, was concealed. These resolutions were introduced into the Kentucky legislature by John Breckinridge and adopted by that body on November 16, 1798. A month later the Virginia legislature passed similar, but less radical, resolutions drafted by James Madison but introduced by John Taylor of Caroline.

The political character of the Virginia and Kentucky Resolutions has been so emphasized that their significance as a restatement of civil liberties in America has not been properly recognized.[10] In the Kentucky Resolutions Jefferson made an important point that has relevance today, namely that the civil liberties are so closely related that whatever violates one "throws down the sanctuary which covers the others." Thus he stated the doctrine of "the entering wedge" in the assault on liberty, which he was later to cite in his

[9] See J. M. Smith, *Freedom's Fetters: the Alien and Sedition Laws and American Civil Liberties* (Ithaca, N.Y., 1956).
[10] Adrienne Koch and Harry Ammon, "The Virginia and Kentucky Resolutions . . .," *William and Mary Quarterly*, Third Series, V (April 1948), 145–176.

criticisms of the Supreme Court for its gradual sapping and mining of the Constitution.

These documents were written at a time when Americans believed in a social compact, or contract, among citizens, as forming the true basis of government. According to this view, sovereignty was divided by the federal Constitution between the states and the central government. The question who should determine the violations of the compact, the Constitution, whenever the federal government should encroach upon the rights of the states had not yet been decided. Marshall's decision of *Marbury* v. *Madison,* establishing the right of judicial review by the Supreme Court was not rendered until 1803. Jefferson and Madison maintained in their resolutions that in the absence of an umpire between the states and the federal government, the states or the people had this power—in the words of the Kentucky Resolution, "That the government created by this compact was not made the exclusive or final judge of the extent of powers delegated to itself." [11]

The Virginia and Kentucky Resolutions restated the theory that the federal government was a government of strictly limited and delegated powers. The Alien and Sedition Acts, they asserted, were unconstitutional and therefore null and void. They called upon the sister states, or "co-states," to remonstrate and secure the repeal of the obnoxious laws. These resolutions were a protest against the trend toward centralization, or a "general consolidated government." The Virginia and Kentucky Resolutions represented the appeal of a minority against the tyranny of a majority. They reflected the fear of the Southern states that the central government would be controlled by the commercial interests of the North, which would use their power to injure the agricultural interests of the South. This fight of Jefferson and Madison to preserve the federal character of the central government was not a disunion movement, for both men were loyal to the Union. Rather, the Republicans had a strong suspicion that the Federalists were trying to change the original character of the central government. The people should be aroused, they believed, to resist the first attempt to convert the Federal government into a highly centralized and powerful institution. Jefferson and Madison were therefore fighting for a limited national government, or constitutionalism.

None of the states responded favorably to the Virginia and Kentucky Resolutions. Several of the Northern states definitely said that the Supreme Court, and not the states, was the proper agency to determine when infractions of the Constitution had been made by Congress. In rebuttal, the Kentucky legislature, on February 22, 1799, passed some additional resolutions, in which for the first time the word *nullification* was used. The core of the second Kentucky Resolutions was the statement "That the several states who formed that instrument [the Constitution] being sovereign and independent, have the unquestionable right to judge of the infraction; and, *That a nullification of those sovereignties, of all unauthorized acts done under the color of*

[11] See E. D. Warfield, *The Kentucky Resolutions of 1798* (New York, 1887).

that instrument is the rightful remedy." [12] The Virginia and Kentucky resolutions are important documents in Southern political theory, for the compact theory of the Constitution that they expounded contained the germs of the South Carolina nullification movement and of the secession doctrines.

Although Jefferson, and Southerners in general, were fond of using constitutional arguments in defense of their positions, the Virginia leader was quite aware of the economic realities of politics. In a letter to Philip Mazzei in 1796, in which he shrewdly analyzed the economic alignment of the two parties, he described the Republican party as containing "the whole landed interest and a great mass of talents," and the Federalist group was portrayed as "an Anglican monarchical aristocratic party, merchants, speculators, holders of bank stock and government bonds, and timid men." [13] Jefferson's characterization of his own party as representing the whole of the agrarian interest was not strictly correct, for many of the aristocratic planters of the Tidewater were Federalists.

Nevertheless, the Republican party appealed powerfully to farmers and small planters in the Southern states. In Virginia, Jefferson had been a representative of the back country farming interest and of the dissenters against the conservative Tidewater planters. Hamilton's financial measures and his doctrine of the loose construction of the Constitution were regarded by these agricultural groups as hostile to their economic interests and as favoring a "moneyed aristocracy." Furthermore, Southern farmers had a reasonable distrust of centralizing power in a distant government (the program of the Federalists), which in a day of slow travel and communication could not have an adequate understanding of local conditions and needs, but which might exercise a dangerous power of interference with their lives. Such a limitation of the powers of government that the Jeffersonians advocated could be safely practised at this time, for the United States was fortunate in having no powerful armed neighbors, whose menace would require a large degree of centralization of the powers of government.

Although the Republican party derived its greatest support from the South, it was powerfully aided by some Northern leaders of factions out of power and representatives of the underprivileged classes. In 1800 Jefferson and Aaron Burr were elected president and vice-president over the Federalist candidates, John Adams and Charles C. Pinckney. Jefferson was not a sectional leader; indeed, he abhorred geographical parties. In his Cabinet he appointed Albert Gallatin from Pennsylvania, and Levi Lincoln, Henry Dearborn, and Gideon Granger from New England. Jefferson had the wonderful power of phrasing the ideals of his youthful party, reminding one in this respect of Woodrow Wilson, but he also knew the practical art of organizing the forces of opposition into a victorious party. In truth, he was

---

[12] H. S. Commager (ed.), *Documents of American History* (New York, 1963) I, 155, 184.
[13] Lipscomb and Bergh (eds.), *Writings of Thomas Jefferson*, IX, 335–336.

much more than the brilliant expounder of Southern economic interests, for he realized the dignity of human nature and the rights of personality of even the humblest individual. He has frequently been portrayed as a dreamer and a theoretical person, but in the long view of history he has proved to be more practical than Alexander Hamilton, the cynical "realist," for he based his political philosophy on a sounder and more optimistic view of human nature.

The election of 1800 has often been called a peaceful revolution. The Republicans believed that they had overthrown an aristocratic monarchical group in control of the government and restored a republican regime. Jefferson walked to the Capitol from his boardinghouse to be inaugurated instead of riding in state in a coach attended by liveried servants. Thus he symbolized his belief in republican simplicity as contrasted with Federalist ceremony and aristocratic attitudes. As president he discarded the practice of seating guests at the dinner table of the White House in accordance with their rank or importance and instituted the democratic principle of pellmell. Even in his negligence and simplicity of dress he dramatized his belief in republican simplicity. Once he offended the pompous English minister, Anthony Merry, who was dressed in diplomatic uniform, by receiving him clad in slippers without heels.[14] Jefferson's emphasis on the fact that clothes do not make the man was illustrated by a vivid description of his appearance written by a New England Senator, William Plumer:

> In a few moments after our arrival a tall, high-boned man came into the room. He was dressed, or rather undressed, in an old brown coat, red waistcoat, old corduroy small-clothes much soiled, woolen hose, and slippers without heels. I thought him a servant, when General Varnum surprised me by announcing that it was the President.[15]

Yet Jefferson was an aristocrat, not of the European model, but a republican aristocrat. He had the tastes of an aristocrat. He gave elegant dinners at the White House, with the aid of his French chef. His generous hospitality is indicated by the fact that his wine bill for the first year in office was $2,800. The critical Senator Plumer has described a delightful dinner with the President in which eight different kinds of wine were served, including a Tokay that cost a guinea a bottle. Jefferson on this occasion was well dressed, with a new black suit, silk hose, clean ruffled linen, and hair highly powdered. Furthermore, the man presiding at the table (he was a widower at this time) was the most brilliant conversationalist in America. Jefferson loved music, architecture, and the collecting of fine books. Although he hated useless dogs, he loved birds—he brought to live with him in the White House a pet mockingbird that would perch on his shoulder or finger. Like most of the

---

[14] Henry Adams, *History of the United States During the Administration of Thomas Jefferson* (New York, 1930). Book II, 366.
[15] William Plumer, *William Plumer's Memorandum of Proceedings in the United States Senate, 1803–1807* (New York, 1923).

Southern gentry, he delighted in fine horses, frequently riding his beautiful saddle horse "Wildair" about the streets of Washington.[16]

Jefferson was the product primarily of the Enlightenment of the eighteenth century and of Virginia plantation influences. He was not unique among the plantation gentry, for many of the liberal aristocrats of his period were very much like him, differing from him principally in degree rather than in quality. It was the fashion in the eighteenth century for men to be versatile, and Jefferson became the most versatile of our presidents. He was an accomplished violinist until in middle life he broke his right wrist, which caused him to give up his violin playing and to learn to write with his left hand. His talents included the art of practical invention, which enabled him to devise an improved type of plow, a polygraph for writing several copies of a letter, the swivel chair, later to become the throne of bureaucrats, and numerous gadgets for his home at *Monticello*. He was a collector of American Indian vocabularies and was one of the first paleontologists in the United States, studying the fossils of prehistoric animals. In politics, he was not only a skilled diplomat and a practical statesman but America's leading political philosopher. He was also one of the finest amateur architects of this country. His literary skill was exhibited in his political pamphlets, his *Notes on Virginia* (1784), his inaugural address, his *Anas,* his *Parliamentary Manual,* and his enormous correspondence.[17] President John F. Kennedy paid homage to his versatility and culture when he wittily observed at a dinner at the White House honoring America's Nobel Prize winners: "Never has there been so much talent assembled in this room since Thomas Jefferson dined here alone."

Jefferson's versatility, however, may not have been as deeply based as his extravagant admirers have claimed. We know that there was little originality in his composition of the Declaration of Independence, which was strongly influenced by the writings of John Locke. Indeed, Jefferson's mind was empiric and practical, which tended to make him an opportunist. His character and personality were so complex that, as a modern biographer has observed, his portrait cannot be painted in broad brush strokes of black and white. He was always a relativist, not an absolutist, even in respect to his cherished principles of freedom of speech and adherence to the Constitution.[18]

Another recent biographer also has pointed out that despite his pleasant nature, Jefferson had a deep reserve that could not be penetrated, for he "kept a tight rein on his emotions." [19] Perhaps the best insight into Jeffer-

---

[16] Jefferson's private personality is charmingly portrayed in Sarah N. Randolph, *The Domestic Life of Thomas Jefferson* (New York, 1871); see also Daniel J. Boorstin, *The Lost World of Thomas Jefferson* (New York, 1960), for his scientific interests.

[17] *Jefferson's Notes on the State of Virginia* [1784] ed. by T. P. Abernethy (New York, 1963) was his only published book.

[18] Dumas Malone, *Jefferson the President: First Term, 1801–1805* (Boston, 1970), 226.

[19] M. D. Peterson, *Thomas Jefferson and the New Nation* (New York, 1970) 29.

son's many-sided nature is afforded by his epitaph, in which he wrote down the achievements for which he wished to be remembered.

> Here was buried Thomas Jefferson,
> Author of the Declaration of American Independence
> Of the Statute of Virginia for Religious Freedom,
> And Father of the University of Virginia.

The "revolution of 1800" was not so profound a change as has been depicted. Actually, it was the transfer of the power of the central government from the control of a commercial aristocracy into the hands of a landed aristocracy. Jefferson formulated the theory of a republican form of government, but the practice of this theory was largely left to the succeeding generation. The psychology of the common man toward the government was not greatly changed until the Jacksonian movement of the 1820's and 1830's. The victory of the Republicans in 1800 arrested only temporarily the growing centralization of the Federal government, and it is significant that much of the Federalist program was retained. Indeed, Jefferson did not indiscriminately discharge Federal officeholders, but steered a middle course between preserving a nonpartisan civil service and the later spoils system.[20]

The theory of politics held by the agricultural South was admirably stated by Jefferson in his first inaugural address, March 4, 1801. In broad outlines he sketched the ideal of a laissez-faire government—"a wise and frugal Government, which shall restrain men from injuring one another, shall leave them otherwise free to regulate their own pursuits of industry and improvement, and shall not take from the mouth of labor the bread it has earned." For the defense of the state he proposed to rely on the militia of the standing army, and he upheld the supremacy of the civil over the military authority. In foreign affairs the nation should pursue a policy of peace and no "entangling alliances." His first inaugural address was permeated with the spirit of reconciliation with the Federalists, who had so bitterly attacked him. He declared that although the will of the majority must prevail, the rights of minorities must be protected.

In his conduct of foreign affairs, despite his recommendation of avoiding foreign alliances, Jefferson was not isolationist. He had the modern concept that nations, having a common feeling for democracy and a similar ideology, should support each other by moral, political, and economic means short of war. When the French overthrew their absolute monarchy, Jefferson wrote to George Mason: "I look with great anxiety for the firm establishment of the new government in France, being perfectly convinced that if it takes place there it will spread sooner or later all over Europe. On the contrary a check there would retard the revival of liberty in other countries. I consider

---

[20] See Leonard D. White, *The Jeffersonians, a Study in Administrative History*, 1801–1829 (New York, 1951); and Noble E. Cunningham, Jr., *The Jeffersonian Republicans in Power, Party Operations, 1801–1809* (Chapel Hill, 1963).

the establishment and success of their government as necessary to stay up our own and to prevent it from falling back to that kind of a half-way house, the English constitution." [21] Later he anticipated the Good Neighbor policy of Franklin Delano Roosevelt in proposing "a cordial fraternization" between the republics of Latin America and the United States.

Although Jefferson was an ardent pacifist who neglected the navy, he was a pragmatic rather than a doctrinaire pacifist, as indicated by his declaring war on the Barbary states of Africa (1801–1805) rather than paying tribute to prevent them from attacking American ships. But when England and France violated American rights on the high seas, and particularly in 1807 when the British warship *Leopard* in seeking deserters from the navy fired on our frigate *Chesapeake* and impressed some of our seamen, the president restrained his country from a declaration of war. Instead, the Republican Congress passed the unwise Embargo Act, which prohibited United States vessels from leaving the harbours of the country for foreign ports.

Jefferson's record as president in his first term contrasts greatly with conditions in the modern presidency. He got along extremely well with Congress, which he respected as truly representing the people whose will should be enacted. He sought to restore to the government "the spirit of 1776," which meant to him elimination of internal taxes, a government of drastic economy, the rapid payment of the national debt, and the preservation of civil liberties. One of the greatest contrasts of his administration with modern practice was that he took very little part in the campaign for his reelection in 1804. He suffered deeply from the libels against him, especially the accusation that he was the father of mulatto children born on his plantation, but he never publicly replied to them, although he did reluctantly sanction some prosecutions of Federalist libels in the state courts.[22]

Franklin Delano Roosevelt drew much of the support for his liberal program from the underprivileged classes of the cities. Jefferson, on the other hand, who had seen the evils of Paris, compared the mobs of large cities to sores on the body politic, unsuitable raw material to make good citizens in a republic. Pre-eminently the leader of the Southern agrarians, Jefferson placed great faith in the virtue and judgment of small, independent farmers, who were property owners as contrasted with the proletariat of the cities. He wished to keep America rural as long as possible in order to prevent the duplication of the unhappy conditions of the mature countries of Europe. American yeoman farmers and planters might temporarily be misled by propaganda, he believed, but the returning good sense of the people would correct their mistakes. Strangely, Jefferson seldom used the words *democratic*

[21] Gilbert Chinard, *Thomas Jefferson, the Apostle of Americanism* (Boston, 1946), 494–495.
[22] Fawn Brodie in *Thomas Jefferson: An Intimate History* (New York, 1974) accepts these accusations as true, but they cannot be proved or disproved, and even if he did beget seven mulatto children during 38 years following the death of his wife, what bearing does this have upon his statesmanship?

and *democracy,* but referred to the American experiment of government as "republican." The word *Democratic* as applied to the political party that Jefferson founded was first used alone as the party label in 1844.

The Southern planters and farmers, who desired a decentralized government, found a spokesman in Jefferson. If the South had possessed a more balanced economy, undoubtedly there would have been less emphasis on states' rights in the history of that section. Over and over again crops up the fear of Southerners that a strong central government would be controlled by the Northern states, which would pass adverse legislation against Southern interests, particularly in regard to slavery and the tariff. The South, therefore, advocated a strict interpretation or construction of the Constitution to confine the Federal government to its delegated powers. In addition to this fear Jefferson had another strong reason for favoring localism in government. An ardent admirer of the New England town meeting, he urged the Southern states to divide their counties into wards, or "ward-republics" he called them, which would enable every citizen to participate in direct government. He believed that if political power was kept largely in the hands of the states and of the local communities the people would have an opportunity to watch their officials more closely and thus prevent corruption.

The democratic leader of 1800 and the democratic leader of 1936 found a Supreme Court hostile to their policies, and therefore they tried to curb its power. Jefferson's attempt to reform the judiciary by the initiation of impeachment proceedings was motivated particularly by his opposition to the centralizing tendency of the Supreme Court. This attack on the independence of the judiciary failed when the trial of Justice Samuel Chase in 1805 resulted in acquittal despite the fact that the Republicans had the requisite majority in the Senate to convict. Jefferson continued, however, to oppose a Supreme Court that was "independent of the Nation," and therefore he proposed that, instead of the tenure of the judges being for life, their appointments should be renewed every four or six years. Indeed, Jefferson's writings give strong support to a modern questioning of the wisdom of judicial review.[23]

The great Virginian was a firm advocate of majority rule, not merely of the original majority who drafted the Constitution, but of the continuing majority. He appealed to young men in all ages by declaring that "the earth belongs in usufruct to the living; that the dead have neither power nor rights over it. . . ."[24] Literally, he held that each generation should make its own laws and not be bound by the dead hand of the past—a generation being twenty to thirty-four years. He was youthful in spirit also in his flexibility, in adapting himself to changed conditions. During the War of 1812 he became convinced that the United States must give up the ideal of a rural Arcadia and develop a more balanced economy by manufacturing enough

[23] See H. S. Commager, *Majority Rule and Minority Rights* (New York, 1943).
[24] Clement Eaton, "The Jeffersonian Tradition of Liberalism in America," *South Atlantic Quarterly,* XLIII (January 1944), 2–5.

goods to be independent of Europe. On his plantation of *Monticello* he himself had erected a nail factory. He took great strides away from his former doctrine of the negative, laissez-faire state by proposing that after the public debt had been liquidated the surplus Federal revenues should be used to build national roads and canals and to support a national university.

Jefferson's political philosophy was derived partly from his experience during the fermenting period of the American Revolution and partly from the insemination of liberal European thought. The works of the English democratic thinkers of the seventeenth and eighteenth centuries, such as those of John Locke, Algernon Sidney, and Bolingbroke, as well as the writings of the Scotsman Lord Kames, had a profound influence on the development of his political philosophy. With the exception of Montesquieu's *Spirit of the Laws,* French political writings do not seem to have greatly affected him. After he had matured his philosophy of life, he spent five delightful years as American minister to France, where he acquired such a decided taste for French wines, music, and cookery that homely old Patrick Henry is reported to have said, "Tom Jefferson has abjured his native vittles." Instead of succumbing to French influences, however, his experiences and observations in France served chiefly to strengthen him in his robust Americanism. Later in his career the Physiocrats and Ideologues, especially Destutt de Tracy, appealed to him, because some of their philosophy clarified and confirmed certain ideas he himself had evolved through his experience and observation.

Jefferson was the most effective exponent of intellectual liberty that America has produced. Uniformity of opinion or of religion, he believed, is neither possible nor desirable any more than is the standardization of face or stature. The masses of the people tend to be intolerant of critics or persons who disagree with their prejudices in vital matters. Dissent gives them a sense of insecurity. Likewise, dictatorships cannot permit an uncensored press or an untrammeled radio. The lovers of liberty, on the other hand, have always been concerned with the protection of minority rights and the preservation of freedom of expression. The preservation of the right of holding heterodox opinions is a perennial problem in a democratic government, for the tyranny of the majority is more formidable, as the great Catholic historian Lord Acton observed, than the tyranny of the minority. In our own time this fact has been demonstrated by the attempts to suppress the "subversive propaganda" of those opposed to capitalistic society, by the spy hunt of the Congressional Committee on Un-American Activities, by the doctrine of "guilt by association," and by the tactics of Senator McCarthy in terrorizing public officials with the charge of communism.

The use of the force of civil government to bring about a uniformity of opinion Jefferson regarded as a violation of the rights of personality and as producing hypocrisy. In the preamble to his famous Virginia Statute of Religious Freedom he declared that the civil government should interfere with the expression of opinions only when they "break into overt acts against peace and order." Let the government practice toleration, he urged, for truth will prevail over lies and propaganda provided free argument and debate are allowed, "errors ceasing to be dangerous when it is permitted freely to contradict them." Only by zealously guarding civil rights, especially the freedom of speech, of religion, and of assembly, he thought, could the right of dissent by individuals and minorities be maintained. Thus the minority would have the opportunity, through debate and persuasion, to become the majority controlling the government.

Jefferson's record in respect to civil liberties contained some startling inconsistencies. In his support of freedom of religion, he never wavered, but in the fields of politics and university education his practical actions at times deviated from his liberal theory. In his prosecution of Burr in 1807 and in his resolute enforcement of the Embargo Acts he ruthlessly disregarded civil liberties. Especially "un-Jeffersonian" was his attempt to guard the minds of young college students from doctrines that he regarded as pernicious. Hume's history of England he thought was an elegant account but a dangerous one because of its Tory principles and because it was "so plausible and pleasing in its style and manner, as to instill its errors and heresies insensibly into the minds of unwary readers." [25] Consequently he endeavored to put into the hands of American youth a censored version published by an Englishman named John Baxter, but he could not persuade a publisher to print such a denatured Hume in an American edition. Furthermore, he advocated that all the professors of the University of Virginia be allowed to select their own textbooks, except the professor of law and government who should be required to use texts that would properly inculcate in the students the principles of Jeffersonian democracy.

This leader of the early Republicans was too great a realist to believe that political democracy could flourish in a soil of tremendous inequalities of wealth. He concluded that, although an equal division of property was impracticable, "legislators cannot invent too many devices for subdividing property." [26] Believing that the small landholders were the most precious part of the state, he wished to see the United States remain a land of modest fortunes, in which the government should assist the weaker members of society to acquire a reasonable share of property, and reduce bloated fortunes by indirect government action. His sympathy for the poor man is revealed in a letter he wrote to Marquis de Lafayette, urging the latter to travel incognito through France to observe the living conditions of the people. "You must ferret the people out of their hovels as I have done," he wrote, "look into their kettles, eat their bread, loll on their beds under pretence of resting yourself, but in fact to find if they are soft. You will feel a sublime pleasure in the course of this investigation, and a sublimer one

[25] Leonard W. Levy, *Jefferson and Civil Liberties, the Darker Side* (Cambridge, Mass., 1963), 144.

[26] P. L. Ford (ed.), *The Writings of Thomas Jefferson* (New York, 1892–99), VII, 35.

hereafter when you shall be able to apply your knowledge to the softening of their beds or the throwing of a morsel of meat into their kettles of vegetables." [27] An example of this disinterested love for humanity was his smuggling of some Italian rice in his pockets through the customs in order to introduce a superior variety into the Southern states. His zeal for human welfare caused him to think of practical means of lessening the drudgery of life. He proposed, for example, the installation of small steam engines in the homes, run by the kitchen fire to pump water for household use and fire protection.

It is the fate of many great men, including Jefferson, to evoke an uncritical hero worship that obscures their faults and limitations. A balanced portrait of Jefferson, therefore, would have to note that at times he avoided frankness and above-board conduct, causing his enemies to accuse him of dissimulation and to nickname him "Saint Thomas of Cantingbury." [28] He also lacked a well-developed sense of humor such as distinguished President Lincoln and the late President Kennedy. Although radical in thought at times and surprisingly violent in his private correspondence, but not in public utterance, he was opportunistic like Franklin D. Roosevelt. Nor was he much of a radical in action after he came into power. Indeed, he adopted a considerable part of the Hamiltonian program that he had attacked and after he became the leader of a political party he did nothing constructive in attacking the greatest social evil of his age, Southern slavery.

Jefferson's reputation has had a curious fluctuation of popular favor and neglect.[29] In the presidential election of 1804 his popularity was at its height, when he carried every state in the Union except Connecticut and Delaware, but at the end of his administration he became very unpopular because of the Embargo. Jeffersonian ideas underly the democratic movement of the Jacksonian era. When the proslavery argument reached its full bloom in the decade of the 1850's, however, the ruling class in the South scrapped his natural rights theory and dismissed the Declaration of Independence as glittering generalities. Although his native section repudiated much of his liberalism, holding nevertheless to his states'-rights doctrine, Jefferson attracted new followers and popularity in the North among the abolitionists and Republicans. Lincoln's speeches and writings are saturated with Jeffersonian thought. Following the Civil War, the Southern people regarded Lee, not Jefferson, as their greatest man after Washington. During the Populist revolt of the 1880's and 1890's, the shirt-sleeved leaders of the farmers, such as Tom Watson of Georgia, appealed to the magic name of Jefferson as the champion of the common man.

Then the fame of the philosopher-statesman subsided, to be revived once

[27] Bernard Mayo (ed.), *Jefferson Himself, the Personal Narrative of a Many-Sided American* (Boston, 1942), 143–144.

[28] A. J. Beveridge, *Life of John Marshall* (New York, 1916–1919), III, 362–364.

[29] See Merrill D. Peterson, *The Jefferson Image in the American Mind* (New York, 1960).

more by historical biographers in the decade of the 1920's and later by the political needs of the party of Franklin Delano Roosevelt. Ironically, the opponents of the Roosevelt administration, especially the Liberty League, likewise claimed Jefferson to be on their side, pointing to him as the advocate of states' rights and of a laissez-faire government and as disapproving of a third term of president. The rise of Hitler and the Fascist ideology also led to the exaltation of Jefferson as the supreme exponent of democracy and Americanism. Since 1932 the American people have been reminded of this superb liberal leader in many ways, by a Jefferson coin, a Jefferson stamp, by the speeches of the New Dealers, by the building of a marble memorial to him on the tidal basin at Washington, and by the publishing of his entire writings. More recently, however, in this era of strong-flowing nationalism the reputation of the great Virginian has again somewhat diminished. A modern poll of seventy-five prominent American historians and writers (most of whom live above the Mason-Dixon line) rated Jefferson below Lincoln, Washington, Franklin Delano Roosevelt, and Woodrow Wilson in the cadre of great presidents.[30]

The party Jefferson helped to found and that Southerners dominated for so long a period has been regarded as peculiarly the champion of states' rights within the United States. The doctrine of states' rights was not a monopoly of the South, however, for it was frequently used as a defense mechanism by different sections of the country to protect their interests against a hostile majority in control of the federal government. Suspicion is aroused concerning the sincerity of this plea of states' rights by the fact that when the exponents of states' rights obtained control of the federal government they lost their enthusiasm for their cherished doctrine. Even Jefferson and Madison, authors of the Virginia and Kentucky Resolutions, when they became president abandoned their extreme states'-rights position, to which they were so devoted as leaders of a faction out of power. The acquisition of Louisiana in 1803, which is discussed in the following chapter, is an example of Jefferson's flexibility or opportunism in departing from his principles of states' rights and strict construction of the Constitution.

The trend of the Republican party after 1801 from its adherence to states' rights led to a split in its ranks. The group that became disgruntled at the leadership of Jefferson were called the "Old Republicans," because they were staunchly loyal to the doctrine of states' rights and the strict interpretation of the Constitution.[31] The outstanding political leaders in this clique were John Randolph of Roanoke, John Taylor, William Branch Giles, and James Monroe of Virginia. The speaker of the house, Nathaniel Macon of North Carolina, joined the discontented faction, probably because of his ruralism. He

---

[30] Arthur M. Schlesinger, Sr., "Our Presidents: A Rating by 75 Historians," *New York Times Magazine*, July 29, 1962.
[31] See N. K. Risjord, *The Old Republicans: Conservatism in the Age of Jefferson* (New York, 1965).

idealized an agrarian society where men did not live close enough to each other to hear their neighbor's dogs barking. This group of Old Republicans was sometimes called "tertium quids," or a third something, neither loyal Jeffersonians nor Federalists.

In addition to their devotion to the original principles of the Republican party, some of the leaders had personal grudges against the President. Monroe had been chagrined by the failure of Jefferson to submit to the Senate a treaty he had made with England. Randolph had been humiliated by his mismanagement of the impeachment of Justice Chase, for which he illogically blamed Jefferson. The "Quids" bitterly attacked Jefferson and his cabinet for the settlement of the Yazoo Fraud question, by which 5 million acres of land were appropriated to satisfy the claims of bona fide purchasers of land from the Yazoo companies. In 1808 the "Quids" supported Monroe as a candidate of the party for president in opposition to Madison, Jefferson's choice.

Of the opponents of the Jefferson administration, John Randolph of Roanoke was the most feared. He was the greatest master of satire and invective that the South has produced. Reared on the plantation *Bizarre,* a scion of the aristocratic Randolph family, he carried the individualism, pride, and arrogance of the Southern planter to the extreme limits of caricature. He was remarkably precocious as a youth but so unstable that he left both William and Mary College and Princeton without completing his studies. In 1799 he was elected to Congress at the age of twenty-six and within two years he had been chosen chairman of the Ways and Means Committee, which made him leader of the Republicans in the lower house of Congress. In 1805 he had a quarrel with Jefferson, following the Chase impeachment fiasco, and from this time on, he became the Great Opposer—vehemently attacking the administration in the Yazoo Fraud, in the attempt to acquire West Florida, and in the passage of the Embargo Act. He violently condemned the maintenance of a standing army, proposing to rely for the defense of the country upon the militia. Also he was one of the early Southern "watchdogs over the Treasury." Unavailingly he tried to prevent a declaration of war against England in 1812 as well as the adoption of nationalizing measures of the Republicans after the Treaty of Ghent. In 1820 he was one of the most extreme opponents of the Missouri Compromise. During a long career of various inconsistencies, there was one fixed principle from which he never deviated, a fanatical devotion to states' rights.

John Randolph was the outstanding eccentric of the Old South. He presented a strange appearance, with his slender legs, like pipe stems, his projecting chin, dark, sad eyes, wrinkled face, and high, feminine voice. He did not need to shave, and he seems to have been impotent sexually. Always unhappy, with frail health and jangled nerves, he lashed at his enemies with a mordant tongue and was ready to fight a duel at the least insult. He would appear in Congress booted and spurred, carrying a riding whip, and followed by his dogs. Although he had a scorn for common people and for political democracy, this perverse aristocrat was an enthusiastic supporter of Andrew

Jackson for president. Jackson repaid his support shrewdly by sending the troublemaker as minister to Russia, where the severe climate ruined his delicate health. There was an appealing humane side in the nature of this Virginia planter. Once he was asked who was the most superb orator he had heard. He promptly replied, "A slave. She was a mother and her rostrum was the auction block." [32] In later life he was afflicted with periods of insanity. He died in 1833, leaving a will that emancipated his four hundred slaves.

More important than Randolph as an intellectual expounder of the doctrines of states' rights was John Taylor of Caroline County, Virginia. This Southern planter had a passionate love for agriculture and the way of life based on it. Although he was a senator for a brief period, he avoided officeholding and devoted his strong mind to writing pamphlets and books and fashioning a political philosophy suited to the agrarian interests of the South. Taylor violently opposed the centralization of political power in the Federal government because he believed that such power would be used by the Northern majority to exploit the South. In 1788 he opposed the ratification of the Federal Constitution by his native state, and ten years later he proposed to Jefferson the idea of forming a Southern Confederacy. Jefferson discouraged such a disunion movement, reminding Taylor that the oppressive Federalist rule would be temporary and that free governments always breed dissenting groups, for which secession was not the right remedy.

Taylor ardently supported Jefferson's early policies, even the purchase of Louisiana. But he refused to change his principles when the majority of his party followed a nationalistic course.[33] Joining the "Quids," he supported Monroe for president in opposition to Madison, Jefferson's choice. In his prolix pamphlets and books, such as *An Inquiry into the Principles and Policy of the Government of the United States* (1814), *Construction Construed* (1820), and *Tyranny Unmasked* (1822), he attacked the establishment of a national bank, the increase of the public debt, and the enactment of a protective tariff as a surrender of the federal government to the Northern capitalists. John Marshall's decisions whittling down the powers of the states alarmed and incensed him. He pointed out the economic bases of political parties and warned the South of the danger of a moneyed aristocracy controlling the central government. Taylor's plea for a balanced government, in which the rights of the states were preserved, became more popular in the antebellum South as that section realized more clearly its minority position in the Union.

John Taylor attempted to preserve those conditions in his native region that had produced "the great generation" of Southerners. Paramount among these economic and social determinants was the maintenance of an independent and dignified life of agriculture as conducted by country gentlemen.

[32] W. C. Bruce, *John Randolph of Roanoke, 1773–1833* (New York, 1922), II, 251.
[33] Henry H. Simms, *Life of John Taylor* (Richmond, 1932); and E. T. Mudge, *Social Philosophy of John Taylor of Caroline* (New York, 1939).

Slavery was regarded as essential to this way of life, but it was a paternalistic type, in which the blacks were considered members of the family. The kind of education that these leaders had was also influential in the formation of their poised and capable personalities. The generation of Jefferson, Madison, and Monroe conceived of education as a process of developing the complete gentleman—an unspecialized, Renaissance type of education.[34] Their age, moreover, was one of republican aristocrats, trained for public service in the justice of the peace system, the militia, and the legislatures. These Southern country gentlemen were on the whole permeated with a strong sense of *noblesse oblige,* clearly aware that rights and privileges demanded a corresponding sense of responsibility. With the exception of Patrick Henry, they were not self-made men but were born to high position.[35] Scorning demagoguery in politics, they developed a more philosophical outlook, a larger view, than did the sectional-minded leaders of the era of Jefferson Davis. Perhaps the most important elements in the rise of this remarkable group of Southern leaders were their exposure to the Enlightenment, with its devotion to reason, and their participation in the birth of a new nation based on great liberal ideas.

[34] See Richard Beale Davis, *Intellectual Life in Jefferson's Virginia, 1790–1830* (Chapel Hill, 1964).
[35] Dumas Malone, "The Great Generation," *Virginia Quarterly Review,* XXIII (Winter 1947), 108–122.

10

The Creoles Become Southerners

CONTRARY to a prevalent misconception, the Creoles were persons of Latin extraction born in the colonies without any admixture of Negro blood.[1] There were two types of Creoles in the South, the Spanish in Florida and Texas and the French in Louisiana and lower Alabama. The military and governmental center of the Creoles in Florida was St. Augustine, founded in 1565, the oldest town in the United States, from which radiated Catholic missions into the hinterland as far north as Guale ("Wallie") or coastal Georgia and the sea islands.[2] After the Franciscan missions were destroyed by Indian revolts and attacks from South Carolina during Queen Anne's War, Spain showed a remarkable indifference to her remote settlements in Florida. Chiefly soldiers and priests came to the flowery peninsula and no Protestants, heretics, or Jews were allowed to enter the Spanish colonies. The settlement at St. Augustine was maintained primarily to assert Spanish ownership of Florida and to provide a military base for the protection of the Bahama Channel, through which the treasure fleet from Mexico sailed to Spain. It is indicative of the inert policy of Spain that the chief motive for establishing the western outpost of Pensacola in 1698 was not any ambition toward expansion but merely to prevent the French from seizing a strategic location.

Under Spanish control (which was interrupted for twenty years during the English occupation, 1763–1783), the Creoles of Florida lived a somnolent and backward existence. They failed to develop a valuable export commodity or to advance beyond a frontier civilization. Nevertheless, it is unhistorical to perpetuate the old stereotype of the Spaniards in the New World, the so-called black legend, which vastly exaggerates the Spaniard's intolerance, laziness, pride, hostility to innovation, lack of local self-government, and cruelty toward the Indians. It must be remembered that Florida was on the periphery of the Spanish empire in America and that at the center a remarkable colonial civilization arose in such cities as Mexico City, Lima, and Havana. Since Florida represented a frontier outpost, it is not surprising that after this region was acquired by the United States in 1821 the remains of Spanish culture were relatively slight.[3]

[1] George Washington Cable, *The Creoles of Louisiana* (New York, 1884). Joseph Tregle, Jr., "Early New Orleans Society: A Reappraisal," *Journal of Southern History*, XVIII (1955), 20–36, maintains that the term *Creole* was applied to anyone, black or white, French-speaking or English-speaking, who was a native of Louisiana.
[2] See J. T. Lanning, *The Spanish Missions of Georgia* (Chapel Hill, 1935).
[3] See John A. Caruso, *The Southern Frontier* (Indianapolis, 1963); and Herbert Bolton, *The Spanish Borderlands* (New Haven, 1921).

The attempt of France to establish an empire on the Gulf coast, on the other hand, has left enduring effects upon the deep South. The voyage of La Salle from Canada down the Mississippi River to its mouth in 1682 formed the basis of the French claim to the land, which they named Louisiana. La Salle failed in the attempt to plant a colony at the mouth of the great river, but one of his followers, a mendacious priest named Father Louis Hennepin, revived the interest of the French in colonizing this remote region by publishing a book, *New Discovery* (Utrecht, 1698), which was widely read in Europe. In this book he claimed to have discovered the mouth of the Mississippi two years before the memorable voyage of La Salle. French secret agents erroneously reported that the English were preparing an expedition under the guidance of Father Hennepin to seize the mouth of the Mississippi River to forestall French occupation. The French Minister, Count de Pontchartrain, sent out an expedition in 1699 under the Sieur de Iberville to found a colony at this strategic place. This Canadian soldier located his colony, not at the mouth of the Mississippi, but to the eastward at Old Biloxi (now Ocean Springs) in the present state of Mississippi. In 1702 the settlement was moved to a site on the Mobile River, and eight years later it was transferred to the location of the modern city of Mobile.

The dominant figure in the early history of Louisiana was a younger brother of Iberville, the Sieur de Bienville. Only twenty-one years of age in 1701, when he was placed in charge of the Louisiana colony, he governed it at intervals for over forty years.[4] He became an adept in Indian diplomacy, studied the languages and characteristics of neighboring tribes, and treated them with frankness and bonhomie. His greatest achievement was the founding of New Orleans in 1718, whose site, one hundred miles above the mouth of the Mississippi River, he had selected the previous year at a place "having one of the finest crescents on the river."

During the early years of Louisiana, King Louis XIV, engaged in war, paid little attention to his far away colony on the Gulf coast. In 1712 he turned over the responsibility of the colony to a rich merchant, Antoine Crozat, who was given a monopoly of its trade with the exception of beaver furs. The appointment of Sieur Antoine de la Mothe Cadillac, the founder of Detroit, as governor failed to bring prosperity to the province, and Crozat became so disappointed at the lack of financial profits from his investment that in 1717 he surrendered his charter to the king.[5]

After the failure of Crozat's monopoly, a Scottish speculator, John Law, in 1717 organized the Company of the West, which was given a monopoly of trade and the right to work the supposed gold and silver mines of Louisiana. In return for the privileges of its charter, the company agreed to trans-

[4] See Grace King, *Jean Baptiste le Moyne, Sieur de Bienville* (New York, 1892).
[5] See Marcel Giraud, *Histoire de la Louisiane, 1698–1715: Le Regne de Louis XIV* (Paris, 1953); vol. I trans. and published by Louisiana State University Press (Baton Rouge, 1973) and the older work, Francis Parkman, *Pioneers of France in the New World* (Boston, 1907).

port six thousand white colonists and three thousand slaves to Louisiana. Here, however, was the rub. It was difficult to get substantial French peasants to emigrate. Consequently, the Company of the West (later entitled Company of the Indies), in its eagerness to obtain human material for its colony, sent over many worthless and vicious settlers, men and women picked up from the streets of Paris, from prisons, houses of correction, and hospitals. The agents of the police of Old Orleans collected prostitutes and vagrants, in order to send them to swell the population of its namesake in the New World.[6] In 1718 the Company transported over eight hundred colonists without proper provision for feeding them. They were dumped upon the shores of Louisiana, and Governor Bienville had a difficult time absorbing them into his weak colony. Few were willing to work as agricultural laborers, and no mines of silver and gold were discovered. Among the worthless rabble that came over was a group of substantial German peasants who settled twenty-five miles above New Orleans, on the "German coast" of the Mississippi River.[7] The most productive immigrants brought into the colony by the Company were large numbers of black slaves. Stock was sold to the public through a remarkable campaign of advertising that puffed up this remote region as an earthly paradise. A wild orgy of speculation in its stock followed in France, known as the Mississippi Bubble. Law exercised such a great fascination, even hypnotic power, over the French people that he deluded all classes, from perfumed noblemen to his own coachman.[8]

In 1720 the Mississippi Bubble burst, one of the most famous swindles in history. The glowing dreams of quick profits that the specious Scotsman had conjured up in the minds of French "suckers" were not realized. Indeed, Louisiana remained an unprofitable colony, a financial loss to the French treasury, as long as France held it. When Law's dazzling stock manipulations failed, he fled from France penniless, and a large number of French people suffered bankruptcy as a result of placing confidence in him. In 1731, after a disastrous Indian war, the Company of the Indies surrendered its charter, and Louisiana reverted to a royal colony.[9]

One of the potent reasons for the failure of the French to thrive in Louisiana was their inability to win and hold the friendship of neighboring Indian tribes. In order to overawe the hostile Natchez, Cadillac had established Fort Rosalie, at Natchez. When these savages killed some French travelers, an expedition was sent against them that was called by Gallic wits "La Guerre aux Poules," or "The Chicken War," because the chief spoils were some captured chickens. In 1729 the Natchez massacred the garrison and settlers at Fort Rosalie. The French retaliated the following year by a

[6] D. M. Quynn (ed.), "Recruiting in Old Orleans for New Orleans," *American Historical Review,* XLV (October 1940), 832.

[7] J. H. Deiler, *The Settlement of the German Coast of Louisiana* (New York, 1904).

[8] Georges Oudard, *Amazing Life of John Law* (New York, 1928); and Pierre Heinrich, *Louisiane sous la Compagnie des Indes* (Paris, n.d.).

[9] G. M. Wrong, *The Rise and Fall of New France* (New York, 1928), 2 vols.

grim war that liquidated this brave and warlike people. The remnants of the defeated nation fled for refuge to the Chickasaw Indians in the present state of Tennessee. Ten years afterward Bienville began a war against the Chickasaw that ended in failure. He was so chagrined over its result, as well as depressed by ill health, that he resigned his governorship and left for France, never to return to Louisiana.

The last important Indian trouble that the French in Louisiana experienced was with the Choctaw, a powerful tribe inhabiting the present states of Mississippi and Alabama. The French regarded these Indians as their property, and in 1736 they built Fort Tombecbé on the upper waters of the Tombigbee River in Alabama to maintain their ascendancy over them. A faction of the Choctaw, however, under the leadership of Rouge Soulier (Red Shoe) was alienated from the French and sought trade connections with the English. Red Shoe had greatly resented the seduction of his favorite wife by a Frenchman and determined to secure vengeance. In 1746, during King George's War, the followers of Red Shoe killed the French traders among them.[10] The English seized this opportunity to send James Adair, an Indian trader who subsequently wrote a *History of the American Indians* (1776), to extend their influence over the disaffected Choctaw. This effort was frustrated, however, by the assassination of Red Shoe the next year by a pro-French warrior. There followed a fratricidal war between the pro-English and pro-French factions of the Choctaw nation. The Louisiana authorities cynically encouraged this civil war, which eventually resulted in the establishment of exclusive French influence over the Choctaw. By the Grandpré treaty of 1750 these Indians agreed to expel all English traders and to continue to make war against the Chicksaw, inveterate enemies of both the Choctaw and the French.

The ineptitude of the French of Louisiana in handling Indian affairs contrasts with the success of the Canadian French in dominating the Algonquin tribes. Two adverse economic factors, however, contributed to the signal failure of the Louisiana colony to develop a lucrative Indian trade. Beaver furs from the Illinois country that were shipped down the river to New Orleans spoiled on account of the warm climate. Furthermore, the French could not secure manufactured goods to use in the Indian trade as cheaply as their English competitors.

Louisiana suffered from a bad governmental system. The administration of the province was divided between the royal governor, who had charge of military defense and Indian relations, and the *ordonnateur,* or intendant, who had charge of finances and justice, assisted by a superior council in which the people were represented by six of the principal inhabitants. The two executive officers were supposed to serve as a check on each other. They were to act jointly in matters relating to commerce, agriculture, and the increase of

[10] L. A. Gipson, *British Empire in America Before the American Revolution* (New York, 1946) IV, chap. 4.

population. This duplex system of government led to innumerable quarrels and the hampering of efficient administration. At times the wives of the intendant and of the governor waged bitter social wars, posting lampoons against each other on the street corners. Nor did this system check the spread of corruption among the officials, for most of them came to Louisiana to exploit their jobs in order to return, well-laden, in the words of Gayarré, the Creole historian, "to their cherished native country, to the beautiful France, which they could not forget." [11] Such a governor was the Marquis de Vaudreuil, who for ten years, from 1743 to 1753, ruled Louisiana with a splendor, luxury, and pomp that were a faint reflection of the reign of Louis XIV in France. Unfortunately, this gay and magnificent governor was a corruptionist, who made illegal profits out of his office. Like the neighboring colony of Florida, Louisiana did not enjoy political freedom. The inhabitants had no control over their government; everything was decided in France or by the royal officials. The laws were the customs of Paris, which did not provide a jury system. Even prices at the market were regulated by the intendant.

The French in Louisiana, however, did not establish the feudal system of landholding that predominated in Canada. The arable land was divided into little farms, consisting of a frontage of one arpent (182 feet) on the river and 40 arpents deep. Also some large estates cultivated by slave labor were established. The fertile alluvial soil of the Mississippi River valley was protected from inundation by the erection of levees that finally attained a height of twenty or thirty feet; New Orleans was protected by a levee as early as 1729. The chief crops of the Creole farmers were tobacco, indigo, and rice. Although sugar cane was introduced into Louisiana from Haiti by the Jesuits in 1751, it did not become an important crop until the close of the century.

In order to control the numerous slaves a black code was promulgated (1724). The *Code Noir* contained some humane provisions, such as laws forbidding masters to work their slaves on Sunday or holidays or sell young children from their mothers or torture their slaves. Furthermore, all slaves were required to be instructed in the Catholic religion, and emancipated slaves were to enjoy the same rights and privileges as freeborn persons. On the other hand, this slave code placed numerous harsh restrictions on the servile population to prevent insurrection and ordered runaway slaves to be branded with a fleur-de-lis on one shoulder and to have their ears cut.

The chief cause for the feeble expansive power of France was the lack of an invigorating stream of immigrants. As in Spanish Florida, Jews were prohibited from immigrating into the colony, and, in general, Protestants also were excluded. Thus France failed to utilize some of her best emigrating stock, the French Huguenots, who would have entered French colonies if permitted. Since the Catholic population of France had little desire to emi-

[11] Charles Gayarré, *History of Louisiana* (New Orleans, 1885), 4 vols.; see also Alcée Fortier, *History of Louisiana* (New York, 1904), 4 vols.

grate to a wilderness country, the Crown resorted to various expedients to increase the colonial population. Prisoners were set free if they would marry prostitutes and go to Louisiana. Abbé Prévost's novel *Manon Lescaut,* published in 1732, relates the story of a beautiful but immoral girl who was transported from a French jail along with others of "the frail sisterhood" to be married by the settlers. In 1728 the king sent over a shipload of virtuous maidens, each provided with a casket of clothes (hence they were called "casket girls"), to be married to the French colonists. Early marriages, boys at eighteen and girls from twelve to fourteen years of age, were encouraged. Soldiers were granted honorable dismissals to become permanent settlers in the country.

The expansion of Louisiana was motivated by military, trade, and imperial considerations, rather than by a drive for agricultural exploitation. During Cadillac's administration, St. Denis was sent in 1713 to establish a French fort on the Red River at Natchitoches. The following year he attempted to open a trade across Texas with the inhabitants of northern Mexico, but he was arrested, his goods were confiscated, and he was imprisoned in Mexico City. He managed, however, to secure his release and to resume his position as commandant of Natchitoches. Here he developed a remarkable influence over the Western Indians, who admiringly called him "Big Legs," and established a profitable trade between Natchitoches and the Spanish Southwest. Indeed, the French avoided any serious conflicts with their Spanish neighbors either on their eastern or western frontiers, because of the lack of ambition of the Spaniards, the vast vacant spaces between the centers of French and Spanish colonization, and the friendliness of the ruling families of those two nations.

The far-flung colony of Louisiana, despite its great potentialities, languished under French rule. Neglected by the royal government, it did not thrive by its own efforts. An inflated currency tended to paralyze commercial activity. In the decade of the 1750's only a half dozen ships a year came from France to the port of New Orleans, as contrasted with the flourishing commerce of the English island of Barbados, which employed two hundred and twenty vessels in 1748. The colony had few exports to send to France in return for manufactured goods. The tobacco was of inferior quality to the Chesapeake Bay staple; lead mining failed, partly on the account of the distance of the mines from New Orleans; indigo, the chief staple, was exported in small quantities. The weakness of the Louisiana colony was exhibited during the French and Indian War, when it remained practically passive during that life and death struggle for empire.

At the end of the French and Indian War, France was willing to abandon her unprofitable colony of Louisiana. By the secret treaty of Fontainebleu in 1762 she ceded Louisiana west of the Mississippi and the Isle of Orleans to Spain, her ally in the war, as a consolation prize for the loss of Florida to the English. The Creoles of Louisiana were greatly perturbed at this surrender of their colony, not only because of attachment to France but because they feared the effect of the exclusive Spanish trade laws. Spain was very slow in taking possession of her new province. Not until the spring of 1766 did a Spanish governor, Don Antonio de Ulloa, arrive with an escort of ninety soldiers. His haughty and aloof manners, his proclamation that the Spanish trade laws must be obeyed, and his disagreement with the Creoles over the redemption of the inflated paper currency finally provoked a rebellion. In 1768 Don Antonio was forced to flee, and the excitable Creoles proclaimed their loyalty to France.

The Spanish officials of Carlos III then debated whether to retain Louisiana or offer to return it to France. The decision was to keep it as a buffer colony for Mexico and to gratify Spanish pride. Furthermore, these officials resolved to make an example of this rebellious colony by a severe punishment. In 1769 Don Alexander O'Reilly, a limping Irish general, who had fought for Spain in the war of the Austrian Succession, was sent to Louisiana with a strong force of soldiers to put down the insurrection. The leaders of the revolt were executed or imprisoned, and Spanish authority was firmly established. Although the Creole inhabitants called him "Bloody O'Reilly," he sought to reconcile the French population to Spanish rule by conciliatory measures, by appointing Frenchmen to office, and by establishing in New Orleans the Cabildo, a council and court for the colony. Spanish administration was very venal; the local offices were purchased or in some cases inherited.

Nevertheless, the government of Louisiana under Spain was more efficient and unified than the French administration had been. Despite the fact that Spanish law forbade trade with the English, this trade was winked at by the governors. By the Grand Pragmatic of Free Commerce in 1778, Spain liberalized her colonial policy, abolished the system of convoyed fleets, and permitted trade between Louisiana and all the ports of France, Spain, the colonies, and the United States. Thus in "the last cycle" of Spanish rule in the New World, elements of freedom and common sense were permeating the old exclusive Spanish policy.[12] Moreover, Governor Bernardo de Gálvez aided the American cause during the Revolution by allowing the Americans to purchase supplies in New Orleans and by the capture from the British in 1779–1780 of Natchez and Mobile.[13]

During the Spanish period of Louisiana history, two new elements of French stock were added to the population. In 1764 the first group of Acadian exiles arrived, ten years after the expulsion from Acadia. The emigration was small, for according to a census taken in 1787 there were only 1,587 Acadians in Louisiana. These people were poor peasants, most of them illiterate, and far different from the sentimental picture of them in Longfellow's "Evangeline." They settled permanently in the bayou region south-

[12] Herbert I. Priestley, *The Coming of the White Man, 1492–1848* (New York, 1929), chap. 7; and John W. Caughey, *Bernardo de Gálvez in Louisiana, 1776–1783* (Berkeley, 1934).

[13] J. W. Caughey, *Bernardo de Gálvez in Louisiana, 1776–1873* (Gretna, La., republished, 1972).

west of the Mississippi River, especially along La Fourche and Bayou Teche. Here they were called Cajuns by the Americans. Preserving the dialect of Normandy, modified by the incorporation of English and Louisiana Creole words, they formed a backward and unprosperous people, comparable to the "poor whites" of the English colonies.

The last important French element to immigrate to the Southern region were Santo Domingo planters and their families. In 1791 the mulattoes of this Caribbean island began a revolutionary movement that stirred up the black slaves and resulted in the massacre of many of the French-speaking planters. The Santo Domingo master class who survived fled to Louisiana and also to Charleston. It is estimated that over ten thousand of these refugees entered the United States and Louisiana, some of them bringing their slaves. Many of these planters were cultivated and art-loving and were responsible for starting the French theater in New Orleans. The Santo Domingans contributed teachers of French, musicians, pastrymakers, fencing masters, and wigmakers to the art of pleasant living in the South.

The Spanish rule of Louisiana was mainly a military occupation; few Spaniards except officials and soldiers emigrated to the new colony. The French Creoles, even opulent sugar planters, were largely illiterate, uniformly Catholic in religion, and inclined to be indolent, and unambitious. The women were described as vivacious, beautiful as Georgian women, with red lips and white teeth, their complexions lighter than those of the men, but their beauty vanished early. The houses of the Creoles were made of cypress logs with steep roofs and were raised seven or eight feet above the ground. Galleries, or porches, were built on all sides of the typical one-story houses. In New Orleans drainage of the unpaved streets was in open sewers after the medieval fashion. The city suffered at intervals from yellow fever and was generally unhealthy. The citizens enjoyed the privilege of going to a French theater and of hearing operas, but culture was confined to a small class. Indeed, Louisiana did not have a newspaper until 1794, when the *Moniteur de la Louisiane* was established. The population of New Orleans shortly before the United States acquired the province was approximately twelve thousand people, black and white; Lower Louisiana had about sixty thousand inhabitants, exclusive of Indians; Upper Louisiana (Missouri) had about ten thousand.[14]

In October, 1800, Napoleon Bonaparte forced Spain to cede him the province of Louisiana by the secret treaty of San Ildefonso, President Jefferson did not learn of the existence of this secret treaty until May, 1801. He wrote to the American minister in Paris, Robert R. Livingston, "the day that France takes possession of New Orleans . . . we must marry ourselves to the British fleet and nation." [15] On October 16, 1802, the Spanish intendant at New Orleans, apparently acting under pressure of the French, refused to

[14] J. A. Robertson, *Louisiana under the Rule of Spain, France, and the United States, 1785–1807* (Cleveland, Ohio, 1911), I, 71, 149–150, 170, 172.
[15] Lipscomb and Bergh (eds.), *Writings of Thomas Jefferson*, X, 313.

American vessels the right of deposit, which had been previously granted. The West was deeply aroused over the prospect of losing its outlet for the Mississippi River trade. The time for action had come. Jefferson determined first to use diplomacy, to try to buy the island of Orleans, on which the city of New Orleans was located, and West Florida. James Monroe was sent as envoy extraordinare to cooperate with Livingston to effect this object. The American representatives were authorized to offer as high as 50 million francs ($10,000,000) for New Orleans and the Floridas.

Before Monroe arrived (April 13, 1803) Napoleon, through his foreign Minister, Talleyrand, offered to sell the whole of Louisiana. The reasons for this swift change of policy were that the French dictator planned to renew the war with England, and Louisiana would then be an easy prey for the British navy. Also Napoleon had failed to recover the control of France over the island of Santo Domingo, a vital part of his project of re-creating a French colonial empire in the Western Hemisphere. He had sent his brother-in-law, General Leclerc, with a formidable army to the island, but Leclerc had to contend with dauntless Negro guerrillas led by the "Black Napoleon," Toussaint L'Ouverture. After he had captured the Negro leader and sent him as a prisoner to France, he still could not conquer the people of Santo Domingo, who were aided by the terrible scourage of yellow fever, which decimated the French army and killed Leclerc himself. Against the proposed sale of Louisiana, Lucien and Joseph Bonaparte bitterly protested to their brother in an interview during which he was taking a perfumed bath. The Little Corsican replied to their patriotic outbursts by a violent splashing in the bathtub that covered them with foam and water and caused their precipitate treat.

When Talleyrand made the offer to our representatives to sell the whole of Louisiana, Livingston and Monroe jumped at the opportunity, afraid that the fickle emperor would change his mind. The treaty was signed April 30, 1803, surrendering this imperial realm to the United States for 80 million francs, or approximately $14,500,000. The Constitution of the United States did not expressly give the president and Congress the right to purchase foreign territory, an obstacle that caused great concern to Jefferson and the Republicans, believers in strict interpretation of that document. Jefferson proposed a constitutional amendment to make legal the purchase of Louisiana, but Livingston pointed out that Napoleon might change his mind and that it was highly expedient to conclude the bargain as soon as possible. Jefferson then suppressed his constitutional scruples and urged the Senate to ratify the treaty and Congress to appropriate the money, disregarding "metaphysical subtleties." [16] Finally the treaty was ratified by the Senate over the opposition of the Federalists, and Louisiana was formally transferred to the United States, December 20, 1803.

The treaty provided that the inhabitants of Louisiana should become citi-

[16] P. L. Ford (ed.), *Writings of Thomas Jefferson* (New York, 1899), X, 7.

zens of the United States and enjoy all the rights and privileges of that status and the protection of their religion. In 1804 Congress created the territory of Orleans, with its capital at New Orleans, and later the upper part of the vast region purchased from France was organized into Louisiana Territory, with its capital at St. Louis. At first the president exercised autocratic authority over the territory of Orleans, but he appointed a mild and benevolent governor, W. C. C. Claiborne, twenty-eight years old, a Jeffersonian leader in Tennessee.[17] The denial of the privileges of American citizens to the inhabitants led to a petition of protest to Congress, drafted by Edward Livingston, a younger brother of the minister to France, who had emigrated to New Orleans. Congress then amended the law regulating the government of the territory by granting an elective legislature and a delegate to Congress. Not until 1812, however, when Louisiana was admitted as a state in the Union, did the inhabitants enjoy "all the rights, advantages, and immunities of citizens of the United States."

Although the purchase of Louisiana insured the loyalty of the West to the United States, this acquisition did not quench the desire of the frontiersmen to seize further territory from the Spaniards. Wrote the Kentucky leader John Adair to James Wilkinson, December 10, 1804: "Mexico glitters in our Eyes—the word is all we wait for." [18] In 1805 a serious threat of war with Spain arose, during which the inhabitants of Kentucky and Tennessee were eager to attack the Mexican provinces. In that year, Vice-President Aaron Burr, defeated for governor of New York and discredited in the East by his fatal duel with Hamilton, went down the Ohio and Mississippi rivers to New Orleans to explore the possibilities of turning Western feelings to his advantage. On his way he was cordially received by such prominent leaders as Henry Clay, ex-Senator John Brown, and Senator John Adair in Kentucky, Andrew Jackson in Tennessee, and Edward Livingston and the Catholic bishop of New Orleans. His chief friend and conspirator in the West, however, was James Wilkinson, governor of the Louisiana Territory and commander of the American army in the West.[19]

A brilliant opportunist, Burr was apparently ready to resort to any scheme that would bring him money and power. To different persons this plausible intriguer told different stories about his objective. He approached the English and Spanish ambassadors with proposals to revolutionize the Western part of the United States and to incite secession movements in Kentucky, Tennessee, and especially Louisiana, whose inhabitants were discontented with the rule of Governor Claiborne, but these intrigues seem to have been motivated only by the desire to extort money. He may have had in mind a plan to lead a filibustering expedition against Spanish territory in the

[17] See Dunbar Rowland (ed.), *Official Letter Books of W. C. C. Claiborne* (Jackson, Miss., 1917), 6 vols.
[18] T. R. Hay and M. R. Werner, *The Admirable Trumpeter, a Biography of General James Wilkinson* (New York, 1941), 219.
[19] See W. F. McCaleb, *The Aaron Burr Conspiracy* (New York, 1903).

Southwest, predicated on the imminence of a war between Spain and the United States. The elimination of the danger of war in 1806, however, caused the supple adventurer to shift his objectives. Obtaining money from Harman Blennerhassett, a guillible Irishman who lived on an island in the Ohio River, and from Joseph Alston, his South Carolina son-in-law, he purchased a large tract of land on the Ouachita River in Louisiana. Here he planned as one of his enterprises to found a colony that might become a base for an attack against Mexico. Another immediate objective, according to the findings of a modern historian, was to lead a filibuster expedition against Spanish West Florida, seizing Baton Rouge and Mobile.[20]

In August, 1806, Burr set forth from Philadelphia on a second mysterious trip to the West. Before his departure he sent cipher dispatches by messengers, Dr. Erich Bollman, Samuel Swartwout, and Peter V. Ogden, to Wilkinson and Livingston, which indicate that he planned to incite a revolution in Louisiana and then invade Mexico by way of the Sabine River. While he was in Kentucky in early December he was indicted for treason by the United States district attorney Joseph Hamilton Daveiss. Defended by Henry Clay, he was acquitted by the grand jury amid great applause of the courtroom crowd, who thought his object was to attack Spanish possessions.

Whatever Burr's real designs were, he was betrayed by his confederate James Wilkinson. This unscrupulous adventurer decided in the summer of 1806, before Burr's expedition had started, to betray his fellow conspirator. Alarmed by the unfavorable publicity of Burr and doubting his success, he used the occasion to extract money from the Spaniards and also to win Jefferson's favor by posing as a great patriot. Instead of provoking war with Spain over the hostile demonstrations of that nation against the Western frontier as the conspirators' plan called for, he concluded an agreement setting up a Neutral Ground between the Sabine River and the Arroyo Hondo. Then he sent a note to President Jefferson from New Orleans warning of a treasonable plot concocted by Burr.

On November 27, Jefferson issued a proclamation announcing that a military expedition against the dominions of Spain was being prepared on the western waters and ordering all American citizens to withdraw immediately from such a criminal enterprise. The governor of Ohio ordered the seizure of the ships assembled at Blennerhassett's Island intended for transporting the conspirators; but a small party led by Comfort Tyler escaped on the night of December 10 in several boats that had not been captured. Burr did not join the expedition until it had reached the mouth of the Cumberland River. When the flotilla of nine boats, containing less than one hundred men, entered Mississippi Territory later in January of the following year, Burr fled, was arrested, and subsequently tried in Richmond, Virginia, before a Federal Circuit Court presided over by Chief Justice Marshall. The Federalist judge was

[20] T. P. Abernethy, "Aaron Burr in Mississippi," *Journal of Southern History*, XV (February 1949), 921; and *The Burr Conspiracy* (New York, 1964), and F. I. Philbrick, *The Rise of the West, 1754–1830* (New York, 1965).

highly prejudiced against Jefferson and issued a subpoena to the president's prosecuting attorney for the delivery to the court of a letter from James Wilkinson of November 12, 1806. Exercising executive prerogative, Jefferson sent the letter, though deleted of certain material he regarded extraneous, and Marshall accepted it. This episode set up the practice of "executive privilege" to which President Nixon referred when he refused to turn over certain tapes in the Watergate affair.[21]

In this famous trial Marshall narrowly interpreted the definition of treason as given in the Constitution, ruling out constructive treason.[22] Jefferson was eager to convict Burr, apparently for political reasons, and in the trial his Attorney General, William Wirt, made an eloquent speech arraigning Burr on the charge of treason. Nevertheless, the plausible adventurer, who conducted his own legal defense, was acquitted of the charge of treason. This verdict, on the basis of evidence presented, seems to be just although there is strong reason to believe that Burr had treasonable intents.

The acquisition of the Louisiana Purchase territory had added to our population the Creoles, who have made distinctive contributions to the pattern of Southern civilization. Although they have been overwhelmed numerically by the immigration of the English since 1803, they still constitute an important and colorful minority in the cities of New Orleans and Mobile and in the surrounding country. Their language has survived in the lower South for well over two hundred years, but in the twentieth century it has been steadily losing ground; members of the younger generation prefer to speak English and are rapidly forgetting their mother tongue. The Creoles have tended socially to keep to themselves and did not mingle freely with the Protestant "Americans." This fact, as well as the lack of a democratic system of education, partly explains their failure to contribute many eminent leaders to the nation.[23]

The French Creoles have made important contributions to legal institutions in Louisiana. Their Black Code was adopted by the Spanish rulers of the province and later by the Americans when Louisiana was acquired by the United States. For many years Louisiana was the only Southern state that prohibited the sale of slave children under ten years of age from their mothers. The Civil Code of the state, adopted in 1825, the work of Edward Livingston and two Creole jurisconsults, continued the Roman law of French and Spanish regimes as the fundamental law of the state. Eighty per cent of the provisions of this code were taken verbatim from the Code Napoléon. Louisiana was the only state in the Union whose law was based on the Roman law rather than on the English common law.[24] The courts of antebellum

[21] See the controversy between Gary Wills and Dumas Malone over the subpoena in *New York Review of Books*, May 2, May 16, and July 18, 1974.

[22] See Edward S. Corwin, *John Marshall and the Constitution* (New Haven, 1919), chap. 4.

[23] See Henry M. Brackenbridge, *Views of Louisiana* (Baltimore, 1817).

[24] See W. B. Hatcher, *Edward Livingston, Jeffersonian Republican and Jacksonian Democrat* (Baton Rouge, 1940).

Louisiana were conducted in the two languages spoken by the people. In the twentieth century Louisiana furnished a chief justice of the United States, Edward White, whose doctrine, "the rule of reason," may have been affected by his Catholic heritage and his training in Louisiana law.

During the French and Spanish occupation of Louisiana, the Catholic Church was firmly rooted. The clergy were under the jurisdiction of the Bishop of Quebec, who placed the Capuchins in charge of lower Louisiana, and the Jesuits were made supreme in upper Louisiana and the Illinois country. The Jesuits, however, tried to secure a foothold in New Orleans, which resulted in a resounding war between the two orders. In 1727 some Ursuline nuns sailed to New Orleans, where they took charge of the hospital and founded a girls' school. Their convent on Chartres Street, built in 1731, is one of the oldest buildings in the Mississippi Valley. The Catholic church was responsible for introducing whatever education was given to the Creole youth. During the Spanish regime an attempt was made (in 1789) by Father Antonio de Sedella to introduce the Inquisition in order to crush all heretics in the colony, but this emissary of the Inquisition was expelled by the governor.

The French have made enduring contributions to Southern agriculture and practical arts. The Creoles introduced sugar cane into the lower South, and in 1795 Etienne de Boré discovered a method of granulating sugar from Louisiana cane syrup that laid the foundations for the great sugar plantations of antebellum days. Also the French began the practice of building levees to prevent the Mississippi River from flooding the plantations and the city of New Orleans. They developed the lead mining industry in Missouri and were foremost in exploring the Mississippi Valley.

Many useful words have been incorporated in the American language from the speech of the French inhabitants of the Gulf coast. From the French of Louisiana the following words have been borrowed: *bayou, levee, crevasse, chute, bureau, depot* (which the Negroes in the South still use in preference to the more dignified term *railroad station*), *picayune,* and *lagniappe,* referring to the pleasant custom of tradesmen giving their customers something extra beyond their purchase, an additional yam, or fig, or flower as a sign of good will. The French of the Missouri country were noted fur traders, from whom, as well as from the French settlers from the North, were derived such words as *prairie, batteau, pirogue, rapids, portage, voyageur, cache, gopher,* and *brave* for Indian warrior. The French Creoles developed a patois in which they orally transmitted proverbs, folklore, and songs, such as "Belle Amerikaine," "Un Pauvre Hobo," and "Jolie Blonde."

The Creoles also contributed a hedonistic element to the society of the lower South. The carnival of Mardi Gras, which comes before Lent, was a colorful pageant and a time of merriment that has continued to be observed in New Orleans and Mobile to the present day. The city of New Orleans became the pleasure metropolis of the Mississippi Valley, although its reputation as a city of sin flourished only after Louisiana became a part of the United States. Orange wine, absinthe, the delicacies of frogs' legs, bouillabaisse, poulet Creole, Creole gumbo, and pralines were distinct French Creole contributions to the art of good food and drink. The Creoles also developed an institution of concubinage with beautiful octoroon and quadroon maidens, and masked balls added gaiety to the worldly life of the Latin Quarter. Americans who came down the Mississippi were shocked at the Creole Sundays, when the Sabbath day was devoted to pleasure and commerce. Furthermore, these Latins were passionately fond of gambling, lotteries, and dancing. French dancing and fencing masters taught the unsophisticated Americans these continental arts.[25]

The Creoles of Louisiana developed a literature and furnished the picturesque material for an important school of local color that developed after the Civil War. Charles Gayarré, who wrote a somewhat romantic history of Louisiana in the decade of the 1850's, was not only the outstanding Creole writer but probably also the greatest historian produced by the antebellum South.[26] The Creoles, including Creole Negroes, composed French poetry and dramas. In the decades of the 1870's, 1880's, and 1890's the Creole civilization was portrayed by George Washington Cable, Kate Chopin, Grace King, and Lafcadio Hearn. These writers described the architecture, customs, and characteristics of Old Louisiana. Cable especially presented the tragedy of the mixture of white and Negro blood. Their stories and romances recreated the flavor of a semitropic civilization affected by Negro slavery and by the Latin temperament.[27]

The passing of French culture from Upper Louisiana forms a little-known but fascinating chapter in the social history of the Southwest. St. Genevieve was begun in 1735 as the shipping point of the lead mining district of Missouri, and St. Louis was founded in 1764 by Pierre Laclede, the agent of a French fur trading company. This town became the center of the fur trading activities of the West, and French Creole trappers dominated the fur trade of the hinterland and the Rocky Mountains. When the United States took possession of the Missouri Territory in 1804, the Creoles dreaded the American occupation, fearing that their complicated land titles might not be respected and distrusting the democracy of the newcomers. The mass of the *habitants* were unambitious, hedonistic, and illiterate, but the small upper class, including the Chouteau family of St. Louis, for example, were better educated than the Americans, possessing good libraries and reading the writings of the French freethinkers.[28] Some of these aristocrats owned large

[25] See Clement Eaton, *The Growth of Southern Civilization 1790–1860* (New York, 1961), chap. 6.
[26] See Clement Eaton, *The Waning of the Old South Civilization* (New York, 1969), chap. 3, "The Culture of the Old South: Its Greatest Historian."
[27] See Howard Mumford Jones, *American and French Culture* (New York, 1927); and Grace King, *Creole Families of New Orleans* (New York, 1921); and Lyle Saxon, *Old Louisiana* (New York, 1929).
[28] Harvey Wish, "The French of Old Missouri (1804–1821): A Study in Assimilation," *Mid-America*, XXIII (July 1941), 167–168.

plantations, tilled by slave labor, while others had gained affluence from the fur trade, the lead mines, and merchandising.

The coming of the Americans wrought a revolution in this civilization of Old Missouri, for the 6,000 Creoles and Negro slaves reported by the Spanish census of 1799 were overwhelmed by the inrush of the Americans that increased the population of the territory to 66,586 by 1820. The horizontal log cabin of the American frontiersman superseded the French log cabin built of vertical logs; French geographical names were corrupted or displaced; the Gallic Sunday with its gaiety was frowned upon by the intolerant Protestant settlers; in 1808 the *Missouri Gazette,* the first newspaper of the region, was published in English; by 1821, when Missouri became a state, much of French culture had been erased and the Creoles were rapidly being assimilated by American civilization. Nevertheless, faint traces of bygone French culture survive in Missouri to this day.

11

The War Hawks and Expansion

FLORIDA, the land of the Spanish Creoles, was coveted by Southern slave-holders. To acquire it, as well as Canada to the north, became one of the objects of "the expansionists of 1812," but lust for more territory was not the main cause of the War of 1812, as a prominent school of earlier historians thought. The war, which was largely brought on by the pressure of Southern and Western congressmen, seems to have been an act of folly from the view-point of Southern interests. It was, as a whole, an inglorious war for the United States and did not accomplish the objectives of its Southern propo-nents. Rather, it increased the power of the central government and con-tributed largely to the growth of New England manufactures and a high tariff policy, both of which developments were later violently opposed by the South.

It is a moot question how important individual leaders are in provoking or restraining the war fever. The personality of President Madison is particu-larly significant in studying the drift to war in 1812. A Tidewater Virginian, born at Port Conway in 1751, he was graduated from the College of New Jersey (Princeton), where he studied Hebrew and theology, intending to be-come a minister. His early career was marked by a high idealism. When Madison entered politics, he refused to follow the Southern custom of solicit-ing votes by treating the sovereign voters with liquor. Madison was a brilliant scholar, but he was unsuited to be president during the critical years preced-ing the War of 1812 or to be a successful war leader.

Small in stature, stiff and cold in general society, but capable of telling smutty stories at the dinner table after he had liberally partaken of wine, Madison lacked the charisma of a popular leader. His wife Dolley, although of North Carolina Quaker background and seventeen years younger than he, made up for his social deficiencies, for she is noted as a charming, vivacious hostess of the White House. Henry Clay is reported to have said of Madison and Jefferson that Jefferson had more genius but Madison had more common sense and prudence. Madison has been accused of vacillation during the war crisis of 1812, but Congress itself was more vacillating than he. The ap-parent weakness of Madison's foreign policy was owing partly to the lack of a strong armed force that would make European nations respect us. More-over, he weakened his administration by appointing one of the most incom-petent cabinets in American history. Unlike Jefferson, who had been a real leader dictating quietly the party program, Madison lacked the political art

185

James Madison (1751–1836) by Rembrandt Peale. (Courtesy of Thomas Gil-
crease Institute of American Art and History, Tulsa, Oklahoma)

and seems to have had little influence on Congress.[1] If he had been a strong
leader, it is quite likely that the United States would have avoided a needless
war.

[1] The personality of Madison is sympathetically portrayed by Irving Brant in his six-
volume biography; see especially vol. 5, *James Madison, the President, 1809–1812*
(Indianapolis, 1956), chap. 30, and vol. 6, *James Madison, Commander-in-Chief,
1812–1836* (Indianapolis, 1961). He portrays a more vigorous wartime leader than

Dolly Madison (1751–1836), wife of James Madison. (Courtesy of Alderman Library, University of Virginia)

When Madison became president, he inherited a problem of maintaining the rights of the United States on the high seas. Great Britain was fighting to survive against the imperialist ambitions of Napoleon. In this fierce struggle American neutral rights were violated by both belligerents, Great Britain by her Orders in Council, setting up a blockade of the coast of Europe controlled by Napoleon, and France by the Berlin and Milan Decrees that declared a paper blockade of the British Isles. Madison continued Jefferson's policy of attempting to preserve peace by diplomacy and economic coercion.[2] Since England and France were almost equally culpable in violating our neutral rights, there was abundant reason to declare war against France as well as England. Indeed, the sympathy of Americans should have been with England in her struggle to preserve her freedom against the ruthless military dictator Napoleon, as John Randolph observed. But anglophobia was strong among the dominant Republicans, and France had not impressed American seamen, whereas Great Britain had been a serious kidnaper of our citizens, impressing

this volume does. See also Ralph Ketcham, *James Madison, a Biography* (New York, 1971).
[2] For the diplomacy preceding the war, see Samuel F. Bemis, *A Diplomatic History of the United States* (New York, 1955); and Bradford Perkins, *Prologue to War; England and the United States, 1805–1812* (Berkeley, 1961).

over six thousand American seamen, a number that popular rumor magnified to over ten thousand. Moreover, the Westerners believed that the British in Canada incited the Indians on the frontier to hostilities and furnished them with guns and ammunition, a charge the British denied. Just at this time Tecumseh organized the Indians of the Ohio Valley to resist the advance of the American pioneer and sought the aid of the Southern Indians. The real cause for Indian warfare, however, was not British instigation but a determination of the Indians to save their hunting grounds from the rapacious Westerners.

In the congressional elections of 1810 and 1811 a number of young representatives were sent to Washington who were resolved to uphold the rights and honor of the United States, which they believed were violated by the British Orders in Council. A group of these ardent patriots from the South and the West boarded at the same tavern and were called "the war mess." Their leader was Henry Clay of Kentucky, thirty-four years of age, who was elected Speaker of the House of Representatives in a period when the lower house of Congress was more respected and powerful than the Senate. These young men bitterly criticized the "if policy" of Madison, his failure to assert vigorously American rights against the British and the French. They came chiefly from the frontier regions or the back country of the South and gained the name "War Hawks," a term applied to them by their Federalist opponents because of their advocacy of war with England. Clay used his power as Speaker to appoint War Hawks on the important committees of the House of Representatives, and his eloquent voice was exerted to arouse Americans to a declaration of war against Great Britain as an obligation of honor and as necessary to preserve our export trade.

In addition to Clay from Kentucky came Richard Mentor Johnson, one of the most vociferous of the War Hawks. Born at Beargrass, Kentucky, he had three brothers slain by the Indians. He was a colorful figure, indeed, noted in Congress for disdaining such effeminate apparel as a cravat and for shocking conventional morality by having a Negro mistress, Julia Chinn, who bore him two daughters. During the course of the War of 1812 he was reputed to have killed Tecumseh, which led to his nickname "Tecumseh Johnson." [3] From Tennessee came Felix Grundy, a brilliant criminal lawyer and practical politician, and also John Sevier, the old frontiersman and Indian fighter. Georgia sent two War Hawks to Congress in the persons of the belligerent, red-headed George M. Troup and William H. Crawford. The ablest delegation of War Hawks was a brilliant trio from South Carolina, John C. Calhoun, Langdon Cheves, and William Lowndes. The last was a remarkably tall young man (six feet six inches in height) with golden hair and low voice, gifted in intellect and in winning friends. If the preponderance of war sentiment was in the West and in the newer parts of the South, the

---

[3] See Leland W. Meyer, *The Life and Times of Colonel Richard M. Johnson of Kentucky* (New York, 1932).

Tidewater area also had some prominent advocates of war, such as Secretary of State James Monroe, and the old Jeffersonian leader, Nathaniel Macon of North Carolina.[4]

The motives that led the War Hawks to demand a war with England were a remarkable mixture of idealism and material considerations. In the first place, these youthful legislators—"Young America"—believed that the United States should take a bold and manly stand against insult and oppression. Madison and "the regular troops" of the Republican party, led by Albert Gallatin, realized that the United States was totally unprepared for war and tried to restrain the rash and headstrong enthusiasm for war of the young leaders. However, the War Hawks were expressing deep social forces of their section, especially for expansion.[5] Kentucky wished to expand at the expense of Canada, but there was considerable sentiment south of the Bluegrass State also to add Canada to the United States in fulfillment of Manifest Destiny. Clay held out the prospect of an easy conquest of Canada, which, he boasted, the Kentucky militia alone could accomplish. Furthermore, the Westerners were desirous of eradicating the power of the British in Canada to instigate attacks on the American frontier, or in Clay's eloquent words, "to extinguish the torch that lights up savage warfare." Yet his correspondence indicates that he was much more concerned over Great Britain's flagrant violations of American rights and the need to uphold American honor than by a desire for expansion.[6] It is strange that the issue of defending American rights on the seas should be brought forward so urgently as the cause for war in 1811–1812 when this grievance was less serious and humiliating then than it had been several years earlier.

In addition to a desire to uphold national honor, the Southern states were affected by two powerful economic motives in their advocacy of war. The lower South was eagerly desirous of seizing Florida, which controlled the outlets of several important Southern rivers. Florida was weakly defended by Spain, an ally of England. John Randolph declared that the motive for the War of 1812 was "agrarian cupidity." Not only was there the urge of southward expansion but also, prior to the war, the Southern farmers were suffering from a decline in the price of their agricultural exports. They be-

---

[4] For a perceptive discussion of the War Hawks, see a group of articles by Reginald Horsman, Alexander DeConde, Roger Brown, and Norman K. Risjord in *Indiana Magazine of History*, LX (June 1964), 121–126. Horsman examines the votes in Congress on war measures and concludes that there were approximately 30 out of 142 members of the House of Representatives that voted in 1811–1812 for war measures and spoke enthusiastically for a declaration of war; the great majority of these were from the South and the West. Brown maintains that the term *War Hawk* is misleading and points out the extreme reluctance of Congress to declare war; it took six months to persuade the members to take the drastic step.

[5] Julius W. Pratt, *Expansionists of 1812* (New York, 1925).

[6] Clement Eaton, *Henry Clay and the Art of American Politics* (Boston, 1957); J. H. Hopkins and M. W. M. Hargreaves (eds.), *The Papers of Henry Clay* (Lexington 1959), I.

lieved that British interference with foreign commerce was responsible for this loss. Nathaniel Macon declared, "We must either prepare to maintain the right to carry our produce to what market we please, or to be content without a market." [7]

The war advocates acted with considerable inconsistency in preparing the country for the approaching war. There were less than seven thousand men in the regular army, and the navy of sixteen ships was ridiculously small in comparison with the naval power of Great Britain. The War Hawks voted for a large increase in the army, which could be used in the conquest of Canada and the Floridas, but some of the most ardent patriots, such as Johnson and Grundy, opposed a large expansion of the navy, which would be useless in fighting Indians or conquering the interior lands of Florida and Canada. Moreover, the War Hawks were very solicitous not to throw cold water on the martial fervor of the South and West by heavy taxation to pay for the prosecution of an expansionist war.

Madison finally yielded to the martial spirit of the South and the West. The old charge that he was forced by the War Hawks to recommend war as a price of renomination for president, however, is untrue, for he was nominated by a Congressional caucus unanimously two weeks before his war message. On June 1, 1812, Madison sent his message to Congress, citing the outrages that would justify a war against England—impressment of American seamen, violation of the three-mile limit of our shores, paper blockades, Orders in Council, and the suspicion of British instigation of Indian outrages. He said nothing in the war message about other great driving forces of the war fever in the South and the West, such as expansionist feeling, anglophobia, and resentment over the foreign export situation.

The vote on a declaration of war, June 18, 1812, revealed that the country was seriously divided in opinion. In the Senate the vote for war was nineteen to thirteen, but in the House of Representatives the vote was seventy-nine in favor and forty-nine opposed. A majority of the congressmen from New England, New York, and New Jersey—the maritime sections of the country—voted against a declaration of war. It is a strange paradox that the two sections of the country, the West and the South, that had few ships and sailors and therefore had suffered least from the British violation of the freedom of the seas were precisely the regions eager for war, whereas New England was bitterly opposed to this vindication of the national honor. In Congress, Ohio, Kentucky, Tennessee, Georgia, and South Carolina voted unanimously for war, Maryland was divided six to three, and coastal Virginia and North Carolina were prowar, the Piedmont antiwar. There was one intensely Southern congressman, John Randolph of Roanoke, who made a

[7] W. H. Goodman, "The Origins of the War of 1812; a Survey of Changing Interpretations," *Mississippi Valley Historical Review*, XXVIII (September 1941), 184; see also Bradford Perkins (ed.), *The Causes of the War of 1812: National Honor or National Interest?* (New York, 1962).

violent speech against our entry into a war with England, in which he pointed out that by attacking England we were aiding Napoleon, the enslaver of Europe.

The United States seems to have blundered into war. British public opinion demanded the repeal of the obnoxious decrees against American neutral commerce, but delay in revoking the Orders in Council was caused by the assassination in May, 1812, of Prime Minister Perceval. On June 16, however, Lord Castlereagh, the foreign minister, announced that the Orders in Council would be suspended. It is possible that if a cable had existed at that time, the American Congress would not have declared war against England. The revocation of the Orders in Council actually took place five days after the declaration of war by the United States.

Three military campaigns were fought in the South during the War of 1812, the British invasion of the District of Columbia and Maryland in 1814, the Creek campaign of the same year, and the battle of New Orleans, January 8, 1815. Kentucky volunteers played an important part in the victories of the American armies on the northwest frontier. William Henry Harrison, a Virginia aristocrat, who had been governor of Indiana Territory, commanded the American troops at the victory of the Thames River in lower Canada (1813). Another Southern officer, Winfield Scott of Virginia, won the battles of Chippewa and Lundy's Lane (1814), which were across the Canadian border not far from Buffalo, New York.

It was fortunate for the unprepared and disunified American nation that England had her hands full fighting Napoleon during the early years of the war.[8] In April, 1814, Napoleon was forced to abdicate his throne, thus releasing a number of veteran British troops for use in the American war. In June, 1814, a force of four thousand, five hundred British regulars under General Robert Ross was sent from Bordeaux to the Chesapeake Bay country. Ross landed at Benedict, Maryland, forty miles from Washington and marched unopposed along the Patuxent River until he came to the village of Bladensburg, about five miles from the capital. Here he was opposed by approximately six thousand green militia under the incompetent General W. H. Winder and a naval detachment under Commodore Joshua Barney. The British sent a shower of Congrieve rockets among the untrained militia, terrifying them. Consequently, they fled in the direction of Washington, with the British regulars running after them, giving rise to the nickname of "the Bladensburg races" (August 24, 1814). The British officers arrived at the White House in time to eat the dinner prepared for the hastily retreating President and Mrs. Madison. After burning the White House, the Capitol, and the public buildings, the victorious army retired. In an attack on Baltimore, they were repulsed, and General Ross was killed. Fort McHenry,

---

[8] An excellent study of the War of 1812 is A. L. Burt, *The United States, Great Britain, and British America* (New Haven, 1940); see also H. L. Coles, *The War of 1812* (Chicago, 1965), and J. K. Mahon, *The War of 1812* (Gainesville, Fla., 1972).

which defended the sea approaches to the city, was too strong to be captured. Its defense inspired the composition of the national anthem, "The Star Spangled Banner," by Francis Scott Key of Maryland.

The instigation to hostilities by Tecumseh and the disgraceful surrender of Detroit early in the war by General William Hull had the effect of encouraging the Upper Creek Indians, called Red Sticks, to attack the Southern frontier. In August, 1813, they captured Fort Mims at the junction of the Alabama and Tombigbee rivers, scalping and killing the five hundred men, women, and children in the Fort. Andrew Jackson, major general of Tennessee militia, was ordered to lead an army against the Red Sticks and administer severe punishment. At this time he was in bed suffering from a pistol wound inflicted in a tavern brawl in Nashville. Nevertheless, he arose from his sick bed, carrying his arm in a sling, and took command of the undisciplined militia. He maintained a stern discipline over this force, suppressing a mutiny by using part of his army to keep another part from returning home. In March, 1814, he attacked the main town of the Red Sticks at Horseshoe Bend on the Tallapoosa River, near the present city of Montgomery, and killed all but about fifty of an estimated number of eight hundred warriors as well as making prisoners of five hundred squaws and children. He then built Fort Jackson at the juncture of the Coosa and Tallapoosa rivers, where he dictated a treaty by which the Creeks surrendered more than 20 million acres of choice land in southern Georgia and Alabama. The Southern Indians never forgot the merciless vengeance of "Long Knife," as they called Jackson.[9]

Jackson's campaign against the Creeks was followed by the most dramatic event of the war, the battle of New Orleans. The British sent an expeditionary force of seven thousand, five hundred veterans of the Napoleonic war, under the command of Sir Edward Pakenham, brother-in-law of the Duke of Wellington, to capture New Orleans. The defenses of this city had been badly neglected, but on December 1, 1814, the masterful Jackson was placed in charge of the forces guarding the city, consisting of between six thousand and seven thousand Kentucky, Tennessee, and Louisiana militia. Two colorful elements among this motley army were four hundred Negro soldiers and the pirates of Barataria, who had infested the Gulf coast. The leaders of the pirates were Jean and Pierre Laffite, who were offered tempting rewards to aid the British, which they patriotically refused, and Dominique You, who rendered effective service as an artillerist.[10]

Instead of going up the Mississippi, the British took an unexpected route by Lake Borgne across the swamps to New Orleans. On January 8, 1815, the main battle took place, lasting less than half of an hour, at Chalmette's plantation a few miles from New Orleans. Showing his contempt for Ameri-

[9] See Marquis James, *Andrew Jackson, the Border Captain* (Indianapolis, 1933).
[10] See Jane L. De Grummond, *The Baratarians and the Battle of New Orleans* (Baton Rouge, 1961).

can soldiers, Pakenham ordered a frontal assault on Jackson's improvised fortifications, made partly of cotton bales and dried mud, which could be reached only by crossing a deep ditch. Jackson ordered his men to hold their fire until the redcoats were in easy range, but it was less the accuracy of their marksmanship than the terrible havoc wrought by the grapeshot of the American artillery that won the incredible battle.[11] The British, charging in close order, were mowed down by Jackson's militia and artillery, Pakenham was killed, and the British lost two thousand men, killed and captured. The American loss was only thirteen soldiers killed in this most spectacular victory ever won by an army of the United States. However, this victory had no military significance, for it was fought two weeks after the peace treaty had been signed at Ghent, Belgium. Again, if a cable had existed at that time, the battle would never have been fought, and very likely Andrew Jackson would later not have been elected president.

But this victory over John Bull made an important contribution to Americans' pride in the nation, as exhibited in the song "The Hunters of Kentucky":

> But Jackson he was wide awake,
>   And was not scar'd at trifles,
> For well he knew what aim we take
>   With our Kentucky rifles.
> So he led us down to Cypress swamp,
>   The ground was low and mucky,
> There stood John Bull in martial pomp
>   And here was old Kentucky.
> Oh Kentucky, the hunters of Kentucky!

The Treaty of Ghent, which was signed on Christmas Eve, 1814, was an inglorious peace treaty, for it was silent about the original American grievances of impressment and interference with our neutral trade. In fact, the British representatives came to the conference with the demeanor of a conquering nation, actually demanding a cession of American territory. The South and West were represented on the United States peace commission by Henry Clay. The American delegation made the mistake of taking a house together in the old Belgian town of Ghent. The gambling, swearing, drinking, and late hours of Henry Clay caused dissension, especially shocking the austere Puritan member, John Quincy Adams. Adams was determined to secure the right of New Englanders to continue to fish off the Grand Banks of Newfoundland, but was less concerned in preventing the British from obtaining the right to navigate the Mississippi. Clay, on the other hand, had no interest in fish for New Englanders but was determined to exclude the British from the Mississippi River. He succeeded in "saving the Mississippi River" exclusively for the citizens of the United States. The main result of

11 John William Ward, *Andrew Jackson, Symbol for an Age* (New York, 1962), 16–27.

the Treaty of Ghent was to restore the status quo. Yet the War of 1812 had some effect in producing economically and spiritually a Second Declaration of Independence from England. The only tangible gains the South derived from this war for expansion were the appropriation of much of the land of the Creeks after their crushing defeat, the bloodless conquest of Mobile in 1813 by General James Wilkinson, and the making of a presidential candidate, Andrew Jackson.

During the five years following the Treaty of Ghent the Southern states reached a peak of national feeling, from which there began a recession in 1820 that continued until long after the Civil War. Part of this enthusiasm for the nation was an afterglow of the war feeling. The disloyal example of New England, culminating in the Hartford Convention, impressed Southerners with the virtue of being patriotic. The executive branch of the Federal government was controlled by Virginia presidents until 1825, a factor in Southern satisfaction with the central government. Moreover, the westward movement, following the conclusion of the War of 1812, tended to produce a more nationalistic outlook. The abolitionist movement had not yet arisen to foment bitter sectional discord.

The nationalistic trend in the South after the war was shown in the support of a protective tariff by a number of Southern congressmen. The war had actually benefited the rebellious New England states more than any other section by the encouragement it gave to the rise of manufacturing. With the conclusion of peace English manufacturers "dumped" cheap goods that had accumulated on the American market, thus endangering the existence of infant American industries. To prevent this catastrophe, Congress passed the protective tariff of 1816. The bill was introduced by William Lowndes of South Carolina and was vigorously supported by his colleague John C. Calhoun. The vote of the Southern states in Congress on the tariff of 1816 was twenty-five for the measure and thirty-nine against. These congressmen and Henry Clay supported the enactment of a protective tariff, because they had visions of the development of Southern manufacturing and furthermore believed that such mills would increase the demand for cotton and raise its price. There were already small textile factories arising in the Carolinas, Kentucky, and Georgia. In 1810 North Carolina had fifty-six small mills and Georgia ninety-one. Also a strong motive for the considerable Southern support of a protective tariff in 1816 was the desire to make the country economically free of foreign nations. By 1820, however, the Southern states realized that a protective tariff was against their interest, and therefore in that year they voted overwhelmingly against an effort to raise the tariff. From this time on, the South, in general, voted against protective tariffs with the exception of special groups, such as the sugar planters, the iron interests, and the hemp growers and manufacturers.

The South also displayed its nationalistic feeling in supporting the chartering of the Second National Bank. In 1816 a committee with Calhoun as the leading member drafted a bill creating a national bank, in which both the government and private investors held the stock. This bank was given the privilege of keeping the government deposits without paying interest, but it was required to transfer government funds without charge. The charter was to run for twenty years and granted the institution the privileges of issuing bank notes, acceptable for government dues, and of establishing branch banks in the states. President Madison signed the bill despite the fact that he had opposed Hamilton's First National Bank as unconstitutional. Two prominent Southerners, John Randolph of Roanoke and John Taylor of Caroline, refused to follow the new trend of the Republican party toward nationalism but fought strenuously against the chartering of this powerful financial institution.

During this period of nationalism, Calhoun introduced his "Bonus Bill" in December, 1816, to use the bonus of $1,500,000 that the Second National Bank paid for its charter to build national roads and canals. He advocated this bill as a military measure, to provide roads for defense and as a means of binding the rapidly growing country into a strong union. He had no constitutional scruples in regard to his proposal, for he believed that such expenditures were authorized by the "common defense" and "general welfare" clauses of the Constitution. The "Bonus Bill" passed Congress but was vetoed by Madison on his last day of office. In the vote in the House of Representatives the Southern states were nearly evenly divided, with a slight preponderance against the bill.

The South did receive the advantage of obtaining one great national road built with federal funds, the so-called National Road, which began at Cumberland, Maryland, on the Potomac River in 1811 and by 1818 was completed as far as Wheeling, Virginia. The eastern end of the road was so heavily used that it began to wear out by 1822, when a bill was introduced into Congress to establish toll gates and use the toll receipts for the repair and upkeep of the road. It passed Congress, but was vetoed by President Monroe as unconstitutional. Monroe's veto message marks a return to the strict construction of the Constitution held by the early Republicans, the victory of a rigid theory over the interest of the nation.

In 1820 Monroe was re-elected president with only one dissenting vote.[12] There was no opposition party worthy of the name, for the Federalist party had practically disappeared. The Republican party, dominated by Southern leadership, had changed greatly since its victory in 1800. In the course of twenty years it had abandoned much of its devotion to strict construction of the Constitution and had adopted some of the salient policies of the Federalists. The last of the Virginia dynasty, President Monroe, promulgated the "Monroe Doctrine" of 1823, one of the greatest documents in the history of American nationalism.

[12] See W. P. Cresson, *James Monroe* (Chapel Hill, 1946); and George Dangerfield, *The Era of Good Feelings* (New York, 1952), and Harry A. Ammon, *James Monroe: The Quest for National Identity* (New York, 1971).

The War of 1812 temporarily checked the westward movement of population, but after the conclusion of peace there developed so extensive a migration of settlers into the region beyond the mountains that the period from 1815 to 1836 is rightly called The Great Migration. One reason for this expansion was the crushing defeat of the Creeks by Jackson in 1814 and the large land cessions extorted from them. The advance guard of this folk movement to the rich lands of the Southwest was formed by pioneer farmers who built log cabins and cleared the land by the process of girdling. Most of this group were seminomadic, restless "movers," who sold their pioneer clearings to more substantial farmers and once more moved westward. Many of these pioneer farmers were cattle and hog raisers who used the public domain for their range. The cattle and hogs did not have to be fed and sheltered during the winter months, as in the North. The more substantial farmers and planters who removed to the Southwest frequently sent out sons or neighbors to spy out the land and report on fertile sites for farms. There was a tendency for groups to settle this new country, a group of neighbors, a congregation, or a large family and its relatives. The rapid filling up of the Gulf area and the lower Mississippi Valley is indicated by the dates at which states in this region were admitted into the Union, Louisiana in 1812, Mississippi in 1817, Alabama in 1819, Missouri in 1821, and Arkansas in 1836.

The flow of population from the upper South to the old Northwest had considerable influence on American political history. In the first quarter of the nineteenth century many Quakers from Virginia and North Carolina migrated across the Ohio River to escape living in a slave country. Thus they removed valuable antislavery elements from the South and weakened the cause of liberalism in that region. Along with the Quakers went many poor farmers of the Southern upland stock. Among this group was the family of Abraham Lincoln, who moved from Kentucky first into Indiana, living in a "half-faced" log cabin, and then to Illinois. These Southern settlers had found by experience in their native region that the soil was most fertile where the trees grew tallest. Consequently, they avoided the rich prairie lands north of the terminal moraine line, made by the retreating glaciers of geologic ages, and confined their settlement to the region of the hardwoods in southern Ohio, Indiana, and Illinois. Many of them were quite illiterate and in Indiana their crude speech caused them to be called "Hoosiers." After the Jacksonian movement arose they usually voted the Democratic ticket. Some of them had favored the introduction of slavery into Illinois and Indiana when the latter became states. So formidable was the movement to establish slavery in Illinois in 1822–1824, during the agitation for the revision of the Constitution, that it was defeated only by the strenuous campaign of Edward Coles, a friend of Jefferson, who had emigrated from Virginia to avoid living in a slave state.[13] The southern parts of Ohio,

[13] See Ralph L. Ketcham, "The Dictates of Conscience: Edward Coles and Slavery," *Virginia Quarterly Review*, XXXVI (1960), 46–62.

Indiana, and Illinois traded with the lower South via the Mississippi River, and until 1850 they might be regarded as a part of the Greater South. During the Civil War this region contained numerous Southern sympathizers, called Copperheads.

The migration of Southerners was directed as a rule along isothermal lines, to regions where the climate, soil, and the type of crops grown were similar to those of their old home. Consequently, the westward movement advanced along parallel lines of latitude into contiguous areas. The presence of river systems as means of transportation also affected the westward flow of population. In 1850 over 142,102 natives of Virginia were living in the upper Southern states of Kentucky, Tennessee, and Missouri, 155,978 in the old Northwest, and only 38,311 in the lower South. The slaves of the lower South were far more frequently natives of "Old Virginia" than the free settlers. Maryland sent very few of her native sons to the deep South. In North Carolina the trend of the southward movement of population was about equally divided between the upper and the lower South, 103,315 natives of the state living in 1850 in the former region, and 107,912 in the latter. South Carolina and Georgia were the chief contributors of population to the young states of the Southwest. Missouri at the time of the great debate over its admission was settled largely by people from the upper South, whereas Arkansas was a child of Tennessee. Texas also received a large contingent of settlers from this state. In Louisiana a remarkable number of New Yorkers settled, largely because of the commercial attraction of New Orleans. In general, the emigrants to the lower South seem to have come predominantly from the Piedmont region rather than the Tidewater area. The westward movement of population into the Mississippi Valley was stimulated by boom times, such as the periods 1813–1819, 1833–1837, and 1853–1857, and noticeably slackened during times of depression.[14]

One of the best examples of these emigrating planters was Colonel Thomas Dabney of *Elmington,* in the Tidewater district of Virginia. Dabney lived in a fine old ancestral house, endeared by many memories, but the worn-out tobacco lands of the estate could no longer support the elegant life of former days. Accordingly, in 1835 he decided to sell *Elmington* and transfer his slaves to richer land. His fast-expanding family—his wife bore him sixteen children—demanded an ampler income than *Elmington* could supply. Before he abandoned his native state he was given an elaborate testimonial dinner at which Governor John Tyler presided. With his two hundred slaves, he set out overland to his new home in Hinds County, Mississippi, forty miles east of Vicksburg. Here he had purchased the lands of several farmers, which he combined into a plantation that ultimately contained four thousand acres. The pioneer farmers invited him to house-raisings and logrollings, but when he came with a gang of Negroes and

[14] William O. Lynch, "The Westward Flow of Southern Colonists before 1861," *Journal of Southern History*, IX (August 1943), and F. L. Owsley, "The Pattern of Migration and Settlement of the Southern Frontier," ibid., XI (May 1945), 147–176.

directed them from his horse while wearing gloves, they resented his aristocratic manners.[15]

The westward march of the cotton planter was attended by a great rise in
land prices. Under the Harrison Land Act of 1800 a settler could buy land
from the federal government on credit. The minimum amount of land sold
to a buyer was three hundred and twenty acres (in 1804 reduced to one
hundred and sixty acres) and the minimum price was $2 an acre. The poor
man could thus easily acquire a farm, for he was required to pay only the
first installment of 50 cents an acre, after which he could begin to plant a
cotton crop, paying the remainder of the purchase price within four years.
Public land was sold at auction, and land offices for the sale of the southwestern lands, released by Indian treaties, were located at Milledgeville,
Georgia, and Huntsville and Cahaba, Alabama. Wild speculation raised the
prices of the virgin lands of the Southwest until the panic of 1819 temporarily held up the westward movement of settlers. During this period of migration, a picturesque settlement of French exiles, some of them former officers
in Napoleon's army, founded Demopolis on the Tombigbee River (1817),
where they attempted to cultivate olives and vineyards for wine-making.

In 1820 the federal government changed the land law by abolishing the
credit system, but the minimum price of government land was reduced to
$1.25 an acre. The auction system was retained, however, and settlers were
allowed to surrender the land that they could not pay for and were given full
title for the amount that their installments covered.[16] Nevertheless, the substitution of the cash system for the credit system did not seem to restrain
speculation successfully. Settlers borrowed paper money from the "wild cat"
banks and the "pet banks" of the decade of the 1830's. In July, 1836, President Jackson issued his Specie Circular, which announced that only gold
and silver coin would be accepted for land payments. This executive order
precipitated the panic of the following year. In 1836 the sale of public lands
reached the peak of 20 million acres, but the depression years that followed
reduced the sales of the public domain by 1841 to 1 million acres.

When the United States acquired Missouri by the Louisiana Purchase,
there were already several settlements in the region, notably St. Louis, St.
Charles, and New Madrid. The latter, located on the west bank of the
Mississippi opposite the mouth of the Ohio, had been founded in 1789 by a
Pennsylvania land speculator, George Morgan. Following the conclusion of
the War of 1812, population flowed into this wild country, so that by 1818
the territory had attained the population of the sixty thousand people requisite for admission into the Union. Accordingly, in that year Missouri Territory applied for admission as a state, and in February, 1819, the Committee
on Territories reported such a bill to the House of Representatives. At this

[15] See Susan Dabney Smedes, A Southern Planter (New York, 1890).
[16] See R. M. Robbins, Our Landed Heritage: The Public Domain, 1776–1936 (Princeton, 1942).

point Representative James Tallmadge, Jr., of New York introduced an amendment to the bill, prohibiting any further immigration of slaves into the proposed state and providing for the emancipation of those born into slavery thereafter. Such children of slave parents, however, could be held to service until they had attained the age of twenty-five years.

The principal motives behind this Northern attempt to restrict the expansion of slavery seem to have been political rather than humanitarian considerations. The North had long resented the three-fifths federal ratio that gave the South representation in Congress for its slaves.[17] Indeed, the Southern states had twenty more Representatives in the lower house of Congress than they would have had if only white population had been counted. Senator Rufus King of New York, leader of the free soil men in the Senate, pointed out that under the unfair rule of slave representation, the votes of five Southerners were equal to those of seven Northerners in selecting both the president and members of the House of Representatives. Up to this date a balance had been maintained in the Union of an equal number of free and slave states. The admission of Missouri as a slave state would upset this equilibrium in the Senate. It is to be noted, however, that in 1820 the free states had a great preponderance of votes in the House of Representatives, 105 representatives, as compared with only 81 from the slave states.

One of the most acrimonious debates in the history of Congress took place over the Tallmadge amendment. The chief spokesmen of the Southerners were Senators John Tyler of Virginia and William Pinkney of Maryland. Tyler admitted that slavery was an evil to be eradicated, but he argued that the evil would be ameliorated by the distribution of the slaves over a wide area, which would lead to better treatment of them. Pinkney, one of the foremost orators of his age, denied that Congress had the right to place restrictions on the admission of states into the Union, a practice that would reduce the Union to a league between giants and dwarfs rather than between equals. The Tallmadge amendment was passed by the House of Representatives, but rejected in the Senate.[18]

In February, 1820, a compromise, proposed by Senator Jesse B. Thomas of Illinois, was adopted. According to this arrangement, Missouri was admitted as a slave state, but slavery was prohibited in the remainder of the Louisiana Purchase territory north of a line of latitude 36° 30′, which was the projection of the southern boundary of Missouri. At the same time the sectional balance in the Senate was maintained by admitting Maine as a free state. Thus the *first* Missouri Compromise bill passed Congress. A factor in securing the passage of this act was a fear on the part of some of the Northern Republicans that the Old Federalist party would be revived on the antislavery issue, and consequently they voted for a compromise. The

[17] A. F. Simpson, "The Political Significance of Slave Representation, 1787–1821," *Journal of Southern History*, VII (August 1941), 314–342.
[18] Glover Moore, *The Missouri Controversy, 1819–1821* (Lexington, 1955).

Southern representatives were almost equally divided over the acceptance of the compromise, thirty-eight for, and thirty-seven against it, the extreme states' rights men opposing the settlement.

A constitution for the new state was drawn up in a convention at St. Louis in the summer of 1820 and submitted to Congress for approval. Unfortunately, it contained a provision authorizing the legislature to exclude free Negroes and mulattoes from entering the state. This provision caused a storm of protest from the Northern members of Congress. At this juncture Henry Clay came forward and was influential in the adoption of the *second* Missouri Compromise. The legislature of Missouri gave a pledge that it would never pass a law that would deprive citizens of other states of the privileges and immunities granted under the federal Constitution. Such a pledge, however, could not be binding, except morally, upon later legislatures. With this understanding, the president proclaimed the admission of Missouri as a state on August 10, 1821.

The debate on the Missouri Compromise is a landmark in the growth of sectionalism in the United States. It created a sense of unity among the slave states, the embryo of Southern nationalism, for they realized the need of a phalanx to oppose the rising antislavery sentiment of the North. Thomas Jefferson at *Monticello* was so alarmed by the great sectional struggle over the admission of Missouri as a slave state that he wrote: "this momentous question, like a fire. bell in the night, awakened and filled me with terror. I considered it at once the knell of the Union." On account of this struggle over slavery, the old statesman feared a cleavage between the North and South along a geographical line "recurring on every occasion and renewing irritations, until it would kindle such mutual and mortal hatred, as to render separation preferable to eternal discord." [19] What Jefferson predicted was realized in the future—the rise of "the irrepressible conflict."

The North won this first round of the sectional battle. The Northwest, which had previously been in alliance with the South, joined the Northeast and voted preponderantly for Tallmadge's Amendment, thus shifting the balance of power. Also the principle of curbing slavery in the federal territory was established. Although the area in the Louisiana Purchase territory above the 36° 30′ line was much greater than the portion allotted to the expansion of slavery, most Southerners believed that the interdicted territory was barren and unsuited to the expansion of slavery. Moreover, thirty-four years later that part of the famous document containing the phrase that slavery should be "forever prohibited" was repealed. .

While Congress was debating the admission of Missouri into the Union, the President negotiated a treaty for the purchase of Florida. Florida had been coveted by Southerners, including the Virginia dynasty of Presidents, for many reasons. It was regarded as included within "the natural boundaries" of the United States and as necessary to give our county control of the

[19] Lipscomb and Bergh (eds.), *Writings of Thomas Jefferson*, XIV, 247–249.

Gulf of Mexico. Some of the large Southern rivers had their outlets in the Spanish-controlled coasts of West Florida. This weakly held colony, moreover, had become a decided nuisance to the inhabitants of the southern border of the United States. Runaway slaves found refuge in this territory, and it harbored predatory Indians who were a constant menace to Southern farmers and planters. The cotton planter eager to find fresh lands for his staple, cast avaricious glances on the valuable agricultural lands in this region preempted by the lackadaisical Spaniards.

Shortly after the Louisiana Purchase, our minister, Robert Livingston, asserted that our title included West Florida as far as the Perdido River, which flowed to the east of Mobile Bay. Jefferson and Monroe adopted this pleasant conception of the treaty, but Spain indignantly denied that Louisiana included West Florida. The Louisiana Purchase treaty was ambiguous, for it ceded to the United States the province of Louisiana with the same boundaries that it had when France possessed it and when Spain had control of it. In French possession, prior to the transfer to Spain in 1763, the province extended east to the Perdido River. In that year, however, England acquired Florida from Spain, and divided the province into East Florida and West Florida, with a western boundary of the Mississippi and Iberville rivers. Thus Louisiana in Spanish hands from 1763 to 1783 extended no further eastward than the Mississippi and Iberville rivers. After the Floridas were restored to Spain in 1783, the Spanish government attached the administration of West Florida to the royal governor at New Orleans.

In 1804 Congress passed the Mobile Act, placing the disputed territory, including Mobile, in a customs district, an assumption that led to a violent protest from the Spanish government. The following year James Monroe was sent to Europe on a special mission to obtain West Florida. He tried to put pressure on the weak Spanish government to yield, but Godoy, the prime minister and paramour of the queen, who had acquired the pompous title Prince of the Peace, refused to surrender. The key to a successful extortion of West Florida from the Spanish was the powerful French emperor and his venal minister, Talleyrand, who understood only the language of military force or of money. Jefferson decided to resort to the latter unscrupulous means of gaining Napoleon's aid in acquiring the coveted land. Accordingly, in December, 1805, he sent a secret message to Congress asking for an appropriation of $2 million to be used for this purpose. He hoped to persuade the French emperor to put pressure upon the unwilling Spanish government to yield this morsel of territory to the United States. The appropriation was voted in February, 1806, but the political situation in Europe changed and frustrated this attempt to win a land that Jefferson claimed already belonged to us by right.

West Florida was annexed to the United States by the medium of force rather than by sinuous diplomacy. After Napoleon began to dominate Spain by placing his brother Joseph Bonaparte on the Spanish throne, the American inhabitants of the western part of Florida feared that France would try to extend its rule over this Spanish colony. Accordingly, some of the large planters called the West Florida Convention (July 25, 1810) to secure control over the weak Spanish government. They attempted at first to reach a compromise agreement with the Spanish commandant, but when this failed, Philemon Thomas, the military leader, seized the fort at Baton Rouge (September 23), and the Convention declared West Florida free and independent of Spain.[20] They erected the first lone star republic, having a flag of blue woolen cloth with a silver star, and applied for annexation to the United States. A month later President Madison issued a proclamation that annexed not only the little republic between the Mississippi and the Pearl rivers but also the territory of the Gulf coast to the Perdido River. Mobile, nonetheless, continued to be held by the Spaniards. It was not until after the War of 1812 had begun that the United States obtained possession of this Creole town. An expedition led by General James Wilkinson captured Mobile in April, 1813, the only piece of territory gained by the war. When Louisiana was admitted to the Union in 1812, that part of Florida between the Mississippi and Pearl rivers was incorporated in the new state.

In 1811 an Indian agent of the United States on the southern border, General George Matthews, attempted to seize East Florida for his government by instigating a revolution against the Spanish in that province. Some gunboats of the United States were ordered to the Atlantic coast of Florida, ostensibly to prevent the smuggling of merchandise and of slaves into the country. Also two hundred soldiers were dispatched to the East Florida border. With such a show of force and with the connivance of the Secretary of State, James Monroe, General Matthews established contacts with the leaders of a revolutionary party, especially John McIntosh, who called themselves the "patriots." Matthews, who had been a Revolutionary soldier and a former governor of Georgia, was a colorful figure, almost illiterate, but full of energy and rashness despite his seventy-two years. He was aided by the imperialistic natives of Georgia, who were eager to liquidate the Spanish rule in Florida. On March 18, 1812, the "patriots" captured Amelia Island and then laid seige to St. Augustine, supported by the United States troops. After the hullabaloo raised by the John Henry papers (revelations of a British intriguer who tried to start a secession movement among the New England Federalists), Monroe decided to repudiate Matthews, and he was dismissed as agent in April, 1812. The siege of St. Augustine by American troops, however, was not abandoned until the following September, and the captured territory was not given up until Congress had twice refused to approve the occupation.[21]

Spain continued to hold East Florida with a relaxed and nerveless grasp by means of three weak garrisons, at Pensacola, St. Marks, and St. Augustine.

[20] Thomas P. Abernethy, *The South in the New Nation, 1789–1819* (Baton Rouge, 1961), chap. 13.
[21] Isaac J. Cox, *The West Florida Controversy, 1789–1813* (Baltimore, 1918), chaps. 9–11.

Runaway slaves had built a fort on the Apalachicola River, called Negro Fort, where they defied capture. On Amelia Island, above St. Augustine, there was a nest of pirates under Gregor MacGregor. British agents, such as Lieutenant Colonel Edward Nicholls, circulated among the Creek and Seminole Indians of the southern border. Criminals frequently escaped across the border. Florida was indeed a nuisance to the United States.

As a consequence of Indian hostilities on the southern border, President Monroe ordered General Andrew Jackson to raise some militia and chastise the offending Indians. In 1818 Jackson crossed the international boundary line in hot pursuit of marauding Indians. When they fled for protection to the Spanish fort of St. Marks, he seized the fort and hanged several Seminole chiefs. He was unable, however, to catch one of the principal Seminole leaders, Billy Bowlegs, whose village lay on the Suwannee River. Warned by a Scotch trader and friend of the Indians, Alexander Arbuthnot, Bowlegs escaped to the Everglades. Jackson then arrested Arbuthnot as well as a young soldier of fortune, Robert Ambrister, who was employed by the Scotch trader, as instigators of Indian warfare. Arbuthnot had aroused the anger of Jackson by telling the Indians that Jackson's treaty of 1814 with the Creeks was no longer valid and by offering to furnish hostile Indians with gunpowder. Jackson ordered a trial by court martial of these two British subjects and executed them. Arbuthnot, a white-haired old gentleman, was hanged from the topsail yard of his trading vessel, the *Chance,* and the young adventurer, Ambrister, was accorded the honor of being shot by a firing squad. Then Jackson marched to Pensacola, drove out the Spanish garrison, and raised the American flag above the fort. Thus this American general had violated international law and trampled upon the rights of both Spain and England.

Many Americans of the South and the West hailed Jackson as a hero for his high-handed conduct. But British public opinion was so inflamed over the affair that Lord Castlereagh had some difficulty in preserving peaceful relations with the United States. Furthermore, Henry Clay made a spirited speech in Congress, condemning Jackson's arbitrary and dangerous course. The latter defended himself by declaring that he had received authority from President Monroe for his action through a private correspondence with a Tennessee congressman, John Rhea. Monroe, on the other hand, denied that he had given Jackson authority to seize Spanish forts and hang British citizens. The Cabinet considered the problem of disciplining Jackson. The secretary of war, John C. Calhoun, advocated the trial of the unruly general by court martial, but Secretary of State John Quincy Adams stoutly upheld Jackson's conduct, and no action was taken. Furthermore, resolutions introduced into Congress censuring Jackson for his Florida invasion were defeated. Pensacola and St. Mark's, nevertheless, were returned to Spain.

Indirectly, Jackson's invasion of Florida was responsible for Spain's decision to turn over the troublesome province to the United States. Before the irruption of the headstrong general into Florida, Adams had been negotiating without success for the purchase of East Florida. He now had a trump card. He declared that Spain should police her border efficiently and that if the United States were forced to send another expedition into Florida against the Indians, American soldiers would remain. Furthermore, he demanded payment of the claims, amounting to approximately $5 million, of American citizens against Spain.

The Spanish government was not as solicitous to retain Florida as to prevent the United States from recognizing the independence of the revolted Latin-American republics. The Spanish officials realized that as long as they delayed selling Florida, the government of the United States would be cautious about recognizing these rebellious colonies of the mother country. Henry Clay and others in Congress were vigorously demanding that the United States should recognize these young republics. The invasion of Florida, however, frightened Spain, which now decided to accept the inevitable and sell Florida rather than lose it by force.

The treaty transferring Florida to the United States was signed February 22, 1819, by Adams, representing the United States, and De Onis, the Spanish ambassador at Washington. By its terms Spain agreed to surrender East Florida and recognize the legality of our occupation of West Florida. In return, the United States assumed the claims of its citizens against the Spanish government and surrendered our contention that Texas was a part of the Louisiana Purchase. The Sabine River was agreed upon as the western boundary of Louisiana.

Hoping to prevent the United States from recognizing the revolted republics of Latin America, the Spanish government delayed ratifying the treaty. Finally in 1821 the transfer of Florida to the United States was consummated. Monroe appointed Jackson to be the first military governor of the new province. The general proved to be an unfortunate appointment, for he was surprisingly sensitive over questions of punctilio and became involved in quarrels with the retiring Spanish governor. Disappointed in the lack of jobs for his friends and relatives, he soon resigned from this unpleasant position.

At the time of its acquisition by the United States, the population of East Florida was estimated at fifteen thousand people and of West Florida at five thousand people, mostly poor whites and frontiersmen. The territory did not attract many American settlers for a number of years. Land titles were dubious as a result of Spanish claims, and during the decades of the 1830's and 1840's the United States army was engaged in a long and costly war against the Seminole Indians. Florida was divided economically and socially into three distinct sections: East Florida, including the area east of the Suwannee River, with St. Augustine as its center, where sugar and oranges were produced; Middle Florida, with Tallahassee as its center, settled after 1825 by Southern cotton planters; and West Florida, with Pensacola as its center of population. Florida under the rule of the United States did not prosper much more than it had under the control of Spain. Indeed, Florida did not become a state until 1845, when it was admitted into the Union to balance the free state of Iowa.[22] The movement for statehood was strong among the inhabitants of the Tallahassee district, but the bitter sectional feelings of East Florida caused its leaders to propose the separation of the territory by the Suwannee River and the admission of only the western portion as a state, the eastern part remaining a territory until a later date, when it should become the separate state of East Florida.

The civilization of the Spanish Creoles has influenced the pattern of life in the lower South chiefly through the avenues of Texas and New Orleans rather than from the original base of Spanish settlement in Florida. The destruction of the Spanish missions in Florida, Georgia, and South Carolina eradicated the influence of mission architecture on the South Atlantic states.[23] In St. Augustine, however, there remain a few relics of Spanish occupation: a baroque Spanish cathedral; the old Spanish fort of San Marcos (now christened Fort Marion), built of coquina stone, or a formation of coral and sand quarried from St. Anastasia Island; the picturesque stone gate of the vanished wall about the town; the unpretentious Spanish governor's house, used as a post office by the Americans; the Treasury; and several old houses, such as the Geronimo Alvarez House. In another quarter of the South, the San Antonio valley of Texas, there are five Spanish missions, including the famous Alamo, which preserve the traditions of Spanish architecture.

The most important and numerous monuments of Spanish architecture in the South are to be found at New Orleans. Contrary to a common impression, the architecture of the old quarter of New Orleans is not primarily French but Spanish. The old French city of Bienville and of "the Grand Marquis," Vaudreuil, was destroyed by disastrous fires in 1788 and 1794, respectively. The principal public buildings were rebuilt in Spanish style by the generosity of the wealthiest citizen of New Orleans, Don Andres Almonaster. The picturesque Cabildo (City Hall), which stands on Jackson Square—formerly Place d'Armes—the Charity Hospital, and the Capuchin Convent were built by him. Many of the houses of the Vieux Carré are of Spanish architecture, constructed of stucco, painted in many pastel colors, with patios in the rear, balconies of wrought or cast iron, and long windows protected from the burning sun by shutters.

To the Spanish settlers in the New World Southern agriculture owes much. The Spaniards introduced many plants, fruits, vegetables, and domestic animals into America. They were responsible for bringing the sweet orange to Florida, which had originally grown in China and had been carried to Spain by the Moors. From Europe they transported to their American colonies wheat, sugar cane, rice, alfalfa, "mission figs," apples, apricots, lemons,

[22] Dorothy Dodd, *Florida Becomes a State* (Tallahassee, 1945).
[23] See John Bartram, "Diary of a Journey through the Carolinas, Georgia, and Florida," *Transactions of the American Philosophical Society*, New Series, XXXIII, Part I, 51–55; William Bartram, *Travels Through North and South Carolina, Georgia, East and West Florida* (Philadelphia, 1791).

cherries, pears, and walnuts. Certain flowers, such as geraniums, red carnations, and lilies, came over on Spanish caravels. Domesticated bees, called by the Indians the "white man's flies," were brought over for honey and to pollinate certain European flowers, such as apple blossoms. When the Spaniards arrived, the American native horse, whose bones have been found in the tar pit of the Rancho la Brea in Los Angeles, had become extinct. But some of the Spanish horses escaped and propagated the wild horses of the Western plains. Although the American continent had millions of buffalo, there were no native cows. Spanish cattle escaped, however and became the ancestors of the wild long-horned cattle of Texas.

The Spanish settlers of the Southwest have enriched the American language in many ways. The terminology of the cattle country is Spanish, because the cowboys were taught much of their skill in handling cattle by the Mexican *vaqueros*. The American cowboy adopted the costume of his Mexican predecessor, the wide-brimmed sombrero, the chaps, the lariat, and even the Mexican saddle. The lingo of the cattle country, the use of the rodeo, the remuda, the practice of branding cattle, the corral, all were inherited from the Spanish-American cattlemen. Many words of common usage in the Southwest, such as *canyon, tornado, mesa, plaza, adobe, burro, patio, presidio, peon, poncho, bronco, desperado, calaboose,* and *vamoose* were derived from the Spanish language. Also the American miner profited from Spanish pioneering efforts in the Southwest. The young republic of the United States adopted the Spanish piece of eight, or milled dollar, as the basis of our coinage. Our debt to Spanish mining adventures is reflected in such words of Latin origin as *bonanza, placer, eldorado,* and *vigilante.* A study of Spanish words incorporated in the speech of the United States reveals the fact that the Spanish in Texas and the Southwest had a greater significance in American civilization than the Latin element in Florida. The reason for this development was that the Spaniards in Florida were always numerically weak, and when the province was acquired by the British and later by the United States, most of the Spanish inhabitants moved away.

Homes in
New Orleans.

Walnut Hall,
near
Lexington,
Kentucky.

The Maturity of the
Plantation

THE TRAVELER in the antebellum South was impressed by the wide spaces of woodland between the lonely houses and cleared fields. He observed also the zigzag rail or Virginia worm fences around these fields. The rails for these fences were split from logs by means of wedges and hickory or butternut mauls, such as Abraham Lincoln used. The long-continuing tradition of the frontier made it necessary for every farmer to defend his fields from ranging cattle. Not until after the Civil War did another philosophy of fences prevail, one where the cattle raiser was required to confine his cattle and prevent them from eating the crops of his neighbor.

Very noticeable were the differences between Northern and Southern agriculture, particularly the fact that the planters were engaged in producing crops for foreign export. A large number of Southern farmers, however, were employed in the same type of agriculture, subsistence farming, as prevailed above the Ohio and the Mason-Dixon line. Southern agriculture was further differentiated from Northern agriculture by the widespread development of the plantation, with its gang system of labor based on black slaves. The plantation was variable in size but frequently consisted of one thousand to one thousand, five hundred acres of land. Its size was limited by the walking distance of an hour or so from the slave quarters to the most distant fields. The relative proportions of the different types of plantations are indicated roughly by the Census of 1850, which lists 74,031 cotton plantations (producing more than 5 bales), 2,681 sugar plantations, including the smallest, 15,745 tobacco estates producing 3,000 pounds or more, 8,327 hemp plantations, and 551 rice plantations, each raising 20,000 pounds and over.[1]

The distribution of the different types of plantations was determined by geographic fitness. The locale of the rice district was a narrow strip of coastal South Carolina and Georgia and a spur in southeastern North Carolina. The sugar-growing region was almost exclusively confined to Louisiana below the Red River and to a few valleys in Texas. The tobacco kingdom covered the upper South, including Missouri. Hemp as a staple crop was grown almost entirely in Kentucky and Missouri. The Cotton Kingdom spread over an

[1] J. D. B. De Bow (Supt.) *Compendium of the Seventh Census* (Washington, 1854), 178.

208

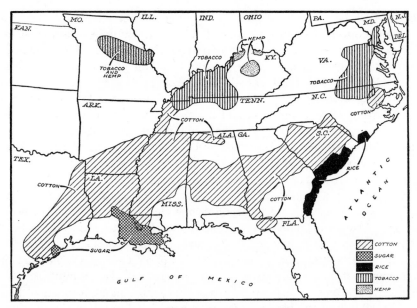

Staple Crops of the South in 1860

imperial realm, which extended as far north as the southern part of North Carolina, and the Mississippi Valley districts of Tennessee, and Arkansas, and as far west as eastern Texas. Although the large plantation was the rule in the cultivation of rice and sugar, both cotton and tobacco in the nineteenth century could also be profitably grown by small farmers. The farms of the yeoman who were engaged in subsistence agriculture were scattered throughout the South, but they were concentrated in the border states and the Piedmont region.

A social revolution occurred in the Southern states as a result of the enormous expansion of cotton culture. The earliest known homes of cotton were Africa and India, where it was woven into cloth—calico, named after the city of Calicut; madras, named after Madras; and muslin from the Orient named after the Moslems. It was introduced into Spain by the Moors, and Columbus brought back cotton from the Bahama Islands. This fiber was also manufactured into cloth by the Aztecs of Mexico and the Incas of Peru. During the colonial period small quantities of the plant were grown, but it did not become a major crop in the South until after the invention of the cotton gin in 1793. There were two main kinds of cotton cultivated in the South, the long-staple variety, used in fine fabrics, and the short-staple variety. Long-staple cotton not only had a greater length than the short-staple species, but its glossy black seed could be detached from the lint far more easily than the green seed of the short-staple variety.

Unfortunately, the long-staple type of cotton could be grown only in a restricted area, the sea islands that fringed the coast of South Carolina and

Georgia and the adjacent littoral. This superior strain of cotton, often called sea-island cotton, was introduced about 1786 into Georgia from the Bahama Islands by Loyalist refugees. The export of this valuable fiber reached its peak in the decade of the 1820's, when 11 million pounds a year were sent abroad. Sea-island cotton had certain disadvantages, the small yield per acre of only one hundred and fifty pounds, the failure of the boll to open fully, thus retarding the picking of it, and the need of skillful handling. The short-staple variety, on the other hand, had the advantage of being a hardy plant that could be grown on the uplands and the interior of the South. It made a fine replacement for the dying indigo industry, as soon as a machine was devised to gin or separate the fiber from the seed.[2]

The need for a cotton gin was supplied by a versatile Yankee inventor, Eli Whitney. Shortly after graduating from Yale College at the age of twenty-seven, Whitney took passage on a ship for the South to secure a position as a tutor. On the ship he met the vivacious widow of General Nathanael Greene, who invited him to visit her at *Mulberry Grove,* a plantation near Savannah that had been given to the general by the grateful people of Georgia. Here he was inspired to experiment with making a practical gin by hearing the talk of the planters about the need for a machine to separate the lint from the green cotton seed. In the spring of 1793 he completed the model of a machine, which, operated by hand, would do the work of ten men, or by horsepower, the work of fifty men. It was a simple mechanism consisting of rollers equipped with wire teeth that rotated against a hopper box constructed of slats. The revolving rollers tore the cotton from the seed, leaving the seed in the hopper. When the rollers became clogged with the lint, Mrs. Greene suggested cleaning them with a broom, a homely device that gave Whitney the idea of adding another cylinder equipped with brushes that revolved in an opposite direction and with greater speed than the wire-teeth roller.[3]

Whitney formed a partnership with Phineas Miller, Mrs. Greene's manager and future husband, to exploit the invention, which was patented March 4, 1794. They hoped to reap a golden harvest by retaining a monopoly of the cotton-ginning business, exacting a toll of one third of the cotton ginned by their machines. But the simple construction of the machine, which could be made by any competent blacksmith, frustrated this design for a monopoly. Improvements were made by other inventors, such as Hodgin Holmes, a mechanic of Augusta, Georgia, who received a patent May 2, 1796, for a gin that substituted iron disks for the wooden rollers with wire teeth. Planters and businessmen disregarded the patent rights of Whitney, and Southern jurors would not convict the infringers. Although some of the Southern states

[2] See Alfred G. Smith, Jr., *Economic Readjustment of an Old Cotton State, South Carolina, 1820–1860* (Columbia, 1958).
[3] See Jeannette Mirsky and Allan Nevins, *The World of Eli Whitney* (New York, 1952).

contributed considerable sums of money to Whitney and his partner, the latter spent much time and money in protecting their patent rights and gained little profit from the invention.

Preceding the invention of the Whitney gin, the Industrial Revolution had begun in England, based on a series of inventions of machines to spin cotton and woolen thread and weave it into cloth in factories. This technological revolution coincided roughly with a great explosion of population in Europe during the last part of the eighteenth and the early part of the nineteenth century, which opened up an enormously expanded market for clothing.[4] Thus the Whitney gin, the textile machinery inventions, and the population explosion of Europe (the latter a significant event long neglected by historians) gave the South the golden opportunity of rapidly creating the Cotton Kingdom.

In 1790 an Englishman, Samuel Slater, introduced the cotton mill, operated by water power, into the United States at Pawtucket, Rhode Island. Following the conclusion of the War of 1812, cotton factories, aided by a protective tariff, began to multiply in New England. Consequently, the English and American textile factories were hungry for Southern cotton. This demand was increased later by the invention in 1846 of the sewing machine, by Elias Howe, which was perfected by Isaac M. Singer in the decade of the 1850's.

The cultivation of cotton was admirably suited to the gang labor of slaves, because the low height of the plant made it easy for an overseer to supervise the slaves, who could not hide from his gaze.[5] The chief limitation of the cotton crop was that it required a long growing season, at least two hundred days free from killing frosts. Consequently, the antebellum cotton belt did not extend into Virginia, Kentucky, except for the extreme western part, Maryland, or Missouri. As late as 1825, Virginia planters experimented with cultivating cotton, but they abandoned the attempt after a trial. Although the cotton belt had a northern limit, its extension westward was prevented only by barren soil or lack of sufficient rainfall. The production of cotton was also restricted by the fact that a gang of slaves could plant and cultivate a much larger acreage of the valuable staple than they could pick, and it was difficult to secure extra laborers during cotton-picking time. If the South could have developed a practicable mechanical picker, such an invention would have enormously lightened the work on a cotton plantation and would have considerably reduced the number of slaves needed. But this invention did not appear until the twentieth century, chiefly because the bolls of the cotton plant ripen at different times.

[4] See William Langer, "Europe's Initial Population Explosion," *American Historical Review*, LXIX (October 1963), 1–17.

[5] A splendid description of the raising of cotton in the South is given by U. B. Phillips, *Life and Labor in the Old South* (Boston, 1929), and first-hand observations by a Northern traveler in Arthur M. Schlesinger, Sr. (ed.), *The Cotton Kingdom . . . by Frederick Law Olmsted* (New York, 1953).

Picking Cotton in South Carolina. (Courtesy of United States Forestry Service)

The varied activity that was pursued on a typical cotton plantation is illustrated by the plantation journals that have survived. One of these manuscripts, the journal of W. S. Hyland, who owned a plantation near Warrenton, Mississippi, reveals the amazing amount of work obtained from the slaves during the cotton-picking season.[6] There were from 20 to 25 cotton pickers, men, women, and children, on the plantation during the years 1847–1861, working under an overseer. The hands began picking cotton about August 20 and continued until the early part of January, picking over the fields from three to five separate times. The best slaves averaged over 300 pounds a day at the height of the season. In 1852 "Little Mary" led the gang of cotton pickers, picking 2,073 pounds of cotton in a week of six days, and one slave, Bob, picked 540 pounds on October 6, 1856. The plantation produced about 150 bales of cotton, the bales varying in weight but averaging 450 pounds.

[6] Journal of W. S. Hyland, MS owned by T. D. Clark of the University of Kentucky; for a fascinating account of the raising and picking of cotton on a Louisiana plantation, see Solomon Northrup, *Twelve Years a Slave* (Buffalo, 1854), chap. 12.

A Cotton Steamboat. (Edward King, *The Great South*, p. 304)

The plantation had its own gin, which was operated by slaves. In addition to the money crop, cotton, the plantation produced an ample supply of corn, meat, pumpkins, sweet potatoes, and peas. The labor record shows that very little time was lost by sickness of the slaves, although there was an epidemic of diphtheria that took a heavy toll of the lives of the children, and the deaths of several mature slaves from consumption and pneumonia are recorded. The slaves on this plantation worked a full day on Saturday, and when rain prevented them from picking cotton they were employed in such other work as gathering and shucking corn, gathering potatoes, sewing, and repairing the worm fences.

The method of cultivating cotton in the antebellum South tended to exhaust the soil, especially because of the failure to practice an intelligent rotation of crops and to check soil erosion. Consequently, the cotton planters began a steady march westward to acquire virgin soil, leaving a wake of desolate and abandoned countryside. These abandoned lands were often called in the later antebellum period "Gone to Texas" farms. The advance of the cotton planters toward the setting sun has been compared to the devastating effect of an army invading a peaceful land. The first stage in the westward retreat (or advance) of the cotton planters was the extension of cotton culture into the Piedmont area of the Atlantic seaboard states. This advance brought the plantation system and slavery into the back country, thus tending to unify the back country and the Tidewater. It can be illustrated by the rapid progress of slavery into the Piedmont counties of South Carolina. In 1790 slaves constituted only one fifth of the population of this region, but by 1830 the black population of this region nearly equaled the white.

Meanwhile, cotton and slavery were expanding into the rich bottom lands of the Gulf area. The old, impoverished soils of the Atlantic seaboard could not compete with the fresh, incredibly fertile lands of the Gulf states. The Atlantic seaboard states, however, still produced the major part of the cotton crop up to 1830, but by 1835 the Gulf states had far outstripped the Atlantic states in the production of the fleecy staple. From this date to the Civil War the Gulf states and Arkansas produced three fourths of the crop grown in the United States. In 1859 the record crop of 4,541,285 bales was grown in the land of Dixie. The weight of the bale in the Southwest, where baling presses and screws prevailed, was approximately five hundred pounds, but in the Atlantic seaboard states the weight was around three hundred pounds. On the eve of the Civil War considerably over three fourths of the Southern cotton crop was sent to Europe. Cotton provided approximately 60 per cent in value of the exports of the United States.[7]

The profits from green-seed cotton grown on virgin soil were at first very alluring. In 1801 the price was 44 cents a pound, and on rich soil a bale an acre was grown. In these early years the lucrative returns from growing cotton with slave labor was demonstrated by Wade Hampton who raised six hundred bales of cotton on six hundred acres of his plantation near Columbia, South Carolina. His crop was valued at $90,000. The price of cotton declined rapidly, however, so that in 1811 it brought only 8.9 cents a pound, and in 1812, when news of the declaration of war against England reached the lower South, the price broke disastrously. Thus early were revealed the evils of dependence on a foreign market. Overproduction began to plague the cotton producers, and they never developed a sensible crop control plan that would adjust the supply to the demand. Prices fluctuated violently, in the decade 1839–1849 dropping to prices below the cost of production, but in the decade preceding the Civil War, rising to profitable levels of 11 and 12 cents a pound.

Whereas cotton was the money crop of the lower South, tobacco was the cash crop of the farmers of the upper South. In the nineteenth century the center of tobacco growing shifted to the Piedmont. By 1840 little tobacco was raised in the Virginia and Maryland Tidewater, and this region, once dominated by great tobacco plantations, was reoccupied by yeoman farmers. This movement was caused partly by the exhaustion and erosion of the soils in the

[7] The classic study of Southern agriculture is Lewis C. Gray, *History of Agriculture in the Southern United States to 1860* (New York, 1941), 2 vols.; also excellent is Paul W. Gates, *The Farmer's Age: Agriculture, 1815–1860* (New York, 1960); and J. C. Bonner, *A History of Georgia Agriculture, 1732–1860* (Athens, Ga., 1964).

older region, but also it was accentuated by the fact that tobacco in this later period could be cultivated most profitably on small farms. In the Virginia–North Carolina tobacco district the typical farm contained only five and one half acres in tobacco, which required the work of two hands. The cultivation of tobacco crossed the mountains and spread into Kentucky, Tennessee, Ohio, and Missouri, casting a dark shadow over the prospects of the Atlantic seaboard, for such dispersion resulted in tremendous overproduction and lower prices. By 1843 the Western surpassed the Eastern states in the production of the royal weed, and by the middle of the nineteenth century Kentucky yielded nearly as much tobacco as Virginia.

The raising of tobacco required a great expenditure of labor. The first step was to prepare the seed beds by burning over the ground to destroy the seed of weeds and then to sow the extremely minute tobacco seed. In the late spring the young plants were transplanted from the beds to the fields. Not only was it necessary to kill the weeds and fast-growing Johnson grass by frequent plowing and hoeing, but the plants also had to be "topped" by an experienced person, they had to be "suckered," or the subordinate leaves removed, and a ceaseless warfare against the fat green tobacco worms had to be waged. After the tobacco matured, it was cut and hung on poles in tall, log tobacco houses, where it was "cured" or dried by slow fires and smoke. It was now ready to be packed in hogsheads, which during the colonial period contained about one thousand pounds of tobacco but through most of the antebellum period approximately one thousand four hundred pounds. Then came the problem of transportation to market, either by boat down the rivers or by rolling the hogsheads along the poor roads. Before the tobacco could be exported it had to be inspected at warehouses by officials appointed by the governor. In colonial days all condemned tobacco had to be burned, but this requirement was abandoned in 1805 in Virginia and in 1817 in North Carolina.

Up to 1840 most of the tobacco raised in the South was exported. The British purchased 40 per cent of the tobacco exported from Virginia, the French 20 per cent, the Italians 15 per cent, and the North Europeans, 25 per cent. From 1800 to 1860 the British government placed a heavy duty on tobacco, 3 to 4 shillings a pound, equivalent to an ad valorem duty of 900 per cent. The assumption, which has been current in American economic history, that the exports of tobacco declined following the outbreak of the Revolution until about 1840 has been challenged by a modern scholar.[8] He points out that this error was based on the statistics of the exports of hogsheads, which changed in weight. The record production of tobacco in the Southern colonies was attained in the five years preceding the Revolution; then there was a decline; a spurt of exports in 1790–1792, however, surpassed the colonial record; and in eight different years before 1840 exports exceeded those of 1792, the banner year of the eighteenth century. It is true

[8] Joseph C. Robert, *The Tobacco Kingdom, Plantation, Market, and Factory in Virginia and North Carolina, 1860* (Durham, 1938).

that tobacco production in the Virginia district did not exceed colonial production until the decade of the 1830's, but there was a large expansion in the crop of the states across the mountains. So great was the increase in the cultivation of tobacco during the last decade of the antebellum period that production in Virginia and Kentucky was doubled and in North Carolina was tripled. The record year for the export of cured tobacco from the United States was 1859, when twice as much tobacco was exported as the colonial amount.

The growing of tobacco in North Carolina and Virginia was revolutionized by the discovery of a new variety, "Bright Yellow Tobacco." This discovery was accidentally made by Stephen, a young slave employed as blacksmith and overseer on the farm of Abisha Slade in Caswell County, North Carolina. In 1839 this intelligent Negro youth discovered a method of curing a new type of tobacco by using charcoal as fuel. The product, "Bright Yellow Tobacco," it was also found, grew not on rich botton lands but on poor, silicous soil. In the decade of the 1850's, the Slade brothers developed and publicized the technique of cultivating and curing this variety, which was sold for four times the price of ordinary dark tobacco. Thus in the last decade of the antebellum period a new type of fancy tobacco was developed, which was at first used as the ornamental cover of plug tobacco, but after the Civil War became the basis of the great cigarette industry.[9]

The price that the farmer received for his tobacco fluctuated violently according to the law of supply and demand. It was difficult to control the quantity of tobacco grown, partly because of an eighteen-month interlude between the planting of the crop and the marketing of it. Also the weather played a tremendous and ominous role in the prosperity of the tobacco country. Consequently, most of the planters were distinctly weather-conscious, as their diaries show. Freshets, hail, storms, droughts, and hostile insects ruined crops and raised prices. On the other hand, a bountiful and gracious Nature produced such bumper crops that prices cascaded downward. Prices ranged from 3½ cents a pound in the early 1800's to a high point of 14½ cents in 1816 after the war with England, to 7.8 cents just prior to the Civil War. Great overproduction in the last few years before secession caused gloomy thoughts concerning the future of their money crops to shadow the minds of the tobacco growers.

A crop that competed with tobacco in Kentucky and Missouri was hemp. In colonial days the British government had tried to encourage the growing of this fiber so essential to the shipping industry by offering bounties of £6 per ton, but little hemp was exported. Hemp and flax were grown widely in the frontier regions of the South, where they were used in making coarse cloth. In Kentucky, hemp was cultivated for commercial purposes principally in the Bluegrass region of Lexington and the districts around Louisville and Maysville (burley tobacco did not become the money crop of the Bluegrass until after the Civil War). A magnificent description of the growing and

[9] See Nannie M. Tilly, *The Bright Tobacco Industry, 1860–1929* (Chapel Hill, 1948).

harvesting of hemp in Kentucky is contained in James Lane Allen's novel *The Reign of Law*. The hemp seed were sown broadcast over the plowed field, growing up in slender stalks that attained a height of ten feet or more. After the crop was ripe it was reaped by cutting with a hemp knife. The substance of the hemp that held the fibers was then allowed to rot, and the stalks were broken by a crude hand machine. As a result of the protection afforded by the tariff and the high prices of 1826–1828, the production of hemp expanded greatly in the Bluegrass region of Kentucky, in middle Tennessee, and in Missouri. Henry Clay, who had married the heiress of a hemp-growing family, became a powerful advocate in Congress of tariff protection that was needed in competition with the superior water-rotted Russian hemp, Manila hemp, and Scottish hemp bagging. Since hemp bagging and bale ropes were used on the Southern cotton bales, the demand of the hemp growers and manufacturers for tariff protection clashed with the interests of the cotton growers.

The failure of the Kentucky hemp growers to supply heavy cordage for the navy is a fascinating story of the bureaucratic mind of the navy and of the independent nature of Southern farmers. The Kentucky growers prepared their fiber for the market by the dew-rotting process, which was satisfactory for cotton bagging and for bale rope but not for the tarred rope used by the navy. The stronger and more flexible water-rotted variety was imported from Russia and was used by the navy throughout the antebellum period. Congress tried on numerous occasions to encourage the production of water-rotted hemp for the navy as a patriotic measure, but its efforts were defeated by the inflexible bureaucracy of the navy and by the inertia and conservatism of the American hemp growers. The navy did send agents into the hemp-growing region, but it gave them little authority and usually refused to buy Kentucky water-rotted hemp unless it was sent for inspection to the national rope factory at the Charlestown Navy Yard in Massachusetts. Accordingly, the agents were unable to procure much Kentucky hemp that would meet the specifications of the navy. An ardent propagandist for persuading the Kentucky and Missouri farmers to adopt the water-rotted process in preparing hemp was David Myerle, who exhausted his fortune in this missionary work but was frustrated by a variety of factors. In 1852 a navy yard and rope factory were established by Congress at Memphis, but although the factory had the finest machinery in the world, it received little Southern hemp and was abandonded two years later. Some of the reasons given for the apathy of the Kentuckians toward producing water-rotted hemp were that it smelled badly, and ignorant farmers thought it spread disease, that the Kentucky water pools were needed for their cattle and blooded horses, and that some Kentucky hemp that had been sent to the Charlestown Navy Yard had been unfairly rejected by the Yankees, thus discouraging further shipments.[10]

The depletion of the fertility of the soils of the tobacco region in the

[10] See James F. Hopkins, *A History of the Hemp Industry in Kentucky* (Lexington, Ky., 1951).

eighteenth and the early nineteenth centuries stimulated the planters to study scientific agriculture. George Washington led the way in trying to rehabilitate his plantation *Mount Vernon*. Not only did he read the works of the English agricultural reformers, such as Jethro Tull's *The Horse-Hoeing Husbandry,* but he practiced a more intelligent rotation of crops, introduced new crops, particularly turnips, lucern (alfalfa), and chicory, and imported an Arabian stallion to improve the breed of horses. The king of Spain sent Washington a pedigreed jack, "Royal Gift," and Lafayette later sent him a jack from Malta to produce mules. All his reforming efforts, however, availed little, for he had neglected *Mount Vernon* during the long period of time that he was in the public service. Twenty-five years after his death a neighbor described the condition of this former regal estate like this: "a more widespread and perfect agricultural ruin could not be imagined." Jefferson also was ardently interested in improving Southern agriculture, making many experiments, but *Monticello,* with its abandoned old fields, was sold after his death to Lieutenant Uriah Levy for $2,500. Yet Jefferson's son-in-law, Thomas Mann Randolph, who had assumed the management of *Monticello,* pointed the way to the future by introducing into the Piedmont the new method of contour plowing, that is, plowing horizontally along the hills, following their curvatures, which was to become an efficient method of checking erosion.

Agricultural reform in Virginia and Maryland was preceded by a great rise in the price of wheat caused by the Napoleonic wars. Also the price of tobacco reached a nadir during the period of the embargo and the War of 1812. Consequently a shift began from a reliance on the soil-exhausting crop of tobacco to wheat. Furthermore, intelligent planters were studying methods of increasing the fertility of soils. In 1784 John A. Binns, of Loudon County, Virginia, experimented with gypsum, or plaster of Paris, as a fertilizer, resulting in the spread of the use of gypsum in the years following the War of 1812. A pioneer work on Southern agriculture was written by John Taylor of Caroline County, Virginia, *The Arator,* which was published in book form in 1813. He advocated rotation of crops, deep plowing, and especially the use of vegetable material for manures.[11]

The greatest agricultural reformer of the Old South was without doubt Edmund Ruffin of Virginia. After studying the chemistry of soils, he concluded that much of the exhausted arable lands of the upper South had acid conditions that must be neutralized before they could become highly productive. His remedy was to apply marl, a fine shell deposit found in eastern Virginia, to neutralize acid soils. This doctrine he expounded in his *Essay on Calcareous Manures,* published in 1833. In this year also he founded the *Farmers' Register,* to advocate the new cult of the use of marl and scientific methods of farming. He made his plantations, *Coggin's Point* on the James River and *Marlbourne* on the Pamunkey River, laboratories for agricultural

---

[11] See Clement Eaton, *The Growth of Southern Civilization, 1790–1860* (New York, 1961), chap. 8, The Renaissance of the Upper South.

experiment, demonstrating the practical value of his ideas by enormously increasing his production of corn and wheat. His fame spread, and he was invited by North Carolina, Georgia, and South Carolina to conduct agricultural surveys in those states and give his expert advice concerning the renovation of their agriculture.[12]

In the decade of the 1830's the agricultural revolution in the upper South was well on its way. Agricultural societies were founded to exchange information on the best methods of farming, and fairs were held that awarded prizes for superior agricultural products and livestock. Fielding Lewis of Fredericksburg began to use lime instead of marl to neutralize acid soils, with excellent results, an example that was followed by the aristocratic planters in the James River Valley, the Harrisons at *Brandon,* Hill Carter at *Shirley,* and others. John Cocke of *Bremo* urged his fellow Virginians to turn away from the cultivation of tobacco and grow wheat and clover and to abolish the overseer system. Mules were gradually substituted for the slow-moving oxen or the horses of the colonial period. Mules became the ideal draft animal for the Southern plantation, because they were strong, fast at the plow, tough and capable of withstanding the abuse of the slaves, and long-lived. The cradle was substituted for the scythe in reaping wheat. Above all, the work of the reformers rescued Southern agriculture from the control of illiterate and routine-ridden overseers and made farming a serious profession, worthy of study for gentlemen. So significant was the agricultural renaissance based on wheat instead of tobacco and on scientific cultivation that Virginia and Maryland were enjoying a new agricultural prosperity in the last decade of the antebellum period.[13]

The agricultural revolution in the lower South occurred later than the Maryland and Virginia renaissance and differed in several respects from its predecessor. Agricultural reform in the cotton belt was led by a group of planters and farmers in middle Georgia, especially in Hancock County. The reform began partly as a result of low prices for cotton in the decade of the 1840's. Georgia had suffered seriously from the emigration of its young men to the West, from the depletion of its soils by erosion, and from the unintelligent cultivation of cotton. Furthermore, the Georgia land lottery, by which 30 million acres of fresh land in the territory from which the Indians had been removed were presented free to Georgia farmers by a lottery system, had encouraged the abandonment of land instead of the practicing of thrifty agriculture. The reformers of Hancock County, organized into a Planters' Club, determined to stay on their farms and increase their value. Accordingly, led by David Dickson, they developed improved strains of cotton seed, checked erosion, bred quality livestock, introduced such new crops as grasses,

---

[12] See Avery O. Craven, *Edmund Ruffin, Southerner . . .* (New York, 1932).
[13] Avery O. Craven, *Soil Exhaustion As a Factor in the Agricultural History of Virginia and Maryland, 1606–1860* (Urbana, 1932), and Kathleen Bruce, "Virginia Agricultural Decline to 1860: A Fallacy," *Agricultural History* (January 1932), VI, 2–13.

peaches, and strawberries, and adopted more intelligent methods of utilizing slave labor. In 1844, when the price of cotton sank to the lowest point it had ever reached, a Georgia planter, Dimos Ponce, proposed a crop control plan of reducing the acreage of cotton that was quite similar to the New Deal plan of the decade of the 1930's. However, he could not secure the cooperation of the individualistic farmers of the South to put his proposal into operation. Southern farmers tried to increase production by the importation of guano (after 1845) from islands off the coast of Peru and by the use of cotton seed, which had formerly been thrown away, as fertilizer. The efforts of the planters and farmers of Georgia to reform agricultural practices of the cotton belt spread to the lower South. Georgia became known as the "Empire State of the South." [14]

The experiments of Southern planters in growing new crops, in improving the breed of livestock, and in developing scientific methods of agriculture have never been properly appreciated. Thomas Spalding owner of most of Sapelo Island, Georgia, was an example of a planter who was a constant experimenter, seeking to diversify Southern crops. He tried to revive silk culture in Georgia, to develop olive orchards, and to introduce sugar culture in this state.[15] Other planters experimented with different strains of cotton, sent peaches to the New York market, introduced Angora goats from the Orient, and studied methods of conserving the soil through drainage, deep plowing, rotation of crops, and fertilizers. They read papers before numerous agricultural societies, were active in agricultural fairs at which prizes were awarded, and patronized the agricultural periodicals that were founded below the Mason and Dixon line.

Most notable of these publications were *The American Farmer* of Baltimore, founded by John Skinner in 1819, the *American Turf Register and Sporting Magazine,* also edited by Skinner, which contributed much to improving the breed of American horses, and the *Southern Agriculturist* of Charleston. Joseph Bond, a progressive cotton planter of Georgia, sent the *Soil of the South* (published in Columbus, Georgia) to each of his six overseers. The *American Cotton Planter* of Montgomery, Alabama (1853–1861), was edited by a physician, Dr. Noah B. Cloud, who advocated a more diversified economy for the South by growing more grain, raising more stock, and manufacturing textiles from cotton. Another physician, Dr. M. W. Phillips of *Log Hall,* Mississippi, edited the *South-Western Farmer* of Raymond, Mississippi, in which he also advocated the diversification of crops as well as the moral culture of the slaves through *oral* instruction in religious truths. Finally a New Yorker, Dr. Daniel Lee, became the editor of a flourishing publication in Augusta, Georgia, *The Southern Cultivator* (founded in 1843), which had attained a circulation of ten thousand subscribers by 1852. It is interesting

[14] J. C. Bonner, "Genesis of Agricultural Reform in the Cotton Belt," *Journal of Southern History,* IX (November 1943), 473–500.
[15] See E. M. Coulter, *Thomas Spalding of Sapelo* (Baton Rouge, 1940).

to observe that he was converted to the opinion that Southern slavery was "upon the whole a good thing," [16] He became the first professor of agriculture at Franklin College (the University of Georgia), holding a chair established in 1854 by a philanthropist.

Some of the largest fortunes from the pursuit of agriculture were accumulated by the rice planters. The richest of the Carolina rice planters was Nathaniel Heyward, who referred to his rice plantations on the Combahee River as "gold mines." In 1805, during the Napoleonic wars, when rice brought a higher price than at any subsequent time before the Civil War, he made a net profit of $120,000 on his rice plantations. When he died in 1851, he had acquired 17 plantations and 2,087 slaves making him the largest slaveholder of the South. His goal in life seemed to have been to amass slaves continuously and multiply plantations.

Rice planting was not an occupation for the poor man. It required a considerable capital outlay to build the dikes and flood gates along the rivers, to erect the pounding mills that removed the husks and polished the rice, and to maintain large gangs of slaves.[17] The rice plantations of the Carolinas and Georgia were based on economy of concentrated slaveholdings. Governor William Aiken, for example, had a rice plantation on Jehossee Island which had a labor force of 700 slaves. The English actress Fanny Kemble, who married one of the rice grandees of South Carolina, Pierce Butler, kept a journal of her residence on the rice plantation of *Butler's Island* in 1838–1839. She has left a bitterly prejudiced account of slavery and the life of a rice planter.[18] Later she obtained a divorce from her husband, and Butler's fortune fell on evil days, so that after the panic of 1857 he was forced to sell his slaves at auction, 429 men, women, and children, bringing $303,850.

On the other hand, the portrait of an ideal rice planter, James Hamilton Couper on *Hopeton,* on the Altamaha River, has been drawn by the English geologist, Sir Charles Lyell, who has written perhaps the fairest travel account of the Old South. Couper was educated at Yale and by travel in Europe, during which he studied the diking system of Holland. Unlike most Southerners, he kept superb plantation records, which are now preserved in the Southern Collection of the University of North Carolina. He arose at six o'clock in the morning and planned his day on the basis of a strict economy of precious hours. The *Hopeton* plantation employed five hundred slaves of various ages and both sexes. Lyell reported that the Negroes on the plantation lived in neat and comfortable cottages and that they usually received

[16] A. L. Demaree, *The American Agricultural Press, 1819–1860* (New York, 1941), 374; see also E. M. Coulter, *Daniel Lee, Agriculturist: His Life, North and South* Athens, Ga., 1972).

[17] See D. C. Heyward, *Seed from Madagascar* (Chapel Hill, 1937); and J. H. Easterby, *The South Carolina Rice Plantation As Revealed in the Papers of Robert F. W. Allston* (Chicago, 1945).

[18] See Frances Kemble, *Journal of a Residence on a Georgian Plantation*, ed. by John A. Scott (New York, 1961).

Unloading Rice Barges in South Carolina.

Negro Cabins on a Rice Plantation. (Edward King, *The Great South*.)

more food than they could eat. Each prime hand produced about four and one half barrels of rice, each barrel containing five hundred pounds, which sold at prices ranging around 3 or 4 cents a pound. The slaves were managed by a white overseer and a Negro driver who had been the son of a Moham- medan prince of the Foulah tribe. The tasks of the slaves were often com- pleted in five hours. The Negroes were allowed to raise and sell chickens, to sell their catch of fish, and to make cypress tubs and canoes, the latter selling for $4. Punishments were rare. The *Hopeton* plantation, indeed, was a splendid example of paternalism.[19]

The rice industry in South Carolina did not expand very much after the close of the eighteenth century. A major factor in this lack of growth was the competition of cotton, made possible by the Whitney gin. Nevertheless, the rice industry on the Atlantic seaboard reached the high point of its develop- ment in the middle of the nineteenth century, which was also the heydey of slavery, but thereafter it declined. In the antebellum period, the Carolina planters began to process their rice at mills in Charleston instead of on the plantations. They also developed "Carolina Gold Rice," which was superior both to the Oriental and the Mediterranean rice. During the Civil War many of the rice plantations were ruined, their labor forces were scattered, and the mansions of the planters were destroyed by Sherman's army. The rice culture of the Atlantic seaboard never recovered, partly because of the competition of rice lands in Louisiana, Arkansas, and Texas. A series of tropical storms, especially the great one of 1906, destroyed the surviving rice plantations. The abandoned fields relapsed into a state of wild nature, covered with water and reeds, and some of them were converted by wealthy Northern sportsmen into game preserves.

Sugar cane was introduced into Louisiana from Santo Domingo by Jesuit priests, but only syrup was at first produced. After the great slave insurrec- tions in the West Indian island in 1791–1795, Louisiana became the refuge for many of the French sugar planters, who brought with them their knowl- edge and skill in the cultivation of sugar cane. They arrived at a fortunate time, for the failure of the indigo crop as a result of the ravages of insects made the planters eager to find a new crop. In 1795 Etienne de Boré, who had been trained as a soldier in France, met this need by discovering a prac- ticable method of granulating sugar from Louisiana cane juice. His first crop sold for $12,000 and yielded a profit of $5,000, pointing the way to riches in Louisiana. But sugar cane was an exotic in this region, for the growing season did not permit it to attain full maturity, as it did in the West Indies. The cane in the Caribbean Islands is normally a twelve-month crop, but the killing frosts of Louisiana prevented it from maturing and confined the crop to the southern part of the state. In 1817 Louisiana planters introduced from the Philippines ribbon cane, which matured a month earlier than the West Indian

[19] See Sir Charles Lyell, *A Second Visit to the United States of America* (London, 1849), 2 vols.

variety. In the West Indies the cane crop did not require replanting for a dozen years, but in Louisiana, for lucrative returns, it had to be planted every three years. Furthermore, the yield from the same acreage was only half as large as in the West Indies, sometimes only one third. Consequently, Louisiana sugar could compete with the West Indian product only because of the protection of the American tariff and the remarkably fertile soil of the delta region of the lower Mississippi Valley.[20]

By 1849 the expansion of the sugar country in Louisiana reached its height of 1,536 plantations, declining as a result of consolidation to 1,308 in 1859. Efforts were made to extend the area of sugar cane growing into Georgia, Florida, and the Carolinas, but the climate of the more Northern region was not suited to it, and the profits from cotton were greater than those from sugar except in years of low prices for cotton. The cultivation of sugar cane did expand successfully into eastern Texas, where forty plantations were established on the Brazos and other rivers along the last decade of the antebellum period.

The cane was planted by laying the stalks in a furrow and covering them with a plow or a hoe. From the joints of these stalks sprouted the new cane. One fourth to one fifth of the crop had to be saved for replanting—placed in mattresses covered with dirt. The stalks grew higher than a man by the late summer, before the fatal frost fell. Just before the frost was due, the cane was cut by Negro slaves with a cane knife, and the leaves were stripped. The grinding season then began, a time when slaves worked eighteen hours a day and on Sunday as well as on weekdays. After harvesting, the cane was run through rollers that extracted the juice, but fully a third of the juice was reabsorbed by the bagasse (crushed cane) and lost to the planters. The cane juice was boiled, which evaporated the water in the juice, and was clarified by slaked lime; from this process came brown sugar and the by-product, molasses. White sugar was made in refineries, which were usually located in the city.

The equipment on the sugar plantations after the 1830's, when the old horse-driven mills were largely abandoned, was quite expensive, requiring a capital outlay of $12,000 to $14,000. The sugar machinery on large plantations was run by steam engines. The boiling process in open cauldrons required two or three cords of wood for each ton of sugar, but the invention of the vacuum pans greatly reduced the cost of fuel. In 1843 Norbert Rillieux, a brilliant Creole Negro, developed a process of using vacuum pans and evaporators that made whiter and finer sugar than that boiled in kettles. The sugar was stored in large hogsheads of one thousand pounds, which were frequently made by Negro artisans on the plantation.

The sugar plantation was really a capitalistic enterprise, and the sugar planters were businessmen as well as planters. For successful operation the

[20] See J. Carlyle Sitterson, *Sugar Country, the Cane Sugar Industry in the South, 1753–1950* (Lexington, Ky., 1953).

Cutting Sugar Cane in Louisiana. (Edward King, *The Great South*, p. 83)

Breaking Hemp in the Bluegrass Region of Kentucky. (Courtesy of J. Winston Coleman, Jr.)

industry required big plantations, and a much larger proportion of prime field hands, strong sturdy men, was employed than on the cotton plantations. *Magnolia* plantation, in Plaquemine parish, forty-six miles below New Orleans, was a good example of the large sugar plantations, and fortunately its Plantation Journal is preserved in the Southern Collection of the University of North Carolina. This estate consisted of 2,213 acres, of which 950 acres were in cultivation. It had a frontage of two and one third miles on the Mississippi River, which was prevented from flooding the plantation by a high levee. In 1856 it had a working force of 118 adult slaves, of whom 72 were males. In 1861 *Magnolia* produced 1,800 hogsheads of sugar, which placed it fourth in production among the Louisiana plantations. The sugar sold for 7½ cents a pound, and the estate made a gross income from the sale of sugar and molasses of $148,000.[21]

Although huge profits were attained in certain years by the sugar planters, there were various expenses that cut down profits. In fact, the production of these plantations varied tremendously from year to year largely because of the wavering prices and the vicissitudes of the weather. The expansion and contraction of sugar growing were facilitated by the fact that the raising of sugar and cotton could be interchanged in the border sugar parishes. When the price of sugar fell below the margin of profit, some of the planters shifted to cotton growing. An early frost might curtail the crop or a crevasse in the levee might ruin the labor of a season or of years. Cholera or yellow fever might decimate the valuable slaves on the plantation.

In 1854 Frederick Law Olmsted, a Northern traveler, made some intelligent observations concerning the sugar plantations in Louisiana. The owner of a large plantation bought on credit declared that success at operating a sugar plantation was like betting on a throw of dice. The year before Olmsted arrived, the planter had been lucky and had made a crop in which the molasses alone paid all his expenses, and the sale of the sugar brought him 25 per cent on his investment. Many planters went heavily into debt in acquiring plantations with the proper equipment and an adequate force of prime slaves. A few bad crops following each other would throw into bankruptcy a sugar planter who had bought his land on credit. Olmsted cites a profit of over 10 per cent in a favorable year on a plantation with an investment of $147,000.[22] Each slave, who on the average cultivated approximately five acres, produced 5,000 pounds of sugar and 125 gallons of molasses. The molasses sold for 18 cents a gallon and the sugar for 5½ cents a pound, making an earning of $297.50 for each hand. The peak of the production of Louisiana sugar was attained in 1853–1854, when nearly 450,000 hogsheads were produced, a record yield in the antebellum period. Yet this bountiful crop brought con-

[21] J. C. Sitterson, "Magnolia Plantation, 1852–1862: A Decade of a Louisiana Sugar Estate," *Mississippi Valley Historical Review*, XXV (September 1936), 197–210.
[22] Frederick Law Olmsted, *A Journey in the Seaboard Slave States* (New York, 1856), 656–673, 686–688.

siderably less money to the planters than the crop of 1859–1860, which was approximately one half smaller.

The expenses on a sugar plantation were usually higher than those on a cotton plantation. Most sugar plantations produced only a part of the food needed for the slaves. Consequently, they imported considerable quantities of pork, rice, cowpeas, beef, and corn. Also some plantations, such as *Magnolia,* bought the lumber and coal used in the manufacture of sugar from Mississippi flatboatmen. The proprietor had to purchase mules and horses at intervals to replenish his stock. Moreover, large supplies of cheap clothing for the Negroes, agricultural implements, doctor's bills, the cost of freight, the factor's commission of 2½ per cent, and the services of a skilled white sugar-maker and an engineer reduced the net profits derived from the sale of sugar and molasses.

Profits on sugar plantations were possible because of high protection given to the industry by the tariff laws. From 1821 to 1832 there was a specific duty of 3 cents a pound on brown sugar and 4 cents on white sugar—equivalent to an ad valorem duty on crude sugar of around 60 per cent. This munificent protection was reduced to 2½ cents in 1833 and during the decade of the 1850's to less than 1 cent per pound on raw sugar. From 1848 to 1861 the ad valorem protection of sugar was 30 per cent. The sugar planters maintained that sugar could be produced profitably in the West Indies for 3 cents a pound but in Louisiana for not less than 5½ cents a pound. They justified the tariff by pointing out that internal trade with the rest of the Southern states and the Ohio Valley in the purchase of pork, corn, tobacco, and so on, consumed three fifths of the money derived from sugar.

The sugar planters of Louisiana were frequently wealthy and cultured men. Duncan F. Kenner, for example, was sent to Miami University in Ohio and then spent four years of study and travel in Europe. He was active in politics and was a student of the scientific method of growing sugar. During the Civil War this large slaveowner was an advocate of emancipating the slaves in order to secure European recognition. William J. Minor of Natchez, Mississippi, an example of the absentee sugar grower, owned three large plantations in Louisiana containing nine thousand three hundred acres and four hundred slaves, property worth approximately $1 million. His plantations nearly doubled their value in the last decade before the Civil War, although the annual net return on the valuation of the property was only 5½ per cent.[23] Minor studied at the University of Pennsylvania and loved books. Like many of the wealthy sugar planters, he was a Whig, in favor of a protective tariff on sugar and opposed to secession. His rules for his overseers were a model of justice and of understanding human nature. The McCollam

---

[23] J. C. Sitterson, "The William J. Minor Plantation: A Study in Ante-Bellum Absentee Ownership," *Journal of Southern History,* IX (February 1943), 59–74; "Lewis Thompson and his Louisiana Plantation, 1848–1888: A Study in Absentee Ownership," in Fletcher Green (ed.), *Essays in Southern History* (Chapel Hill, 1949).

brothers, who had a plantation called *Ellendale,* were examples of self-made sugar planters. When they acquired *Ellendale* in 1851 for $50,000 it was plastered with twenty-six mortgages, but by 1860 they had developed a plantation worth $150,000, largely through shrewd management. They, too, were Whigs, who sent their children to college and lived the good life. Nevertheless, there were drawbacks to living on a sugar plantation, such as the unhealthiness of the climate in the lowlands, the mosquitoes that "nearly eat you up," breaks in the levees, loneliness, and the tribulations of slave labor.

In contrast to the planters, the small farmers of the South were engaged principally in growing food crops.[24] This absorption in subsistence agriculture can be attributed to their lack of transportation facilities (for many of the small farms were remote from navigable streams or from highways and railroads), to their location in the uplands or regions unsuitable to the growth of staples, to lack of capital, and other factors. The typical farmer raised corn, rye, barley, oats, and wheat. In the coastal plain he might cultivate a patch of sweet potatoes or of peanuts largely to feed hogs or raise sorghum for molasses. He supplemented his crops of grain with raising livestock in small numbers. In the cotton and tobacco districts the small farmers frequently raised a bale of cotton or a small quantity of tobacco for the purpose of obtaining money to buy sugar, salt, powder, and lead. In a modern study of farmers in antebellum Mississippi, the author found that in a representative sample of counties less than 7 per cent of the cotton produced in 1860 was raised by nonslaveholders.[25]

The main crop of the farmers was corn, which was easy to cultivate and admirably suited to the Southern climate and soil. This cereal was far more extensively cultivated than cotton below the Mason-Dixon line. Even in Mississippi, the heart of the Cotton Kingdom, only a bale and a half of cotton per person was produced in 1860, whereas thirty-five bushels of corn were raised for each inhabitant of the state. From this grain the farmers made corn pone, hoe cakes, grits, roasting ears, and they fed their stock. The mountaineers converted this cereal into corn liquor, called bald-face whiskey. which was a potent alcoholic beverage. A single farmer could cultivate thirty acres of corn and obtain thirty bushels an acre from fertile soil as well as harvest a crop of cowpeas planted between the rows. Corn sold for 52 cents a bushel in 1840 and 95 cents in 1859. In 1849 the Southern states produced 60 per cent of the corn grown in the United States, but ten years later the proportion had declined to 52 per cent of the national yield, a result of the opening of the vast cornfields of the Middle West. The largest corn-producing states of the South were Kentucky, Tennessee, and Virginia.[26]

[24] See Blanche Henry Clark, *The Tennessee Yeoman, 1840–1860* (New York, 1941); and Frank L. Owsley, *Plain Folk of the Old South* (Baton Rouge, 1949).
[25] Herbert Weaver, *Mississippi Farmers, 1850–1860* (Nashville, 1945), 100–101; see also John H. Moore, *Agriculture in Ante-Bellum Mississippi, 1850–1860* (New York, 1958); and Charles S. Davis, *The Cotton Kingdom in Alabama* (Montgomery, 1939).
[26] Donald L. Kemmerer, "The Pre-Civil War South's Leading Crop: Corn," in *Agricultural History,* XXIII (1949), 236–239.

Wheat was another important crop of the yeoman farmer. It was grown extensively in the upper South, but it did not thrive in the lower South. Furthermore, cornbread was the staple of Southern diet, and bread made from flour was regarded as a luxury. With inadequate scientific knowledge the wheat farmer had to struggle at times against the ravages of the Hessian fly and of such diseases as smut and rust. He learned, nevertheless, to increase the production of his crop from six bushels an acre in Tidewater Virginia at the beginning of the nineteenth centry to twelve or fifteen bushels on an average in the decade of the 1830's, as a result of the introduction of clover as a cover crop and of plaster to increase fertility. Wheat was grown in Maryland, Virginia, and North Carolina as a staple crop by many large planters, as well as by the yeomen. Virginia was the leading wheat-producing state of the South, and Richmond and Baltimore were two of the largest centers in the United States for milling flour. During the sixty years of the antebellum period the average price for wheat was $1.14 a bushel, but just before the Civil War it sold for $1.40 a bushel.

The Southern states surpassed the Northern states in the raising of livestock during the antebellum period. In 1860 the fifteen Southern states had approximately three eighths of the population of the nation, including the Negroes. Nevertheless, the South could boast of owning 90 per cent of the mules in the country, 60 per cent of the swine, nearly 45 per cent of the horses, 52 per cent of the oxen, and more than one half of the poultry. Although the South had 40 per cent of the dairy cows of the country, it produced less than 20 per cent of the butter and only 1 per cent of the cheese made in the United States. The slaves, in general, were not fed on dairy products, except buttermilk, and the absence of ice and the lack of near markets discouraged the production of milk and butter in extensive quantity. The Southern farmers also failed to take proper care of their hogs or to breed for quality. The typical Southern hog was a plebeian animal, often called a razorback, who roamed in the woods and meadows, shifting for himself.[27]

The concept of the Southern states devoting their agricultural energies to a one-sided cultivation of staple crops for export omits the role of the yeoman farmers. Although some areas of large plantations, such as the sugar-producing district, imported a considerable proportion of their food and livestock and even bales of hay, the South as a whole supplied its own food, with a surplus to spare. Most cotton planters raised bountiful crops of corn, and those planters who purchased corn and meat for their slaves justified this practice on the ground that the labor of the slave was more valuable in producing staple crops.[28] Nevertheless, it has been observed by a penetrating

---

[27] See Paul C. Henlein, *Cattle Kingdom in the Ohio Valley, 1783–1860* (Lexington, Ky., 1959), and Eugene D. Genovese, *The Political Economy of Slavery: Studies in the Economy and Society of the Slave South* (New York, 1965), chap. 5.

[28] A case history of a successful cotton planter in the black belt of Alabama who tried to make his plantation produce adequate food for his slaves and failed is recorded by W. T. Jordan, *Hugh Davis and His Alabama Plantation* (University, Ala., 1948), chap. 6.

student that the South as a whole practiced a less diversified type of agriculture in 1860 than in 1850.[29] During this decade cotton was bringing high prices, and according to the census reports there was a decline within the decade in the per capita production of such basic food materials as corn and hogs, although wheat production increased.

A constant criticism that has been made of Southern agriculture was its excessive devotion to one crop, such as cotton, and the consequent failure to diversify its agriculture. However, there were strong economic reasons to condone this persistence in the one-crop economy, which became even more dominant after the Civil War. The lack of adequate transportation facilities was a vital factor in the rule of King Cotton. Cotton was easy to transport along the rivers, dirt roads, and railroads of the South; it did not spoil waiting for transportation or for a market, as wheat or corn might. To experiment with perishable crops was a risky business before the days of the refrigerated cars. Furthermore, merchants and factors who furnished credit to farmers frequently insisted on the planting of cotton.

The factors, or commercial agents of the planters, were the key figures in the marketing of the staple crops.[30] They were often Northerners or Englishmen who had countinghouses or warehouses in the leading Southern ports and inland shipping towns. To them the planters sent their staple crops to be sold either to buyers of Northern or English houses or forwarded directly to Liverpool or New York. The factor was a versatile man of business in an agrarian society who performed many different services for the planter in addition to selling his crops. He purchased or sold slaves for his client, arranged for the hiring of slaves or the placing of the planter's children in distant schools, gave advice concerning the condition of the market or the advisability of selling or withholding his crop, and bought for his client a large proportion of the plantation supplies.[31]

The factorage system was a development in the specialization of labor in the South. The planter was relieved of the responsibilities of selling his crop and buying his supplies and could, therefore, devote his energies to the problems of slave management and the production of staple crops. But he frequently paid a high price for the services of the factor. The cotton factor received not only 2.5 per cent commission for selling the staple crops but also charged a commission varying from 2.5 per cent to 10 per cent for buying supplies for the plantation. From the planter's balance on his books the factor also deducted a standard rate for insurance, storage, drayage, weighing, mending, and so on, in some instances receiving a rebate from the business firms supplying these services. Some of the rice planters, however, such as Robert F. W. Allston, established such favorable connections with

[29] R. R. Russel, *Economic Aspects of Southern Sectionalism, 1840–1861* (Urbana, Ill., 1924), 203.
[30] See H. D. Woodman, *King Cotton and Its Retainers* (Lexington, Ky., 1968).
[31] For the portrait of a successful factor in the South, see Clement Eaton, *The Mind of the Old South* (Baton Rouge, 1967), chap. 3, The Commercial Mind: The New Orleans Merchant, Maunsel White.

their factors that they rendered many miscellaneous services for the privilege of handling the sale of, the rice. Indeed, one of the modern studies of the rice factor indicates that he realized only a moderate profit from his transactions with the planters and did not unduly exploit his strategic position.[32]

The factor performed a valuable service in furnishing credit to the planter until his crops were harvested. Bishop Leonidas Polk, for example, received an advance of $25,000 from his factor on his growing sugar crop. One of the more serious indictments against the factor has been that he exploited the planter by charging exorbitant rates of interest. The antebellum period was an era of high interest rates in various sections of the country. Planters paid as much as 12 per cent or more for loans during times of depression. On the other hand, the papers of Elisha F. King, one of the wealthy planters of the black belt of Alabama who usually had a favorable balance in his accounts with the numerous factors he employed, show that he paid only 2.5 per cent interest on loans from his factors and that he received a similar rate of interest for his surplus money kept on deposit by them. The planter used the factor as a means of providing a checking account, against which he issued drafts or due bills in settling debts or purchasing Negroes and land.[33]

The old view of the factor as an outrageous exploiter is a one-sided picture, based primarily on the papers of the planters. The much-aligned factor has received more favorable treatment than is usually accorded him in a monograph on Ebenezer Pettigrew, an enlightened grain planter of eastern North Carolina. Pettigrew sent his wheat to New York, his corn to Charleston, and his forest products—lumber, shingles, and staves—to Norfolk or Baltimore. The firm of New York factors with whom he dealt had branches in the North Carolina ports of Edenton and Plymouth. The factors often saved money for the planter by their advice when to sell and buy, based on an elaborate crop-reporting system, which furnished information about the effects of drought, floods, and disease on growing crops. Some of these commercial agents were vertical factors, who not only did a commission business —but also owned wholesale stores, ships, ropewalks, brick kilns, and so on. The factors tried to get the best prices for the staples of their patrons and the fact that many of them went into bankruptcy may throw some light on whether they exploited the planter. The exorbitant freight rates for shipping staples to New York seem to have been a much greater grievance of the planters than the factors' commissions. Pettigrew tried to free himself from vassalage to grasping ship owners by building his own schooner, *Lady of the Lake,* which proved to be very successful. Only a few planters, however, adopted this device to eliminate excessive transportation rates.[34]

The occupation of the gentleman farmer in the antebellum South was in

[32] J. H. Easterby, "The South Carolina Rice Factor As Revealed in the Papers of Robert F. W. Allston," *Journal of Southern History,* VII (May 1941), 160–172.

[33] See Ralph H. Haskins, "Planter and Cotton Factor in the Old South; Some Areas of Friction," *Agricultural History,* XXIX (1955), 1–14.

[34] Bennett H. Wall, "Ebenezer Pettigrew, an Economic Study of an Ante-Bellum Planter," Doctoral dissertation, University of North Carolina, 1947.

some respects a delectable avocation. But it is a mistake to think of the life of the average Southern farmer as an independent one. If he grew staple crops for export, foreign wars might cut off his markets and overproduction cause his bountiful crops to bring ruinous prices. American farmers were individualists who never worked out a plan to control production and ensure fair prices. The Southern farmer, moreover, was a hostage to Nature, with no insurance against the destruction of his crops by drought, hail, storms, and injurious insects. Epidemics might carry off his valuable slaves, or the slave might run away. Although insurance was occasionally taken out on the lives of slaves, this practice was not generally followed. Fortunately, the Mexican boll weevil had not crossed the Rio Grande at this period to devastate the cotton region. If this plague had come before the Civil War instead of a half century later, one is tempted to speculate whether this would have led to an early emancipation of the slaves. The Atlantic seaboard farmer had to meet the competition of the virgin soils that had been recently opened in the Southwest. Enlightened planters, such as Senator James Barbour of Orange County, Virginia, the owner of 20,000 acres of land, sought to raise the standard of farming by innovative methods, but the great majority of yeoman farmers stubbornly pursued the traditional methods. Rather than change their habits, many of them chose to emigrate to the fertile Southwest, where they pursued their old habits of wasting the soil.[35] All Southern farmers, except for the sugar and hemp planters, believed themselves to be exploited by the Federal protective tariff. Most of them were in semi-vassalage to their factors, who sold the crops for them and advanced credit at high rates of interest. Finally, a majority of planters and farmers had to rely on the reluctant and often inefficient labor of slaves, who were a constant source of exasperation to their master unless he adopted a philosophy of fatalism or resignation, although the inefficiency of the slaves as laborers in the fields, as will be shown in the next chapter, has been exaggerated by racist writers.

[35] J. B. Boles (ed.), *America: The Middle Period, Essays in Honor of Bernard Mayo* (Charlottesville, 1973), chap. 10, "James Barbour, A Progressive Farmer of Ante-Bellum Virginia."

13

Slave Labor—Was It Profitable?

THE STUDY of American Negro slavery has a new relevance today, for it lies at the roots of the great struggle for racial equality in the United States at the present time. The institution of slavery in the Old South was not merely a means of human exploitation but a system of race control and relationships. In the land of Dixie, as in other parts of the world, such as South Africa, where black men have dwelt in considerable numbers within white societies, there has arisen the mysterious chasm of race and color. DuBose Heyward, in his vivid story "Porgy," has portrayed the subtle psychological sense of differentness the Negro feels toward the white man, his ways, and his God. The white man, on the other hand, has often wondered what the Negro was thinking and feeling. On April 13, 1861, Mrs. Chesnut observed in her famous diary that the outward demeanor of the Negro servants seemed to be unchanged by the war, and she could not fathom their real feeling, whether they were genuinely apathetic "or wiser than we are; silent and strong, biding their time?" [1] Small children do not seem to be aware of the barrier of race. Moreover, the realization of a common humanity between whites and blacks becomes keener as the Negro elevates himself by education and the acquisition of wealth, and as the white man meets him on intellectual and artistic levels. But in the Old South the barrier of race, lurking fear of insurrection, and the repulsion at the thought of amalgamation immeasurably strengthened the chains of slavery.

The Negro slave was the answer to the expanding Cotton Kingdom's need for a large supply of cheap agricultural labor. The original source of supply of black labor for Southern agriculture, the African slave trade, was closed by the legislatures of most of the Southern states during and following the Revolution. At the time of the Federal Constitutional Convention, Georgia, alone among the Southern states, permitted the importation of slaves from Africa, and in 1798 Georgia prohibited the maritime slave trade. In 1808 the African slave trade, which had been tolerated for the preceding twenty years as a result of one of the compromises of the Constitutional Convention, was prohibited by Congress. Humanitarian reasons for this closure of the African slave trade were bolstered by economic motives, the fear that further importation would decrease the value of slaves already held and would lead to an overproduction of staple crops. Furthermore, the introduction of large numbers of Africans would increase the danger of servile insurrection. In

---

[1] Mary B. Chesnut, *A Diary from Dixie* (New York, 1929), 38.

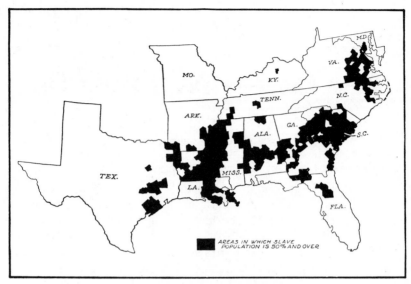

The Black Belt in 1860

South Carolina a long-continued debate occurred between the wealthy conservatives, who were opposed to reopening the slave trade, and the radicals, led by a Charleston merchant, Alexander Gillon, who favored the resumption of this cruel traffic. The legislature was finally persuaded in 1803 to legalize the importation of Negroes from Africa and the West Indies. For the next four years there occurred a hectic importation of slaves for speculation and for sale in the state as well as in other parts of the South. During this period South Carolina brought in nearly forty thousand Negro bondsmen, absorbing such a large portion of capital that it affected business enterprises.[2]

After 1808 slaves from Africa or the West Indies could be brought into the United States only by smuggling. In 1820 Congress tried to stop smuggling by declaring the maritime slave trade piracy, which exacted a penalty so severe that juries were reluctant to convict offenders; only one violator of the law, the New England Captain Nathaniel Gordon, was hanged—in 1862. The United States entered into a treaty with England in 1842 for a joint patrol of the west coast of Africa to suppress the nefarious traffic, but anglophobia prevented an agreement to allow British warships to search suspicious American vessels. Although these slavers, owned almost entirely by Northerners or foreigners, engaged extensively in the slave trade between Africa and Brazil and Cuba, they seldom attempted to land slaves in the Southern states. In 1858 the *Wanderer,* owned apparently by C. A. L. Lamar of Georgia, a notorious advocate of the opening of the African slave trade, landed between three hundred and four hundred Africans on the Georgia

[2] See Elizabeth Donnan (ed.), *Documents Illustrative of the Slave Trade to America* (Washington, 1930–35), 4 vols.

coast near Jekyll Island.[3] This flagrant violation of federal law caused Jacob Thompson, Secretary of the Interior, to dispatch a special agent, Benjamin Slocumb, to investigate rumors that slaves were being smuggled into the Southern states. Slocumb traveled over the South, but could not find anything to substantiate the rumors; he reported that Southern sentiment as a whole was very hostile to the smuggling of slaves or to the revival of the African slave trade.[4] This finding is contradictory to the conclusion of the Negro historian W. E. B. DuBois, who greatly exaggerated the extent of smuggling slaves into the United States in his Harvard doctoral thesis on the suppression of the African slave trade.[5] It is significant that the census takers of 1870, who cannot, however, be relied upon for strict accuracy, could find only about two thousand Negroes in the United States that admitted African birth. U. B. Phillips in his study *American Negro Slavery* has declared that "these importations were never great enough to affect the labor supply in appreciable degree."[6]

The closure of the African slave trade made the upper South the nursery of surplus slaves. When the slave trade ended legally, approximately 1 million slaves were in the United States to produce the future laborers of the South, who in 1860 numbered about 4 million. The invention of the cotton gin and the westward movement of population into the Gulf region led to the growth of a flourishing internal slave traffic between the upper and lower South. The oldest tobacco-producing states had a large surplus of servants to sell to the eager cotton planters of the deep South. The extent of the internal slave trade has been greatly exaggerated by earlier writers on the subject. Robert Fogel and Stanley Engerman in their recent thorough study of the economics of American Negro slavery have concluded that 80 per cent of the slaves taken to the Southwest were transported, not by slave traders, but by emigrating masters. Only an average of three thousand slaves a year were sold from East to West from 1810 to 1860, the greatest periods of the internal slave trade being in the decades of the 1830's and 1850's. New Orleans (by far the largest slave market in the lower South) had a law requiring the registration of slave sales in order to acquire legal title.[7] From these statistics it appears that less than 10 per cent of the slaves sold involved the separation of husbands and wives from each other, and that the sales of children under thirteen years of age represented 9.5 per cent of the total sales. Many of these

---

[3] For the fascinating story of the *Wanderer,* see T. H. Wells, *The Slave Ship* Wanderer (Athens, Ga., 1967).

[4] W. S. Howard, *American Slavers and the Federal Law* (Berkeley, 1963).

[5] W. E. B. DuBois, "The Enforcement of the Slave Trade Laws," *Annual Report of the American Historical Association for the Year 1891* (Washington, 1892), 173; also *The Suppression of the African Slave-Trade to the United States* (New York, 1896).

[6] U. B. Phillips, *American Negro Slavery* (New York, 1918), 147; Philip P. Curtin, *The Atlantic Slave Trade; A Census,* estimates the number of slaves smuggled into the U.S. as about one thousand a year.

[7] Robert W. Fogel and S. L. Engerman, *Time on the Cross: The Economics of American Negro Slavery* (Boston, 1974), I, 49–50.

children were orphans. These figures tend to lessen the horror of the internal slave trade as portrayed in the abolitionist stereotype and by neo-abolitionist writers.[8]

The slave trade was conducted by a group of men called "Nigger traders," who made considerable fortunes from the traffic. There is disagreement among observers as to whether Southern society looked down upon these merchants of men.[9] The tradition is that Southerners despised the slave traders, and that, although they associated with them freely in business transactions, they did not accept the slave traders socially. Nevertheless, some successful slave traders occupied respectable positions in Southern society. Nathan Bedford Forrest, the celebrated cavalry leader of the Confederacy, was a slave trader of Memphis whose profits exceeded $50,000 annually. In 1858, Forrest was elected alderman of Memphis. In Charleston, Louis de Saussure and Thomas Norman Gadsden, both of whom came from aristocratic families, were prominent slave traders, although they called themselves by euphemistic titles, such as "auctioneers," "brokers," "commission merchants." De Saussure had a beautiful home on the Battery and derived an income of nearly $11,000 from commissions in the slave trade. The most eminent slave-trading firm in the South was Franklin and Armfield, with buying headquarters at Alexandria in the District of Columbia and selling depots at Natchez, Mississippi, and New Orleans. Isaac Franklin married the daughter of a Presbyterian preacher, built a beautiful mansion in the Nashville Basin, and left an estate of $750,000.

The slaves who were sent to the lower South were usually young men and women in their early twenties, in other words, "prime fieldhands." They were given new suits of clothes and oiled or "spruced up" for the auction. Buyers examined them carefully, especially their hands, needed for picking cotton, and their backs to see that they were free from the scars of frequent whipping. They were transported to the lower South either in coastal ships or overland by slave coffles, in which the men were manacled and the women and children followed unfettered. Occasionally slaves who were being transported by sea seized control of the ship and steered into a West India port, as was the case of the *Creole,* in 1841, which entered Nassau, where the slaves were liberated. The upper South tried to get rid of their vicious and intractable Negroes by selling them to the slave traders doing business with the lower South. Consequently, the states of the lower South passed legislation against the introduction of criminal slaves and required a certificate of good character with each slave imported for sale. Indeed, these states pur-

---

[8] See William Calderwood, "How Extensive Was the Border State Slave Trade? A New Look." *Civil War History,* XVIII (1972), 42–55.

[9] Frederic Bancroft, *Slave-Trading in the Old South* (Baltimore, 1931) challenged the traditional view that slave traders were detested and W. H. Stephenson, *Isaac Franklin, Slave Trader and Planter of the Old South* (Baton Rouge, 1938) tends to support Bancroft's position, but there is too much contrary evidence to accept it uncritically. Bancroft was highly prejudiced, and some of his conclusions are discredited by recent scholarship.

sued a vacillating course of prohibiting the introduction of slaves for the purpose of sale and then repealing such legislation.

The worst feature of the internal slave trade was the breakup of Negro families. Only Louisiana and later Alabama, by an act of 1852, had laws prohibiting the sale of a child under ten years old from its mother. None of the Southern states prohibited the separation of husband and wife by sale. The numerous sheriff sales of bankrupts and the division of slaves in wills formed constant threats to the forcible separation of Negro families. This separation of slave families was one of the unhappy consequences of the westward movement. White families were also broken up, frequently forever, by the migration of younger sons to the West. On the other side of the balance sheet it must be noted that Southerners made an effort to prevent the separation of Negro families and that many of the wills specifically stipulated that slave families should not be divided or sold out of the state, the country, or even out of the family.

The prices of slaves tended to vary in proportion to the price of cotton. In 1860, however, the cost of slaves was out of all proportion to the profits obtained from cotton, for prime fieldhands were selling from $1,200 to $1,800 while cotton was selling for 11½ cents. In 1800, when cotton was bringing 36 cents, prime field hands cost only $400. The price of slaves was booming in 1858–1859, when Pullman and Betts, "Auctioneers for Sale of Negroes," at Richmond, Virginia, gave the following quotations: "No. One Men bring $1500 to $1550, No. One Girls $1300 to $1350; Boys & Girls from 10 years old to 14 years sell better than we ever saw them sell, 4 feet Boys $500 to $550, Girls the same, and so on increasing as they go up in size and likeliness" (MS in possession of the author).

The price of black servants had approximately quadrupled during a period of sixty years, but cotton had declined to one fourth its price at the opening of the nineteenth century. Part of this discrepancy in the ratio of cotton and slave values may be accounted for by the fact that slaves could produce more cotton per hand in 1860 than in 1800. During the last decade of the antebellum period, moreover, there was a tremendous speculation in property in slaves, a veritable "Negro fever," which artificially increased their value. Other reasons for this factitious value of slaves were the social distinction involved in owning slaves and the inflationary movement produced by the mining of California gold. During the last decade of the antebellum period there was a dearth of hands for the rapidly expanding agricultural region of the Southwest, and new demands for labor were opening in the development of tobacco factories, iron works, construction of railroads, and mining. These facts tended to modify the old rule that the price of slaves was dependent on the price of cotton. The purchase price of slaves began to be based on the hiring wages. At the close of the eighteenth century a prime slave could be hired for $70 a year, plus board and medical expenses, but in 1860 slave factory hands were hired for $200 to $225 annually and agricultural hands for $150 a year.

The high cost of slaves in the last decade of the antebellum period had certain unfortunate results. It led to a movement for reopening the African slave trade in order to furnish the small farmer with black labor. It was argued that the reopening of the foreign slave trade would democratize the system of Southern slavery and lead to the solidarity of the South in the defense of its "peculiar institution." In 1856 Leonidas Spratt, an editor of South Carolina, was one of the outstanding propagandists for this move. He had the support of Governor James H. Adams of that state and of certain prominent publicists, such as De Bow of *De Bow's Review* and Edward Pollard, a journalist of Virginia. In 1859 the Southern Commercial Convention at Vicksburg adopted resolutions in favor of reviving the African slave trade. A minority led by Henry S. Foote published a protest, pointing out that the slave states of Virginia, North Carolina, Kentucky, and Missouri were unrepresented at the convention and that the proposal "has been mainly sustained in this body by avowed disunionists. . . ."[10] The states of the upper South, which had a surplus of slaves to sell, were opposed to the agitation for the reopening of the African slave trade. They maintained that the revival of the maritime slave trade would increase the danger of servile insurrection and would be accompanied by great cruelty. The large planters in general tended to oppose a movement that would depreciate the value of their slave property.

There were three types of organization of slave labor: the task system, the gang system, and the system on small farms. The task system was in general use in the rice and sea-island cotton districts and in the hemp country, where tasks were assigned to each laborer to be completed within a day. In the rice districts slaves often finished their tasks before two or three o'clock in the afternoon and enjoyed the leisure of the rest of the day. In the tobacco, short-staple cotton, and sugar districts the gang system prevailed, in which the gang worked under an overseer. The field slaves under this system worked from sunrise to sunset, with a two-hour rest period in the middle of the day. These long hours of work were standard practice of the time, for the white farmers and factory hands of New England also worked from "dark to dark." In the lower, but not usually in the upper South, on large plantations a Negro driver aided the overseer in superintending the slaves. He set the pace of work and was responsible for seeing that the slaves did not do slovenly work. He acted also as a policeman in the Negro quarters and often did the whipping, in the presence of the overseer, when slaves needed disciplining.[11]

The small-farm type of slavery is illustrated in the early life of Booker T.

[10] J. D. B. *De Bow's Review,* XXVII (1859), 470.
[11] Slavery on the large plantations is described by C. S. Sydnor, *Slavery in Mississippi* (New York, 1933) and in documents in Clement Eaton, *The Leaven of Democracy, the Growth of the Democratic Spirit in the Time of Jackson* (New York, 1963), Parts IV and VI; Ina Van Noppen (ed.), *The South, a Documentary History* (Princeton, 1957; and Katherine Jones (ed.), *The Plantation South* (Indianapolis, 1957), and U. B. Phillips and J. D. Glunt (eds.), *Florida Plantation Records* (St. Louis, 1927).

Washington, who was born a slave on a farm near Roanoke, Virginia, in 1858 or 1859. His master, James Burroughs, lived with his wife and thirteen children in a two-story log house. He owned two female slaves, forty and forty-one years of age, a man twenty-two years old, and four children. Booker's mother was the cook for the farm and lived with her three children in the log kitchen. The little mulatto boy and his brother and sister slept on a bed made of rags on the dirt floor. Booker's only garment was an uncomfortable flax shirt, but this was not unusual; indeed many of the "pickaninnies" ran about the plantations naked. The farmer and his sons worked with the slaves in the fields, cultivating the crops of wheat and corn. Although the slaves do not seem to have been well fed or clothed during the war period, there was a friendly feeling between them and the white family, and a whipping was a rare event. Some of the small farmers, however, were hard taskmasters who sought to get as much labor out of their slaves as possible. Frederick Douglass's experience in being hired to a small farmer in Maryland who had the reputation of a "slave breaker," or harsh disciplinarian, indicates that slavery on a small farm could be grimmer than on the large commercial plantations of the Southwest.[12]

The abolitionists popularized the idea that the slaves on the large plantations of the lower South were deliberately worked to death.[13] Although it may be true that slavery had harsher features on some of the large "factory plantations" of the Southwest than on the typical farm of the upper South, the evidence does not warrant such statements of barbarity. In addition to the caricature of Southern slavery by the abolitionists, the planters of the upper South blackened the reputation of the lower South in order to use the threat of selling a slave "down the river" for disciplinary purposes. Mark Twain has vividly described, in *Puddin'head Wilson,* the terror of the slaves of being sold "down the river."

Modern research has dispelled some of the false conceptions of the slavery regime propagated by the abolitionists, who generalized isolated cases of cruelty as typical of the treatment of the slaves.[14] The slaves had a wonderful

[12] See Samuel R. Spencer, Jr., *Booker T. Washington and the Negro's Place in American Life* (Boston, 1955), Louis R. Harlan, *Booker T. Washington, the Making of a Black Leader, 1856–1901* (New York, 1972), and Frederick Douglass, *Narrative of the Life . . . of an American Slave* (Boston, 1845).

[13] For a presentation of views of slavery by the abolitionists, see Dwight Dumond, *Antislavery: The Crusade for Freedom in America* (Ann Arbor, 1961); and Louis Filler, *The Crusade Against Slavery 1830–1860* (New York, 1960), the latter a well-balanced work.

[14] Realistic modern studies of slavery in the different states include, besides Sydnor's study, R. B. Flanders, *Plantation Slavery in Georgia* (Chapel Hill, 1933); R. H. Taylor, *Slave-Holding in North Carolina* (Chapel Hill, 1926); J. Winston Coleman, Jr., *Slavery Times in Kentucky* (Chapel Hill, 1940); Orville W. Taylor, *Negro Slavery in Arkansas* (Durham, 1958); J. G. Taylor, *Negro Slavery in Louisiana* (Baton Rouge, 1963); James B. Sellers, *Slavery in Alabama* (University, Ala., 1950); Chase C. Mooney, *Slavery in Tennessee* (Bloomington, 1957); and Edward Phifer, "Slavery in Microcosm: Burke County, North Carolina," *Journal of Southern History,* XXVIII

power of passive resistance, which tended to prevent overwork. Frederick Law Olmsted estimated that the Southern slave did about half the work of the average white farmhand in the North.[15] On the cotton plantations of the lower South the evidence indicates that the slaves did a very moderate amount of work. The records show that during the cotton-picking season, the average quantity of cotton picked per hand was one hundred and fifty pounds a day, although superior slaves could pick three hundred and fifty to five hundred pounds a day. In the postwar South the average amount of cotton picked by Negroes remained virtually the same as in antebellum days.[16] Furthermore, the average acreage of cotton and corn cultivated by a prime Negro hand, eight acres of cotton and four of corn, was not excessive. On the sugar plantations of Louisiana the slaves labored very hard during the grinding season, but they liked this phase of their work better than their less strenuous occupations, for during this period they were given extra food, abundant coffee, and drams of liquor. The accusation that slaves in the lower South were killed by cruel treatment and inhuman work is refuted by vital statistics of the plantations. The slaves of *Magnolia* plantation in Louisiana, for example, more than reproduced themselves during the decade 1852–1862. In the 5 years preceding the Civil War there were only 11 runaways from the plantation out of a labor force of 118 slaves, and most of them were back at work within a week.

In addition to working for their masters in the fields slaves were often hired out as servants in town, factory hands, laborers in building railroads, steamboat hands, miners, and skilled mechanics. Henry Clay wrote to his overseer in 1833, instructing him to rent one of his slaves, provided the latter gave his consent. "If Messrs. Bruce and Gratz," he directed, "will give $120 for Abraham, and he is willing to go, you may hire him to them." [17] This practice of getting the slave's consent for hiring or even for sale was not uncommon in the Old South. John W. Coleman, hemp manufacturer of Woodford County, Kentucky, stipulated in his contracts for hiring slaves: "I am to treat said men well, feed, and clothe them, and pay taxes and physicians' bills, etc., and return them well clothed." [18] In some of his con-

---

(May 1962), 137–165; H. A. Trexler, *Slavery in Missouri, 1804–1865* (Baltimore, 1914). See also Avery Craven, *The Repressible Conflict 1830–1861* (University, La., 1939), chap. 2; John Hope Franklin, *From Slavery to Freedom: A History of American Negroes* (New York, 1973); and Julia H. Smith, *Slavery and Plantation Growth in Antebellum Florida, 1821–1860* (Gainesville, 1973).

[15] See Arthur M. Schlesinger, Sr. (ed.), *The Cotton Kingdom . . . by Frederick Law Olmsted* (New York, 1953); Olmsted noted that it took four house servants to do the work of one in the North, p. 9.

[16] See Charles S. Sydnor, *Slavery in Mississippi* (New York, 1933); for a different view, see Solomon Northrup, *Twelve Years a Slave* (Buffalo, 1854).

[17] "Memo. of H. Clay for Mr. Martin made the 20th of Sept., 1833," MS owned by J. Winston Coleman, Jr., of Lexington, Kentucky.

[18] Contract of John W. Coleman with John McQuiddie, December 29, 1831, John W. Coleman MSS, 1828–1833, owned by J. Winston Coleman, Jr.

tracts for slave labor he promised to pay the slave $5 a year as a reward for good behavior. In the 1840's and 1850's owners were able to hire out their slaves for annual rents, averaging 12 to 15 per cent of their value.

The practice of hiring slaves was especially prevalent in the upper South. In Richmond there were slave-hiring brokers, such as Lewis and Robert Hall, whose papers in the Huntington Library vividly illuminate the practice of slave hiring. Letters to these agents show that they charged masters 7.5 per cent for arranging the hire of slaves. A striking characteristic of the letters of masters to the slave-hiring brokers is the humanitarian concern they show not only for the health of the slave but for considering his wishes and trying to secure good treatment for him. In many cases hiring represented an intermediate stage between freedom and bondage for the slaves. In the tobacco factories of Virginia, for example, the slave hired hands worked during a ten-hour day according to the task system and were paid for overwork, so that most slaves earned for themselves a bonus of at least $5 a month and some $20. Moreover they enjoyed many privileges that the slaves of the plantation did not have, such as receiving sums of money to find their own sleeping quarters and meals. In the cities the hired slaves from the country became more sophisticated, and insensibly the bonds of slavery were loosened. Indeed, slavery appeared to be breaking down in the cities at the close of the antebellum period.[19]

The growing expensiveness of hired slave labor had a part in a more humane treatment of hired slaves, such as occurred in the iron industry of Virginia. The iron industry employed the task system, which allowed greater flexibility in dealing with the slaves. The owner of slaves would as a rule hire out their slaves only to employers for whom the slaves consented to work. The ironmasters found that, because of severe competition for hired slaves, it was folly to abuse their workers, for an unsavory reputation was a distinct handicap in obtaining slave laborers. Also, they found it wise to practice the incentive system. Accordingly, slaves who finished their tasks could earn money by extra work, being paid for this work at the same rate that white labor was compensated. As a result of this policy a large proportion of the hired slaves in the Virginia iron industry, especially those who had acquired skills or served in a supervisory capacity, earned considerable sums of money, which they expended for luxuries—coffee, sugar, fancy clothes—and even a few put their money in savings banks.[20] Charles B. Dew has found in the records of ironmasters of Virginia that not only did they practice the incentive system, but they tried to preserve the black family as

[19] Clement Eaton, "Slave-Hiring in the Upper South: A Step toward Freedom," *Mississippi Valley Historical Review*, XLVI (1960), 663–678.
[20] See Charles B. Dew, "Discipling Slave Ironworkers in the Antebellum South: Coercion, Conciliation, and Accommodation," *American Historical Review*, vol. 79 (April, 1974), 393–418; also "David Rose and the Oxford Iron Works: A Study of Industrial Slavery in the Early Nineteenth-Century South," *William and Mary Quarterly*, XXXI (April, 1974), 189–224.

a working unit so that fathers taught their skills to their sons. Negroes with a remarkable range of skills were quite common and were often employed as supervisors and in other responsible positions; Abram, the slave in charge of the blast furnace at Oxford Iron Works near Lynchburg, Virginia, for example was described by his master as a Negro of unblemished character, of great good sense, and of "untarnished" honor.

The problems involved in slave hiring are illustrated by the experience of the Tredegar Iron Works of Richmond, the largest iron manufacturing company in the South. Some of the slave hands were owned by the company, but over half were hired, at rates ranging from $100 a year in 1849 to $175 a year in 1860. The incentive system was employed with very favorable results as was the practice of many of the plantations. The Negro laborers of the company were taught the skills needed in the iron industry by white mechanics imported from the North. In 1847 this situation led to a strike by the white mechanics, who demanded that slaves should not be used in the skilled processes of puddling and rolling. Joseph R. Anderson, president of the company, replied that he would not relinquish his constitutional right to employ or discharge anyone at his pleasure and notified the white strikers that they had discharged themselves. After this event, Anderson began more extensively to employ slaves, who made satisfactory employees. White mechanics, however, were reluctant to teach Negroes their acquired skills in the iron industry, for they feared that the Negroes would later usurp their jobs. Despite Anderson's innovation of using Negro labor in the skilled processes of the iron industry, there occurred a marked decline by the end of the 1850's in the proportion of slaves employed by the Tredegar Company. Such a decline does not seem to have been the result of inefficiency of Negro workers but rather to the sharp increase in the hiring prices of slaves.[21] Although the use of slaves in the Tredegar Iron Works after they were trained cut costs by 12 per cent, Tredegar's cost of slave labor in producing manufactured iron was still far more expensive than the cost of free labor in Northern rolling mills and three times more expensive than such labor in the European iron industry—truly a remarkable paradox.

The great majority of hired slaves were domestics, many of whom lived in the cities and towns. Only 5 per cent of the Southern slaves were employed in industry, and of these only one fifth were hired, whereas four fifths were owned by the industries, which presumably would seek to take care of their valuable human chattels.[22] Furthermore, the lot of a small minority of slaves was ameliorated by their being allowed to hire their time from the master by paying a stipulated sum each week after which the slave was free to engage his services, often those of skilled craftsmen, to others at a considerably higher rate. This practice was discouraged by laws, which, however, were

[21] Charles B. Dew, *Ironmaker to the Confederacy: Joseph R. Anderson and the Tredegar Iron Works* (New Haven, 1966).
[22] R. S. Starobin, *Industrial Slavery in the South* (New York, 1970), 11.

frequently laxly enforced or evaded. One of the slave girls of Charles Colcock Jones fled the plantation to Savannah and sought to hire herself as a domestic without a written permit. Charles Colcock, Jr., a lawyer in Savannah, described the situation in respect to slaves hiring their time in this city: "There are, you may say, hundreds of Negroes in this city who go about from house to house—some carpenters, some house servants, etc.—who never see their masters except at pay day, live out of their yards, hire themselves without written permit, etc." [23] This comment illustrates an important fact about Southern slavery, namely, that it was much milder than the laws indicate.

Students of Southern history have differed over the question of the vitality of slavery on the eve of the Civil War.[24] The answer to this complex problem requires an evaluation of the profitableness of "the peculiar institution." It is true that there were important considerations other than economic in perpetuating slavery, such as the need to retain it as a mechanism of social control, the desire for tractable domestic servants, so essential to comfort in a warm climate, and the political value of keeping the Federal three-fifths ratio. Nevertheless, it seems reasonable to conclude that the main consideration in preserving slavery was its economical profitableness, either actual or presumed.

Slave labor often was reluctant labor, because there were relatively few incentives for zealous work in such a system of exploitation. Hostile observers maintained that slaves often went through the motions of labor but accomplished about half the work of a farmhand in the North. Yet white men working in a hot climate also did less work than white laborers in the more stimulating climate of the North. Furthermore, the slaves who worked beside the numerous small slaveowners tended to slow down the labor of the whites and make them less efficient. Since slave labor was based on routine, it was difficult for Southerners to practice scientific or diversified agriculture.[25] This fact contributed to the condition by which the South became wedded to a one-money crop, leading to overproduction and low prices.

Despite the fact that slave labor was unpaid, it was in many respects an expensive form of labor. The cost of supervision of the Negro slaves was excessive. A large proportion of the slaves were too old or too young for hard work. Even in a state such as Mississippi, which imported from the upper South a large proportion of prime fieldhands, a planter was fortunate

---

[23] R. M. Myers (ed.), *The Children of Pride: A True Story of Georgia and the Civil War* (New Haven, 1972), 241.

[24] For a discussion of this subject, see Clement Eaton, *The Growth of Southern Civilization, 1790–1860* (New York, 1961), chap. 3; and Harold D. Woodman, "The Profitability of Slavery: A Historical Perennial," *Journal of Southern History*, XXIX (August 1963), 303–325.

[25] See Eugene D. Genovese, *The Political Economy of Slavery: Studies in the Economy and Society of the Slave South* (New York, 1965), chap. 2, "The Low Productivity of Southern Slave Labor: Causes and Effects."

if 60 per cent of his slaves could be classified as "hands." Each plantation carried an overhead expense of virtually old age pensions and of sickness and unemployment insurance, as well as the cost of rearing Negro children. Too many slaves were withdrawn from productive labor in the fields to act as household servants. In some of the large slaveholding families each member enjoyed the services of a maid or valet. These favored individuals of the master class prided themselves on not lifting their hands to do any menial work. Southerners maintained that black slaves were unsuited to the use of machinery and that they broke or misused high-priced agricultural machines. Consequently, the South could not use its manpower to the best advantage by the introduction of machinery and labor-saving tools. Yet the picking of cotton, the main occupation of slaves, has been a hand process until rather recently.

A large proportion of Southern capital was tied up or "frozen" in slaves, thereby reducing significantly the amount available for industrial enterprises. Souhterners fell into a vicious practice of investing in slaves to produce more cotton to buy more slaves and land. Indeed, the value of personal property in the Southern states (chiefly slaves) far exceeded the value of real estate; in South Carolina the ratio was nearly three to one. The immobility of Southern capital invested in black chattel property was one of the greatest drawbacks to the use of slave labor. In times of depression, the planter could not reduce his labor force nor could he shift his capital easily to other forms of investment.

The most eminent student of American Negro slavery, U. B. Phillips, believed that at the close of the antebellum period only those slaveholders who lived in the very fertile districts of the South and who had extraordinary managerial ability "were earning anything beyond what would cover their maintenance and carrying charges. . . ." [26] His view has the strong support of one of the large planters of South Carolina, Joel R. Poinsett, first minister to the Mexican republic (after whom the poinsettia flower (which he introduced from Mexico, is named). In a private letter, October 14, 1844; he wrote:

> I have long been of opinion, that Slave labour is too unprofitable in farming districts to be long maintained there. By the operation of their principles and none other, Slavery has been gradually abolished in the Northern and Eastern States. Its northern confine is now Maryland; but it is fast wearing out there and is destined to recede from that state and from Virginia and North Carolina where that description of labour is becoming

[26] Phillips, *American Negro Slavery* (New York, 1918), see especially chap. 19. This eminent student's conclusion as to the unprofitability of slavery was shared by C. S. Sydnor, C. S. Davis, *The Cotton Kingdom in Alabama* (Montgomery, 1939); and C. W. Ramsdell, who maintained that by 1850 slavery in its advance west had reached its natural limits "The Natural Limits of Slavery Expansion," *Mississippi Valley Historical Review* XVI (1929), 151.

daily less profitable and less necessary. Even in the upper districts of the South States the same principle is at work. It is found more profitable in this region to hire Labour at seed time and harvest than to maintain it the year round; and the slaves are sent to the cotton growing countries either within or without the state. In either case the mass of the population, of the white population I mean, of the Atlantic slave states will have no sympathies or interests in common with those of the slave owners and will not be disposed to make the great sacrifices which a separation from the free states and the maintenance of an independent government will require at their hands.[27]

On the other hand, some modern writers have questioned the assumption that slavery in the Old South was economically unprofitable and that slave labor on the plantation was less efficient than white labor. Dr. Lewis C. Gray, in his monumental *History of Agriculture in the Southern United States to 1860,* found that slave labor was efficient, even expert, on the well-managed plantations. Slave labor, under the system of incentives and punishments practiced on these plantations, he maintained, was probably more productive than free Negro labor in the modern South. Competent observers in the antebellum South expressed the opinion that slave labor was more efficient than the free Irish labor or the services of the native whites that were available. The relative difference in wages paid to hired white labor and the price of slave labor indicates no marked superiority in value of the free labor available. Slavery had a superior advantage over free labor in that it provided a stable labor supply, free from strikes. Under competent plantation management slave labor had an "irresistible ability to displace white labor" in competition for rich soils accessible to markets.[28] This competitive advantage of slave labor arose primarily from the low subsistence level of the slave—a melancholy evidence of human exploitation.

Accordingly, Dr. Gray has maintained that slavery in the South was economically a strong and vital institution in the years before the Civil War. There was no danger in 1860 of its being discarded because of a lack of fresh, fertile lands. Railroads were opening up new sources of fertile land suitable for exploitation by slave labor. Furthermore, slaves were being successfully used in the tobacco factories of Richmond and could be trained to use machinery, as some low country textile mills found when they integrated white and Negro workers. Slaves may have been overcapitalized in 1860, Gray admits, but this was only a temporary phenomenon that would have adjusted itself, just as stocks and bonds that are overvalued today.

The popular theory today, called "revisionist," maintains that Southern plantation slavery was a profitable form of business enterprise. Two Harvard economists, influenced by Keynesian economics, have maintained that slavery

[27] Joel R. Poinsett Papers, MSS Library of Congress vol. XVI, p. 159.
[28] L. C. Gray, *History of Agriculture in the Southern States to 1860* (Washington, 1933), I, 474.

was profitable in the Cotton Kingdom both on rich lands and poor lands, in the latter case the profit coming from rearing and selling slaves. Predicating a life expectancy of thirty years for a twenty-year-old slave, they estimate that the return from his labor in producing cotton on the majority of plantations and farms was between 4.5 per cent and 8 per cent, which compared favorably with contemporary investments in railroads and New England municipal bonds.[29]

Moreover, the records of some outstanding planters point to the profitableness of slavery under good managerial ability. A study of the papers of Elisha F. King, a planter of the black belt of Alabama, shows how a poor man rose to become a wealthy planter, owning 8,000 acres of land and 186 slaves, expanding his possessions through buying on credit and by intelligent management.[30] The career of King could be matched many times in the antebellum South. There were lordly planters, such as Samuel Hairston of Pittsylvania County, Virginia, who owned nearly two thousand slaves and was reputed to be the largest slaveholder in the South in the last decade of the antebellum period; self-made men, such as Joseph Davis of Mississippi, who produced over three thousand bales of cotton some years, and wealthy sugar planters whose incomes exceeded $100,000. Henry Clay, writing from New Orleans, February 16, 1831, in favor of tariff protection for sugar, maintained that the sugar planters did not receive an average of more than 5 or 6 per cent profit on capital invested in sugar plantations, which is a good profit according to modern standards.[31] In addition to the profits from staple crops, the slaveholders obtained a good living out of their farms— hams, fresh eggs, chickens, milk and butter, fruit, the use of horses tended by slaves for pleasure and transportation, and other satisfactions, especially domestic servants—that cannot be measured in dollars and cents and are, therefore, left out in computing profits from plantation slavery.[32] That there was an increase in prosperity among slaveholders as well as nonslaveholders, as reported by census statistics, 1850–1860, may throw some light on the debatable question of the profitability of slavery.

The view that plantation slavery was an unprofitable institution and for that reason alone would have died out in the course of a few decades without the violent surgery of the Civil War has been vigorously attacked by a group of modern historians; they seem to have the best of the argument. The most

---

[29] Alfred Conrad and J. R. Meyer, "The Economics of Slavery in the Ante-Bellum South," *Journal of Political Economy*, LXVI (1958), 95–130.

[30] W. T. Jordan, "The Elisha F. King Family, Planters of the Alabama Black Belt," *Agricultural History*, XIX, 9 (July 1945), 152–162.

[31] Calvin Colton, *The Life, Correspondence, and Speeches of Henry Clay* (New York, 1864), IV, 294.

[32] T. P. Govan, "Was Plantation Slavery Profitable?" *Journal of Southern History*, VIII (November 1942), 513–535. Govan argues that interest earned for the payment of plantations, as well as the wages of management, should be regarded not as an expense but as part of the profit from plantation slavery.

convincing of these investigators are Robert W. Fogel and Stanley L. Engerman who in a recent study conclude that, instead of being inefficient, Negro slavery was more efficient in agriculture than free labor, because of the advantages of large-scale organization. They maintain that the typical Southern slave fieldhand was not lazy and inept but that he was harder working and more efficient than his white counterpart in the South. They attribute much of the present unfavorable view of the antebellum Negro as a laborer to the report of Frederick Law Olmsted, whom they maintain was a racist who formed his opinion of the inefficiency of slave labor on his first visit to the South in 1853 during the slack season and from reports of prejudiced Southerners.[33] Yet Olmsted was not alone among outsiders in denigrating slave labor and this view harmonized with contemporary beliefs that slave labor, being forced labor, was bound to be inefficient.

By using statistics and cliometric methods, Fogel and Engerman arrive at the startling conclusion that Southern plantation agriculture, as a whole, using an equivalent amount of land, labor and capital, was nearly 40 per cent more efficient than Northern agriculture. The newer plantations of the Southwest, because of large-scale operation, were 28 per cent more efficient than the plantations of the old Southern states. A further advantage that plantation slave labor had over free labor was the greater use of women and children in the working force, 67 per cent of all slaves were in the labor force. Undoubtedly productivity of slave labor was increased by the incentive system whereby masters offered inducements for good labor, such as monetary rewards, holidays, and feasts, which, these writers maintain, was normal practice, rather than the exception.

However profitable plantation slavery may have been to individual slaveholders during good times when cotton and tobacco were bringing satisfactory prices, paradoxically, slavery was bad for the general welfare of the section. Indeed, slavery prevented the development of a society of consumers (since the slaves consumed a minimum of goods) and thereby contributed to a low level of economy. Morover, the retention of this primitive system of forced labor had an adverse effect on capital accumulation, morals, and education of the masses, and led to the suppression of freedom of speech and the press. Roswell King, who for nineteen years supervised the vast estates and the seven hundred slaves of Pierce Butler in coastal Georgia, discussed the evil effects of slavery on the South in a conversation with the actress Fanny Kemble, who had married Butler, which she reported in her highly prejudiced antislavery *Journal of a Residence on a Georgian Plantation in 1838–1839*. King, who was of New England parentage and a man highly

---

[33] R. Fogel and S. L. Engerman, *Time on the Cross: The Economics of American Negro Slavery* (Boston, 1974), I, 219–223. They believe that this false opinion of the inefficiency of Negro labor in slavery times has been carried over to modern times. See also R. K. Aufhauser, "Slavery and Scientific Management," *Journal of Economic History*, XXXIII (1973), 811–24; for a recent analysis of Olmsted's travel accounts, see Laura W. Roper, *F.L.O.: A Biography of Frederick Law Olmsted* (Baltimore, 1974).

respected for his shrewd judgment and integrity, said, according to Fanny Kemble: "I hate slavery with all my heart: I consider it an absolute curse wherever it exists. It will keep those states where it does exist fifty years behind the others in improvement and prosperity. . . . As for it being an irremediable evil—a thing not to be helped or got rid of—that's all nonsense; for as soon as people become convinced that it is their interest to get rid of it, they will soon find the means to do so, depend upon it." [33] One of the evils that King did not mention but Fanny Kemble did, namely that "Mr. Butler's paragon overseer" had propagated several mulatto children on the plantation. One of the great paradoxes of the South was that those slaveholders who clearly saw that slavery was an evil, nevertheless, kept their slaves, because they saw no practicable way to emancipate them without the action of the whole community or state.

[33] Frances Anne Kemble, *Journal of a Residence on a Georgia Plantation,* ed. by J. A. Scott (New York, 1961).

14

The Nature of the Southern Slave System and of the Slave

IN 1975 it is still difficult for the historian to view slavery—"the peculiar institution" of the Old South—in an objective light. For the United States is engaged in a great struggle to secure the recognition of the full rights and dignity of its Negro citizens, who over a hundred years ago were enslaved. It is also difficult for the modern historian in considering slavery to free himself from the prepossessions of his time and refrain from being a moralist in passing judgment on the "sins" of a bygone generation. Yet it is the true function of the historian to use his imagination and knowledge of sources to understand an institution of a past epoch in its own setting rather than judge it by the standards of his own age. He then will see that Southern slavery was an immensely complex thing that was remote from the streotype of general cruelty presented by the abolitionists as well as the romantic legend of happy slaves.

The history of slavery from the point of view of the Negro remains to be told. Contemporary Negro accounts of the institution are mainly those of escaped slaves, who were not typical of the mass of slaves, and whose stories were usually written or edited by abolitionists for propaganda purposes.[1] An important body of evidence, the reminiscences of twenty-three hundred ex-slaves who were interviewed in 1936–38 by W.P.A. workers, is contained in the seventeen volumes of these interviews in the Library of Congress.[2] The majority of blacks interviewed were children during the slavery regime and probably did not experience the most severe side of slavery. Also the un-

---

[1] The most valuable of pre-Civil War narratives are Rayford Logan (ed.), *Memoirs of a Monticello Slave* (Charlottesville, 1951); Robin Winks (ed.), *An Autobiography of the Reverend Josiah Henson* (Reading, Mass., 1969); Frederick Douglass, *My Bondage and My Freedom* (New York, 1955); Solomon Northrop, *Twenty Years a Slave* (London, 1853); and Lunsford Lane, *The Narrative of Lunsford Lane* (Boston, 1848).

[2] A selection of these interviews has been published by Norman R. Yetman (ed.), *Life Under the "Peculiar Institution": Selections from the Slave Narrative Collection* (New York, 1970), and George P. Rawick (ed.), *The American Slave: A Composite Autobiography* (Westport, Conn., 1972), 19 vols.; also B. A. Botkin, *Lay My Burden Down, a Folk History of Slavery* (Chicago, 1945), and John B. Cade, "Out of the Mouths of Ex-Slaves," *Journal of Negro History* XX (July 1935) have recorded testimony of ex-slaves.

trained interviewers were largely white women, and there were relatively few black interviewers.[3] The results of the interviews are ambiguous. Many of the former slaves recalled kind masters and good living conditions, whereas others told of the cruelties of the institution—miscegenation, severe whippings, tortures, separation of families in the slave trade, excessive work, and inadequate food and clothing. Thus, from the extant testimony of the slaves, one must conclude that the treatment of the slaves by masters was as varied as human nature, and that the picture of the institution presented by many white sources, such as the letters and diaries of the planters and the observations of travelers, as humane and paternal is subject to a serious question.

Some insight into slave psychology, but not much insight into life in their quarters, is to be found in plantation records and the papers of the planters. Toward whites the slaves acted the role of deference dictated by their situation, but at the same time the black house servants adopted the aristocratic attitudes of the masters and assumed airs of dignity, acquired courteous manners, and became shrewd observers of the white man's psychology. Many slaves developed a hereditary regard for their masters, but when the opportunity came during the Civil War to flee to the Union lines even the most trusted house servants surprised their masters by abandoning them. Contrary to conventional ideas today, the Negro family in slavery was often held together by warm affectionate feelings and the parents tried to instruct their children. According to incomplete records of the Freedman's Bureau, cited by John Blassingame, approximately a third of the slave marriages were broken up by the masters.[4] The slave had many resources to protect himself from abuse in addition to the violent ones of arson, runaway, sabotage, and insurrection; not only was he protected to some degree by the community but by the custom of the country, which it was unwise for the planter to violate; once the slaves on a plantation had determined the amount of labor they would do, it was useless to try to obtain more.

Undoubtedly there were many instances of brutality and crime in the treatment of slaves by their owners. Drunken masters and sadists at times perpetrated horrible crimes on their black dependents. However, these cases of abnormality were perhaps no more typical of the slave regime than are the lurid accounts of crimes reported in the daily newspapers of today. The Southern laws protected the Negro from wanton cruelty or mayhem, prescribing the death penalty for deliberately murdering a Negro servant. The force of this law was weakened, however, by the fact that slave testimony

[3] An analysis of the interviews with surviving slaves in the 1930's has been made by C. Vann Woodward, "History from Slave Sources," *American Historical Review,* **79** (April 1974), 470–481; also John W. Blassingame has written a critical essay, in which he points out the serious deficiencies of the W.P.A. slave narratives: "Using the Testimony of Ex-Slaves: Approaches and Problems," which has been accepted for publication by the *Journal of Southern History.*
[4] John W. Blassingame, *The Slave Community: Plantation Life in the Ante-Bellum South* (New York, 1972), 90.

was not valid against a white man in the courts of law.[5] Furthermore, if a servant was killed by his master or overseer during the administration of moderate correction, neither was punishable. Nevertheless, public opinion in the South was a powerful factor in preventing the mistreatment of Negroes. A cruel slavemaster was ostracized by the community. Finally, it was decidedly to the economic interest of the master to treat his slave well, preserve his health, and secure his cooperation, even though some men in mistreating their slaves disregarded their own true economic interest.

Counterbalancing the stories of cruelty to be found in some of the slave narratives are the papers, diaries, and plantation records of countless planters who treated their slaves paternally. These documents tend to refute a recent tendency of historians of a presentist liberal point of view to exaggerate the cruelty of Southern slavery—a reaction to the romanticization of the institution by older writers as well as a response to the civil rights crusade. The true picture of the treatment of the slaves lies between the two extremes of romanticization and of moral indignation.[6] The best side of slavery was presented by the thousands of benevolent planters such as Charles Colcock Jones of Georgia, whose letters together with those of the family have recently been published—a major contribution to the social history of the antebellum South.[7] Jones undoubtedly was an exceptional planter. He was

[5] J. C. Hurd, *The Law of Freedom and Bondage in the United States* (Boston, 1858–62), 2 vols.

[6] Two contrasting views of Southern slavery are presented by U. B. Phillips, a native of Georgia, in an able study, *American Negro Slavery* (New York, 1918) based on a deep knowledge of the sources but weakened by a racist bias and too benign a view of Southern slavery, and Kenneth Stampp, in *The Peculiar Institution: Slavery in the Ante-Bellum South* (New York, 1956), also based on the sources, presented a stark and exaggerated picture of slavery. Stampp's study starts from the premise of "the basic irrelevance of race." He maintains that there was no justification for enslaving Negroes in the South because of the hot climate or the supposition that Negroes were immune from the diseases that made work on the plantations of the lower South so hazardous. Actually the slaves suffered severely from malaria, hookworm, yellow fever, and cholera. Stampp discards the idea that paternalism or public opinion furnished much protection from cruelty for most of the slaves. He asserts that the overwhelming majority of the slaves were not contented with bondage but longed for freedom. Masters who were willing to emancipate their slaves were exceedingly few; despite the fact that bondsmen were "troublesome property" and that many slaves made the lives of their masters miserable by their efforts to sabotage slavery, especially by passive resistance, the masters clung to their human property. In general, he holds that Negroes were overworked on the plantations, poorly clad, inadequately housed, and received the minimum of medical care. Whenever economic interest clashed with human rights, notably in the breakup of families through the slave trade, human rights were usually sacrificed. Instead of plantation slavery serving as a school in Christianity and the rudiments of civilization, as Phillips maintained, Stampp holds that Southern slavery "merely took away from the African his native culture and gave him in exchange little more than vocational training." He concludes somberly, but inaccurately: "In 1860 the peculiar institution was almost precisely what it had been thirty years before" (p. 28).

[7] R. M. Myers (ed.), *The Children of Pride: A True Story of Georgia and the Civil War* [the Charles Colcock Jones family letters] (New Haven, 1972).

well educated, having studied at Phillips Academy at Andover, Massachusetts, and at the Princeton Theological Seminary, and as a Presbyterian minister had a deep commitment to religion. He and his wife owned 129 slaves, distributed on three plantations in eastern Georgia. His education in the North did not diminish his ardent support of slavery. He searched the Scriptures for justification for the institution, and, of course, found what he was seeking. In the twelve hundred letters printed of the approximately six thousand letters extant, not once is there mention of whipping the slaves. Dr. Jones supervised the operation of the plantations, but he had able and faithful Negro foremen. The master and mistress treated their black dependents as organic members of the family, and the latter reciprocated with a genuine interest in the welfare of the white family. Dr. Jones would buy from his slaves the hogs, cotton, and corn that they had raised. He was also concerned for the spiritual welfare of his slaves and built a chapel for them and conducted Sabbath schools to educate them in religious truths. In 1842, in an effort to arouse Southern slavemasters to their duty to attend to the spiritual life of the slaves, Dr. Jones published in Savannah *The Religious Instruction of the Negroes in the United States,* in which he advocated only *oral* instruction, chiefly from a *Catechism* that he also had drawn up.

From the letters of the Jones family one would judge that their slaves were contented, cheerful, and willing workers. The slaves, according to the letters, often sang melodiously in chorus, to the great delight of the white family; "these are not the voices of poor downtrodden humanity," one of them observed. When Charles, Jr., would write from Harvard College, he would end his letters, "Howdy for all the servants." The good treatment of the slaves by the Joneses can be seen from the fact that during the Civil War when there was an exodus of slaves from the surrounding plantations, most of the Jones slaves remained faithful. Yet there were shadows on the life of this warm, affectionate family of slaveholders, such as the apparent necessity of selling an unprincipled slave family, the murder of a newborn slave baby by the mother, who was tried and punished by confinement in jail for eight days and ninety lashes of the whip, the death from natural causes of admirable slaves, such as Beck, "that intelligent fine young woman," and the birth of a mulatto baby, the offspring of a young man employed as an amanuensis by Dr. Jones to copy a religious book that he was writing.

The utilization of the labor of slaves and their treatment as human beings in the Old South have been studied principally from the records of large plantations, which are easily accessible. Our view of Southern slavery, therefore, may be modified when our knowledge of the institution as administered by the farmers and small planters, who seldom kept records or journals, has been enlarged. Nearly half of the slaves in the South did not live on the large plantations, laboring under the overseer system, but were owned by small masters.[8] In 1860, 47.6 per cent of the Southern slaves were owned

[8] See Richard Hofstadter, "U. B. Phillips and the Plantation Legend," *Journal of Negro History,* XXIX (April 1944), 109–125.

by men who had fewer than twenty slaves and some authorities hold that two-thirds of the slaves worked under the supervision of blacks. In the upper South the percentage of slaves owned by small slaveholders was much higher, 61.7 per cent, but in the lower South, only 38 per cent of the slaves belonged to this class of slaveholders. The testimony of the Southerners themselves indicates that the conditions of slavery were more humane on the farms and small plantations, where the dark-skinned worker escaped the overseer system and came into frequent contact with the owner, than was the case on the large estates. Nevertheless, the observations of the Northern traveler and agricultural writer Solon Robinson discloses that on many of the large plantations of the lower South the slaves were given better medical care, larger quantities of food, and better housing than the slaves of small masters in the upper South.[9] Also, the old idea that slaves were more harshly treated and harder worked on the plantations of the Southwest has been largely discredited by modern studies, particularly by Abigail Curlee in a Ph.D. dissertation, University of Texas, 1932, entitled "A Study of Texas Slave Plantations, 1822 to 1865."

The distinction that existed between the field slaves and the house servants has been exaggerated. The latter, numerically small, fared much better than the field slaves. They worked less, were better fed and clothed, and came more in contact with the refining influences of the master's family than did the field slaves. Yet the house servants were usually old or young Negroes who were not suitable for field labor. Frequently, on the large plantations there was a superfluity of domestic servants, so that their tasks were light. The Charles Colcock Jones family of five, for example, had twelve house, garden, and stable slaves. Often the household servants, especially the Negro mammies, developed a real affection for their masters and mistresses, which was warmly reciprocated. Moreover, the house servants acquired a keen sense of pride both in their market value and in belonging to "quality folks," and they looked down on "poor white trash." Yet most Southerners did not realize how deeply felt and widespread was the desire of the slaves for freedom, and when the opportunity was given to them by the approach of the Union army, "faithful" house servants as well as field servants deserted in droves. The "moment of truth" had arrived for the masters, but they reacted by accusing the slaves of ingratitude.[10]

A large element in the happiness of the slaves was the food supply. The evidence indicates that, in general, the slaves were given a nourishing diet but one without much variety. The general rule on slave plantations was to

[9] Herbert A. Kellar (ed.), *Solon Robinson, Pioneer and Agriculturist* (Indianapolis, 1937), I, 454–456; II, 213, 289–302. No one has ever made a scholarly study comparing the living conditions of the poor whites with those of the slaves, but on the physical level their lot in life seems to have been fully as hard as that of the slaves.

[10] Eugene Genovese in a manuscript entitled "Roll, Jordan, Roll: Afro-American Slaves in the Making of the Modern World," which he graciously permitted the author to read, has made this point. See also Bell Wiley, *Southern Negroes, 1861–65* (New York, 1953).

furnish each slave three or four pounds of hog meat weekly. This ration of meat, as far as quantity was concerned, is better than the rationing of two and one half pounds of meat or less per week in the United States during World War II. The slaves were also given a peck of cornmeal each week, and in some districts they were given a pint of molasses a week. These were standard food supplies issued to slaves by the masters, but the slaves were usually allowed to supplement this diet by cultivating vegetable gardens. Also they obtained fish from the rivers, caught rabbits in homemade traps, and hunted the opossum at night with dogs and axes to cut down the tree on which these tasty animals took refuge. Food was cheap in the antebellum South, so that slaves hired to railroad companies in Mississippi were boarded for 15 cents a day. On the plantations at Christmas time the Negroes frequently were given a small supply of whiskey and a feast. Slaves were often allowed to raise hogs and chickens, for the possession of such property was a good insurance policy against their running away.

Frederick Law Olmsted cites a report to Secretary of the Treasury Walker of forty-eight Louisiana planters, who wished to influence the government to maintain the tariff on sugar, that the cost of food and clothing for a working hand was $30 for an entire year, from which this Northern writer inferred that the cost was 5½ cents a day.[11] Yet this calculation does not include the supplies of food grown by the slaves themselves, their little vegetable gardens, the poultry and hogs they raised. The planters needed strong and sturdy slaves for the successful growing and manufacture of sugar, and it was essential that they should be well nourished. The law of Louisiana required that meat should be given to the slaves daily, the only state in the South to have this requirement. The Creole planters were reported to treat their slaves less humanely than the American planters and to evade compliance with the meat law. Not all planters were as intelligent as William J. Minor, whose slaves were allowed to cultivate an acre per family for their personal use. On his several plantations in Louisiana they were permitted to keep chickens and to retain the money they made from selling both chickens and eggs.

The slaves were housed in cabins that were entirely inadequate, according to modern standards, for good health and morality, but were probably as good as those that white laborers in the South had.[12] The slave quarters on the big plantations consisted of a village, usually on a wide street with a row of cabins on each side, with the house of the white overseer at the end of the street. These one-room cabins were almost invariably overflowing with blacks. Estimates made of the housing of slaves in Mississippi indicate that, on the average, four or five slaves occupied a cabin; for example, 28 houses were provided for Jefferson Davis's 113 slaves at *Brierfield,* 76 houses for the 355 slaves of his brother, Joseph E. Davis, and 104 houses for the 452 slaves of William N. Mercer. These cabins had large open fireplaces at which

[11] Olmsted, *A Journey in the Seaboard Slave States* (New York, 1856), 686, 688.
[12] Foley and Engerman, Time on the Cross, I, 115–116.

the cooking was done. The slave cabins of the antebellum period would compare favorably with the houses occupied by many of the Negroes in the modern South. In the antebellum period thousands of farmers lived in log cabins no more commodious for their large families than the slave houses.

As to clothing, the house servants often wore the cast-off finery of their masters. The field slaves were issued annually two summer suits, two winter suits, one straw hat, one wool hat, and two pairs of shoes. Most of the slaves went barefoot in summer, as did many of the poor whites. The Negro children wore only one garment, a shift, or an abbreviated nightgown. Sometimes they ran around the plantation nude. (The author recalls a little Negro playmate on a farm in North Carolina who wore only one piece of clothing, a cap of many colors.) The Negro women were given linsey-woolsey or calico to make dresses, and they delighted in materials of gaudy colors. On many plantations the Negro women who were unfit for fieldwork wove homespun cloth, which was used to clothe the slaves.

The planters tried to protect the health of their human property. They and their overseers often acted in the capacity of amateur doctors, using a family medical book and a medicine chest. Cholera, yellow fever, smallpox, chills, colds, dysentery, whooping cough, and measles were the chief ailments that affected the slaves. To combat these diseases the planters purchased quantities of castor oil, calomel, liniment, quinine, and ipecac. On many of the large plantations there were slave hospitals, and often the white mistress of the plantation cared for sick slaves. Doctors were employed on some plantations at a yearly rate to attend to the sick slaves. Childbearing slave mothers were allowed a month of absence from field labor, and after they returned to work they were permitted to leave the fields at intervals to nurse their babies. The mortality rates of black babies, as well as white babies, were both very high in the Old South. Yet the mortality of mature Negroes in Mississippi, for example, was only slightly higher than that of whites.[13] Reliable estimates place the number of days that slaves lost from work throughout the year owing to sickness as an average of twelve days. Planters tended to protect their slaves from dangerous and unhealthy work. Irishmen were often employed in unhealthy jobs, such as digging ditches and handling the bouncing cotton bales that were loaded on the steamboats. If a Negro slave worth $1,500 were killed, that was a grave loss indeed, but it did not make much difference to society if an Irishmen were killed.

Discipline on the large plantations was maintained primarily by the overseers, but a large proportion of the planters dispensed with overseers and used Negro foremen or drivers. One of the most frequent complaints of the Old South was the difficulty of finding good overseers. The principal causes for this condition were the low social status of the overseer, the insecurity of

---

[13] See William D. Postell, *The Health of Slaves on Southern Plantations* (Baton Rouge, 1951); and Bennett W. Wall, "Medical Care of Ebenezer Pettigrew's Slaves," *Mississippi Valley Historical Review*, XXXVII (1950), 451–470.

tenure, and the poor salary he received, which varied from $120 to $600 a year.[14] Stewards or managers of several plantations, however, received salaries of $1,500 or more. The ambitious overseer tried to achieve a reputation for himself by striving to make as many bales of cotton for the owner as possible, regardless of the welfare of the slaves. The planters were concerned to prevent the overdriving of the slaves, a factor that led in the antebellum period to the substitution of a fixed salary for the overseer instead of compensation by a share of the crop, which had prevailed in the colonial period. If an overseer was too harsh, he would cause the slaves to run away from the plantation, thus causing a considerable financial loss to the owner. On the other hand, if he was too lenient, the slaves would neglect their work, malinger, and become insubordinate. Other serious faults of overseers that impaired their authority were drunkenness, frequent absences from the plantation, and immorality with the Negro women. The experience of Benjamin L. C. Wailes, an intelligent planter of the Natchez area, in paying overseers bonuses for large crops proved unsatisfactory in that they neglected other affairs of the plantation and, because of their hustling ways, often caused the slaves to run away.[15]

Most large plantations had strict rules to guide the overseer in his management of the slaves. The overseer was sometimes restrained by the instructions of the owner never to flog a slave while he was in anger and to limit his punishment to fifteen lashes. The Negro driver was often the instrument of inflicting corporal punishment, but only in the presence of the overseer. The principal punishment of Negroes was flogging, which was in accordance with the penological practice of the age. Slaves were seldom placed in jail for crimes, and frequently escaped the serious punishment that was given to white criminals. The chief recourse of the slave for protection from cruelty was to appeal to the master, but on absentee or large plantations this safeguard was seldom available.[16] A remarkable set of rules for the management of the plantation *Beaver Bend,* on the Cahaba River in Alabama, contains the humane provision "that each and every slave shall communicate to the master all things proper to be known, in the master's judgment, especially such as have reference to his food and its supply, his clothing, or the deficiency thereof, his punishment, the quantity and cause thereof, the existence of any known immorality and the parties engaged in it, etc." [17]

The fact that the slave system rested partly on force is seen in the need of frequent whippings. The diary of a Louisiana cotton planter, Bennet H.

---

[14] See John Spencer Bassett, *The Southern Plantation Overseer As Revealed in His Letters* (Northampton, Mass., 1925).

[15] Charles S. Sydnor, *A Gentleman of the Old Natchez Region, Benjamin L. C. Wailes* (Durham, 1938), 297–299.

[16] See U. B. Phillips and J. D. Glunt (eds.), *Florida Plantation Records* (St. Louis, 1927), 2 vols.

[17] W. T. Jordan (ed.), "System of Farming at Beaver Bend, Alabama, 1862," *Journal of Southern History, VII* (February 1941), 80.

Barrow, shows a realistic picture of whipping on a large plantation. Barrow was a successful planter, in good years selling his cotton crop for more than $20,000. He secured excellent cooperation from his slaves and had few runaways. He rewarded the faithful for good work by giving them frequent holidays throughout the year, treating them to a special dinner, giving outstanding workers an extra suit of store-bought clothes, providing them with whiskey for a dance, and donating a money gift before Christmas. He expressed strong disapprobation of a jury clearing a man from the charge of murder who had flogged a slave to death. "Went to town—man tried for Whipping a Negro to Death—deserves death—Cleared!" [18] He also spoke with disgust of a neighbor planter who had the reputation of being a cruel master. Yet Barrow maintained firm discipline over his own slaves by a variety of punishments. Sometimes he devised punishments that would make the slave ridiculous to his fellows, such as exhibiting the culprit on a scaffold with a red flannel cap on his head, making some "rascally" Negroes wear dresses or wash clothes, imprisoning a Negro in the plantation jail on weekends and holidays. The most common penalty for misdeeds was whipping. Slaves were flogged for picking trashy cotton, for laziness, for keeping themselves or their cottages filthy, or for running away. His diary shows that he engaged in whipping two or three times a week. Certainly the muscles of his right arm must have become habituated to this frequent exercise of punishing his slaves. However, Barrow was not a typical master.

The loss of the services of black labor as the result of slaves fleeing from the plantation was less than one might expect. In 1860, according to census reports, only 803 slaves escaped to the North, hardly any of them from the lower South. In all parts of the South slaves occasionally ran away from the plantations because they feared a whipping for some dereliction, or because of a labor strike of a group of slaves against a harsh overseer, or, most frequently, to escape from being sold to the lower South or to revisit their old home places and see their relatives after they had been sold to a distant master. Often these slaves would return of their own accord after they had been absent for a few days, hiding in the woods or swamps. The chief loss from flight of slaves out of the land of Dixie fell upon the border states. There were professional "nigger catchers" in the South who at times used bloodhounds to trail the fugitive, but the usual method of recovering absconding slaves was to run advertisements in the newspapers, such as the following:

> Ranaway from the subscriber, living at Crab Orchard, Ky., last June, a
> negro man named *Grandison*, about 24 years of age, very black, wears

---

[18] Edwin A. Davis (ed.), "Bennet H. Barrow, Ante-Bellum Planter of the Felicianas," *Journal of Southern History*, V (November, 1939), 439; see also his *Plantation Life in the Florida Parishes of Louisiana 1836–1846, As Reflected in the Diary of Bennet H. Barrow* (New York, 1943).

large whiskers, and is lame in one of his ankles. He is a preacher . . . (offers reward of $400; also advertises for capture of two other Negro men).[19]

After the runaway reached the Ohio River or the Mason-Dixon line he was frequently aided by the Underground Railroad to arrive in Canada. This organization to assist slaves to escape was composed of Quakers and other ardent abolitionists, whose reputed president was the Quaker Levi Coffin of Cincinnati. They established stations or hiding places for the slaves, often the attics of their homes, at distances of a day's journey. They gave the fugitive food and instructions how to reach the next place of refuge.[20] The fleeing slaves traveled at night, with the North Star as their guide. Some of the most devoted "nigger stealers" who aided them were Delia Webster, the New England schoolteacher who purchased a farm in Kentucky along the Ohio River with abolitionist funds, Calvin Fairbank, a Northern preacher in Lexington, Kentucky, who claimed that he had "liberated forty-seven slaves from hell," and the Southern-born Reverend John Rankin, who operated one of the most active stations across the Ohio River at Ripley, Ohio.[21] The Negro historian George Williams declared that the Underground Railroad served as a safety valve for the institution of slavery, for it aided the most dangerous slaves, the natural leaders of insurrection, to escape.

The dangers inherent in the slavery regime in the South were revealed by occasional outbreaks of insurrection and countless rumors of slave plots. Starting back in colonial times, when wild Africans were intruded into Southern society, the fear of insurrection occurred at intervals throughout the history of slavery. The stereotype of the Negro as a docile worker, in contrast to the untamable Indian, has been questioned by some modern students. In 1791–1795 the South was frightened by the horrible massacres of the whites by the black slaves of Santo Domingo. Five years later there was consternation among the people of Richmond when they discovered a plot to destroy the city by slaves under the lead of "General" Gabriel Prosser. This slave plot led to the formation of a little standing army at the Virginia capital and a movement to colonize free Negroes on the western frontier.

One of the strangest and most terrible examples of mass hysteria that ever occurred in the United States took place in Charleston in the summer of 1822. Denmark Vesey, a free Negro carpenter, who had purchased his freedom with money obtained by winning a $1,500 lottery, was accused of organizing a conspiracy among the Negroes of this city to undertake an insurrection. Vesey was a remarkable Negro who could read and who was believed to have been incited to plot to obtain the freedom of the slaves by

[19] Lexington *Observer and Reporter*, May 12, 1849.
[20] Larry Gara, *The Liberty Line: The Legend of the Underground Railroad* (Lexington, 1961), concludes that free Negroes were far more important than white sympathizers in aiding slaves to escape.
[21] J. Winston Coleman, Jr., *Slavery Times in Kentucky*, 197–202, 216.

reading passages from the Bible and the antislavery speeches made in Congress during the Missouri Compromise debates. His reputed accomplices also belong to the urban Negro elite—Monday Gell, who hired his time from his master and kept a harness shop on Meeting Street, Peter Poyas, a skilled ship carpenter, Bacchus Hammett, and Gullah Jack, a sorcerer. There existed in the city among the whites an element of tension, for normally the Negroes outnumbered the whites 14,127 to 10,653, and in the summer many of the whites were away at resorts. The white man's fear of the Negro is a mysterious thing (the author can remember rumors of race riots in his native city of Winston-Salem that stirred up irrational fears). When a slave reported to his master that an insurrection plot had been formed, the people of Charleston fell into a panic of fear, which caused them to do savage acts under the guise of law. Thirty-five slaves were hanged and thirty-four were deported on the basis of the flimiest of evidence. The court of respectable citizens who tried the cases published *An Official Report of the Trials of Sundry Negroes, Charged with an Attempt to Raise an Insurrection in the State of South Carolina . . .* (Charleston, 1822), which has been accepted by historians as a true report. But an able scholar has recently shown that the report is highly suspect, and he believes that "there is persuasive evidence that no conspiracy in fact existed." [22]

The complacency of the Southern people was further disturbed in 1829 by the discovery of the circulation within the South of an incendiary pamphlet, *Walker's Appeal to the Colored Citizens of the World.* This violent publication was written by a North Carolina free Negro, David Walker, who had emigrated to Boston. Copies of this pamphlet were brought to some of the Southern ports for the purpose of circulating them among the blacks. The alarm created by this insurrectionary document resulted in the passage in 1830 of laws prohibiting the teaching of slaves to read or write in North Carolina, Georgia, and Louisiana, in 1831 in Virginia, and in 1834 in South Carolina.[23]

The most momentous of all the slave revolts occurred in August of the following year, the Nat Turner Insurrection in Southampton County, Virginia. Nat Turner was a slave preacher who cultivated an atmosphere of mystery and prophecy and wielded great influence over the blacks. Although he was well treated by his master, he conceived of a plot to lead the slaves in a revolt to win their freedom. From reading the Bible, especially the Book of Revelation, Turner had derived fanatical ideas that caused him to see

[22] See Richard C. Wade, "The Vesey Plot: A Reconsideration," *Journal of Southern History*, XXX (May 1964), 150; John Lofton, *Insurrection in South Carolina: The Turbulent World of Denmark Vesey* (Yellow Springs, 1964), and R. S. Starobin (ed.), *Denmark Vesey: The Slave Conspiracy of 1822* (Englewood Cliffs, N.J., 1970) who concludes the trial was grossly unfair and was designed to terrorize the black inhabitants.
[23] Clement Eaton, "A Dangerous Pamphlet in the Old South," *Journal of Southern History, II* (August 1936), 323–334.

visions of black and white angels fighting. The insurrection was rendered more bloody by the fact that Turner's followers broke into the wine cellars of their masters and fortified themselves with copious draughts of peach and apple brandy. Before the revolt was suppressed, over sixty whites as well as many innocent Negroes had been killed.[24]

The Nat Turner Revolt was the last important insurrection in the Old South. Nevertheless, the Southern whites continued to be frightened by numerous reported conspiracies. In 1835 a number of Negroes and whites were executed as a result of a wave of hysteria that swept Mississippi caused by an alleged plot of John A. Murrell, "the land pirate," and his confederates to start a slave insurrection. Frances Gaither, in the novel *The Red Cock Crows,* has drawn a faithful picture of the operation of vigilance committees at this time in condemning whites and Negroes to death, impelled by an incredibly violent fear of servile uprising. In 1856 and 1860 rumors of servile plots spread throughout the South, causing the death of many unfortunate Negroes. These were presidential election years, filled with political excitement in the South over the rise of the Republican party. Such dark rumors, when investigated, were usually found to be false, yet they did much to produce at times a pathological state of feeling among the Southern people.[25]

Although the Southern newspapers on occasions tried to suppress rumors of servile insurrection, in political campaigns they tended to magnify them, blaming the Northern abolitionists as responsible for instigating the slaves to rebel. The "jittery" state of public opinion was revealed by the John Brown Raid of 1859. Not a single slave arose to aid this band of Northern fanatics who brought pike heads to distribute among the slaves. Nevertheless, the Southern people were deeply stirred by fear and passion over this incident. The results of actual revolts or conspiracies, both real and imagined, were to impose more drastic restrictions on slaves and free Negroes as well as to limit the freedom of the press and speech in the South.

After the discovery of the David Walker pamphlet and after the Nat Turner Revolt, the South modified its slave code to secure stricter control over the Negroes. A paramount motive in establishing this new rigor was the fear that the abolitionists would stir the slaves to revolt or run away. After the black code had been perfected in the decade of the 1830's, slaves could not legally be taught to read and write, except in Maryland, Kentucky, Tennessee, and Arkansas; they were prohibited by law from leaving their plantations without a written pass; in the cities as well as on the plantation they were required to be in their houses when the curfew rang, usually at nine o'clock; Negro preachers were prohibited from exhorting their brethren

[24] See W. S. Drewry, *The Southampton Insurrection* (Washington, 1900); J. C. Carroll, *Slave Insurrections in the United States, 1800–1861* (Boston, 1938), and H. I. Tragle, *The Southampton Slave Revolt of 1831: A Compilation of Source Material* (Amherst, 1971).

[25] See Clement Eaton, *The Freedom-of-Thought Struggle in the Old South* (New York, 1964), chap. 3, The Fear of Servile Insurrection.

unless a white person were present; slaves could not own firearms, horses, horns, or drums or give medicine to a white person; they could not legally be employed in printing offices; and they were prohibited from assembling in crowds for dancing or even for funerals without the presence of a white man.

A patrol of white men was established to enforce these laws. The patrols consisted of a captain and three other members, who were appointed at the militia muster or by the county court. They were required to patrol the county once every two weeks, or oftener in times of emergency. Among their duties were the searching of the Negro cabins for firearms and the flogging of slaves found on the roads at night without a pass. Often the patrols were manned by poor whites who got drunk (although it was illegal to drink on patrol) and unmercifully beat Negroes who came across their path. The patrol also captured runaways, for which they received $6 per capture. The fear of the slaves of the patrol was expressed in the cry, "Run, nigger, run! the patter-rollers will ketch you!" [26]

Furthermore, the black codes of the Southern states prescribed a special set of laws for dealing with slave crime and slave relations with the whites. Slave marriages had no legal validity. City ordinances prohibited Negroes from smoking on the streets or riding in hacks, and they were required to yield the streets in passing to whites. Death was the penalty for rebelling or plotting to rebel; slaves executed by the state for crimes were paid for by state funds; slaves were not tried usually by a jury but by an informal court of justices of the peace.[27]

The draconic laws of the black code were laxly enforced, however, particularly the laws relating to the patrol and to the teaching of slaves to read and write. Joseph Turner, editor of *The Countryman,* published on a plantation near Eatonton, Georgia, declared in 1862, when there was some agitation to repeal the law prohibiting the teaching of Negroes to read: "the law is obsolete, and never has prevented a negro [sic] who desired it from learning to read. I have never known a case of punishment for its violation." [28] Southern legislators were in the habit of making extreme laws for emergencies, which were later tempered by the good-natured or the inefficient practice of the Southern people and the liberality of court decisions. Indeed, the laxity of the Southern states in enforcing laws was not confined to the slave code. The Southerner tended to have a cavalier attitude toward laws restraining his personal liberty and to rely upon himself rather than the courts to punish insults and injuries, while at the same time he strenuously insisted upon strict adherence to the federal Constitution.

Recent studies have compared the conditions of slavery in Cuba and Brazil with those in the Southern states but with different conclusions. Frank

[26] See H. M. Henry, *The Police Control of the Slaves in South Carolina* (Emory, Va., 1914).

[27] See Helen T. Catterall (ed.), *Judicial Cases Concerning American Slavery and the Negro* (Washington, 1926–36), 4 vols.

[28] *The Countryman*, Turnwold, Putnam Co., Georgia, Dec. 1 and Nov. 17, 1862.

Tannenbaum and Stanley Elkins maintained that slavery in Latin America was a milder institution than in the Southern states, owing largely to the influence of the Catholic church. Actually there was little difference between the two societies in the conception of the status of the slave; by law he was both a person and property. The Catholic clergy in Brazil were not active in the abolition movement, according to the researches of Carl Degler, and only a small proportion of the Brazilian slaves were married by the Church. Moreover, the disruption of the slave family by the internal slave trade was as great in Brazil as it was in the Southern states, there being no law to prevent it until 1869. Similar situations existed in Brazil and the United States in regard to the rights of a slave to hold property; both societies in practice, though not in law, recognizing this right with respect to chickens, hogs, the slaves' garden produce, and articles they manufactured on their own time—but in the South, not firearms. The laws in Brazil with regard to slaves were as laxly enforced as they were in the South, but Brazil had no legislation, as did the Southern states, requiring Negroes to emigrate after manumission. Indeed, Brazil was more liberal as to manumission than the Southern states, with the result that whereas in the South the number of slaves was sixteen times the number of free Negroes, in Brazil it was only three times. On the other hand, there was less rebelliousness of slaves in the South than in Brazil, owing partly to the fact that Brazilian slavery depended on the long-continued African slave trade, while Southern slavery expanded by the reproduction of slaves. Accordingly, the ratio of slave men and women was approximately the same in the South but was greatly unbalanced in Brazil. Carl Degler has concluded that slavery was actually milder in the South than it was in Brazil, but that the Latin country accepted blacks in its society far more readily than in the United States.[29] It is a significant fact that the South was the only area of the Western Hemisphere where the slave population grew in numbers without receiving fresh supplies from the African slave trade.[30]

So much scholarship has been lavished recently on the study of slavery that the important study of the free Negro has been neglected. The plight of the free Negroes of the Old South was tragic. The majority of them were located in the upper South, particularly in Maryland, where the free colored population of 84,000 nearly balanced the slave population. The Southern states having the smallest number of this class in 1860 were Mississippi, with only 773, and Arkansas with 144. The freedmen tended to congregate in the towns and cities, but the considerable free Negro population of North Caro-

---

[29] Carl Degler, *Neither Black Nor White: Slavery and Race Relations in Brazil and the United States* (New York, 1970).

[30] C. V. Woodward, in *American Counterpoint: Slavery and Racism in the North-South Dialogue* (Boston, 1971), chap. 3, offers several explanations for this phenomenon, but to the author it indicates strongly that the Southern slaves were treated more humanely than elsewhere in the Western Hemisphere—with nourishing food, moderate labor, good health care, and a proper balance of the sexes.

Frederick Douglass (1817–1895), a Maryland slave who became a great man.

lina was mainly rural. Many of this class were the offspring of illicit relations between whites and blacks. According to Southern laws a person with only a slight admixture of Negro blood in his veins, in North Carolina as much as one sixteenth and in Virginia as much as one fourth, was classified as a Negro; marriage between a Negro and a white was prohibited; and illegitimate mulatto children followed the status of the mother. The antebellum laws in this respect were more liberal than the laws of some Southern states in the twentieth century; for example, the modern Virginia statute that defines a Negro as a person having any quantum of Negro blood, and the North Carolina legislation that permits marriage between whites and persons of Negro descent to the third generation inclusive, but until very recently prohibited children with any Negro blood whatsoever in their veins from attending white schools.[31]

In addition to origin by birth from a free mother, the free Negro class was derived from the emancipation of slaves. During and after the American Revolution, Southern masters were influenced by the liberal philosophy of natural rights as well as by the decline of the tobacco trade to free their slaves, particularly by will. In 1782 Virginia passed a liberal manumission law, but in 1805 reversed her policy and made the emancipation process very difficult by requiring the immediate removal of the freedmen from the state. Tennessee also abandoned her generous manumission policy in 1831 by ordering the immediate removal of the freed Negro from the state. Kentucky, by an act of 1851, was one of the last Southern states to require the removal of the slave after emancipation.

Various restrictions stood in the way of the manumission of slaves. In order to prevent masters from liberating old and infirm slaves for the sake of escaping financial responsibility, the Southern states usually required that consent for the emancipation of slaves must be obtained from county courts. In Georgia slaves could not be emancipated after 1801 except by the act of legislature, although they could be freed by will outside of the state. Some of the Southern states, Virginia, for example, had laws that held that if an emancipated slave did not leave the state within twelve months, he was liable to be sold by the state into slavery. In the later antebellum period such legislation made it practically impossible for most masters to free their slaves, not only on account of the financial cost, but also because some of the Northern states prohibited the immigration of free Negroes (notably Indiana, Illinois, Oregon, and, until 1849, Ohio). Nevertheless, some masters evaded the law by allowing their slaves to live as virtually free persons.

The free Negro in a slave society was an anomaly bitterly resented by the whites. Joel Chandler Harris, in his story "Free Joe and the Rest of the World," has portrayed the pathos and isolation of the free rural Negro in a world of black slaves and whites. In the town he was hated and feared as a competitor by white artisans and mechanics. Southerners regarded free Negroes as the most vicious members of their race, as potential leaders of insurrection. Calhoun in his report to Congress on a bill for preventing the circulation of incendiary publications maintained that free Negroes were found more frequently in jails than any element of the population. Slave-owners believed that the free Negroes tended to corrupt the slaves, sold liquor to them, were thieves and the receivers of stolen property, and set a bad example of idleness.

After the discovery of the David Walker pamphlet and the excitement produced by the Nat Turner Revolt, the legal position of the free Negro in the South deteriorated greatly. In Georgia and Florida he had to have a

---

[31] See C. S. Mangum, Jr., *The Legal Status of the Negro* (Chapel Hill, 1940).

white guardian, and in other states where there was no such legal requirement he usually secured some white friend to defend him. He had to register
with the county officials; his testimony in the courts, save in Louisiana, was
invalid against whites; in some states he was prohibited from preaching to
Negroes; he was not allowed to buy or sell liquor; and he was subject to
curfew laws. His freedom of movement and of assembly was severely limited,
and except in Kentucky, Tennessee, and Maryland, it was illegal to teach
free Negroes to read and write. He was constantly in danger of being kidnapped and sold.[32]

Nevertheless, the harsh laws of the free Negro code were only spasmodi-
cally enforced, and many free Negroes who legally should have left the state
of emancipation remained unmolested. In addition to this laxness of law enforcement, the lot of the free Negroes had other redeeming features. The
right of jury trial was not denied to him, and he could sue in the courts. He
was permitted to vote in Tennessee until 1834 and was not disfranchised in
North Carolina until by the action of the Constitutional Convention of 1835
—then by the surprising vote of 66 to 61. Prior to that time it is possible
that the free Negroes held the balance of power in some of the eastern
counties and towns of the state. In certain of the eastern counties free Negro
orphan children were taught to read and write under the apprentice laws,
just as were white orphans.

The great majority of free Negroes were employed as domestic servants
and agricultural laborers, but there was a considerable proportion of skilled
workers among them. In Virginia, for example, there were 4,224 free Negro
blacksmiths and 3,728 shoemakers listed in the census of 1860. Free Negroes
had almost a monopoly on certain occupations, such as the barber's trade,
from which they have been driven since the Civil War by the white man.
Free Negroes in the South accumulated money as merchants, hotelkeepers,
and planters. The year 1830 marks the zenith of the ownership of slaves by
free Negroes, most of such slaves being purchased in order to protect relatives, but others for exploitation as agricultural labor. An interesting case of
the ownership of slaves by free Negroes was the purchase of an eloquent
slave preacher by the Pleasant Green Baptist Negro church of Lexington,
Kentucky. When the slave preacher was put up for auction in the settlement
of an estate, a friendly white Baptist congregation purchased him for their
black brethren, who, in turn, paid for him on the installment plan by taking
the Sunday collections to the white deacon.[33] The free Negroes of Virginia
shared in the revival of prosperity of that state after 1830, so that they
owned as much land on the eve of the Civil War as the whole of the race held

[32] For admirable studies of the free Negro, see, J. M. England, "The Free Negro in
Ante-Bellum Tennessee," *Journal of Southern History, IX* (February 1943), 37–58;
J. H. Franklin, *The Free Negro in North Carolina, 1790–1860* (Chapel Hill, 1943);
and J. H. Russell, *The Free Negro in Virginia, 1619–1865* (Baltimore, 1913), and
H. E. Sterx, *The Free Negro in Ante-Bellum Louisiana* (Madison, 1972).

[33] William M. Pratt, Diary, Jan. 1, 1856, MS in the University of Kentucky Library.

in the state in 1890. From 1790 to 1850 the proportional growth of the free Negro element in the upper South was greater than either the white or slave population, and despite the deterioration of their legal status during this period, they improved and strengthened their economic position in Southern society.

Although black and white relationships in the South were legally rigid, in actual practice there were some remarkable variations in the status of Negroes. One of the most notable teachers in North Carolina was John Chavis, a free Negro who conducted schools for white children at Raleigh and Hillsborough, teaching the sons of Chief Justice Henderson and such eminent men as Governor Charles Manly and Senator Willie P. Mangum. Also white congregations at times listened to eloquent Negro preachers. Negro women often suckled the children of aristocratic white families. Moreover, among the free Negroes of Louisiana were some wealthy and cultivated persons who had been educated in Paris and who owned large plantations tilled by black slaves. A collection of poetry by Louisiana Negroes, representing seventeen authors, was published in 1845 by Armand Lanusse under the title *Les Cenelles, Choix de Poésies Indigènes.*[34]

The diary of a free Negro of Natchez, William Tiler Johnson, which has recently been discovered, reveals the large measure of freedom and economic opportunity that a very exceptional Negro could enjoy in a Southern state. Johnson, the son of a white father and a mulatto mother, operated three barber shops and owned 1,500 acres of land and eight slaves. In one year he made sixteen loans totaling $2,000 to white men. A Negro sport, he bet on the horse races, bought liquor, spent money on lascivious pleasure, went to the theater, and gambled with cards. He subscribed to four or five Mississippi and Louisiana newspapers as well as to the sporting magazine *The Spirit of the Times,* the *New York Mirror,* and the *Saturday Evening Post.* In 1851 he was murdered by a white man after he had won a lawsuit against the latter involving the boundaries of his plantation.[35]

Not only did free Negroes gravitate toward the towns and cities but many slaves joined them as workers and domestics, frequently hired from the neighboring plantations. In the urban centers, slaves were able to live a freer life and had more opportunities to develop their minds and personalities than were available to their rural brethren. They enjoyed better food, clothing, quarters, and recreation than the bondsmen on the plantations. They mingled with the free Negroes, who often could read, and thus became more sophisticated; they frequently evaded the laws relating to assembly and prohibiting the sale of liquor. Since most of the slaves that were hired into the cities and

[34] See R. L. Desdunes [a Creole black], *Our People and Our History* (Baton Rouge, 1973), chap. 2.
[35] W. R. Hogan and E. W. Davis (eds.), *William Johnson's Natchez, the Ante-Bellum Diary of a Free Negro* (Baton Rouge, 1951). The white man who killed him escaped punishment because the only witnesses to the murders were blacks, who could not legally testify against a white.

towns were domestics there was a considerable preponderance of women over men among the urban slaves. In many subtle ways life in the cities relaxed the bonds of slavery, and accordingly masters became reluctant to hire their valuable human chattels in the urban centers for fear that they would be ruined or spoiled as slaves. Consequently, beginning in the late 1830's, a remarkable decline occurred in the proportion of slaves in the Southern towns and cities. In Charleston, for example, the Negroes in 1820 exceeded 58 per cent of population, but forty years later the slaves formed approximately only one third of the inhabitants; in New Orleans the slaves in 1860 numbered only one in seven of the residents, whereas in the early part of the century they had formed a large part of the population; in Louisville the Negro people had decreased from approximately one fourth of the population in 1830 to only 10 per cent in 1860.[36] Part of this decline was owing to the rising cost of slave labor and the availability of cheap white immigrant labor.

The greatest indictment of the South's treatment of the Negro in the antebellum period was not that of cruelty but of keeping him in a state of pupilage.[37] Thus he could not develop his potential and demonstrate that he was not inherently inferior to the white man, as Southerners of that period almost universally believed. Southerners attributed the peculiar characteristics shown by the slaves to an inherent nature different from that of the whites or to their African heritage. It has become increasingly clear, however, that most of these characteristics were owing to the institution of slavery. A recent scholar has observed that prisoners in the German concentration camps after a period of conditioning developed characteristics somewhat similar to those of Southern slaves.[38] The childlike nature, the irresponsibility, the tendency to steal, the loose morals, the matriarchal society, the indolence, the proneness to flattery and obsequiousness, even the loud guffaws, were to a large degree caused by slavery.

This view of the plantation slave as a "Sambo" has been vigorously combatted by some modern scholars and clearly represents only a partial truth.[39] Now that the Negro has so signally proven his ability in recent years, it is obligatory for the historian to take a new look at the slave in his antebellum environment. The letters and diaries of planters and plantation records often discredit the stereotype of the typical Southern slave as being a lazy, unreli-

36 See R. C. Wade, *Slavery in the Cities, The South, 1820–1860* (New York, 1964).

37 Frederick Jackson Turner, *The United States, 1830–1850: The Nation and the Sections* (New York, 1935), 167–168, admirably presents this point of view.

38 Stanley Elkins, *Slavery: A Problem in American Institutional and Intellectual Life* (Chicago, 1959), and D. B. Davis, *The Problem of Slavery in Western Culture* (Ithaca, 1966).

39 See Kenneth M. Stampp, "Rebels and Sambos: The Search for the Negro's Personality in Slavery," *Journal of Southern History*, XXXVII (August 1971), 367–392; and Clement Eaton, *The Mind of the Old South* (Enlarged ed., 1967) chap. 9, The Mind of the Southern Negro: The Remarkable Individuals.

able, obsequious individual. Instead, they tell of some slaves who were so intelligent that the masters consulted them as advisers on plantation policies, slaves who were competent overseers, slaves who made real progress in developing skills, slaves who had a passionate attachment to the plantation —the good earth—and a pride in the crops. In the papers of Ebenezer Pettigrew, a planter of eastern North Carolina, for example, are found records of remarkable Negroes.[40] The letters of the Charles Colcock Jones family of Georgia also tell of admirable Negro slaves such as Andrew, who directed the work on the Maybank plantation and of whom a neighboring planter who occasionally visited the plantation reported: "Andrew is such an intelligent man—and one of principle—it is a pleasure to see to his work." [41] The noted agricultural reformer Edmund Ruffin had a very intelligent black overseer, "Jem" Sykes, whom he mentions in his diary as follows: "I have been amused to hear, from Mr. Sayre [his son-in-law who took over the management of the Ruffin plantation], of some of the remarks of Jem Sykes, the foreman, (& my former overseer) about the crops & the land. He is full of glorification and boasting, & exaggerates the truth." [42]

In industry, also, the Negro had many opportunities to advance in skill and develop his latent ability. Numerous plantations had slave mechanics and carpenters, some of whom were hired in the cities. In fact, the competition of slave mechanics was so threatening to white mechanics that they petitioned the legislatures, as previously noted, to protect them from this competition, without success except in Georgia. One of these remarkable slaves was Horace, the bridge builder in Alabama, whose master out of gratitude for his work in constructing bridges throughout the black belt had the legislature pass a law in the 1845–46 session emancipating Horace and thereafter employed him as a free artisan. Two notable slaves who were employed in the cypress lumber industry in Louisiana, Simon Gray and James Matthews, even "bossed" white employees and were entrusted with money by their master, Andrew Brown, the magnate of the lumber industry in the Southwest. But with the coming of freedom, John H. Moore observes, "these Negroes lost their unusual opportunity to rise above the ranks of manual labor in this branch of industry in the old Southwest. From mid-1863 onward all positions of authority were reserved only for whites." [43]

It is a delight to the researcher in Southern history to come across these remarkable Negroes in the slave regime. Edmund Ruffin, who wrote of his descent into a coal mine in Virginia, mentioned a slave foreman of a mine

[40] The Pettigrew Papers are in the Southern Collection of the University of North Carolina. B. H. Wall of Tulane University has made some valuable unpublished researches into the lives of individual slaves as revealed in these papers.
[41] R. H. Meyers (ed.), *The Children of the Pride*, 353.
[42] W. K. Scarborough (ed.), *The Diary of Edmund Ruffin* (Baton Rouge, 1972), 186–87.
[43] John Hebron Moore, *Andrew Brown and Cypress Lumbering in the Old Southwest* (Baton Rouge, 1967).

whom the master gave complete charge of the slave force. The master was so pleased with the slave's performance that he emancipated him and thereafter paid him wages of $200 a month to continue to manage the mine.[44] When Sir Charles Lyell visited the Hopeton Plantation in Georgia in 1846, he was surprised to see the rank held by the black mechanics. "When these mechanics come to consult Mr. Couper [the master] on business," he wrote, "their manner of speaking to him is quite as independent as that of English artisans to their employers. Their aptitude for the practice of such mechanical arts may encourage every philanthropist who has had misgivings in regard to the progressive powers of the race—." [45] Ex-Governor James H. Hammond of South Carolina declared in an address in 1849 opposing the use of slaves in industry, "whenever a slave is made a mechanic he is more than half freed." [46]

In assessing Southern slavery within the context of its own time rather than that of the twentieth century, we must recognize that it was a mixture of good and evil. As Thomas Hardy wrote: "All things merge in one another— good into evil, generosity into justice, religion into politics. . . ." We do not know, for example, the latitude of the slave system, how many ambitious and able slaves scattered through the plantation districts and in the cities advanced in skills, knowledge, and status despite tremendous handicaps. But their anonymous existence warns us against accepting the neoabolitionist, Marxist stereotype of an institution that was actually composed of infinitely varied relationships. Although the statement of the eminent authority U. B. Phillips that slavery was a school for training the Negro in the ways of civilization was only partially true, it was a fairer assessment than the stark indictment of a modern historian that it was a school from which the slave did not graduate.

[44] E. L. Schwaab (ed.), *Travels in the Old South, Selected from Periodicals of the Time* (Lexington, 1973), 2 vols., II, 310–316.
[45] Sir Charles Lyell, *A Second Visit to the United States of North America* (New York, 1849).
[46] R. S. Starobin, *Industrial Slavery in the South* (New York, 1970), 208.

15

The Middle Class and the Disadvantaged

IN THIS AGE of awakening interest in the common man, historians have begun to turn the spotlight of research away from the life of the gentry to the plain people of the Old South. Contrary to the romantic stereotype, these historians have discovered that the typical Southerner was an unostentatious farmer, cultivating a small acreage of land with his own hands or with the aid of a few slaves. In Tennessee, for example, two thirds of the heads of agricultural families in 1860 tilled farms containing less than two hundred acres. In North Carolina, approximately 70 per cent of the farms at this time were under one hundred acres. Even in Louisiana, which has been regarded as the paradise of the large planter, approximately two thirds of the agricultural properties were farms of less than one hundred acres. This large proportion of small farmers is partly explained by the fact that many humble Creole families refused to sell their farms to neighboring planters and that on the death of the father the farm was subdivided among the numerous sons. In Mississippi, 60 per cent of the agricultural owners had less than one hundred acres of improved land.

Perhaps the most significant fact about the yeoman farmers of the Old South was that they owned their land. Investigations of land ownership in the decade 1850–1860 reveal a surprising proportion of the farmers of the Old South who owned their farms.[1] In Alabama, which may be taken as representative of the lower South, 74 per cent of the farmers owned their land in 1850, a high degree of proprietorship that was increased to 80 per cent ten years later. In the Sugar Bowl parishes of Louisiana, 80 per cent of the farming population owned their land. A similarly independent, land-owning status of the yeoman farmers existed in the upper South, where there was about the same proportion of free landowners as in the lower South. In contrast, the farm tenants of the South in 1930 constituted 57.3 per cent of the farm population, and in states such as Georgia and Mississippi, the percentage rose to 65.6 per cent and 66.1 per cent, respectively, an unwholesome condition, the reverse of the situation in 1860. The widespread ownership of land in the Old South gave to the farmer a sense of independence and self-respect and apparently provided the economic basis for a democratic policy.

Such statistics make it necessary for us to revise traditional ideas of

---

[1] See F. L. Owsley, *The Plain Folk of the Old South* (Baton Rouge, 1949), and Herbert Weaver, *Mississippi Farmers, 1850–1860* (Nashville, 1945).

Southern society during the antebellum period. It is clear from the study of land tenure that there existed a large body of yeoman farmers below the Potomac who constituted a true middle class. A school of historians centered at Vanderbilt University have made large claims for this class, maintaining that they enjoyed a remarkable prosperity in the decade 1850–1860, during which they increased their holdings both of land and slaves, and that small farms and plantations were frequently side by side, the yeoman ploughing as fertile soil as his rich planter neighbor.[2]

This last conclusion challenges the Phillips-Gray thesis of a large degree of segregation of the planters and yeoman farmers. According to this older view, the small farmers and poor whites were driven by the advance of the plantation from fertile soils into areas of poorer soils.[3] Slave labor was uneconomical on poor land and even on rich land with inadequate communications to market. Certainly the maps of the distribution of slaves and of staple-producing areas show that the slaves and the vast majority of the plantations were concentrated in the rich soil areas and along the river valleys. The yeoman farmers, on the other hand, were most numerous in the uplands—the Piedmont region of the upper South, the hill regions of east Tennessee, northern Georgia, Alabama, and Mississippi—as well as in the poorer soils of the coastal region. This fact does not invalidate a conclusion that frequently planters and farmers lived in juxtaposition, for in contiguous areas the soil is often of unequal fertility. Furthermore, there was considerable fluidity in Southern society so that yeomen did acquire fertile land and become planters.

The dynamics of Southern slavery seems to have been in the direction of greater concentration of slaves into fewer hands rather than the reverse trend of a wider distribution of slave property. In 1850 approximately one third of the Southern people belonged to slaveholding families, but by 1860 the proportion had declined to slightly over one fourth of the white population. A case study of Greene County, Georgia, for example, shows a remarkable decline of the white populations by 1840 as the plantations and the number of slaves increased. The nonslaveholders, tenants, and unsuccessful farmers tended to move farther west.[4]

This emigration was particularly active in the Atlantic seaboard states in the decade of the 1830's. During this decade South Carolina's population stood almost stationary, registering according to the federal census a gain of only 0.47 per cent. North Carolina had a rate of increase of only 2.54 per

---

[2] F. L. and H. C. Owsley, "The Economic Basis of Society in the Late Ante-Bellum South," *Journal of Southern History*, VI (February 1940), 24–45; B. H. Clark, *The Tennessee Yeomen, 1840–1860* (Nashville, 1942); H. L. Coles, "Some Notes on Slave Ownership and Land Ownership in Louisiana, 1850–1860," *Journal of Southern History*, IX (August 1943), 380–394; percentages based on sampling.

[3] U. B. Phillips, "The Origin and Growth of the Southern Black Belts," *American Historical Review*, XI (July 1906), 798–816.

[4] A. F. Raper, *Tenants of the Almighty* (New York, 1943), 32.

cent and Virginia 6.7 per cent as compared with 8.6 per cent, 12.79 per cent, and 15.12 per cent respectively in the previous decade. The lower South, on the other hand, was increasing in population by huge ratios during these decades, but after 1840 there was also constant emigration from the Gulf states to Arkansas and Texas. The nomadic farmers and planters had practised the same type of soil butchery here as in the older states. Accordingly, after the land had begun to wear out and erosion had carried away much of the topsoil, they abandoned their farms. The ever-recurring movement of the covered wagons, pulled by oxen and horses, filled with women, children, grandparents, and "household plunder," was a melancholy sight on the dusty roads of the Old South.

The question of how important in the whole economy of the South was the middle class of farmers as compared with the planter group remains an unsolved problem. William E. Dodd, in his study of the lower South, has pointed out the tremendous and unwholesome concentration of wealth in the hands of a small planter class.[5] The Vanderbilt studies, on the other hand, emphasize the wide distribution of land ownership in the lower as well as in the upper South and the apparent prosperity of the yeoman farmers during the last decade of the antebellum period. The quality of land that a farmer tilled was more important than the number of acres he owned. The fact that the planters tended to monopolize the soils of high fertility and the farmers those of inferior quality meant that the planters in the rich black belts produced the "lion's share" of the money crops, cotton, sugar, and rice.[6] The yeoman farmers, on the other hand, although they owned their little farms, lived a low standard of existence on a hog and corn economy.

With the exceptions of rice and sugar for export, the yeoman farmers raised the same crops as did the planter. Despite the economic advantages of the slave plantation, part of the Southern cotton crop was grown by small farmers. This group, however, was engaged principally in cultivating subsistence crops, such as wheat, corn, oats, and sweet potatoes, and sorghum cane. In the cotton and tobacco districts the typical farmer planted as a rule several acres in cotton or tobacco that furnished him with money to buy goods from the store and pay taxes. To process his small cotton crop for the market he used the planter's gin and press and to grind his corn and wheat, the planter's gristmill, paying a toll of a portion of the grain. The Creole small farmers, in addition to cultivating corn, sweet potatoes, the sorghum

[5] W. E. Dodd, *The Cotton Kingdom* (New Haven, 1919), 24; a recent study strongly supports this thesis of planter economic and social dominance, concluding that the planters monopolized to a great extent not only the good land, the slaves, and cotton production but also the political leadership. R. B. Campbell, "Planters and Plain Folk: Harrison County, Texas, as a Test Case, 1850–1860," *Journal of Southern History,* XL (August 1974), 369–398.

[6] Fabian Linden, "Economic Democracy in the Slave South: An Appraisal of Some Recent Views," *Journal of Negro History,* XXXI (April 1946), 140–189, a severe criticism of the Owsley school.

cane, raised perique tobacco and a type of rough rice that was different from and sweeter than Carolina rice.

The small farmers also raised a large number of livestock. The landscape of the small farms of the Old South was animated by the grunting of numerous lean hogs, expressively dubbed "razor-backs," which found their own food by rooting in the forests and fields. The yeoman farmer raised a relatively larger proportion of cattle and sheep than did the large planter, often using the public lands for grazing and allowing his cattle largely to feed themselves, even in winter.[7] They were kept tame by placing cakes of salt for them to lick in the neighborhood of the house. Often a substantial yeoman, particularly in the pinelands and mountainous areas, appeared to belong to the "poor whites" because of lack of visible wealth, having only a few acres of corn or cotton, but actually he owned unsuspected wealth in the cattle that were hidden in the woods. The advance of plantation agriculture caused a decline in the production of livestock, for slavery was not especially suited to the raising of cattle.[8]

The overwhelming majority of the yeoman farmers lacked the capital to invest in slaves. A sampling of Mississippi counties in 1860 reveals that 51.56 per cent of the agricultural operators possessed no slaves and that approximately 20 per cent more of the farmers owned less than ten slaves.[9] In Alabama only one third of the families were slaveholders, and of this minority one half owned less than five slaves. In North Carolina on the eve of the Civil War nearly three fourths of the families owned no slaves, and of the small minority who were slaveholders 70.8 per cent owned less than ten slaves. The yeoman farmers who acquired a few slaves usually worked beside their black servants in the fields. Many of the nonslaveholders aspired to acquire slaves, not merely for the purpose of securing laborers or to aid their hard-worked wives, but also for the sake of social prestige. Nevertheless, in the upper South, at least, there was little distinction made in social intercourse between slaveholders and nonslaveholders belonging to the same economic level. Furthermore, in this region there was no dishonor or lessening of respect involved in working in the fields.

A large proportion of the overseers came from the yeoman class. Although the planters have drawn a very unfavorable picture of the overseers as a class, many of them were sons of substantial farmers and even of planters, young men "on the make," who wished to earn money for buying land and Negroes. In the census records of Hancock County, Georgia, for example, of the 139 overseers listed, 42 lived in the homes of the planters and 20 were sons of planters. Jesse Belflowers, the overseer of the rice plantation

[7] Frank L. Owsley, *Plain Folk of the Old South* (Baton Rouge, 1949), chap. 2.

[8] Eugene D. Genovese, *The Political Economy of Slavery: Studies in the Economy and Society of the Old South* (New York, 1965), chap. V, takes issue with Owsley over whether there was a flourishing livestock industry in the lower South, maintaining that, because of poor quality, there was "an excess of animals and a shortage of meat."

[9] Herbert Weaver, *Mississippi Farmers, 1850–1860* (Nashville, 1945).

Chicora Wood for twenty-four years, was a respectable yeoman whose yearly salary was increased from $300 at the beginning of his service to $1,000 after he had attained experience. William K. Scarborough, who made a statistical analysis of overseers, concluded that "the number of illiterate overseers was relatively insignificant," yet their spelling was erratic.[10] The overseer's position in the Old South was difficult, for very often the sole test of his success was the number of bales of cotton to the acre he could raise. Consequently, there was little incentive for him to take care of the land or slaves. His tenure was insecure, and there was a constant turnover in overseers. The job of managing black slaves required a combination of qualities that was hard to find. He was a rare overseer, indeed, who, like Garland Harmon of Georgia, wrote articles for agricultural magazines and zealously strove to preserve his employer's soil.[11]

It is difficult to find journals and letters of nonslaveholders that give a realistic picture of the life of the yeoman farmer. One of these rare records is a manuscript account of Newton Knight, leader of the Unionists of Jones County, Mississippi, by his son.[12] Jones County is in the pineland belt of southern Mississippi, a region of small slaveless farmers, in which a movement arose during the Civil War to detach the county from the Confederacy and, according to popular legend, establish the "Free State of Jones." Knight, a poor farmer boy, did not receive any schooling in his youth but worked hard on his father's farm. When he was nineteen years old he married, erected a log cabin, and cleared some land for cultivating corn and sweet potatoes. The people of his community marketed their produce, chickens, wood, and grain, at Shubuta, Mississippi, transporting them by oxen, whose slow progress consumed six days going and coming. In such a rural society many articles had to be made by hand. Knight, for example, made shoes for his neighbors and helped them to build log cabins. These yeoman families cooperated with each other in various ways, such as logrollings, corn huskings, and quilting parties. They attended camp meetings, barbecues, and stump speakings. Newton Knight was a primitive Baptist, who seems to have represented the strong streak of puritanism to be found in the yeoman class of the Old South. Quiet in demeanor, "strictly business," a person who "did not believe in any kind of foolishness," he had a grim and violent side to his nature that led him to kill a Negro. Despite his lack of education (he was finally taught to read and write by his wife) he was a natural leader in his community. Since he resolutely refused to fight against the Union in the Civil War, he was made a hospital orderly by the Confederates. The passage of the "twenty nigger law" [sic], exempting owners of twenty slaves from military

[10] W. K. Scarborough, *The Overseer: Plantation Management in the Old South* (Baton Rouge, 1966), 65.
[11] J. C. Bonner, "The Plantation Overseer and Southern Nationalism," *Agricultural History, XIX* (January 1945), 1–11; and J. S. Bassett (ed.), *The Plantation Overseer as Revealed in His Letters* (Northampton, Mass., 1925).
[12] MS in Department of Archives, Louisiana State University.

service, and the plundering of his community by Confederate cavalry caused him to desert and take the leadership of a guerrilla band of Unionists in the southern part of the state.

Another rare manuscript that affords an intimate glance into the life of a yeoman farmer of the Old South is the diary, 1838–1846, of Ferdinand Steel of Grenada, Mississippi.[13] He and his brother raised five or six bales of cotton, which they prepared for market by using the gin of a nearby planter, paying a toll of one eleventh of the ginned cotton. He arose at five o'clock in the morning, said his prayers, fed two horses and milked three cows, worked until noon, rested two hours and then worked until sundown. In the evening he studied his books for a few hours, and then after family prayers retired to bed. He did not think that cotton was a suitable crop for yeomen to raise; he believed that it would be better to concentrate on corn and wheat. His chief amusements were going to church, especially attending the singing school, and hunting deer and wild duck. He was more puritanical even than Newton Knight. A believer in the literal word of the Bible, Steel ascribed to Providence constant interference in human affairs, and his goal was to be "ready" to die and enter heaven. Strangely, his diary is silent on slavery and says very little about politics, suggesting that religion and the hard struggle to make a living were much important to the yeoman farmer than either slavery or politics.

The will books in the county courthouses give a valuable insight into the lives of the plain people of the Old South. The will of Barbary Keistler of Rowan County, North Carolina, May, 1856, for example, shows the personal possessions of an old lady of German extraction who could not read or write but signed her name by making her mark. To her two sons she bequeathed $31 in cash, her bed and bedding, a commode, a spinning wheel, a reel, a wash pot, a bucket, a chest, a bake oven, a cupboard, a skillet and a frying pan, and her clothes to be divided among her daughters-in-law.[14] The bill of sale of the personal property of Arnett White of Fayette County, Kentucky, September, 1849, included property valued at $937.03, which included a feather bed, quilts and blankets, a dining table, a bureau, a carpet, churn, crocks, kettles, six silver spoons, one dozen tumblers, a castor stand, a rifle, a saddle and bridle, four hoes, two hay forks, a grain cradle, a hemp brake, stretchers, hackles, a quantity of hemp and corn, two stacks of rye, seven head of cattle, fourteen horses, two sheep, ten hogs, and a large boar. The worldly possessions of a more substantial slaveholding farmer of the Bluegrass region of Kentucky, Daniel B. Kay, as recorded in his will of June, 1854, included: one hundred and sixty acres of land valued at $50 an acre, eight slaves, sixteen horses, twelve silver spoons, eight fine mahogany chairs,

---

[13] MS owned by Edward M. Steel, Jr., of West Virginia University. For a portrayal of the life of the yeomen and poor whites, see Clement Eaton, *The Mind of the Old South* (Baton Rouge, 1967, revised and enlarged ed.), chap. VII, The Southern Yeoman: The Humorists' View and the Reality.

[14] MS in the Courthouse of Rowan County at Salisbury, North Carolina.

one pair of cut-glass decanters, one rocking chair, as well as receipts for hemp stored in a warehouse and loans bearing interest.[15]

The monotonous life of these yeoman farmers of the Old South seems very drab to modern eyes. Most of them lived in log houses of the type called "dog-run cabins," consisting of two rooms united under the same roof but with an open space or "breezeway" between them. The boys and girls slept in the loft under the roof. The huge fireplace was equipped with pots, pans, and cranes for cooking. The furniture was largely homemade, the lye soap was homemade, gourds were used for dipping drinking water from the wooden pail; in fact, these homes of the yeoman farmers were symbols of a large measure of economic independence. Working from dawn to dark, they accepted the niggardly rewards of their toil and the manifold blows of nature with fortitude, even quiet desperation.[16] Although the generations of farmers that came after the Civil War suffered most keenly from the inheritance of eroded and exhausted soils, the small farmers of the Old South also were often victims of barren land, whose symbol of barrenness was the brooms-edge. No historian has portrayed so realistically and poignantly as has Ellen Glasgow in the novel *Barren Ground,* the effect of impoverished soil on Southern men and women who unimaginatively accepted their fate, stubbornly opposed to "new-fangled ways," such as experimenting with different crops and new methods of agriculture that might have liberated them.

Nevertheless, the plain people of the Old South had their distinctive amusements, which are richly illustrated, with some exaggeration, by the Southern humorists. In such stories as "Polly Peablossom's Wedding" by John Basil Lamar, *Major Jones's Chronicles of Pineville* by William Tappan Thompson, *Fisher's River Scenes and Characters* by Harden E. Taliaferro, "Taking the Census" by Johnson Hooper, and "The Big Bear of Arkansas" by Thomas Bangs Thorpe are delineated the diversions of the common man. Here one may vicariously enjoy with the yeoman his zest in breakdown dancing, in singing folk songs, in attending camp meetings, in going to the county court, in getting drunk, in hunting with his hounds, in practical joking, in shooting at a target for the prize of a beef, and in attending barbecues and corn shuckings.

The yeomen of the South, particularly the mountain whites, have made a valuable contribution to American music and to the literature of ballads and folk songs. Traditional English and Scottish ballads survived in the Appalachians, often modified by the Southern environment. There were lively tunes played by mountain fiddles, such as "Money Musk," "Leather Breeches," "Old Joe Clark," "Sally Good'n," "Weevily Wheat," and "Skip to My Lou." There were melancholy songs about the frustration of life, such as "Barbara Allen." Some of the most creative songs of the Southern uplands were the white spirituals, which expressed the deep religious emotion of a frontier people, dominated by a solemn reverence and an appreciation of the mystery

[15] MS in Courthouse of Fayette County at Lexington, Kentucky.
[16] See Bell I. Wiley, *The Plain People of the Confederacy* (Baton Rouge, 1943).

of nature. The favorite theme was the longing for heavens, the "promised land," in such songs as "Roll! Jordan, Roll!" In the country churches group singing was directed by a leader with a tuning fork, the group often using songbooks with notes of four shapes. The most popular of these songbooks compiled and in part composed by Southern men were the *Kentucky Harmony* (1815) by Ananias Davisson, *The Southern Harmony* (1835) by William ("Singing Billy") Walker of South Carolina, and *The Sacred Harp* (1844) by Benjamin F. White of Georgia.[17]

An insight into the mentality of the Southern farmers is afforded by the almanacs of the time. These publications, which were sold generally by country stores, ranked next to the Bible as the chief reading matter of the plain people. Not only did they predict weather but they were also a mine of practical information. Some of them gave the names of members of Congress and of the state legislature, the time of the meeting of the county courts, prices of cotton, temperatures throughout the year, schedules of sunrises and eclipses, jokes, anecdotes, advice about making good butter, getting rid of chinch bugs, mending china, and recipes. Most of the antebellum almanacs followed the example of Benjamin Franklin's *Poor Richard's Almanac* in including axioms of conduct, encouraging the middle-class virtues. *M'Carter's Country Almanac, Calculated for the Carolinas and Georgia* for the year 1836 published at Augusta, Georgia, gives this advice: "Humble wedlock is better than proud virginity." In the *Christian Almanac for Georgia and South Carolina,* 1830, is an unconsciously amusing article on "Eminent Early Risers," citing examples of great men who arose early in the morning. *Richardson's Virginia and North Carolina Almanac* for 1854 published at Richmond, contains this bit of folklore:

> When the peacock loudly bawls,
> soon we'll have both rain and squalls.

Perhaps the most valuable contribution of the almanacs was their encouragement to scientific agriculture. One of the most famous Southern almanacs was *Affleck's Rural Almanac,* published by Thomas Affleck of Washington, Mississippi, in connection with the advertisement of his Southern Nurseries. Affleck was a significant agricultural reformer in the lower South who used his almanac as a medium for agitating for more scientific agriculture in this region. Especially did he urge farmers to diversify their crops instead of overproducing cotton and to keep businesslike records of their agricultural operations. Other almanacs, such as the *Western Farmer's Comprehensive Almanac,* published at Louisville, Kentucky, had brief articles on the management of cattle, rules for overseers, the use of manure, the proper time to sow seeds, crop rotation, and miscellaneous agricultural information.

In addition to the yeomen and the small planters, the middle class com-

---

[17] G. P. Jackson, *White Spirituals in the Southern Uplands* (New York, 1913).

prised a large proportion of the merchants and professional men, dwelling principally in the towns and villages. Hundley, in his analysis of Southern society in 1860, placed in this middle class the "half-fledged" country lawyers, doctors, preachers, and teachers of "Old Field" schools.[18] The smallness of this class illustrates the overwhelming dominance of rural conditions; for example, according to the census of 1850, Alabama had only 15 professors, 30 editors, 570 lawyers, and 1,264 physicians in a population of approximately 320,000 whites and approximately the same number of Negroes. At the same date Mississippi had 16 professors, 34 editors, 570 lawyers, 1,109 teachers, and 1,217 physicians to serve a white population of 295,718 people as well as the huge horde of slaves.[19] In North Carolina, the professional class on the eve of the Civil War formed about 4 per cent of the total number of persons classified as to occupation by the Census Bureau.

The urban class in the South, those living in towns of over four thousand inhabitants, was a very small fraction of the population, only 7.8 per cent. At the apex of this urban society was a small group of retired or nonresident planters who had moved to town. Here they built imposing mansions of the Greek Revival style and through overseers supervised their outlying plantations. Closely associated with these "nabobs" were the lawyers, doctors, ministers, teachers, and editors. A large proportion of the income of the professional class was derived from services for the slavocracy. Moreover, the merchants and professional people were dominated by the agrarian ideal, causing them to aspire to own plantations and to acquire slaves. A modern study of a Georgia county in the Piedmont has disclosed that over 54 per cent of the professional class owned slaves and that this group enjoyed a greater average wealth than did the merchant class.[20] Except in some of the large seaports, the merchants ranked socially below the professional class.

What shall we say of the lazy, provincial life of a typical villager of the Old South, whose chief excitement was to watch a dog fight and who prided himself on his accuracy in squirting tobacco juice through his teeth at a distant spittoon? No better description of the vacuity of the life of the small villagers of Georgia can be found than in a letter from Alexander H. Stephens among the 115 bound volumes of his manuscript papers in the Library of Congress, written on July 20, 1852. On this somnolent day Stephens rode from *Liberty Hall* to the nearby village of Crawfordville and critically observed the activities of the villagers. At Gee's grocery, he found some of the villagers sitting on the porch playing or watching two games of "drafts" (checkers) that were in progress, the clerk and the village doctor participating in the game while the storekeeper watched through the window. Finding no interest in such idle waste of time, he passed on, but seeing old Billy Littler sitting on his piazza, he stopped to talk with him; then he went

[18] D. R. Hundley, *Social Relations in Our Southern States* (New York, 1860).

[19] J. D. B. DeBow (Supt.), *The Seventh Census of the United States: 1850*, pp. 428–429, 455, 481.

[20] J. C. Bonner, "Profile of a Late Ante-Bellum Community," *American Historical Review*, LXIX (July 1944), 672.

to the cobbler's shop and ordered a pair of shoes made; later in the day he returned to Gee's store and there saw the same villagers still playing and spitting tobacco juice. "What a dull day!" he commented.[21]

Among the villagers were usually some skilled laborers who were often paid higher wages in the South than in the North. Solon Robinson in 1849 reported that a cotton factory in South Carolina paid its thirty-five hands, some of whom were ten years old, an average wage of $1.90 a week, whereas a machinist was paid $9.00 a week. In 1860, a carpenter was paid per day without board $1.50 in North Carolina, $2.15 in Alabama, $2.47 in Mississippi, $1.65 in Indiana, as compared with the national average of $1.85. In New Orleans, a skilled laborer received as a rule $2.00 a day, whereas an unskilled laborer was paid $1.00 a day, and on the plantations only 50 to 75 cents a day.

In the cities the white mechanics bitterly resented slave competition. On occasions, they went on strike when Negro mechanics were employed to work beside them. Sometimes they resorted to mob violence, such as the beating of Frederick Douglass by the ship mechanics of Baltimore. Such prejudices against the Negro mechanic, prevailed in the North as well as in the South. The mechanics agitated at various times for legislation excluding Negro mechanics from the cities, and in some cases succeeded, such as the enactment of a Georgia law, in 1845, forbidding black mechanics or masons, slave or free, from making contracts for the erection or repair of buildings, or the master of slave mechanics from making such contracts. On the plantations, however, much of the skilled labor required for agricultural operations and for the needs of the planter was furnished by slave mechanics, masons, carpenters, coopers, and blacksmiths.

The skilled workmen of the Old South were too individualistic and perhaps too isolated to form effective trade unions and develop a strong sense of class solidarity. In the large cities they organized mechanics associations, which were incorporated by the legislature, but often the purposes of these organizations were to furnish mutual aid to each other or to form lyceums for intellectual improvement rather than for purposes of striking or of regulating the price of labor. The printers seem to have been the most active branch of skilled labor in organizing genuine trade unions, particularly in Augusta, Georgia, and New Orleans. The Typographical Society of New Orleans was founded as early as 1835, and after disbanding several times was firmly established in 1852 by Gerard Stith, who was later elected Mayor on the American ticket. The strongest of the early unions in the Crescent City was the Screwmen's Benevolent Association, or the union of the stevedores for the cotton ships. Their union paid mutual sick benefits of $3 a week and secured high wages for its members.[22]

---

[21] Cited by Clement Eaton, *The Waning of the Old South Civilization* (paperback ed. New York, 1969), 8–9, chap. I, The Southern Folk on the Eve of the Civil War.
[22] Roger Shugg, *Origins of Class Struggle in Louisiana* (University, La., 1939), 114–115.

The workingmen of the South lived rather insecure lives, such as was the lot of laborers in other parts of the nation.[23] In the cities open gutters, privies, and unprotected wells were sources of pollution and disease. In this individualistic age there was little control over callous landlords. Also the Irish laborers who worked on the railroads and dug ditches were sadly exploited. Their labor was handled by a contractor, who provided them with liquor but paid them very low wages to do the dangerous and unhealthful work from which slaves were protected. The mechanic class and the day laborers bore all the burden of the risks of their occupation, because the common-law doctrine that prevailed in America relieved employers from liability for accidents unless they were directly responsible for the accident. The many hardships of the laboring class are illustrated in a very racy auto-biography written by one of them, *The Life and Travels of John Robert Shaw, The Well Digger* (Lexington, Kentucky, 1807). After service in the Revolutionary army Shaw traveled in Kentucky digging wells, splitting rails, and working with drovers. Despite many vicissitudes he acquired property and a measure of prosperity, freeing himself from thralldom to liquor and becoming a shouting Methodist.

In the Southern towns and cities the artisans and laboring class were re-cruited to a considerable extent from foreign immigrants. The large rural districts of the South, on the other hand, were not an inviting region to foreigners; indeed, for every eight immigrants who settled in the North, only one located in the South. The reasons for this avoidance of the land of Dixie were that the principal shipping lines to America terminated in the Northern ports, industrial opportunities also were greater in the North, and the lands of the West were better advertised and more accessible. In the South, on the other hand, competition with slave labor was a deterrent (although this factor has been overemphasized), and the techniques of cultivating Southern staple crops were unfamiliar to European immigrants.

The horde of immigrants who poured into this country in the decade of the 1850's, therefore, sent only a small contingent into the Southern states. Moreover, perhaps 90 per cent of this group settled in the coastal and river towns, New Orleans being the great port of entry for them. The foreign-born in the Southern towns and cities were usually artisans, shopkeepers, cabmen, and specialized laborers, such as workers in the construction of railroads. Despite the overall picture of a relatively small proportion of foreigners in the South, such cities as Baltimore in 1860 had a 24.71 per cent foreign-born population, Richmond 23 per cent, and Mobile 24 per cent. In Charleston 30 per cent of the white population belonged to this category, and in Natchez there were 1,186 foreign-born in a population of 4,680 persons, the Irish numbering 571, the Germans 256. The foreign element in Louisville and Memphis was over one third of the population of those cities, in New Orleans

[23] See Clement Eaton, *The Growth of Southern Civilization 1790–1860* (New York, 1961), 162–169.

40 per cent, and in St. Louis 59.76 per cent. Although some of the great Northern cities, such as Chicago and New York, had a foreign-born population of approximately 50 per cent, the percentages of many Southern towns were not far behind the ratio of most Northern urban communities.[24]

Separated by a deep chasm from the respectable yeoman class was a peculiar class of people called "the poor whites." These people were not only extremely poor in worldly goods but existed on the fringe of society. The poor, both the rural and the urban poor, have been greatly neglected by historians. Antebellum society neglected them because it believed in the Bible statement that the poor you will always have with you. Moreover, instead of the modern ideology that environment is largely responsible for men being poor and backward, antebellum Southerners believed as did New Englanders that individuals themselves were responsible for being poor, depressed, and for being criminals. But the number of the "poor whites" in the social structure of the Old South was greatly exaggerated by the abolitionists in order to make a stronger case against the debasing effects of slavery. Travelers also tended to confirm this impression, because they failed to distinguish between "the poor whites" and the yeoman farmers, and because they often carried with them in their mental luggage the stereotype of the South that had been created by antislavery writers. The existence of a class of "poor whites," however, was recognized by the Southerners themselves, who called these unfortunate people, comparable to the slum dwellers of the North, such opprobrious names as "hillbillies," "peckerwoods," "dirt eaters," "clay eaters," "poor white trash," "tackies," "piney woods folk," and "crackers." The last epithet was probably derived from the habit of these poor people of reducing their corn to meal by cracking it with a pestle, or possibly the term originated from the long whips that the drivers of ox carts "cracked" over the backs of their plodding animals. The number of the "poor whites" [the landless rural population] probably did not exceed 20 per cent of the white population of the South.

It was formerly thought that the "poor whites" were descended from the indentured servant class and the transported convicts of colonial days. The modern explanation of their status, however, is that they were "stranded frontiersmen" who became victims of their isolated environment.[25] They were as a rule located in the regions of poor soils, especially "the pine barrens," and the mountains. There were some "poor whites" occupying infertile pieces of land between the plantations who were regarded as nuisances by the planters, because they sold liquor to slaves and received stolen property. Consequently, the planters tried to get rid of such objectionable neighbors. Environment was not alone the cause of the "poor white" class,

[24] See Ella Lonn, *Foreigners in the Confederacy* (Chapel Hill, 1940).

[25] A. N. J. Den Hollander, "The Tradition of 'Poor Whites,'" in W. T. Couch, *Culture in the South* (Chapel Hill, 1935), 403–431; Horace Kephart, *Our Southern Highlanders* (New York, 1913); and S. McIlwaine, *The Southern Poor-White* (Norman, 1939).

but the contempt of the upper classes for these underprivileged people was a factor in their debasement.

Indeed, many complex forces explain the existence of "the poor whites," who incidentally were not confined to the South. Doubtless some of "the poor whites" arrived at their lowly position in life because they desired to escape the law or wished to live a freer life in a semifrontier region, whereas others were unfortunate in the struggle for existence, became bankrupts, drunkards, or suffered from poor heredity. Travelers in the South were impressed by the indolence not only of the degraded class but of many villagers, a lethargy that cannot be attributed to climate alone. It is probable also that the abolitionists were partly right in blaming the slavery system for the creation and continuation of this class. Slavery tended to produce a monopoly of the richer soils by the planters and the more fortunate yeomen, and it retarded the diversification of industry in the South that would have given the landless class larger opportunities for productive work.

Modern students recognize that among the most important causes of the shiftlessness and laziness of the poor whites were disease and lack of a proper diet. The most serious of these diseases were hookworm and malaria,[26] which also affected to a lesser degree the yeomen and the planters. The poor whites lived frequently in regions of sandy soil, which was most congenial to the hookworm parasite, and furthermore, the majority of these poor people did not wear shoes. The hookworm enters the body through the feet, passes along the bloodstream to the intestines, where it adheres to the walls by a hook on its body. There it lays numerous eggs and drains the human body of energy. For generations Southern energy was dissipated by this disease that was probably brought to America by African slaves. Although hookworm did affect the Negroes in the South, they seem to have attained some immunity from the disease, so that they were not so frequently the victims of its ravages as were the whites. Not until the twentieth century were the Southern people freed from this great incubus. In 1902, Charles W. Stiles, a zoologist in the employ of the federal government, made a trip through the South, during which he discovered the great havoc wrought by the disease. He thereupon began a crusade to free the South from this destroyer of human energy. In 1908, the Rockefeller Sanitation Commission for the Eradication of Hookworm was created as a result of the efforts of a North Carolina reformer, Walter Hines Page. John D. Rockefeller gave over $1 million to this cause of rehabilitating the South by eliminating the scourge of disease. Twenty years after the Rockefeller Commission had begun its work, over 7 million people had been treated, largely by a simple remedy, a purging of the patient with thymol and epsom salts. Today hookworm has practically disappeared from the South.

[26] Paul H. Buck, "The Poor Whites of the Ante-Bellum South," *American Historical Review*, XXXI (October 1925), 44–46. The origin of the poor whites has not been adequately investigated, and some of them may have been the product of a traditional society. See Elmora Mathews, *Kin ·and Neighborhood in a Tennessee Ridge Community* (Nashville, 1965).

The appearance and habits of the "poor whites" bore testimony to their diseases and lack of a balanced diet. Tallow-faced, they were melancholy in aspect, thin and emaciated, frequently with bleary eyes and very wrinkled faces. The women, who did most of the drudgery, married at extremely early ages and by the time they were thirty years of age looked like old women. The teeth of the poor whites were almost wholly uncared for, and they relied upon patent medicines or homemade remedies instead of doctors for the cure of disease. Their poverty-stricken aspect and outlandish clothes caused them to be laughed at as "tackies." One of the peculiar habits of the poor whites was eating clay, which in many became an addiction. The habit also existed among the slaves, its cause unknown, perhaps in the beginning arising from the pangs of hunger. The habit continued as a social habit, such as smoking, and still lingers in parts of the South.[27]

The "poor whites" were not primarily agriculturists but were hunters, fishermen, and stock raisers. Frequently squatters on the public land, they disdained sustained labor in the fields. Usually, they had a few razorback hogs and some lean cattle that roamed through the woods subsisting on wire-grass. A small patch of cotton and corn was cultivated, chiefly by the women, to provide a little money for buying snuff, powder, lead, salt, sugar, and coffee. The diet of the family was monotonous. In addition to the game that was killed, the "poor whites" lived mostly on corn and hog meat. In some regions sweet potatoes were used for a multitude of needs—as a food in the forms of roasted potatoes, sweet potato pie, and sweet potato coffee, or as an intoxicant in home brew, and the vines of the sweet potato were used for mattresses and to feed the stock. From their corn the "poor whites" made corn pone and "big hominy" and distilled it into corn whiskey. The men were frequently drunkards. The piney woods folks were almost invariably illiterate and highly supersitious. The Bible was a sealed book to them and their religion was of a primitive, fundamentalist type.

The most deplorable aspects of the "poor whites" were their lack of ambition and their shiftlessness. Yet they had a type of pride that caused them to disdain begging and they would not work at any job of domestic or menial service. Furthermore, they regarded themselves as being superior to the slaves whom they hated and whom they wished to keep in bondage as long as the latter remained in the South. Many of the "poor whites" had a psychology that appears almost incomprehensible in this age of "go-getters," bulldozers, and lust for gadgets and material goods. They had "an ideology of non-success," for success would elevate them and separate them from their neighbors and blood kin who acted as a protective agency.[28] In common

[27] R. B. Twyman, "The Clay Eater: A New Look at an Old Southern Enigma," *Journal of Southern History*, XXXVIII (August 1971), 439–448.
[28] Bertram Wyatt-Brown, "Religion and Formation of Folk Culture: Poor Whites of the Old South," L. F. Ellsworth, Jr. (ed.), *The Americanization of the Gulf Coast, 1803–1850* (Pensacola, Fla., 1972), 20–33; and "The Antimission Movement in the Jacksonian South: A Study in Regional Folk Culture," *Journal of Southern History* XXXVI (November 1970), 501–529.

Georgia Crackers. (Edward King, *The Great South,* p. 372)

with the poor subsistence farmer, most of the "poor whites" were opposed to missionary societies, both domestic and foreign; to temperance societies, which would restrict one of their chief pleasures and psychological outlets; to educated preachers, and to Sunday Schools, both of which were of Northern origin. The poor usually wedded members of the same church, a common practice also among the upper class; the type of church to which one belonged had an important bearing on one's status in the community.

The mountain whites dwelling in the secluded valleys of the Appalachian Mountains have been called "our contemporary ancestors." They preserved the language and even some of the ballads and folklore of the seventeenth-century immigrants. They were frontiersmen who remained after the frontier had passed by, hunting bear and deer and raising cattle for subsistence. Occasionally, they drove their oxen hitched to covered wagons down to the towns to dispose of their distilled whiskey, apples, chestnuts, and cabbage. It is a mistake to think of all the mountain people as "poor whites." Although there were some individuals among them, especially squatters, who belonged to this category, a considerable proportion of them owned land and cattle and should be classified with the yeomen. Indeed, these mountaineers were a proud and independent people who hated the soft ways of civilization, and outsiders were "furriners" to them. Their primitive ideas of government and justice caused them to carry on vendettas or feuds, in which they held responsible for murder not merely the criminal but his family or clan. After the Civil War they shot revenue officers who attempted to come into their lonely valleys and coves to collect the federal revenue tax on their distilled whiskey. Olmsted found some of these Southern highlanders antislavery in sentiment, but the majority seldom saw a Negro and had no desire to free the slaves.

Close to the poor whites in the economic scale were the agricultural laborers, who were hired by the farmers and planters particularly during harvest. Their wages were largely determined by the competition of the hiring of slaves. In 1860 the average wage paid for a farmhand with board was $10.37 a month in North Carolina, $21.41 a month in Alabama, $16.66 a month in Mississippi, $13.71 in Indiana, and in the United States the national average was $14.73. Without board the daily wage in North Carolina was 77 cents, the lowest in the nation, in Virginia, 81 cents, in Louisiana, $1.39, in Indiana, 98 cents, in Alabama, 96 cents, and in the United States, $1.11.[29] Prime slaves were hired in the tobacco factories of Virginia for approximately $18 a month, with board, and on the plantations of Louisiana for as much as $30 a month. The working hours of the white agricultural laborers were from sunrise to sunset. The planters and farmers preferred to hire Negro slaves rather than the poor whites, for they regarded the white laborers as shiftless and inefficient.

In addition to the agricultural laborers there were several other landless groups in the country, the woodchoppers along the Mississippi River who received $50 a month for providing the steamboats with fuel, the Irish ditch-diggers on the sugar plantations, hired to do unhealthy and dangerous work, and the tenants. The last generally tilled the old fields of the planters that had been abandoned as too sterile to waste slave labor on them. Living a marginal existence, they were usually in debt to the planter or the country storekeeper. Indeed, the tenant system did not originate after the Civil War as a result of the freeing of the slaves but was a prewar institution for white workers, particularly in the regions of worn-out soil. The emancipation of

---

[29] U.S. Bureau of the Census, *Statistics of the United States* (*Including Mortality, Property, etc.*) *in 1860* (Washington, 1866), 512.

the slaves and the disruption of the economy of the Old South, however, enormously expanded the use of the tenant system.

Although poor and rich alike were subjected theoretically to a harsh criminal code derived largely from the common law of England, the poor bore the brunt of it. During the first half of the nineteenth century, however, the Southern states slowly humanized their criminal codes and procedures. The medieval punishments of flogging, branding, the pillory, dismemberment, and public hangings were retained throughout the antebellum period, but imprisonment for debt was gradually abolished. The first constitution of Alabama (1819) prohibited imprisonment for debt, and in 1823 Georgia forbade the imprisonment of debtors except in cases of fraud and concealment of property. North Carolina and South Carolina were among the most conservative of the Southern states in abandoning old attitudes toward criminals. In South Carolina, 165 offenses were capital crimes in 1813; 22 were punishable by death as late as 1850. The *Revised Code* of North Carolina of 1855 abolished the death penalty for housebreaking in the daytime, for the second offense of bigamy, for forgery, horse-stealing, embezzlement by servants, and malicious burning of public bridges, but retained this extreme penalty for 17 crimes, including arson, sodomy, murder, castration, infanticide, the second offense of circulating incendiary publications, and stealing free Negroes from the state. As a consequence of the severity of the law, juries were reluctant to convict—in South Carolina, for example, only 39 per cent of the defendants tried by jury in the antebellum period were convicted, whereas in 1950 more than 90 per cent of those indicted were pronounced guilty.[30]

Kentucky, by contrast, was one of the most progressive of the Southern states in the treatment of criminals. In 1798 this state adopted a penal code that provided for capital punishment for only one crime committed by free persons, murder, and during the following year established a penitentiary at Frankfort. Kentucky also experimented with the system of separate cells for criminals modeled after the famous Auburn, New York, prison, where the prisoners worked together in the daytime under the rule of silence. Overcrowding of the Frankfort prison led to the abandonment of the solitary confinement system, but under the able administration of the superintendent, Joel Scott, the rule of silence was enforced and a prison textile factory was founded. Unfortunately, Joel Scott in 1825 leased the labor of the convicts of the state for five years, paying the state $1,000 a year. Thus, he became the first lessee of convict labor in the South and started a practice that became one of the greatest evils of the New South.[31]

Most of the Southern states tried to make their prison systems economically self-sustaining. In 1817 Georgia established a penitentiary where the

[30] Jack K. Williams, *Vogues in Villainy: Crime and Retribution in Ante-Bellum South Carolina* (Columbia, S.C., 1959), 85.
[31] F. G. Davenport, *Ante-Bellum Kentucky, a Social History, 1800–1860* (Oxford, Ohio, 1943).

prisoners carried on various trades. From 1845 to 1862 Alabama leased the labor of criminals in her penitentiary to private contractors, a pernicious practice followed by Northern as well as Southern states. A successful textile factory was established in the penitentiary at Jackson, Mississippi, which furnished supplies to the Confederate armies. Enlightened reforms were inaugurated by some of the Southern states, such as by the Baltimore prison that had separate quarters for women prisoners and employed a chaplain, by the Richmond prison that was the first in the United States to use honor badges and the grading system as incentives for good behavior, and by Tennessee's precedent in 1836 of rewarding good behavior in prison by lessening the term of service.[32]

On account of a parsimonious policy in regard to taxation, North and South Carolina did not have penitentiaries until after the Civil War. In 1846 a proposal in North Carolina to establish a state penitentiary at a cost of $100,000 was overwhelmingly voted down. In South Carolina enlightened men, such as Governor William Aiken and the Greenville editor Benjamin F. Perry advocated establishing a penitentiary, but the people were so conservative that the Senate voted down the proposal in 1849. On the eve of the Civil War Florida, Arkansas, and the two Carolinas were the only Southern states that did not have state penitentiaries. In these states the detention of criminals was left to the counties, which operated inadequate jails.

Another humanitarian cause that made considerable progress below the Mason-Dixon line was the enlightened care of the mentally diseased. In colonial days insane people were regarded as possessed by devils and were either chained in jails and poorhouses or allowed to wander at large unsupervised. Urged by the enlightened Governor Francis Fauquier, the legislature of Virginia in 1773 established an insane hospital at Williamsburg. For fifty years it remained the only state hospital for the insane in the United States. During the first half of the nineteenth century the conception of insanity as a disease that could in many cases be cured by proper care began to spread. The second state institution in the United States exclusively for the insane was established by Kentucky in 1824. Four years later South Carolina was the third state to provide an asylum for the mentally disordered and for epileptics.

The crusade for a more humane treatment of insane people was powerfully aided by the activities of the celebrated Massachusetts reformer Dorothea L. Dix.[33] This devoted woman traveled throughout the United States speaking before state legislatures and lobbying to get bills passed establishing insane asylums. In 1847–1848 she came to Tennessee and North Carolina, where she exposed the wretched conditions in the care of

[32] Blake McKelvey, *American Prisons, a Study in American Social History Prior to 1915* (Chicago, 1936).

[33] H. E. Martin, *Dorothea Dix: Forgotten Samaritan* (Chapel Hill, 1937); and Norman Dain, *Concepts of Insanity in the United States 1789–1865* (New Brunswick, N.J., 1964).

the mentally ill, many of whom were confined in attics, log cabins, poor-houses, and jails, and other pauper lunatics were let out to the lowest bidder. As a result of the crusading zeal of this Northern woman these states were aroused to vote appropriations for erecting insane asylums. The institution at Raleigh, North Carolina, which was opened in 1853, was appropriately named "Dix Hill" in honor of the reformer. Before the outbreak of the Civil War all the Southern states except Florida had established insane asylums, although the Alabama and Texas institutions did not receive patients until 1861. The census reports indicate that only a small proportion of the insane were cared for in these state institutions. Nevertheless, during the latter part of the antebellum period, instead of being confined with chains like animals in jails and poorhouses, the mentally sick were being treated in a more enlightened fashion.

The obligation of the state to care for the deaf, dumb, and blind was tardily performed by most states. In Georgia a remarkable eccentric, John Jacobus Flournoy, who was himself handicapped by deafness and incoherent speech, presented a petition to the legislature in 1833 urging the state to educate its deaf and dumb citizens. The legislature responded by appropriating $3,000 for sending some of these dependent persons to the American School for the Deaf at Hartford, Connecticut, founded in 1817 by the great humanitarian, Thomas Gallaudet, but only three of those selected to go were willing to venture to this distant retreat.[34] As early as 1824 Kentucky had founded a school for the deaf and dumb at Danville, which followed the methods used by the American Asylum at Hartford, and in the decades of the 1840's and 1850's other Southern states started similar institutions. Schools were also established for the education of the blind in which the students were taught to read Braille as well as to learn arts and crafts. Yet, according to census reports, only a small fraction of these variously handicapped persons in the South received care and training in state institutions. There was far less reliance on the government in the rural society of the Old South and more on the family for aid to the unfortunate than has been the practice in recent times.

Although the South, dominated by a laissez-faire philosophy, neglected the poor and the disadvantaged, it could claim the virtue of being a relatively open society. Especially in the Southwest, considerable mobility existed between the social classes. The rise of overseers and yeoman farmers to the status of planters was an outstanding illustration of the fluidity and social mobility in the young society of the Southwest.[35] Ephraim Beanland, overseer for James K. Polk, for example, showed what an enterprising overseer could do for himself and family in elevating a humble man to a higher economic and social status. Emigrating to the Southwest, he acquired slaves

[34] E. M. Coulter, *John Jacobus Flournoy, Champion of the Common Man in the Ante-Bellum South* (Savannah, 1942).
[35] J. S. Bassett (ed.), *The Southern Plantation Overseer, as Revealed in His Letters* (Northampton, Mass., 1925).

and a section of land and became a successful and respected planter and his children obtained honored positions in the new society. Some overseers also improved their social status by being elected to local office, such as sheriff or tax collector, whereas others married their employer's daughter and thus inherited plantations.

A striking characteristic of this movement from a lower to a higher class in the South was the transforming power of Southern society to develop new standards of gentility in men of humble origin. Olmsted noted that young men who elevated themselves by starting as overseers [or yeoman farmers] frequently saved their wages, acquired "a valuable stock of experience and practical information," and as a result of intercourse with their employers "developed somewhat of gentlemanly bearing." [36] Also, Charles Colcock Jones, Jr., in a letter to his father described the progress of a self-made man in Savannah from being desperately poor to becoming head of the city bar, acquiring along the way the manners and polish of an aristocrat. Judge Law, he wrote, is "an accomplished gentleman of the old school, remarkably uniform and urbane in his manners and noted for his courtesy to brother members of the bar . . . the experience of that of many of the prominent men of our country." [37]

The best illustration of social mobility in the Old South was the remarkable rise of men of humble birth to high political position despite the large concentration of wealth in the hands of the planters. Indeed, many of the leading statesmen of the Old South came from the yeoman class, such as Andrew Jackson, John C. Calhoun, Alexander H. Stephens, George McDuffie, Albert Gallatin Brown of Mississippi, Joseph E. Brown of Georgia, and Andrew Johnson. The first governor of Virginia elected by the people (1851) was Joseph Johnson, who had been a poor boy without formal schooling, and the governor of the proud Old Dominion in 1861 was John Letcher, the son of a butcher. Jefferson Davis's first cabinet as Confederate president had a decidedly plebeian complexion, with only two members of aristocratic background. The cabinet included John H. Reagan, who had served briefly as an overseer, Judah Benjamin who rose from a poor Jewish family, Christopher Memminger who had been reared in an orphanage, and Stephen Mallory, whose mother had kept a boardinghouse, and also the president and the vice-president were of yeoman stock.

Because Southern society was a relatively open society serious class antagonism did not develop.[38] Indeed, there was no peasant psychology in the South. The yeomen were often kinsmen of the planter, and kinship even to remote cousins was a strong bond in the Old South. The farmers

---

[36] Frederick Law Olmsted, *A Journey in the Back Country, 1853–1854,* with a new introduction by Clement Eaton (New York, 1970), 161.

[37] R. M. Myers (ed.), *The Children of Pride: A True Story of Georgia and the Civil War* [the Charles Colcock Jones family letters] (New Haven, 1972), 275.

[38] Clement Eaton, "Class Differences in the Old South," *Virginia Quarterly Review* (Summer 1957).

also often used the planter's gin to prepare his cotton for market, his gristmill to grind his corn, and he sold some of his grain and food products to the planter. Only "the cotton snobs" or some of the nouveau riche planters of the Southwest notably assumed airs before the yeoman.[39] In fact, the planters cultivated the good will of the farmers to obtain their votes. As a rule, the yeomen did not envy the planters for having slaves when they did not, for they themselves hoped to own slaves and many of them did. There were some demonstrations of class feeling, but, in general, it took the form of sectionalism, such as the conflicts between the hill country of northern Alabama and the rich plantation area of the black belt.[40] Although the mountain whites and some of the yeomen of the Piedmont were Unionists in the Civil War, the great mass of yeomen united loyally with the planters to defend the institution of slavery.

[39] D. R. Hundley, *Social Relations in our Southern States* (New York, 1860).
[40] Clement Eaton, "Social Structure and Social Mobility in the Old Southwest," L. C. Ellsworth, Jr. (ed.), *The Americanization of the Gulf Coast, 1803–1850* (Pensacola, Fla., 1972), 53–67.

16

The Hero of the Common Man

THE EXPANSION OF SLAVERY and the great folk movement into the Southwest in the decades of the 1820's and 1830's coincided with the remarkable growth of practicing democracy in the South. This rise of the common man in political power was symbolized by the person of Andrew Jackson. No leader of the democratic masses in American history has possessed so colorful and masterful a personality as he. He became an authentic folk hero— the type of man the common people have always admired, an out-of-door personality, a man of direct action, a military hero. Arising from plebeian origins, he had the extroverted tastes of the frontier, the prejudices, the religion, and the sense of values of the common people, which enabled him to understand their psychology. Although he was shrewd, he was not an original thinker, nor was he expert in the handling of ideas, and he lacked the gift of eloquence. Like Washington and Jefferson, he seems to have lacked a developed sense of humor, a trait that has proved so valuable to popular leaders in establishing a bond of union with ordinary men.

Jackson's appearance as well as his highly individual personality were striking. Tall and slender, he impressed observers with the dignity, even courtliness of his bearing. His great mane of white hair, rising perpendicularly, gave the impression that no comb had ever smoothed it to conventional order. His blue eyes were usually kindly and filled with "an expression of melancholy gravity," but at times they blazed with anger, and he was easily aroused.[1] A person of violent hates and loyalties, he was the storm center of controversy. No man ever occupied the White House that had a stronger will or was more decisive than "Old Hickory," as his soldiers called him. This Tennessee planter and soldier was a deeply sentimental person, whose devotion to his wife Rachel was equal to any romantic passion described in the sentimental novels that were so popular in his time.[2] Although he had no children, he was extremely kind to the children with whom he came into contact, and he was mild and indulgent toward his adopted son, Andrew Jackson, Jr., who caused him great trouble by his incompetence and extravagance. Although democratic in manners, he was never folksy, and he might be described as a one-generation aristocrat.[3]

[1] Harriet Martineau, *Retrospect of Western Travel* (London, 1838), I, 161–163.
[2] See Clement Eaton, *The Leaven of Democracy: The Growth of the Democratic Spirit in the Time of Jackson* (New York, 1963), Intro.
[3] See Richard Hofstadter, *The American Political Tradition and the Men Who Made It* (New York, 1948), chap. 3.

Andrew Jackson in his prime (1767–1845), by Rembrandt Peale. (Courtesy of Kirby Collection, Lafayette College)

Jackson has been accused of being an opportunist, of having no political philosophy, only rich and stubborn prejudices, and of exercising a dangerous military power in government. It is true that he was often autocratic and prejudiced, but his intuitions or sympathies placed him on the right side of the great issues of his day, whereas the most intellectual statesman of his time, Calhoun, took the wrong course. A combination of a Southerner and a Westerner, he had the notable virtue of being national in outlook in a period when sectionalism was growing. On becoming the leader of the forces known as "Jacksonian democracy," his public career was deeply intertwined with the political development of the Old South.

Born in 1767 in the border region between North and South Carolina, "the garden of the Waxhaws," he was the product of the American frontier. His Scotch-Irish parents were poor, humble people, and his mother was early left a widow. When he was thirteen years old he participated in the Revolutionary battle of Hanging Rock. He acquired an enduring hatred of England as a result of his military experience, which included capture by the British and a sword cut when the indomitable youth refused to clean a British officer's muddy boots. His mother died as a martyr while nursing American soldiers on a prison ship in Charleston harbor, and he was left alone in the world at the age of fourteen years. In the back country he developed into a self-willed and turbulent youth, a "redhead," fighting at the least insult, fond of cock fights, and vehement in the use of oaths. From his grandfather in Ireland, a linen weaver and merchant, he inherited a modest sum of money, which he squandered in Charleston, betting on the horse races and throwing dice. Here he may have acquired the ceremonious manners of Southern aristocrats that later distinguished him as well as his lifelong passion for horse racing. Although he obtained only a smattering of learning, he taught school for a short while and then studied law in the office of Spruce Macay of Salisbury, North Carolina. In this backwoods village he continued his dissipated life, "slicking" his mane of reddish hair down with bear's grease and playing such crude practical jokes as inviting the leading prostitute of the town to a ball of which he was the manager.[4]

In 1788 he emigrated to the growing village of Nashville, Tennessee, where he hung out his shingle as a young lawyer. Possessing precisely the type of personality suited to frontier conditions, he arose rapidly in this community. At the age of twenty-nine he was elected Tennessee's first representative in Congress (1796), and then became successively United States senator and judge of the Supreme Court of Tennessee. His success arose partly from his connection with the land-speculating Blount faction in Tennessee politics, but perhaps more from his iron will, courage, scrupulous regard for honor, and common sense. A crucial step in his career was his election by the officers of the state militia to the position of major general (1802), which he won over John Sevier by one vote. His whole military career and later election to the presidency may have depended upon this victory.

One of the best insights into Jackson's personality might be afforded by a glance at his dueling activities. On May 30, 1806, he challenged Charles Dickinson, a prominent planter, to a duel as a result of bitter words between

---

[4] The most colorful biography of Jackson is by Marquis James, *Andrew Jackson: The Border Captain,* and *Andrew Jackson, Portrait of a President* (Indianapolis, 1933–1937); see also James Parton, *Life of Andrew Jackson* (New York, 1861), 3 vols.

the two men over a race track dispute. Because of the Tennessee law forbidding dueling, they crossed over the state line into Kentucky, where they fought a fatal duel. Dickinson was noted for his consummate skill with a dueling pistol and was regarded an almost infallible shot. On this occasion the principals stood facing each other at a distance of eight yards, pistols pointing to the ground. At the command "Fire!" Dickinson quickly aimed at his opponent's heart but his bullet only wounded Jackson in the shoulder. Then the relentless Jackson slowly aimed at his opponent, who was standing with folded arms, and pulled the trigger. The hammer stopped at half-cock, but he coolly recocked the pistol and killed his enemy. John Spencer Bassett in his *Life of Andrew Jackson* has branded this unmagnanimous episode as "little less than murder," a deed that lessened Jackson's political influences.[5]

Seven years later, when he was forty-six years old, he engaged in a rough and tumble fight with the Benton brothers. This undignified affair arose out of a duel between Jesse Benton and William Carroll, in which Jackson served as a second for the latter. The duel turned out to be an uproarious farce. After Jesse had fired and missed Carroll, he tried to present as small a target as possible to his opponent's return shot by bending low and pulling his coat tightly around his body. As a result of this stance, an amusing accident occured. Carroll's bullet traversed Benton's back and wounded his buttocks. Thus Jesse became the laughingstock of all Tennessee. The humiliated man transferred some of his bitterness of soul arising from this episode to Jackson, who had acted as Carroll's second. Gossip aggravated the ill feelings between the Benton brothers and Jackson, so that the latter threatened to horsewhip Thomas Hart Benton on sight. Consequently, when Jackson saw Tom Benton standing in the doorway of a tavern in Nashville, he started after him with his riding whip. In the fracas that followed Jesse, rushing out of the barroom to save his brother, shot Jackson in the shoulder. Later the Bentons and Jackson were reconciled and Thomas Hart, as a senator from Missouri, became an ardent supporter of Jackson's administration.

Jackson's incredible victory at New Orleans in 1815 made him a national hero and a potential candidate for the presidency. During Monroe's last term there was a hectic scramble among ambitious politicians to win the succession to the presidency. The Federalist party had virtually disappeared, and new parties were forming. In the presidential campaign of 1824 the Southern states produced five of the six candidates, William H. Crawford from Georgia, John C. Calhoun and William Lowndes from South Carolina, Henry Clay of Kentucky, and Andrew Jackson from Tennessee. The only Northern candidate was John Quincy Adams from Massachusetts, the best educated of the political rivals.

Of the chief aspirants to the office of president, Jackson alone depended largely on a reputation of military glory. Moreover, he had shown little fit-

---

[5] J. S. Bassett, *Life of Andrew Jackson* (Garden City, 1911), I, 64, although old, is still probably the best biography.

ness to be the executive of a democratic nation. While he was ruling New Orleans following his famous victory he continued martial law after the need for it no longer existed, and when a Creole member of the legislature freely criticized his acts, he had the audacious member arrested and tried by court martial. He also refused to honor a writ of habeas corpus by Judge Hall and even expelled this upholder of law from New Orleans. Later the judge returned to the city, summoned Jackson before his court, and fined him $1,000 and costs. His unauthorized invasion of Florida in 1818, his hanging of Arbuthnot and shooting of Ambrister, and his arbitrary conduct as governor of Florida cast serious doubts on his wisdom as an administrator. Indeed, his career had been violent, and Jefferson was right when he observed that Jackson had an autocratic temperament that caused him to disregard constitutions and laws. Jefferson was reported to have declared that although Jackson was an able military chieftain, he was utterly unfit for the presidency, this man whose passions were terrible.

It is difficult to determine how much personal ambition motivated him to run for this high office. Although he professed that he was through with public life after his fiasco as governor of Florida, he subscribed in 1822 to twenty newspapers from all sections of the country—a significant detail. He seems to have been stirred to go after the presidency by a group of Tennessee politicians, the so-called Nashville Junto, including his neighbor, William B. Lewis, and Senator John H. Eaton, John Overton, and Felix Grundy. These men groomed the Old Hero for the presidency, arousing his sleeping ambition and subtly enlisting his violent personal animosities. Although these men had originally favored the election of Clay, they saw an opportunity to use the popularity of the old general to advance their political and economic interests in Tennessee. Accordingly, they urged him to become a candidate— without any expectation that he could win.[6] It is one of the ironies of American politics and of human nature that the public welfare is often advanced by such selfish individuals seeking personal advantage. Thus, this coalition of Tennessee politicians with their eye on the promotion of their petty interests launched Andrew Jackson into national politics to become the great champion of democracy.

The presidential campaign of Jackson in 1824 was cleverly managed. Contrary to a common misconception of Jackson, he often heeded the advice of his friends, and he himself was an astute politician. He was very shrewd in not advancing a clear-cut set of proposals, or a constructive platform, but in relying upon his popularity as a military hero. Furthermore, his personality was the kind that the plain people admired, a self-made man with not too much book learning and with the earthy tastes of the common man. In 1822 the legislature of Tennessee nominated Jackson for president. Jackson gained popularity in the North by his Grass Hat letter of May 17, 1823, written to

[6] Charles G. Sellers, Jr., "Jackson Men with Feet of Clay," *American Historical Review*, LXII (April 1957), 537–551.

a Pennsylvania protectionist who had sent Mrs. Jackson a grass bonnet. In this letter he expressed approval of a protective tariff. A step in developing his campaign was his election to the Senate in 1823 by the Tennessee legislature. Here he voted for internal improvements and the tariff of 1824, votes that strengthened his candidacy. Also a convention at Harrisburg, Pennsylvania, March 4, 1824, declared in his favor, designating Calhoun as candidate for vice-president. After this blow Calhoun decided not to run for the presidency but to be content, for the time being, with attaining the subordinate office. Henry Clay, advocate of "the American System" of protective tariff and internal improvements, divided with Jackson the support of the West.

The candidate who was most feared by all was William H. Crawford, secretary of the treasury under Madison and Monroe, and ambassador to France. This dynamic man, of powerful physique and skilled in reading human nature, had been born and educated in Virginia but had removed to Georgia.[7] Here he became the leader of the radicals or the states' rights school. He was nominated for the presidency by the Congressional Caucus, a move that probably injured him, because this method of nominating candidates was propagandized as undemocratic by his rivals. In North Carolina a People's Ticket was formed to defeat this candidate made odious as the choice of the caucus. The People's Ticket was a coalition of the enemies of Crawford, pledged to support whichever candidate proved to be the strongest and most likely to defeat the Georgia stateman. The Jackson men were finally able to capture the People's Ticket, carrying the western section of the state and the undeveloped portions of the East bordering on Albemarle and Pamlico sounds.[8]

When the electoral vote was counted, it was found that Jackson had received the largest number of votes, but no candidate had obtained a majority of all the votes cast. Consequently, the House of Representatives was forced to make a decision, voting on the three highest candidates, Jackson, Adams, and Crawford. Clay had been last in the electoral vote, and was thus eliminated. However, he was placed in the strategic position of being able to throw his strength to the candidate of his choice and thus virtually determining who should be president. Courted by both sides, Clay decided in favor of Adams and persuaded the Kentucky delegation in Congress to vote for the New Englander. Shortly before the election took place, a Pennsylvania Congressman, George Kremer, who was regarded as somewhat of an eccentric, notorious for wearing a leopard coat, made the charge that a corrupt bargain had been formed between Clay and Adams. He asserted that Clay had agreed to throw his support to Adams in return for a promise by the latter to appoint Clay secretary of state. Subsequently the Kentuckian

---

[7] See C. C. Mooney, *William H. Crawford, 1772–1834* (Lexington, Ky., 1974).
[8] See A. R. Newsome, *The Presidential Election of 1824 in North Carolina* (Chapel Hill, 1939).

was made secretary of state by President Adams, an appointment that seemed to substantiate the charge that the New Englander and "Harry of the West" had participated in an unscrupulous intrigue to secure the election of Adams. Jackson believed this accusation and, spurred by vindictive feelings, was determined to become a candidate four years later to unseat the beneficiary of a "corrupt bargain." [9]

During this campaign of 1828 "Old Hickory" kept silent on national issues. Indeed, the campaign was one of bitter personalities designed to attract the votes of the unthinking electorate. The old charge of a corrupt bargain between Adams and Clay was used effectively, and Adams was accused of having introduced gambling tables in the presidential mansion because he had installed billiard tables in the White House at his own expense. On the other hand, Jackson's enemies made fun of Rachel, his wife, who smoked a corncob pipe and was semi-illiterate. Especially, they made malicious remarks about his marriage to Rachel before she had obtained a legal divorce from her former husband, a mistake that had to be rectified by performing a second ceremony two years after the original marriage. His opponents also printed coffin handbills to advertise the fact that during the war against the Creek Indians he had ordered the death of six mutinous militiamen. A modern student of the election of 1828 has concluded that Jackson's victory was owing, not so much to the Jackson image as hero of the common man, although that was important, but to the organization of political machines in the states by aggressive politicians.[10] Chief among these were Martin Van Buren and the Albany Regency, expert political brokers, and James Buchanan of Pennsylvania, politicians whose states were decisive in the election. Jackson and Calhoun as vice-presidential candidate swept the South and West as well as Pennsylvania and New York to pile up an electoral majority of 178 to Adams' 83.

The inauguration of Jackson as president on March 4, 1829, was truly a symbol of the rise of the common man. Jackson treasured the myth of Jefferson riding on horseback to his inauguration and tying his horse with his own hands. He, too, wishing to demonstrate his belief in republican simplicity, walked from his tavern to the inauguration ceremonies, where he read his address. It was a conciliatory document, designed to dispel the fears of many citizens aroused by his previous turbulent and autocratic career. He proclaimed himself an advocate of states' rights, strict economy and the extinguishment of the public debt, a judicious protective tariff for the sake of national independence, and, ironically, a humane Indian policy. Declaring himself opposed to large standing armies, he held that "the bulwark of our defense is the national militia." After the inaugural a reception

[9] For a discussion of this episode, see Clement Eaton, *Henry Clay and the Art of American Politics* (Boston, 1957).
[10] Robert V. Remini, *The Election of Andrew Jackson* (Philadelphia, 1963), chap. 6, Triumph of the Politician.

was held in the White House during which the realistic democracy had little respect for the furniture and rugs of the presidential mansion. "King Mob" trampled with muddy boots on the carpets and stood on the damask seats of the chairs to see the Old Hero. In fact, Jackson was mobbed by ardent democrats who wanted to shake the hand of the victor of the battle of New Orleans. Finally, bowls of punch were placed on the White House lawn to lure the democracy out of the house, and the president escaped through a back window. Jackson entered the presidential mansion alone, for his wife had died shortly before the inauguration. His close friend, William B. Lewis, lived with him in the White House (much like Harry Hopkins in Roosevelt's administration), and Emily Donelson, who had married the nephew of his wife, presided over his social occasions.

Jackson realized the great power of public opinion in a democracy. Consequently, he cultivated newspaper editors, who formed an important group in the so-called Kitchen Cabinet, or his informal coterie of advisers, whom wits represented as meeting in the White House pantry and there deciding the fate of the nation. He made Francis P. Blair, a Kentucky journalist, the editor of the administration organ, the Washington *Globe*.[11] Whenever he wished to influence public opinion, he or his lieutenants would write a communication, and Jackson would order, "Give it to Bla-ar!"—(Blair). Amos Kendall, another Kentucky editor, was also an important member of the Kitchen Cabinet, later appointed postmaster general. A ghostly figure who seldom appeared in public, he was often a dominating influence in the president's strategy. Jackson's official cabinet was a rather weak body of men, with the exception of the secretary of state, Martin Van Buren. The cabinet appointments were divided between his own friends and the followers of Vice-President Calhoun, with whom there was a silent understanding that the vice-president should succeed the Old Hero after one term.

The source of Van Buren's influence over Jackson remains somewhat a mystery. The tall, angular Tennessean, with his forthright methods, seems hardly compatible with the suave New York politician called "the Little Magician." Yet Van Buren was an opportunist who studied the character of "Old Hickory" and treated him with unfailing tact. Probably Jackson also admired Van Buren's sagacity as a political manipulator. Observing that the planter-President liked to exercise by horseback riding, Van Buren acquired a horse and often his plump little figure could be seen bobbing up and down on his horse as he rode beside the stern old man. Southerners as a whole never liked Van Buren, regarding him as a designing New York politician. But Jackson declared that he was remarkably frank and guileless and "one of the most pleasant men to do business with I ever saw." [12]

[11] See W. E. Smith, *The Francis Preston Blair Family in Politics* (New York, 1933), 2 vols.
[12] John Spencer Bassett (ed.), *Correspondence of Andrew Jackson* (Washington, 1926–31), IV, 108–109, and 260.

Van Buren strengthened Jackson's attachment to him by his tactful conduct in the amazing Peggy O'Neale affair. Shortly before the president appointed his close friend, John H. Eaton, to the Cabinet as secretary of war, the Tennessee Senator had married Peggy O'Neale Timberlake, whose father conducted a tavern in which Eaton roomed. Peggy was a beautiful, vivacious woman, who sometimes served drinks at her father's bar, and gossip was rife concerning the relations between the Senator and the sexy barmaid. Jackson, aware of the talk of the capitol, forthrightly advised his friend to marry the woman or change his boardinghouse. After the marriage, most of the official society of Washington, led by Mrs. John C. Calhoun, the vice-president's wife, snubbed the lady of questionable virtue. Never did knight in armor rush to the defense of a lady in distress more gallantly than did Jackson to defend the wife of his friend. Over this social feud, he held a Cabinet meeting that the cartoonists delighted to portray. Proclaiming Peggy a pure woman, as chaste as snow, he tried to force the members of his official family to receive her socially. But though he could defeat redcoats and Indians and master men, he was vanquished by the ladies; even his hostess, Emily Donelson, left the White House rather than yield. The occasion gave Van Buren a golden opportunity to win the heart of the determined Old Hero, for being a widower and unencumbered by female protocol, he became especially attentive to the snubbed lady.

At his suggestion Jackson reorganized his cabinet in 1831, purging it of the Calhoun members and appointing Eaton governor of Florida and later minister to Spain, where the lovely Peggy played a brilliant role in Spanish society. Van Buren was at the same time appointed minister to England, but the Senate rejected him through the deciding vote of Vice-President Calhoun. Thereupon Jackson was more than ever determined to make the "Little Magician" vice-president in 1832 and his successor at the following election.

The New York leader had a bond of agreement with the South in a mutual support of the states' rights doctrine. Indeed, he had been a zealous promoter of William H. Crawford, the preeminent champion of states' rights in the South, and had shifted to the Jackson camp only after the Georgia statesman had been eliminated from the political arena by sickness. But below the Mason-Dixon line, "the Red Fox of Kinderhook," and his cohorts, such as Colonel James A. Hamilton, son of Alexander, Silas Wright, and William L. Marcy, who were sensitive to the labor vote of the North, were distrusted. With the rise to power of Van Buren, Southern and Western influences on the administration tended to dwindle.

Although Jackson did not initiate the democratic movement of the 1820's and 1830's, he seized leadership of the movement and rode the groundswell of the democratic revolt.[13] The rise of the common man to political power

[13] The varying interpretations of Jackson as a democratic leader are considered by Charles G. Sellers, Jr., "Andrew Jackson versus the Historians," *Mississippi Valley Historical Review*, XLIV (March 1958), 615–634.

Cartoon of Andrew Jackson, his Cabinet and Peggy O'Neale (Mrs. John H. Eaton). (Courtesy of Library of Congress)

was accelerated by the War of 1812, which shook American society out of the old grooves, developed a new sense of nationality, and stirred the discontent of the common people. Following the conclusion of the war there was a widespread shift of population from the East to the West. Never before had such a large proportion of the American people lived under frontier conditions; at least half the population of the United States in 1828 was living under such conditions. Thus the influence of the American frontier on politics, which has contributed to the growth of a democratic spirit, was probably at its height during this period.[14] Furthermore, the Industrial Revolution led to a labor movement that encouraged the common man to assert himself politically. The growth of the factory system, nevertheless, did not affect the Southern section of the country very deeply, except in the indirect fashion of enormously stimulating agricultural production for export markets and thus revivifying slavery, which exerted an aristocratic influence. The democratic upheaval of the late 1820's and 1830's followed a decade of political apathy on the part of the American people during the administrations of President Monroe. The passing of the "Virginia dynasty" and the emergence of new leaders, however, resulted in violent political activity.

The rise of Jacksonian democracy within the Southern states cannot be explained in terms of a simple formula.[15] In the Atlantic seaboard states, local conditions and sectionalism frequently produced revolts against the control of the conservatives and the Tidewater aristocrats. The Panic of 1819 had political repercussions especially in states such as Kentucky, where a fight over inflationary and stay laws produced a great schism between conservatives and radicals, the latter joining the party of Jackson.[16] A brilliant student of the age of Jackson has discounted the influence of the frontier on the rise of the democratic movement in the decades of the 1820's and 1830's and has emphasized the role of the working class in the Northern cities.[17] Below the Mason-Dixon line, however, this influence seems negligible, whereas the existence of frontier conditions in a large part of the South was undoubtedly an important catalyst of democracy. In the whole country there was a cultural lag between democratic theory and democratic practice. A reaction was due to occur in order to close up the gap between theory and practice.

Jackson became the champion of the interests of the common people partly as a result of circumstances. During his early career, when he was fighting for money and power in Tennessee, he was allied with the upper classes. Eager

[14] Frederick Jackson Turner, *The Rise of the New West, 1819–1829* (New York, 1906).

[15] See Marvin Meyers, *The Jacksonian Persuasion* (Chicago, 1957); John William Ward, *Andrew Jackson, Symbol for an Age* (New York, 1962); and Harold C. Syrrett, *Andrew Jackson: His Contribution to the American Tradition* (Indianapolis, 1954).

[16] C. S. Sydnor, *The Development of Southern Sectionalism, 1819–1848* (Baton Rouge, 1948), chap. 5.

[17] Arthur M. Schlesinger, Jr., *The Age of Jackson* (Boston, 1945); for a criticism of his thesis, see Joseph Dorfman, "The Jackson Wage-Earner Thesis," *American Historical Review*, LIV (January 1949), 64–77.

for capital, he developed many financial interests, such as operating a general store, earning money by his race horses and by his lawyer's fees, conducting a large plantation with slave labor, and speculating in land. Some of his ruthless Indian treaties were made in the interest of land speculators. In 1820 Jackson vehemently opposed Felix Grundy's bill for the establishing of a state loan bank to furnish relief to the debtors suffering from the panic of 1819. The following year he supported Edward Ward, the aristocratic candidate for governor, against William Carroll, champion of the people. Modern research indicates that Jackson was a conservative in Tennessee politics, and that the real champion of democratic reforms in that state was not Jackson but his opponent, Governor William Carroll, a former nail merchant with an affable personality, who remained governor from 1821 to 1835.[18]

Jefferson had attempted to establish a liberal republican form of government led by gentleman farmers. The type of democracy that bears the name of Andrew Jackson, on the other hand, was a realistic democracy with all its virtues and defects. It emerged before Jackson became a candidate for president. A recent study of voting records in the states shows that there was a far higher rate of voting before 1824 than had previously been realized. Before Jackson was elected president in 1828 manhood suffrage had been attained in all of the states, with the exception of Rhode Island, Virginia, and Louisiana. The presidential election of 1828 brought out more than double the number of voters that had participated in the previous election, constituting 56.3 per cent of the electorate, six states turning out at the polls over 70 per cent of the electorate. Nevertheless, in some elections before 1824 ten different states had exceeded this percentage. The appearance of "the new domocracy" in overwhelming numbers at the polls occurred after the Jackson period, in 1840, when 78 per cent of the electorate voted, and in 1844, when nearly 75 per cent voted.[19]

Until the Jacksonian movement the common people seemed to have been content to have the upper classes rule. But by 1828 the psychology of the plain people toward their government had changed, and they wished for direct participation in the government and for the elevation of a man of their choice into the presidency. In that year the common men came to the polls, demagogic oratory flourished, party slogans, party workers and organizers who had an eye on the plums of office got out the vote. The campaign was personalized. This new type of democracy, composed of the farmers of the West, the yeomen and small planters of the South, and the labor vote of the North, was violently partisan and had little interest in the protection of intellectual liberty or the rights of minorities, which had ennobled the brand of

[18] Thomas P. Abernethy, "Andrew Jackson and Southwestern Democracy," *American Historical Review,* XXXIII (October 1927), 64–77.
[19] Richard P. McCormick, "New Perspectives on Jacksonian Politics," *American Historical Review, LXV* (January 1960), 288–301, and Chilton Williamson, *American Suffrage,* chaps. 8 and 11, point out that contrary to the Turner thesis, suffrage reform in the East was not significantly influenced by the Western states.

democracy that Jefferson had advocated. It was a rough and tumble movement that resulted in the elevation of pushing, mediocre men to office. Their
leader Andrew Jackson, had a personality that was autocratic instead of being
truly democratic, and he lacked an interest in fundamental *social* reforms.

"Jacksonian democracy" had its roots in Jeffersonian ideas; but it translated democratic theory into practice, extending democratic principles to the
national government. It was decidedly more radical than Jeffersonian democracy and less concerned with quality government. Under "Jacksonian democracy" rotation in office was put into practice. This political device was
based on the assumption that one citizen was as good as another and that the
duties of government should be made so simple that any honest citizen with
common sense could administer a public office successfully. The spoils system
was transferred from state politics to the national government. Yet Jackson's
removal of federal officeholders has been grossly exaggerated, for he removed
in the first year of his administration only about one fourth of the incumbent
federal officeholders. A large measure of political democracy was realized by
the creation of the nominating convention for president, introduced by the
Anti-Masonic party in 1831, manhood suffrage, first adopted by the frontier
states, then extended to the older states, the substitution of popular election
of state officials for the old method of selection by the legislature or by appointment, the removal of property qualifications for officeholding, and the
election of presidential electors in all the states, except South Carolina, by
the people instead of by the legislature.

Jackson's Indian policy is a good example of his sympathy with the point
of view of the frontiersmen and of the common people of the South. He
accepted the frontiersman's estimate that the only good Indian was a dead
Indian, and he was zealous in robbing Indians of their land by treaties imposed by force or by chicanery. The removal of the Indians from the South
was a tragic but inevitable result of westward expansion. In 1825 President
Monroe announced as one of his last official acts a policy of the removal of
the eastern Indians to an Indian territory beyond the Mississippi River, a
policy that his secretary of war, Calhoun, had advocated. The country
selected was the region west of the Arkansas-Missouri state lines, an area
that was believed unsuited to agricultural expansion as a result of Major
Stephen Long's report of "The Great American Desert." It was believed that
the Indians could reside permanently in this area, the present state of Oklahoma, undisturbed by the cupidity of the white man. To Jackson fell the
burden of carrying out this policy of removal authorized by Congress in 1830.
Treaties were made with the various tribes for exchanging land in the West
for their hunting grounds in the Eastern states and for their peaceable emigration. Jackson and his successor, Van Buren, had little trouble in removing
the Northern Indians, but the "Five Civilized Tribes" in the South offered
powerful resistance to surrendering their homeland.

The most formidable resistance was made by the Cherokee of Georgia and
the Seminole of Florida. The Cherokee had made great advances in the art

of civilization. They had become successful farmers and in some cases tilled cotton plantations with slaves. One of their brilliant leaders, the crippled Sequoyah, whose father was a white man, had invented an alphabet for the Cherokee language, and a newspaper, the *Cherokee Phoenix,* had been established at their capital, New Echota. In 1827 they had organized a government with a written constitution that denied the jurisdiction of the state of Georgia and established a state within a state.[20]

In addition to this repudiation of the sovereignty of Georgia, there was another powerful reason for the removal of the Cherokee, the greed of Georgians for their land. The Cherokee had the double misfortune of owning some fertile cotton land and of having gold discovered in their territory. In 1802 the state of Georgia had given up her claims to Western lands on condition that the Federal government extinguish the Indian title to the lands within her borders. The federal government, however, was slow in taking the Indians' land away from them by treaty, although President John Quincy Adams did negotiate in 1825 the Treaty of Indian Springs with Chief McIntosh of the Creek tribe for the surrender of a large area of land in Georgia. This treaty was rejected by the Creeks, and McIntosh was killed, but the next year a new treaty resulted in the cession of a considerable portion of the Creek land. The Cherokee, however, announced in 1824 that they would sell no more land to the whites.[21]

During this period of controversy the truculent, redheaded governor of Georgia, George M. Troup, threatened to expel the Indians from the state by force if the federal government failed to act. In 1828 Georgia extended her laws over the Cherokee nation. Two years later, a Cherokee named Corn Tassel committed a murder and was arrested by Georgia officials and brought to trial before a state court. The Cherokee nation hired the eminent lawyer William Wirt of Baltimore and appealed to the Supreme Court to protect their treaty rights in the famous case of *Cherokee Nation* v. *State of Georgia* (1831). The Supreme Court ordered the state of Georgia to appear before its tribunal to defend the case, but the governor refused to heed the subpoena, and Corn Tassel was speedily hanged. The majority of the Supreme Court held that the Cherokee were not a foreign nation but a domestic dependent nation in a state of pupilage, and that they were not competent to appear as a party to a suit against a state in the tribunal of the Supreme Court. Therefore, the motion for an injunction restraining Georgia from executing its laws within Cherokee territory was refused.

In 1832, the Supreme Court decided another case, *Worcester* v. *Georgia,* which was more favorable to the Cherokee cause. The legislature of Georgia had passed a law making it illegal for white persons to reside in the Cherokee territory without a license from the state and without taking an oath of allegiance to Georgia. Some New England missionaries violated this law and eleven of them were arrested and convicted. Samuel A. Worcester and Elizur

---

[20] See Marion L. Starkey, *The Cherokee Nation* (New York, 1946).
[21] See Grant Foreman, *Indian Removal* (Norman, Oklahoma, 1932).

Butler, two of the condemned men, appealed to the Supreme Court. Georgia again refused to appear before this tribunal. The Supreme Court then ruled that the Georgia law in question was a violation of the Constitution, which had given to Congress the right to regulate intercourse with the Indians. Worcester and Butler were declared entitled to their freedom, but Georgia disdained to obey the mandate of the Supreme Court in favor of the missionaries and the Cherokee. President Jackson, however, refused to use his executive authority to enforce the decision of the highest federal court. Jackson's inaction in this case was inconsistent with his policy toward South Carolina when the state nullified a Federal law. Jackson is reputed to have said, "John Marshall has made his decision, now let him enforce it." Jackson was restrained from moving against the recalcitrant state for fear that Georgia would join South Carolina in the nullification controversy and influence other states to join, and for this reason also the missionaries decided not to prosecute their case.[22]

In December, 1835, the Cherokee, finding that Jackson would not protect them or enforce the decision of the Supreme Court, yielded to their hard fate. They signed a treaty ceding their lands east of the Mississippi for $5.5 million and received a larger amount of land in the Indian territory than they had held in Georgia. A Southerner, Joel R. Poinsett, who was secretary of war in Van Buren's administration, supervised their painful removal in 1838. The Cherokee were passionately devoted to their beautiful homeland, with the graves of their fathers, and the long journey to the setting sun was a "Trail of Tears" to them. Poinsett selected another Southerner, General Winfield Scott, to command the troops that escorted the more than twelve thousand Cherokee to their new home. Instead of giving the contract for furnishing supplies and transportation to white contractors, the War Department awarded the contract to the leading chief, John Ross, who aided greatly in the peaceful removal of the tribe. Nevertheless, at least one fifth of them died on the way as a result of various hardships and diseases. The Cherokee living in the Great Smoky Mountains of North Carolina were not removed, and some of them remain on reservations in that state to this day.

By the treaties of Dancing Rabbit Creek and Pontotoc (1830–1832), the Choctaw and Chickasaw gave up their homeland in the northern part of Mississippi that contained fertile cotton lands. Like the Cherokee, the Choctaw and Chickasaw emigrated to the territory beyond the Arkansas-Missouri line now included in the state of Oklahoma. Here they had to change their habits and modes of life to fit a strange environment. By 1840, the forced emigration of the Southern Indians to the West was largely completed, resulting in the removal of about sixty thousand Indians.[23]

[22] See E. A. Miles, "After John Marshall's Decision: *Worcester* v. *Georgia* and the Nullification Crisis," *Journal of Southern History*, XXXIX (November, 1973), 519–544.

[23] See Angie Debo, *A History of the Indians of the United States* (Norman, Oklahoma, 1970) and A. H. Derosier, Jr., *The Removal of the Choctaw Indians* (Knoxville, 1970).

The Seminole Indians of Florida refused to abandon their hunting grounds and fought bitterly against federal troops from 1836 to 1842. This "nation" was a branch of the Creeks who had emigrated into Florida at the beginning of the eighteenth century, and their name in the Creek language meant "runaways," or "separatists." One of the chief reasons for their fierce struggle to remain in their native haunts was that many fugitive Negroes who had mingled their blood with the tribe were living among them, and in the process of removal, they might be reclaimed by white masters. Furthermore, the Seminole were incensed by the unscrupulous action of United States agents in negotiating a treaty for removal with only a few chiefs. For years these Indians fought the United States regulars and Florida militia in a war characterized by inefficiency and barbarism, costing the United States over $20 million.[24] Protected by the labyrinths of the Everglades and ably led by the gallant mixed-breed Osceola, the Seminoles were remarkably successful in frustrating the efforts to remove them. Finally, some of their chiefs, including Osceola, were captured while they were approaching under a flag of truce and were imprisoned at Fort Moultrie, on Sullivan's Island in Charleston harbor. Here young Osceola died mourning over the fate of his people. Approximately four thousand of the Seminole were finally removed to the Indian territory, but a remnant has survived in Florida to the present day.

One of Jackson's most significant actions that affected the South was the destruction of the Second National Bank. This institution, with its headquarters in Philadelphia, had twenty-seven branches scattered throughout the country, exercising a powerful control over the rising American economy. Nicholas Biddle, the president, was an imperious man who had an arrogant disdain of politicians and believed that his business was above the law. His great financial institution had been given valuable special privileges by its charter of 1816, especially the monopoly of keeping the government's deposits, which averaged $7 million, without paying interest, and the exclusive privilege of issuing bank-notes that were valid for government dues. The Bank was hated by many in the South and West because of its sound money policy, yet it had also powerful friends in these regions, particularly in South Carolina, where a huge block of its stock, 40,674 shares, was held.[25]

Partly because of an unfortunate personal experience with banks, Jackson was strongly prejudiced against the Second National Bank, but more importantly, he sensed the fact that a huge monopoly supported by the government was inconsistent with democracy. In no sense was he hostile to business enter-

[24] See James W. Silver, *Edmund Pendleton Gaines* (Baton Rouge, 1949), chaps. 4 and 8.

[25] See R. C. H. Catterall, *The Second Bank of the United States* (Chicago, 1903); and G. G. Van Deusen, *The Jacksonian Era, 1828–1848* (New York, 1959). Van Deusen shows that the Bank was not really a monopoly, holding only one third of the nation's bank deposits, p. 63; H. R. Smith, *Economic Aspects of the Second Bank of the United States* (Cambridge, Mass., 1952), points out that its note circulation was about one fifth of the total circulation of the country.

prise, and in seeking to deprive the Second Bank of its favored position with the government he was not trying to regulate Big Business, as Franklin D. Roosevelt sought to do in the 1930's. Recent studies of the Bank fight indicate that it was fundamentally a struggle to preserve equality of economic opportunity to small entrepreneurs—in other words, the competitive, free-enterprise system. The allies of Jackson were not so much the agricultural class but the state banks and the small-business men.[26]

Jackson's hostility to the Bank was revealed in his first message to Congress, in which he declared that both the expediency and constitutionality of the institution were doubtful. His Cabinet, however, was divided over the wisdom of tackling this powerful financial institution, and Jackson himself wavered at first in his course in regard to the Bank. The charter of the Bank would not expire until 1836, but Nicholas Biddle was persuaded by his agent in Washington and by Senators Henry Clay and Daniel Webster, whose retaining fees as attorneys for the Bank were "refreshed" at intervals, to apply for a recharter early in 1832, a presidential election year. Clay, planning to be a candidate, wished to make the Bank question a leading issue of the campaign. The recharter bill passed Congress, but Jackson vetoed it in a fighting message, written largely by Amos Kendall and by Roger B. Taney, his attorney general.

In this message Jackson portrayed the Second United States Bank as possessing a dangerous potential of influencing elections. He appealed to the prejudices of the common people by denouncing the recharter bill as an attempt to "make the rich richer and the potent more powerful" by granting to the wealthy class exclusive privileges denied to "the humble members of society—the farmers, mechanics, and laborers." [27] He cleverly aroused the prejudices of the common people also by pointing out that a substantial portion of the stockholders were foreigners. Adopting the strict interpretation of the Constitution, he argued that the Bank was unconstitutional, despite a decision of the Supreme Court to the contrary. Indeed, he held that the president and the Supreme Court had equal rights in deciding on a question of constitutionality affecting his action as president.

In the ensuing election Jackson, with Van Buren as his running mate, won a smashing victory over Clay. Only South Carolina of the genuinely Southern states refused to vote for him, although the border states of Kentucky, Maryland, and Delaware voted for Clay. Jackson interpreted the election as a mandate from the people to destroy the Bank. Despite a report of a Congressional committee that the Bank was sound, he determined to remove the deposits of the national government from it before the expiration of its charter. The cabinet was divided over the wisdom of this radical move, and

---

[26] See Bray Hammond, *Banks and Politics in America from the Revolution to the Civil War* (Princeton, 1957); and Thomas P. Govan, *Nicholas Biddle, Nationalist and Public Banker, 1786–1844* (Chicago, 1959).

[27] J. D. Richardson, *A Compilation of the Messages and Papers of the Presidents, 1789–1897* (Washington, D.C., 1901), II, 590.

Jackson had to remove two secretaries of the treasury, one by promotion and another by dismissal, in order to appoint to this office a man who would carry out his will. The new secretary of the treasury, Roger B. Taney, executed the policy of weakening the Second National Bank by depositing no more government funds in its vaults and by drawing out gradually the government reserves through means of checks for disbursements. The new depositories for government money were a group of fifteen state banks selected by the secretary of the treasury, known as "pet banks." As a punishment for the removal of the deposits from the National Bank, the Senate under Clay's leadership passed an unprecedented resolution of censure against the president. However, Senator Thomas Hart Benton, after repeated efforts, succeeded in January, 1837, in getting the Senate to expunge the famous censure from its journal.

The destruction of the Second National Bank by Jackson has been evaluated by the great American historian Frederick Jackson Turner as follows: "The severance of official connection between the national government and the capitalist was one of the most important steps in American history. Thenceforth, the industrial interests were obliged to act by underground methods and by the lobby." [28] The victory for an untrammeled economy was further extended when Roger B. Taney, whom Jackson had appointed to succeed John Marshall as chief justice, wrote the decision in the Charles River Bridge case (1837), striking down an old monopoly.

Despite its salutary political effects, the immediate economic consequences of the veto of the recharter bill were pernicious, for the destruction of the Bank, which had acted as a stabilizing influence on the economy, contributed greatly to the banking evils that followed. The veto and the removal of the deposits gave, in effect, the green light to the speculation and unsound banking practices that speeded the panic of 1837. Accordingly, some students have felt that the sounder course for Jackson and Congress to have pursued would have been to preserve the bank and firmly regulate it in the public interest.

A policy of the Southern agrarians had been to keep the national government on a course of strict economy. One of the most cherished objectives of Jackson, which had also been a cardinal policy of Jefferson, was to pay off the national debt before he retired from office. In 1835 he succeeded in accomplishing this purpose, and for the first and last time in American history the Federal government was practically free from debt. The Treasury had accumulated a large surplus of money as a result of the huge land sales and receipts from the protective tariff policy. In 1836 Congress ordered the distribution of this surplus among the states in installments, theoretically as loans, but actually as gifts. Some of the Southern states wasted this money in unwise programs of internal improvement, but North Carolina, whose

[28] Frederick J. Turner, *The United States, 1830–1850: The Nation and the Sections* (New York, 1935), 407–408.

share was $1,433,757.39, devoted most of this gift to establishing free public schools.

Speculation was rife at this time throughout the country, and economic conditions were brewing a panic. The tremendous inflation that was occurring was registered in the South by the sharp rise in the price of cotton and slaves. Cotton rose from 7.5 cents in 1830 to 15.2 cents per pound at New Orleans in 1836, the highest price since the boom of 1818. When deflation came as the result of the panic, delayed in the South until 1839, the price dropped to 7.9 cents, reaching the nadir of 4.7 cents in 1844. At the close of 1836 prime slaves were selling for $1,100 in Virginia and $1,300 in Louisiana, marking an advance of nearly 400 per cent since the end of the eighteenth century. Deflation in the decade of the 1840's reduced their value by almost one half.

This inflation was accompanied by a tremendous speculation in public lands, encouraged by the state banks, which issued banknotes without adequate specie basis and lent money recklessly. One of the virtues of the Second National Bank had been that it had maintained a stable uniform currency, partly by forcing state banks to keep a reasonable reserve of specie to pay their banknotes. The destruction of this institution by Jackson had released a brake on the activity of the state banks in inflating the currency. Contrary to the sentiment of the frontier region, from which he had come, Jackson favored a hard-money policy. He was sustained in this policy by Senator Thomas Hart Benton of Missouri, who was appropriately nicknamed "Old Bullion." Accordingly, the president, alarmed by the inflationary movement, issued his Specie Circular of July 11, 1836, requiring the payment of hard cash for government land. This measure, designed to strike a blow at speculators and protect the common man against the "non-resident proprietorship" of the public lands, precipitated a disastrous panic that did much to ruin the administration of his successor, Martin Van Buren.[29]

On March 4, 1837, Jackson retired from public life to his plantation near Nashville, *The Hermitage,* where he lived until his death in 1845. His career is inseparably connected with the growth of political democracy and the cause of nationalism in the South. It is true that his course as president was not consistently nationalistic. Influenced by Martin Van Buren, he had taken the states' rights point of view in vetoing the Maysville (Kentucky) Road Bill in 1830. By adhering to a strict construction of the Constitution in this instance, he delayed the desirable development of a network of national roads uniting the various sections of the country. He also adopted the states' rights view in the controversy of Georgia with the national government over the removal of the Cherokee. More than any other president, with the exception of Franklin Delano Roosevelt, he polarized the political elements of the nation around his powerful and partisan personality.[30] It was during his ad-

[29] See Reginald C. McGrane, *The Panic of 1837* (Chicago, 1924), 600–661.
[30] See W. O. Lynch, *Fifty Years of Party Warfare, 1789–1837* (Indianapolis, 1931), chap. 6; and Claude Bowers, *Party Battles of the Jackson Period* (New York, 1922).

ministrations that the democratic doctrine of the instruction of senators by the legislatures was reduced to a partisan instrument to get rid of the opposition.[31]

Nevertheless, Jackson was one of the greatest of Southern nationalists. By his firmness he contributed powerfully to crushing the nullification movement in South Carolina and asserting the authority of the national government. An ardent expansionist, just before his retirement as president, he signed the proclamation recognizing the independent republic of Texas. Furthermore, he gave the country real leadership, immensely strengthening the powers of the presidency, especially by his courageous use of the veto power. The veto power had been applied only nine times by all the presidents who had preceded Jackson, but he alone vetoed twelve bills of Congress. Other presidents had vetoed bills because they regarded such bills as unconstitutional or defective technically, but Jackson also vetoed bills he regarded as unwise or against the interest of the people. In foreign affairs, he raised the prestige of the nation by his "shirtsleeve diplomacy," which, for example, forced France to pay the American spoilation claims dating from the Napoleonic wars. His most deplorable weakness was his encouragement of violent partisanship in American politics.

After his death Jackson's name continued to be a symbol of loyalty to the Union. His staunchest disciples who outlived him, President James Knox Polk, Thomas Hart Benton, Sam Houston, and the Francis Preston Blair family, carried forward the torch of nationalism. By a curious reversal of fate, the Whig party, which had so bitterly fought Jackson in his lifetime, became the strongest force below the Mason-Dixon line to preserve national sentiment. In times of national crisis, such as in 1850 and 1860, the firmness of Jackson in suppressing nullification was an inspiriting example to the upholders of the Union. It was the tragedy of the South that this section failed to hold to the Jackson tradition of nationalism but followed sectional leaders such as Calhoun, Rhett, and Yancey into secession.

[31] See Clement Eaton, *The Freedom-of-Thought Struggle in the Old South* (New York, 1964).

The Two-Party System
of the Old South

IN CONTRAST to "the Solid South," which developed after the Civil War, the antebellum South had a vigorous two-party system. Jackson's autocratic measures as president and his violent partisanship produced a strong coalition against him, the Whig party. Formed in 1834, this party took the name *Whig* from the English party label of those opposed to the king. Indeed, cartoonists drew caricatures of Jackson as "King Andrew I," wearing a crown and holding a sceptre in his hand. A nucleus of the new party was the group who called themselves National Republicans and who had voted in 1832 for Henry Clay for president. Another element that joined the party was the more extreme Nullifiers, who resented Jackson's stern repression of South Carolina. Other discontented persons who entered the ranks of the opposition were ambitious officeseekers, those who were disgusted with the spoils system, and the advocates of internal improvements by the Federal government who had been alienated by the Maysville Turnpike veto. Also many Southerners who disliked the influence of Van Buren over the "Old Hero" revolted from administration leadership. The disintegration of the Anti-Masonic party, which had nominated William Wirt of Baltimore for president in 1831, resulted in some of the members going over to the Whigs. Perhaps the most important factor in the formation of the Whig party in the South was the opposition of conservatives to Jackson's bank policy.

The Jacksonians claimed to be the inheritors of the Jeffersonian tradition, with its emphasis on the protection of human rights as opposed to property rights. They elevated the sovereignty of the people and majority rule as their cardinal principles. The Whigs, on the other hand, were identified with the protection of property rights and the advancement of the interests of the business community. Consequently, they were more solicitous for the protection of minority rights. Some of the aristocratic Whigs, in their franker moments, spoke of the common people as "the rabble" and rejected scornfully the doctrine of natural rights and the equality of man. Indeed, the majority of the party carried on the Federalist tradition of broad construction of the federal Constitution and an economic program in the interests of the capitalists. In contrast, the Jacksonians, who had the support of the plain people in the South and the laboring vote in the North, wished to restrain by a strict interpretation of the Constitution the powerful industrial groups who sought special favors from the government. Nevertheless, since parties in America are seldom homogeneous but contain both liberal and conservative wings, many humble people belonged to the Whig party; and, vice versa, the Democratic party in the South eventually became the vehicle of the slave power. Furthermore, a considerable number of Southern Whigs believed in the narrow interpretation of the Constitution and were rightly called State Rights Whigs.[1]

The rise of the Whig party in Tennessee is especially interesting, because this state was the home of Jackson. One of the earliest of the Tennessee Whigs was the frontiersman and wit David Crockett. This picturesque Indian fighter had been elected in 1827 from western Tennessee to Congress, where he amused his colleagues by his eccentricities and Irish wit. His motives for opposing Jackson, under whom he had fought Indians, were probably a strong sense of independence and jealousy of the fame of Tennessee's favorite son. His opposition to Jackson became pronounced after the latter had removed the government deposits from the National Bank, which incidentally had loaned money to Crockett. The Whigs utilized the opportunity to play up this representative of Tennessee as the opponent of Old Hickory, and in 1834 invited him to make a tour of the North, arranging enthusiastic receptions and public dinners for him. They intimated that he should run for president, and the immense egotism of Crockett caused him to swallow this flattery. Crockett's name was used as author of a Whig campaign volume satirizing Van Buren, entitled *Life of Martin Van Buren* (1835), but the ghost writer was a Georgia Congressman, Augustin S. Clayton.

Crockett did not develop an important personal following, nor was he as significant in the formation of the Whig party in his native state as Hugh Lawson White of Knoxville and John Bell of Nashville. White had been an Indian fighter and a judge of the Supreme Court of the state, a man highly respected in Tennessee. He was a strict constructionist, who did not differ greatly in his principles from Jackson. Indeed, he was a friend of the president until 1831, when Jackson tried to persuade him to resign from his position as United States Senator and accept an appointment as secretary of war in order to permit John H. Eaton to enter the Senate. White refused and became very resentful of the dictatorial manners of the Jackson administration. Moreover, he seems to have resented the growing ascendancy over the president of Van Buren and of the Kitchen Cabinet (whom he called "small men").[2] John Bell represented the conservative business interests, and moreover, he became hostile to Jackson, who had opposed his political ambitions. Under the leadership of these men, Tennessee shifted (in the years 1834–

[1] For the origins of the Southern Whig party, see A. C. Cole, *The Whig Party in the South* (Washington, 1913); E. M. Carroll, *Origins of the Whig Party* (Durham, 1925); H. H. Simms, *Rise of the Whigs in Virginia, 1824–1840* (Richmond, 1929); and Paul Murray, *The Whig Party in Georgia, 1825–1853* (Chapel Hill, 1948).

[2] L. P. Gresham, "The Public Career of Hugh Lawson White," *Tennessee Historical Quarterly*, III (March-December, 1944), 308.

1836) from an overwhelming support of the Jacksonian party to the Whig camp and remained normally a Whig state as long as that party had a vital existence.[3]

The Whig party in Tennessee seems to have been fostered both by personal animosities and by local needs. East Tennessee desired particularly internal improvements at the expense of the federal government, whereas middle Tennessee, containing the Bluegrass basin of Nashville, demanded favorable banking facilities, both of which measures were advocated by the Whig party. Hence a curious coalition of aristocrats and yeomen arose in this state for mutual advantage. The Whigs of East Tennessee had a powerful advocate in "Parson" W. G. Brownlow, editor of the Knoxville *Whig,* who hated abolitionists but loved the Union intensely. Not all of the plain people of this mountainous area, however, voted the Whig ticket, for the Democrats had some plebeian leaders, such as Andrew Johnson of Greeneville, who had been a tailor's apprentice.

A map delineating the location of Whig and Democratic strength in the South shows some very significant correlations. In the lower South the Whigs were strong in the rich delta country and alluvial valley areas of the Mississippi River. Natchez, for example, was the stronghold of conservatism and Whigism in Mississippi; the hostility of the frontier districts to this aristocratic area led, as early as 1822, to the removal of the capital from Natchez to Jackson. The sugar planters of Louisiana supported the Whig party, because it stood for a protective tariff. In Alabama the Whigs were clustered in the black counties along the Tennessee River—the Huntsville district—and in the black belt in the middle of the state, of which Montgomery was the center. The Whigs in Alabama normally elected about one third of the representation both in the legislature and in Congress. Only once in Alabama's history were they able to elect the governor. In Georgia the frontier counties, the hill counties of the northern part of the state, were pro-Jackson or Democratic, but the cotton area of middle Georgia became Whig under the leadership of the redheaded, belligerent Governor George M. Troup, who formed the States' Rights party, which joined the national Whig organization.[4]

There was an aphorism concerning the black belt of the lower South to the effect that wherever you found rich soil, there you would find a cotton bale, and sitting on the bale would be a Negro, and nearby would be a Whig in a silk hat. The great planters joined the Whig party, believing it to be the conservative party, careful of property interests—the broadcloth party. A close correlation existed between Whig strength and high concentration of slaves, high land values, and low illiteracy rate of the white population. The Democrats, on the other hand, were strong in the pine barrens and areas of high illiteracy of the white population, of low land values, and of small proportion

[3] Powell Moore, "The Revolt against Jackson in Tennessee, 1835–1836," *Journal of Southern History,* II (August 1936), 334–359.

[4] Paul Murray, "Economic Sectionalism in Georgia Politics, 1825–1855," *Journal of Southern History,* X (August 1944), 293–307.

of slaves.[5] Varina Howell, as a girl seventeen years old in Natchez, wrote to her mother of her first impression of Jefferson Davis whom she was to marry, "Would you believe it, he is refined and cultivated, and yet he is a Democrat!" [6]

These generalizations do not apply to South Carolina or to the upper South. Recent scholarship has also thrown doubt on the Whig party's being a class party. A study of the elite in the Nashville area shows that the wealthy and the prominent were almost equally divided in their allegiance to the Whig and Democratic parties. Many prominent men through the South were Democrats or Whigs because of family tradition or friendships rather than political conviction.[7] South Carolina became solidly Democratic. For a short while after the nullification struggle Calhoun acted with the Whigs. However, the Whig party with its program of a protective tariff, its conservatism on agitating the slavery question, and its broad nationalistic outlook was not a promising vehicle for the Carolinian's views or ambitions. Consequently, he returned to the Democratic party in 1837 by accepting Van Buren's proposal of an independent treasury for the Federal government. The leadership of the Whigs, such as it was, fell to the highly cultivated W. C. Preston, who dared to oppose Calhoun's course on Abolitionists' petitions and the bank issue.

In the upper South the Whig party appealed to the business interests as well as to the large conservative planters. Kentucky and Maryland usually voted for the Whig candidates, partly because of the magnetic influence of Clay, but also because of the hemp interests of Kentucky, which demanded tariff protection, and the commercial interests of Maryland that needed stable banks. Kentucky, however, was pro-Jackson in sentiment as late as 1831, choosing eight Jacksonian and four National Republican congressmen in that year, although curiously the Clay men won control of the state legislature.[8] The Bluegrass in the center of Kentucky, the Pennyroyal on the southern border, both rich agricultural areas, and a group of poor counties in the southeast above Cumberland Gap became Whig constituencies. The Democratic strongholds were the mountainous northeast, the tobacco counties in the extreme west, and a block of counties in the hump of the Ohio River where the German and Irish immigrant influence was felt.

In Virginia, the constant Whig areas were the Tidewater and the counties along the Great Kanawha River, where the salt, iron, and woolen industries

[5] See T. H. Jack, *Sectionalism and Party Politics in Alabama, 1819–1824* (Menasha, Wis., 1919).
[6] Varina H. Davis, *Jefferson Davis, Ex-President of the Confederate States of America, A Memoir* (New York, 1890), I, 192.
[7] B. W. Folsom II, "The Politics of the Elites: Prominence and Party in Davidson County, Tennessee, 1835–1861," *Journal of Southern History*, XXXIX (August 1973), 359–378.
[8] John Coffin, "A History of the Whig Party in Kentucky," unpublished M.A. thesis, University of Kentucky Library, chap. 2, p. 39.

of western Virginia were located. The Whigs were strong in the towns and cities, especially Richmond and the Lynchburg area, where the business interests were powerful. The consistent Democratic districts of Virginia were the upper Shenandoah Valley counties, where the small German farmers were dominant and the southwestern part of the state, also largely occupied by yeoman farmers. The Piedmont area was normally Democratic, but it had a strong Whig element. The Whig leaders, such as Abel P. Upshur and Benjamin W. Leigh, were aristocratic in political thought and were strong believers in states' rights.

In North Carolina the distribution of Whig strength has mystified many scholars. The back country and mountainous areas of the state were Whig, whereas the Tidewater, with the exception of the region of the Albemarle and Pamlico sounds, was Democratic. The area around Albemarle Sound hoped for Federal aid to construct an ocean inlet into the Sound and eliminate the necessity for the long and dangerous trip to Ocracoke Inlet to the south. The western district of North Carolina was also attracted by the Whig program of federal aid to internal improvements. Moreover, a deep antagonism existed between the West and the planter aristocracy of the East, who had long opposed an equitable representation of the West in the legislature. When the eastern planters supported the Democratic party, partly held in line by the influence of Nathaniel Macon, the yeomen and mountaineers of the West took the opposing side. The leadership of the Whig party was aristocratic, including such men as Governor John Motley Morehead, Senator Willie P. Mangum, William A. Graham, vice-presidential candidate in 1852, and George E. Badger, secretary of navy in the Harrison and Tyler administrations. The Whigs agitated for the calling of the Constitutional Convention of 1835, which gave the people the right to elect the governor and rectified the inequality of representation between the East and West. Consequently the numerically stronger West was able to elect Whig governors from 1835 to 1850.

The parties during the 1830's and 1840's were so evenly matched that, as a modern scholar has expressed it, "it was rare for any southern state to be regarded as absolutely safe for either party." [9] The Whigs had a slight margin of 2.4 per cent superiority over their opponents in the four presidential elections from 1836 to 1848. This situation of keen competition between the parties, which completely disappeared in the "Solid South" after the Civil War, tended to make voters more loyal to the party than to the section. Indeed, during the virulent party warfare of this period many Whigs bitterly hated and distrusted Democrats, and vice versa. Until 1848 Southerners were divided primarily by economic issues, such as banking and financial policies, rather than sectional issues (if one can ever separate economic from political considerations). On the economic issues the Whig party in the South was led

[9] Charles G. Sellers, Jr., "Who Were the Southern Whigs?" *American Historical Review* (January 1954), 335–346.

by urban businessmen, lawyers, and the staple-producing planters. Senator John Bell of Tennessee was a good example of Southern Whig leaders—an urban lawyer from Nashville and the privileged Bluegrass section of the state and a businessman who acquired large iron mining interests on the Cumberland River (his mines were operated by slave labor).[10] The role of the lawyers in the Whig party is indicated by the fact that from 1833 to 1843 nearly three fourths of the Southern congressmen were lawyers, whereas only 55 per cent of the Democrats belonged to this profession.

Although they held conservative views in regard to democracy, the Whigs might appropriately be described as the party of material progress and nationalism in the United States. They had definitely a more modern view of the functions of government than their opponents, for they thought that the government should actively promote the general welfare by protective tariffs, internal improvements, a stable currency, sound credit, and the chartering of corporations. The Jacksonians, on the other hand, believed in a relatively "do-nothing government," the strict construction of the Constitution, hard money, loose banking laws, and the Independent Treasury, which represented an abandonment of the function of the government of regulating the currency. Their strong point was a greater sympathy for the common man, as evidenced by their championship of greater political reform and by Van Buren's order in 1840 establishing a ten-hour day on public works.[11]

The greatest leader of the Whigs was Henry Clay, who stands almost as a symbol of that party. Clay was born in 1777 in Hanover County, Virginia, fifteen miles north of Richmond, the son of a Baptist preacher. He received very little schooling in his youth, and all through his career he suffered from the lack of a sound education. Later in life he liked to picture himself as having suffered as a poor boy, "the mill boy of the slashes," which was a political asset, but actually his family lived in a comfortable frame structure and owned eighteen slaves. One of the important influences on his life was the oratory of Patrick Henry, the great man of Hanover County. His family moved to Richmond, where he became a clerk in a store and later an amanuensis of Chancellor George Wythe, who had a crippled hand. After studying law and being admitted to the Virginia bar, he emigrated in 1797 to Lexington, Kentucky. Here he became the leading criminal lawyer of the state primarily because of his ability as an orator. His marriage to Lucretia Hart, the daughter of a wealthy hemp manufacturer, tended to identify him with the ruling class of planters and hemp manufacturers.[12]

Clay had a personality well suited to success in the youthful state of Ken-

---

[10] Joseph H. Parks, *John Bell of Tennessee* (Baton Rouge, 1950).

[11] G. G. Van Deusen, "Some Aspects of Whig Thought and Theory in the Jacksonian Period," *American Historical Review, LXIII* (January 1958).

[12] For the career of the Kentucky statesman, see Bernard Mayo, *Henry Clay, Spokesman of the New West* (Boston, 1937); G. G. Van Deusen, *Life of Henry Clay* (Boston, 1937); Clement Eaton, *Henry Clay and the Art of American Politics* (Boston, 1957); and Hopkins and Hargreaves (eds.), *Papers of Henry Clay.*

Henry Clay (1777–1852), attributed to the Kentucky painter, Matthew Jouett (1783–1827). (Courtesy of University of Kentucky Department of Art)

tucky. Tall, six feet one inch in height, with small gray eyes, and brown hair that became prematurely white, he had the gift of winning friends and influencing people, especially by his wonderful oratorical voice. His warm and genial nature attracted friends to him, and his love of pleasure was another bond of union with the mass of men. He was fond of drinking Kentucky whiskey, playing cards, gambling, dancing, and being the lion at White Sulphur Springs in Virginia and Olympian Springs in Kentucky. Some of his characteristics are reflected in his many nicknames, "The Cock of Kentucky," "Prince Hal," "Harry of the West," "the Western Star," "the Western Hotspur," and to the Jacksonians, "the Judas of the West."

On his estate *Ashland,* outside of Lexington, he raised hemp and fine cattle, horses, and mules. He is credited with introducing Hereford cattle into America in 1817, and he imported merino sheep and jacks of high pedigree into the Bluegrass. That he not only delighted in agriculture but also had a good practical knowledge of farming is shown by an extensive memorandum for his overseer, in which he directs the rotation of crops, corn, wheat, oats, clover, and hemp and orders the sale of 50 hogs and some fat mules. A list he drafted of his taxable property for 1851 included *Ashland,* containing 510 acres of land, valued at $40,800, *Mansfield,* 125 acres, valued at $6,250, 35 horses and mules, 1 stud horse, "Yorkshire," 2 jennies, and 6 head of cattle.

His agricultural interests brought him directly into contact with the institution of slavery, to which he bore a curiously inconsistent relationship. In his early career he had written letters for the *Kentucky Gazette* urging the gradual emancipation of the slaves, but this opposition to the dominant institution did not prevent him from buying, owning, and selling slaves. In 1799 he owned one Negro, but the year before he died he had acquired thirty-three taxable slaves, valued at $9,600, and "17 Black tithes under equalization," namely children, valued at $2,000.[13] His will revealed his antislavery feelings, however, for it provided that the issue of his female slaves born after January 1, 1850 should be free, males at twenty-eight years of age, females at twenty-five, that they should be taught to read, write, and cipher, and that they should be sent to Liberia.[14]

In politics Clay began his career as a youthful Jeffersonian of the Virginia school of Wythe and Thomas Ritchie, editor of the *Richmond Enquirer,* but after 1815 he shifted to a Hamiltonian position. The explanation may lie partly in a new orientation of outlook following his marriage, in his adherence to the economic interests of the hemp growers and businessmen of Lexington, and in his strong enthusiasm for American nationalism, stimulated by the War of 1812. Furthermore, his association with wealthy commercial men as attorney for the Second United States Bank undoubtedly contributed to his new political philosophy. He borrowed heavily from wealthy businessmen in the North, notably $20,000 from John Jacob Astor, a loan he continually renewed until his political friends came to his rescue in 1845 and paid off a part of his debts. Clay's enemies regarded him as an opportunist without political principles, but the author's reading of his career from the great mass of his papers collected at the University of Kentucky and now being gradually edited and published does not confirm this unfavorable view of him. He seems to have been a patriot and very sincere in seeking to improve the economic strength and general welfare of the nation. In this ob-

[13] "Henry Clay, List Taxable Property for 1851." MS owned by J. Winston Coleman, Jr., of Lexington, Ky.
[14] "Last Will and Testament of Henry Clay, July 10, 1851." MS in Fayette County Court House. Edited by Clement Eaton and published in University of Kentucky Libraries *Bulletin,* No. I (Lexington, Ky., 1949).

jective his name will always be connected with the "American System," which aimed at national self-sufficiency.

The "American System" was designed primarily to encourage American manufactures and the economic growth of the country by a protective tariff. In support of this policy, Clay made a notable argument in Congress in 1824 justifying such a policy by "the home market theory." Unfortunately, Clay's "American System" did not harmonize with the Southerners' concept of the economic interest of their section. Since the South was predominantly an exporting, agricultural region, a high tariff was regarded as an instrument for exploiting the South for the advantage of the North. It was natural, however, that Clay should become an advocate of a protective tariff, because the hemp-growing and wool-producing interests of Kentucky demanded tariff protection. Another reason why the "American System" was distasteful to the South as a whole was that it required a liberal construction of the Constitution to sanction Federal appropriations for internal improvements, and the South regarded a strict construction of the Constitution as more suited to its interests.

As the struggle between rival sections began to develop, Clay sought to form an alliance between the West and the North. Not only was he a champion of the National Bank and of a protective tariff, measures desired by the Northern business interests, but also he sided with the North in the opposition to the annexation of Texas, and after 1820 he was opposed to the extension of slavery. His advocacy of the distribution scheme, which the South opposed, was also popular in the Northern states. According to this project the price of western public lands was not to be lowered, but the proceeds from the sale of government lands were to be distributed among the states according to population after 10 per cent had been donated to the state in which the lands lay. This proposal would favor the thickly populated states of the North and deprive the Federal government of a valuable revenue, thus necessitating the maintenance of a high protective tariff. Clay hoped to get the support of the West for this measure, which would provide money for internal improvements, but the West preferred a policy of cheap lands, such as Thomas Hart Benton's Graduation Bill, and the preemption of land for squatters, to Clay's panacea.[15]

No man ever desired to be elected president more ardently than did Henry Clay. He was almost a perennial candidate for that office, but he failed to win for a variety of reasons. An eloquent orator and possessing a magnetic personality, he unfortunately had no military record, and twice his party rejected him for a candidate who had the glamour of a military hero. Furthermore, the Kentuckian was not on the popular side of many of the great controversies of his day. In a period of the rising power of the common man, he sought to advance the business interests, the money power of the North. Moreover, he failed to appreciate the ardent desire of his section to expand.

[15] See George R. Poage, *Henry Clay and the Whig Party* (Chapel Hill, 1936).

His antislavery sympathies, revealed signally at the close of his career by the Pindell letter of 1849 urging the adoption of a plan of gradual emancipation, proved to be an element of weakness in his political career, for he was distrusted by the extremists of both sections.

His solutions of the great problems of his era were compromises, a role that caused him to be called "the Great Pacificator." Compromise was a natural policy for a representative of Kentucky, a border state, and was a sound method of preserving a Union composed of sections with clashing economic interests. It is a significant fact that Clay's successor in the Senate, the Whig leader J. J. Crittenden, was also a compromiser. Clay's constant defeats in the presidential races caused tears to flow down the cheeks of the respectable and educated classes. The deep affection in which he was held by the Whigs is expressed in the remark of a charming young woman, Ellen McCollam, the wife of a Louisiana planter, who ate gumbo with the old statesman at a party in 1844 and found him a fascinating person, "What a pity such a man should ever die." [16]

The motley elements that composed the Whig party were unable to unite on a presidential candidate in 1836. Various state legislatures nominated their favorite sons—Webster nominated by Massachusetts, William Henry Harrison by Ohio, and Hugh Lawson White by Tennessee and Alabama. The strongest of these candidates in the South was White. In the election he carried Tennessee and Georgia, Senator Willie P. Mangum of North Carolina received the electoral vote of South Carolina, and Harrison developed surprising strength, winning Maryland, Delaware, and Kentucky. Van Buren, despite his unpopularity below the Mason-Dixon line, was in general supported by the politicians and some influential Southern editors, such as Thomas Ritchie of the Richmond *Enquirer*. Aided by the powerful federal patronage wielded by Jackson, he won the election. The Democratic candidate for vice-president, Richard Mentor Johnson of Kentucky, did not receive a majority of the electoral vote but was chosen by the Senate, the only time in our history that such a method of election was necessary.

In 1840 the Whigs rejected their most eminent leader, Henry Clay, and nominated William Henry Harrison as their standard-bearer. In order to placate Southern Whigs and gain state's rights support, Senator John Tyler was nominated for the vice-presidency. The Whigs contained so many heterogeneous elements that they were unable to agree on a platform and therefore dispensed with that formality. Harrison was born in the fine old plantation house of *Berkeley* on the James River in Virginia and was educated at William and Mary College. He had been territorial governor of Indiana, in which position he had been aggressive in taking land away from the Indians by treaty. Much of his fame was based on his record as an Indian fighter at the battle of Tippecanoe (1811), in which he won a dubious victory, and

[16] J. C. Sitterson, "The McCollams: A Planter Family of the Old and New South," *Journal of Southern History*, VI (August 1940), 357.

on his career as a general in the War of 1812. An aristocrat by birth and rearing, he lived in an imposing mansion at North Bend, Ohio. Nevertheless, he became the beneficiary of an amazing political hoax that represented him as a man of the plain people. A Democratic newspaper of Baltimore sneered at the old gentleman by declaring that he would be content to live in a log cabin on a pension of $2,000 a year, drinking hard cider, and studying moral philosophy. The Whig newspapers and orators took up this myth and exploited it.

During the presidential campaign of 1840 the mass of voters were deluded by slogans and juvenile electioneering devices. Enthusiastic devotees wearing coonskin caps held torchlight processions and, rendered hilarious by hard cider, sang such songs as the "Hard Cider Quick Step." In the villages and towns log cabins were erected at Whig headquarters where barrels of hard cider were always on tap. Whig orators practiced the art of demagogy. In campaigning for Harrison, Webster apologized for not being born in a log cabin but condoned his mistake by declaring that his brother had been born in such a humble dwelling. Clay simplified the issues of the campaign by declaring that it was a contest between palaces and log cabins, between champagne and cider.[17]

Martin Van Buren, the Democratic candidate, the son of a tavern keeper, and descended from indentured servants, was represented as an aristocrat who had no sympathy for the common man. Orators with vivid imaginations pictured him as lavishing great sums of money on luxurious appointments at the White House. He anointed his whiskers with cologne, they said, he wore corsets to reduce his figure, and even his dish rags had lace on them. "Van, Van, is a used-up man!" they shouted, while they emphasized the military glory of their candidate by the slogan "Tippecanoe and Tyler too!" Such a campaign of hurrah and tomfoolery, reinforced by the effects of the Panic of 1837 on the party in power, resulted in a landslide for the Whigs, whose candidates were elected by a majority of 234 to 60 electoral votes.

When Harrison was inaugurated as the first Whig president at the age of sixty-eight, he tried to demonstrate that he was no feeble old man and recklessly exposed himself to inclement weather. Furthermore, he was besieged by a horde of officeseekers who exhausted his strength. Such excessive strain resulted in sickness and death after serving a month as president. He was succeeded by the Vice-President, John Tyler, who retained Harrison's cabinet, headed by the great Northern Whig, Daniel Webster.

The accession of Tyler to the Presidency brought to the surface the main division among the Southern Whigs—the State Rights wing of the party and the Clay or National Whigs. Tyler was the leader of the States' Rights faction, a strong believer in the strict interpretation of the Constitution. A former Jackson adherent, he had joined the Whig party primarily because of Jackson's action in the nullification controversy. He was a Virginia aristo-

---

[17] See Robert G. Gunderson, *The Log-Cabin Campaign* (Lexington, Ky., 1957).

crat, born on the plantation of *Greenway* in the Tidewater, the son of a former governor of the state. He was graduated at the precocious age of seventeen from William and Mary College. Tall, with a high forehead and unusually long nose, possessing courteous manners, he had a pronounced feeling of family and state pride as well as a stubborn sense of consistency. Among presidents, he holds a record that will probably never be surpassed, namely of being a prolific father, with a brood of fourteen children.[18]

After the death of Harrison, Clay assumed that he would be the power behind the throne. Accordingly, he set forth the program of the Whig party in a series of resolutions that he introduced into the Senate on June 7, 1841. These proposals for legislation to carry out Whig objectives included the repeal of the Subtreasury system of Van Buren's administration, the establishment of a National Bank, the adoption of a higher protective tariff, and the enactment of his Distribution Bill. The Distribution Bill had passed Congress in 1833 but did not become a law because of a pocket veto by Jackson. Clay was able to force his Distribution Bill through Congress in 1841, but it was a fruitless victory. Owing to Southern pressure, an amendment had been added to the original bill, which prohibited the distribution scheme from going into effect if the tariff should be raised beyond the 20-percent level fixed by the Compromise Tariff of 1833. Since the tariff was increased above this ceiling in the next year, Clay's pet bill became inoperative. The important land act of the Tyler administration was the Preemption Act of 1841, a victory for the frontier, which allowed any citizen to preempt one hundred and sixty acres of the public domain at the price of $1.25 an acre.

The dramatic break between Tyler and the majority of his party occurred over the issue of rechartering a national bank. The President accepted the repeal of the Independent Treasury Act, or the Subtreasury, but balked on the re-establishment of a National Bank, which the Whigs ardently desired. He seemed willing to accept a central bank that could establish branches in the states, but only with the previous consent of the states involved. Clay's first bill for the chartering of a National Bank was vetoed. In order to cater to Tyler's strict construction views, the Whigs drafted a new plan for a bank, which they called a Fiscal Corporation, but he also vetoed this bill. The Whigs then became thoroughly disgusted with their recalcitrant president and held a Congressional caucus, which expelled him from the party. In protest of Tyler's recreancy to party principles, all of his cabinet resigned except Daniel Webster, who gave as his excuse for remaining that he was negotiating a treaty with England, the Webster–Ashburton Treaty. Actually, Webster was hostile to Clay, his rival for leadership in the party, and he had no desire to increase the ascendancy of the Kentucky Hotspur by following his lead.

[18] See Oliver P. Chitwood, *John Tyler, Champion of the Old South* (New York, 1939); and Robert Seager III, *And Tyler Too; A Biography of John Tyler and Julia Gardner Tyler* (New York, 1963).

Tyler retained the allegiance of a small fraction of the Whig party, consisting mainly of Southerners. Henry A. Wise of Virginia became the leader of this "corporal's guard" in Congress who remained loyal to the discredited president. Thus the Whig party was split into two warring factions shortly after they had won a great victory at the polls.[19]

The formation of the Whig party had the virtue of giving the South a vigorous two-party system. Following the passage of the Kansas–Nebraska Bill of 1854, the Whig party virtually disappeared as a national party, but strong opposition to the Democratic party in the South did not cease. The Whig party deserves praise because of its devotion to the preservation of the Union. When the slavery controversy arose, its leaders, such as Henry Clay, John Bell, and the two younger leaders, Alexander H. Stephens and Robert Toombs of Georgia, sought to prevent the agitation of this dangerous question and to preserve national feeling. For this reason, also, the Whigs, in general, opposed the expansionist program of the Democrats and the Mexican War. Finally, the majority of the Whigs held to the doctrine of the liberal interpretation of the Constitution, which is much closer to the view of our own day, and which, if it had prevailed, would have contributed to strengthening the nation and developing its resources.

By 1850 the common man in the South had attained a large measure of *political* democracy, a development that had been aided by the two-party system. In the early years of the republic the Southern states had been ruled by a slaveholding aristocracy. A fundamental step toward realizing political democracy was made in 1792, when Kentucky in its first constitution discarded property qualifications both for voting and for holding office. Georgia also advanced rapidly toward political democracy, in 1798 removing its previous requirement of paying a tax to vote and by 1824 allowing the people to elect all their officers, including the governor and the judges. In 1810 South Carolina yielded to the pressure of her up-country population and granted white manhood suffrage. By 1810 Maryland also had provided for manhood suffrage and had instituted other democratic reforms, such as the adoption of the written ballot instead of the viva voce method of voting, the abolition of plural voting, and the elimination of property qualifications for officeholding. Alabama and Missouri, admitted into the Union in 1819 and 1821, placed no property restrictions on voting or holding office, although in order to qualify to become a member of the legislature in Missouri, the payment of state taxes was required. Thus before the emergence of the Jacksonian movement, considerable progress had been made toward democracy within the Southern states.[20]

The Jacksonian movement further accelerated the growth of democracy below the Mason-Dixon line. When Mississippians drafted their first consti-

---

[19] See G. G. Van Deusen, *The Jacksonian Era*, chap. 8, The Advent of "His Accidency."
[20] Fletcher M. Green, *Constitutional Development of the South Atlantic States, 1776–1860* (Chapel Hill, 1930), chaps. 4 and 5.

tution, contrary to the dogmas of frontier historians, they made a conservative constitution, which required the governor to own six hundred acres of land or $2,000 of wealth and members of the lower house of the legislature to possess one hundred and fifty acres of land or $500 of wealth. Furthermore, no person who denied the existence of God or of a future state of rewards and punishments could hold office in the commonwealth, and voting was restricted to those who paid a state tax and were enrolled in the militia. Stirred later by Jacksonian democracy, the sovereign people held a constitutional convention in 1832 and removed all property qualifications on voting or officeholding and even provided for the election of judges by popular vote. In Tennessee a constitutional convention in 1834 abolished the undemocratic features of the first constitution of the state, which had confined voting to landowners and had placed property qualifications on officeholding. In Maryland the aristocratic electoral college, which had chosen the state senators, was abolished by "the revolution of 1837."

The Jacksonian movement failed to make any great headway in Virginia, however, until 1850. The Western counties demanded the calling of a constitutional convention, for they resented the unjust system of representation in the legislature whereby the smaller Tidewater counties with much less white population were given the same number of representatives as the more populous Western counties. The Tidewater aristocrats were unwilling to surrender their minority control over the legislature, because they feared that democratic reforms would enable the Western counties to impose heavy taxation on the slaveholding East and also vote taxes for internal improvements and schools. Consequently the constitutional convention of 1829–1830, which was attended by the most eminent men of the state, including ex-Presidents Madison and Monroe, Chief Justice Marshall, and John Randolph of Roanoke, was dominated by the conservatives.

Accordingly, the constitution of 1830 did not remove property qualifications from voting, although it extended the suffrage to leaseholders and housekeepers. It was estimated that after the adoption of the new constitution thirty thousand out of one hundred fifty thousand white men continued to be excluded from voting.[21] The Piedmont counties were given greater representation in the legislature, but the refusal to adopt the white basis for representation caused the Western counties to remain discontented. Indeed, there were many threats of the dismemberment of Virginia that came from beyond the Blue Ridge.

The western section of North Carolina, which was underrepresented in the legislature, forced the calling of a constitutional convention in 1835. This body adopted some valuable reforms, such as the election of the governor by popular vote, the abolition of borough representation, and the removal of discrimination preventing Catholics from holding office. The new con-

---

[21] C. H. Ambler, *Sectionalism in Virginia from 1776–1861* (Chicago, 1910), 138, and Federal Census of Virginia, 1830.

stitution substituted the word *Christian* for *Protestant* in the old constitution, which had declared that "no person who shall deny the being of God, or the truth of the Protestant religion or the divine authority of either the Old or New Testament" should be permitted to hold office in the state.[22] Jews continued to be disqualified from officeholding in North Carolina until 1868. Although the convention of 1835 retained a property qualification on voting for state senators, it placated the western section of the state by abolishing the old system of equal representation of counties, regardless of size and population. The new constitution adopted Federal population, or the three-fifths ratio, as the basis of representation in the House of Commons and the amount of taxes paid as the basis of representation in the Senate.

The power of the aristocracy continued to be strongly entrenched in South Carolina and Louisiana, more so than in any other states of the Union. In 1808 a compromise was made between the Tidewater and the up-country of South Carolina by which half of the lower house of the legislature, which consisted of 124 members, represented property—slaves and land—as registered by taxation. Thus the lowland aristocracy was able to prevent legislation hostile to their interests from being passed by the white democracy. In 1860 South Carolina was the most aristocratic state in the nation, the only one that continued to choose presidential electors, the governor, and state officials by the legislature and to require a high property qualification for its chief executive. Thus statewide elections were not held in South Carolina, only elections in local units, the largest being the congressional district. The constitution of Louisiana of 1812 was also aristocratic in tone, requiring the governor and the members of the legislature to own considerable land and voters to pay a tax. Although the revised constitution of 1845 granted manhood suffrage, Louisiana remained under the rule of gentleman planters, aided by the change in the constitution in 1852, making total population the basis of representation in the legislature.[23]

During the decade of the 1850's another reform movement liberalized the governments of the less democratic Southern states. The Virginia constitutional convention of 1850, called as a result of the pressure of the West, granted complete manhood suffrage, provided for the election of the governor and the county officials by the people, and abolished plural voting. It refused, however, to adopt the white basis for the apportioning of representation in the lower house of the legislature, which was demanded by the West.[24] Missouri, already a relatively democratic state, extended the power of the people in 1850 by providing for the election, instead of the appoint-

[22] *Proceedings and Debates of the Convention of North Carolina Called to Amend the Constitution of the State* (Raleigh, 1836), Appendix, p. 416.

[23] See Roger W. Shugg, *Origins of Class Struggle in Louisiana, A Social History of White Farmers and Laborers During Slavery and After, 1840–1875* (University, La., 1939), chap. 5.

[24] See Clement Eaton, "Henry A. Wise, A Liberal of the Old South," *Journal of Southern History*, VII (November 1941), 487–490.

ment, of judges. In North Carolina, David S. Reid ended the long rule of the state by the aristocratic Whig leaders when he won the election as governor in 1850 on a platform of abolishing the property qualifications of fifty acres of land for voting in senatorial elections, a reform adopted seven years later.

The voting records of the Northern and Southern states throw some light on the comparative democracy of the two sections. Modern studies reveal a striking similarity between the North and the South in the exercise of the franchise. In 1820, during the time of President Monroe, when the one-party system prevailed, a national apathy toward voting existed, only seventeen votes being cast for presidential electors in Richmond, for example, and only fifty-two in Newport, Rhode Island.[25] The real contest in the Jackson-Adams campaign of 1828, however, brought out a greater vote. Nevertheless, in Georgia the percentage of the white population who participated in the election was only 6.3 per cent, the exact percentage that obtained in Connecticut. Although more than 10 per cent of the white population in Alabama voted in this election, slightly over 5 per cent both in Virginia and Massachusetts and approximately 8 per cent in Tennessee participated in the election. By 1860 these percentages had increased in Virginia to 13.7 per cent, in Massachusetts to 15 per cent, and in Tennessee to 17.4 per cent.[26] Since the Whigs and Democrats were almost evenly matched in the South, the existence of a genuine two-party system was an element of democracy. Furthermore, during the Jacksonian period, it was a habit in the South for the legislature to instruct the United States senators of the state how to vote. Most senators obeyed orders, but some senators, such as John Tyler, resigned rather than sacrifice their political principles.[27]

After the democratic movement of the Jacksonian period, undignified methods of electioneering arose, and the new leadership tended to be less cultured and less independent of public opinion. Although it would seem that on the eve of the Civil War remarkable progress had been made in the South since the time of Jefferson in realizing political democracy, it is unwise to generalize too confidently concerning the democratic status of the Old South. A distinction should be made between the Southwest and the older Atlantic seaboard states, especially in regard to county government and the apportionment of representation in the legislature. In the older part of the South and in Kentucky, the colonial system survived in county government,

[25] C. S. Sydnor, "The One-Party Period of American History," *American Historical Review*, LI (April 1946), 439–451.

[26] Fletcher M. Green, "Democracy in the Old South," *Journal of Southern History*, XII (February 1946), 3–24. These figures, which seem to contradict the statistics of voting given in the discussion of Jacksonian democracy in Chapter 16 are based on total white population rather than on the estimated white electorate, which was used in the previously cited study. The two can be roughly harmonized by considering the average white family as consisting of five persons, of whom only one voted.

[27] See Clement Eaton, "Southern Senators and the Right of Instruction," *Journal of Southern History*, XVIII (August 1952).

at least until 1850, and in some instances until the Civil War.[28] The lives of the citizens were affected in many ways by the ruling oligarchies of the counties—the justices of the peace. These local officers met in the courthouse four times a year to try important cases and to transact administrative and legislative duties. There were on an average about thirty-five justices to a county, but only a small minority attended courts except on important occasions. In Virginia the justices of the peace were appointed by the governor upon the recommendation of the county courts until 1851, after which date they were elected by the people. This undemocratic method of appointment of these officials was followed by Kentucky, the child of Virginia. In both of these states also the power of the gentry was strengthened by the viva voce method of voting, which remained intact throughout the antebellum period. In North Carolina the justices of the peace continued to be appointed by the governor upon the recommendation of the General Assembly, which in practice resulted in the appointment of those candidates recommended by the county representatives. Since the justices of the peace appointed most of the local officials, the effect of this practice was the short ballot for the people of the county. A genuine progress toward democratizing local government, however, took place in the newer states of the South between 1820 and 1850, so that by the latter date eight out of thirteen Southern states had given the voters control over the county officials.[29]

In respect to state government, Alabama, Mississippi, Tennessee, Texas, and Missouri, all lying west of the Appalachian Mountains, had become technically democratic by 1850. In these states the governor was elected by the people, manhood suffrage existed, no property qualifications were imposed on officeholding, the county governments were democratic, and particularly important, the apportionment of the legislature was on the basis of white population. Yet the creation of democratic machinery does not seem to have been followed by important social reforms for the common people, such as vigorous educational programs, fair taxation, good roads, and control over banks. Too often the sons of the plain people who arose to influential political positions forgot their lowly origins and became zealous agents of the vested interests and the ideology of the slavocracy. The antislavery controversy tended to divert attention from state issues. Furthermore, in many counties courthouse rings or cliques and influential families controlled the local governments and the representatives in the legislature.[30] The political power of a family was demonstrated in Arkansas, where the "Johnson Family" virtually ruled the state from its admission into the Union to 1860.

---

[28] See R. M. Ireland, *The County Courts in Antebellum Kentucky* (Lexington, Ky., 1972), and R. A. Wooster, *The People in Power: Courthouse and Statehouse in the Lower South* (Knoxville, Tenn., 1969).

[29] Charles S. Sydnor, *The Development of Southern Sectionalism*, chap. 2.

[30] W. B. Hesseltine has observed, "the real central theme of Southern history seems to have been the maintenance of the planter class in control." "Some New Aspects of the Pro-Slavery Argument," *Journal of Negro History*, XXI (January 1936), 14.

An important criterion in determining whether the state government was controlled by an aristocracy or by the people was the basis used in apportioning representation in the legislature. The presence of a large slave population in the South, in some states over half of the population, made this question of the principle of apportionment extremely significant. If slaves were counted as freemen or at three fifths of their number in the allotment of legislators, obviously the planter group and the black belt would have much more power than if the white basis were adopted. In North Carolina, Georgia, and Maryland (until 1852) federal population, or the three-fifths ratio, was the basis of apportionment. In Louisiana and Maryland (after 1852) total population was the basis of apportionment, the most undemocratic measure of all, because Negro slaves were thus counted at their full number. In South Carolina representation in the legislature was based on a combination of white population and taxes, and in Virginia the white basis was rejected in 1850 in favor of a compromise, or mixed basis, of white population and taxes. In addition to slave representation, some Southern states practiced an undemocratic discrimination against the cities, especially New Orleans, Louisville, and Baltimore, by refusing to give them a fair proportion of representatives in the legislature.

The taxation policies pursued by the Southern states, furthermore, indicated undue power over the government by the planters or the slavocracy. The Southern people during the antebellum period conceived of the state as a laissez-faire institution and were reluctant to vote money for schools or social services. Consequently, prior to the panic of 1837 taxation was remarkably low. Many of the states, however, acquired large bonded debts when they departed from laissez-faire principles in establishing banks and undertaking internal improvements, and as a result taxes were sharply increased during the latter part of the antebellum period. In several of the Southern states rudimentary income and inheritance taxes were adopted at this time, but by far the main source of revenue was the general property tax, which in Virginia, for example, constituted 90 per cent of the total amount of tax collected during the decade of the 1850's. All the Southern states, except Arkansas, imposed poll taxes, usually 50 cents or $1, but payment of the tax was not a prerequisite for voting as it became in the postbellum period.

The planters were able to secure especially light taxation of their slaves. The chief form of taxation of this type of property was a poll tax, such as the Alabama tax in 1852 of $1 on slaves from fifteen to thirty years old, 80 cents on those from thirty to forty years old, and 50 cents on those from forty to fifty years old. In Virginia after 1850 slaves under twelve years of age paid no taxes, and those over that age were assessed at no higher than $300 per individual. In North Carolina on the eve of the Civil War land was taxed $1.50 per $1,000 valuation, but slaves, regardless of value, were taxed only by a poll tax of 50 cents. The small amount of taxes paid by the large planters is illustrated by some specific examples recorded in 1849 by Solon

Robinson. In Louisiana, Thomas Pugh, one of the largest planters, paid only $200 taxes on his plantation of *Madewood,* containing 3,000 arpents of land and 201 slaves, assessed at $206,265.[31] A plantation near Society Hill, South Carolina, containing 4,200 acres, valued at $63,000, was taxed $70, and 254 slaves, assessed at $89,000 were taxed $193.04.

The light taxes on slave property caused considerable discontent to arise in the Western counties of the Atlantic states and among the towns and cities. A public-spirited slaveholder of Wake County, North Carolina, Moses Bledsoe, led a movement in 1856 to tax all property, slaves as well as land, ad valorem. Three years later the Raleigh Workingmen's Association took up the issue, and a newspaper, the *Ad Valorem Banner,* was founded to agitate the cause. In 1860 the Whig candidate for governor, John Pool, waged his campaign largely on this issue of advocating ad valorem taxation. He was defeated, and the question of fair taxation of slaves was pushed into the background by the coming of the Civil War.[32] At the same time the yeomen of western Virginia were becoming more class-conscious and entering into politics against the slaveholders. In the Secession Convention of 1860 the Western delegates proposed an amendment to the constitution equalizing taxation and abolishing the system of partiality in taxing slave property. Even in South Carolina, the citadel of Southern aristocracy, there arose on the eve of the Civil War an ominous demand from the up-country and the workingmen of Charleston for a democratic reform of the state constitution. But the agitation of the secession issue diverted attention from state politics and social injustice to the absorbing questions of Federal relations and Southern nationalism. Thus the privileged position of the wealthy slaveholders was not disturbed by an incipient revolt of the submerged classes, such as came after the Civil War, in the Tillman movement, and in the overthrow of the Bourbons.

[31] H. A. Kellar (ed.), *Solon Robinson, Pioneer and Agriculturist, 1825–1845* (Indianapolis, 1936).
[32] C. O. Norton, *The Democratic Party in Ante-Bellum North Carolina, 1835–1861* (Chapel Hill, 1930); C. H. Ambler, *Francis H. Pierpont, Union War Governor of Virginia and Father of West Virginia* (Chapel Hill, 1937).

18

Calhoun and States' Rights

THE GROWTH of sectionalism in the nation from 1820 to 1861 is the dominant political theme of the period. Increasingly the South began to realize the implications of its minority status in the nation and to rely on states' rights as a means of protection. The South as "a conscious minority" could follow several paths of development, one that led to Southern nationalism, another to find allies in the North within the national parties, and a third to seek defense for its way of life by constitutional amendments. All of these methods were advocated by different groups below the Mason-Dixon line. Senator John C. Calhoun sought to defend Southern interests by strengthening the federal character of the central government, by forming an alliance with the West, and finally in desperation, by forming a Southern bloc and seeking constitutional amendments protecting the South.

Calhoun was a complex personality, not "the cast-iron man" whom Harriet Martineau described, but a flexible person who adjusted himself to the changing economic interests of the South while he thought he was moved only by a devotion to "principle." [1] Indeed, the key to Calhoun's life is to be found in understanding these remarkable changes. The supreme tragedy of his life was not the wreck of his political ambitions through the intrigue of Van Buren, but the fact that despite his genuine love for the Union he was led to advocate measures that tended to destroy it. The circumstance that prevented Calhoun from being a truly national statesman was the existence of slavery in the South. After the close of the nullification struggle he devoted his life to the preservation of this archaic institution. But into this cause that seems so ignoble to us today Calhoun carried a paradoxical love of liberty—a belief in the freedom of the Southern people to determine their way of life within a decentralized government. He was not primarily a champion of property interests; actually, he never aspired to make money as an end of life, and he decried the money-making passion prevalent in the North; to him honor was far more important, and in this aspect of his personality he was very Southern. [2]

Calhoun was the intellectual leader of the proslavery South, formulating the political theories that rationalized its economic interests. He did not

[1] Harriet Martineau, *Retrospect of Western Travel,* quoted by Clement Eaton (ed.), *The Leaven of Democracy: The Growth of the Democratic Spirit in the Time of Jackson as Experienced by the American People and Witnessed by Foreign Visitors* (New York, 1963), 78.
[2] Francis J. Grund, *Aristocracy in America* [1839] (New York, 1959), 279–280.

originate, however, the doctrines he so ably advocated, for they were implicit in the political, social, and economic trends of the beleaguered South. Not only was he a one-man "brain trust" for the solution of the problems of his section but he also became the South's greatest agitator and propagandist for Southern unity against the antislavery forces of the North. Yet a modern reader may wonder whether the oratory and the great forensic battles in the Senate that Calhoun waged against Clay and Webster in behalf of states' rights were really significant. When Congressmen voted, they usually voted for their interests regardless of the scintillating swordplay of words.

The young Calhoun is an attractive figure in the portrait gallery of the South's heroes. Born in the back country of South Carolina, near Abbeville, in 1782, he developed into an angular young man, six feet two inches in height, with a superabundant mane of dark hair, deep-set hazel eyes, high cheek bones, strong jutting chin, and a wide mouth. His family belonged to the Scotch-Irish yeomanry who had emigrated from Pennsylvania into the frontier country of the Carolinas. From his Scotch-Irish forbears he had inherited some dominant traits that clearly marked his career as a statesman. He was serious in temperament, lacking in humor, and an aggressive fighter in the political arena, but never descending to fight a duel. Chaste in private life—he never sowed wild oats—he was incorruptible in public life.[3]

Calhoun matured late. Until he was nearly nineteen years old he worked on his father's farm side by side with his slave companion, Sawney. He then decided to get an education, and with all the deep seriousness of his nature he studied two years in the log cabin academy of Moses Waddel at Appling, Georgia, entered the Junior Class at Yale College, was graduated with highest honors from this New England institution in 1804, and prepared for a law career by studying in the famous school of Judge Tapping Reeve at Litchfield, Connecticut. In 1811 he married an heiress of the lowland aristocracy of South Carolina and in that year entered Congress, joining the ranks of the War Hawks.

In the early part of his career Calhoun deserved great praise. "Calhoun," John Quincy Adams wrote on October 15, 1821, "is a man of fair and candid mind, of honorable principles, of clear and quick understanding, of cool self-possession, of enlarged philosophical views, and of ardent patriotism. He is above all sectional and factious prejudices more than any other statesman of this Union with whom I have ever acted." [4] In his speeches before Congress he refused to follow the custom of his period of indulging in florid oratory and artificial gesticulation. He relied upon close reasoning, logical argument, lucid statement, and sincerity to convince his audience.

[3] For a critical estimate of Calhoun's personality, see W. H. Meigs, *Life of John C. Calhoun* (New York, 1917), II, chap. 3; Margaret L. Coit, *John C. Calhoun, American Portrait* (Boston, 1950); and Gerald M. Capers, *John C. Calhoun, Opportunist; a Reappraisal* (Gainesville, Fla., 1960).

[4] Allan Nevins (ed.), *Diary of John Quincy Adams, 1779–1845* (New York, 1928), 265.

Monroe appointed him secretary of war, in which position he demonstrated fine ability as an administrator. He reorganized the department to a high degree of efficiency, eliminated corruption, fought earnestly for an adequate system of fortifications and a strong army.[5] One of his most admirable policies was his humanitarian Indian policy, by which he sought to civilize the dependent tribes and protect them from exploitation by the powerful fur interests.

The point to be emphasized about the young Calhoun was his ardent nationalism.[6] His career as a War Hawk has already been discussed. During the period following the War of 1812 he voted for the nationalistic program of a protective tariff, the establishment of the Second National Bank, and the Bonus Bill for internal improvements. In speaking on the Bonus Bill, February 4, 1817, he declared that he was "no advocate for refined arguments on the constitution. The instrument was not intended as a thesis for the logician to exercise his ingenuity on. It ought to be construed with plain, good sense. . . ." [7] Later, Calhoun sought to attract the West into an alliance with the South by favoring a land policy that would appeal to the West, even to the extent of granting the public lands to the states to be used for internal improvements.

One of the weaknesses of Calhoun was his intense craving to become president, but he was a man of high principles who would not stoop to unscrupulous means to attain his end. At the height of his career he received a disastrous political blow from which he never recovered. He incurred the bitter enmity of Jackson, an unrelenting hostility that blasted his favorable prospects of attaining his heart's desire. The master architects in defeating Calhoun's ambition were a cabal of Van Buren's friends, intent on making "the Little Magician" the successor of Jackson. The Peggy O'Neale affair had done much to elevate Van Buren in the good graces of the president and to sow distrust of Calhoun in his mind. The breaking point, however, did not occur until May, 1830, when Jackson received proof that the South Carolina statesman had favored a court martial in 1818 to try him for his Florida invasion.

For years Jackson had believed that Calhoun had defended him on that occasion in Monroe's cabinet. Calhoun had allowed the vindictive general to hold this illusion.[8] At a strategic moment in the developing rivalry between Van Buren and Calhoun to succeed to the presidency, a group of Van Buren's friends devised a plot to alienate Jackson completely in his support of the formidable South Carolinian. It was a complicated intrigue, engineered by friends of both Jackson and Van Buren, especially Major William B.

[5] See W. Edwin Hemphill (ed.), *The Papers of John C. Calhoun*, II [1817–1818] (Columbia, S.C., 1963).
[6] Calhoun's early career has been admirably described by C. M. Wiltse, *John C. Calhoun, Nationalist, 1782–1828* (Indianapolis, 1944), vol. I of a three-volume biography.
[7] R. K. Crallé (ed.), *The Works of John C. Calhoun* (New York, 1853), II, 192.
[8] For a defense of Calhoun in this episode, see C. M. Wiltse, *John C. Calhoun, Nullifier, 1829–1839* (Indianapolis, 1949).

Lewis and James A. Hamilton, son of the famous Alexander. The ultimate stage of the plot was reached when Jackson was shown a letter from William H. Crawford, who had been in Monroe's cabinet, revealing that in 1818 Calhoun had advocated a court martial for the obstreperous general. The Old Hero was now thoroughly aroused by this evidence of what he regarded as Calhoun's duplicity. He sent the Crawford letter to Calhoun for his denial or confirmation. The latter replied in a fifty-two-page letter, not denying the charge, but observing that this revival of an old and forgotten controversy at this time was an intrigue. The breach between these two leading Southern statesmen became public when the correspondence between them was published early in 1831. The consequences of this quarrel, based on such petty grounds, became far-reaching and tragic, for Calhoun lost his chance to become President, and possibly the course of American history may have thereby been changed.

In the latter part of the 1820's South Carolina, in common with the older Atlantic seaboard states, was suffering an economic decline, a phenomenon that has been called "the rural depression." [9] Cotton sold at the peak of 29.5 cents a pound in June, 1825, thus stimulating heavy planting for the next season, but the price of the staple dropped to 12 cents a pound in 1826 and 9.3 cents during the following year. It was natural that the planters should seek to find some cause for their economic suffering—a scapegoat. Instead of blaming themselves and their forebears for wasteful agriculture that took no thought of the future, and instead of considering the factor of overproduction, they hit upon the protective tariff as the cause of their distress. The tariff was prejudicial to the economic interests of the planters, but the main reasons for their inadequate returns from agriculture were the exhaustion of their soils and their inability to compete in cotton production with the rich virgin soils of the new Southwest.

The policy of a protective tariff, begun in 1816, had led to increases in the customs duties, until in 1828 the Tariff of Abominations stirred deep resentment in the South. Even before this unjust law was passed, Robert J. Turnbull had written letters in the Charleston *Mercury*, entitled "The Crisis," protesting violently against the high tariff policy and threatening secession. Dr. Thomas Cooper, president of the University of South Carolina (then called South Carolina College), declared that the time had come for the people of his adopted state to calculate the value of the Union to themselves. In 1828 a committee of the South Carolina legislature had published an ominous document of warning to the North, entitled the *South Carolina Exposition and Protest*. Calhoun was the author, but this fact was kept secret.[10]

[9] Avery O. Craven, *The Coming of the Civil War* (New York, 1942), chap. 3.
[10] The older standard studies of the nullification movement are D. F. Houston, *A Critical Study of Nullification in South Carolina* (Cambridge, 1896); and C. S. Boucher, *The Nullification Controversy in South Carolina* (Chicago, 1916); but they have been superseded by W. W. Freehling, *Prelude to Civil War: The Nullification Controversy in South Carolina, 1816–1836* (New York, 1965).

The Carolina leader had radically changed his attitude toward the tariff since 1816. At that time he thought that his native state could develop manufactures under the protection of such a law and thus obtain a more balanced economy. But the years had demonstrated the fallacy of his youthful optimism, and he now believed that the agricultural section of the nation was being exploited by the industrial section through the tariff. In 1827 came the turning point in his public attitude to the protection, or subsidizing, of manufactures. The introduction of the Woolens Bill into the Senate brought forward again the issue of tariff protection. The division of yeas and nays on this measure was equal, which forced him as president of the Senate to cast the deciding vote—a negative vote. In New England Webster had also made a remarkable reversal in his stand on the tariff as the economic interest of his section shifted.

During the next year, yielding to the pressure of lesser political leaders in his state, Calhoun drafted an elaborate argument against the constitutionality of the tariff in the *South Carolina Exposition and Protest*. In this document he pointed out that the South exported two thirds of all domestic products sent to foreign nations by the United States—chiefly cotton, tobacco, rice, sugar, and naval stores. In return for these exports, England and other European countries sent manufactured goods that were taxed at the customs ports for the benefit of New England and the Middle States manufacturers. He observed also that the tariff of 1828, which averaged 45 per cent ad valorem, deprived the South of cheap manufactured goods and thus increased the cost of the production of cotton. Furthermore, this bill was imposed by a two-thirds majority on the one third of the population who produced two thirds of the exports of the country. He proclaimed that the inhabitants of the South were "the serfs" of the tariff system, which extracted $16,650,000 annually from them in duties, whereas the national government disbursed to the South less than $2 million annually. Thus the South was being ruthlessly exploited by the North.[11]

What was the remedy? Not secession, as the radical leaders, Dr. Thomas Cooper, Robert J. Turnbull, and Robert Barnwell Rhett, had suggested. Disunion was abhorrent to Calhoun at this time. His remedy was what he liked to call "State Veto," but others called nullification. This legal doctrine was derived primarily from the Virginia and Kentucky Resolutions of 1798, the last of which had declared that the several states had the right to nullify an unconstitutional law. The South Carolina statesman took a more extreme step of declaring that a single state could nullify a federal law it regarded as unconstitutional. The federal government, he maintained, was merely the agent of the states, created by the Constitution, and it could not act legally beyond its written instructions in the compact, or contract, of the Constitution. In the case of grand clashes between the state and the federal government over a question of the interpretation of the Constitution, there

[11] Crallé (ed.), *Works of John C. Calhoun*, vol. VI.

was no common umpire (the Supreme Court could not be considered such, since it was a party of the federal government). Each state, therefore, had a right to judge whether the federal government had violated the Constitution. To arrest the operation of an unconstitutional law it was necessary for a specially elected convention to exercise the sovereignty of a state.

Calhoun did not take an active part in the nullification movement until the summer of 1831. The crisis in his career as a national statesman seems to date not from 1828 but from his quarrel with Jackson, which blasted his immediate prospects to become president. His authorship of the *Exposition* was then made public, and on August 28, 1832, he gave a definitive statement of his views on nullification in the "Fort Hill Letter" (*Fort Hill* was the name of Calhoun's home near Pendleton in the up-country of South Carolina). In this document he made important qualifications of the doctrine as expounded by the extremists. He recognized an appeal beyond the sovereign state, namely, a three-fourths majority of the states—the ratifying power of the Constitution. If an amendment conferring upon the Federal government the disputed power should be ratified, the dissatisfied state must submit or leave the Union. Calhoun did not believe that a state could nullify a Federal law and remain within the Union. Even in this modified form the nullification doctrine seems to be an impracticable instrument that would permit a state to refuse to obey a national law that it did not like and thus paralyze the action of the Federal government in carrying out the will of the people.

Calhoun refused to recognize that the Constitution had changed since 1789. Actually a new concept of the nation had risen that reduced the power of self-determination, or sovereignty, of the individual states. The framers of the Constitution and the Americans of 1789 believed that sovereignty could be divided and that the Constitution gave sovereignty to the national government in some departments of political action and to the state government in other fields. But Calhoun accepted a new definition of sovereignty expounded by the English theorist John Austin that sovereignty was indivisible, for the ultimate power of decision cannot be divided. This idea was wittily expressed by John Randolph of Roanoke, who compared sovereignty to a woman's virtue, observing that it was just as absurd to ask a state to surrender part of her sovereignty as to ask a woman to surrender a part of her virginity.

The *South Carolina Exposition* was a statement of South Carolina's grievances and a warning, which was considered and published by the legislature but not formally adopted. The state now waited to see what would be the policy of the new administration in regard to the unjust and oppressive tariff legislation. Since Jackson considered himself a native of South Carolina and was a cotton planter and a slaveowner, the Carolinians expected sympathy and aid from him. In January, 1830, Senator Robert Hayne delivered a magnificent speech in the Senate, seeking to form an alliance between South and West, and defending the South Carolina doctrines, to which Webster replied, asserting national supremacy. In the following April at the Jefferson anniversary dinner, designed to promote the South-West alliance, Jackson gave a toast that was a sharp warning to those hotheaded Carolinians who might attempt the nullification of a federal law—"Our (Federal) Union—it must be preserved!" Calhoun replied with a nobler toast: "The Union—next to our liberty, most dear. May we always remember that it can only be preserved by distributing equally the benefits and burthens of the Union." [12]

The first effort to call a convention to nullify, in the autumn elections of 1830, was defeated. Two years later, however, a new tariff law was enacted that continued the high level of duties that had exploited the South. The North rejected a compromise, and Jackson refused to veto. South Carolina decided that the time to resist had arrived. By a two-thirds majority the legislature summoned a convention at Columbia and voted (November 24, 1832) that the Tariff Acts of 1828 and 1832, being unconstitutional, were null and void. The nullification ordinance was to go into effect February 1, 1833, after which date no federal duties could be collected in South Carolina ports and no appeal from the state courts to the Supreme Court of the United States in regard to the tariff was permissible. The adoption of the nullification ordinance was preceded by a bitter fight between the nullifiers, led by Robert Y. Hayne, George McDuffie, and James Hamilton, Jr., and the Unionists led by such cool-headed men as James Louis Petigru, Daniel E. Huger, Joel R. Poinsett, and Benjamin F. Perry, editor of the *Greenville Mountaineer.*

South Carolina appealed to her sister states below the Mason-Dixon line to join in this movement of resisting the oppression of the federal government. But not a single other Southern state came to her aid by nullifying the obnoxious tariff law. Georgia, however, proposed a Southern convention. Disaster then faced South Carolina, especially since Jackson privately announced that he would hang nullifiers on the trees of the state as traitors. Publicly he issued a proclamation written mainly by his secretary of state, Edward Livingston, declaring nullification to be a destruction of the Union, which he would not tolerate. South Carolinians then began to prepare for defending the homeland from the invasion of Federal forces.

In this crisis Calhoun resigned the vice-presidency and was elected to the Senate by the South Carolina legislature. His journey from his plantation at *Fort Hill* to the national capitol has been compared to Luther's journey to the Diet of Worms. Calhoun did not know whether Jackson would order his arrest for treason when he arrived in Washington or permit him to take his seat in the Senate. In the Senate he spoke earnestly in defense of his native state, but his words had little effect. Henry Clay stepped forward and offered a compromise tariff bill, gradually reducing the tariff duties for a period of nine years, until by July 1, 1842, they should stand at a revenue basis of 20 per cent. Privately Clay told his friends that one Congress could not bind later Congresses—a Machiavellian line of argument.

[12] R. R. Stenberg, "The Jefferson Birthday Dinner, 1830," *Journal of Southern History,* XIV (August 1948), 331–356.

In the meanwhile the South Carolinians had postponed the date of the operation of nullification. On March 1, 1833, the Clay compromise tariff, as well as a "Force Bill," giving the president authority to employ the armed forces of the United States to collect the customs in the disaffected state, were passed. South Carolina then repealed the nullification ordinance, but as a last gesture of defiance, nullified the Force Act, Actually, South Carolina had won in the nullification controversy, for she had accomplished her object of forcing the lowering of the tariff. At the same time the doctrine of nullification received a fatal blow, since South Carolina had been isolated in her struggle against the Federal government. The problem of the state veto has been revived in the twentieth century on a broader scale in the Council of the United Nations, where it remains as difficult a question to solve as in the time of Calhoun.

Recently historical scholarship has thrown a new light on the nullification struggle. By analyzing the forces supporting nullification and those opposed to it, a revisionist historian has concluded that the struggle was not merely over the tariff but was also precipitated by a deep-seated fear that the growing power of the North threatened the existence of slavery and, therefore, the Federal government had to be curbed by establishing the right of a state to nullify hostile legislation.[13] The economic decline of the short-staple cotton planters of the Piedmont did not extend to the rice and sea-island cotton planters of the coastal plain; the primary concern of the latter was in warding off federal legislation that might endanger slavery. The yeomanry of the up-country violently opposed nullification, as did the merchants of Charleston, who did so with moderation. Civil war threatened South Carolina; the nullifiers raised twenty-five thousand volunteers, the Unionists eight thousand. When this danger was averted by the repeal of the nullification ordinance, a new occasion for civil war arose over the passage by the legislature of a test oath for officeholders, especially militia officers, of allegiance to the state. The issue was one of ideology and semantics, whether the nullifiers could impose an oath of "paramount" allegiance to the state. A compromise oath was finally passed in 1834, but the Supreme Court of the state declared it unconstitutional. The scars of the nullification struggle profoundly affected the South Carolina mind during the remainder of the antebellum period.

Calhoun regarded his nullification, or state veto, doctrine as a Union-saving device that would allay sectional discontent by protecting minority rights. Gradually the former War Hawk lost his enthusiasm for broad national measures and placed the interests of his section above those of the nation. After the subsiding of the nullification movement, he was aroused to a defense of Southern interests by the rise of the Northern abolition movement. The South Carolina statesman was one of the foremost Southern leaders in working for legislation to quarantine his section from the abolition contagion. He appealed to the Northern states to suppress their antislavery societies and the antislavery press. From Congress he demanded that rules

---

[13] See Freehling, *Prelude to Civil War,* especially chaps. 3, 4, 9.

be adopted that would prevent the reception of antislavery petitions by Congress—the most thoroughgoing type of gag resolution—and legislation authorizing the Southern states to exclude from the mails publications regarded as incendiary. He believed that slavery was not a national but a local problem that should be exclusively handled by the people of the Southern states, who understood the Negro and who were directly affected by the race problem.

Calhoun had a remarkably prophetic intelligence. Not only did he foresee the War for Southern Independence but he also predicted that a civil conflict to free the slaves would result in the Negroes becoming, not slaves of individual masters, but slaves of the community. His clairvoyant genius made him gloomy, like Cassandra, for he never quite lost his early nationalism and his love of the Union, which he believed to be in grave danger from the antislavery "fanaticism" of the North. His constant advice to his section was to meet the enemy (the Northern antislavery men) "on the frontier." Making concessions to the abolitionists would not satisfy them, but lead to bolder encroachments on the rights of the South and to more intolerable insults. Therefore the proper course for the South to pursue was not to yield an inch of Southern rights. In order to protect their vital interests, Southerners must give up their party loyalties and unite in an unbreakable phalanx. Realizing that the South's relative strength in the Union was ebbing each day on account of the rapid growth of the North in population and economic resources, he warned that the cause of the South would be lost by pursuing a temporizing course. "If there must be an issue," he said in 1836, "now is our time. We never can be more united or better prepared for the struggle, and I, for one, would much rather meet the danger now, than turn it over to those who come after us." [14] A few years later, he reiterated this advice: "The true policy is to take bold ground and force an issue as soon as possible."

During these years of agitating to arouse the Southern people to realize the dangers of the abolition movement. Calhoun was not unmindful of his frustrated presidential aspirations. After his return to the Democratic fold during Van Buren's administration, he aspired to win the presidency by forming an alliance between the South and the West. Such a powerful partnership would curb the menace of the industrial Northern states and might elevate him to the presidency. In 1843 he launched his candidacy by publishing a campaign biography he himself wrote, but he induced Representative R. M. T. Hunter of Virginia to assume the paternity of this anonymous panegyric. In April, 1844, his appointment as secretary of state in Tyler's Cabinet gave him a splendid opportunity to win a large political following by championing the annexation of Texas, but he muffed his chance by his foolish Lord Aberdeen letter, in which he maintained that annexation of this region was needed to protect Southern slavery.

---

[14] Crallé, *The Works of John C. Calhoun,* II, 486; see Eaton, *Freedom of Thought in the Old South* (Durham, 1940), chap. 6.

John C. Calhoun (1782–1850). Photograph by Matthew Brady. (Courtesy of Library of Congress)

His claim to be more than a sectional statesman was bolstered by his renewed interest in internal improvements. On this issue primarily he hoped to base an alliance between the South and West. In 1845 he was invited to attend a Southern Convention at Memphis. Here he proposed a great east and west railroad that would connect Memphis and Charleston, a more appealing project to Southerners than Robert Y. Hayne's plan of a line uniting Charleston and Cincinnati. At this convention he returned to his earlier idea of obtaining the aid of the federal government in undertaking internal improvements. He announced his doctrine that the Mississippi River and its tributaries were so vast that they should be regarded as an inland sea, and therefore they formed a proper object for the expenditure of federal funds for the improvement of their navigation. Thus Calhoun anticipated some of the aspects of "regional planning," which as a developed program lay far ahead in the next century.

Although he had opposed the Mexican War, he was determined that the South should be treated fairly in the distribution of the spoils. Consequently he powerfully resisted the adoption by Congress of the Wilmot Proviso (first introduced in 1846), which would have excluded slavery from any territory acquired from Mexico. He elaborated the doctrine that the Constitution protected the establishment of slavery in all Federal territories. Only when a territory had attained the status of a state could it exclude slavery, and Congress had no power to pass legislation prohibiting Southerners from entering the common domain of the nation with their slaves.

When California in the autumn of 1849 drafted a constitution forbidding slavery and applied for admission to the Union, Calhoun was greatly alarmed by this threat to the preservation of the sectional equilibrium in the Senate— a safeguard to slavery. He sought to form a Southern bloc in Congress to protect Southern rights. For this purpose he composed an "Address of the Southern Delegates in Congress to Their Constituents," which presented the dangers that menaced his section from the antislavery crusade and urged Southerners, regardless of party loyalties, to unite to resist encroachment on their rights by the North. As early as 1845–1847 Calhoun had attempted to organize a third party based on Southern rights, by which he may have hoped to elevate himself into the presidency via election in the House of Representatives.[15] When the efforts to form a Southern third party and a Southern bloc in Congress failed, he agitated for the calling of a Southern convention, which resulted in the assembly of the Nashville Convention of 1850 (discussed in a later chapter). His last days were spent feverishly trying to alarm and unite the South in order to arrest "the aggression of the North." The only hope for the continuance of the Union, he believed, was for "the South to present with an unbroken front to the North the alternative of dissolving the partnership or of ceasing on their part to violate our rights. . . ." [16]

[15] J. S. Rayback, "The Presidential Ambitions of John C. Calhoun, 1844–1848," *Journal of Southern History,* XIV (August 1948), 331–356.

[16] J. F. Jameson (ed.), "Correspondence of John C. Calhoun," *Annual Report of the American Historical Association for 1899* (Washington, 1900), II, 765. Letters to Calhoun have been edited by Chauncey S. Boucher and R. P. Brooks, "Correspondence Addressed to Calhoun." *Annual Report of the American Historical Association for 1929* (Washington, 1931).

After Jefferson, Calhoun was the ablest political philosopher produced by the Old South. His ideas of a correct government were formed very much as the political theory of Aristotle was devised, by rationalizing the status quo of the political state in which he lived. Slavery was a social institution Southerners regarded of paramount importance, and it must be protected against an aggressive antislavery movement based in the Northern states. The South was overwhelmingly agricultural, whereas the industrial interest of the North was becoming increasingly powerful. Politically, the South was a minority group in the nation. How was this section to protect itself within the framework of the Union against a numerical majority that was bent on using its power in Congress to injure the economic interests of the South and its way of life?

Calhoun devoted his magnificent powers of analysis and logic to forge a weapon of defense, a political theory that fitted the needs of the Southern planters. Beginning with a concept of human nature quite different from the romantic idealism of Jefferson or the pessimism of Hamilton, he held that human nature is neither black nor white, but gray—a medium view of human beings. Men are dominated, he thought, by their selfish interests, so that it is essential for a democratic government to provide protection to the minority from the selfishness of the majority. His view of human rights was based on a frank repudiation of the Declaration of Independence, with its equalitarian doctrines. He declared that men are unequal and that liberty is the reward of ability and achievement. Therefore, liberty must not be thrust upon men, but they must earn it by acquiring the ability to govern themselves. Such ideas he expressed in lucid prose in his essays. *A Disquisition on Government* and *A Discourse on the Constitution and Government of the United States,* written at the close of his career and published posthumously.

Calhoun's most significant contribution to political theory was made in dealing with the problem of protecting minority rights against a numerical majority. He was only the most prominent of a group of Southern political thinkers who rationalized the status quo of their section into a political theory. Abel P. Upshur, a Tidewater Virginian, in his *A Brief Enquiry into the True Nature and Character of Our Federal Government* (1840), also gave a remarkable analysis of the dangers of majority rule, maintaining that the tyranny of a majority is more destructive of liberty than the tyranny of the few. Calhoun developed an abhorrence for the uncurbed rule of the majority, declaring that the word *democrat* was usually applied to "those who are in favour of the government of the absolute numerical majority to which I am utterly opposed and the prevalence of which would destroy our system and destroy the South." [17] Although this aspect of Calhoun's political thought fits into an antidemocratic tradition, he was nevertheless a great defender of constitutionalism, an opponent of the totalitarian state, which has a modern validity.

[17] Jameson (ed.), "Correspondence of John C. Calhoun," 399–400.

One means of preserving minority rights advocated by Calhoun was the strengthening of the doctrine of states' rights, a defense mechanism used by minorities in the North as well as the South. In support of this time-honored device, he proposed the doctrine of the concurrent majority, or of the concurrent voice. The Carolina statesman had observed the working of this formula in the government of his native state. The power of the numerical majority in South Carolina was checked by a compromise in the constitution by which the minority of wealthy slaveholders in the eastern parishes controlled the Senate, which could veto legislation unfavorable to their property interests, whereas the upland areas of the state, in which the slave interest was weak, was given control of the lower house of the legislature.

Calhoun advocated the application of the doctrine of the concurrent majority to fundamental controversies between the states and the federal government. He held that in all great clashes between the national government and a state, or group of states, the will of the numerical majority should not be put into force unless the minority consented or concurred. He cited historical examples of this principle, such as the working of the jury system, the consuls in the Roman republic, and the Polish diet. He believed that in a nation composed of sections with divergent economic interests the doctrine of the concurrent majority should be exercised in order to preserve liberty. The power to check the numerical majority from adopting an unjust course was needed as a Union-saving device, for it would cause the leaders of a dominant section to be more conciliatory and more cautious in disregarding the rights of weaker sections. In other words, fair compromise would be the basis of an enduring marriage between the sections.

The theory that Calhoun proposed for the protection of minority rights sounds admirable, but it had great practical weaknesses. His agency for the operation of the doctrine of the concurrent majority was the state veto of legislation that was deemed unconstitutional. Ignoring the function of the Supreme Court of judicial review, he maintained that a state had the right to hold up the execution of an unconstitutional law until three fourths of the ratifying states—the amending power—could pass on the controversy between the Federal government and the aggrieved state. South Carolina successfully applied this doctrine in the nullification crisis, and Northern states practically nullified the Fugitive Slave Act of 1850 by passing Personal Liberty Acts. Nevertheless, Calhoun's doctrine of a state interposition appears impractical as a working instrument of government. At the close of his life he offered another solution of the problem of protecting the South as a conscious minority, namely, the creation of a dual executive for the federal government, a Southern president and a Northern president, each having a veto power over legislation hostile to the interests of either section.[18]

[18] Valuable expositions of Calhoun's political theory are found in W. E. Dodd, *Statesmen of the Old South* (New York, 1911); Gaillard Hunt, *John C. Calhoun* (Philadelphia, 1908); J. T. Carpenter, *The South as a Conscious Minority, 1789–1861* (New York, 1930); and Louis Hartz, *The Liberal Tradition in America: An Interpretation of American Political Thought Since the Revolution* (New York, 1955).

Calhoun in his later career became reactionary, rigid in his fixed ideas, absorbed in political abstractions. But his political theorizing was devoted to the practical task of forging intellectual weapons to protect Southern economic and social interests. Ideas are, in reality, the most powerful of political weapons, which pass by a process of osmosis, or seepage, into the current of political life. The politicians need the slogans, the simplified dogmas, and the imaginative symbols that the intellectuals create. Calhoun furnished these ideas for his section. He was a conservative, however, fearful of the leveling or reforming spirit, and the champion of landed capital against industrial capital. He regarded the rise of Northern capitalism to dominant power in the federal government as a great menace to the economic interests of the "cotton capitalists" of his section.[19] He believed that the interests of this minority group within the South were also the interests of all Southern people. His argument in behalf of minority rights thus broadened into a defense of the agricultural interest against the exploitation of the industrial interest, which was largely localized in the Northern states. Consequently, there is a definite link between the gaunt, defiant Calhoun of 1850 and the Southern Agrarians of 1930, who in a provocative book, *I'll Take My Stand,* fought a quixotic battle against the industrialization of the South.

The strongest criticism of Calhoun and the Carolina political leaders is that they turned the attention of the people away from progressive reforms within the state to fighting national political issues over slavery. Benjamin F. Perry, the South Carolina Unionist, was sagacious in his comment: "What might not South Carolina now be if her Calhouns, Haynes, McDuffies, Hamiltons and Prestons had devoted their great talents and energies to the commercial and internal improvements of the State, instead of frittering them away in political squabbles, which ended in nothing?"[20] The reforms that South Carolina desperately needed were an enlightened system of public schools, good roads, manufactures, a penitentiary for criminals, railroads, and democratic changes in government, such as the abolition of the over-representation of the lowland parishes in the legislature and of the aristocratic method of choosing the governor and presidential electors. Perry as editor of the *Greenville Mountaineer* and later of the *Southern Patriot,* and as a member of the South Carolina legislature fought bravely for these reforms, but Calhoun was the dictator in South Carolina from 1832 to 1850, and he thwarted all the efforts toward progressive reforms within the state, for he did not wish South Carolina to be distracted by bitter internal fights. Rather, Calhoun was determined to preserve the unity of the state and devote its harmonious energies to fighting the battles for slavery in Congress and in presidential elections.

Calhoun's great weakness as a political philosopher was also the error of his section and to a lesser degree of the America of his time—racism. He saw

[19] See Richard N. Current, "John C. Calhoun, Philosopher of Reaction," *Antioch Review* (Summer 1943), 223–234.
[20] L. A. Kibler, *Benjamin F. Perry, South Carolina Unionist* (Durham, 1946), 302.

the Negro as a permanently inferior person in American society and he had no plans to ameliorate slavery or gradually elevate the Negro. He perceived the slave primarily as property, in the form of an unpaid laborer who was essential to the production of the South's great staple, cotton. Calhoun's inveterate racism seems in great contrast to the general kindness and consideration of his nature that he displayed toward his family and relatives, especially to his daughter Anna. She adored him, sitting in the gallery of the Senate to hear his intellectual speeches, writing letters to cheer his loneliness, nursing him when he was sick, and discussing politics with him. In the largely lost history of Southern feminism before the Civil War, Anna Calhoun stands out as an example of the Southern woman who could combine feminine qualities with a profound interest in politics. She was very much like her father in mind—indeed C. M. Wiltse, a Calhoun biographer, calls her a carbon copy of her father—although in her small stature and vivacious, pert, witty personality she was different. Although Calhoun's wife, Floride, took no interest in politics, his daughter, Anna, was a spirited Southern partisan who impressed Northern statesmen with her ability to defend the Southern cause. Moreover, Calhoun's thoughtfulness for the welfare of his family extended to his consideration for his slaves, who were housed in substantial stone quarters. He was concerned with their health and granted them cotton patches, the produce of which they sold for their own profits. Calhoun illustrated the paradox of the kind master, who nevertheless upheld slavery.

This inconsistency, common to the great majority of Southern slaveholders, can be explained, at least partially, by the existence of a different "blind spot," or insensitivity, from the "blind spot" in modern society. Calhoun, like his compatriots, believed that slavery was so interwoven with the institutions of the South that to destroy slavery would be equivalent to the destruction of the social order of the South. Slavery was the one issue, therefore, on which the South could not compromise; yet the essence of his concurrent majority theory rested on compromise.

Madison and Jefferson had believed that in the American society the majority would constitute a fluctuating condition, so that the minority would have a chance to become the majority. But on this point Calhoun had a sense of realism for he perceived that the antislavery, industrial majority that the South faced in 1850 would dominate the nation for a long time, far beyond his day. It was here, on the question of the continuance and the expansion of slavery, that his theory of the concurrent majority broke down, for both sections were intransigent. Although the doctrine of the concurrent majority seems today to be a bizarre and academic theory, for a considerable period during the twentieth century it actually became a powerful but unarticulated force in American politics. The Southern minority in the Senate was able to block the enactment of legislation by the majority through the operation of the party system, through the use of the filibuster, through the two-thirds rule in the Democratic party convention, and especially by con-

Anna Calhoun, daughter of John C. Calhoun. (Courtesy of Professor Ernest Lander, Jr., Clemson University)

trolling powerful Senate committees as a result of the seniority method of appointing chairmanships.[21]

What is Calhoun's significance today? Calhoun spoke for the right of self-determination of a section against centralization—to him this meant liberty—but there was and is another fundamental right of the nation that balances his point, namely the preservation of human liberty. The great Catholic historian Lord Acton has observed that one truth is often balanced by an opposing truth; one can rightly act only in behalf of the larger truth. Does Calhoun's doctrine of the concurrent majority and its corollary of "state interposition" have any vital application to the modern problem of protecting minority rights? Was his warning against great centralization the voice of wisdom? The answer must be that although his means were invalid and he was wrong in the particular issue upon which he waged his fight for minority rights, his end was just. Calhoun's warnings against a naïve faith in the justness or wisdom of majority rule has tended to make American political theory more sophisticated. His contribution to posterity was to educate the people of the United States to recognize the need of protecting minority rights, which in the course of our history has often been forgotten.

[21] See David M. Potter, *The South and the Concurrent Majority* (Baton Rouge, 1972).

19

Exuberant Imperialism—
A Southerner's War

THE OCCUPATION of Texas by Southerners seemed to be manifest destiny. The initiator of this movement was not a Southerner, however, but an elderly Connecticut Yankee, Moses Austin. Possessing a restless, adventurous nature, Austin shifted from place to place until he located in the lead mining district of Missouri, where he became a Spanish subject and made a fortune in lead mining. Later he lost his fortune in a bank failure, a catastrophe that impelled him to seek new adventures in Spanish territories. In 1820 he traveled to San Antonio and received permission from the Spanish authorities to lead an expedition of three hundred American settlers into Texas, provided they were Catholics. Moses Austin died the following year, but his son, Stephen, twenty-seven years old, prevailed upon the new republic of Mexico to confirm the grant made to his father.[1] Thus young Austin became an *empresario,* or contractor, to colonize American settlers in Texas. He himself was given a huge grant of land, and the settlers were granted one labor (177 acres) of farming land and a league (4,428 acres) of grazing land for each head of a family. The *empresario* was also allowed to charge his colonists a fee for his services; Austin charged 12½ cents an acre for cotton lands. In the early years of Texas colonization Austin exercised autocratic powers of government, but he was an able and just administrator. He was the most prominent of a small group of *empresarios* who were commissioned by the Mexican government to bring population into the vast, vacant expanses of Texas.

By 1835 approximately twenty-five thousand Americans as well as three- or four thousand slaves had settled in this border province. The American settlers were supposed to become Catholics, but this requirement was evaded, and in 1834 religious toleration was established by law. The most important lure for immigration was the abundance of cheap cotton lands in the river valleys of eastern Texas. Most of the colonists were respectable citizens, Southern cotton farmers with their slaves, but some were rough characters who moved one jump ahead of the sheriff. "Gone to Texas" frequently had an ominous meaning. Nativity studies of the Census of 1860 indicate that

---

[1] Eugene C. Barker, *Life of Stephen F. Austin, Founder of Texas, 1793–1836* (Nashville, 1925).

Tennessee contributed more settlers to this Southwestern frontier than any other state, with Alabama ranking second.

The danger of encouraging a large-scale American immigration into Texas was early revealed to the Mexican government by the Fredonian Revolt. An American *empresario* named Haden Edwards had a quarrel with the Mexican government that led to the annulment of his land grant. Thereupon he led a revolt of American settlers in 1826 and established the Fredonian Republic in the eastern part of Texas, near Nacogdoches. The United States refused to recognize or aid the tiny American republic, and Stephen Austin cooperated with Mexican troops in suppressing the rebellion. This uprising, however, alarmed the Mexican government, which believed that the United States had incited the leaders. Suspicion was heightened by the fact that before and after the revolt, both President John Quincy Adams and President Andrew Jackson had tried to buy Texas.

After the Fredonian Revolt the Mexican authorities began a policy of restricting settlers from the United States. In 1829 the Mexican government promulgated a decree forbidding slavery. This reform resulted in such a storm of protest by the American colonists that Texas was exempted temporarily from the decree. The next year the Mexican government forbade any further immigration of American colonists into Texas, but this law was never effectively enforced. The old Spanish exclusive policy of trade was revived, so that heavy duties made trade with the United States almost prohibitive. In 1831 military garrisons of convicts were established in Texas to control and overawe the Americans. Also the province of Texas was joined to the neighboring province of Coahuila, which was dominated by corrupt Mexican officials. Although most of the restrictions were evaded by the Americans, they served to irritate them and to develop a spirit of independence.[2]

In 1832 the first Texan revolution began, not for independence, but for reform. The immediate occasion for hostilities was friction over the enforcement of the Mexican tariff at Brazoria. In the same year Santa Anna led a rebellion against the Mexican government, offering a program of liberalism. He promised the Texas revolutionists that if they would accept his rule, he would grant them the reforms they desired. Urged by Stephen Austin, they accepted the fair promises of the Mexican leader and laid down their arms. Austin then went to Mexico City to present the three demands of the Americans: tariff reform, repeal of the restriction of American immigration into Texas, and the separation of Coahuila and Texas. After Santa Anna had attained power, however, he threw off the mask of liberalism and became a typical despot. He made facile promises of reform to Austin, but no legislation was passed to carry out these promises.[3] The American leader was arrested on his way back to Texas and thrown into prison because of an indiscreet letter he had written.

[2] R. N. Richardson, *Texas, the Lone Star State* (New York, 1943).
[3] See Wilfred H. Calcott, *Santa Anna: The Story of an Enigma Who Was Once Mexico* (Norman, Oklahoma, 1936).

In 1835 relations between Texas and Mexico had become so strained that the Texans began a second revolt. The revolt originated at Anahuac, at the head of Galveston Bay, over a disturbance in connection with the unequal collection of customs and practical jokes on the guards. At first the Americans hoped that the Mexican liberals would join them in an effort to reform the despotic Mexican administration, which had recently discarded the federal system of government. Since this cooperation was not secured, the Texans decided to strike for independence.[4] Only by a declaration of independence could they hope for financial support and active sympathy from the United States. In a convention at Washington, Texas, March 2, 1836, the Texans drew up a declaration of independence, based on the doctrine of natural rights and the fact that Santa Anna had overturned the federal system of government.

The Texans suffered two tragic defeats in the early part of the war. In February, 1836, a small band of 187 volunteers under Lieutenant Colonel William B. Travis were defending the church-fortress of the Alamo in San Antonio. Although they had ample warning that Santa Anna was advancing upon them with an army of between six- and seven-thousand men, they were foolhardy enough to remain in this dangerous position. Among the defenders of the Alamo were James Bowie, brother of the inventor of the bowie knife, and David Crockett, the famous frontiersman. Colonel Travis, a native of South Carolina and a lawyer by profession, issued a high-flown proclamation "To the People of Texas and all Americans in the World," appealing for aid and announcing the determination of the Texans to die rather than surrender. However, only thirty-two men, from Gonzales, joined the beleaguered garrison. On March 6, 1836, the Mexican army assaulted the Alamo and killed every man of the garrison. Approximately half of the brave defenders were recent arrivals from Tennessee, Kentucky, and Alabama. One authority on the Texan Revolution has suggested that this fact goes far to explain the savage treatment of "the foreigners" by the Mexican commanders.[5] The tragedy of this heroic fight aroused the Texans to avenge their slain comrades; "Remember the Alamo!" became their battle cry. The disaster of the Alamo was soon followed by the massacre of the American garrison at Goliad. Their commander, James W. Fannin, had delayed in obeying orders to evacuate the town. When he finally began a retreat, his little army was surrounded by the Mexican troops. Faced by overwhelming numbers, he de-

---

[4] Frederick Merk writes that the old idea that the Texas revolution was "an uprising against Mexican tyrrany is unfounded," *Slavery and the Annexation of Texas* (New York, 1972), 180. Holman Hamilton in reviewing it in the *Journal of Southern History* wittily observed: "If Justin H. Smith in 1911 was a fifty-four-year-old revisionist, Mr. Merk in 1972 was an eighty-five-year-old re-revisionist, demonstrating that tendencies in those directions are not confined to youth."

[5] William C. Binkley, *The Texas Revolution* (Baton Rouge, 1952), 96–97. Binkley estimates that out of approximately seven hundred men killed by the Mexicans in the spring of 1836, less than one fifth were residing in Texas when hostilities began the year before.

Sam Houston (1793–1863). (Courtesy of Library of Congress)

cided to surrender and trust to the mercy of the foe. The victorious General José Urrea wished to treat his prisoners with clemency, but he was overruled by Santa Anna, who ordered the massacre of the Texans, 234 in number.

The person who devised the strategy of victory for the rebels was Sam

Houston, who the day after the disaster at the Alamo took command of the Texan army of 374 men. This dynamic leader was born in Virginia, but his family had emigrated to the wilderness of Tennessee when he was a youth. Young Houston fought in the War of 1812 under Andrew Jackson, who became his lifelong hero. In the frontier state of Tennessee Houston had a rapid rise as a lawyer and politician, being elected governor at the age of thirty-four (1827). But his promising career ended disastrously as a result of his marriage to a girl eighteen years old, who accepted Houston, twice her age, because of the ambitions of her family. Several months after the marriage she left his home, creating a scandal in which public opinion condemned him. Dramatically, he resigned his office as governor and went to live with the Cherokee Indians, who gave him the names "The Raven" and "The Big Drunk." In 1832 he moved to Texas, where he became an advocate of independence.[6]

For thirty-seven days Sam Houston retreated before the enemy until he reached the San Jacinto River. Near a ford of this river, twenty miles from the recently founded village of Houston, he intercepted a portion of the Mexican army under Santa Anna returning from an unsuccessful raid to capture the provisional government at Harrisburg. The two armies were approximately equal in numbers, about 1,200 men each.[7] It is significant that half of the Texan army had recently arrived from the United States. On April 21, 1836, the Texan army surprised completely the Mexican force and won the decisive victory of San Jacinto. The Texans lost 16 men killed and 25 wounded, including Houston, who had his right leg shattered. The Mexicans, according to the fantastic figures of the Texans, lost 630 killed, 208 wounded, and 730 made prisoners, which was 300 more Mexicans than were present on the battlefield. Among the captured was General Santa Anna, whom the Texans were eager to kill on the spot, but Houston saved him by persuading his men that the Mexican leader would be more valuable to the Texan cause alive than dead. Consequently, the captive Santa Anna sent orders to other Mexican generals to retire and made a secret treaty recognizing the independence of Texas with the Rio Grande boundary. However, this treaty was repudiated by the Mexican government, which for the next nine years refused to recognize the independence of Texas. In fact, the Mexican army as late as 1842 twice invaded Texas and captured San Antonio.

Following the victory of San Jacinto the Texans adopted a democratic constitution and elected Houston president of the republic. Not long after they had won their independence, a proposal of annexation to the United States was adopted by a vote of six thousand to one hundred, and a minister, W. H. Wharton, was sent to Washington. The South was eager for the annexation of this region, because it offered a field for the expansion of the

[6] See Marquis James, *The Raven; a Biography of Sam Houston* (Indianapolis, 1929); and M. K. Wisehart, *Sam Houston, American Giant* (Washington, D C., 1962).
[7] C. E. Castaneda, *The Mexican Side of the Texas Revolution* (Dallas, 1928).

cotton kingdom and slavery. Moreover, perhaps as many as five slave states could be carved out of this imperial domain and thus afford a reserve of future slave states to keep the balance of power in the Senate. The Texan government offered two sections of land (one thousand two hundred eighty acres) to any American volunteer who served for one year in the Texan army. New Englanders, who since 1803 had opposed westward expansion, were hostile to the annexation of Texas, because they regarded it as a "slaveholder's conspiracy." The year of Texan independence was a presidential election year in the United States, and President Jackson, although he favored the eventual annexation of Texas, opposed any hasty action, because he feared that his advocacy of annexation might jeopardize the chances of Martin Van Buren to be elected President. Consequently, the Texan appeal for annexation was rebuffed. But in 1837 just before Jackson retired from office, he officially received the minister of the "Lone Star Republic," and under authority from Congress recognized its independence.

During the next nine years Texas was a sovereign state with its capital located (after 1839) at Austin on the western edge of settlement. The constitution contained a provision limiting the president's term to two years and making him ineligible to succeed himself. Consequently, during the interim, when the veteran Houston was disqualified from serving as executive, Mirabeau Lamar acted as the pinch hitter. This masterful Georgian was a versatile person, being a romantic poet, a soldier, and a statesman. Lamar had grandiose ideas of the future of Texas, which had an area larger than France. Opposing annexation to the United States, he dreamed of extending Texas to the Pacific Ocean.[8] In 1841 he organized an expedition to capture Santa Fe on the east bank of the upper Rio Grande, territory claimed by Texas. The capture of this old Mexican town promised not only an expansion of territory but also money, which was badly needed, and the diversion of the Santa Fe trade to Texas. Furthermore, the people of Santa Fe seemed desirous of joining the new republic. The expedition consisted of two hundred seventy volunteers, as well as some merchants and government officials, including George W. Kendall, editor of the New Orleans *Picayune,* who wrote a vivid account of the adventure. The expedition was poorly planned and the leaders had no knowledge of the best route to Santa Fe. The men suffered terrible privations crossing the plains in a journey of one thousand, three hundred miles and were reduced to eating their horses. Whenever they came to a prairie dog town they would assault it with impetuous ardor. The governor of New Mexico, Manuel Armijo, easily captured the famished men, who heard the Spanish officers debate whether to kill them on the spot or send them to Mexico City. Finally they decided to send them on foot to the Mexican capital, where the survivors were imprisoned.[9]

[8] See H. P. Gambrell, *Mirabeau Buonaparte Lamar: Troubadour and Crusader* (Dallas, 1934).

[9] W. C. Binkley, *The Expansionist Movement in Texas, 1836–1850* (Berkeley, 1925).

About 1840 a famous military unit, the Texas Rangers, was organized to guard the frontier. This picturesque body of men, which included the boyish "Big Foot" Wallace, was under Captain John Coffee Hays and had headquarters at San Antonio. Later they were commanded by the famous Ben McCulloch, who became a prominent Confederate general. These mounted troops carried an ideal weapon for fighting on horseback, the Colt revolver, patented in 1836 by Samuel Colt, a Connecticut Yankee. In fact, one of the earliest models of this revolver was called "the Texas" and was used in the "Lone Star Republic" about 1839. It was without a trigger guard, a defect that was remedied by the Walker Colt (1842), named after Captain Samuel Walker of the Texas Rangers. During the Mexican War the Texas Rangers demonstrated the value of the Colt revolver, inducing General Zachary Taylor to order these weapons for his army.[10]

On the whole, Lamar's administration was unsuccessful. His Indian wars, his foreign adventures, and the effect of the Panic of 1837, which reached Texas three years later, ran the Texas debt up close to $8 million. As a consequence, Texas bonds depreciated so that they became worth only 15 cents on the dollar. The paper currency of the republic, called "red backs," in 1841 declined in value to 10 cents on the dollar. One of Lamar's extravagances was the Texas navy of seven warships, which was acquired to prevent Mexico from invading Texas by sea. In 1839 he sent this fleet to Vera Cruz bearing James Treat, a diplomatic agent. Treat was authorized to offer Mexico $5 million if that state would recognize the independence of Texas with the Rio Grande as a boundary. When the Mexican Congress indignantly refused to entertain the proposal, the Texas navy was used in aiding a rebellion of Yucatan against the central Mexican government. Furthermore, Lamar pursued a harsh policy toward the Indians, determined to expel most of them from the republic and open up additional fertile lands for settlement. When Houston returned to the presidency in 1841, however, he tranquilized the Indian frontier and undertook a policy of financial retrenchment.

The population of Texas expanded rapidly during the period of the Republic and even more rapidly after annexation. In 1847 it had a population of one hundred forty-two thousand, exclusive of Indians, but including thirty-nine thousand Negroes. After the winning of independence, a considerable proportion of the Mexican population, particularly the more prominent citizens, left the principal town of San Antonio. The atmosphere of this raw frontier state was vividly contrasted with the civilization of the older Atlantic states.[11] Land speculation was the rage, and pistol fights on the streets of the towns and villages were common. Mary Austin Holley, the sister of Stephen Austin, reported in 1838 that the seat of government, Houston, was the scene of vice, where scoundrels and criminals gathered;

[10] Walter Prescott Webb, *The Texas Rangers* (New York, 1935).
[11] For an excellent discussion of internal conditions in Texas, see W. R. Hogan, *The Texas Republic, a Social and Economic History* (Norman, 1946).

also prime Negro slaves were in such demand that they were being hired at rates four times ($400) the normal rate in other Southern states.[12] Young George Denison from Vermont who went to San Antonio to teach (1854) was amazed at some of the mores of this town, especially the smoking of women, who "used chalk on their face an inch thick," and the fact that only specie was used for currency (the law prohibited the establishment of banks).[13] By 1860 the population of Texas had grown to 602,432, of whom 12,443 were Mexicans and 20,553 were German immigrants.

The Germans were the most valuable of the foreign stocks. The center of German settlement was New Braunfels, on the Guadalupe River between Austin and San Antonio, founded in 1845 by Prince Carl of Solms-Braunfels, agent of the Adelsverein, or Society for the Protection of German Immigrants in Texas. This organization, led by German noblemen, was founded at Mainz on the Rhine in 1844 for the purpose of concentrating German colonization to the United States in Texas. In 1845, four thousand German immigrants came to Texas, but more than one thousand died of disease, especially malaria and dysentery. The Germans in Texas became a thrifty and prosperous group, cultivating their cotton fields without the aid of slaves, teaching their children handicrafts as well as reading and writing, thus setting a good example to their neighbors. Dr. Ferdinand Roemer, who has written the best travel account of early Texas (1849), pointed out the virtues of this new country, particularly the cheap and fertile land, the fluidity of society, and the freedom of trade. He observed that skilled workers were not restricted by guilds as in Europe but that a man might be a jack-of-all-trades, for example, a combination of doctor, baker, apothecary, and horse trader.[14]

In 1839 France, and, in the next year, England recognized the independence of Texas. England was very much interested in obtaining a protectorate over Texas, for she saw the great advantage of monopolizing Texas cotton and securing a supply of this raw material free from the control of the United States. Also the antislavery group in England hoped to abolitionize Texas, an objective that would endanger Southern slavery. In 1843 Great Britain, whose capitalists had considerable investments in Mexico, brought about an armistice between that country and Texas. Sam Houston cleverly played Great Britain against the United States, arousing the fears of the latter that John Bull would dominate Texas and practicing "coquetry."[15] The Southerners, moreover, were alarmed by the rumor that S. P. Andrews

[12] Mary Austin Holley to Mrs. Sayres, March 21, 1838. Mary Austin Holley Letters, 1808–1846, MSS in University of Texas Library, copies in University of Kentucky Library.
[13] George Denison to his sister, April 21, June 6, 1855, George Denison Papers. MSS in Library of Congress.
[14] Ferdinand Roemer, *Texas: With Particular Reference to German Immigrations* (San Antonio, 1935).
[15] A. W. Williams and E. C. Barker (eds.), *The Writings of Sam Houston* (Austin, 1938–1941), IV, 467–468.

of Houston, Texas, had persuaded the British government to finance a plan to abolish slavery in Texas.

Another circumstance that made the United States more favorable to annexation was the influence of the Texas bondholders in the United States. Texas was in a chronic state of penury. In order to secure money, the government had made large bond issues that were sold in the United States, especially in the Middle States. Nicholas Biddle, former president of the United States Bank, wrote a forceful letter in favor of annexation, pointing out that if Texas was not annexed by the United States, it would drift into the sphere of British influence. Also the Lone Star Republic had given land scrip to Americans who had fought for independence or had defended the state from Mexico. This scrip was extensively purchased by Northern speculators, who urged the annexation of Texas in order to advance their speculations. Jay Cooke, the great Philadelphia financier, believed that the Texas bondholders in the North exerted enough influence to decide the closely contested question in Congress.

The chief reasons why the United States had rejected the Texan appeals for annexation were (1) the fear that if the United States annexed Texas war with Mexico would result and (2) the opposition of the antislavery element in the country. Mexico had given warning that she would declare war against the United States if Texas were annexed. John Quincy Adams, the leader of the antislavery opposition to the acquisition of Texas, pursued a curiously inconsistent policy. While he was President he tried to buy Texas, but in July, 1838, after he had become an antislavery man, he led a filibuster in Congress for three weeks against the resolution of Waddy Thompson of South Carolina for the annexation of Texas. He popularized the idea that the move to acquire Texas was a slaveholder's conspiracy. The same charge was made by the abolitionist Benjamin Lundy in a pamphlet entitled *The War in Texas*. Actually the expansion of slavery had little to do with the settlement of Texas.[16]

President John Tyler was an ardent advocate of the annexation of our southwestern neighbor. Alarmed by reports of British intrigue with regard to Texas, he ordered his secretary of state, the Virginian Abel P. Upshur, in the autumn of 1843, to begin negotiations for a treaty of annexation with the Lone Star Republic. President Houston, however, assumed an indifferent attitude as a result of his negotiations with England. He was on the point of getting England and France to force Mexico to recognize Texan independence and to guarantee it. He therefore demanded the protection of the United States army during negotiations, and pointed out the unfavorable position of the republic in case the United States Senate rejected the proposed

---

[16] For the controversial role of slavery in the annexation of Texas, see Frederick Merk, *Slavery and the Annexation of Texas* (New York, 1973), which to some degree supports the old charge of "a slave power conspiracy," especially in regard to propaganda.

treaty. Tyler's representative in Texas, W. S. Murphy, gave Houston the assurance of military protection against Mexico by the United States during the negotiation of a treaty. Upshur was killed, however, February 28, 1844, while he and a presidential party were inspecting the battleship *Princeton*. He and several Cabinet officers were standing near the huge gun "Peacemaker" during an exhibition. The gun blew up and killed the secretary of state and the secretary of the navy, thus interrupting the negotiation of the treaty.

In Upshur's vacant place Tyler appointed Calhoun. Although he disliked the Carolina statesman, he was forced to make this appointment by a maneuver of Henry A. Wise, Congressman from Virginia, who was a dominant force in the Tyler administration. Calhoun made a serious blunder in replying to Lord Aberdeen, the British secretary of foreign affairs, who had declared that the British government was exerting its efforts for the general abolition of slavery throughout the world. The Carolinian's letter to Lord Aberdeen has been called by Edward Channing "the supreme example of Southern provincialism." [17] Calhoun maintained that slavery was a positive good and cited the miserable examples of free Negroes in the United States as a proof. He declared that the Southern states could not permit Texas to become abolitionized and a refuge of fugitive slaves. Therefore, he urged the necessity of annexing Texas as a safeguard to the civilization of the South. Calhoun's Aberdeen letter played an important role in the defeat in June, 1844, of the treaty that he and Upshur had so laboriously negotiated.

The question of the annexation of Texas was then thrown into the arena of politics, to be decided by the presidential election of 1844. The Southern Whigs as a group were opposed to the annexation of Texas, for the dominant element of the party consisted of men of large property interests who feared that annexation would lead to a war with Mexico and would intensify the controversy over the expansion of slavery. Henry Clay, who expected to be nominated as the candidate of his party, wished to avoid the explosive issue in the campaign.[18] So did Van Buren, the potential candidate of the Democratic party. In the spring of 1842 Van Buren went on a Southern tour, during which he stopped by *The Hermitage* to see the aged Jackson, but he made a more significant visit to Lexington, where he conferred with his rival, Henry Clay. Although there is no positive evidence to establish the conclusion, it was believed that Clay and Van Buren agreed to eliminate the Texas question from the coming campaign. Later the two politicians published letters on the same day sidetracking the question of the annexation of Texas. Clay wrote his famous "Raleigh (North Carolina) Letter," April 17, 1844, opposing the annexation of Texas "at the present time." He declared that annexation would lead to war with Mexico and that it would not be of

---

[17] Edward Channing, *A History of the United States* (New York, 1921), V, 543.
[18] See Clement Eaton, *Henry Clay and the Art of American Politics* (Boston, 1956), chap. 10.

advantage to the South, because climate and geography would prevent more than two of the possibly five states to be carved from Texas from becoming slave states. Van Buren's letter in the Washington *Globe* opposing annexation lost him the support of Andrew Jackson and the Democratic nomination.

In the Democratic convention of 1844 at Baltimore, Van Buren's enemies succeeded in reviving the two-thirds rule, which had first been adopted in 1832. This rule stated that no candidate could be nominated unless he received a majority consisting of two thirds of the delegates of the convention, a procedure that was continued by the Democratic party until 1936. Van Buren had a majority of the delegates, but he could not command the necessary two-thirds majority to be nominated. As a consequence of this impasse, the Democrats chose the first surprise, or "dark horse," candidate in our history, James Knox Polk of Tennessee. He owed his nomination to the advocacy of Andrew Jackson. The old political dictator wrote a letter favoring the selection of Polk, because the latter was an ardent expansionist. Gideon J. Pillow, Polk's law partner, read this letter in the convention at the strategic time. The news of Polk's nomination was flashed to Washington, forty miles away, by the telegraph, the first time this invention had been used in a presidential campaign. The Whigs tried to belittle the Democratic candidate by the question "Who is James K. Polk?"

Nevertheless, Polk had had an honorable career in national politics. Although he was born in Meckenburg County, North Carolina, his early life was spent in the Duck River Valley of Tennessee, to which his father had moved. He was a graduate of the University of North Carolina, where he attained first honors in classics and mathematics. In Tennessee and in Congress he became a devoted follower of Andrew Jackson and one of his chief lieutenants in the bank fight. From 1835 to 1839 he served as Speaker of the House of Representatives, where he refused to be goaded into a duel by his enemies. Later, he redeemed Tennessee from Whigery by his successful campaign for governor in 1839. He was a very methodical, self-controlled individual, who kept a diary. Serious and conscientious, he drove his frail body unmercifully, working at the job of president until the late hours of night and taking only six weeks' vacation during his four years of office. Perhaps one reason his abilities were unappreciated by his generation was that he was not an orator.[19]

The platform of the Democratic party expressed the strong mood of imperialism that was rising in the West and the lower South. It cleverly demanded "the reoccupation of Oregon and reannexation of Texas," referring in the latter case to the surrender of our claim to Texas in 1819. The slogan "Fifty-four Forty or Fight!" served notice that the Democrats demanded all the western coast of Canada up to the Alaskan boundary of 54°40′. President Tyler was persuaded by some leading Democrats, including Andrew Jackson, to withdraw from the presidential race so that the forces behind

[19] Charles G. Sellers, Jr., *James K. Polk, Jacksonian, 1795–1843* (Princeton, 1957).

James Knox Polk (1795–1849). Photograph by Matthew Brady. (Courtesy of Library of Congress)

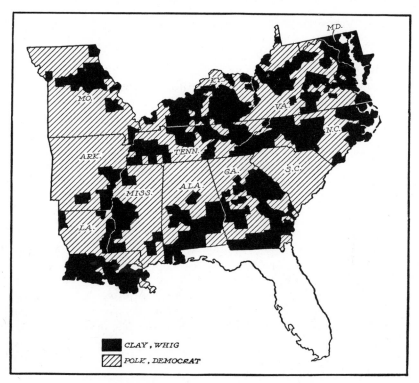

The Presidential Election of 1844 in the South

expansion would not be divided in the election. Henry Clay realized too late the strong sentiment in the country for expansion. He tried to straddle the question of the annexation of Texas by his "Alabama Letters" (July), in which he wrote that he approved the acquisition of Texas if annexation could be accomplished without war and without dishonor.

In the election Clay won the upper South (with the exception of Virginia) but lost the important abolitionist state of Ohio. The crucial blow to his candidacy was the vote of New York State, which decided this fateful election. Here Polk won by the slight majority of 5,106 votes. The explanation given both in textbooks and scholarly works is that the Whig candidate lost New York because of his straddle in the "Alabama Letters," causing many antislavery Whigs to vote for the candidate of the Liberty party, James G. Birney, another Kentuckian, who polled 15,812 votes in this pivotal state. Birney's candidacy may have had some influence on the election, but a more important cause than the Liberty party, a recent study indicates, was the nativist sentiment against the Whig candidate.[20] Actually, the Liberty party's vote in this election was virtually the same as in a state election during the

[20] Larry D. Stanly, "New York As a Pivotal Point in Henry Clay's Presidential Aspirations, 1839–1844," M.A. thesis, University of Kentucky, 1964.

preceding year. In the national voting, Polk, the candidate of western expansion, obtained a mere plurality of the popular vote and was therefore a minority president; in the South as a whole he had only a very slight popular majority over Clay.

After the election, Tyler considered that the people had given the government a mandate to annex Texas. He wished to snatch the glory of this achievement before he retired from office. Accordingly, in a message to Congress he suggested quick action on the annexation of the coveted land by a joint resolution of Congress. This procedure required only a majority vote of both houses; the negotiation of a treaty, on the other hand, would have to be ratified by a two-thirds majority vote of the Senate. His plan was adopted, and shortly before he left office, Tyler signed the joint resolution offering annexation to the United States. The vote on annexation in Congress was very close, twenty-seven to twenty-five in the Senate, and one hundred twenty to ninety-eight in the House of Representatives. By the terms of this offer Texas would enter the Union as a state; also she would be allowed to keep her public lands but must pay the debts of the Lone Star Republic; as many as four additional states might be carved out of this huge territory with the consent of Texas, and she must abolish slavery north of the Missouri Compromise line. On July 4, 1845, the people of Texas in a convention accepted annexation under these conditions with only one dissenting vote.

The election of Polk brought to the head of the federal government a Southern imperialist. Polk's appearance and manner were unimpressive, but beneath his quiet reserve there was great tenacity of will and force of character. Since the publication of his frank and manly diary, historians have revised their former low opinion of him and now recognize that he was one of our stronger presidents.[21] The mantle of old Andrew Jackson who died at at *The Hermitage* in the year of Polk's inauguration was conferred upon him, and he carried on the robust nationalism of Old Hickory at a period when the trend of the South was away from nationalism to a sectional course. His militant nationalism was expressed in his first message to Congress, December 2, 1845, in which he reasserted the Monroe Doctrine. This reassertion of the Monroe Doctrine, after a long period of quiescence, has been evaluated by modern students as second in importance only to the original promulgation of the doctrine of President Monroe. But Polk's most enduring claim to fame is that he enormously expanded the boundaries of his country, giving to the United States control of the Pacific coast. Indeed, he became our greatest expansionist president.

The election of 1844 was one of the most important elections in the history of our country. The victory of Polk strengthened the dominance of the South in the control of the Democratic party. From 1844 to the election of

[21] The latest biography, Charles Sellers, *James K. Polk, Continentalist, 1843–1846* (Princeton, 1966), dilutes this judgment, portraying Polk as disingenuous, narrowminded, and stubborn.

Lincoln every candidate elected was either a Southerner or a "doughface," a Northern man with Southern sympathies. The ascendancy of the South is revealed by its dictation of the tariff policy of the country. Polk's secretary of the treasury, Robert J. Walker, former Senator from Mississippi, wrote the Walker tariff of 1846. It was essentially a tariff for revenue instead of protection, but it placed high ad valorem duties on luxuries, such as alcoholic liquors, cigars, and spices. The tariff duties were still further decreased in 1857, when the Southerner, Howell Cobb, secretary of the treasury, secured one of the lowest tariffs the nation has ever enjoyed.

Polk was determined to take from Mexico the provinces of California and New Mexico, peaceably if he could, forcibly, if he must. He hoped to rob our weak neighbor to the south politely and with the solace of money. He did not want a war, partly because it might produce a military hero who would be a presidential candidate, and it would involve heavy taxation. Although he was a Southern slaveholder, he does not seem to have been motivated in the acquisition of territory by the desire of bolstering Southern slavery. Rather, he was the spokesman for the expansionist mood of the country, the agent of manifest destiny.

Mexico had been a bad neighbor. One of our grievances against her was her refusal to pay the claims of American citizens for damages. But Mexico had a greater grievance against us—the annexation of Texas, which the Mexicans considered had been wrested from her during the Texas Revolution by recent arrivals from the South (a charge that had much truth). When annexation was consummated, therefore, Mexico broke off diplomatic relations and recalled its ambassador.

In order to restore relations, to secure payment for our claims, some of which were just and some padded, and to buy California, President Polk sent John Slidell, a prominent Louisiana politician, as minister plenipotentiary to Mexico City.[22] In the fall of 1845, the Mexican government had agreed to receive a diplomatic representative, but by the time Slidell arrived, public opinion had become so incensed against the United States that the government did not dare to receive him and refused to do so on the basis of a technicality. The fundamental reason for this insult to the United States was that the Mexicans had learned that Slidell's real mission was to buy California and New Mexico. He was authorized by President Polk to offer as much as $30 million for this vast region. To proud Mexicans, this attempt to mutilate the national domain must be resisted with scorn. Furthermore, the Mexicans were not averse to war with the United States, for they had a contemptuous opinion of our military ability and believed that they could defeat the hated gringos.

Such was the background of the war with Mexico. The immediate occasion for hostilities was our annexation of Texas and the arrogant claim of Texas to the boundary of the Rio Grande. The Mexican government had

[22] See L. M. Sears, *John Slidell* (Durham, 1925).

never recognized the independence of Texas, and annexation seemed to be the culmination of a plot by the United States to seize the territory from its legitimate owners. The aggressive Texans claimed the Rio Grande to be their southern boundary, and the United States assumed this claim. Actually, the province of Texas had not extended beyond the Nueces River, and Mexico's position was well founded that the southern boundary of Texas was the Nueces River. The flimsy nature of the American claim was indicated by the fact that Slidell was authorized to offer the Mexican government $5 million to recognize the Rio Grande as the rightful boundary between the United States and Mexico. When Mexico refused to receive Slidell, on January 13, 1846, Polk ordered General Zachary Taylor, who was stationed with an army at the older part of Corpus Christi, located on the north bank of Nueces River, to move down to the Rio Grande.

In a cabinet meeting on Saturday, May 9, Polk stated that he intended to send a war message to Congress on the following Tuesday. His secretary of the navy, George Bancroft, the historian, advised that the United States should wait until Mexico committed some definite act of hostility. Polk planned, nevertheless, to ask Congress for a declaration of war on the basis of Mexico's refusal to pay American claims and her rejection of our minister, John Slidell. These claims amounted to only $3,208,314.96, as determined by a United States commission after the war was over. Fortunately, for Polk's purpose, that afternoon he received the news that a skirmish had taken place north of the Rio Grande between the army of Taylor and Mexican troops in which sixteen American soldiers had been killed. The next day he was busily engaged, with time out to attend church, in composing his war message. A conscientious churchgoer, he recorded in his diary his regret that he had "to spend the Sabbath in the manner I have." [23] His message to Congress now had in his eyes a moral justification. Mexican troops he declared had invaded our territory and had "shed American blood upon the American soil . . . war exists, and, notwithstanding all our efforts to avoid it exists by the act of Mexico herself." [24] Congress responded by declaring war against Mexico on May 13, 1846, by a vote of 174 to 14 in the House of Representatives and 40 to 2 in the Senate.

Nevertheless, Polk did not have a unified country behind him in the prosecution of this war. The Mississippi Valley states and Texas supported this war of disguised conquest with enthusiasm; in fact, Tennessee sent so many volunteers that it was called "the Volunteer state." New England, on the other hand, was hostile to a war that would provide territory for the expansion of slavery and decrease her influence in the nation. Moreover, the older Southern states along the Atlantic seaboard were not as ardent for war as

[23] Allan Nevins (ed.), *Polk, the Diary of a President, 1845–1849* (New York, 1929), 86.
[24] J. D. Richardson, *A Compilation of the Messages and Papers of the Presidents, 1789–1897* (Washington, 1901), IV, 442.

were the Southwestern states. Especially were the Southern Whigs, who included many large slaveholders and owners of great plantations, dubious about this war of conquest waged by a Democratic administration. Alexander H. Stephens, later to be vice-president of the Confederacy, joined hands with Abraham Lincoln in opposing the prosecution of an imperialistic war. The great Calhoun also spoke out against this developing imperialism, because he foresaw that the territory owned by Mexico for which we were fighting was unsuited to the expansion of slavery. He believed, moreover, that the mongrel population of the region we hoped to conquer would tend to break down the color line, and that the war would strengthen the central government. He said, "Mexico is forbidden fruit; the penalty of eating it would be to subject our institutions to political death." [25]

Polk had selected General Zachary Taylor, sixty-one years of age, to lead the invading army. Born in Virginia but reared in Kentucky, Taylor had spent a long period of his life on the American frontier. He was a very homely old gentleman, whose dark brown face was deeply lined and whose sturdy body supported a corpulent stomach. He looked and dressed the part of a plain farmer, and he was fond of talking about crops and his Mississippi cotton plantation tilled by many black slaves. An Illinois volunteer described him as short and heavy, with pronounced face lines and gray hair, and as wearing "an old oil cap, a dusty green coat, a frightful pair of trousers and on horseback looks like a toad." [26] Despite Taylor's unmilitary bearing, he was loved by his soldiers, who called him "Old Rough and Ready." In battle he constantly exposed himself on his white horse to the enemy fire and even fought on foot with his soldiers.

Taylor had little difficulty in defeating the Mexican armies that opposed him. Crossing the Rio Grande, he captured Matamoros, on the south bank of the river, and after a courageous fight, the fortified city of Monterrey in northeastern Mexico. He was now becoming a military hero, and Whig newspapers were mentioning him as a presidential candidate. Accordingly, the Democrats wished to minimize his glory by dividing military honors with another general. The president planned to send an army by sea from New Orleans to Vera Cruz that would march overland to capture Mexico City. Unable to find a competent Democratic general for the command of this second expeditionary army (he desired to appoint the bombastic Senator Thomas Hart Benton), he was forced to appoint General Winfield Scott, a Whig, whom he disliked. By the end of March, 1847, Scott had captured Vera Cruz and was marching overland to the rich and delightful capital of Mexico.

The Mexican War was fought in a loose and undisciplined fashion, largely by volunteers. Lieutenant A. P. Hill of Virginia, fresh from West

[25] R. K. Crallé (ed.), *The Works of John C. Calhoun* (New York, 1853), IV, 308.
[26] Holman Hamilton, *Zachary Taylor* (Indianapolis, 1941), 238; see also Brainerd Dyer, *Zachary Taylor* (New York, 1946).

Point, kept an interesting diary of his participation in the Mexican campaign, seeking martial glory.[27] He found the Mexican soldiers lacking in stubborn resistance, so that most of the time he was pursuing Mexicans as though he were engaged in an old-fashioned fox hunt in Virginia. Nor did he find this war to be glorious; rather it was disgusting to see the lack of discipline of the volunteers. He witnessed them sacking a Mexican town, and the next day he saw them on the march wearing beautiful shawls that they had taken and carrying miscellaneous booty with them. Half of the troops were drunk on Mexican *aguardiente*. The bites of the fleas were terrible, and food was scarce and unappetizing, facts that hardly compensated for the smiles of beautiful but unpatriotic senoritas.

The great superiority of the Mexican army in numbers was no match for the enterprising American volunteers, as was proved in the Battle of Buena Vista.[28] In February, 1847, the Mexican president and general, Santa Anna, started north to attack Taylor's army occupying Saltillo. Polk had stopped Taylor's victorious advance and ordered him to send the greater part of his forces to join Scott's army. His army had thus lost most of its best young officers, including Robert E. Lee, Ulysses S. Grant, and George Meade. Taylor decided to meet the assault of Santa Anna at the pass of La Angostura, a mile and a half from the ranch of *Buena Vista,* which gave the name to the fierce battle between the Americans and the Mexican army that took place on February 22–23, 1847. Santa Anna's army outnumbered the American army more than four to one, but he was ignominiously defeated and fled in the vanguard of his retreating soldiers. At this battle, a Southern officer, Colonel Jefferson Davis of the Mississippi Rifles, arranged his men in a V formation and played a decisive role in the Mexican defeat. He became known as the hero of Buena Vista, and ever afterward he thought of himself as a military expert.

Meanwhile General Scott was marching from Vera Cruz to Mexico City, a distance of two hundred fifty miles, through a difficult terrain and a hostile population. Scott was a Virginian educated at William and Mary College. He was a large and powerful man with a leonine countenance, and in striking contrast to Taylor, loved pomp and military show. In his naïve delight in resplendent uniforms, he bore some resemblance to German Air Marshall Goering, and he was called "Old Fuss and Feathers." Despite his foibles, he was a student of military science, an able general, and he conducted a skillful campaign against the Mexican armies. He asked for twenty thousand soldiers for this expedition, but received only ten thousand effectives with which to conquer a nation of 6 million people. Part of the time his army had to live off the country, and in addition to the Mexicans he had to combat

[27] Unpublished manuscript in possession of the late William J. Robertson, Savannah, Georgia.
[28] See Otis A. Singletary, *The Mexican War* (Chicago, 1960) for an interesting account of the military history; consult also Robert S. Henry, *The Story of the Mexican War* (Indianapolis, 1950).

yellow jack, the dread disease of yellow fever. After winning the battles of Cerro Gordo, Chapultepec, and Churusbusco, Scott entered Mexico City on September 17, 1847.[29]

In Scott's expedition to Mexico City traveled Nicholas P. Trist, Virginian, chief clerk of the State Department, who has been described as "a diplomat with ideals." [30] President Polk had sent him to conclude at the earliest possible moment a peace that would give to the United States the territory that the expansionists coveted. At first General Scott violently resented the presence of this agent of the president. But eventually the two Virginians, both vainglorious and both mighty warriors, one with the sword and the other with a copious pen, were reconciled. The administration then became dissatisfied with Trist and ordered him home, partly because he had not followed his instructions and was not sufficiently greedy for Mexican territory. Trist decided to disregard his recall and seized the opportunity to make a treaty with the Mexican government. Delay might have led to internal chaos in Mexico, so that no responsible government could have been found with whom to negotiate, and the war would have been prolonged. Consequently, he negotiated the Treaty of Guadalupe Hidalgo, February 2, 1848, when he had no legal authority to do so. The president was furious at Trist for his disobedience, but he accepted the treaty because he feared the development of an irresistible movement to annex all of Mexico.[31] The terms of this treaty gave to the United States the Rio Grande boundary and the vast territory of California and New Mexico. In return, the United States agreed to assume the claims of American citizens against the Mexican government and to pay Mexico $15 million.

The Mexican War was an adventure in imperialism of the South in partnership with the restless inhabitants of the West. It was provoked by a Southern president and fought largely by Southern generals and by Southern volunteers. It furnished the training school of practical experience for most of the Confederate and Union officers who participated in the Civil War. It gave to the United States a vast territory, with a Pacific front, that inevitably turned the face of the nation toward Oriental adventure and commerce. One of the most important consequences of the Mexican War was that it precipitated a great sectional struggle between the North and the South over the status of slavery in this territory, a controversy that eventually led to the Civil War.

According to the view of historians under the influence of the abolition tradition, the Mexican War was a war of conquest, unjustified morally. But such able historians as Edward Channing, and Justin H. Smith, who has written the classic history of *The War with Mexico,* have held that the war

[29] See Charles W. Elliott, *Winfield Scott, the Soldier and the Man* (New York, 1937).

[30] L. M. Sears, "Nicholas P. Trist, a Diplomat with Ideals," *Mississippi Valley Historical Review, XI* (June 1924), 85–98.

[31] J. D. P. Fuller, "The Slavery Question and the Movement to Acquire Mexico, 1840–1848," *Mississippi Valley Historical Review, XXI* (June 1934), 31–48.

was just. They have maintained that it was practically impossible to obtain satisfaction from Mexico in regard to American claims except by forcible means. The United States was entirely free from blame in annexing Texas, whose independence had been maintained for nine years and recognized by England and France.[32] Both Smith and Channing argued also that Spain and Mexico had held California and New Mexico for years without developing these provinces. It was desirable from the standpoint of civilization that the land should not lie idle but should be seized by a vigorous people who could make use of it. A weak point in the American apology for the Mexican War was the contention that the Rio Grande was the legitimate boundary line of Texas. When Polk ordered Taylor to move from Corpus Christi to the north bank of the Rio Grande, he was invading the territory of a neighbor at peace with us. Although the approximately $118 million that the United States spent in acquiring the coveted territory was a cheap price, many times repaid by the gold of California discovered in the very year of the treaty of Guadalupe Hidalgo, the manner in which we obtained this territory nevertheless left a heritage of bitterness and distrust of the powerful United States among the weaker Latin-American republics.

During and for some years after the Mexican War the doctrine of Manifest Destiny was strong in the Western and Southern states. One phase of this expansionist sentiment was the attacks on Latin-American countries by filibuster expeditions. William Walker, a native of Tennessee, led expeditions into lower California and Sonora in northern Mexico in 1853, and later this small "gray-eyed man of destiny" made himself dictator of Nicaragua. He tried to secure Southern support by proclaiming the legality of slavery in Nicaragua and by triumphal tours of the Southern states. New Orleans became a center of filibuster expeditions in the decade of the 1850's, directed especially against Cuba. Governor John A. Quitman of Mississippi, a Northern man who had settled at Natchez, was an ardent promoter of filibuster expeditions to acquire more slave territory. Perhaps the most arrogant phase of the Manifest Destiny Doctrine was the so-called Ostend Manifesto of 1854, in which three American ministers, two Southerners and the doughface James Buchanan, advised President Pierce's secretary of state that this country should offer Spain a huge sum for Cuba, teeming with slaves, and if Spain refused the offer, the United States would be justified in seizing the island.[33] Although the pro-Southern Pierce administration repudiated the Ostend Manifesto, it did the Southern cause serious harm in arousing fear in the North of Southern imperialism to acquire additional foreign territory for slave states.[34]

[32] Samuel F. Bemis, *A Diplomatic History of the United States* (New York, 1955), also justifies the American position, pp. 243–244.

[33] H. S. Commager, *Documents of American History* (New York, 1963), I, 334–335.

[34] Frederick Merk in his study, *Manifest Destiny and Mission in American History* (New York, 1963), which to a large degree supersedes Albert K. Weinberg, *Manifest Destiny; a Study of Nationalist Expansionism in American History* (Baltimore, 1935),

Although President Buchanan, as well as some Northern Democratic leaders advocated the acquisition of Cuba, undoubtedly the greatest support for expansion into the Caribbean came from politicians of the lower South. Senator John Slidell of Louisiana in 1859 introduced his Cuba bill, providing for the appropriation of $30,000,000 for negotiations to buy the rich slave island, but because of lack of support he withdrew his bill. The Southern advocates hoped to make several slave states out of the island as a political counterbalance to Northern superiority in Congress. Yet Southerners as a whole were restrained in their desire for tropical expansion by their foreboding that such a program would present a serious race problem and would weaken the free system of our constitutional government. In a speech at the State Fair of Augusta, Maine, Senator Jefferson Davis declared in September, 1859, that although it was probably undesirable to incorporate the whole of the North American continent into the United States, it was the manifest destiny of our country to establish a protectorate over the continent and adjacent islands. Nevertheless, he was opposed, he said, to incorporating into the Union, countries "densely populated with a different race" from ours, for he believed that the United States had grown great by keeping its Caucasian blood pure.[35]

Economic factors, as well as the overriding issue of secession in the decade of the 1850's were destined to nullify the Southern drive to acquire new slave states in the Southwest and in the Caribbean.[36] The major result of "manifest destiny" and the Mexican War undoubtedly was the vast expansion of U. S. territory, which was to have a permanent bearing on the future of the nation, making this country a Pacific Ocean power. A secondary consequence was the reopening of an old wound, namely a bitter divisive debate over slavery in which the changed attitude of both the Northern and Southern people was ominously revealed.

---

distinguishes two periods of Manifest Destiny sentiment in the South. "In 1846–8," he writes (pp. 210–211), "the South had shown only a limited enthusiasm for Manifest Destiny." In support of this generalization he cites the Southern lack of enthusiasm for carrying out the campaign slogan "54° 40′ or Fight" and the opposition of Calhoun and Alexander H. Stephens to the all-America idea; the center of enthusiasm for Manifest Destiny then, he holds, was in the states of New York and Illinois. In 1860, the attitude of the sections was reversed, the South becoming the supporter of "a Caribbeanized Manifest Destiny," especially in respect to Cuba.

[35] Dunbar Rowland (ed.), *Jefferson Davis Constitutionalist: His Letters, Papers and Speeches* (Jackson, Miss., 1923), III, 313.

[36] See R. E. May, *The Southern Dream of a Caribbean Empire, 1854–1861* (Baton Rouge, 1973). Mr. May has convinced me that the movement for expansion into the Caribbean had considerably more support in the South than I had expressed in the second edition of my *A History of the Old South* (New York, 1966), p. 335.

Changing Attitudes Toward Slavery

THE ARGUMENT that Southerners evolved to justify the institution of slavery is one of the great rationalizations that the human mind has conceived. Like the philosophy of the Scholastics of the Middle Ages, it was a product of many minds, a remarkable intellectual achievement, finely articulated, and based on the far-reaching assumption that Negroes are innately inferior to whites. Before the rise of the proslavery argument large numbers of Southerners, especially in Virginia, did not subscribe to this faith in the rightfulness and permanence of slavery. There was, indeed, a time when Southerners in general apologized for the existence of human bondage in their region—a period extending from the American Revolution to the middle of the decade of the 1830's.

The development of a liberal attitude toward the emancipation of the slaves during this period was explained in part by economic considerations. The exhaustion of tobacco lands and the shift to wheat growing gave to the upper South a surplus of slaves. Slavery was becoming decidedly unprofitable in this region until the invention of the cotton gin in 1793 restored the value of slaves. Washington declared that he had twice as many working Negroes on his estate as could be profitably employed. John Randolph of Roanoke wittily described the economic burden of supporting slavery during this period by remarking that, instead of masters advertising for runaway slaves, the slaves would be advertising for the arrest of fugitive masters.

In addition to economic motives, the natural-rights philosophy of the Revolutionary period predisposed Southerners to a desire for gradual emancipation. One of the earliest persons in America to link the right of Negroes to freedom with the Declaration of Independence was the wealthy South Carolina merchant and planter Henry Laurens, who became president of the Continental Congress in 1777 and 1778. In writing to a son in England, a student of law there, on August 14, 1776, he expressed his abhorrence of slavery as an institution that was in conflict with the golden rule of Christianity. He was planning, therefore, he declared, to manumit some of his slaves and cut off the entail on the remaining servants. But such a bold step, he anticipated, would encounter the opposition of the society in which he had been reared, and might cause his children to reproach him for having deprived them of so much of his estate.[1]

---

[1] This letter, edited by Richard B. Morris, has been published by the Anthoensen Press of Portland, Me.

368

A considerable number of Southerners freed their slaves by will during this period. George Washington set an example by emancipating his slaves by will, so did John Randolph of Roanoke later, and Jefferson was prevented from adopting a similar course by his financial bankruptcy. The wills of emancipation indicate that the liberal planters were disturbed by the inconsistency of holding slaves and subscribing to the equalitarian doctrines of the Declaration of Independence. Most of the prominent Virginia leaders, such as Patrick Henry, George Wythe, and James Madison, condemned slavery as an institution that should be eradicated from a free America. George Mason, the proprietor of beautiful *Gunston Hall* on the Potomac, and the master of three hundred slaves, declared slavery to be an infernal school of tyranny for the future leaders of the South, which caused slaveholders to lose sight of "the Dignity of Man which the Hand of Nature had planted in us for great and useful purposes." [2] Furthermore, the most enlightened planters, such as Jefferson, realized that slavery had a pernicious effect on the white population, degrading manual labor, encouraging pride and arrogance, and exposing children to the corrupting influence of licentious slaves.

Holding these liberal views, these Southern planters were nevertheless inhibited from action by the tremendous power of property interests, by their low estimate of the Negroes' capacity, and by the need to preserve slavery as a police measure. Even Jefferson doubted that the Negro was genetically equal to the white man, and he was certainly unwilling to risk his political position by openly championing the cause of emancipation.[3] Consequently, modern scholarship has shown that when it came to active support of measures to free the slave, those Virginians of the generation before 1830 were very conservative.[4] However, they did not look on slavery as a permanent institution as did the succeeding generation, but as one that would gradually die out over a long period of time.

The grave problem in emancipating slaves was what to do with the freedmen. Practically all Southerners believed that the process of liberation should be gradual and that the freedmen should be colonized, which would entail a staggering cost. St. George Tucker of William and Mary proposed in 1796 a plan of gradual emancipation based on liberating all female slaves at birth, and in 1824 Jefferson proposed what seems to me a reasonable solution, a

[2] George Mason, Papers, 1766–1788. Bancroft Transcripts, pp. 85–89. MS in New York Public Library, cited in Eaton, *The Freedom-of-Thought, Struggle in the Old South* (New York, 1964), 19.

[3] In opposition to this leftist, revisionist position, William Freehling observes that Jefferson and the Founding Fathers were, as to the short view, pragmatists, practicing the art of the possible, but in the long view, did a great deal to advance emancipation, especially by closing the slave trade in 1808, which the Constitution permitted to 1808 but did not require after that date. "The Founding Fathers and Slavery," *American Historical Review,* LXX (February 1972), 80–93.

[4] This analysis conflicts with views expressed in the author's first book, *Freedom of Thought in the Old South* (Durham, 1940); but see R. McColley, *Slavery and Jeffersonian Virginia* (Urbana, Ill., 1973).

federally financed "post nati" plan of emancipation. Several of the Southern states repealed their colonial laws forbidding the manumission of slaves except for meritorious services adjudged by the governor and council or the county court, and now permitted the emancipation of slaves provided the owner gave guarantees that the freedmen would not become public charges. The experiences of planters who emancipated their slaves, however, were frequently unfortunate. In 1791, Robert Carter of *Nomini Hall* emancipated more than five hundred slaves by a plan of gradually freeing groups over a period of twenty years. He tried to rent small patches of land to them, but this practice was not an economic success. The neighbors protested that the freedmen stole and abused their freedom and corrupted the slaves. Ironically, two of Carter's sons, whom he had sent to the Baptist College in Rhode Island (Brown University) in order that they might escape the immoral influence of slavery, tried to frustrate the noble experiment of their father. When Carter liberated his slaves he was influenced by the teachings of the Baptist and Swedenborgian churches, but laso, it is to be noted, the price of slaves had reached the bottom of a twenty-year decline in this last decade of the eighteenth century.[5]

The Quakers of the upper South were the principal Southern group that tried to do something practical about removing slavery. Those planters who apologized for slavery, as a rule, made no positive efforts toward eradicating the institution. Since slavery had not originated in their generation, they were willing for its removal to be left to the gradual operation of time. But the Quakers, who loathed the element of force in human relations, actively sought to dissolve the institution. One method they adopted was the use of antislavery propaganda through the press. In 1819 Elihu Embree founded *The Emancipator* at Jonesborough, Tennessee, the first antislavery newspaper in the South. Benjamin Lundy, a saddlemaker who worked in Wheeling, Virginia, established in 1821 the *Genius of Universal Emancipation* at Baltimore, Maryland. In North Carolina flourished the Quaker newspaper the *Greensborough Patriot,* which as late as 1834 championed the cause of freeing the slaves.

To agitate for the removal of slavery, the Quakers organized abolition societies. Since they were close to slavery, they were practical enough to urge the gradual rather than the immediate abolition of the peculiar institution and the amelioration of slavery by repealing the laws against the education of the slaves. Charles Osborn, a Quaker preacher born in Guilford County, North Carolina, was the pioneer organizer of manumission societies in Tennessee (1814–1816). After he had emigrated to Mount Pleasant, Ohio, he published an antislavery newspaper as early as 1817. By the year 1827, fifty antislavery societies, with a membership of three thousand, were reported in North Carolina, twenty-five in Tennessee, and eight in Virginia—a much greater number of antislavery societies than existed in the North. In addition to this

[5] Louis Morton, *Robert Carter of Nomini Hall* (Princeton, 1941).

method of attacking the institution of slavery, the Quakers formed free produce societies, pledged not to use products of slave labor, and became operators in the Underground Railroad. The antislavery sentiment in the South was weakened greatly as many of the Quakers emigrated to free territory beyond the Ohio River in the first three decades of the nineteenth century. In 1834 the last meeting of the North Carolina Manumission Society was held at Marlborough, and in 1860 only about fifteen hundred Quakers were left in the state.[6]

Most Southerners believed that if the slaves were freed and remained in the South a race conflict would follow and Southern civilization would be destroyed. Jefferson, Clay, Calhoun, and practically all Southern leaders believed that the removal of the freed Negro was indispensable to a scheme of emancipation. In 1817 the American Colonization Society was founded at Washington, D.C., to solve this problem by transporting freed Negroes to Africa. Liberals saw in the movement an encouragement to kindly masters to free their slaves, whereas conservatives supported the colonization society as a means of strengthening slavery by removing the objectionable free Negroes already present in the South. The society, composed largely of Southerners, elected Bushrod Washington, a nephew of the Revolutionary hero, as the first president. In 1819 agents were sent to the west coast of Africa and acquired from the native chiefs large areas for a colony, which was named Liberia, "land of freedom," and its capital, Monrovia, in honor of President Monroe. Not until 1847, however, did Liberia become a republic with a Negro as president.

The American Colonization Society failed miserably in its larger purposes. It was unable to persuade the Federal government to give financial support to its adventure. Sections of the colony were set aside for Negro groups from various Southern states, such as Mississippi in Liberia, Maryland in Liberia, and Kentucky in Liberia. Agents were sent throughout the South to obtain funds and emigrants, and a magazine, the *African Repository,* was published in Washington as a means of propaganda. In Mississippi the society raised approximately $100,000, and the legislature of Maryland pledged its credit to the amount of $200,000 to aid in the colonization of Maryland Negroes. Some benevolent planters provided in their wills for the emancipation of their slaves and transportation to Liberia. Despite the efforts of the American Colonization Society, a relatively small number of Negroes were sent to Africa, 571 from Mississippi, for example, and 1,363 from North Carolina. The Society transported a total of over 15,000 Negroes between 1821, when the first contingent was sent, and 1860. So prodigious was the Negro birthrate that this number was a pitiful fraction of the increase of black babies born in slavery during this period. Thus, colonization proved utterly impractical, not

[6] H. M. Wagstaff (ed.), *Minutes of the North Carolina Manumission Society, 1816–1834* (Chapel Hill, 1934); and S. B. Weeks, *Southern Quakers and Slavery* (Baltimore, 1896).

only because of the invincible birthrate of the Negro but also because of the cost and difficulties of transportation to Africa. The American Colonization Society was branded by the abolitionists as a proslavery device to get rid of the free Negro, but after 1831 slaveholders gave it slight support.[7]

The Southern Negroes themselves had no enthusiasm to return to their ancient home in the Dark Continent. Having become accustomed to American food, climate, and civilization, they dreaded going to a strange land. Many of those who did emigrate to Liberia died from tropical disease. The interior tribes were hostile and dangerous. Some of the Negroes who emigrated wrote discouraging reports to their masters and brethren in the United States—that the Negroes had farms usually no larger than five acres, which they tilled with the hoe without the aid of horses and mules, lived in bamboo houses in a wilderness, and "tell Uncle pleasant that we have snakes here 15 to 20 feet and can Swalow a man, Dear, or a hog with ease." [8] Even to this day Liberia is not an attractive asylum to the American Negro. Sleeping sickness, malaria, hookworm, and dysentery make life precarious. The American Negroes and their descendants have enslaved the interior tribes until as late as 1930. Moreover, they developed the idea that manual labor was degrading and a caste system arose—the descendants of slaves were copying the patterns of the white masters.

In January, 1831, William Lloyd Garrison began the publication in Boston, Massachusetts, of *The Liberator,* the first newspaper in the United States devoted to *immediate* abolition of slavery. This New England printer and journalist was a natural agitator who espoused many other reforms in addition to the abolition of slavery. Always an enthusiast, Garrison reversed the life process of many men who are liberal in youth but become conservative in middle life; as a young man Garrison was a strong conservative, an ardent Federalist, a scorner of democracy, who was later to become a radical. He had worked for a short time with Benjamin Lundy on the latter's antislavery newspaper in Baltimore, but he knew practically nothing of slavery from observation or experience. Nevertheless, he and his followers indulged in the most bitter attacks against the moral character of the slaveholders in language so extreme that they injured their cause, both in the North and the South. The platform of *The Liberator* was immediate emancipation of the slaves without any compensation to slaveholders. Since the federal Constitution sanctioned slavery, Garrison condemned it as a compact with Hell and urged his followers not to vote or have anything to do with this inquitous government. Indeed, he made slavery a great moral issue, upon which he would neither speak with moderation nor accept compromise. In 1857 he and

[7] P. J. Staudenraus, *The African Colonization Movement, 1816–1865* (New York, 1961), for numbers, see p. 251.
[8] Moses Jackson, Kentucky in Liberia, to Eliott West, Nicholasville, Ky., March 22, 1846. MS in Wilson Collection, University of Kentucky Library. Another letter in the collection, on the other hand, from Robert Johnson to Thomas Dolan, August 20, 1846, refers to Liberia as "that country where I am known as a man and the only country in which the colored man enjoys undisturbed liberty."

his followers held a Secession Convention at Worcester, Massachusetts, to advocate that the *Northern* states should secede from the union with slave-holders.[9]

The abolition movement in the North was soon organized into very vocal and active societies. The New England Anti-Slavery Society was founded by Garrison in 1832, and during the next year the American Anti-Slavery Society was started in New York City. The New York group of abolitionists until recently has been neglected by historians, but it contained such effective agitators as the wealthy merchants Lewis and Arthur Tappan, William Jay, the son of Chief Justice John Jay, and Gerrit Smith, the millionaire of Peter-boro.[10] The Northern abolitionists were profoundly influenced by the English antislavery crusade, which had led to the abolition of slavery in the British West Indies in 1833. From the reformers across the Atlantic were learned most of the techniques used in advancing the antislavery cause in the United States. The New England and New York societies published tons of lurid and fervid antislavery publications that they sent through the mails to leading men in the South. Although the New York group adopted as their slogan "immediate emancipation," they interpreted this term to mean that "measures looking toward ultimate emancipation be immediately begun"—which was a reasonable program that Jefferson might have approved.

Less spectacular than the Eastern abolitionists, but tremendously influential, was the Ohio group, led by Theodore D. Weld. The publication of the correspondence of Weld, the Grimké sisters, and of James G. Birney as well as modern studies of the abolition movement have called attention to this group.[11] Although Garrison remained in Southern eyes the symbol of the antislavery movement, it is possible that the Midwestern band of abolitionists accomplished more effective work in converting Northerners to the cause than did the Garrisonians.[12] The midwestern group arose out of the great religious revivals conducted in the decade of the 1820's by Charles Grandison Finney. These Western abolitionists applied the technique of religious revivals to the abolitionist crusade, emphasizing the point that Southern slavery was a moral sin. Weld compiled a terrible tract called *American Slavery As It Is,* composed of recitals of abnormal and sensational incidents of Southern slavery that he had culled from newspapers and antislavery literature.[13] Oberlin College, founded in 1833, in Ohio, became the center of Western

[9] John L. Thomas, *The Liberator, William Lloyd Garrison, a Biography* (Boston, 1963); and Walter M. Merrill, *Against Wind and Tide: A Biography of William Lloyd Garrison* (Cambridge, Mass., 1963).

[10] See B. Wyatt-Brown, *Lewis Tappan and the Evangelical War Against Slavery* (Cleveland, 1969).

[11] G. H. Barnes and D. L. Dumond (eds.), *Letters of Theodore Dwight Weld, Angelina Grimké, and Sara Grimké, 1822–1848* (New York, 1934), 2 vols.; and D. L. Dumond (ed.), *Letters of James Gillespie Birney, 1831–1857* (New York, 1938), 2 vols.

[12] G. H. Barnes, *The Anti-Slavery Impulse, 1830–1848* (New York, 1933).

[13] Benjamin P. Thomas, *Theodore Weld, Crusader for Freedom* (New Brunswick, N.J., 1950); R. O. Curry and J. D. Cowden (eds.), *Slavery in America; Theodore Weld's American Slavery As It Is* (Itasca, Ill., 1972).

abolitionists as well as one of the first American colleges to admit Negro students.

The abolitionists started out by attacking the institution of Southern slavery, but soon began a violent and indiscriminate denunciation of Southerners and their way of life. They built up a stereotype of slavery and of Southern society that modern historians have found difficult to dispel. The abolitionists blamed all the backwardness of the region, the illiteracy of the people, the exhaustion of the soil, and the lack of industrialization on slavery and upon slavery alone. The abolitionists painted the South as a land where masters made female slaves their concubines and enslaved their mulatto offspring. The whip never ceased to sear the flesh of their trembling bond servants, for Southerners were cruel and coarse in all the relations of life. The slave trade and the separation of families were a constant staple of their exaggeration. The existence of a substantial middle class of yeoman farmers in the South was ignored, and members of the nonslaveholding class were portrayed as debased creatures. In politics, the Slave Power was envisaged as always on the aggressive, striving to pollute free soil and exclude honest laborers from the North from settling on the public domain. In short, the abolitionist propaganda was a black-and-white type of ideology.[14] Their libels of Southern civilization naturally aroused the deepest resentment and intolerance below the Mason-Dixon line. Furthermore, with few exceptions, notably the millionaire abolitionist Gerrit Smith, the abolitionists did not advocate the only fair and practical step toward accomplishing their objective, namely, the use of federal funds to aid in compensating the owners of slaves for their loss of property as a result of adopting the abolition program.

Southerners made the mistake of thinking of all abolitionists in terms of the extremists. But there were many types of abolitionists and some were admirable persons.[15] The Civil Rights struggle of the 1960's and 1970's and the protestors against the Vietnam War have created an atmosphere that is favorable to a new evaluation of the abolitionists, the agitators for reform of over a hundred years ago. Moreover, the recent findings indicating the profitability of slavery and, accordingly, its vitality on the eve of the Civil War have added a new justification for the crusade of the abolitionists. Like Socrates' gadfly the abolitionists stung the apathetic Northern masses to a realization of the evils of slavery. Although it is true that some of them were bigoted and self-righteous, and yearned for the martyr's crown, the majority

---

[14] Valuable studies of the abolitionists and their propaganda are Louis Filler, *The Antislavery Crusade, 1830–1860* (New York, 1960); H. H. Simms, *A Decade of Sectional Controversy, 1851–1861* (Chapel Hill, 1942); D. L. Dumond, *Antislavery: The Crusade for Freedom in America* (Ann Arbor, 1961); and Betty L. Fladeland, *James Gillespie Birney: Slaveholder to Abolitionist* (Ithaca, 1955), and Louis Ruchames, *The Abolitionists: A Collection of Their Writings* (New York, 1963).

[15] See Martin Duberman (ed.), *The Antislavery Vanguard: New Essays on the Abolitionists* (Princeton, 1965), and W. H. and J. H. Pease (eds.), *The Antislavery Argument* (Indianapolis, 1965).

of the abolitionists were high-minded men and women who were stirred deeply by humanitarian and religious feelings.[16] The Transcendental movement, too, had an influence on some of the New England abolitionists. Also, not to be neglected, was the important part the Negro played in the abolition movement, especially the speeches before Northern audiences of escaped slaves who detailed the horrors of Southern slavery and who published their autobiographies with much help from white abolitionists. By far the most prominent and eloquent of the Negro abolitionists was Frederick Douglass, an escaped Maryland slave, who became editor of the abolitionist newspaper *The North Star* and after the Civil War was appointed minister to Haiti. In addition to advancing the antislavery cause, the abolitionists rendered a valuable service in initiating the woman's rights movement and in upholding freedom of petition, speech, and the press in the United States. The abolitionists were only a vocal minority among the antislavery men of the North; thousands opposed the expansion of slavery in the federal territories, not because of any moral fervor, but because they were anti-Negro in sentiment and wished to save the land for whites only.

The abolition movement led to one of the most violent struggles in the history of the nation to suppress civil liberties.[17] Some of the worst offenses against civil liberties occurred in the Northern border states during the decade of the 1830's. Here abolitionists were mobbed countless times and denied their constitutional rights of free speech and freedom of the press. In 1835 they discovered an effective means of advertising their cause by linking it to the cause of civil liberties. They began the strategy of presenting petitions to Congress to abolish slavery in the District of Columbia. Southern Congressmen maintained that such petitions should not be received, on the ground that Congress had no jurisdiction over domestic slavery. On the other hand, Northern Representatives, as a group, believed that the antislavery petitions should be received, for the freedom of petition, one of the sacred rights of a democracy, was involved in this issue. The chief presenter of the abolitionist petitions, which came in a flood in 1835–1837, was John Quincy Adams, the ex-president, who was now serving as a Congressman from Massachusetts. In this new role as the introducer of antislavery petitions, Adams maintained, perhaps insincerely, that he was not an abolitionist but was fighting for the freedom of petition. This bald-headed, irascible, and satirical New Englander enjoyed taunting the long-haired orators from the South, and his activities in Congress increased the atmosphere of bitter hatred between the sections. The South was not lacking in violent champions, chief of whom was Henry A. Wise of Virginia, who replied to Adams in kind, and who led a secession of

---

[16] See David Donald, *Charles Sumner and the Coming of the Civil War* (New York, 1970), and M. L. Dillon, "The Abolitionists: A Decade of Historiography, 1959–1969," *Journal of Southern History* XXXI (November 1969), 500–522.

[17] Clement Eaton, "Mob Violence in the Old South," *Mississippi Valley Historical Review*, XXIX (December 1942), 351–370.

Southern Congressmen from the House of Representatives in 1836 when William Slade of Vermont caustically attacked Southern slavery.[18]

On account of Southern pressure, the lower house of Congress in 1836 adopted the Gag Resolution. Introduced by Henry L. Pinckney of South Carolina, this resolution provided that the House of Representatives should technically receive the abolition petitions, but that such petitions should immediately be laid on the table, without referring them to a committee and without debate. The Gag Rule was continually renewed until it was repealed in December, 1844. The Gag Rule of 1840 read, "That no petition, memorial, resolution or other paper praying the abolition of slavery in the District of Columbia, or any State or Territory, or the slave trade between the States or Territories of the United States in which it now exists, shall be received by the House, or entertained in any way whatever." [19] This rule was finally abandoned when Northern allies withdrew their support and when some Southerners realized that it was doing more harm than good to their cause. Southern chauvinists who insisted on a rigid rejection of abolitionist petitions in Congress did the South a great disservice by alienating the sympathy of many sincere lovers of democracy in the North who were indifferent to the reform of abolishing slavery.

Another flaming issue that involved civil liberties was the right of the abolitionists to use the federal mails to forward their publications into the Southern states. In the summer of 1835 a mob in Charleston, South Carolina, supported by ex-Governor Robert Y. Hayne, entered the post office and destroyed several sacks of mail containing abolition literature. The whole South was aroused to the menace of the circulation of abolition publications below the Mason-Dixon line. It is an established fact that the abolition societies of the North had adopted a concerted plan in 1835 to flood the South with antislavery pamphlets, newspapers, and periodicals. These publications were addressed to white people to persuade them to abandon slavery, but Southerners believed that the abolitionists designed their publications to foment servile insurrections. A small minority of the slaves could read, some of whom were taught illegally by their masters. It was feared in the South that the lurid antislavery literature would fall into the hands of some brooding Nat Turner who would lead a slave revolt.

In a message to Congress, December, 1835, President Jackson recommended that Congress pass a law prohibiting the circulation through the mails in the Southern states of "incendiary publications intended to instigate the slaves to insurrection." [20] Calhoun was opposed to such a law that would enhance the power of the Federal government. Instead, he introduced into the Senate early in 1836 a bill that would accomplish the object of erecting a

---

[18] Clement Eaton, "Henry A. Wise and the Virginia Fire Eaters of 1856," *Mississippi Valley Historical Review*, XXI (March 1935), 495–512.

[19] *Congressional Globe*, VII (26th Congress, 1st Session) p. 150.

[20] J. D. Richardson (ed.), *A Compilation of the Messages and Papers of the Presidents, 1789–1897* (Washington, 1907), III, 176.

cordon sanitaire against the entry of abolition literature into the South. His bill would have made it illegal for Northern postmasters to receive and forward abolition publications to those states whose laws prohibited the circulation of such publications. This bill failed to pass Congress, but a policy of federal censorship of the mails, preventing the free circulation of abolition publications in the South, was adopted unofficially by the Postal Department. With impunity, individual postmasters in the South refused to deliver abolition literature. A series of Postmasters General, from the days of Amos Kendall in Jackson's Cabinet to Joseph Holt in Buchanan's Cabinet, permitted this extralegal censorship of the mails. No attempt was made to discriminate between literature that was a rational discussion of the evils of slavery and that which comprised incendiary appeals to violence. Thus, a genuine blockade was set up that protected the minds of Southern whites from the contagion of abolitionist arguments as well as kept the slaves from being inflamed to dissatisfaction or revolt by emotional antislavery literature.[21]

The development of an elaborate argument justifying slavery began in the South before the rise of the abolition movement. South Carolina was the cradle of the proslavery argument, which originated as early as 1789. In the Palmetto State the economic and social humus was most suited to the growth of an intellectual defense of slavery. South Carolina had inherited its type of slavery and its attitudes toward the Negro from the rich sugar island of Barbados. Moreover, rice culture was peculiarly adapted to the use of slave labor. The Negroes who worked in the rice fields were blacker and closer to Africa than the slaves of the upper South. Many of the Gullah Negroes, indeed, had been imported during the period when the state reopened the African slave trade, and they needed stricter control than the slaves of the upper South who had been habituated to the white man's society for a considerable period of time. Also the prevalence of malaria in the swampy, coastal region of South Carolina and Georgia caused the wealthy planters to flee from the miasmic lowlands during the spring and summer seasons, leaving the blacks and the overseers to the tender mercies of disease-bearing mosquitoes. It was natural that South Carolina should have discarded the apologetic tone of defending slavery, and that, in such leaders as Senator William Smith, Whitemarsh B. Seabrook, and Dr. Thomas Cooper, president of South Carolina College during the decade of the 1820's and early 1830's, should have produced some of the early exponents of slavery as a positive good. Later, in 1852, the great classic of slavery defense. *The Pro-Slavery Argument,* containing essays by the South Carolinians, William Gilmore Simms, Chancellor William Harper, James H. Hammond, and others, was published at Charleston.[22] Was this elaborate rationalization of a great social evil motivated by the desire to convince nonslaveholders in order to preserve planter control, or

---

[21] Clement Eaton, "Censorship of the Southern Mails," *American Historical Review,* XLVIII (January 1943) 266–380.
[22] See W. S. Jenkins, *Pro-Slavery Thought in the Old South* (Chapel Hill, 1935).

was it evoked to quiet the conscience of Southern slaveholders, or was it a recognition of the moral power of world opinion?

In the upper South a pioneer in producing an able argument in defense of slavery was Thomas Roderick Dew. He was a young professor at William and Mary College who had recently returned from study in Germany. In 1832 he published a pamphlet, *Review of the Debates in the Virginia Legislature of 1831 and 1832,* in which he refuted arguments for the emancipation of the slaves made in the Virginia legislature following the Nat Turner revolt. Dew based his polemic partly upon his study of Aristotle, who had justified Greek slavery as a recognition of the natural inequality of man. In addition to deriving a justification of slavery from the order of nature, Dew pointed out that the Bible sanctioned this ancient institution. These philosophical arguments were buttressed by the economic argument, namely, the lucrative profits obtained from the internal slave trade and the immense property loss that emancipation would entail.[23]

One of the most powerful arguments in the proslavery dialectic was the alleged support of the Bible, for the overwhelming majority of Southern people were firmly indoctrinated in a belief in the sacredness of the literal word of the Bible. The apologists of slavery drew their arguments chiefly from the Old Testament, which described a primitive society among the Jews in which the patriarchs held slaves. They also maintained that slavery was ordained by God as a punishment of Canaan, son of Ham, from whom, they affirmed without reliable evidence, the Negroes were descended. In the New Testament the defenders of slavery pointed to the advice that the Apostle Paul had given to a fugitive slave to return to his master as well as Christ's silence in regard to this contemporary institution.

The Baptist, Methodist, and Presbyterian churches in the South, which had condemned slavery in their pioneering period, gradually became proslavery as their congregations grew wealthier and more attached to the vested interests of Negro slavery. Leading Southern ministers, such as J. H. Thornwell, B. H. Palmer, Thornton Stringfellow, H. B. Bascom, and William A. Smith, wrote books and delivered sermons showing that the institution was approved by God. In 1844 the general conference of the Methodist Episcopal church requested Bishop James O. Andrew of Georgia to cease his episcopal duties until he had disposed of his slaves acquired by a second marriage. This incident led to the separation of the Southern churches from the national organization and the formation at Louisville in 1845 of the Methodist Episcopal Church, South. During the same year, the Southern Baptists, incensed over the refusal of the national missions board to employ a slaveholder as a missionary, organized the "Southern Baptist Convention."

A myriad of arguments were adduced to show that slavery was needed as a social discipline. If the slaves were emancipated, the proslavery argument maintained, they would be uncontrollable, refusing to work, stealing, and

[23] Eric L. McKitrick (ed.), *Slavery Defended: The Views of the Old South* (Englewood Cliffs, N.J., 1963).

committing other crimes. The example of the shiftless free Negro was brought forward as a solemn warning against a wholesale freeing of the blacks. The poor whites and mechanics feared the consequences of competition with hordes of emancipated Negroes. The massacre of the whites in Santo Domingo and the great decline of agriculture in Jamaica after emancipation were cited as proofs of the dangers of emancipation. Religious apologists maintained that the Negro had benefited tremendously from slavery, for he was transported from the barbarism of Africa and was civilized and Christianized in America.

Demagogues raised the bogey of social amalgamation if the slaves were freed and allowed to remain in the country. Deeply rooted in Southern psychology was a fear that the emancipation movement would break down the barriers set up to preserve a pure white race in the South. The census of 1860 clearly indicated that racial antipathy was not enough to prevent considerable miscegenation, for approximately 10.4 per cent of the slaves in the United States were mulattoes.[24] The presence of mixed blood among the free Negroes was striking, approximately three fourths of the free Negroes having an admixture of white blood. New Orleans was notorious for the concubinage system by which Creoles maintained mulatto and quadroon mistresses.[25]

The emphasis in the Old South on the biological inferiority of the Negroes bears some resemblance to the Nazi ideology of race. Most Southerners took it for granted that the Negroes constituted a permanently subordinate race, inferior to the white man in intellect, character, and physiology—a childlike people. Dr. Josiah C. Nott, a physician of Mobile, Alabama, strengthened the ethnological argument justifying slavery by his theory of the plural origin of the races. In 1854, with the collaboration of the archaeologist, George R. Gliddon, he published his work *Types of Mankind,* in which he maintained that mankind did not have a common progenitor but that the Negro and the white man were separately created species.[26] This theory, which denied the unity of mankind did not win general acceptance in the South, because it conflicted with the Biblical account of the origin of man. Reverend John Bachman of Charleston, South Carolina, confuted the pluralists in his volume *The Doctrine of the Unity of the Human Race* (1850), and Dr. John Wesley Monette of Mississippi wrote a manuscript entitled "The Causes of the Variety of the Complexion and Form of the Human Species," in which he affirmed the primitive unity of the races and explained racial differences as caused by environment and climate. One of the degrading effects of the proslavery argument that has continued into our day was the emphasis on the basic inferiority of the Negro to the white man.

In the last decade of the antebellum period the proslavery argument ac-

[24] The definition of a mulatto was a person of mixed blood, having as little as one eighth of white blood.
[25] J. H. Blassingame, *Black New Orleans, 1860–1880* (Chicago, 1973), maintains that many of these liaisons were common-law marriages.
[26] See William R. Stanton, *The Leopard's Spots: Scientific Attitudes toward Race in America, 1815–1859* (Chicago, 1960).

quired a militant leadership under Henry Hughes of Port Gibson, Mississippi, William J. Grayson, collector of the port of Charleston, and George Fitzhugh, a Virginia lawyer. Hughes wrote a defense of slavery in 1854 entitled *A Treatise on Sociology,* in which the word *sociology* was first used in the title of an American book. It is interesting to note that the proslavery argument led to pioneering efforts, however prejudiced, in developing the science of sociology. Hughes maintained that the advance of civilization in the South had essentially changed Southern slavery, although he produced no valid evidence for his conclusion. He held that slavery had advanced to warranteeism, which gave to the master a trusteeship over the slave and the ownership of the slave's labor only and not of his body. Convinced that slavery was a positive good, he was a strong advocate for reopening the African slave trade under an apprenticeship system. In 1856 Grayson published a vigorous poem, "The Hireling and the Slave," defending Southern slavery as a paternal institution far more humane than the wage slavery of New England.

Fitzhugh's important contribution was to focus attention on the evils of Northern capitalism, which the abolitionists had ignored in their zeal to reform their Southern brethren. He proclaimed "the failure" of free society, for the condition of the laboring class in the industrial states, he asserted, was worse than that of the Southern slave. Slavery, he maintained, was a wholesome and natural institution for free *white* workers as well as black slaves. He predicted that the North would experience the diseased symptoms of competitive society prevalent in Europe, strikes, the rise of socialism, and the degradation of the laboring class, whereas the South with its harmonious labor system would become the conservative balance wheel of the nation. In the land of plantations the slaves were cared for during sickness, old age, and in times of economic depression, whereas in the North wages were barely enough to sustain life, child labor of the worst type prevailed, and the workers were ruthlessly exploited by capitalists in a form of wage slavery. These arguments were propagated in *De Bow's Review,* in Southern newspapers, and in two paradoxical books, *Sociology for the South, or, the Failure of Free Society* (1854), and *Cannibals All! or, Slaves Without Masters* (1857).[27] Fitzhugh was not a deep or original thinker, deriving many of his ideas from Carlyle and the English reviews, but he was primarily "a propagandist of the Old South." He did a great deal of harm by exacerbating the relations between the North and the South.

One of the significant phases of the proslavery argument was the repudiation of the philosophy of liberalism.[28] Senator James H. Hammond of South Carolina denounced the Declaration of Independence with its doctrine of the equality of men as a fallacious and glittering generalization. On the contrary, he declared that men were naturally unequal and that Negro slavery furnished

[27] See introduction by C. V. Woodward (ed.), in George Fitzhugh, *Cannibals All; or, Slaves Without Masters* (Cambridge, Mass., 1960).
[28] W. G. Bean, "Anti-Jeffersonianism in the Ante-Bellum South," *North Carolina Historical Review*, XII (April 1935), 102–124.

"a mudsill" for a white democracy. Calhoun supported this argument in behalf of slavery, contending that the Southern slaves freed the master class from drudgery and allowed them the leisure to cultivate the art of politics and refined living. Thus Southern society was idealized as being a Greek democracy, resting on a base of slave labor. The Whig leader Abel P. Upshur and later Fitzhugh flatly rejected the romantic liberalism of Thomas Jefferson in favor of a thoroughly conservative and aristocratic caste system. But they misrepresented public opinion in the South, which was devoted to a decentralized white democracy. When Fitzhugh proclaimed an irrepressible conflict between the free form of society and the slave system, which would be resolved by the extension of slavery into the North, he represented only a distinct minority of Southerners. By his extreme editorials in the Richmond press he furnished Seward and Lincoln with the ammunition for their famous speeches on "the irrepressible conflict" and "the House Divided" doctrine that alarmed Northern workers and small farmers.[29]

A modern scholar has asked the pertinent question, to whom was the proslavery propaganda of the 1840's and 1850's addressed? It certainly did not try to convince the Northerners, for such an attempt would be like Don Quixote tilting against the windmills. Nor was it primarily designed to convince the nonslaveholders, of whom few could be expected to read it, because they were illiterate or had no interest in such propaganda. Was it designed to quiet the consciences of the slaveholders themselves? There is good reason to believe that this was one object of the propaganda. Another reason was undoubtedly the natural reaction of a people to defend themselves ideologically when attacked. David Donald has suggested that some of the most prominent Southern defenders of slavery were motivated by similar psychological drives as some of the leading abolitionists, namely, that they had failed in their early lives to attain the distinction that they desired and to which they felt they were entitled by the prominence of their families. Accordingly, they sought to distinguish themselves as champions of a cause—the proslavery cause.[30]

Modern liberals, and even the independent-thinking William Faulkner in his novels, have expressed the belief that Southerners of the antebellum period had "a guilt complex," or as Faulkner conceived it, a curse rested upon the land because of slavery and the treatment of the Negro. In a letter to Calhoun in 1849, Governor James H. Hammond wrote that the discussion of the abolition question (by revealing the rightness of slavery) had "eased nearly every conscience in the South about holding slaves."[31] Although some

[29] See Harvey Wish, *George Fitzhugh, Propagandist of the Old South* (Baton Rouge, 1943).

[30] David Donald, "The Pro-Slavery Argument Reconsidered," *Journal of Southern History*, XXXVII (February 1971), and *Lincoln Reconsidered: Essays on the Civil War Era* (New York, 1956), chap. 2.

[31] J. H. Hammond to Calhoun, February 19, 1849. Boucher and Brooks (eds.), "Correspondence Addressed to John C. Calhoun, 1837–1849," *Annual Report of the American Historical Association, 1929*, p. 1192.

humanitarians, such as Mary Minor Blackford of Fredericksburg, an ardent colonizationist, remained unconverted, the evidence seems overwhelming that the average Southernerner was convinced that the Bible sanctioned slavery —and in that generation in the South such an assumption alone was sufficient justification.[32] One of the finest Southerners of the antebellum period, W. C. Preston, ex-senator of South Carolina and former president of South Carolina College, wrote to Waddy Thompson, a prominent political leader of Greenville, South Carolina, while he was visiting in Virginia in 1857, that he had read a defense of slavery by the Reverend Thornton Stringfellow, a Baptist minister of the state. He urged Thompson to get the book and read it, for it was "vastly the best work I have ever read on the subject, especially the *Scriptural*. It has wrought a change in my views which has been worrying me all my life." [33] When a cultivated and fair-minded Southerner such as Preston, or a Northerner serving Southern pastorates such as Woodrow Wilson's father, could be convinced of the rightfulness of slavery in the decade of the 1850's what can one say of the ready acceptance of this point of view by the great majority of poorly educated yeomen and planters? [34] If Southerners had a guilt complex concerning the Negro, it was not primarily over the sin of slavery but the sin of miscegenation.[35] Some of the erring planters, such as Benjamin Watkins of Virginia, felt so troubled in conscience over begetting mulatto children from slave mothers that they tried to atone for their conduct by freeing their mulatto children as well as the slave mothers in their wills.[36]

Opposing the overwhelming propaganda of the proslavery argument was a small group of Southern liberals or dissenters.[37] No one will ever know the strength of the antislavery sentiment in the South during the period 1831–1861. The representatives of this viewpoint were either persons of tender conscience or critical-minded individuals who were able to free themselves from traditional views. Probably most of the antislavery people maintained their silence because of prudence. The relatively few outspoken opponents of slavery, of whom records have been preserved, were chiefly members of the

[32] See L. Minor Blackford, *Mine Eyes Have Seen the Glory* (Cambridge, Mass., 1954).
[33] W. C. Preston to Waddy Thompson, August 10, 1857, J. H. Hammond Papers, MSS, South Carolina Library, Univ. South Carolina.
[34] Rev. Joseph R. Wilson, father of Woodrow Wilson, published *Mutual Relation of Masters and Slaves As Taught in the Bible* (Augusta, 1861), a sermon ardently defending slavery. A. S. Link, "Woodrow Wilson: the American As Southerner," *Journal of Southern History*, XXXVI (February 1970), 3–17.
[35] Eugene Genovese has made the valid observation that the South had a "guilt culture," owing primarily to their stern religion rather than to any sense of sin over slavery. Indeed, many Southerners looked upon slavery as a duty and a burden, and they had a hereditary regard for their slaves. Genovese, "Roll, Jordan, Roll," a manuscript being prepared for publication.
[36] B. E. Steiner (ed.), "A Planter's Troubled Conscience," *Journal of Southern History*, XXVIII (August 1962), 343–347.
[37] See Carl N. Degler, *The Other South: Southern Dissenters in the Nineteenth-Century* (New York, 1974).

professional class, preachers, college professors, lawyers, and literary men.[38] With regard to geographical distribution, they were located principally in the upper South, where Negroes were decidedly less concentrated than in the deep South.

A turning point in the development of the Southern mind was reached in 1831–1832, after the shock of the Nat Turner insurrection. The great debate over emancipation that took place in the Virginia legislature following that event brought forward a number of Southern liberals. In the course of the discussion eloquent speeches were made by young men, such as Charles J. Faulkner, James McDowell, and George W. Summers, attacking the evils of slavery and urging the adoption of a plan of gradual emancipation. They based their arguments on the danger of servile insurrection, the economic decline of Virginia, which they blamed on slavery, and the pernicious effects of the "peculiar institution" on the whites. Unfortunately, they were unable to agree on a practicable plan of emancipation and deportation of the freed Negroes. Sectionalism also played an important role in the development of antislavery sentiment in Virginia, for the western part of the state believed that the slaveowning planters blocked the progress of the West. Consequently, an antislavery resolution introduced by William B. Preston from the West received the unanimous support of the Western delegates. Only nine votes from the combined Tidewater and Piedmont, however, were cast in its favor, including the vote of Jefferson's grandson, Thomas Jefferson Randolph. The measure was lost by seventy-three negative votes against fifty-eight affirmatives votes.[39] After this defeat of the liberals, there was a strong conservative reaction in Virginia that lasted until the surrender at Appomattox.

After 1832 those Southern liberals who protested against the continuance of slavery as a perpetual institution met strong social disapproval. Their position in the South was rendered more difficult by the rising tide of resentment against the Northern abolitionists. A South Carolina editor, young Maynard Richardson, opened the columns of his paper, the Sumterville *Southern Whig,* in 1832 "for a *liberal* and *guarded* discussion of slavery" and printed an antislavery article, but his boldness met such a storm of opposition that he yielded to public sentiment.[40] Jesse Burton Harrison, educated at Harvard, published a reply to Dew's celebrated proslavery pamphlet entitled *Review of the Slave Question* (Richmond, 1832), in which he made a noble appeal for freedom of discussion of the grave problem and the adoption of a plan of gradual emancipation, but he too retreated into silence.[41]

[38] Clement Eaton, *The Freedom-of-Thought Struggle in the Old South,* chap. XI.
[39] J. C. Robert, *The Road from Monticello: A Study of the Virginia Slavery Debate of 1832* (Durham, N.C., 1941).
[40] W. W. Freehling, *Prelude to Civil War: The Nullification Controversy in South Carolina, 1816–1836* (New York, 1965), 83–85.
[41] Eaton, *The Mind of the Old South* (Baton Rouge, Enlarged ed., 1967), chap I, The Young Reformers of 1832.

At Danville, Kentucky, James G. Birney, a planter who was converted to the antislavery cause by Theodore D. Weld, tried in 1836 to establish an anti-slavery newspaper, *The Philantropist,* but was prevented from doing so by hostile demonstrations and forced to transfer the publication of his paper to Cincinnati. In North Carolina Daniel R. Goodloe, converted to the anti-slavery cause by reading the Virginia debates of 1831–1832, attacked slavery from an economic point of view in a pamphlet entitled *Inquiry into the Causes Which Have Retarded the Accumulation of Wealth and Increase of Population in the Southern States* (1844). One of the most significant of the antislavery publications by Southerners was *An Address to the People of West Virginia, Shewing [sic] that Slavery is Injurious to the Public Welfare,* published in 1847 by Dr. Henry Ruffner, president of Washington College at Lexington, Virginia. Dr. Ruffner attacked slavery as a wasteful and un-sound system of labor that had caused many of the sons of Virginia to emi-grate to free soil.

Two concerted efforts were made by liberals in the upper South after the Virginia debate to secure the adoption of a plan of gradual emancipation. In 1834, when a constitutional convention met in Tennessee, memorials for the adoption of a scheme of gradual emancipation were presented that were signed by 1,804 persons, chiefly from East Tennessee. A report was finally adopted by the convention, admitting that slavery was an evil: "To prove it to be a great evil is an easy task, but to tell how that evil can be removed is a question that the wisest heads and the most benevolent hearts have not been able to answer in a satisfactory manner." [42] Nothing was done, how-ever, to free the state from the incubus of an admitted evil, primarily because of the race problem—the blind spot of Southerners in being unable to visu-alize a society of free Negroes and whites living together to the mutual ad-vantage of both races. [43]

The liberals of Kentucky were similarly frustrated in 1849, when a con-stitutional convention met. An antislavery newspaper, *The Examiner,* was established in Louisville to influence public opinion to send delegates to the convention who would vote for the gradual abolition of slavery in Ken-tucky. [44] An Emancipation Meeting at Bowling Green, Kentucky, on May 12, 1849, proclaimed that although the group was opposed to "disturbing the right of Masters to their slaves now in being in Kentucky," its members desired a clause in the new constitution utterly prohibiting the further intro-

---

[42] *Journal of the Constitutional Convention of 1834* (Nashville, 1834), 87–88.

[43] Chase C. Mooney, "The Question of Slavery and the Free Negro in the Tennessee Constitutional Convention of 1834," *Journal of Southern History, XII* (November 1946), 486–509.

[44] *The Examiner* was opposed to the Northern abolitionists. It published a plan of emancipation proposed by W. L. Breckinridge, based on freeing all slaves born after 1850 at the age of twenty-five and sending them to Liberia. *The Examiner,* March 3, 1849. A file, February 10, 1847, to March 3, 1849, is owned by the Wisconsin His-torical Society.

duction of slaves into the commonwealth. This document also declared that all slaves emancipated in the state should be removed to Africa or elsewhere, and finally that a time should be fixed in the new constitution "when the people may vote on prospective emancipation, and declare whether they desire to rid our beloved commonwealth, in a convenient and reasonable time, of the institution of slavery." [45] It was signed by forty-one citizens and ordered to be distributed by means of handbills. Also, a state emancipation convention was held at Frankfort and was attended by many slaveholders. Despite the fact that ten thousand votes were cast in the state for the election of antislavery delegates, not a single antislavery candidate was elected. In this year also the proslavery faction succeeded in repealing a law of 1833 prohibiting the bringing of slaves into the state for sale. Furthermore, shortly after the convention adjourned the liberal *Examiner* perished for want of financial support.

No account of Southern liberalism would be complete without recording the crusading efforts of John Hampden Pleasants and Samuel Janney of Virginia. During a brief interim of freedom of discussion enjoyed by the press after the shock of the Nat Turner insurrection, Pleasants wrote brilliant editorials in the Richmond *Whig* urging the emancipation of the slaves. In 1846 he was killed in a duel by a rival editor, the son of Thomas Ritchie, who had accused him of being an abolitionist. Janney, the leader of the Virginia Quakers, published essays in the Leesburg *Washingtonian* in 1849 attacking slavery, for which he was tried on the charge of violating Virginia law by maintaining that "owners had no right of property in their slaves," but he was acquitted.[46]

In Kentucky, Cassius Marcellus Clay, the son of an aristocratic planter of Kentucky, sacrificed a promising career in politics to advocate the gradual emancipation of the slaves. Clay had been educated at Yale, where he was deeply attracted to the antislavery cause by hearing William Lloyd Garrison speak. Nevertheless, he did not become a militant antislavery man until he had a political quarrel in 1840 with Robert Wickliffe, called "the Old Duke," the largest slaveholder in Kentucky, whose son he defeated for representative in the legislature.[47] In 1845, Clay began the publication of an antislavery newspaper at Lexington that bore the name of *The True American*. Clay's main emphasis in attacking slavery was that it prevented the growth of industry in the South, which became a cliché, for actually slaves were widely used in industry—textiles, the iron industry, tobacco and hemp factories, and

[45] MS in the Thomas Henry Hines Papers, University of Kentucky Library; Clement Eaton (ed.), "Minutes and Resolutions of an Emancipation Meeting in Kentucky in 1849," *Journal of Southern History*, XIV (November 1948), 541–545.

[46] Patricia Hickling, "Gentle Agitator: Samuel M. Janney and the Antislavery Movement in Virginia, 1842–1851," *Journal of Southern History*, XXXVII (May 1971), 159–190.

[47] David L. Smiley, *Lion of White Hall, the Life of Cassius M. Clay* (Madison, Wis., 1962), and Eaton, *The Mind of the Old South*, chap. 6.

Cassius Marcellus Clay
of *White Hall* near
Richmond, Kentucky.
Antislavery crusader
and Minister to Russia
during the Civil War.
(Courtesy of The New
York Public Library,
Astor, Lenox and
Tilden Foundations)

many other industries.[48] Anticipating the attack of a mob, Clay fortified his
printing office with an arsenal of cannon and rifles and placed a keg of
powder with a fuse attached to it that could be used to blow up the office
in case it was invaded by ruffians. Clay had published his antislavery newspaper only a few months when a huge assembly of citizens resolved that no
abolition organ should be tolerated in Kentucky on the principle that *salus
populi suprema lex.* A committee was appointed who, while Clay was sick,
entered the amateur fortress of *The True American,* dismantled the presses,
and sent them to Cincinnati. A similar fate of suppression by a mob occurred
in 1859, when William Bailey, a Northern mechanic, established the *Free
South* at Newport, Kentucky, devoted to a policy of organizing the Southern
nonslaveholders to use their votes to exterminate slavery.

[48] See R. S. Starobin, *Industrial Slavery in the Old South* (New York, 1970), *passim.*

North Carolina produced three valiant critics of slavery during the last decade of the antebellum period. Benjamin Sherwood Hedrick, after study at Harvard, became a professor of chemistry at the University of North Carolina. During the presidential campaign of 1856 he expressed his free soil views by announcing that he would vote for Fremont. The Raleigh *Standard* launched a campaign to drive him from the state, which succeeded, for he was dismissed from the faculty of the University. Reverend Eli Washington Caruthers was forced to resign his position as pastor of a Presbyterian church at Greensboro, North Carolina, in the summer of 1861 because of his antislavery views. The most significant opponent of slavery that the state nurtured was the writer Hinton Rowan Helper, a representative of the yeoman class of the Piedmont.[49]

In 1857 Helper published in New York City *The Impending Crisis of the South,* in which he tried to show that the South was far inferior to the North in economic productivity and general civilization as a result of the burden of slavery. Using the statistics of the Census of 1850, he made invidious comparisons. He stated, for example, incorrectly that the Northern hay crop alone was worth more than all the cotton, rice, tobacco, and hemp produced in the fifteen slave states. (Southerners replied to this spectacular statement by observing that their warm climate permitted their cattle and horses to graze a large part of the year and that the production of hay was really a drain on the economic energies of the Northern people.) He also developed the view that the slaveholding oligarchy had conspired to keep the poor whites in a dependent, illiterate condition. With considerable accuracy he may be called the Karl Marx of the nonslaveholding whites whom he tried to arouse to a sense of class consciousness. Although he was an immediate abolitionist, he hated the Negroes, whom he regarded as the competitors of the poor whites.[50] Like the Georgia pamphleteer John Jacobus Flournoy, Helper was a Negrophobe, a bitter expulsionist, urging the wholesale shipping of the Negroes to Africa. *The Impending Crisis* was published as a campaign document for the Republican party, and it became a crime in the South to circulate it.

Southern liberalism had little apparent effect in counteracting the victory of the proslavery argument. But the numerous efforts of enlightened planters to ameliorate the harsh featurers of slavery must be reckoned as a part of Southern liberalism. The aristocratic planter William H. Fitzhugh of *Ravensworth,* in Virginia, adopted a plan of gradually training slaves for the responsibilities of free men, preparatory to liberating them. He settled some of his slaves as tenants on small farms. They paid him a rent for the land and for the stock he furnished, but nothing for the hire of their time. The net profits

---

[49] See Hugh Bailey, *Hinton Rowan Helper: Abolitionist—Racist* (University Ala., 1965), and Eaton, *The Mind of the Old South,* chap. 8.

[50] A bitter race feeling toward the Negroes existed also among the whites in the North. See Leon F. Litwak, *North of Slavery: The Negro in the Free States, 1790–1860* (Chicago (1961).

of this arrangement were set aside for the purchase of their freedom and to send them to Liberia.[51] Jefferson Davis and his millionaire brother Joseph adopted on their Mississippi plantations a rudimentary form of self-government for their slaves, with slave courts, and with incentives for working industriously and earning money. A great planter of Virginia, John Hartwell Cocke of *Bremo*, had some of his slaves taught by a Negro teacher and sought to prepare them for the responsibilities of freedom before he liberated them and sent them to Liberia.[52] John McDonogh, the famous merchant of New Orleans, allowed his slaves to earn their freedom by overtime work on Saturday afternoons. Some benevolent Southerners, such as Charles Colcock Jones of Georgia, tried to improve the moral and spiritual side of the Negroes by zealous efforts to give them religious instruction. Also, it is a commentary on the changed attitude of many Southerners of the later antebellum period that they seldom referred to their Negro bondsmen as "slaves" but used such terms as *servants, hands,* and *my people.* In the adoptiton of this nomenclature there seems to be revealed a kinder feeling toward their dark-skinned dependents than the use of the more brutal word *slave* would imply. Or were Southerners ashamed of the stark use of this word?

The endeavors of the Southern liberals and the abolitionist crusade, however, accomplished practically nothing toward revising the black code in the direction of greater humanity. The most progressive step that the Southern states could have taken toward attacking a great social evil was to have repealed the laws that virtually prevented individuals from emancipating their slaves. The refusal to make this concession was a great mistake, for by individual emancipations a more liberal spirit might have been generated in Southern society as a whole. At the close of the antebellum period nothing had been effected to prevent the sale of husbands from their wives, and only Louisiana and Alabama had laws prohibiting the sale of children under ten years of age from their mothers. All the Southern states, except Maryland, Kentucky, Tennessee, and Arkansas prohibited the teaching of slaves to read and write. The disability of slaves and of free Negroes, except in Louisiana, to give testimony against white persons in the law courts also remained an unjust practice of the Southern states. Thus the Negro was left poorly protected from cruel or unscrupulous white men, for the force of public opinion was not an adequate substitute for justice in the courts. The failure to revise the slave code, to ameliorate the conditions of Negro bondage, or even to permit the realistic discussion of emancipation, and the refusal of the border states to take any constructive steps toward gradually removing slavery add up to a dark outlook for the cause of Southern liberalism on the eve of the Civil War.

---

[51] *The African Repository*, **III** (August 1827), 185.
[52] See Clement Eaton, *The Mind of the Old South* (1967), chap. 1.

The Southern Way of Life

SERENE WHITE MANSIONS, aristocratic planters, ladies descending graceful staircases in crinoline skirts, slave gangs singing in the cotton fields, and the fragrance of moonlit gardens form a tenacious stereotype of the Old South. Such scenes of glamour and ease for the privileged class actually existed in those areas of the South possessing rich soil and accessibility to markets. This romantic stereotype, however, omits from the landscape the large middle class of farmers, the barefoot women, the log cabins, and the sweaty toil of white men under the hot sun. In actuality, three fourths of the white population of the antebellum South did not belong to slaveholding families, and the typical home was not a *Mount Vernon* or a *Tara Hall* but a log cabin or a modest frame cottage. The stereotype has taken certain real aspects of Southern society, especially the life of the small class of large planters, and has generalized and exaggerated them so that they appear to be typical of the South as a whole.[1]

The romantic image of the Old South is a creation of a number of forces. The abolitionists made a contribution to this distortion by propaganda that represented the land of Dixie as inhabited chiefly by haughty aristocrats, debased "poor whites," and black slaves. The picture of an aristocratic society below the Potomac was also elaborated by the Southerners themselves. Passionately fond of reading Sir Walter Scott's novels, they tended to idealize their anachronistic society in terms of medieval chivalry. After the Civil War the psychological need of a compensation for bitter defeat and poverty led to the rise of reminiscences and of romances, such as those of Thomas Nelson Page, James Lane Allen, and John Esten Cooke, idealizing the splendid days "befo' the war." This romantic legend has been perpetuated by more recent scenario writers and novelists, notably Stark Young in *So Red the Rose* and Margaret Mitchell in *Gone with the Wind*.

The true profile of the antebellum South, however, has been recovered from the exaggerations both of the abolitionists and of the romancers by the researches of modern historians. Especially valuable in this work of restoration have been the unpublished reports of the manuscript Census of 1860, which clearly indicate that the South of slavery days was predominantly a region of small independent farmers. Indeed, the social pyramid bulged

[1] See Francis P. Gaines, *The Southern Plantation, a Study in the Development and Accuracy of a Tradition* (New York, 1924); and William R. Taylor, *Cavalier and Yankee, the Old South and American National Character* (New York, 1961).

Belle Helene, Ascension Parish, Louisiana. Home of Duncan Kenner, great sugar planter and Confederate diplomat.

greatly at the sides, and the social structure was flexible enough to permit the movement of the sons of numerous poor men to a higher economic and social status.

At the apex of the social pyramid were the planters. According to the arbitrary classification of the census bureau, the planter status was based on the ownership of 20 or more slaves engaged in agriculture. The accurate definition of a planter, however, should also include the ownership of a considerable acreage of land, a minimum of between 500 and 1,000 acres, of which at least 200 were in cultivation. The census of 1860 reported a surprisingly small number of "planters," only 46,274 persons, most of whom were heads of families, owning as many as 20 slaves. Out of this privileged group, only 2,292 persons belonged to the large planter classification, that is, persons owning as many as 100 slaves. In the whole land of Dixie, the census officials of 1860 reported finding only 1 slaveholder, an individual in South Carolina, having as many as 1,000 slaves, and only 13 persons owning between 500 and 1,000 slaves. The large slaveholders, thus, were very few in number and comparable to the millionaires of modern America.

This small privileged class of planters tended to think of themselves as "the South"; they confused their narrow class interests as identical with the welfare of the whole South. Unlike the Northern agriculturists, they cherished the concept of the country gentleman living in the style of an English squire of the eighteenth century—a powerful formative ideal in the Old South. Nonetheless, many of the planters were self-made men, caught up by the restless spirit of America, which drove them to buy more land and more slaves on credit in order to grow more cotton and sugar, the profits of which were used, not to pay off their mortgages, but to purchase more black laborers. Frequently, they moved from one exhausted old plantation to a fresh one located in a cruder but more fertile region of the Southwest. Thus these "movers" lost the cultural accumulations and the satisfactions of the more static English squires who quietly lived on inherited estates that they passed on to their sons and grandsons. Some of these large planters belonged to the class of nouveau riche, whom D. R. Hundley, an amateur sociologist of the Old South, described as "cotton snobs." [2]

The landholdings of the larger planters were not as a rule consolidated, but scattered among half a dozen or more plantations. Indeed, it was a more efficient practice to operate units of about one thousand acres in the production of cotton or sugar and of about five hundred acres in the cultivation of rice. Each of these agricultual units utilized approximately fifty to sixty slaves under an overseer, but some of the largest planters employed a steward or superintendent to supervise their overseers. The wealthier planters, such as the powerful Wade Hampton family of South Carolina, often invested their surplus profits in the virgin lands of the Southwest. Thus they became absentee owners who administered their distant possessions through overseers guided by an elaborate set of rules for disciplining the slaves. Yet the relative number of absentee planters has been exaggerated. The great majority of planters supervised their own slaves, usually with the help of drivers or Negro foremen. Fogel and Engerman in their recent study of the economics of American Negro slavery found that, as a rule, masters lived on their plantations and managed them; less than one in six planters who owned between sixteen and fifty slaves employed an overseer, only one out of four of masters owning between fifty and 100 slaves employed an overseer, and less than a third of the great slaveholders owning more than one hundred slaves used the services of an overseer.[3] These revealing figures dispel much of the glamor of the plantation legend.

Instead of generalizing about the daily lives of the planters, several case histories are cited as being more informative. In Virginia, the journal of John A. Selden, who had purchased the famous colonial estate of *Westover,* on the James River, gives a faithful mirror of the activities of a wheat

[2] D. R. Hundley, *Social Relations in Our Southern States* (New York, 1860).
[3] R. W. Fogel and S. L. Engerman, *Time on the Cross, Vol. I, The Economics of American Negro Slavery* (Boston, 1974); see also the estimate of W. K. Scarborough, *The Overseer: Plantation Management in the Old South* (Baton Rouge, 1916), p. 10, that only 11 per cent of the planters who owned between ten and fifty slaves employed overseers.

planter.[4] During the period of agricultural depression from the Revolution to 1830, many of the Virginia and Maryland planters turned from cultivating tobacco to wheat growing and diversified farming. Selden was a practical farmer on a large scale, who personally supervised the various operations of planting wheat, corn, oats, turnips, and clover, the plowing and hoeing of the crops, and the harvesting and sale of them. In 1858 he made twenty-one and one half bushels of wheat per acre, which he described as "the best average I have heard of," and killed ninety-eight hogs for meat. During the next year he harvested five thousand eight hundred bushels of wheat, which he sold in Richmond for $1.50 a bushel. Selden, however, did not have to worry about being in the high bracket of an income tax; he paid his taxes for the year 1858 in full, amounting to only $244.51. In his abbreviated journal, as published by John Spencer Bassett, Selden does not mention whipping his slaves, of whom he owned sixty-three in 1861, nor does he seem to have been troubled by runaways or excessive sickness among his black laborers. At harvest time he employed extra agricultural labor, paying them 62½ cents and 75 cents a day, a scale of wages that should be evaluated in terms of the price of wheat, at $1.50 a bushel, and of the price he paid for chickens, at about 15 cents apiece.

With his ample income Selden purchased such luxuries as a silver tea set for $320, a silver egg cup, and a frock coat, and employed two teachers, an academic teacher and a music teacher, each of whom received $250 a year. He frequently visited by stage the White Sulphur Springs, was a member of the Richmond Whist Club, and on one occasion gave a dinner party for fifty-two persons. He was a public-spirited citizen, active in the Virginia Central Agricultural Society, serving as a justice of the peace without remuneration, and using his slaves to keep his share of the public roads in repair, one of the public services rendered by farmers and planters that partly explains the low taxes paid in money.

The papers of the Allston family of *Chicora Wood,* on the Pee Dee River in South Carolina, afford an excellent view of the life of the rice planter. *Chicora Wood* lay in the Georgetown District, the heart of the rice country, located north of Charleston. Here the slaves outnumbered the whites six to one. After graduating from West Point Military Academy, Robert F. W. Allston began to combine the career of a large planter with participation in politics, becoming governor of the state in 1856. Like many planters, he expanded his broad acres and his slave force by purchasing on credit, a practice that contributed heavily to his ultimate financial ruin. Eventually, he acquired seven plantations, containing over 4,000 acres of land, of which about one fourth was rice land. *Chicora Wood,* his home plantation, contained 922 acres. His slaves increased in number from 42 Negroes in 1820 to 590 in 1864, the year of his death. From his combined plantations he pro-

[4] J. S. Bassett (ed.), *The Westover Journal of John A. Selden* (Northampton, Mass., 1921).

duced a bumper crop in 1859 of 2,581 barrels of rice, each barrel containing 600 pounds. He estimated that the profits of rice planting under favorable circumstances were 8 per cent, "independent of the privileges and perquisites of the plantation residence." [5] Certainly he was able to live in the style of a gentleman, to own a splendid town house in Charleston, and to escape from the danger of malaria by going to the resort, Pawley's Island, or to his house in the dry pineland region.

Allston had a fine sense of noblesse oblige that distinguished the best members of the Southern aristicracy. As a member of the South Carolina legislature, he was an ardent champion of an elementary public school system that would be attended by all classes, the establishment of a normal school "with a model school attached," and increased taxation for schools. He maintained a scholarship at South Carolina College, and was president of the Winyah Indigo Society, which operated a school for the poor in Georgetown District. He was a prominent vestryman in the Episcopal Church, and he treated his Gullah slaves with genuine paternalism. Nevertheless, he was strongly in favor of the continuance of slavery, the abolition of which, he declared, would cost him the loss of half of his property.

An insight into the life of the large planters of the deep South is afforded by the diary of Bennet Barrow of West Feliciana Parish in Louisiana. Becoming disgusted with overseers, Barrow supervised his own plantation of five thousand arpents (an arpent was almost equal to an acre) with the aid of a Negro foreman. He worked hard at his vocation of farming, getting excellent performance from his two hundred slaves by a combination of rewards and of rather frequent whippings. He was impatient with slovenly work in the fields and occasionally his temper flared up, as when he broke his sword cane over the skull of a Negro. He carefully supervised the health of his slaves, acting as an amateur doctor. His life as a planter was a rhythm of routine of work, varied by hunting, fishing, attending dances, and going to horse races. He planted about seven hundred fifty acres of cotton and three hundred acres of corn. In 1840 he sold his cotton crop for approximately $20,000, but despite his lucrative returns he was continuously in debt, caused in part by a habit of endorsing the notes of his relatives and friends. In politics he was a Whig, opposed to the "man worship of Andrew Jackson" by the Democrats, but in 1844 because of his ardent wish to see Texas annexed to the United States, he voted for Polk.[6]

The sugar planter of Louisiana was usually a large operator, for the production of sugar required expensive machinery. On the eve of the Civil War the wealthiest sugar planter in Louisiana was John Burnside, an immigrant from North Ireland, who had obtained his capital as a merchant in New

[5] J. H. Easterby (ed.), *The South Carolina Rice Plantation As Revealed in the Papers of Robert F. W. Allston* (Chicago, 1945).
[6] E. A. Davis, *Plantation Life in the Florida Parishes of Louisiana, 1836–1846, As Reflected in the Diary of Bennet H. Barrow* (New York, 1943).

Orleans. Burnside had six thousand acres of continuous cane fields, and his sugar plantations and slaves, numbering more than one thousand, were valued at $2 million. Judah P. Benjamin, the Confederate statesman, was another example of a city man, a lawyer, who purchased an interest in a sugar plantation, *Bellechase,* and introduced the most modern methods of making sugar, such as discarding the old "open kettle" process of boiling the cane juice and using vacuum pans. Benjamin popularized the new scientific techniques in articles in *De Bow's Review,* 1846–1848. He would retire from the turmoil of the city to *Bellechase* on weekends, until he lost the plantation as a result of a flood breaking through the levee and a financial disaster in endorsing the note of a friend.

The more aristocratic type of sugar planter was illustrated by John Hampden Randolph of distinguished Virginia lineage, whose family had emigrated to the deep South when he was a boy. Randolph changed from being a modest cotton planter to a sugar planter about 1846, while the price of cotton was in a slump and the sugar industry was expanding. Although he was forced to borrow much money, he became very prosperous, increasing his number of slaves from 23 in 1842 to 195, 20 years later. His *Forest Home* plantation in Iberville Parish (2,000 arpents), produced a crop of 540 hogsheads, which together with his molasses sold for $36,225.26 net. Randolph continued to carry on genteel Virginia traditions in his home in the fertile Southwest. He employed tutors to teach his children the classics and dancing and music masters to give them the accomplishments of polite society. He sent his daughter to a girl's school in Baltimore and one son to the University of Virginia and another to Van Rensselaer Polytechnic in New York. He took frequent trips for pleasure, enjoyed hunting, subscribed to several newspapers, and purchased books, such as Audubon's *Birds of America,* for which he paid $166.67. His taste for magnificence was expressed in building the beautiful home of *Nottaway* in the Virginia style, with fifty rooms and such luxuries as a White Ball Room and an apparatus for gas illumination (1859). He retained his expensive property after the Civil War and continued to live in an aristocratic style until his death.[7]

From travel accounts one gains the impression that many of the planters particularly of the Southwest did not live nearly as well as thrifty farmers of the North, although their property was much greater. The major reason for this state was that they were usually "land poor," with their capital frozen in land and slaves. Consequently, they lacked the ready cash to buy some of the comforts of life the Northerner enjoyed. Frederick Law Olmsted noted the absence in their homes of such things as good reading lamps, good furniture, thermometers, bathtubs, and other equipment. Some of the owners

---

[7] P. S. Postell, "John Hampden Randolph, A Louisiana Planter, "*Louisiana Historical Quarterly,* XXV (1942), 149–223; for other descriptions of life on the large plantations, see Katharine Jones (ed.), *The Plantation South* (Indianapolis, 1957); and Clement Eaton (ed.), *The Leaven of Democracy* (New York, 1963).

of numerous slaves and large plantations lived in log cabins and ate a monotonous diet of hog, hominy, and execrable coffee.

The flavor of life of the Southwestern planter is contained in the rollicking poem of General Albert Pike, who came from Massachusetts to Arkansas as a young tutor and served in the War for Southern Independence as an officer leading Indian troops:

> Now all good fellows listen, and a story I will tell
> Of a mighty clever gentleman who lives extremely well
> In the Western part of Arkansas, close to the Indian line;
> Where he gets drunk once a week on whiskey and immediately sobers
>   himself up completely on the very best of wine,
> A fine Arkansas gentleman
> Close to the Choctaw line!

> This fine Arkansas gentleman has a mighty fine estate,
> Of five or six thousand acres or more of land, that will be worth a great
>   deal some day or other, if he don't kill himself too soon, and will
>   only consent to wait;
> And four or five dozen negroes that would rather work than not;
> And such quantities of horses, and cattle, and pigs, and poultry, that he
>   never pretends to know how many he has got;

> This fine Arkansas gentleman makes several hundred bales,
> Unless from drought or worm, or a bad stand, or some other damned
>   contingency, his crop is short and fails:
> And when it's picked and ginned and baled, he puts it on a boat,
> And gets aboard himself likewise, and charters the bar, and has a devil
>   of a spree, while down to New Orleans he and his cotton float.
> This fine Arkansas gentleman
> Close to the Choctaw line.

In contrast, Henry Barnard described in 1833 the gracious manner of living at *Shirley* on the banks of the James, where he enjoyed a rich feast enlivened by champagne and wines of various sorts, held at the fashionable hour of three o'clock in the afternoon.[8] The diary of the rice planter John Berkeley Grimball also depicts a cultivated, elegant aristocracy. Grimball dined with a group of men—the elite of Charleston—on June 13, 1832. His host served a many-course dinner, consisting of turtle soup and turtle steaks, a fine fish, a leg of boiled mutton, a hammock of venison, vegetables, sauterne, Madeira, champagne, Stilton cheese with bread and butter and Porter, bananas, oranges, pineapple with olives, and sherbet. He recorded the menu of such fashionable dinners "because they are given by men of acknowledged taste" and would furnish "hints" to guide him in giving

[8] Bernard C. Stenier (ed.), "The South Atlantic States in 1833 as Seen by a New Englander," *Maryland Historical Magazine*, XIII (December 1918), 317–328.

aristocratic dinners himself. He listed for the Confederate tax his ownership of silver plate worth $800, three gold watches, and a piano valued at $150.[9]

How the lesser gentry of the South lived is vividly depicted in the diary of Benny Fleet, who grew up on the plantation *Green Mount,* in eastern Virginia. His remarkable diary begins on January 9, 1860, when he was 13 years old and ends when he was killed in Confederate uniform at the age of 17. His father was a doctor, a justice of the peace, and the owner of the 3,000-acre plantation, *Green Mount,* which was roughly equivalent in size to Madison's *Montpelier.* Approximately 50 slaves raised the crops of wheat and corn, which were the staples of the plantation. Benny himself sometimes plowed with the slave hands and did other work on the plantation. His relations with the Negroes were friendly and informal, for slavery at *Green Mount* was a paternal institution. Religion played an important role in the life of this family that had departed from the Episcopal faith of earlier generations to join the Baptist church. The Fleets combined the Puritan with the Cavalier traditions. Fond of visiting, hospitable, enjoying dances, home-made wine and the reading of novels, they were nevertheless strong supporters of the church.

The Fleets had the Southern idea of honor, which made them look down upon those who were forced into the army by the draft, and they made quite a distinction between "gentlemen" and the common people.[10] The Fleet family illustrated the class consciousness that existed in certain areas of the South, particularly in the Tidewater and Delta regions. But the vicissitudes of the Civil War tended to break down the caste system where it existed. Kate Stone, the daughter of a wealthy Louisiana planter, found it quite ironic, with her aristocratic ideas, to have a brother serving as a private in a Confederate company whose officers included a livery stable keeper, an overseer, and a butcher.[11] On the other hand, Captain Charles Colcock Jones, Jr., wrote to his parents that his Chatham Light Artillery Company of Savannah, Georgia, had enlisted only gentlemen to the manor born.

Southerners were hypersensitive about their honor. To accuse a gentleman of untruth, insult him, or attack his honor was to provoke a duel. An elaborate etiquette was evolved in regard to sending a challenge and in making preparations for the encounter. One did not fight a duel with a person who did not belong to the category of a "gentleman," but avenged an insult from such a person by caning or horsewhipping him. Challenges were frequently settled by explanations or the good offices of antidueling associations, such as the Camden (South Carolina) Anti-Dueling Association, which prevented a duel between James H. Hammond, later a Senator, and an abusive

[9] Diary of John Berkeley Grimball, June 13, Oct. 15, 1832, Nov. 13, 1862. MS in Southern Collection, University of North Carolina.
[10] Betsy Fleet and Clement Eaton (eds.), *Green Mount: A Virginia Plantation Family during the Civil War* (Lexington, 1962).
[11] J. Q. Anderson (ed.), *Brokenburn, the Journal of Kate Stone, 1861–1868* (Baton Rouge, 1955).

Congressman. Most Southern states passed laws against the practice of dueling, but such legislation was unenforceable against the mores of the people. The Kentucky statute of 1852 punished dueling or carrying a challenge by imprisonment or a heavy fine and by disfranchisement and disqualification from holding office for a period of seven years. When William L. Yancey, Representative from Alabama, fought a duel with Congressman T. L. Clingman of North Carolina, the legislature of Alabama passed a special law exempting him from disqualification from officeholding under the Alabama law against dueling. The editor of the Greenville (South Carolina) *Mountaineer,* Benjamin F. Perry, who had killed a rival editor in a duel, condoned this evil practice by saying: "When a man knows that he is to be held accountable for his want of courtesy, he is not so apt to indulge in abuse. In this way dueling produces a greater courtesy in society and a higher refinement." [12] Many a high-minded man recognized the evil of dueling and yet accepted a challenge of a duel in order to escape the odium of being regarded a coward and thus lose his influence in society.

Along with the code of honor, the practice of hospitality was part of the mores of Southerners. Hospitality was supported in part by the rural Southerner's keen sense of family, of kinship widely extended, which gave rise to the term "kissing cousin." Economic conditions also favored the growth of hospitality—the scattered farms and plantations that produced loneliness, the bad roads, the abundance of food, a superfluity of domestic servants on the plantations, and the lack of decent taverns.[13] The antebellum Southerner, curiously, bore some resemblance in characteristics to the desert Arabs who make a fetish of hospitality, honor, and virility.

One of the most attractive virtues nourished by aristocratic plantation society was the practice of chivalry, an ideal that seems virtually extinct in modern industrial America. Chivalry led to the formation of a code of gracious manners, slightly formal and artificial it is true, but recognizing the dignity of human personality. Gentlemen in the Old South were forever getting up from comfortable seats in stage coaches, railroad cars, and public gatherings to give "ladies" a seat. The chivalric or romantic ideal dictated that women should be highly feminine and that they should look up to the male as the protector and the oracle of wordly wisdom. The women in the Old South were shielded from hearing profane or sexy language, and convention required them to blush at the mention of sex.

The Southern "lady" dressed in the romantic vogue, wearing crinoline skirts, reducing her waistline by stays, wearing her hair in curls or in the

[12] L. A. Kibler, *Benjamin F. Perry, South Carolina Unionist* (Durham, 1946), 135.
[13] Paton Yoder in "Private Hospitality in the South, 1775–1850," *Mississippi Valley Historical Review*, XLVII (December 1960), 424, 452, minimized the practice of hospitality to strangers in the South, except, significantly, to itinerant preachers; but it is the opinion of the author that the majority of respectable country folk were ashamed not to invite an acquaintance, or even a stranger, to sit down to a meal, although it often was only a gesture.

Grecian style of headdress, and shading her delicate white complexion from the sun by wearing bonnets and carrying parasols. Southerners strongly condemned the feminist movement in the North, abhorring such vagaries as women speaking in public or wearing the ridiculous costume invented by Miss Amelia Bloomer, editor of *The Lily*. An insight into the attitude of the best Southern men toward women is afforded by Calhoun's letter to his daughter, Anna: "I am not one of those who think your sex ought to have nothing to do with politicks. They have as much interest in the good condition of their country, as the other sex, and though it would be unbecoming them to take an active part in political struggles, their opinion, when enlightened, cannot fail to have a great salutary effect." [14] Two of the most prominent leaders in the feminist and antislavery movements, Sarah and Angelina Grimké, were reared in South Carolina, but they pursued their reforming crusades in the North. Southern women of the upper class were taught in academies or by governesses such subjects as French, music, sewing, Latin, English, art, and polite manners. Among the oldest colleges for woman in the nation were the Moravian College at Salem, North Carolina (first a seminary, 1802, and later a college), and Wesleyan Methodist College at Macon, Georgia, founded in 1836.

The diary of Mrs. Isaac H. Hilliard gives a vignette of the blissful life of a sugar planter's wife. In February, 1850, Mrs. Hilliard of Grand Lake, Arkansas, visited the plantation of Bishop Leonidas Polk on Bayou La Fourche in Louisiana, which was a model of paternalism. The Bishop paid a rector $300 to preach to his three hundred and seventy slaves, and on Sunday afternoons the young Negroes were catechised. The grounds of his estate had an outer hedge of Cherokee roses, and his garden was fragrant with orange trees and with pyramids of Picayune roses. He had an extensive and rare library as well as a collection of prints brought from Italy. Mrs. Hilliard wrote with envy concerning the leisure of the mistress of *Leighton:* "She has a faithful nurse (negro) to whose care she abandons her babies entirely. Only when she has a fancy to caress them does she see them. Eight children and cannot lay to their charge the loss of a single night's rest. In another department she is equally fortunate in having a housekeeper who gives out, regulates, and is everything she ought to be." [15] Also the Polk girls were taught by a white governess. Yet four years later, this idyllic life came to an end when *Leighton* was surrendered to creditors.

The romantic attitude of the age toward women had its obverse side in narrowly constricting their activities. Their functions were to marry early, stay within the sphere of the home, raise numerous children, and uphold the religious tradition. Mrs. Basil Hall, a Scottish traveler, observed at Charleston: "Women are just looked upon as house-keepers in this country."

[14] J. F. Jameson (ed.), "Correspondence of John C. Calhoun," *Annual Report of the American Historical Association for 1889* (Washington, D.C., 1900), II, 315–316.
[15] MS in Department of Archives, Louisiana State University.

She also protested against the vile custom at social gatherings in the South of women herding together and men segregating themselves. At Darien, Georgia, she commented, "there appears to be no sympathy between the sexes. They have no subjects of conversation in common." [16] She was told by James Couper, a great planter of this region, that the only hope for a man to obtain a rational companion for a wife was to marry a young girl and cultivate her mind. Mrs. Couper was married when she was sixteen.

Despite the romantic tradition, the majority of Southern women spent laborious lives, cooking, preserving fruits, making clothes for the family, milking, gardening, and bearing children. Even the mistresses of large plantations had many responsibilities in managing the inefficient household servants, in attending the sick slaves, and in supervising the domestic industries, such as weaving cloth and making soap. Sara Williams, a New York girl who came in 1855 as a young bride to *Clifton Grove,* a turpentine plantation in eastern North Carolina, found that her mother-in-law worked harder than any Northern farmer's wife she knew. The Negro slaves, she observed, were, in contrast to the mistress, "certainly not overtasked on this plantation." [17] Many duties were the lot of the great majority of the plantation mistresses, but the teen-age girls on the whole lived gay and leisurely lives, free from domestic work. Kate Stone, who grew up on the plantation *Brokenburn,* in Louisiana with its one hundred and fifty slaves, was probably typical of the daughters of the large planters, spending her days in visiting, riding horseback, reading novels, and sewing.[18] Indeed the diaries, reminiscences, and letters of antebellum Southern ladies, notably Mrs. James Chesnut, Mrs. Clement C. Clay, Mrs. Jesse Burton Harrison, Mrs. Roger A. Pryor, Mrs. Maria Fleet, and Mrs. Catherine Edmondston, mirror a delightful and refined social life that was enjoyed by the upper classes.[19]

A realistic picture of the life of the mistress of a large slave plantation in the lower South is mirrored in the remarkable collection of letters of the Charles Colcock Jones family of Georgia previously quoted. The master drew this intimate sketch of his wife: "She rises about six in the morning; takes her bath, reads, and is ready for family worship about seven; then breakfasts with a moderate appetite and enjoys a cup of tea." [20] Then she put on her sunbonnet and India-rubber gloves and worked with the slaves in the garden;

[16] Una Pope-Hennessy (ed.), *An Aristocratic Journey: Being the Outspoken Letters of Mrs. Basil Hall Written during a Fourteen Months' Sojourn in America, 1827–1828* (New York, 1931), 212, 230.

[17] J. C. Bonner (ed.), "Plantation Experiences of a New York Woman," *North Carolina Historical Review, XXXIII* (July 1956), 384–417.

[18] John Q. Anderson (ed.), *Brokenburn, the Journal of Kate Stone, 1861–1868* (Baton Rouge, 1955).

[19] Anne F. Scott, in *The Southern Lady; From Pedestal to Politics, 1830–1930* (Chicago, 1970), has done much to deglamorize the legend of the antebellum Southern woman.

[20] R. M. Myers (ed.), *The Children of Pride: A True Story of Georgia and the Civil War* (New Haven, 1972), 35.

Sally Ward, a Kentucky belle. (Courtesy of Speed Museum, Louisville, Kentucky)

hoeing, planting, and pruning for nearly two hours; supervised the kitchen; and devoted herself to cutting out, fitting, and sewing clothes for the family and slaves; retired for an hour or two after dinner; and made her appearance dressed for the evening and entertained visitors sitting in rocking chairs on the piazza. She enjoyed the sea breeze, the glories of nature, the sunset, and her flowers; the whole family loved nature and the plantation as few Northerners in cities love their homes. She kept up her mental improvement with reading good books and delighted in hearing her daughter sing and play on the piano. She was more puritanical than many Southern ladies of her class, for she did not dance or play cards. She was a wonderful mother to her children in giving them a high sense of values, encouraging them to read the Bible, practice secret prayer, never to travel on Sunday, drink liquor, carry arms about them ("an awful and cowardly practice"), or duel, but always to maintain a high-toned sense of honor. She was kind to the slaves, administered medicine to them, yet she believed abolitionists were fanatics and infidels and that Negroes were incapable of governing themselves.

Southern women were far less emancipated than Northern women. They did not join feminist organizations or agitate for woman's rights, for they were inhibited by the fact that these organizations were closely related to abolition societies and by the prevailing cult of chivalry in the South. Their religious faith and the ridicule of the strong-minded women of the North also had a powerful influence in their rejecting feminist movements. What normal Southern woman would be willing to subject herself to the type of ridicule expressed by the Virginia liberal John Hartwell Cocke? After attending the World Temperance Convention in New York Cocke wrote to William McGuffey of the University of Virginia in 1853, "You have doubtless seen in the newspapers the struggle we had with the strong-minded women as they call themselves in the World Temperance Convention. If you have seen the true account of the matter, you will see that we gained a perfect triumph, and I believe have given a rebuke to this most impudent clique of unsexed females and rampant abolitionists which must put down the petty-coats—at least as far as their claim to take the platform of public debate and enter into all the rough and tumble of the war of words." [21] Accordingly, Southern women continued to suffer without public protest the discriminations against their sex, such as deprivation of the right to vote and the fact that when they married, their husbands controlled their property (although Mississippi had a law passed in 1839 granting married women control of their property and freeing it from liability for their husband's debts). The husband alone was legal guardian of their minor children, and divorce was extremely difficult (South Carolina prohibited it entirely). Women were discriminated against in obtaining a college education, in securing jobs, and in the Victorian double standard of morals.[21a]

But there were some rebels, even if only in their diaries and private letters. Mrs. James Chesnut, Jr., for example, was one, who lived on a plantation near Camden, South Carolina, when she was not peregrinating to far more exciting places such as Columbia and the Confederate capitals of Montgom-

[21] John Hartwell Cocke to William H. McGuffey, Sept., 1853, John Hartwell Cocke Papers, MSS in the University of Virginia Library.
[21a] See Clement Eaton, "Breaking a Path for the Liberation of Women in the South," *The Georgia Review*, XXVIII (Summer, 1974), 187–199.

ery and Richmond. She was bright, witty, married to a Senator of great wealth, but unhappy because she was childless and Southern women looked down on a childless married woman. She saw life from a narrow, aristocratic point of view, and she had more sympathy for the slave than for the poor white. She professes (in her diary) again and again that she hates slavery and that the aristocrats such as the Hamptons and the Prestons were not fighting in the Civil War to preserve it. She writes that in the war the men have all the glory and the honor. In condemning slavery she includes the slavery of Southern women and she resented the necessity of women having to ask their husbands for money—even for "pin money."

But her greatest bitterness at the unjustness of the lot of women was over the Victorian double standard of morals. "Under slavery," she wrote in a famous passage in her diary, "we live surrounded by prostitutes, yet an abandoned [white] woman is sent out of any decent house. . . . Like the patriarchs of old, our men live in one house with their wives and their concubines: and the mulattoes one sees in every family partly resemble the white children." [22] This hyperbolic protest (belied to a great extent by the federal census of mulattoes) finds an echo in the frank manuscript diary of Mrs. Gertrude Thomas, who lived on a Georgia plantation during the Civil War and who wrote that moral conditions in slaveholding families made all Southern woman abolitionists.[23]

European visitors were very much impressed with the Americans' indulgence of their children. The French nobleman De Montlezun, who visited this country in 1816–1817 wrote: "The children of Louisiana, like those of every other part of America, are absolute masters of their fate. The authority of the parents is no restraint at all." The Jesuit scholar Giovanni Grassi, who published his observations of the United States in 1819, wrote, "The observers of American customs have always deplored the fact that the fathers, especially in the South, yield sadly and foolishly to their children whom they seem unable to contradict and whose capricious wishes they do not restrain.[24] The Hungarian exiles the Pulszkys talked with the mistress of a plantation in Louisiana who told them: "Our children are spoiled by our institution. It is very difficult to educate them; they never exert themselves in any way; they always depend on the slaves." [25] Yet Southern youth were passionately fond of hunting and dancing, and in these diversions they were

[22] B. A. Williams (ed.), *A Diary from Dixie, by Mary Boykin Chesnut* (New York, 1949), 215. Modern scholars are skeptical about the published diary, first published in 1909 after the death of Mrs. Chesnut, based on a manuscript that she had copied from her original diary, and then possibly changed by several later editors. See D. Aron, *The Unwritten War: American Writers and the Civil War* (New York, 1973), 251.

[23] M. E. Massey, "The Making of a Feminist," *Journal of Southern History*, XXXIX (February 1973), 9; see also Gerda Lerner, *The Grimké Sisters from South Carolina: Rebels against Slavery* (Boston, 1967).

[24] Oscar Handlin (ed.), *This Was America* (New York, 1964), 134, 142.

[25] Francis and Theresa Pulszky, *White, Red, Black; Sketches of Society in the United States* (London, 1853), II, 273.

extremely energetic. Moreover, there must have been a change in parental discipline toward the end of the antebellum period. Catherine Hopley, an Englishwoman who taught the children of Govenor John Milton on his plantation near Tallahassee in 1860, observed an instance of it in the fact that the slaves were seldom whipped, but the cihldren of the master were flogged frequently.[26] One of the essential qualifications of the teacher in an old field school in the South was that he could be firm in flogging unruly students.

The type of amusements that delight a people indicate the stage of their civilization. The Southerners were an out-of-door people whose recreations reflected that fact. But the upper class also enjoyed more sophisticated indoor entertainments, such as dancing, musical concerts, charades, and the theater. Williamsburg had the first theater in the colonies, established before 1722, but in the nineteenth century theaters and actors were disapproved by great numbers of religious folk. Nevertheless, stock companies were organized in the larger cities of the South in the period 1820 to 1860 and were sustained largely by the visits of Northern and English "stars," such as Fanny Kemble and her father, Joseph Jefferson, Junius Booth, and the famous Irish comedian, Tyrone Power.[27] The two leading promoters of theaters in the South were Joseph H. Caldwell, a British actor who in 1822 established the American Theater in New Orleans, and Sol Smith, a New Yorker, who opened a theater in Natchez as early as 1830 and others later in New Orleans, Mobile, and St. Louis. Smith's entertaining account of his experiences as an actor and manager in the South forms perhaps the most valuable source for studying the theater in this region before 1860.[28] The Creole population established an Opera House and a French-language theater that competed with the English-language theaters. Although Shakespeare's plays were performed relatively more often then than today, the popular taste ran to light comedies, circuses, and farces, and especially to black-face minstrel shows. The founder of minstrel shows in the United States was "Daddy" Thomas D. Rice, a New York theater man. In Louisville, Kentucky, Rice heard an old Negro named Jim Crow, who worked in a livery stable near the theater singing a lively song accompanied by a shuffling dance and step. Rice mimicked the dance and memorized the stanza that formed the chorus of Jim Crow's songs.[29] The name Jim Crow was used long after the Civil War to designate the practice of segregation.

Attending minstrel shows, the theater, and the circus were only a small

[26] [Catherine C. Hopley], *Life in the South from the Commencement of the War, by a Blockaded British Subject* (London, 1863), II, 248.
[27] See J. H. Dormon, Jr., *Theater in the Ante-Bellum South, 1815–1861* (Chapel Hill, 1967).
[28] Sol Smith, *Theatrical Management in the South and West for Thirty Years* (New York, 1868).
[29] Carl Wittke, *Tambo and Bones, a History of the American Minstrel Stage* (Durham, 1930), chap. 1.

part of the Southerner's addiction to pleasure, or the pronounced hedonism of the Southern people as characterized by W. J. Cash, author of *The Mind of the South*. Southerners were not oppressed, as was the hustling Yankee, with the sense of passing of time. A way of life is frequently disclosed by some significant detail of conduct of the people—for instance, A. DePuy Van Buren, a Northern tutor who observed the hospitable planters of the Yazoo Valley of Mississippi in 1858, reported, "The planter takes his time in eating—don't 'bolt it down,' as the Yankees do," and he noted the survival in the South of many traits of old English life.[30]

Travelers from Europe and the North felt that the plantation life developed certain traits in Southerners that differentiated them from Northerners. Henry B. Whipple (later to become Episcopal Bishop of Minnesota) wrote in his travel diary in 1843: "The southerner himself is different from the northerners in many striking particulars. He is more chivalrous, that is to say he has more of the old English feeling common in the days of the feudal system."[31] Some twenty-five years later, another Northerner, John W. DeForest, concurred with Whipple's characterization. An officer in the Union Army who was stationed as a Freedmen's Bureau agent at Greenville, South Carolina immediately after the war, DeForest observed that Southerners exhibited more of the antique virtues than did New Englanders: "they care less for wealth, art, learning and other delicacies: they care more for individual character and honor."[32]

So beguiling was the Southern way of life with its warm climate, semitropical flowers, plentiful domestic servants, and cordiality of the people that most of the Northerners who settled in the South easily adopted Southern ways and Southern attitudes. The census of 1860 revealed that approximately 360,000 Northerners were living in the South; a larger number than the white population of Alabama in 1850 (320,000) or of Mississippi (295,718). A majority of college and university presidents, tutors, and principals of classical academies in the South and a considerable proportion of the professors were Yankees.[33] These transplanted Northerners did not seek to indoctrinate their students by insinuation with antislavery ideas. Most of them were racists like the communities from which they came, and nearly all adapted themselves to the regional mores. Northerners, however, did have a progressive influence on Southern life especially in stimulating the industrialization of the region, for there were many enterprising Northern factors, merchants, and manufacturers living in the South. And some of the prominent orators and political leaders of the South, notably Sergeant Prentiss,

[30] A. DePuy Van Buren, *Jottings of a Year's Sojourn in the South* (Battle Creek, Mich., 1859), 88.

[31] L. B. Shippee (ed.), *Bishop Whipple's Southern Diary, 1843–1844* (Minneapolis, 1937), Dec. 12, 1843.

[32] J. W. DeForest, *A Union Officer in the Reconstruction*, ed. by J. H. Croushire and D. M. Potter (New Haven, 1948), 173, 184.

[33] See Fletcher Green, *The Role of the Yankee in the Old South* (Athens, Ga., 1972).

Colonel Vick of Vicksburg, Mississippi. "A specimen of the noble-looking men grown in the Mississippi valley—six feet four in stature, erect and stately, with the charming courtesy of the old school." (Edward King, *The Great South*, p. 289)

John A. Quitman, Robert J. Walker, and John Slidell, were Yankees. Perhaps the most influential group of Northern settlers in influencing the Southern mind, next to the educators, were the editors and lawyers, who became leaders in their communities.

The Southern way of life (for the aristocracy) was most conspicuously portrayed in domestic architecture and romantic landscape gardening. During the period of the early republic Thomas Jefferson was the dominant influence in architecture. This Virginia aristocrat was a pioneer in introducing into America the Roman revival style of architecture, with its emphasis on the dome, a style admirably suited to the young republic. Jefferson derived his passion for architecture partly from the study of English books on architecture but especially from Palladio, the Italian architect of the Renaissance, whose work on architecture he studied closely. His exquisite taste and skill in architecture were applied in building his home *Monticello,* near Charlottesville, Virginia. Unlike most Southern planters, who located their homes near river banks, Jefferson chose as the site for his residence a high eminence with a magnificent view over the Blue Ridge Mountains and the Fluvanna River below. In 1769 he began the construction of this noble example of domestic architecture, continued building through the Revolutionary War, and did not complete *Monticello* in its final form until forty years later.

This versatile Southerner was the first great American architect, an amateur in the sense that he refused money for his architectural designs, but a professional in competence and skill. In his *Notes on Virginia,* published in 1784, Jefferson preached the doctrine to his fellow Southerners of constructing their homes in a tradition of beauty as well as of utility. He designed or remodeled spacious plantation homes with classic façades for his neighbors and friends in Virginia, *Ash Lawn,* the home of James Monroe, *Farmington,* now the country club of Charlottesville, and *Montpelier,* the residence of Madison. In a period in which there were virtually no professional architects in the South each planter had to design his home or select patterns from architectural books. It is a testimony to the taste and refinement of the Southern gentry that so many of them, John H. Cocke, for example, built such beautiful country homes as *Bremo* in Piedmont Virginia.

Jefferson was prominent in the introduction of neoclassicism into America. While he was minister to France he saw the celebrated Roman building preserved at Nîmes, called Maison Carrée, which he contemplated for hours as a lover looks on his mistress. When he returned to his native Virginia, he brought a design for the capitol at Richmond, copied from the Roman temple at Nîmes, the first use of the classic temple form for an important public building in America (1789). In the planning of the city of Washington and its classic buildings, Jefferson exerted a powerful influence, especially suggesting to Major Pierre L'Enfant the design of placing the Capitol and the president's mansion at opposite ends of a spacious street. He heartily approved of Latrobe's use of tobacco leaves and the ears of Indian corn instead of acanthus leaves for the Corinthian columns in the Capitol's interior.

One of his most distinguished services to Southern architecture was his design of the buildings at the University of Virginia, completed in 1825. He rode almost daily to the site of the University at Charlottesville to superintend the building operations, a round trip of ten miles, and when he was kept at home, he watched the construction with his telescope. The central building was the Rotunda, or Library, with its great Roman dome that dominated a quadrangle of buildings that the eminent authority Fiske Kimball has called the most beautiful ensemble of buildings in America.[34] This group contained the pavilions, or homes, of the professors, the recitation rooms, and the dormitories, forming what Jefferson described as "an academical village." Jefferson wished to present to the students exquisite examples of classic architecture that would influence their later lives in erecting homes and public buildings with good taste. Consequently, the ten pavilions displayed different styles of classical architecture, modeled after Diocletian's baths, the temple of Fortuna Virilis, the theater of Marcellus, and the designs of Palladio. Most of the columns and capitals of the porticoes, Doric, Ionic, and Corinthian, were imported from Italy. In order to conserve brick Jefferson designed the beautiful serpentine walls of the campus, which the students say Jefferson traced while he was drunk.[35]

The type of architecture that ultimately prevailed in the antebellum South was the style of the Greek Revival. This style was based on the design of a Greek temple—the white temple whose rich colors of classical days had been washed during the transit of the centuries. The vogue of the Greek classical style was not confined to the South but prevailed from New England to Louisiana and as far west as Arkansas. The architect most responsible for the development of the Greek revival style in America was Benjamin Latrobe, an Englishman who was appointed architect of the Capitol in Washington in 1803. Latrobe was buried in Southern soil at New Orleans, where shortly before his death in 1821 he had designed the Louisiana Bank.[36] The great popularity of the Greek Revival was influenced partly by the heroic struggle of the Greeks to win their independence from Turkey in the decade of the 1820's. Byron had died as a volunteer in the cause of Greek liberty and had popularized the romantic side of this war. So sympathetic were Southerners to the Greek Revolution that the legislature of South Carolina petitioned Congress to recognize the independence of the little country. Furthermore, the education of gentlemen in America was heavily weighted with the learning of the Greek and Latin classics—a fact that facilitated the growth of the Greek Revival style of architecture.

The adoption of the new mode in building occurred rather late in the South, with the exception of Baltimore on the perimeter of the land of Dixie. Yet in the decade of the 1830's and 1840's it developed great momentum as planters gained wealth from cotton, sugar, and wheat. Men who had been born in a log cabin, such as Andrew Jackson, followed the new style in building imposing mansions fronted by Greek columns. Jackson's home, *The*

---

[34] Fiske Kimball, *American Architecture* (Indianapolis, 1928), 83.
[35] Lewis Mumford, *The South in Architecture* (New York, 1941).
[36] Talbot F. Hamlin, *Benjamin Henry Latrobe* (New York, 1955).

Hermitage, near Nashville, reconstructed in 1835, was built along classic lines. President James K. Polk was buried in a Greek Doric tomb on the grounds of the state house in Nashville, which was likewise built in the classic style of architecture. Also the Polk mansion in Tennessee, called *Rattle and Snap,* built in 1845, was a lofty white residence with a portico supported by ten fluted Corinthian pillars extending two stories high to a pediment.

The houses of the Greek Revival were chiefly constructed of wood, rather than of brick or stone. At times the façade was imposing but the interior was lacking in dignity. The best Southern homes, however, had attractive interiors, with classical marble mantels and beautiful winding staircases. Gay-colored wallpaper succeeded the white paneling of Georgian houses. These homes of the Greek Revival style were not slavish imitations of classic models but contained sensible adaptations to the climate and the way of life of the Southern gentry. They were designed for coolness and spacious living, with a central hallway, through which the breeze could blow, with long windows that were shaded with green shutters, and with high ceilings. Few of these houses had bathrooms, but used toilets detached from the house. The weekly bath on Saturday afternoons was usually taken in a small basin or tin tub. The kitchen, presided over by the black cook, was also frequently detached from the big house, and food was carried to the dining table by barefooted Negro girls. The wide piazzas beneath the Greek porticoes were a distinct improvement on most of the Georgian houses, for they were admirably adapted for pleasant conversation and for hospitality. The appearance of these serene Greek temple façades gave a quiet dignity and an atmosphere of harmonious leisure to the homes of the Southern aristocrats.

The mansions of the Greek Revival style were found especially in the rich and fertile areas of the South. The newer regions of the South, such as the black belt of Alabama and Mississippi, were the sites of large mansions built in the 1830's and 1840's, when this new style had superseded the Georgian houses of the Tidewater.[37] One of the most beautiful of these homes is *Gaineswood,* near Demopolis, Alabama, which had an oval drawing room and a circular balustrade on the roof. In the Natchez district of Mississippi are numerous palatial homes, so large that the modern housewife would shrink from the responsibility of their care. They stand as monuments to the slave aristocracy, in the days before federal income taxes were dreamed of. Every spring are open for public inspection, at a fee, during the so-called Natchez Pilgrimage. In the Kentucky Bluegrass region are found charming one-story classical houses typical of the region, notably *Rose Hill,* a Breckinridge home, and *The Grange,* in Bourbon County, built by a slave trader, Edward Stone, who was killed in 1826 by slaves whom he was transporting "down the river."

One of the most original variations of the Greek Revival style in the South

---

[37] See J. Frazer Smith, *White Pillars; Early Life and Architecture of the Lower Mississippi Valley* (New York, 1941).

is illustrated by the homes of the Charleston aristocrats. These houses faced
a side lawn or garden hidden from inquisitive eyes by high walls. The narrow
end of the house was placed toward the street, and the classic portico, facing
the garden, contained a double-decker piazza. The house gained height by
being placed on an arched basement. The gateways were made of wrought
iron, often in beautiful designs, such as are found before houses in Savannah,
Mobile, and New Orleans. Frequently, in the lower South and along rivers of
Kentucky influenced by intercourse with New Orleans, the Greek classic style
was combined with iron balconies.

Perhaps the most notable Southern architect after Jefferson was Robert
Mills of Charleston. He has been described as "the first native-born American
regularly trained for the profession of architecture." [38] Educated at the College of Charleston, he studied under James Hobart, the Irishman, who lived
in Charleston for a while before he became the architect of the president's
mansion, or the White House. Mills also came under the influence of Thomas
Jefferson, serving as his draftsman for two years, and finally he became a
pupil of Benjamin Latrobe, an innovator of the Greek Revival style in
America. He was chosen the architect for the famous Washington Monu-
ment in Baltimore, a huge Doric column completed in 1829, and he also
designed the great obelisk, 555 feet high, in honor of Washington at the
nation's capital. Mills did some notable work in the classic style in his native
city. His Records Office in Charleston, built in 1826, is one of the first fireproof buildings erected in America. Mills had been greatly shocked by the
fire in Richmond in 1812 that had burned a theater, killing seventy-one
people, including the governor of the state. When he was employed to design
the Monumental Church erected on the site of the theater that had burned,
his attention was drawn to the need of fireproof public buildings. In 1822 he
designed the First Baptist Church of Charleston in the form of a Greek
temple, and later the Jewish Synagogue was built in this style. In 1850 a
beautiful Ionic portico was placed in front of the College of Charleston. Mills
was not only an architect with high ideals, but he was a humanitarian, whose
book, *Statistics of South Carolina* (1826), advocated reforms in the treatment
of criminals, the colonization of slaves, and so on.

Other talented architects of the Greek Revival who worked in the South
were Benjamin Latrobe, William Jay, an Englishman at Savannah, and
Gideon Shryock of Lexington, Kentucky. Jay blended artistically the classic
style with the use of iron balconies. Shryock, the son of a Kentucky builder,
had studied the new style of architecture in Philadelphia. His first important
commission was to build the state capitol at Frankfort, which he designed in
the Greek temple form (1825). Shryock also was the architect of Morrison
Chapel, the principal building of Transylvania University, with its dignified
Doric portico, and the Louisville Bank with its elegant Greek façade. One of
his most beautiful structures was the state capitol of Arkansas, completed in

[38] Talbot F. Hamlin, *Greek Revival Architecture in America* (New York, 1944), 53.

Courthouse at Cheraw, South Carolina. (Courtesy of Library of Congress)

1836. Although this state was dominated by primitive, frontier conditions, its capitol building was modeled after the temple of Minerva in Ionia. All over the South, the shadow of the ancient civilization of Greece rested. In small villages such as Hillsboro, North Carolina, the courthouses were replicas of the exterior of dignified Greek temples; college buildings, such as the group at Washington and Lee University at Lexington, Virginia, Methodist and Baptist churches, banks, spacious plantation homes, such as *Berry Hill* in Virginia, city homes such as *Belo House* in Winston-Salem, state capitols, such as William Strickland's edifice at Nashville, clubs such as Hibernian Hall in Charleston, all were overcome by the regnant taste for classical architecture. Furthermore, the North and the West shared in this enthusiasm, and the victory of the Greek Revival style tended to make the appearance of the sections more alike.

Despite the dominance of the classic vogue, another style of building, the Gothic Revival, attained a minor following in the Old South, Originating in England, this style expressed in architecture the romantic mood that prevailed in the literature of the period. Indeed, the readers of Scott's novels must have found delight in seeing at various places in the South public buildings and private homes constructed in imitation of castles, with stained-glass windows, crenellated walls, and pointed arches, and gables. The old capitols at Baton Rogue and Milledgeville, Georgia, have survived into the twentieth century, reminders of this architectural fad of the antebellum South.

The most prominent Southern architect of the Gothic Revival was John McMurtry, born in 1812, near Lexington, Kentucky. This self-educated architect began his career as a practical builder in the Bluegrass region, where the wealthy planters and successful businessmen of Lexington employed him to construct homes befitting their privileged position in Southern society. McMurtry was taken to England in 1840 by a wealthy resident of Lexington who wished to build a home in the Gothic style. Accordingly, this talented builder had an opportunity to study some of the old castles of England, especially Warwick Castle, and the Tudor manor houses. After his return he constructed during the decades of the 1840's and 1850's some beautiful homes in the Gothic style, especially *Loudoun, Ingelside,* and *Aylesford,* located in and near Lexington.[39] In addition to such adaptations of medieval designs to the American environment, McMurtry also built dwellings in the Greek Revival style, such as the charming *Botherum,* in Lexington. In both styles, the spacious veranda, or porch, contributed much to the art of comfortable living in a warm climate.

It is an error to think that the majority of Southerners, or even of the small planter class, in 1860 dwelt in imposing houses of the Greek Revival style. On the contrary, the typical planter lived in a simple frame house, at times unpainted, without any pretense to architecture. The town and city homes of absentee planters in the cotton belt were often white-pillared mansions with Greek façades so familiar to romance, but their country residences were utilitarian structures, even constructed at times of roughly hewn logs.[40] The houses of the overseers were not much better in many cases than the cabins of the slaves. Moreover, the average yeoman farmer dwelt in a frame cottage or a log cabin, often a double log cabin with a breezeway or "dog run" between the two rooms. The chief reason for the failure of the planters to build attractive and durable homes on the cotton plantations was the air of impermanency about these habitations. Many planters regarded their homes as temporary abiding places until the cream of fertility of the soil had been absorbed and then they would sell out and move farther west to virgin land. Ardent Southern nationalists in the decade of the 1850's protested against the reign of the Greek Revival style and also against the minor Gothic Revival fad, but the antebellum South was in the chrysalis stage of its culture when the Civil War came and was unable to create a genuinely Southern style of architecture or overcome the inertia of imitation.

The Southern way of life included an urban as well as an agricultural style of living. In 1850, when the South contained 32.6 per cent of the nation's free population, it had six of the fifteen largest cities of the country. These cities were located on the periphery of the South on the seacoast and on large rivers—Baltimore, Charleston, Washington, New Orleans, St. Louis, and Louisville. In the decade of the 1830's the cities and towns of the South had an air of decay and dilapidation, but in the decade preceding the Civil

---

[39] Clay Lancaster, *Back Streets and Pine Forests, the Work of John McMurtry* (Lexington, 1956); and Rexford Newcomb, *Architecture in Old Kentucky* (Urbana, 1953).
[40] J. C. Bonner, "Plantation Architecture of the Lower South on the Eve of the Civil War," *Journal of Southern History,* XI (August 1945), 370–388.

The Grand Stairway of *Cooleemee,* near Mockville, North Carolina, characteristic of the homes of the wealthy planters. (Drawing by Margaret Eaton Smithdeal)

War most of them displayed astonishing growth, owing to the prosperity of the Cotton Kingdom and the expansion of steamboat and railroad traffic. Louisville gained in population by 55 per cent, St. Louis by 93 per cent, New Orleans and Savannah by approximately 45 per cent, Memphis by 155 per cent, whereas the population of Mobile, a thriving cotton port, grew from fifteen hundred people in 1820 to thirty thousand in 1850. Solon Robinson described Atlanta in 1851 as "a sort of Jonah's gourd city," which had arisen as a result of railroads. In sad contrast with these flourishing cities, Charleston's population declined and Norfolk stood absolutely stationary during the decade with a population of approximately fourteen thousand, five hundred blacks and whites. Moreover, a number of the Southern cities in 1860 had a larger percentage of foreign-born than most Northern cities, as noted in an earlier chapter.[41]

The Southern cities and towns were different from the Northern ones principally because of the existence of slavery. The stranger could hear the curfew bell at night for the slaves, watch the slave convicts, both men and women, in chain cleaning the streets, observe the miserable huts in which the slaves lived in the alleys and backyards, and sense the apprehension of the citizens over arson by disgruntled slaves and rumors of insurrection. Moreover, the towns were haphazardly laid out, paint for the houses seemed in scant supply (unlike the neat, white New England towns), and sanitation was poor in this era when the germ origin of disease was unknown. Epidemics of Asiatic cholera (introduced in Kentucky in 1833) and yellow fever were devastating, and pest houses for isolating smallpox victims were reminders of this scourge.[42] Open sewers with green scum on them; livery stables with their multitude of flies; privies, despite the use of lime; and polluted wells seriously endangered the health of the citizens. New Orleans had the greatest death rate of any city in the Union. The Southern cities had an array of regulations and inspectors for flour, weights and measures, salt, liquor, markets, and taverns; they had none, however, for meat. By the end of the period the volunteer firemen in some of the large towns had exchanged hand-operated pumps for steam engines and the larger cities had waterworks. The night watchmen were gradually supplemented by day policemen, and the safety of large towns was increased by the introduction of gas lighting for the streets, Baltimore in 1818 being the first American city to light its streets with gaslights. In New Orleans, James H. Caldwell turned from the poorly paid business of theatrical management in 1835 to developing a system for lighting the streets by gas instead of by whale oil lamps, and later made a fortune from establishing gas lighting in Mobile and Cincinnati. A recent scholar has pointed out the similarity of Northern and Southern cities in regard to municipal government; the use of a mayor, who gradually lost

---

[41] See chapter 15, p. 280.

[42] For an expanded discussion of urbanism in the Old South, see Clement Eaton, *The Growth of Southern Civilization, 1790–1860* (New York, 1961), chap. XI, Town Life.

his judicial functions, and a council that represented wards, and in the handling of the various tasks of "urban housekeeping," such as regulating the dogs and hogs on the streets, paving streets, sanitation, and the caring for the poor in almshouses.[43]

In a society composed of diverse elements, is it possible to distinguish "a Southern way of life" or "a Northern way of life?" When one speaks of the Southern way of life, one usually thinks of those aspects of Southern life that were distinctive or different from the North. Actually, the great majority of Southerners lived very much like the subsistence farmers north of the Ohio River and in the Middle Atlantic states. Their style of life has been described in an earlier chapter. But the life of the Southern planter was quite different from that of the upper classes in the North. A fruitful comparison might be made of the Southern aristocrats and the Russian landlords, especially their use of tutors, their attitude toward their dependents, regarding them as children, their old-fashioned libraries of books that they seldom read, their devotion to hunting and fishing and riding horses, their indolence, and the contrasting elements of violence and paternalism in their character.[44] The institution of slavery profoundly affected the character of the Southern master class, encouraging a streak of violence already evident in their frontier background, a cavalier attitude toward observance of the laws, and a different attitude toward manual labor from that of the North. Moreover, slavery contributed greatly to giving the Southern mind a romantic and decidedly conservative cast.

[43] L. P. Curry, "Urbanization and Urbanism in the Old South: A Comparative View," *Journal of Southern History, XL* (February 1974), 43–60.
[44] See especially D. M. Wallace, *Russia* (London, 1877); Roger Dow, "Seichas: A Comparison of Pre-Reform Russia and the Ante-Bellum South," *Russian Review,* VII (1947), 1–5; and Eaton, *The Growth of Southern Civilization, 1790–1860,* 23–24.

Toward a More Diversified Economy

THE SOUTHERN WAY of life had a capitalistic side. Indeed, an eminent historian has called the cotton planters, "cotton capitalists." However that may be, the spirit (or to use a vogue term, the *ethos*) of antebellum Southern society, as Eugene Genovese has pointed out, was not bourgeois in the sense that European and Northern societies were.[1] There were bourgeois elements, of course, represented by the small class of petty village capitalists, the country merchants, the promoters of railroads, the bankers, and the manufacturers.

The activities of one of the petty village capitalists are delineated in the fascinating manuscript diary of Edwin Michael Holt, who kept a store, first on his farm and later in the upland village of Graham, North Carolina.[2] The Holt store in Alamance County was only one of the manifold interests of the proprietor. This embryo capitalist established a cotton factory on Great Alamance Creek, whose hands furnished customers for his store. He was also an enterprising farmer, raising about one thousand, two hundred bushels of wheat and killing and salting about ninety hogs annually. He had a sawmill, a gristmill, and made brick with his slaves, whom he at times hired to construct a railroad. One of his most thriving enterprises was distilling whiskey. During a year in which he was particularly active in attending camp meetings and protracted religious gatherings, Holt made two thousand, eight hundred gallons of whiskey, which he sold for 37 cents a gallon. On December 11, 1846, he jotted down in his diary: "Started wagon to Fayetteville, six barrells of flour, 146 gallons Whiskey, 30# butter."

The country merchant in the South operated on a credit basis. In the fall or spring when he traveled to New York or to New Orleans to buy his fall stock of goods he obtained from the wholesale houses a credit of six months without the payment of interest. His ability to secure credit from the Northern wholesale houses depended on a favorable credit rating, often furnished by local lawyers who collected debts for these Northern firms or by a credit rating agency, such as the famous one operated by Lewis Tappan of New York City, which had agents stationed in the South. In turn, the merchant was compelled to sell goods on credit to his farmer customers, who rarely had cash until they had harvested their crops. A careful student of antebellum

[1] See Eugene D. Genovese, *The Political Economy of Slavery* (New York, 1965) and *The World the Slaveholders Made* (New York, 1969); A. M. Schlesinger, Sr., described the planters as "Cotton Capitalists."
[2] The Holt diary is in the Southern Collection of the University of North Carolina Library.

415

Southern merchants has found that "at least two-thirds to three-fourths of all merchandise purchased by farmers was obtained on credit." [3] For this service the merchant charged his customers a high markup price. He kept a ledger recording the numerous small purchases on credit of each customer. The ledger of William Smith, who owned a store at Smithville, South Carolina, reveals a typical record of few cash purchases; in May, 1841, the ledger showed a total of $455.41 sales, of which only $37 were in cash, and in August of that year only $82.10 were paid in cash out of total sales of $604.27. In the autumn after the crops were sold, the store bills were paid. Some of these debts were also liquidated by the acceptance of produce from the farmers, such as whiskey, country linen, feathers, flaxseed, furs, beeswax, corn, cotton, tobacco, and even knitted socks.[4] The ledgers of stores in the upper South indicate that the people were self-sustaining as far as food was concerned, but ledgers of stores in the lower South, such as those of the Hankinson Store at Yokena, Mississippi, show large importations of barrels of pork, kegs of lard, sacks of corn, and barrels of flour. The ledger of the store of V. E. Martin at Lafayette, Tennessee (1835), shows that it was a rare customer who did not buy wine, whiskey, and brandy, which were frequently sold by the glass; for example, a half pint of whiskey sold for 7 cents.[5] The country merchant often served as postmaster and petty banker, allowing his customers credit on postage and for loans as small as 38 cents.

Some of the exporting and importing merchants of the principal Southern seaports made considerable fortunes from commerce. The most famous of the early nineteenth-century merchants was John McDonogh of New Orleans, a poor Scotch-Irish boy who came from Baltimore to New Orleans in 1800 and gathered an immense fortune in trade and real-estate speculations. Regarded as a miser and eccentric in life, he left his great fortune in 1850 to found schools for poor boys in New Orleans and Baltimore. Judah Touro, the son of a rabbi of Newport, Rhode Island, who humbly began his career in New Orleans by the sale of soap, candles, and codfish, through thrift and shrewdness became a millionaire and devoted his wealth to philanthropies so that when he died the city mourned. The career of John Burnside, a Scotch merchant of New Orleans, illustrates the dominance of the agrarian ideal in the South. After he had made a a huge fortune, he retired from mercantile pursuits, purchased a baronial estate on the Mississippi River, and became the largest sugar planter in the South.

The greatest export port of the South was New Orleans, the "Queen of the Mississippi." Each year at least four thousand flatboats and four hundred and fifty steamboats brought their cargoes to this "agricultural focus." The

---

[3] See Lewis E. Atherton, *The Pioneer Merchant in Mid-America* (Columbia, Miss., 1939) and *The Southern Country Store, 1800–1860* (New York, 1949); also Thomas D. Clark, *Pills, Petticoats, and Plows: The Southern Country Store* (Indianapolis, 1944).

[4] The MS ledger is in the University of Kentucky Library.

[5] MS in the University of Kentucky Library.

Steamboats at the dock in New Orleans. (Edward King, *The Great South*, p. 50)

produce of the Missouri and Ohio valleys—grain, flour, furs and hides, bacon, lead, ore, lumber, whiskey—poured as from a cornucopia into this Southern city. To these products of a cooler climate was added the vast freightage of cotton bales and barrels of sugar from the Gulf region. More than three hundred factors advertised in the *Price-Current,* the trade journal of the city.[6] In 1815 Charleston was the leading cotton export port, with New Orleans close behind, but at the close of the antebellum period the Creole city surpassed Charleston in exports five to one. For nearly a decade beginning in 1834 New Orleans even outranked New York in the value of its exports.[7]

Southern maritime trade was conducted largely around a triangular voyage. The cotton ports shipped their cotton directly to Europe, but the ships returned to New York, bringing imports of European goods. From New York European and Northern manufactures were sent along the coastal route to Southern ports. Another pattern of trade, a right angle, began with the carrying of cotton to New York, where it was exported to Europe. The returning ships then brought imports to the harbor of the great Northern port, and from here manufactured goods were sent to the South and West. The phenomenal rise of the port of New York, according to its most able historian, should be attributed more to Southern trade than to the opening in 1825 of the Erie Canal, which gave an outlet to the wheat, pork, and beef of the Northwest.[8] In 1822 Southern products, rice, cotton, tobacco, and naval stores, made up 55 per cent of the exports of New York port, and as late as 1860 cotton ranked "an easy first in New York's exports." This indirect routing of exports and imports through New York was uneconomic, illogical, and a great indictment of Southern business initiative. The commercial passivity of the antebellum South contrasts with the bourgeois trading enterprise of its colonial period.

The trade of the Southern ports had the disadvantage of being highly seasonal. Cotton was shipped to the port of Liverpool or to New York and Boston beginning in the early fall, with exports subsiding sharply in the spring and summer. The most important reason for this phenomenon was that the Southern planter was not in strong enough financial condition so that he could market his crop in a steady year-round distribution. He was frequently in debt to his factor and had to sell his crop as soon as it was gathered. The result was that the Southern farmers and planters disposed of their crops in a mass movement instead of gradually feeding them into the market. Since they lacked the capital to retard the marketing of their crops, they suffered from the glut of staples in the market, cotton especially, which reduced the prices that they received. Such a seasonal rush to the market also had an adverse effect on the steady development of Southern railroads.

[6] Wendell H. Stephenson, "Ante-Bellum New Orleans As an Agricultural Focus," *Agricultural History* (October 1941).

[7] For a vivid eye-witness description of the shipping at the levee, see L. B. Shippee (ed.), *Bishop Whipple's Southern Diary, 1843–1844* (Minneapolis, 1937); and Harold Sinclair, *The Port of New Orleans* (Garden City, N.Y., 1942).

[8] Robert G. Albion, *The Rise of the Port of New York* (New York, 1939), chap. 4.

Furthermore, there was a great imbalance between exports and imports of the Southern ports. To take an extreme example, Mobile exported $18 million worth of produce in 1851, but imported only $413,000 worth.[9] The ships that carried the cotton bales to Europe did not bring back European imports to Southern harbors, but rather to Northern ports. In 1850 New York imported more than twice as much as she exported (a considerable proportion of these exports being Southern), whereas New Orleans exported nearly four times as much as she imported. In Charleston some of the old streets are paved with cobblestones brought back in ballast by empty or semiempty ships—melancholy reminders that vessels from Southern ports failed to bring back rich cargoes from Europe as in colonial days.

According to the old mercantilistic theory, the Southern ports should have grown rich on this highly favorable balance of trade. Actually, the reverse was true; the Southerners claimed that the North got 40 cents out of every dollar obtained from the sale of cotton. Annually Southern merchants flocked to New York to buy the year's supply of manufactured goods, paying a high middleman's profit to the New York merchant or importer. The Northern businessmen received the profits of insuring cargoes, drayage, broker's fees, freight charges, and high rates of interest. The great Northern city had its agents in all the cotton ports. In 1850 approximately 10 per cent of the white population of Mobile were New York–New Englanders. Indeed, Southerners allowed commercial opportunities to go by default while they used their capital to buy more slaves and more land to produce more cotton, thus reducing the price of their staple by overproduction. One of the important reasons why New York absorbed so much of Southern trade and profits was that the merchants of the great metropolis gave Southern customers long terms of credit (often at a high rate of interest).

Constantly in need of credit to finance themselves until the crops were sold or to buy more slaves and land, Southerners tended to think of banks primarily as institutions to manufacture paper money rather than to serve as depositories of accumulated capital. The hard times in the South and West following the Panic of 1819 stimulated popular pressure for the creation of state banks. When Kentucky yielded to the cries of the debtors for the panacea of cheap money, a dramatic legal battle resulted. In 1820 the legislature chartered the Bank of the Commonwealth of Kentucky, which issued a large supply of banknotes based on public credit without providing an adequate cash reserve for their redemption. These notes, authorized as legal tender for the payment of public dues, were loaned to debtors in amounts not exceeding $2,000 to pay "just debts." Within a short while this cheap paper money declined to half its face value. Moreover, the state supreme court in 1823 declared the stay laws passed by the radical legislature unconstitutional, as impairing the obligation of a contract. Thereupon, the debtor group in the legislature abolished the court of appeals and reorganized the judicial system, setting up a "New Court." The "Old Court," however, refused to abdicate,

[9] Charles D. Summersell, *Mobile, History of a Seaport Town* (University, Ala., 1949).

and for two years two supreme courts functioned within the Bluegrass State. Finally, the "Old Court" party triumphed, and in 1826 the legislature repealed those laws destroying the independence of the judiciary.[10]

The heyday of state banks in the South and West came during the speculative period prior to the Panic of 1837. Jackson's Specie Circular precipitated the panic, which had been brewing for several years. The South, however, did not feel the full impact of the depression until 1839, when the price of cotton dropped disastrously. Then followed a wave of bank failures; internal improvements were left half-finished; and thousands of farmers and planters abandoned their lands and moved farther west, especially to Texas. The price of cotton continued to decline until it reached bottom in January, 1844, selling for 4.7 cents per pound at New Orleans, the lowest price in antebellum history. One of the most lamentable results of this depression was that it led some of the states to refuse to pay their debts. In 1842 Mississippi repudiated $5 million in bonds that had been invested in the bankrupt state bank, and in the same year the territory of Florida followed Mississippi's example.[11] The financial debacle had some good results, nevertheless, especially in producing a movement for banking reforms. Louisiana, for example, established its Specie Reserve System, which required state banks to keep one third of their capital as a specie reserve and limited loans on deposit to ninety days. The Louisiana banking reforms set an example to other Southern states and had considerable influence in the formulation of the National Bank System during the Civil War.[12]

Not only was the economic life of the Old South handicapped by lack of operating capital but the South Atlantic states were also especially retarded until 1850 by the difficulty and slowness of transportation. Joel R. Poinsett, the South Carolina statesman, analyzed the economic ills of his state as, not primarily the result of the exhaustion of its soils or the exploitation of the tariff, but rather the consequence of the lack of adequate transportation facilities. "Any one who has seen our produce making its way through Fairfield or Newberry," he wrote, "the wagons plunging up to the hub in these sloughs of despond, so frequently on those roads obliged to wait upon each other in order to double their teams in the most difficult passes, and toil heavily and slowly along for days together will understand why the produce of the valleys watered by the Mississippi and the tributaries prove so much more valuable to the farmer." [13]

For the vast Mississippi Valley area a new era of transportation had been

---

[10] See A. M. Stickles, *The Critical Court Struggle in Kentucky, 1819–1829* (Bloomington, Ind., 1929).

[11] See Charles S. Sydnor, *The Development of Southern Sectionalism, 1819–1848* (Baton Rouge, 1948); and Thomas P. Govan, "The Banking and Credit System in Georgia, 1810–1860," *Journal of Southern History*, IV (May 1938), 164–184.

[12] See Bray Hammond, *Banks and Politics in America from the Revolution to the Civil War* (Princeton, 1957).

[13] Joel R. Poinsett Papers, vol. 20, p. 7. MSS in Library of Congress.

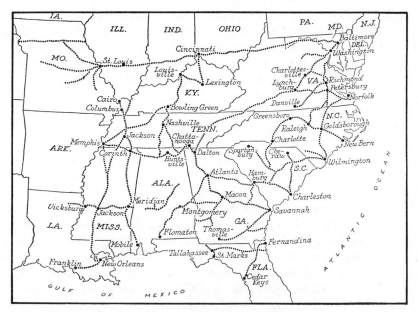

Southern Railroads, 1861

inaugurated in January, 1812, when the steamboat *New Orleans,* a side-wheeler, arrived at New Orleans from Pittsburg on a pioneer trip.[14] Following the introduction of the steamboat, the tempo of transportation in the South was also tremendously increased by the introduction of railroads. The first significant railroad in the United States was the Baltimore and Ohio. Charles Carroll, the last living signer of the Declaration of Independence, dug the first spadeful of earth on July 4, 1828, and by 1853 the railroad had reached its destination at Wheeling on the Ohio River. The economic significance of this railroad is illustrated by the rapid growth of Baltimore, which in 1850 was approximately equal in population to New Orleans, but 10 years later had forged far ahead of the "Queen of the Mississippi," attaining a population of 212,418. After an early period of railroad building in the 1830's, during which Charleston built a line of 136 miles, connecting the city with Hamburg on the Savannah River, making it the longest railroad in the world at that time, the Southern states languished in completing railroads. A second phase of railroad building in the South began in the decade 1850–1860 in which the Southern states surpassed the North in the rate of railroad construction.[15] State, county, and city governments played a dominant role in constructing these iron highways, cooperating with private companies by

[14] See Louis Hunter, *Steamboats on the Western Waters* (Cambridge, Mass., 1949).
[15] See R. S. Cotterill, *The Old South* (Glendale, Calif., 1939); G. R. Taylor, *The Transportation Revolution, 1815–1860* (New York, 1951); and R. C. Black III, *The Railroads of the Confederacy* (Chapel Hill, 1932).

issuing bonds. Cities and counties made large subscriptions to the stock of the companies on the condition that the railroad tracks should pass through them. The most unique of the Southern railroads was the Western and Atlantic, 138 miles in length, between Atlanta and Rossville on the Tennessee River opposite Chattanooga, which was built, owned, and successfully operated by the state of Georgia.[16]

The letter books of John McRae, engineer of the South Carolina Railroad, give intimate glimpses into the peculiar problems of building Southern railroads. Slaves were hired from the adjoining planters to grade the roadbed, their masters being paid $10 to $12 a month for the use of each slave. Malaria seriously hampered construction in the swampy lowlands during the spring and summer. Stockholders were slow in paying installments on their stock, and McRae had trouble in securing rights of way. After its construction McRae wrote in March, 1847, that the South Carolina Railroad was doing an immense business in freight so that the Charleston depot had to be closed for seven days and ten new locomotives had been ordered. In the summer of that year McRae wrote that the citizens of the state had railroad mania, "the people of the up-country and Columbia are in a perfect fever on the Subject of Railroads." But local jealousies interfered with rational planning of railroads. For example, the South Carolina Railroad was not permitted to locate its depot at the Charleston wharves, because of a variety of local interests, including "the fraternity of black barbers," wrote McRae with scorn because they feared that they would be deprived of the opportunity of shaving the passengers as they passed from the cars to the ocean ships.[17]

The remarkable rate of growth of Southern railroads in the last decade of the antebellum period stimulated the development of manufacturing below the Mason-Dixon line, but the greatest spur to the growth of manufacturing was the depression in the cotton economy of the late 1830's and through the 1840's. Manufacturing in the Southern states did not originate in the postwar "New South," when Henry W. Grady and his fellow editors publicized the expansion of cotton mills. Rather, the South had made important progress in industry prior to 1860, which was interrupted by the Civil War and resumed in the decade of the 1880's.[18] The movement of industrialization below the Mason-Dixon line was promoted to some degree by the War of 1812, but was stimulated to a much greater extent by the depression of agricultural staples in the period of 1839–1850.[19]

[16] See U. B. Phillips, *A History of Transportation in the Eastern Cotton Belt to 1860* (New York, 1908), and M. S. Heath, *Constructive Liberalism: The Role of the State in Economic Development in Georgia to 1860* (Cambridge, Mass., 1954).

[17] Letter Books of John McRae, Entries of March 25, June 5, 1847; December 1, 1846, Wisconsin Historical Society Library. There are eighteen MS books, 1845–1864.

[18] Robert S. Cotterill, "The Old South to the New," in George Tindall (ed.), *The Pursuit of Southern History: Presidential Addresses of the Southern Historical Association* (Baton Rouge, 1964).

[19] Herbert Collins, "The Southern Industrial Gospel before 1860," *Journal of Southern History,* XII (August 1946), 386–402.

The progress of manufactures below the Mason-Dixon line was impeded by a number of psychological and physical handicaps. The agrarian ideal caused many Southerners of the antebellum period to hold prejudices against trade and manufacturing and to regard planting and politics as more honorable occupations. Southern capital was largely monopolized in buying more land and slaves. The accumulation of capital needed to start manufactures was retarded also by the indirect method of selling the Southern agricultural staples, which enabled Northern businessmen to exploit the South and which contributed largely to perpetuating the colonial status of that region. Lesser reasons for the industrial lag of the South were the avoidance of this region by European immigrant laborers, the aversion of yeoman farmers to give up the independence of the farm and become "mill hands," the belief that Negroes were not suited to the handling of machinery, and the argument that the rise of manufactures would weaken the slave system and the opposition in the South to the protective tariff. Consequently, in 1860 those states that formed the Confederacy produced slightly less than 10 per cent of the manufactures of the United States (measured in terms of value).

The development of cotton mills in the antebellum South was socially more significant than the rise of any other industry, for it pointed the way to utilizing the labor of the poor whites in factories. The Southern states enjoyed at least three advtantages in the early development of mills. They had excellent waterpower along the fall line, they could procure cheap white labor, and they could obtain clean, freshly picked cotton, undamaged by shipping and exposure.

The most influential promoter of the textile industry of the antebellum South was William Gregg of South Carolina. Trained as a watchmaker and silversmith, Gregg became a successful jeweler in Charleston and Columbia thus obtaining the capital that he later invested in the cotton mill industry. His interest in this industry had been attracted when as a boy he had been associated with his uncle in an unsuccessful venture in cotton manufacturing in Georgia.[20] As early as 1836 he acquired an interest in the Vaucluse Cotton Mill in South Carolina. His revolutionary role in the development of Southern cotton mills began, however, in 1844 as a result of a tour of New England he made to observe the operation of the textile industry in that region. Upon his return, he wrote ten articles for the Charleston *Courier,* entitled "Essays on Domestic Industry," which were published in pamphlet form in 1845. In these essays he preached the new gospel of developing manufactures in the South by utilizing the great reservoir of poor white labor that had hitherto been largely neglected. He advocated confining slave labor to agriculture and to the reclamation of swamps. By bringing the poor whites into the factories, he maintained, not only would their labor be profitably employed but their moral and social condition would be thereby improved.

[20] Thomas P. Martin, "The Advent of William Gregg and the Graniteville Company," *Journal of Southern History,* XI (August 1946), 389–402.

The Southern mills, he thought, should at first confine their efforts to the production of the coarser cotton goods and should import experienced Northern men to aid in starting the factories. He pointed out that by building cotton mills, the South could prevent the emigration of its sons to the West. Furthermore, he did not demand tariff protection for these infant industries, primarily because they specialized in making yarn and the cheaper grades of cloth, which needed protection from New England rather than from foreign nations.

Gregg determined to build a model cotton factory to demonstrate the value of his ideas. In 1846 he constructed a remarkable textile mill at Graniteville, South Carolina, not far from Augusta, Georgia (opened in 1848). It was constructed of granite, "airy and commodious," the grounds landscaped and ornamented with shrubbery and flowers. To house the workers he erected eighty-five cottages in the Gothic style, each cottage provided with a large garden. His mill people, he boasted, lived "under parental care," for they were not allowed to solace their arduous labor with alcohol, they were required by their leases to their cottages to send their children to school, and no children "of tender age," that is, under twelve years old, were worked in the factory.[21] Thus Gregg started the first compulsory school system in the South. He was a benevolent despot, who caught truants from his school and punished them personally, but he also gave them picnics and lectures on politeness and thrift. He required that his employees should be moral and sober, and he prohibited such hedonistic practices as dancing in Graniteville. Gregg's paternalistic policy may have been influenced by the Lowell factory in Massachusetts, but it also carried over plantation traditions into industry and the mill village. Graniteville must have been a very thrifty and sober community, but a dull place in which the sparks of freedom and individuality were smothered.

Graniteville Factory was operated by waterpower. The superintendent and overseers were Northern men, but the labor force was composed of three hundred "piney woods" folk. The operatives were chiefly women and children over twelve years of age, for the older people who came from the hill districts and pine barrens did not have the flexibility to make good mill hands. The employees worked twelve hours a day, the men receiving $4 to $5 and the women $3 to $4 per week. The mill cottages rented from $16 to $25 a year. These wages were very low, but they compared favorably with agricultural wages in the South. It was an era when respectable, churchgoing factory owners both in the North and the South exploited human labor without recognizing any injustice in making large profits and giving their employees a pitiful share of the returns of their labor.

Although there were failures, the well-managed textile mills in the South during the decade of the 1850's paid good dividends. The Graniteville Mill

[21] See Broadus Mitchell, *William Gregg, Factory Master of the Old South* (Chapel Hill, 1928).

in its early years paid a 7 per cent dividend and later as much as 18 per cent. Gregg pointed out that the Southern mills had the advantages over their Northern rivals in securing labor 20 per cent cheaper and cotton at 1½ cents a pound cheaper, and the superiority of bright, freshly picked cotton over shipped cotton. The Southern mills, with few exceptions, manufactured the cheaper grades of cloth, osnaburgs, "nigger cloth," sheeting, and yarn, and their market remained largely below the Mason-Dixon line.[22]

Edwin Michael Holt's mill on the Great Alamance Creek in Piedmont, North Carolina, founded in 1837, might be taken as typical of the small Southern cotton mill. In 1849, it was running twelve looms making sheeting "as good as you ever saw," and selling its goods as fast as they could be made, but the following year the factory was paying very poorly. Indeed, the cotton mill business in the South was often a precarious adventure of capital. A constant menace to the Holt Mill in the summer was low water in the creek, which frequently stopped the mill wheel from operating. In 1853 a French dyer came to Alamance County and was employed by Holt to teach his mill operatives the art of dyeing cloth. Thus the Holt Mill became the pioneer factory south of the Potomac River in introducing colored cotton cloth made by power looms—"the Alamance plaids." By 1861 the Holt Mill had increased from the original start of over five hundred spindles to twelve hundred spindles and ninety-six looms.

The human side of early textile manufacturing in the South is also illustrated by the records of the Holt Mill. The proprietor arrived at the factory early in the morning and left it after the hands had completed their day's work of twelve hours. The proprietor attended strictly to business, eschewing the pursuit of political office, training his sons to be cotton manufacturers with the mottoes, "Stick to business," and, "Put your profits into your business." Since the proprietor was very religious, he stopped the mill at times in order to permit the hands to attend camp meetings and religious revivals. He built tenement houses for them near the factory and sold them goods from his store. At least on one occasion there was a strike resulting from the overseer's "being too tight" with the workers. Very low wages were paid, and the majority of the workers were women and children. Before his death in 1884 this hard-driving capitalist attained the greatest fortune owned by any individual in the state.[23]

The great period in the founding of cotton factories in the South was in the 1840's, when cotton was selling at the lowest price in American history.

[22] One of these exceptions was the Salem, North Carolina, Cotton Mill, established by the Moravians in 1837, which found its best consignee in Philadelphia. Although it failed in 1854, the woolen mill of Francis Fries in Salem, which was in operation by 1840, prospered in manufacturing thirteen varieties of woolen cloth, in carding hatter's wool, and in weaving carpets. Adelaide L. Fries, "One Hundred Years of Textiles in Salem," *North Carolina Historical Review*, XXVII (January 1950), 1–19.

[23] Diary of Edwin Michael Holt, Southern Collection, University of North Carolina Library.

North Carolina affords a good illustration: 32 mills were established in the state during this decade, as compared with only 11 started in the decade of the 1850's.[24] The census statistics on cotton mills in the South in 1860 are highly unreliable, reporting exactly the same number as existed 10 years before—159 in 11 Southern states. Actually, there were many more mills than were recorded by the careless census takers. The largest cotton manufacturing state in the South was Georgia, followed in rank by Virginia, North Carolina, and Alabama. Maryland, which was classified by the census officials with the Middle states, produced considerably more cotton textiles than any of the leading "Southern" states. The expansion of the textile industry in the antebellum South, indeed, should not be overestimated, for the value of cotton goods manufactured by New England in 1860 exceeded the value of the Southern output almost ten times (according to the census), and the single town of Lowell, Massachusetts, had more spindles running than were operating in the whole South. Nevertheless, the Southern states at this time produced one third of the national output of yarn, and Richard Griffin, who has studied the subject more thoroughly than any other scholar, collating various types of evidence, has concluded that the fifteen slave states produced between 20 and 25 per cent of national total of cotton textiles manufactured.

A bad habit that in the America of the nineteenth century was widespread among all classes of society, the chewing of tobacco, created a distinctly Southern industry. President Andrew Jackson injured his frail health by chewing tobacco over a long period of years. The Mormon prophet Joseph Smith received a revelation from God against the use of tobacco by his followers after his wife, Emma, had protested vigorously against the practice of the visiting elders who spit on the cleanly swept floors of their house. Even the most eminent orators, statesmen, and preachers indulged in this minor vice, and there were Southern tobacco-chewers whose prowess in spitting accurately at the targets of distant spittoons resembled the unerring marksmanship of "Wild Bill" Hickok. Cigarettes were not manufactured in the South until after the Civil War, and cigars were made principally in the North. But the habit of chewing tobacco was responsible for the growth of an industry that ranked third in importance among the manufactures of the Old South. Only flour and lumber exceeded in value the finished product of tobacco within the Southern states. The tobacco factories, concentrated in Virginia and North Carolina, were chiefly plug tobacco establishments, 98 per cent of them being devoted to the manufacture of this product and only 2 per cent to the production of pipe tobacco.[25] The manufacture of cigarettes was begun in the South after the Civil War by the Washington Duke family of Durham, North Carolina.

[24] Richard W. Griffin and D. W. Standard, "The Cotton Textile Industry in Ante-Bellum North Carolina," *North Carolina Historical Review*, XXXIV (January 1957), 15–35; (April 1957), 131–164.
[25] See J. C. Robert, *The Story of Tobacco in America* (New York, 1949).

The leading tobacco manufacturer in Richmond during antebellum days was James Thomas, Jr., whose voluminous papers have been acquired by Duke University. This native Virginian was a poor boy who received only a meager education but who had remarkable business ability and industry. He began his tobacco career in 1829 as the agent of the French government in purchasing tobacco in the Virginia markets. Early in the decade of the 1830's he began manufacturing chewing tobacco. By 1850 he had become a large manufacturer whose popular brand, "Wedding Cake," was sold in large orders in England, Germany, Australia and in the distributing centers of New York, Baltimore, and Boston. After the Gold Rush of 1849, he held a virtual monopoly on the trade of chewing tobacco shipped to California. At the close of the antebellum period his factory employed 150 hands and was manufacturing 1,100,000 pounds of chewing tobacco yearly. He was a devout Baptist, who on one occasion entertained sixty preachers during a religious convention in the city. His habit of entertaining Baptist preachers caused the wits of Richmond to call his home "Baptist Hotel." Also he liberally supported the Virginia Baptist Seminary (later named Richmond College).

The growth of the tobacco industry in the upper South was phenomenal. By June, 1860, Virginia and North Carolina factories were producing 61 per cent of all plug, smoking, and snuff tobacco manufactured in the United States. Instead of shipping their raw tobacco abroad, as in former times, these states processed two thirds of the tobacco grown within their boundaries. There had been a steady evolution from small factories to larger units so that in 1860 eighty-five factories, or almost one fourth in the Virginia-Carolina area, eimployed fifty or more hands. Richmond, with its fifty-two factories, was by far the largest tobacco manufacturing city in the United States. The 11 Southern states produced a total of $14,612,442 worth of manufactured tobacco and employed 11,321 male and 2,300 female hands.

The Southern iron industry dates back to early colonial days. Lieutenant Governor Alexander Spotswood in 1716 began mining operations on his huge estate *Germanna,* on the Virginia frontier in the vicinity of the Rapidan River. His labor force at first consisted of Swiss Germans whom he imported, later of seventy Palatine Germans, and finally of Negro slaves. He exported pig iron to England and developed a profitable business of making iron kettles, pots, and pans, which was continued by his family long after his death in 1740. The largest iron mining company in the colonial period was the Principio Company, founded in 1722, which operated four furnaces and two forges in southern Maryland and northern Virginia. Most of the capital was furnished by English partners, but the Washington family and other Southern planters were also interested in this venture. The company owned a huge amount of land as well as a large number of slaves. During the Revolution the English holdings of the company were confiscated and sold by Maryand. In South Carolina the Aera Furnace, located on a creek of the Catawba River, supplied the cannon balls for the defense of Charleston in

1780. In Kentucky the Bourbon Furnace, erected in 1791, made pig iron, which was converted by forges into bar iron for the use of blacksmiths and the making of stoves, flatirons, and cooking utensils for the early settlers of Kentucky. Along the Cumberland River of Tennessee, beginning early in the 1790's, iron furnaces, forges, and bloomeries were developed.

Prior to the founding of Birmingham, Alabama, in 1871, the iron center of the New South, Richmond was the most important iron-manufacturing city below the Mason-Dixon line. Here was located the Belle Isle Iron Works, founded in 1839, which manufactured nails that became famous throughout the land of Dixie. By 1856 this company, its name changed to the Old Dominion Nail Works, was producing over one thousand tons of nails a year. Richmond had the advantage of being located near a coal basin that furnished abundant supplies of cheap bituminous coal. Raw material for the iron-manufacturing industry was obtained from the charcoal-burning furnaces of the Valley of Virginia, which produced a superior grade of iron of great tensile strength. Indeed, the furnaces and forges of the valley had from the early nineteenth century made bar iron for the numerous blacksmith shops of the South.

The greatest iron company of Richmond, and of the South, was the Tredegar Iron Works, which was founded in 1837. The masterful personality behind the success of the Tredegar Works was Joseph Reid Anderson, a graduate of West Point Military Academy, who became sales agent of the company in 1841 and seven years later purchased the business for $125,000. The Tredegar Company secured contracts from the United States government to furnish cannon for the navy. By 1860 the company had sold thirteen hundred cannon to the federal government. The company also manufactured shells, chain cable, rails, and spikes for the expanding railroads, and steam machinery for the Louisiana sugar plantations. The market of this Richmond company was largely in the North, for Southerners were prejudiced against buying homemade iron products. The chief contribution of the company to Southern industrial development was the manufacture of over forty locomotives for Southern railroads. During the Civil War the Tredegar Works played a vital role in Confederate armament, one of the reasons for the stubborn defense of Richmond.[26]

In 1860 the milling of flour and cornmeal still ranked at the top of Southern manufactures. A familiar and picturesque sight on the roads of the upper South was a boy such as the young Henry Clay riding to the gristmill with a sack of wheat or corn to be ground into flour or cornmeal for the subsistence of the family. In the lower South much of the flour consumed was brought from the Northwest down the Mississippi River. Thousands of small gristmills all over the South served local needs, but the tendency was to concen-

---

[26] See Kathleen Bruce, *Virginia Iron Manufacture in the Slave Era* (New York, 1930); and Charles B. Dew, *Ironmaker to the Confederacy: Joseph R. Anderson and the Tredegar Iron Works* (New Haven, 1966).

trate commercial milling in a few urban centers, such as Richmond and Baltimore. At Richmond were located the largest grain mills in the world, a single mill having the capacity of producing one thousand barrels of flour a day. Baltimore was also a great flour-milling city. From these two centers vast quantities of flour were exported to the lower South and to Brazil. According to the Census of 1860, the value of flour and meal produced in the eleven Southern states that later formed the Confederacy, $37,996,470 yearly, was nearly twice as great as the value of the next most important industry of that region, the sawmill or lumber business.

The processing of the forest resources of the South was a highly dispersed industry. Numerous small sawmills were scattered throughout the land of Dixie, operated first by waterpower and then by steam engines, producing over $19.5 million of wood products per year. Yellow pine lumber, live oak timber for ships, cypress shingles, and staves for barrels were cut from the seemingly illimitable virgin forests. Frequently lumbering was a by-product of clearing the land for the purpose of agriculture. The chief export market for the Southern wood products, especially cypress shingles, was the West Indies. The lumber industry in the South employed approximately sixteen thousand persons, the largest labor force engaged in any Southern manufacturing enterprise. The work crews were a mixture of whites, free Negroes, and hired slaves, with no preference as a rule being indicated by employers concerning race, and all workers had virtually the same living conditions.[27] There were also over four thousand persons employed in extracting turpentine from the long-leaf pines of the Carolinas and Georgia—a $7.5 million business. During the 1840's and 1850's an important shift in the naval stores industry took place from producing tar, the principal product of the colonial period, to turpentine. This growth was mainly the result of new uses for turpentine, particularly for illumination in lamps.[28] In 1860 North Carolina still retained its supremacy in the production of turpentine, furnishing 60 per cent of the turpentine produced in the United States.

The taste in the antebellum South for alcoholic beverages had changed since colonial days when the aristocrats had imported wine from Europe and the poorer people had drunk rum brought by New England ships; the hard liquors had supplanted European wines and West India rum. But the conversion of the South to evangelical religion and the rise of the Temperance movement tended to decrease the drinking of alcoholic liquors in this region. In 1860 only $1.75 million worth of whiskey and beer were made in eleven Southern states by 355 establishments. However, Kentucky, incorrectly classified by the Census Bureau with the Western states, had 243 liquor stills

[27] See John A. Eisterhold, "Lumber and Trade in the Lower Mississippi Valley and New Orleans, 1800–1860," *Louisiana History* 71–91 and "Mobile: Lumber Center of the Gulf Coast," *Alabama Review* (April 1973), 83–104; and J. H. Moore, *Andrew Brown and Cypress Lumbering in the Old Southwest* (Baton Rouge, 1967).

[28] See Percival Perry, "The Naval Stores Industry in the Old South, 1790–1868," *Journal of Southern History*, XXXIV (November 1968), 509–526.

and breweries that turned out more liquor than the other 11 Southern states combined.[29] Since these 11 states distilled only 7, 244,414 gallons of whiskey in the national total of 88,002,988, it is reasonable to conclude that Southerners imported much of their whiskey from the North, especially from Cincinnati, the greatest market for whiskey in the the world at that time.

A now forgotten industry that existed in the Old South was the mining of gold. The Federal government derived its entire gold supply for coining money between the years, 1804–1827, from the state of North Carolina. Until the discovery of the precious metal in California in 1848 the Southern states were the chief gold-producing region of the United States. In 1830 Mrs. Anne Royall, the sharp-tongued journalist and rampant feminist, visited the North Carolina gold fields, but she had no good words for the long-tailed, cotton-coated Tar Heels whom she saw poking about like snails in the gold mines using absurd machinery. Over $9 million worth of the glistening metal was extracted from these mines between 1799 and 1860. Gold was also discovered in the foothills of North Georgia on Cherokee lands. A mining rush followed in which at least six thousand gold diggers entered the region. John C. Calhoun owned a gold mine at Dahlonega, Georgia, but it did not make him rich. In 1837 the federal government established a branch mint at Charlotte, North Carolina, and other branches were located at Dahlonega and New Orleans. By 1860 the gold industry of the South had declined so greatly that the mines of that region were producing only about $225,000 worth of bullion annually.[30] But toward the end of the antebellum period the mining of coal exceeded that of gold in importance. Cannel coal, from which coal oil (kerosene) was extracted, was mined in the Charleston area of western Virginia and bituminous coal was mined in the central Virginia counties around Richmond. Numerous companies were chartered, but most of them had a brief existence because of difficult transportation problems.[31]

Throughout the antebellum period the Southern states depended largely upon the North for the manufacture of agricultural implements. Jefferson had invented a scientific moldboard for a plow in 1798, a year after Charles Newbold of New Jersey had made the first iron plow in America. The manufacture of plows, however, was carried on chiefly in the industrial center of Pittsburgh and in Illinois, where John Deere was laying the foundations for

[29] See H. G. Crowgey, *Kentucky Bourbon: The Early Years of Whiskey-Making* (Lexington, Ky., 1971).

[30] F. M. Green, "Gold Mining: A Forgotten Industry of Ante-Bellum North Carolina," *North Carolina Historical Review*, XIV (1937), 1–19; 135–155; E. M. Coulter, *Auraria: The Story of a Georgia Gold-Mining Town* (Athens, Ga., 1956); and Charles E. Rothe, "The Gold Mines of North Carolina," in Eugene Schwaab (ed.), *Travels in the Old South, Selected from Periodicals of the Time*, I, 210, describes the "rocker" process of placer mining.

[31] See Otis K. Rice, "Coal Mining in the Kanawha Valley: A View of Industrialization in the Old South," *Journal of Southern History*, XXXI (November 1965), 393–416.

the largest plow-manufacturing business in the world. A Shenandoah Valley farmer, Cyrus H. McCormick, had patented in 1834 a reaper to harvest wheat, perhaps the most influential invention made by an antebellum Southerner. His invention was not as well suited to the hilly country of the Virginia Valley and the Piedmont as to the level wheat fields of the West, and being a good businessman, he moved to Chicago, near the developing Western wheat belt, where in 1848 he began to manufacture his machines.[32] During the Civil War the McCormick reaper was an important factor in the victory of the North. Obed Hussey also received a patent on a successful reaper, December 31, 1833, but unwisely moved from Cincinnati in the West to Baltimore, where he located his factory. In competition with the McCormick reaper, his business declined so greatly that in 1858 he retired from the contest.

In one branch of manufacture, the making of cotton gins, the South had a monopoly. In 1860 Alabama was the leading state in the Union in the production of cotton gin machinery, and Georgia came second. Daniel Pratt, a native of New Hampshire, was the most successful manufacturer of cotton gins below the Mason-Dixon line. He established a flourishing village at Prattville, Alabama, where in addition to his gin factory he built a cotton mill, a sawmill, and a gristmill. In 1851 he was employing two hundred hands and making annually 600 gins of a superior quality.

The manufacture of hemp in the South was confined largely to Kentucky and Missouri, where the raw material was grown. In 1800 there were four ropewalks in the Bluegrass State, but by 1810 the number had increased to thirty-eight, giving Kentucky the largest number of rope factories in the Union. These establishments were called ropewalks, because in the process of twisting the hemp fibers into ropes the operator, usually a Negro slave, walked to and fro. Instead of manufacturing heavy rope for the navy and for the sailing ships of the merchant marine, which required water-rotted hemp, the Kentucky factories were engaged in making hemp bagging and lighter ropes for the Southern cotton bales, in which the cheaper dew-rotted hemp was used.[33] Kentucky and Missouri had almost a monopoly on this exclusively Southern trade. The papers of John Coleman, a hemp manufacturer near Versailles, Kentucky, show that he hired a number of slave boys to work in his ropewalk, paying approximately $50 a year for the services of a boy. He sent his coils of rope by steamboat down the Kentucky River to a Louisville commission house (or factor), who charged him 5 per cent for selling his product. Also his factor loaned him money at 6 per cent interest and dispatched by return steamboat such articles as bags of coffee, sugar, glassware, and a cask of oysters.

[32] See William T. Hutchinson, *Cyrus Hall McCormick* (New York, 1930–1935), 2 vols.
[33] James F. Hopkins, *A History of the Hemp Industry in Kentucky* (Lexington, Ky., 1951).

In addition to the textile, iron, tobacco, and hemp industries, many small industrial enterprises, such as woodworking shops, cottonseed oil mills, steam compresses, foundries, and brickmaking establishments, arose in the Southern states during the latter part of the antebellum period.[34] Charleston, for example, had a surprising variety of industries, including the making of railroad locomotives, steam engines, and the machinery for steamboats. In 1850 it ranked as the third industrial city of the South, after Richmond, which was first, and New Orleans, second.[35] Despite this modest growth of manufactures that contributed to giving the South greater diversity in its economy, the South remained largely a colonial province to the North and England.

Two thirds of all exports from the United States to Europe consisted of Southern agricultural products, rice, tobacco, sugar, and cotton. Nevertheless, much of the profit from the sale of these staples went into the pockets of Northern businessmen, through the cotton factorage system, the indirect trade with Europe via Northern ports, and the purchase of Northern manufactured goods. Thomas Prentice Kettell, editor of *Hunt's Merchants' Magazine,* attempted to show the various ways in which the South was exploited by the North in a book entitled *Southern Wealth and Northern Profits* (1860). He included in his bill of indictment Federal bounties to fisheries, customs duties, profits of Northern manufacturers on goods sold in the South, profits of importers of European goods, profits of factors, brokers, and commission men, interest charges on money loaned to Southerners, profits on the numerous Southern travelers who patronized Northern resorts, and the money sent northward by Yankee teachers and tutors in the South. He pointed out the folly of agitating the slavery question on the part of the North and thus driving out of the Union Southern customers ["suckers"] who were so profitable to the North.

The protective tariff was regarded by the planters and farmers of the South as one of the means of exploiting their section by the North. This grievance was most irritating in the period 1828–1833. The compromise tariff of 1833, gradually lowering duties, was replaced in 1842 by the Whig tariff, which raised duties. This revival of high protection led to the Bluffton Movement in South Carolina, a second resistance movement, agitated by Robert Barnwell Rhett, but it did not succeed even in South Carolina. In 1846 the Walker tariff began a long period of moderate duties that lasted until the Civil War. Indeed, Southerners controlled the Federal government, so that the tariff of 1857, largely drawn up by Howell Cobb of Georgia, secretary of the treasury, resulted in, as F. W. Taussig observed "as near an approach to free trade as the country has had since 1816." [36] Furthermore, powerful groups in the South, such as the sugar growers of Louisiana, the hemp

[34] A. R. Childs, *Planters and Businessmen, the Guignard Family of South Carolina, 1795–1930* (Columbia, S.C., 1957).

[35] Ernest M. Lander, Jr., "Charleston: Manufacturing Center of the Old South," *Journal of Southern History,* XXXVI (1960), 330–351.

[36] F. W. Taussig, *The Tariff History of the United States* (New York, 1888), 115.

growers of Kentucky and Missouri, and the ironmasters of Virginia and Maryland, were in favor of a protective tariff. The chief injury that the tariff did to the South was to raise the price of manufactured goods purchased from the North. The Southern states did not import foreign goods to the degree that the more urbanized North did. In 1860 the amount of customs duty paid in Southern ports was $7 million, which was only 14 per cent of the total annual duties collected in the United States. The Southern consumers bought principally Northern goods, and competent estimates indicate that the Southern people consumed less than half of their proper proportion of the foreign goods imported into the United States.

In order to liberate themselves from Northern exploitation, the Southerners considered various proposals: the establishment of direct trade with Europe, the development of Southern manufactures, the boycotting of Northern manufactures, the diversification of Southern agriculture, the building of railroads, and the reopening of the African slave trade. How much the growing sentiment of Southern nationalism contributed to the rise of manufactures below the Mason-Dixon line is impossible to measure. In an address entitled "The Industrial Regeneration of the South" (1852) the Honorable J. H. Lumpkin of Georgia urged his section to free itself from dependence on the North by developing its own industries. "Will the South, the chivalrous South, remain longer in a condition of colonial servitude?" he asked.[37] William Gregg, eight years later, appealed to provincial patriotism, especially to the devotion of Southern ladies, to patronize Southern manufactures, but he sadly observed the tendency of Southerners to prefer Northern goods. "Graniteville goods," he wrote, "are more popular in New York and Philadelphia than at home." [38]

The most influential voice in the South to advocate Southern economic nationalism was *De Bow's Review of the Southern and Western States,* founded in 1846. This periodical reflected the interests of the merchants, the planters, and the businessmen of the South. Its editor, James D. B. De Bow, was a South Carolinian, educated at the College of Charleston, who carried the South Carolina doctrines of Southern nationalism to New Orleans. In his magazine he encouraged the development of Southern manufactures, direct trade with Europe, the building of railroads, the patronizing of Southern colleges and health resorts, and the organization of Southern commercial conventions. His *Review* also carried articles on the management and care of slaves, the diversification of crops, and improvements in the cultivation of cotton and sugar. In politics he sought to form an alliance between the South and the West, and after 1858 he acted with the Southern fire-eaters. His magazine became quite prosperous, rivaling *Hunt's Merchants' Magazine* of the North, and it survived both the Civil War and Reconstruction.[39]

[37] *J. D. B. De Bow's Southern and Western Review,* XII (January 1852), 42.
[38] *J. D. B. De Bow's Review,* XXIX (October 1860), 497.
[39] See Otis C. Skipper, *J. D. B. De Bow, Magazinist of the Old South* (Athens, Ga., 1958).

De Bow was quite influential in the deliberations of the Southern Commercial Conventions that were held at intervals between 1837 and 1860 in the leading cities of the South. Such meetings of Southerners from all parts of the land of Dixie were compared by De Bow to the assembly of the Greeks at the ancient Olympic games, because both peoples thus developed a sense of unity and a realization of common aims and grievances. At these meetings many resolution were passed and much oratory was expended, but little was accomplished, except the engendering of ill feeling against the North.

One of the most hopeful proposals made at the Southern Commercial Conventions was to establish a direct trade with Europe.[40] Virginia took the lead in this movement, hoping to restore Norfolk to its pristine glory of colonial days. Governor Henry A. Wise strongly supported this proposal, and in 1856 A. Dudley Mann of Virginia presented a plan of a steam ferry between Norfolk and Milford Haven, England, operated by the construction of four huge steamships of 20,000 tons each, a project estimated to cost $7 million. The Virginia legislature granted a charter to the Atlantic Steam Ferry Company in March, 1858, and a number of prominent leaders of the state subscribed to its stock. Also William Ballard Preston was sent to Europe to advance direct trade with the South. He succeeded in interesting some French businessmen in the project, and the Virginia legislature incorporated in 1858 the Norfolk and St. Nazaire Navigation Company, with a board of directors composed equally of Frenchmen and Southerners. A trial ship, the *Lone Star* was sent out, but the plan failed to mature, partly because the Federal government in 1859 abandoned giving mail subsidies and because of the approach of the Civil War.[41]

Southerners felt keenly their dependence on the North for manufactured goods. It was often asserted that Southerners were rocked in a cradle manufactured in the North, dressed in Northern-made clothes, read Northern books and magazines, used Northern plows and agricultural instruments, sent their children to Northern colleges, and were buried in Northern coffins. Resentment over this economic vassalage to the Yankees was intensified by the rise of the abolition crusade and the attempt to exclude slavery from the territories. After John Brown's Raid in 1859 a strong demand arose to boycott Northern goods. The agitators for Southern nationalism beginning in 1850 proposed commercial nonintercourse with the North. Bills were introduced in state legislatures to levy a tax of 10 per cent on all Northern goods imported into the Southern states. Southern Rights Associations were formed to arouse the people not to patronize Northern resorts such as Saratoga Springs or Newport, not to subscribe to Northern magazines or newspapers, or employ Yankee teachers in Southern schools, or send Southern youth to

[40] See Herbert Wender, *Southern Commercial Conventions, 1837–1859* (Baltimore, 1930).
[41] See Emory Q. Hawk, *Economic History of the South* (New York, 1934).

Northern colleges, or use Northern manufactures. Although the state governments failed to pass drastic laws to carry out such a policy, individuals of extreme Southern feelings did boycott Northern manufactures. The fire-eater Edmund Ruffin wore a suit of Southern manufacture, and Senator Mason of Virginia dramatized Southern nationalism by appearing in a home-spun suit in the national Senate. Lincoln ridiculed such displays by observing that the dignified Senator from Virginia should have come into the Senate barefoot as well as wearing his homespun suit. "If that's the plan," he remarked, "they should begin at the foundation, and adopt the well-known 'Georgia costume' of a shirt collar and a pair of spurs." [42]

In the latter part of the antebellum period the assembly of various planters' conventions represented a promising effort at cooperation to increase Southern prosperity and free the region from its colonial status. In October, 1851, a Cotton Planters Convention at Macon, Georgia, adopted the "Florida Plan" as a means of the planters' controlling the price of their cotton instead of accepting the practice of speculators and manufacturers determining the price. The main idea of the "Florida Plan" was to establish warehouses in which to store cotton and thus to hold the crop from the market when the price was low. Later conventions advocated direct trade with Europe and, notably, the establishment of agricultural colleges. [43]

These various efforts to free the South from its colonial status represent an early form of economic planning. Many of the proposals of the antebellum "regional planners" and of the Southern Commercial Conventions were sound, but they could not be realized by paper resolutions or the facile dreams of orators. The South was rural, conservative, individualistic, and only by a slow process of education or by drastic economic pressures could Southern ways be radically changed. Furthermore, the South was more prosperous in the decade of 1850–1860 than ever before, with cotton selling twice as high as in the preceding decade. If cotton and tobacco had declined disastrously in price at this time, discontent would have aided the reformers and "regional planners." One aspect of the agitation toward economic independence, however, was pernicious—the generation of a bitter anti-Northern feeling in the South. In calling attention to the problems of the South, the Southern Commercial Conventions and the extremists tended to weaken the bonds of the Union.

In addition to their struggle for economic independence, Southerners were also striving for spiritual autonomy that could be attained only by the education of the masses, a progressive press, the development of a native literature, and a Southern-oriented religion—subjects that are considered in the next chapter under the rubric Molding the Southern Mind.

[42] Arthur C. Cole, *The Irrepressible Conflict, 1850–1865* (New York, 1934), 68.
[43] See Weymouth T. Jordan, *Rebels in the Making: Planters' Conventions and Southern Propaganda* (Tuscaloosa, 1958).

Molding the Southern Mind

THE MORES of a society are not fixed and immutable, although they usually change very slowly, especially in a rural society such as existed in the Old South. What causes these changes in the characteristics of a people? Are these changes primarily the result of economic forces, of a religious revival, a shock of a war, or of the powerful and determined personality of an individual, such as that of Mustafa Kemal Atatürk, who revolutionized the mores of the Turkish people during the fifteen years he was president of Turkey after World War I? More recently Chairman Mao with his Chinese version of communism has effected momentous change in the mores and spirit of the People's Republic of China, demonstrating the power of an individual leader to revolutionize a way of life. In the Old South there was no such turnabout, never anything like the rapid change that occurred, for example, in the characteristics of the Israelis after the Six-Day War of 1967. Indeed, the more we learn about the Old South the more it becomes apparent that even the change in the 1830's from apologizing for slavery to justifying it was not so great a shift of sentiment as was formerly thought. Very slowly, dominant forces, notably ineluctable economic pressures, a protracted religious revival, the working out of certain great ideas of the Enlightenment, and the direction that the Romantic movement took, molded the Southern mind into a peculiar cast.

One of the great ideas of the Enlightenment was the education of the people in order for democracy to function. In 1779 Jefferson introduced "A Bill for the More General Diffusion of Knowledge" into the Virginia legislature. He proposed a system of free public school education for all children for three years that would be supported by taxation. The brighter students should be selected to go on to grammar or high schools where they should receive free tuition and board. From the grammar school the most intelligent children should be chosen to be educated at public expense at the College of William and Mary. Thus "the geniuses" were to be raked from the mass of humanity and educated to become leaders of the republic. The essence of this plan was the selection of the natural aristocracy of intellect from all ranks of society and the education of them for the greatest usefulness. A somewhat similar plan for instructing talented children of the poor at public expense and for a gradation of public schools was presented in 1817 to the legislature of North Carolina by the idealist Archibald D. Murphey, called "Father of the Common Schools of North Carolina." Neither proposal, however, was adopted, for both were far ahead of the state of public opinion at the time.[1] Indeed, the free school movement in the South, instead of following the Jeffersonian tradition, was an outgrowth of Jacksonian democracy, of the contagious example of the New England reformers, and of shame over the exposure of illiteracy by the census reports of 1840 and 1850.

More than any section of the country, the South was gravely handicapped in the establishment of free public schools. In contrast to Massachusetts, which had a density of population of 127 inhabitants to the square mile, Southern states such as Virginia and North Carolina had respectively only fourteen and twelve white inhabitants to the square mile. The Southern states also had almost impassable roads during seasons of the least need for the agricultural labor of children. From England there was inherited a tradition that only the upper class or the leaders should be educated. Furthermore, the laissez-faire conception of the role of government prevailed to an exceptionally strong degree in the South, a belief that the state should not assume a function that was regarded as a private duty. The Southern people paid amazingly light taxes, and the planters did not wish to bear the burden of educating the children of the poor. Moreover, many of the farmers had no appreciation of "book larning" and did not demand free schools for their children, whose labor they needed on the farms except during the three winter months. Indeed, the very poor class of whites displayed an apathy toward education and often neglected to send their children to schools when the opportunity for free education existed. One reason for such indifference was the charity feature of most of the free school systems in the South. Consequently, their pride rebelled at the requirement of making a declaration of poverty before their children could receive free schooling. Another important obstacle was the prevalence among them of such enervating diseases as malaria and hookworm.

During the last three decades of the antebellum period the Southern people slowly began to respond to the public school movement that was agitating the rest of the nation. The Federal censuses of 1840 and 1850 of illiteracy in the South was a stimulus to improve the shocking situation. In 1850, according to J. D. B. DeBow, superintendent of the federal census, the Southern states had an illiteracy rate among the native white population of over 20 per cent, as compared to a rate of 3 per cent in the Middle States, and 0.42 per cent in the New England states. In some parts of the land of Dixie, fully one third of the white population was illiterate, unable to read the Bible and signed their names with a cross mark.[2]

Those regions containing few slaves and that were inhabited predominantly by the yeomen advocated public education, but the Tidewater and black belt districts, the location of slave plantations, opposed such reform

---

[1] Charles L. Coon (ed.), *The Beginnings of Public Education in North Carolina, A Documentary History* (Raleigh, 1908), 3 vols.

[2] J. D. B. DeBow (Supt.), *Compendium of the Seven Census* (Washington, 1854), 153.

because they would have to bear the heaviest burdens of school taxation. During the decade of the 1840's, western Virginia found an effective spokesman for free schools in President Henry Ruffner of Washington College who drafted a memorial to the legislature on the subject. The Southern educational campaign was led by some men who had risen from the plain people, such as Andrew Johnson of Tennessee, who had been taught to write by his wife, Christopher Memminger of South Carolina, and Governor Joseph E. Brown of Georgia. Other agitators for free schools, however, were enlightened members of the planter class, notably Governor Henry A. Wise of Virginia, Robert J. Breckinridge of Kentucky, Governor Robert F. W. Allston of South Carolina, and William L. Yancey of Alabama.

The only Southern states that made notable progress in founding free public schools prior to the Civil War were in the upper South—Kentucky and North Carolina. Louisiana had a very progressive system of public schools on paper, but the laws were not carried out.[3] In Kentucky the legislature appropriated over half of the surplus revenue received from the federal government in 1837 as a fund for free schools. At that time approximately one half of the children of school age in the state had never been to school, and one third of the adults could not read and write. In the agricultural depression of the 1840's an effort was made to repudiate the state debt to the school fund, but the fund was saved as the result of a vigorous fight led by the Reverend Robert J. Breckinridge. In 1847 Breckinridge was chosen state superintendent of common schools despite his ardent antislavery views. This member of the Bluegrass aristocracy waged a campaign that led to the adoption by the legislature of a 2-cent tax upon all property in the state for the free common schools, the beginning of state taxation for schools in Kentucky.[4] The Bluegrass State was more progressive then than after 1865.

The leadership of North Carolina among the Southern states in popular education was attained partly as a result of the more democratic society of that state and partly as a result of the agitation of two remarkable men, Joseph Caldwell, first president of the University of North Carolina, and Calvin H. Wiley. Caldwell, a graduate of Princeton, published in 1832 eleven able letters to the people of the state urging popular education. Wiley, born in the Piedmont region of the state, was a Whig lawyer, editor, and member of the legislature. Before Wiley began his crusade for free public schools, North Carolina had adopted a law in 1839 permitting counties to raise taxes for schools. But there was little centralized control of the public school system by the state, a common defect of the educational systems of other Southern states. Studying the reforms of the New England educational leaders, Wiley began a strenuous educational campaign in his native state. In 1852

---

[3] C. W. Dabney, *Universal Education in the South* (Chapel Hill, 1936), 2 vols.
[4] See Frank L. McVey, *The Gates Open Slowly: A History of Education in Kentucky* (Lexington, 1949), chaps. 4 and 5.

the office of State Superintendent of Schools was created, and Wiley was appointed to this position, serving from January 1, 1853, to 1866. He accomplished such a revolution that North Carolina had the best system of public instruction in the Southern states prior to the Civil War. In this most advanced educationally of Southern states in 1860, there were one hundred and fifty thousand children enrolled in more than three thousand schools out of a scholastic population of two hundred and twenty-one thousand. The school term, however, was only four months, and teachers reecived an average of $28 a month.[5]

The Civil War shattered the promising beginnings of free schools in the Southern states. In North Carolina the free schools remained open during that conflict, and the Literary Fund, which had been increased to nearly $2 million, was not diverted to war purposes. After the catastrophe of war the Southern states had to start public school systems anew, with impoverished resources and the great burden of a biracial system. Despite its failure to educate the masses, the antebellum South was not as backward as the mother country of England in realizing the public obligation to educate all the children, for England did not establish a free school system until after the passage of the Forster Education Act of 1870.

In the schools of the South and of the expanding West the two principal textbooks that were used for several generations were Noah Webster's blueback spelling book and McGuffey's *Eclectic Readers*. William H. McGuffey, the author of the celebrated readers, was teaching at Miami University in Ohio when he published his first reader at Cincinnati in 1836. From 1845 until his death in 1873 he was a professor in the University of Virginia. His readers contained selections of literature, oratory, and poetry designed to inculcate morality, patriotism, and devotion to orthodox religion. They also emphasized the cultivation of the virtues Franklin had extolled—thrift, industry, and obedience. They were written for a generation that placed a high value on oratory, and consequently they inspired young boys to become orators. Furthermore, they were illustrated with sentimental pictures, particularly those showing affectionate and humane feelings of children toward animals. The McGuffey *Readers* have been regarded by some authorities as next to the Bible in molding the mind of the plain people of the South and West who had access to few other books.

In the 1840's and 1850's a campaign arose in the South to expurgate the schoolbooks used in that region, which were written mainly by Northerners.[6] An article in *De Bow's Review* (September 1852) pointed out the sectional bias of these Northern textbooks, such as geographies that "devote two pages to Connecticut onions and broom corn and ten lines to Louisiana and sugar." Regarded as particularly dangerous to the minds of Southern youth were the

[5] See Edgar W. Knight, *Public Education in the South* (Boston, 1922).
[6] John Ezell, "A Southern Education for Southrons," *Journal of Southern History*, XVII (August 1951), 303–327.

antislavery sentiments and innuendoes found in such books as *Peter Parley's* histories, Wayland's *Moral Science* (a college text), Gilbert's *Atlas,* and Whelpley's *Compend of History.* The need for textbooks with a Southern point of view was expressed by a writer in *De Bow's Review* as follows: "We believe that southern life, habits, thought and aims are so essentially different from those of the north that here a different character of books, tuition and training is absolutely required." [7] Southern Commercial Conventions urged the necessity of employing Southern men rather than Yankees in the schools, using textbooks written and published in the South, and boycotting all Northern colleges and preparatory schools. The largest textbook publishing and distributing house in the South, Morton and Griswold, of Louisville, Kentucky, employed a writer to adapt the famous *Peter Parley* readers, written by a Connecticut Yankee, for the Southern trade.[8]

The upper class in the South enjoyed reasonably good advantages for giving their children an education. The tutorial system, which had played such an important role among the colonial aristocracy, declined very greatly in the antebellum period, and planters seldom sent their sons to England to be educated, as they had frequently done before the Revolution. Instead of these methods, the chief educational institutions for the upper class became the "old field schools" and the academies. In 1850 the South led the nation in the support of academies, possessing two thousand seven hundred, as compared to two thousand one hundred in the Middle States and one thousand in New England. Such schools emphasized training in the Greek and Latin classics. Many of the masters of Southern academies were Yankees, but some of the most effective of these nurseries of Southern leaders, such as Zion-Parnassus in Rowan County, North Carolina, David Caldwell's "log cabin college" near Greensboro, North Carolina, and Moses Waddel's academy at Willington in South Carolina were taught by Southern ministers. The type of training given in the best of the academies is richly revealed in the manuscript diary of Moses Waddel, 1821–1833, a dynamic schoolmaster, who not only taught throughout the week but preached on Sundays, in addition to supervising his cotton plantation (sometimes picking cotton with his slaves). His academy was conducted with the severity of the ancient Spartans; indiscriminately he flogged the schoolboys and the slaves who did not do their duty. The principal subjects that he taught his students were Latin, Greek, mathematics, religion, and public speaking.[9]

The Southern states concentrated their educational efforts on developing the culture of the upper classes. Consequently, the antebellum South had a larger proportion of college-trained men than any other section of the country. Since the term *college* was loosely used, some of these college graduates

[7] *De Bow's Review,* XIII (September 1852), 260, 262.
[8] The records and papers of Morton and Griswold are in the University of Kentucky library. Peter Parley was the pen name of Samuel Griswold Goodrich, but this name was not used on the readers published by the firm in the decade of the 1850's, for example, *Goodrich's Sixth School Reader,* edited by Noble Butler (Louisville, 1858).
[9] See Moses Waddel, Diary, 1821–1836, MS in the Library of Congress.

probably received little more than a modern high-school education. North Carolina, under the lead of an aristocrat, William R. Davie, was the first state to establish a state university, which opened its doors to students in 1795. Franklin College (the future University of Georgia) was chartered earlier than the University of North Carolina but did not begin instruction until 1801. Although the College of Charleston was incorporated in 1785, it did not develop into a real college until the first quarter of the nineteenth century, and not until 1837 did the city of Charleston assume control over it and make an annual appropriation for its support.[10] Thus it became the first municipal college in the United States. In 1805 South Carolina College was founded at Columbia by the legislature. Thomas Cooper, irreverently called "Old Coot" by the students because of his massive bald head and short, corpulent body, which reminded them of a "cooter," or a terrapin, became president in 1821 and introduced into the college a bold spirit of rationalism and freethinking.[11]

The University of Virginia, which began to function in 1825, became the most influential and liberal of Southern institutions of higher learning. It has rightly been called "the lengthened shadow of Thomas Jefferson," for he fought a desperate fight to secure funds from the legislature to start it, he designed its buildings and campus, and he supervised its curriculum. He introduced the elective system in the choice of studies, and the students were treated as gentlemen by the adoption of the honor system, which had previously been tried at William and Mary College. They were not compelled to go to chapel or attend religious exercises in this institution founded on the "illimitable freedom of the human mind." Jefferson imported the first faculty largely from England and introduced modern languages and scientific courses into the curriculum. Instead of becoming a democratic institution, the school at Charlottesville was patronized chiefly by the aristocratic element of society. Consequently, strenuous opposition arose among the people, particularly in western Virginia, toward levying taxes for the support of this state university, which was granted only the paltry sum of $15,000 a year by the legislature.[12]

The oldest institution of higher learning west of the Allegheny Mountains was Transylvania University at Lexington, Kentucky, founded only six years after the admission of the state into the Union.[13] When Horace Holley, a

[10] See R. D. W. Connor (ed.), *A Documentary History of the University of North Carolina, 1776–1799* (Chapel Hill, 1953), 2 vols.; Daniel Hollis, *University of South Carolina* (Columbia, 1951–1956), 2 vols.; J. H. Easterby, *History of the College of Charleston* (Charleston, 1935), and E. M. Coulter, *College Life in the Old South* (New York, 1928).

[11] George W. Featherstonhaugh, *Excursion Through the Slave States* (New York, 1844), 155–157.

[12] See Philip A. Bruce, *History of the University of Virginia, 1819–1919* (New York, 1920–1922), 5 vols.

[13] For student life at Transylvania University in the early nineteenth century see Clement Eaton, "A Law Student at Transylvania University, 1810–1812," *Filson Club Quarterly,* July 1957.

Boston clergyman, became president in 1818, he dreamed of making this university in the wilderness an American Oxford. During the decade of the 1820's its medical and law schools, founded in 1799, were flourishing, and Transylvania attained a larger enrollment than Princeton and had only four less students than Harvard. Holley's liberalism, however, caused the Presbyterians to wage a virulent campaign against him and finally in 1819 to found a rival institution, Centre College, in nearby Danville, based on strict Calvinistic doctrine. After Holley was forced to resign, the student body declined from an enrollment of 419 in 1826 to 184 in December, 1827. For a while, Transylvania became practically a municipal college and then fell under Methodist influence after Henry Bascom, a prominent Methodist clergyman, was chosen president. In 1837, a faction of its medical school, led by Dr. Charles Caldwell, abandoned Lexington and started the Louisville Medical Institute, which later developed into the University of Louisville. The failure of Transylvania University to fulfill its early promise as a result of religious quarrels and its lack of support by taxation is one of the tragedies in the development of Kentucky and the Old South.[14]

Following the rise of the cotton kingdom, colleges and universities were founded in the lower South. In Louisiana, where the population was divided between Catholic Creoles and Protestant Anglo-Americans, the state subsidized the College of Orleans in the metropolis, which was dominated by the Catholic Creoles, and the College of Louisiana at Jackson, which was patronized largely by Anglo-Americans. The University of Alabama was established at Tuscaloosa in 1831, and seventeen years later the University of Mississippi was founded at Oxford.[15] Also over twenty-five religious colleges arose in the South during the last four decades of the antebellum period. These colleges originated not only as a result of the luxuriant growth of religious sectarianism but also because some of the universities, such as those of Virginia and North Carolina, were dominated by the aristocratic Episcopalians or Presbyterians.

The martial spirit of the South nourished some excellent military schools, particularly the Virginia Military Institute, founded at Lexington in 1839, and the South Carolina Military Academy (the Citadel), chartered in 1842 by the legislature.[16] In 1860 Louisiana State Seminary, located in the Red River Valley, near Alexandria, was opened for instruction. Supported by state appropriations and by the sale of federal land grants, the seminary was a military and classical school patterned after V.M.I. Its first president was William Tecumseh Sherman, later famous as a Union general. When Louisiana seceded, Sherman resigned, and most of the professors and cadets

[14] W. W. Jennings, *Transylvania, Pioneer University of the West* (New York, 1955).
[15] See E. W. Knight (ed.), *Documentary History of Education in the South before 1860* (Chapel Hill, 1949–1953), 5 vols.; also Richard Hofstadter and Wilson Smith (eds.), *American Higher Education: A Documentary History* (Chicago, 1961), vol. I.
[16] John Hope Franklin, *The Militant South, 1800–1861* (Cambridge, Mass., 1956).

entered the Confederate army. In 1860, after the main building had burned, the Seminary was moved to Baton Rouge, where the following year it was converted into Louisiana State University.[17]

Numerous sons of the planters attended schools and colleges in the North. At Princeton nearly half of the students enrolled in 1850 came from the Southern states. Likewise, at the University of Pennsylvania in 1846 a majority of the students were Southerners, principally medical students. Southern political leaders who were educated at Northern colleges included John C. Calhoun, Judah P. Benjamin, and Governor Joseph E. Brown at Yale, William L. Yancey at Williams, Robert Toombs at Union College, Governor Henry A. Wise of Virginia at Washington College, Pennsylvania, Jabez L. M. Curry, the Alabama statesman, at Harvard, President Madison and James G. Birney, candidate of the Liberty party, at Princeton. These Northern institutions do not seem to have had much influence in nationalizing the Southerners who attended them or in producing antislavery critics. During the decade of the 1850's the growth of Southern nationalism led to a campaign to dissuade Southerners from patronizing Northern colleges or preparatory schools where they might absorb pernicious Yankee doctrines. Nevertheless, from 1840 to 1860 Southern students at Harvard and Princeton continued to increase in number. Only at Yale was there a striking decrease. In 1859, after the John Brown Raid, over two hundred Southern medical students left the University of Pennsylvania and enrolled at the Richmond Medical College. In order to provide a Southern university that would teach pure Southern doctrines, especially in regard to slavery, and to train Episcopal ministers, Bishop Leonidas Polk, assisted by Bishop James H. Otey, both of whom were alumni of the University of North Carolina, founded in 1860 the University of the South at Sewanee, Tennessee.[18]

Supplementing the influence of the schools and the colleges upon the Southern mind was the press, which did much to educate the adults and to stimulate a strong interest in politics. Francis J. Grund, an Austrian who settled in the United States and became a journalist, wrote in 1839: "The Southerners are the only people in the Union who study politics as a science, having both the education and leisure for that purpose. The Southern papers, therefore, are, on an average, much better edited than those of the North; though from their higher standard, and the peculiar composition of Southern society, they have comparatively a small number of readers." [19] In the last decade of the antebellum period, however, the circulation of Southern newspapers more than doubled. One of the strongest of the Southern newspapers, the New Orleans *Picayune* had a circulation at the close of the antebellum period of only five thousand, six hundred subscribers for the weekly edition

[17] See Walter L. Fleming, *Louisiana State University, 1860–1896* (Baton Rouge, 1936).
[18] W. M. Polk, *Leonidas Polk: Bishop and General* (New York, 1893), 2 vols.
[19] Francis J. Grund, *Aristocracy in America*, ed. by G. E. Probst (New York, 1959), 193.

and De Bow's *Review* had only two thousand, five hundred subscribers.[20] The Southern newspapers devoted little attention to local news. Instead, they gave elaborate space to debates in Congress, to foreign news, and to letters on political subjects submitted by anonymous contributors.

The antebellum period was an era of personal journalism. The leading newspapers were dominated by powerful personalities, such as Thomas Ritchie, editor of the Richmond *Enquirer,* "Parson" Brownlow of the Knoxville *Whig,* George D. Prentice, of the Louisville *Journal,* and George W. Kendall of the New Orleans *Picayune,* the last two of whom were Yankees, who made their newspapers political arms of the Democratic and Whig parties, respectively. Jefferson, the libertarian, declared: "Our newspapers, for the most part, present only caricatures of disaffected minds. Indeed, the abuses of the freedom of the press have been carried to a length never before known or borne by any civilized nation." And in his old age at Monticello, Jefferson had become so disillusioned by the abuse of the freedom of the press that he read only one newspaper, the *Richmond Enquirer,* "and in that chiefly the advertisements, for they contain the only truths [?] to be relied on in a newspaper." [21] After Jefferson's death, Southern journalism became so partisan and violent that the cartoon of a Southern editor with a quill in one hand and a dueling pistol in the other was not entirely out of line with reality.[22]

If the schools and the press had a profound but imponderable effect in molding the Southern mind, what can be said of the persuasive force of Southern oratory? [23] From the beginning of their schooling, Southern youth were taught that oratory was one of the most important acquisitions of their education, the tool needed to elevate them into politics and leadership and to influence juries. The literary societies in college gave valuable training in this art, and the political campaigns and speeches of lawyers in the county courts presented models. The Southern orators drew their inspirations from the Bible, the classics, Shakespeare, and the farm. Although some of the most noted political leaders of the South, Washington, Jefferson, Madison, and Calhoun were, technically, poor speakers, they were the exceptions, for oratory played an important role in giving a political reputation and influence. One can only be amazed at the sway orators such as Henry Clay, Governor Henry A. Wise of Virginia, and Sergeant Prentiss, an imported

---

[20] Wendell H. Stephenson, "Ante-Bellum New Orleans As an Agricultural Focus," *Agricultural History* (October 1941), 171, 173.

[21] Dumas Malone, *Jefferson the President,* 224–225 and L. W. Levy, *Jefferson and Civil Liberties: The Darker Side* (Cambridge, Mass., 1963), 68.

[22] See Clement Eaton, "The Freedom of the Press in the Upper South," *Mississippi Valley Historical Review,* XVIII (March 1932), 479–499, and F. L. Mott, *American Journalism . . .* (New York, 1941).

[23] See W. W. Braden (ed.), *Oratory in the Old South, 1828–1860* (Baton Rouge, 1970), and D. C. Dickey, *Sergeant S. Prentiss, Whig Orator of the Old South* (Baton Rouge, 1945).

Yankee in Mississippi, had over the poorly educated audiences that they addressed. One reason for such oratorical power was that the South was deeply influenced by the Romantic movement that succeeded the Age of the Enlightenment. Although the classical influence competed with the romantic influence in determining the nature of Southern oratory, the latter easily won the victory. Thomas Hamilton, a British traveler, commented that he heard more Latin quoted in Congress than in the British Parliament, but noted that it was for show and was superficial.

Thomas Jefferson thought that men were more influenced by the printed page than by oratory, but in the Old South with its large number of illiterates and a people not given to reading books and newspapers, we may well doubt this. And the influence of oral speech in shaping Southern opinion was enormously extended by the pronouncements of leading men at informal gatherings at country stores, rural churches, and county courtyards. John William DeForest, agent of the Freedman's Bureau of Greenville, South Carolina, observed: "Every community [of the state] had its great man, or its little great men, around whom his fellow citizens gather when they want information, and to whose monologues they listen with respect akin to humility." [24]

Since Southerners as a whole were not a reading people, one might question whether imaginative literature had any appreciable influence in molding the Southern mind. The answer is, yes, by a process of osmosis, or ideas filtering from the small class of readers down to the majority of the people. The evidence is clear. Although Jefferson, a product of the rationalistic Enlightenment, could not enjoy Sir Walter Scott's high-flown romances, the vast majority of Southern readers were passionately fond of him. Mark Twain's observation that Sir Walter Scott had run the Southern people mad with his medieval romances and contributed to the Civil War was a great exaggeration, but yet it contained some grains of truth.[25] The aristocratic organization of Southern society, with its slaves and manor houses, bore some resemblance to the serfs and chivalry of Sir Walter Scott's novels. Tournaments were actually held in the Southern states, where Southern youths clad as knights on spirited steeds tilted with lances at suspended rings while Southern belles waved them on with fluttering, scented handkerchiefs.[26] Northerners were far too pragmatic to hold tournaments, but even the harsh realities of the Civil War did not stop these romantic spectacles in the South. In her famous diary, Mrs. Chesnut wrote in May, 1864, of her husband's nephew, Johnny, an officer in the Confederate army: "He rode at a tournament in Columbia, and crowned Natalie Heyward queen of love and

[24] John William DeForest, *A Union Officer in the Reconstruction,* ed. by J. H. Croushire and D. M. Potter (New Haven, 1948).

[25] Samuel L. Clemens (Mark Twain), *Life on the Mississippi* (New York, 1903), 308–309.

[26] See R. G. Osterweis, *Romanticism and Nationalism in the Old South* (New Haven, 1949).

beauty." [27] It is ironic, and yet indicates the great vogue of Sir Walter Scott below the Mason-Dixon line, that Frederick Douglass, who did not know the surname of his white father, adopted the name of Scott's hero in *The Lady of the Lake* after he escaped from slavery.

The South has been described by an eminent scholar as a cultural province of the North, at least until 1830.[28] The South imported most of its college presidents, its professors, its books, and its musical instruments from the metropolitan centers north of the Mason-Dixon line. But in the decade of the 1830's, influenced by the danger of the abolition movement and by the tariff controversy, the South became more self-conscious and began to take steps in that direction of cultural independence. Signs of such a development were registered in the appearance in 1832 of J. P. Kennedy's *Swallow Barn*, "the South's first novel of importance," the publication of Edgar Allan Poe's first story in 1833 and William Gilmore Simms's *Guy Rivers* in 1834, and the founding of the *Southern Literary Messenger* at Richmond in the same year.

John Pendleton Kennedy, a Whig lawyer of Baltimore, Maryland, was one of the most significant authors in creating the romantic tradition of the Southern plantation.[29] His *Swallow Barn* gives a mellow picture of the aristocratic society of Virginia about the year 1800, a novel reminiscent of Washington Irving's *Bracebridge Hall*. Kennedy's novel portrays the virtues of the Southern gentry, their openhearted hospitality, their devotion to family tradition, their high sense of honor, and their feeling of paternalism. Although he mildly disapproved of slavery, Kennedy painted a picture of kindly relations between the masters and their black retainers. The romantic vogue in writing novels was also developed by William Alexander Caruthers of Lexington, Virginia, at approximately the same time that Simms began writing his romances. Caruthers, the son of the leading merchant of the Shenandoah Valley, was graduated from the University of Pennsylvania Medical School. He settled as a doctor, first in Lexington, where he advertised that he could cure stammerers, then in New York (1829–1835), and finally in Savannah. He made an important contribution to romanticizing the history of the South by his novels, *The Cavaliers of Virginia* (1835) and *The Knights of the Horseshoe* (1845).[30] Caruther's, however, was a Southern liberal who realized the evils of slavery, especially in injuring the yeomen and poor whites. His most significant novel, *The Kentuckian in New-York* (1834), urged the wisdom of sectional understanding and of good will between the North and the South.

[27] B. A. Williams (ed.), *A Diary from Dixie by Mary Boykin Chesnut* (New York, 1949), 409.

[28] See provocative interpretations by Vernon L. Parrington, *The Romantic Revolution in America 1800–1860* (New York, 1927) and Van Wyck Brooks, *The World of Washington Irving* (New York, 1944).

[29] C. H. Bohner, *John Pendleton, Gentleman from Baltimore* (Baltimore, 1961).

[30] E. C. Davis, *Chronicler of the Cavaliers, a Life of a Virginia Novelist, Dr. William A. Caruthers* (Richmond, 1953).

The most notable novelist of the Old South was William Gilmore Simms. Born in Charleston in 1806, he was the only Southerner who made a good living from the profession of belles lettres in the antebellum period, but not because of the encouragement or patronage of the Southern people. A poor boy in an aristocratic city, he won his way upward from the lowly position of a druggist's apprentice by tremendous energy and ability. After a brief career as a lawyer and a newspaper editor, Simms found his true vocation as a storyteller. His second marriage to the daughter of a Southern planter enabled him to live the privileged life on the plantation of *Woodlands,* with its library of ten thousand volumes. Here and at Charleston he dispensed lavish hospitality and was kind to aspiring young writers. His devotion to the South led him to write apologies for slavery and a history of South Carolina glorifying her past and to take an active part in politics as a champion of secession. Notwithstanding, he never succeeded in obtaining from the aristocracy of his native state the social recognition or the appreciation of his works that he craved. His life had a tragic ending, with the destruction of *Woodlands* during the Civil War, the death of nine of his fourteen children, and the loss of the whole of his fortune.[31]

In 1834 he published his first successful novel, *Guy Rivers,* a romance of the Southern border, and in the following year, *The Yemassee,* portraying South Carolina Indians in a style influenced by both Sir Walter Scott and James Fenimore Cooper. These novels had an immense vogue in the North and in England, but not in the South. Simms was a versatile and amazingly prolific author who would not take the time to rewrite and polish his romances. One of the secrets of the extensive sale of his novels was the strong ingredient of melodrama in them. His finest works, *The Partisan, The Forayers,* and *Woodcraft,* portrayed the Revolutionary War in South Carolina as a social conflict, in which the Tories were recruited largely from the poorer classes who resented aristocratic dominance and pride. Simms loved the South passionately and studied deeply its history. He described the Southern frontier and Southern landscape better than any other literary man of his period.[32] He had an excellent talent for realism, which was exhibited in his description of earthy characters, such as frontiersmen and yeomen. Lieutenant Porgy, lusty gourmand, fighter, and homely philosopher, was one of the best and most vivid portrayals of character in his novels. On the other hand, his delineation of Southern aristocrats, especially highbred ladies, whom he did not know from experience, was highly romantic and theatrical.

---

[31] W. P. Trent, *William Gilmore Simms* (Boston, 1892), is prejudiced and outdated; see the long introduction of C. Hugh Holman to Simms's *Views and Reviews* (Cambridge, 1962); William R. Taylor, *Cavalier and Yankee,* chap. 8; and Clement Eaton, *The Mind of the Old South,* chap. 10, The Romantic Mind.

[32] The best insight into Simms and his literary career is to be found in Mary C. Simms Oliphant et al. (eds.), *The Letters of William Gilmore Simms* (Columbia, S.C., 1954–1956), 5 vols. These editors maintain that Trent in his biography exaggerated the lack of appreciation of Simms by the South Carolinians.

The high point in the composition of romantic literature in the South was attained by the poets Edgar Allan Poe, Thomas Holley Chivers, Henry Timrod, and Paul Hamilton Hayne.[33] The South's most famous literary figure, Edgar Allan Poe, was born in Boston in 1809, but most of the forty years of his life were spent in the South. His mother, an actress, died when he was a child, and he was reared in the home of John Allan, a Richmond merchant. Poe spent a year at the University of Virginia, from which his foster father withdrew him because of his extravagance and gambling debts. He then enlisted in the army and was stationed for a while at Fort Moultrie, Charleston, South Carolina, where he absorbed some of the local color that he portrayed in his short story "The Gold Bug." After a brief term at West Point, from which he was dismissed for neglect of duties, Poe devoted himself to a literary career.[34]

Although his poetry had little patent relation to his early Southern environment, Poe was an ardent Southerner. From 1835 through 1836 he brilliantly edited the South's most distinguished literary magazine, the *Southern Literary Messenger,* founded in Richmond in 1834. As editor he displayed high talents of criticism, refusing to praise weak literary productions because they were written by local talent, and surprisingly, in view of his lugubrious temperament, Poe wrote at times with a hilarious and ironic wit. Not because of his drinking habit or his laziness, for he was a hard worker, but because of his independence of mind, he was dismissed from his editorial job, which paid the munificent salary of $15 a week. A loyal Southerner, Poe resented the conceit of New England writers and their assumption that they had a monopoly on American literature. He injured his literary career by making fun of Longfellow and ridiculing the provincialism of New England, calling Boston the "Frogpond." Poe had the Southern aversion to abolitionists, and he was Southern, too, in his addiction to richness of rhetoric.[35]

Poe was one of the very few Southerners of his period who had a true artist's point of view. He was not concerned with social problems, causes, or politics, but only with sheer beauty. He was obsessed with an interest in the weird, the morbid, and the tragic in life that reflected his melancholy and distraught life, darkened by poverty and an addiction to alcohol. Poe suffered from a complex concerning his dead mother. He believed that the most beautiful thing in the world was a beautiful dead lady, an obsession that colored his highly romantic verse. His poems of love have an ethereal quality, rather than an appeal to sex, such as the unforgettable lines of "To Helen" and the sweet melancholy of "Annabel Lee." Not only was Poe the South's greatest artist in verse but he also became the master technician of the short story in America.

[33] The romantic vogue was especially exhibited by sentimental poems in magazines and newspapers of the period. See B. B. Minor, *The Southern Literary Messenger, 1834–1864* (New York, 1905).
[34] See Arthur H. Quinn, *Edgar Allan Poe: A Critical Biography* (New York, 1942).
[35] Jay B. Hubbell, *The South in American Literature,* 1607–1900 (Durham, 1954), an excellent study, discusses Poe's connection with the South, pp. 528–550.

Almost without exception the Southern poets of this period were highly romantic in writing verse. Among the most romantic was Thomas Holley Chivers of Georgia, who had the inherited wealth to enable him to pursue a literary career. Born in the same year as Poe, Chivers was another lugubrious poet who liked to write about death in in its physical aspects. He received his medical degree in 1830 from Transylvania University, where his manuscript dissertation on the treatment of malaria is preserved, advocating the use of calomel, and ending with an original verse. Chivers' poetry is sensuous— consider his sonnet "To Isa Sleeping Voluptuous As the Summer South at Noon." A long controversy has existed as to whether Chivers plagiarized Poe's works, or if Poe plagiarized the verse of Chivers.[36]

Charleston was the home of the gifted poets Henry Timrod and Paul Hamilton Hayne. Timrod, descended from German stock, lived a poverty-stricken life, supporting himself by serving as a tutor in private families. He wrote some exquisite nature poems, particularly "Spring," which begins:

> Spring with that nameless pathos in the air
> Which dwells with all things fair. . . .

His "Cotton Boll" and "Ethnogenesis" are permeated with a high devotion to the Southern cause. Hayne, a member of the Carolina aristocracy and a graduate of the College of Charleston, abandoned the serious profession of law to cultivate the art of poetry, a calling that doomed him to poverty. He, too, had a sensitive love of nature, expressed in his beautiful "Aspects of the Pines," and a passionate nostalgia for the Old South.

The Civil War interrupted or blighted the careers of three of the most admirable of Southern poets. Henry Timrod volunteered as a soldier in the Confederate army (too poor to buy an officer's uniform) and also served as a war correspondent, injuring his frail body so seriously that he died prematurely in 1867. Paul Hamilton Hayne served as a military aide until he was forced to retire because of illness.[37] Sidney Lanier entered Confederate military service shortly after his graduation from Oglethorpe University and was engaged in blockade-running when he was captured. He was confined in a Northern prison from which he emerged in a terrible emaciated condition, with the germs of consumption, and later died an early death. The Civil War, nevertheless, stimulated the writing of martial poetry, such as "The Sword of Robert Lee" by Father Abram Ryan, a Confederate chaplain, "Little Giffen" by Francis O. Ticknor, and "Maryland, My Maryland!" and "John Pelham" by James R. Randall.

A pleasant relief from the artificial literature of romanticism was furnished by the humorists of the Old South. Unfortunately, they did not act as a

[36] S. Foster Damon, *Thomas Holley Chivers, Friend of Poe* (Durham, 1930); C. H. Watts, *Thomas Holley Chivers, His Literary Career and His Poetry* (Athens, Ga., 1956).

[37] For the last glow of the Southern Romantic movement, see Charles R. Anderson, "Charles Gayarré and Paul Hayne: The Last Literary Cavaliers," in D. K. Jackson (ed.), *American Studies in Honor of William Kenneth Boyd* (Durham, 1944).

solvent of the high-flown romanticism of their section as did Cervantes in Spain, for their work was published chiefly in newspapers and was regarded as trivial and vulgar. The founder of the school of Southern humorists was Augustus Baldwin Longstreet of Augusta, Georgia, descended from New Jersey Dutch stock. He was a versatile man, holding such positions as judge, editor, preacher, college president, and author.[38] Between 1832 and 1835 he wrote humorous sketches describing the mores of the common man of the South, especially on the Georgia frontier, which were first published in his newspaper, the Augusta *State Rights Sentinel,* and later collected in a volume entitled *Georgia Scenes* (1835). A similar vein of humor was exploited by another Georgia editor, William Tappan Thompson (born in Ohio), who wrote *Major Jones's Courtship* and *Major Jones's Chronicles of Pineville,* describing the activities of a naïve Georgia bumpkin.

Much of this semirealistic literature of the Southern frontier was written by newspapermen to entertain their readers or by aristocrats amused by the uncouthness of the cracker. Johnson J. Hooper, a native of North Carolina, who emigrated to Alabama and edited the Montgomery *Journal,* wrote a delightful book entitled *The Adventures of Captain Simon Suggs,* describing the picaresque adventures on the Alabama frontier of a plausible scamp.[39] The captain of a steamboat on Tennessee rivers, George Washington Harris, created some of the most powerful comic stories of the Old South in *Sut Lovingood's Yarns,* "the humor of discomfiture." The humor of the North Carolina back country was culled by Harden Taliaferro in *Fisher's River Scenes and Characters* and by Hamilton C. Jones in such stories as "Cousin Sally Dilliard" and "McAlpin's Trip to Charleston." In the Southwest flourished the tall tale, notably Thomas B. Thorpe's narration, "The Big Bear of Arkansas," and the incredible stores told about David Crockett, about the semimythical character Mike Fink, and the Texan fighter "Big Foot" Wallace.[40] Some of the drollest personalities of the Old South, such as Governor "Zeb" Vance of North Carolina and Judge Dooley of Georgia, remained oral storytellers and wits whose humor has been lost to a great extent.

The literary productions of the Southern humorists are valuable as sources for the social history of the common people, but they must be used with discrimination.[41] They preserve vivid and authentic accounts of camp meetings, horse racing, country weddings, cracker dances, quilting parties, rude fights in which gouging was practised, shooting matches, military drills, gander pullings, snatches of old songs such as "Bingo," and stories about politicians,

[38] John D. Wade, *Augustus Baldwin Longstreet: A Study of the Development of Culture in the South* (New York, 1924).
[39] W. S. Hoole, *Alias Simon Suggs, the Life and Times of Johnson Jones Hooper* (University, Ala., 1952).
[40] An excellent anthology of Southern humor is presented by Franklin G. Meine (ed.), *Tall Tales of the Southwest* (New York, 1937).
[41] Clement Eaton, "The Southern Yeoman: The Humorists' View," in *The Mind of the Old South,* chap. 6.

preachers, practical jokers, horse traders, confidence men, and so on. One of the most valuable works of humor in describing the color and flavor of a vanished period of history is Joseph G. Baldwin's *Flush Times in Alabama and Mississippi* (1853), which portrays the period of speculation in the lower South just before the Panic of 1837. The Negro was seldom used as a subject for comedy by the antebellum humorists, a source of literary material that was unexploited until after the Civil War by such innovators as Irwin Russell and Joel Chandler Harris. Mark Twain, who spent his youth in Hannibal, Missouri, was undoubtedly influenced in his development as a humorous writer by his predecessors, the school of Southern humorists of the antebellum period.[42]

Why did the antebellum South fail (with the exception of some political writings) to produce a significant literature? During the same period New England and the Middle States experienced a flowering of literature and of transcendental philosophy. The answer is complex: the lack of the stimulus of city life, the widespread illiteracy and isolation of the people, a very small reading public that bought books, and the absence of flourishing publishing houses. The main reason lies deeper, however; the Southern planters had a different set of values from the city men of the North or even of villagers such as those of Concord and Salem. The Southern gentry believed that farming was the most delectable occupation in the world when the actual physical exertion and sweaty labor were performed by others, and next to planting they placed politics. One example is the Virginia romantic poet Philip Pendleton Cooke, a man of talent, whose intellectual energies were dissipated, he confessed, by the enticement of the pleasures of out-of-door life, "where I saw more of guns and horses and dogs than of pens and paper. Amongst dinners, barbecues, snipe shooting, riding parties etc. I could not gain my brains into the humour for writing. . . ."[43] The cultivation of letters and fine arts was regarded as a purely ornamental accomplishment rather than worthy of a serious profession. Arts and letters flourish in periods of freedom and innovation, but the antebellum South suppressed not only discussion of slavery but all of the "pernicious isms" that agitated the Northern mind.[44]

More influential than literature or the press or the schools in molding the Southern mind was religion, not as dispensed by theologians or philosophers but by country churches and their evangelical preachers. Particularly after "the Great Revival" of 1800 the Southern people were deeply affected by evangelical Protestantism. This phenomenon should be regarded as an American Crusade to convert the masses to emotional Christianity. Thousands of people in the undeveloped areas of the South had been denied the opportunity to join churches because of the rapid expansion of the frontier across the

[42] See K. S. Lynn, *Mark Twain and Southwestern Humor* (Boston, 1959), who emphasizes the role of Whig writers in creating Southern humor.
[43] J. B. Hubbell, *The South in American Literature, 1607–1900* (Durham, 1954), 506.
[44] Clement Eaton, "The Resistance of the South to Northern Radicalism," *New England Quarterly*, VIII (1935), 215–231.

Appalachian Mountains into Kentucky, Tennessee, and the Ohio Valley. A religious apathy also existed among the older settlements of the Atlantic seaboard partly as a result of the disrupting effect of the American Revolution on the churches and the indifference or skepticism of the upper classes who had been affected by deism.

The revival movement began in Logan County, Kentucky, at the close of the eighteenth century. The outstanding personality in this awakening was a Presbyterian preacher, James McGready, a man "superlatively ugly," with an unearthly voice, and possessing the ability of "running people distracted." The revivals were carried on by a peculiarly American gathering—the camp meeting in the woods. The country people from miles around, after the crops were laid by, came with their families, bringing their provisions with them, and camped in tents or in their covered wagons on the campground for a week of excitement. Thus the tinder was ready for the revival flame that leapt from community to community throughout the South, not subsiding until 1805.

The camp meetings were often scenes of mass hysteria. Preachers in relays would harangue the huge assemblies from their platforms beneath "brush arbors." [45] At Cane Ridge, in Bourbon County, Kentucky, during August, 1801, a crowd estimated at over twenty thousand people attended the greatest of the camp meetings, with eighteen Presbyterian ministers and numerous Methodists and Baptist preachers exhorting. These evangelists concentrated on a technique of frightening people into religion by a description of the horrors of Hell and the torments of damned souls. The more neurotic or sensitive members of the audience became so excited by such preaching and by the deep emotional effect of the camp meeting hymns that they fell into extravagant physical "exercises." Some of them swooned in a trance, and their limbs became stiff and fixed, others "shouted" for mercy, then went into the "dancing exercise." Still others laughed hysterically—"the holy laugh," or grimaced, and some had "the jerks," or babbled in unknown tongues, or barked like a dog, going on all fours. Such fantastic manifestations were condemned by the aloof Episcopalians and the more conservative Presbyterians, but they were welcomed by the evangelists as outpourings of God's spirit. Although revivals and camp meetings occurred in cycles throughout the antebellum period, the violent physical "exercises" were seldom prevalent in the later revivals.[46] One of the most interesting of these later revival movements occurred in the Northern states after the financial catastrophe of the Panic of 1857.

The Great Revival and subsequent revival movements had profound results, both good and bad, on Southern society. Beneath the tumult and excitement of the camp meetings can be discerned the craving of lonely frontier people for human companionship. These religious orgies performed in a

[45] See C. A. Johnson, *The Frontier Camp Meeting* (Dallas, 1955).
[46] See C. C. Cleveland, *The Great Revival in the West, 1797–1807* (Chicago, 1916),

sense the function of the later circus or carnival, bringing excitement and glamor into the lives of isolated farmers and their families, furnishing a much needed social outlet. The camp meetings developed stirring hymns and tunes that affected American music, especially the Negro spirituals. The evangelists influenced Southern oratory in the direction of emotionalism and Biblical illustrations. Some of the camp meetings led to immorality, particularly arising from frequent potations of liquor, and some of the strenuous ministers shattered their nerves by their perfervid exhortations. The Great Revival tended to introduce censorious and ascetic elements into Southern society. The waves of evangelism were an important factor in erasing skepticism from the South and enforcing religious orthodoxy.[47]

On the other hand, the Great Revival led to the rapid expansion of the evangelical churches in the West and South. One admirable result of this religious crusade was a cooperation of Presbyterian, Methodist, and Baptist ministers, a harmony later to be dissolved by the rise of denominational warfare. The Great Revival aided the growth of democracy in the Southern region. The central idea of the revival movements was the democratic concept that an individual was not predestined to Hell or Heaven, as Calvinism taught, but could exercise free will and become "saved." This doctrine fitted well into the frontier psychology of optimism and self-reliance and gave dignity to the humblest human being. The evangelists emphasized the equality of the rich man and the poor man, the fine lady and the frontier woman in her linsey-woolsey dress, in the light of eternity. Also in the church government the common man was given training in the practice of self-government.[48]

In the first quarter of the nineteenth century there were many evidences to indicate that the South was passing through a liberal cycle of its history, marked by a rational attitude toward religion. Among the exponents of religious liberalism of this period were Thomas Jefferson after he had retired from the presidency in 1809, Dr. Thomas Cooper, president of South Carolina College, and Horace Holley, president of Transylvania University. These men, having an optimistic view of human nature, rejected the dogmas of human depravity. They believed that man should use his reasoning faculty fearlessly to investigate the mysteries of religion. Jefferson, for example, advised his grandson to read the Bible with the same detachment and critical faculty that he would adopt in reading Livy or Tacitus. Instead of this attitude resulting in disillusionment and atheism, they believed that the moral law was the natural law of human society. Thus they developed a serenity of mind and a tolerance of variety of opinion that were far different from the complacency of ignorance or a childlike faith in authority. Indeed, the reli-

[47] W. W. Sweet, *Revivalism in America* (New York, 1944); and Clement Eaton, "The Ebb of the Great Revival," *North Carolina Historical Review*, XXIII (January 1946), 1–12.

[48] See J. B. Boles, *The Great Revival, 1787–1805: The Origins of the Southern Evangelical Mind* (Lexington, Ky., 1972), observes that the revival movement began earlier than 1800 and received an impulse from Pennsylvania.

gion of the liberals was ideally suited to form the substratum of a republican type of government.

Religious liberalism in the South received a strong impulse from English exiles who came to America. Of these men, Joseph Priestly, the discoverer of oxygen, was the greatest. Although he did not enter the South but spent the ten years of his life in America within Pennsylvania, he had a remarkable influence on Southern religious liberalism through his writings and his disciples. His book *An History of the Corruptions of Christianity* profoundly influenced Thomas Jefferson, and may have been the decisive factor in the development of Jefferson's serene and rational religious faith. Two followers of Priestly, Harry Toulmin and Dr. Thomas Cooper, both exiles from England, settled in the South. Toulmin became head of Transylvania Academy and later secretary of state of Kentucky, in which position he converted Governor James Garrard to Unitarianism. Thomas Paine was another English exile who attained great prominence in America as a religious radical as well as a political pamphleteer. His *Age of Reason* (1796), attacking orthodox ideas of religion, was widely read in the South. A friend of Jefferson, Paine had shocked conservative Federalists by a bitter letter criticizing President Washington. Undoubtedly the violent attacks made against his religious ideas in the South as well as in the North were partly motivated by rancorous party politics.

Dr. Thomas Cooper had an amazing career of advocating unorthodox ideas in the South. Jefferson tried to secure his appointment to one of the first professorships in the University of Virginia, but he was prevented by the forces of religious intolerance. However, Dr. Cooper became president of South Carolina College from 1821 to 1834, where he stoutly championed freedom of speech and thought. When the discoveries of geology began to disturb some of the orthodox leaders of the churches and colleges, Dr. Cooper fearlessly accepted the findings of science and severely condemned Benjamin Silliman of Yale College, the most eminent teacher of geology in America, for warping natural science to harmonize with the Mosaic account of creation in his college textbook. The book of *Genesis,* Dr. Cooper boldly declared, was a collection of "absurd and frivolous tales," and he warned his readers that it was high time to resist the intermeddling of the clergy and their orthodox adherents with the discoveries of natural science.[49]

At Transylvania University President Horace Holley, a graduate of Yale and a Unitarian minister, exerted a liberal influence in Kentucky for nearly a decade (1818–1827). Holley opposed the doctrine of the depravity of human nature, upheld the Unitarian faith, and sought to overcome the sectarian spirit by preaching a religion of love and catholic tolerance. Furthermore, his genial manner of living, which included card playing and dancing, was a rebuke to the narrow ascetic spirit of evangelical religion.[50] A similar spirit of

[49] Dumas Malone, *The Public Life of Thomas Cooper, 1783–1839* (Columbia, 1961).
[50] Niels H. Sonne, *Liberal Kentucky, 1780–1828* (New York, 1939).

tolerance and of rationalism prevailed in the founding of the University of Virginia, which departed from the practices of colleges both in the North and the South in freeing itself from clerical influence.

One of the evidences of the development of religious liberalism in the South was the growth of the Unitarian church. In 1819 Jared Sparks, the future president of Harvard University and the first editor of Washington's writings, became the pastor of a Unitarian church at Baltimore. Then Unitarianism spread into the cities of the South during the decade of the 1820's and 1830's. The Unitarian church in Charleston developed vigorously under the Harvard-trained minister, Samuel Gilman, who wrote the nostalgic song "Fair Harvard." At Raleigh the leading editor of the state, Joseph Gales, and his intellectual wife Winifred, exiles from England, were propagandizing for the Unitarian faith during the decade of the 1820's and the early 1830's.[51] At Louisville, Kentucky, James Freeman Clarke, another Harvard graduate, while preaching as Unitarian pastor, was chosen superintendent of the public schools of the city. In New Orleans, the Reverend Theodore Clapp, a graduate of Yale, preached to large audiences in an independent church, the building of which was owned by a strange Jewish merchant and philanthropist, Judah Touro, who charged him no rent. With religious ideas quite similar to Unitarian doctrines, Dr. Clapp became an advocate of tolerance toward all classes of people, including Catholics, atheists, and skeptics. He eschewed the brimstone type of sermons and the reliance on supernatural elements common to many of the orthodox preachers.[52]

The liberal phase of Southern religion began to fade in the decade of the 1830's. It had been based on certain rational doctrines, the separation of church and state, and of church and college, the exclusion of the clergy from politics, an emphasis on ethics rather than theology, an unclouded faith in reason as a purifier of superstition, and a belief in the goodness of human nature. The liberal minority, who must fight a never-ending battle against the intolerant mores of the people, was defeated. A great resurgence of religious orthodoxy in the South occurred after 1830 as that section began to regiment thought within its borders to protect powerful vested interests that were threatened by the liberal forces of the period.

This change was indicated by the silencing of progressive religious leaders, especially in the colleges. President Holley was driven from Transylvania University primarily because of his liberalism. In the Holley manuscripts preserved at Transylvania College are notes for sermons and letters that indicate that he believed in the validity of religion "independent of a written revelation." A system of espionage was established by his pious enemies who came to his social entertainments, "like serpents into the Garden of Eden," to

[51] Clement Eaton, "Winifred and Joseph Gales, Liberals in the Old South," *Journal of Southern History,* X (November 1944), 460–474.
[52] John Duffy (ed.), *Parson Clapp of the Strangers' Church of New Orleans* (Baton Rouge, 1957).

gather evidence against him in unguarded moments. The fact that nude female statues were exhibited in his home excited horror. After an attack by the governor before the Kentucky legislature, he was practically forced to resign in 1827, a martyr to the growing intolerance of the churches. He died that year from yellow fever as he was on his way from New Orleans to Boston.[53]

Also the intransigent Dr. Cooper was dislodged from his presidency of South Carolina College in September, 1834. The immediate occasion for his forced resignation was an attack in the legislature because of a pamphlet that he had written against the enactment of laws to stop the carrying of mail on Sundays. In this pamphlet he had declared that avaricious priests had ordained the Sabbath, that Christ had prohibited public prayer, and that payment of the clergy was a pernicious practice. The charges made against him in the legislature bore a curious resemblance to the accusation against Socrates in the fifth century—the promulgation of certain religious opinions "dangerous to the youth and abhorrent to the feelings of the great mass of the community." [54] Perhaps Dr. Cooper would have been guillotined by public opinion long before if he had not been a stout champion of the popular political creed of South Carolina—of states' rights, opposition to abolitionists, and the belief that a protective tariff was unconstitutional. Contemporaneously with the victory of orthodoxy in South Carolina, Jefferson's policy of a secular university at Charlottesville, Virginia, was abandoned. Faculty and students by common consent called chaplains to perform services, regularly chosen in rotation from the different sects.

The Southern clergy were disturbed by the dangers of skepticism arising from the new science of geology. Sir Charles Lyell, about 1830, had pointed out the vast antiquity of the earth and the implications of fossils in the strata of the earth, which seemed to conflict with the account of the creation given by the Bible. Lamarck's theory of the transmutation of the species was also disturbing to those who believed in the Adam and Eve story. However, Darwin's *The Origin of Species* was not published until 1859 and his *Descent of Man* until 1871. Accordingly, the principal struggle between science and religion in the antebellum period was not over the theory of evolution but concerning the findings of geology. The danger of skepticism being produced by the study of science led commencement orators to warn college students against the insidious attacks of science on Christianity. The will of Judge John Perkins of Mississippi endowed a unique chair in the Columbia [S.C.] Theological Seminary, entitled "The Perkins Professorship of Science in Connexion with Revelation" (1861), whose purpose was to teach ministers to defend the faith against the assaults of science. The first Perkins Professor was James Woodrow, the uncle of Woodrow Wilson, who was later dismissed

[53] Charles Caldwell, *A Discourse on the Genius and Character of the Rev. Horace Holley, LL.D.* (Boston, 1828), 218.
[54] Columbia *Telescope*, December 20, 1831; quoted in Clement Eaton, *Freedom of Thought*, 286.

from his position because he believed that evolution was true and did not conflict with the teachings of the Bible.[55] Despite a religious climate hostile to the free development of science, the antebellum South produced some eminent scientists, the geologists, William Barton Rogers and Joseph LeConte and the pioneers in medical science, Drs. Ephraim McDowell (whose statue Kentucky selected together with Henry Clay's statue to go in the Hall of Fame at the Capitol in Washington), Daniel Drake, Marion Sims, and Crawford W. Long, who in 1842 discovered the use of ether as an anesthetic.[56]

By 1860 the reaction against religious liberalism had reached the farthest swing of the pendulum. The Unitarian church had not fulfilled its promise of the decades of the 1820's when Jefferson wrote "I trust that there is not a young man now living in the United States who will not die an Unitarian." [57] Sustained chiefly by New Englanders in the cities, it was moribund on the eve of the Civil War. The prevalent orthodoxy of the South was indicated by the virtual absence of liberal sects below the Mason-Dixon line as registered by the census of 1860. This enumeration listed in the South only 1 of the 58 Swedenborgian churches in the United States, only 24 of the 665 Universalist churches, and only 3 of the 264 Unitarian churches. Although the South did not support a single one of the 17 Spiritualist churches, it did have in Kentucky two Shaker communities that were agitated at times by mystical visions. It is a significant index of the religious uniformity of the South in 1860 that the dichotomy that had existed between the religion of the common people and of the aristocrats in the late eighteenth and the early nineteenth century had been erased. In the latter decades of the Old South the religion of the common people and of the aristocrats had become almost identical in content, a prevailing orthodoxy. The few articulate Southerners who applied a critical spirit to religion, such as the Virginia liberal Moncure D. Conway, or the agricultural reformer Edmund Ruffin, or the Louisiana planter Bennet Barrow, were either ostracized or forced to conceal their unorthodox views.

The growth of a more orthodox spirit in religion within the antebellum South was preceded and accompanied by certain social changes that seem to be related to this religious evolution. In the first place the leaders of a new generation who succeeded the generation of Jefferson, Madison, and Dr. Thomas Cooper lacked as a whole the culture and emancipation of mind that had distinguished the earlier leaders. The older liberalism had originated across the Atlantic Ocean, but had been closely related to the struggle in America to emancipate men politically and religiously. That impulse, how-

[55] Clement Eaton, "Professor James Woodrow and Freedom of Teaching in the South," George B. Tindall (ed.), *The Pursuit of Southern History, Presidential Addresses of the Southern Historical Association, 1935–1963* (Baton Rouge, 1964).

[56] See Clement Eaton, *The Mind of the Old South*, Chap. 11, The Scientific Mind: the Empiric Age.

[57] Clarence Gohdes, "Some Notes on the Unitarian Church in the Ante-Bellum South," D. K. Jackson (ed.), *American Studies in Honor of William Kenneth Boyd* (Durham, 1940), 327.

ever, was largely spent by 1830. As the Age of Reason declined the Romantic movement spread from Europe to America, marking a change in taste and elevating emotion and religious feeling. The Jacksonian movement in politics, which generated violent partisanship and the following of magnetic leaders with their facile slogans, was not conducive to an appeal to reason and a calm investigation of religious dogmas. Insofar as the Jacksonian movement led to the rise of the common man, it strengthened the old religious mores of the American people. Furthermore, the South was subjected to the Great Revival and subsequent waves of evangelism that eradicated the skepticism and deism of an earlier epoch. As the Atlantic seaboard lost direct contact with Europe by the cotton and tobacco trade shifting to Northern ports, the South grew more provincial. The intellectual stimulus of European immigration was also greatly diluted by the fact that immigrants now generally avoided the South, except at the ports and the towns along the Mississippi River. Finally, the defense of slavery against the rising tide of abolitionism and of hostile world opinion desperately required the support of a conservative religion that leaned strongly upon a literal interpretation of the Bible.

Nearly three fourths of the Southern churchgoers in 1860 were Methodists and Baptists.[58] The aristocratic churches of the South were the Episcopal and the Presbyterian, the church of the Scotch-Irish. According to a famous saying in the Tidewater South, there were many ways to go to Heaven, but the gentleman would always choose the Episcopalian way. This church of the gentry remained confined largely to the Tidewater areas of the South and was very weak beyond the Appalachian Mountains. Even in the older areas of the South the Episcopalians represented only about 5 per cent of the church membership. In the lower South some of the most prominent men, such as Jefferson Davis's millionaire brother, Joseph, and Governor Joseph E. Brown of Georgia, belonged to the Baptist and Methodist churches. The Baptist and Methodist churches were dominant in the Piedmont, the mountains, and the piney woods districts of the South. The Methodists expanded rapidly partly as a result of the circuit rider who rode on horseback from one little congregation to another in thinly populated regions. The form of church organization of the Baptists, which gave complete autonomy to the separate churches, was suited to the rural communities of the South. Neither the Methodist nor the Baptist church required educated ministers and were closer to the common people because of their high emotional voltage. Frequently, the Baptist ministers were farmers for six days of the week and on the seventh were preachers who were prohibited from receiving pay. Some of the more extreme Baptists, called Hard Shells, or Primitive Baptists, prac-

[58] For modern studies of the religious sects, see Walter B. Posey, *The Development of Methodism in the Old Southwest, 1783–1824* (Tuscaloosa, 1933); *The Baptist Church in the Lower Mississippi Valley* (Lexington, 1957); and "The Protestant Episcopal Church: An American Adaptation," *Journal of Southern History*, XXV (February 1959), 3–30; Ernest T. Thompson, *Presbyterians in the South, 1607–1861* (Richmond, 1963), I.

used foot washings, violently condemned card-playing and dancing, sang a primitive music led by a leader without the accompaniment of musical instruments, and opposed missionary societies as unscriptural.

Sectarianism, although it indicated the vitality and freedom of American religion, had its bad side. The great South Carolina planter and political leader James H. Hammond wrote to a Georgia planter on April 2, 1850, that his brother Marcellus, who had been reading the works of Swedenborg, strongly condemned "the miserable *sects,* whose bigoted & ignorant selfishness is the curse of the day. We want a universal religion founded on the love of God & of the world—the world, for I so interpret neighbor. Our sectarian religion now rests on fear of the Devil & hatred of all who differ from us." [59] Alexander Campbell, a British immigrant who founded Bethany College in western Virginia, was a notable example of a Southern preacher who sought to eliminate sectarianism, but he ended by creating (with Barton W. Stone) a new sect, the Christian church.

A very significant function of the Protestant churches of the South was the exercise of discipline over the members. This discipline was wielded by church trials and by the penalty of excommunication, which substituted church courts for the temporal courts. The manuscript minutes of the Lulbegrud Baptist church in Kentucky describe a typical procedure of the exercise of church authority over sinning mortals. Whenever a member transgressed against another, the injured person was required to go alone to the offender and tell him of his fault. If the latter refused to do justice, the offended person should then take one or two members of the church with him and try again to settle the difficulty with the offender. If such efforts failed, the church would hear the case, and if the defendant was found guilty, would either censure him, or accept his explanation, or excommunicate him.

The Baptist and Methodist churches excommunicated persons for a variety of offenses, such as "drinking too much licker," failing to attend church regularly, scolding one's husband, abusing one's wife and child, sexual immorality, particularly "having an heir without a lawful husband," swearing, dancing, gambling, quarreling, fighting, and treating one's father badly. One of the most interesting phases of the disciplinary action of the church was manifested in controlling the slave and free Negro members of the white churches. The manuscript record books of some Baptist churches deposited in the University of Kentucky library shows that slaves were excommunicated for stealing, running away from their masters, impudence to their mistresses, and having illegitimate children. In the Providence Baptist (Ky.) Church Record Book, for example, is the sentence of excommunication against Frank, a slave, for the crimes of lying, disobeying his master's commands, and "making too free with women." Also it is recorded, "Mr. Colemans Archebal is Excluded for refusing to hear the Church to answer for his Con-

---

[59] James H. Hammond to W. B. Hodgson. Jan. 24, 1846 Hodgson Papers. MSS in Duke University Library.

duct Shuch [sic] as Carnelly Singing, biting at a horse's nose and report sais that he Swore and Dancest." [60] (Maybe he was full of "corn licker" at the time of such gay conduct.) A record of discipline kept by a Baptist church in North Carolina, 1791–1860, showed five hundred cases tried, of which drunkenness led the list by far, followed in order by quarreling with a member, neglecting to attend services, and sex immorality.[61]

Closely associated with the religiousness of the South was the growth of the temperance movement. This reform harmonized with the evangelical religious spirit that had captured large portions of the South. Prominent political leaders, such as Robert Barnwell Rhett of South Carolina, Governor Henry A. Wise of Virginia, and Governor Joseph E. Brown of Georgia, championed the temperance cause. A group of hard drinkers of Baltimore who were converted to the total abstinence cause by an evangelist started the Washington Movement in 1840 to spread the gospel of cold water by the exhortations of reformed drunkards. The Sons of Temperance, organized two years later at Teetotaler's Hall, New York City, enrolled many members in the Southern states. An effective method that they adopted to stop the drinking of alcoholic beverages was the practice of obtaining pledges of total abstinence. *The Kentucky New Era* of Louisville in 1852 listed 265 temperance societies in the state as well as 80 post offices where 10 or more copies of this temperance newspaper were taken.[62]

In Lexington the battle over outlawing coffeehouses that sold liquor swayed back and forth. On January 1, 1853, the prohibition, or no license, party won the city election. Reverend William M. Pratt of Lexington observed the effect: "On Washington's birthday not one in the workhouse, jail or watchhouse, such an event not known before for years—this is owing to the suppression of the liquor traffic." [63] But the following year the liquor party overwhelmingly defeated the idealists and prohibitionists by electing the city councilmen. The opponents of liquor in Georgia also entered politics and in 1855 cast over six thousand votes for B. H. Overby, a Methodist preacher, the candidate of the Temperance party for governor.

This intermittent struggle over liquor represents one of the paradoxes of Southern life—the conflict between hedonism of the people and an unworldly oriented religion. To many religous folk in the antebellum period indulging in the use of wine and liquors was a "sin," whereas it was not in the colonial period. Along with drinking alcoholic beverages, there were so many other "sins" to avoid—breaking the Sabbath, dancing, card-playing, the "secret vice" of masturbation that was thought to be one cause of insanity, and swearing, to name only a few—as well as the mysterious and unforgivable sin against the Holy Ghost. Many of these "sins," or transgressions against

[60] MS in University of Kentucky Library.
[61] G. S. Johnson, *Ante-Bellum North Carolina: A Social History* (Chapel Hill, 1937).
[62] *The Kentucky New Era*, Sept. 4, 1852.
[63] Diary of William M. Pratt, Jan. 1; Feb. 28, 1853; Jan. 7, 1854.

the law of God, as interpreted by often ignorant and dogmatic preachers, are no longer regarded as sins. So writes the eminent psychiatrist, Karl Menninger, in a recent book, entitled *Whatever Became of Sin?* But the antebellum South, perhaps more so than the North, was a guilt-ridden society, ever conscious of sin and of the temptations of the Devil. Indeed, religion played a much larger role in shaping the Southern mind of 1860 than it does today, a conclusion that the manuscript diaries and letters of the period abundantly illuminate.

The Growing Alienation

THE INTRODUCTION of the Wilmot Proviso in the House of Representatives in 1846 was the signal for a great sectional controversy over slavery. This proviso was a rider attached to an appropriation bill, which declared that any territory acquired from Mexico as the result of the war should be forever free from slavery. The Southern people felt outraged at this proposal, for it placed a stigma upon their peculiar institution and would deny to the South any of the fruits of anticipated victory in a war waged by a Southern President, "Mr. Polk's War," and fought largely by Southern generals and Southern volunteers. The adoption of the Wilmot Proviso would prevent Southerners with their slaves from treading upon the soil purchased by common blood and treasure. Thus high-spirited Southerners felt that the Wilmot Proviso was an attempt to deny to them equality in the Union. It played into the hands of the fire-eaters, or Southern extremists who desired to form a Southern Confederacy.

The outstanding fire-eater of the South was William Lowndes Yancey of Alabama. This agitator, born in Georgia, had spent twelve of his most impressionable years in the North. His father, an able lawyer of Abbeville, South Carolina, and a friend of John C. Calhoun, died when Yancey was a child. His mother married a Yankee schoolmaster, who took the family to Troy, New York, where he became a prominent minister and abolitionist. Young Yancey attended Williams College for three years and then returned to the South to practice law in the office of the strong Unionist Benjamin F. Perry of Greenville, South Carolina. At the close of the nullification controversy he edited a strongly Unionist newspaper, the *Greenville Mountaineer*. When he was twenty-two years old he emigrated to the black belt of Alabama, where he became a planter and editor at Wetumpka. The accidental poisoning of his slaves ended his career as a planter, and he returned to law.

Yancey was a strikingly handsome man, exceedingly proud, and his Northern exile had made him a more pronounced Southerner than his neighbors, even in the matter of dress. His manner was courteous, and the "habitual expression of good humor" on his face hardly comported with the fact that he had killed a man in self-defense and had fought a bloodless duel with the North Carolina Congressman, Thomas L. Clingman. He was the type of individual who scorned compromise. Despite his violent proslavery prejudices, he was a liberal in many respects, fighting for free public schools and for the right of married women to control their property, and advocating the white basis instead of the federal ratio in the apportionment of representatives in the legislature.

The change of Yancey from an ardent Unionist to an equally zealous states' rights advocate poses an intriguing question. The transition was made between 1836 and 1840 and seems to have been motivated by his violent resentment of the activities of the Northern abolitionists and by his belief that only a strict interpretation of the Constitution could protect the South from a dangerous antislavery majority.[1] From 1844 to 1846 he was a Representative in Congress, but he resigned out of disgust at the selfishness of party politics and never afterward did he hold a federal office.

Yancey has been called "the orator of secession." [2] He spoke with absolute candor, in that blend of fire and musical cadence that never failed to enthrall Southern audiences. He made hundreds of speeches at barbecues and political rallies, not in the interest of his personal ambition, or for party success, but with an almost austere devotion to the cause of the South. In 1848 he drew up a set of resolutions that were adopted by the Alabama Democratic Convention, stating the extreme Southern demand, not merely that slavery should be permitted to expand into the common territories of the United States but should be protected by Federal legislation. He sought to arouse the Southern people to realize the dangers to their way of life threatened by the Northern majority. If the Constitution and states' rights could not give the South security within the Union, he favored secession and a separate Southern Republic. In the last decade of the antebellum period, he had no hope that justice would be granted to the South within the Union or that the Constitution would be faithfully observed by the North. For the purpose of agitation, therefore, he founded the League of United Southerners in 1858, and he was one or the organizers of Southern Rights associations. To spread the blessings of slavery to poorer men in the South he agitated for the reopening of the African slave trade.[3]

Robert Barnwell Rhett of South Carolina was another significant and masterful figure among the fire-eaters. The owner of one hundred and ninety slaves, he belonged to the small privileged class of his native state. His deeply religious nature and his frustrations in his political career gave his life an undertone of sadness. He had no taste for the hedonistic ways of the Cavalier; he was vice-president of a Young Men's Temperance Society, secretary of the Charleston Port Society for the promotion of the Gospel among seamen, and he refused, on account of religious scruples, to fight duels. When he failed to attain his political ambitions, he found a haven of solace in his family, who knew that he was a great man. One common characteristic of the fire-eaters was very pronounced in Rhett, an exaggerated sense of honor or pride. At the

[1] A. L. Venable, "William L. Yancey's Transition from Unionism to States Rights," *Journal of Southern History*, X (August 1944), 331–342.

[2] W. G. Brown, *The Lower South in American History* (New York, 1903), chap. 2.

[3] See Clement Eaton, "The Voice of Emotion: William L. Yancey," *The Mind of the Old South* (Baton Rouge, 1967), chap. 11, and John W. DuBose, *The Life and Times of William Lowndes Yancey* (Birmingham, 1892), 2 vols.

age of thirty-seven, he changed his name from the plebian Smith to the aristocratic Rhett. In that year he began his political career in Congress.[4]

John C. Calhoun was Rhett's master and idol. Yet he differed from the great Carolinion, whom he tried to make president, in that he had no love for the Union. One of the most fiery leaders of the nullification movement was this aristocratic South Carolinian, whose slogans were "Liberty" and "The Spirit of '76!" Rhett never diluted his language but spoke out in bold and challenging words. The abolition movement enraged him. In 1838 he proposed that the Constitution be amended in order to protect the rights of the South in regard to slavery, or the Union should be peaceably dissolved. The South must act quickly, for by delay Virginia, Kentucky, and Maryland would gradually get rid of their slaves and become lukewarm in the defense of Southern rights. The Southern states should call a Southern Convention and threaten the North with a dissolution of the Union, as the best fulcrum by which to obtain Southern rights in the Union.

Rhett treasured a bitter resentment against the North because he believed that the North exploited the South by means of the tariff, the merchant marine that carried Southern cotton, and the internal trade that furnished the South with manufactured articles. In 1844 he began an agitation at Bluffton, South Carolina, called the Bluffton movement, to summon a state convention in order to resist the raising of the tariff. Calhoun opposed this radical action because it interfered with his ambitions for himself and for the Democratic party. The movement was regarded as a disunion project, but Rhett explained its purpose to be the reform of the Constitution and to prevent the rise of "a consolidated government." Rhett favored all measures to strengthen the South, especially the annexation of Texas.

When the Wilmot Proviso was being considered in Congress, he hoped that it would pass, because it would afford an occasion for the South to secede. Henceforth, Rhett became an outright disunionist and the agitator for the formation of a Southern republic. He believed that this revolution was to be accomplished by the action of a single state—separate state secession. If South Carolina took the initiative, other Southern states would follow. Like Yancey, Rhett did not believe in compromise, but in forcing the issue between the North and the South. Over his mind hovered the alarming vision of the North growing steadily stronger and the South steadily weaker as the years went by. There was no hope for his native section in following bargaining politicians, nor in waiting until all the Southern states would cooperate to go out of the Union as a body. The South would never secede, he believed, if such a procedure should be followed.

In 1850 Rhett attained one of his ardent ambitions, election to the United States Senate. But the following year South Carolina rejected his leadership by accepting the Compromise of 1850. Then Rhett resigned, "sacrificed his

[4] Laura White, *Robert Barnwell Rhett: Father of Secession* (New York, 1931), 24, 32, 127.

ambition on the altar of liberty." From this time to the eve of the Civil War he was in political retirement. However, his brother, Edmund Rhett, who was in the South Carolina legislature, and his son Robert Barnwell Rhett, Jr., editor of the *Charleston Mercury,* carried on his influence as a Southern fire-eater. In 1860 the triumph of the great fire-eater came with the secession of South Carolina.

Besides the commanding figures of Rhett and Yancey, there were lesser fire-eaters in each Southern state. In Louisiana James D. B. De Bow, a native of South Carolina, the prolific mother of Southern extremists throughout the South, exerted wide influence in developing Southern nationalism through his editorship of *De Bow's Review,* the most important commercial magazine in the South. Another Louisiana fire-eater was Pierre Soulé, a native of France who had emigrated to Louisiana and was elected to the United States Senate, where he became an ardent Southern and proslavery advocate. In Mississippi there was Governor John A. Quitman, born in the North, who became a supporter of filibusters in a movement to acquire slave territory. Jefferson Davis was a fire-eater until the secession crisis of 1860. In Florida David Levy Yulee, a Senator of part Jewish ancestry, was an extreme champion of Southern interests. The fiery Senator Louis T. Wigfall carried the ultra proslavery doctrines of his native South Carolina to Texas. In South Carolina Senator James H. Hammond, the son of a New England schoolteacher, was a potent agitator for a Southern republic until 1860 when he was pessimistic over the Southern states being able to unite. In Georgia Henry L. Benning was the prophet of the necessity of the South to secede because the North would never let the South alone until her slaves were emancipated.

Virginia produced a brilliant group of extreme proslavery publicists, such as Beverley Tucker of William and Mary College, George Fitzhugh, author of *Cannibals All,* Roger A. Pryor, newspaper editor, and Edmund Ruffin. Ruffin was the most fanatical of the Virginia fire-eaters. He had rendered a great service to the whole South in his earlier days by his agricultural reforms. But in the latter part of his life he became a crusader for Southern independence. He spread his doctrines at the Virginia springs, at political rallies, and at agricultural conventions. He developed such a virulent hate of the North that he wore homespun suits rather than patronize Northern manufacturers. When the South was defeated in 1865 he committed suicide.[5]

The fire-eaters were not all of one mind. Some of them, such as Rhett and Ruffin, longed for the independence of the South and hoped that the North would stir the Southern states to secede. Others, such as Jefferson Davis, were secessionists in 1850 but conservative in 1860. They hoped that the North would yield to Southern demands for the protection and expansion

---

[5] The Ruffin Diary, written in a handwriting that is difficult to read, reveals the mind of an extremist who had lost touch with reality, very similar to the mind of an ardent segregationist of today. W. K. Scarborough has edited the first volume of Ruffin's diary (Baton Rouge, 1972).

of slavery. Some Southern leaders, notably Robert Toombs, were opposed to the fire-eaters through most of their careers, but became ardent secessionists in 1860, when they became convinced that there was no hope for the protection of Southern rights within the Union. Some of the most extreme fire-eaters rejected the doctrines of Jefferson and boldly proclaimed their belief in aristocracy. Beverley Tucker explained Virginia's reluctance to follow the lead of the fire-eaters by writing to a fellow extremist in South Carolina, the novelist William Gilmore Simms, that Virginia was "sunk in the slough of democracy, which has no sense of honor." [6] Indeed, all the fire-eaters had an exaggerated and unwholesome feeling for "Southern honor."

How shall we estimate the fire-eaters in the development of Southern history? Were they responsible for the Southern decision to secede from the Union? Every society that is suffering from profound discontents, from social and economic maladjustments, throws up individuals who react more intensely to the situation than the majority of the people. Moderate Southerners felt that the fire-eaters were in the same category as the abolitionists in the North—both groups fanatical and pernicious. It is possible that the fire-eaters in the South and the abolitionists in the North emotionalized sectional controversies so greatly that they prevented the successful application of compromise and sanity to the issues that led to the Civil War. One conclusion is certain, that the fire-eaters could see only one side of a question—the Southern point of view.

Various incidents occurred after the conclusion of the war with Mexico to give the fire-eaters splendid opportunities for agitation. The most dangerous issue threatening the unity of the nation arose over the status of slavery in the territory acquired from Mexico. The North was determined to apply the Wilmot Proviso to this vast new land, or "to monopolize" these common territories, as Calhoun phrased it. At the time Mexico ceded this land to the United States, the Mexican municipal law forbade slavery in any part of the domain. The Carolina statesman maintained that the moment the United States took possession of it, the Constitution, which recognized slavery, applied to it. He deduced from this premise that Southerners had an equal right to immigrate into the common territories with their slaves, a right that could not be canceled by Congress or by a territorial legislature. Although Calhoun had vigorously opposed the Mexican War, he was determined that the South should share equally in the spoils of victory.

This great sectional leader wished to arouse the Southern people to the dangers of Northern aggression on their rights and to unite the South to take a firm stand. Accordingly, early in 1849 he called a meeting of the Southern senators and representatives in Washington. To them he presented his draft of an "Address of the Southern Delegates in Congress to their Constituents," which stated the Southern grievances—violation of the Fugitive Slave Act, constant agitation against the South by abolition societies, the

[6] W. P. Trent, *William Gilmore Simms* (Boston, 1892), 186.

attempt to exclude Southern slaveholders from the territory acquired by the Mexican War. The address urged the Southern states to unite, disregarding party success and party ties, anxiety for which had formerly paralyzed their efforts for self-defense. He hoped to impress the North with the gravity of the crisis produced by the attempt to apply the Wilmot Proviso to the Western territory. The resolute stand of a united section, he declared, would cause the North to pause and calculate the consequences of goading the South to disunion. By this maneuver he hoped to save the Union, or if unsuccessful, to unify the South for secession.[7] Unfortunately for his plans, the Southern Whigs refused to cooperate. They entered the Southern caucus to control it and crush any disunion movement. Not only the Whigs but also some influential Southern Democrats, such as Howell Cobb of Georgia and President Polk, opposed Calhoun's Southern movement as being a dangerous means of increasing sectionalism in the South. Consequently only forty-eight of the eighty-eight members of Congress who attended the Southern caucus signed Calhoun's address. Instead of revealing Southern unity to the North, therefore, it had the opposite effect.

Various proposals were now offered for the settlement of the question of slavery in the territories that threatened to disrupt the Union. President Polk favored extending the Missouri Compromise line of 36°30′ to the Pacific Ocean. Senator John M. Clayton of Delaware proposed organizing the territories in the Mexican cession without Congressional action on the question of slavery, but leaving the decision to the territorial courts and eventually to the Supreme Court. The Calhoun solution was to allow slavery to exist in all territories of the United States, until the territory became a state, at which time a constitutional convention could decide on slavery or freedom. The Western point of view, represented by Lewis Cass of Michigan, advocated letting the people of the territory decide the question of slavery or freedom. This solution was called "squatter sovereignty," later "popular sovereignty." The adoption of the Wilmot Proviso was the solution of the antislavery Congressmen from the Northern states. But the Virginia legislature, which undoubtedly represented the opinion of the South, declared in a set of resolutions that if the Wilmot Proviso should be adopted, the state would not submit to it, even if it involved the last extremity of disunion.

In this explosive situation, Calhoun turned once more to his favorite idea of an all-Southern Convention. Realizing that if South Carolina issued the call for such a meeting, this fact would prejudice numerous Southerners against the convention, he persuaded some of his political friends in Mississippi to extend the invitation. Accordingly, a convention in Jackson summoned all Southern states to send delegates to Nashville on June 1, 1850, to a Southern Convention. Calhoun's instigation was carefully concealed, and the state of Mississippi was regarded as the originator of the Nashville Con-

---

[7] Cralle (ed.), *Works of John C. Calhoun* (New York, 1853–1855), VI, 285–313 (January 15, 1849).

vention. The fire-eaters hoped to use this convention to bring about a secession movement.

In the autumn of 1849 California, which had suddenly received a large accession of population as a result of the gold rush, had applied for admission to the Union with a free-state constitution. President Zachary Taylor had sent agents both to California and New Mexico urging the people of these areas to form constitutions and apply for admission as states. His plan was for California and New Mexico to skip the territorial stage of government and enter the Union as states. Thus he hoped to avoid the agitation over whether the land acquired from Mexico should be organized as free or slave *territories*. Although a large slaveholder, President Taylor was in favor of admitting California as a free state without any concessions or compensation to the South. Southern political leaders were alarmed over this prospect. Until 1850 there had been an equal number of slave states (15) and of free states (15) in the Union, thus maintaining a balance of power in the Senate. As long as this equilibrium was preserved, the South could prevent hostile legislation against slavery from being passed, but the admission of California as a free state would deprive this section of its veto. Furthermore, if the Wilmot Proviso should be applied to the rest of the Mexican cession, as the North demanded, there would be no hope for the South of ever improving its political position by the admission of a slave state. The South was deeply incensed over this attempt of the North to exclude Southerners from emigrating with their slaves into a region "purchased by common blood and common treasure," partly because of its declining strength in Congress.

On January 29, 1850, Henry Clay introduced into the Senate a series of resolutions that embodied a comprehensive compromise of the controversies between the North and South over slavery. At this time Clay was seventy-three years of age and for nearly eight years had been in retirement from political office. His return to the Senate in 1849 was motivated by a sincere love for the Union and a desire to prevent its dissolution. He appealed to both hostile sections to assuage their violent partisan feelings and accept a fair compromise.[8] The debate over his compromise proposals brought forward the most distinguished leaders both of the old and of the new generation. Although these full-dress speeches may not have changed a single vote they educated the country on the issues of the day and gained time for compromise. The barrage of oratory on this occasion was really a debate between geographic sections.

John C. Calhoun delivered the ultimatum of the South. He, too, was an old gentleman, haggard, and disillusioned. He was too ill to speak on March 4, but Senator James M. Mason of Virginia read his written speech to the Senate while Calhoun sat in his chair with half-closed eyes. His passion to be president had now burned to ashes, and he thought only of the safety of the

[8] See Clement Eaton, *Henry Clay and the Art of American Politics* (Boston, 1956), chap. 12.

South, an unchanging South based on slavery. Calhoun warned the North that the bonds of union were snapping one by one, the psychological, emotional, and religious ties. The North was growing stronger every day by the exploitation of the South by tariffs and by a centralized government. He demanded that the North stop its agitation for the abolition of slavery, that the South be admitted to terms of equality in the territories by allowing its citizens to emigrate with their slaves, and that the equilibrium in the Senate between the North and the South be preserved so that the rights of the South, a minority within the Union, could be protected from the Northern majority. He opposed the admission of California with its free-state constitution and advocated constitutional amendments to guarantee Southern rights. Although his speech did not clearly specify the type of constitutional amendments he desired, his last political essay proposed two presidents, like the consuls of Rome, one chosen from the free states and another from the slave states, each having a veto on Congressional legislation. A few weeks later Calhoun died, despairing of the Union and expressing the sentiment, "The great battle must be fought by you younger men . . . *there* indeed, is my only regret at going—the South—the poor South!" [9]

Senators William H. Seward of New York and Salmon P. Chase of Ohio spoke for the Northern antislavery men. In his speech Seward warned the South against trying to pass a more stringent fugitive slave law, for he said public opinion in the North would not support it. He opposed the expansion of slavery in the Western territories, maintaining that a higher law than the Constitution forbade it, namely, moral conscience. For his higher law doctrine he was condemned bitterly in the South. The advocates of the Wilmot Proviso had in mind not only to exclude slavery from the territory recently acquired from Mexico but also to serve notice to the South that any further territorial acquisitions, Cuba, for instance, must be free.

Senator Stephen A. Douglas of Illinois represented the feeling of the West. Douglas did not believe that any of the semiarid territories acquired from Mexico would ever support slavery and therefore abolition on paper would be needless. He was opposed, consequently, to antagonizing the Southern states by the attempt to apply the Wilmot Proviso to the territories. Douglas asserted the doctrine that slavery was a local question, not a national one, and that it depended on local legislation. He favored compromise and granting the South a more effective fugitive slave law. He restated the argument of Lewis Cass for the doctrine of squatter sovereignty.[10]

On March 7, Senator Daniel Webster gave his famous speech advocating compromise. He alone among the prominent speakers did not represent the feeling of his section. Webster maintained that the territories in dispute were not suited to slavery and therefore human bondage would never expand into

[9] "Rhett's Oration before the Legislature of South Carolina, Nov. 28, 1850," J. P. Thomas (ed.), *The Carolina Tribute to Calhoun* (Columbia, S.C., 1857), 369.
[10] See R. W. Johannsen, *Stephen A. Douglas* (New York, 1973).

this region. "I would not take pains," he declared, "uselessly to reaffirm an ordinance of Nature, nor to re-enact the will of God." [11] He urged the North to stop agitating the slavery question, for it would destroy the Union. Thus he alienated the people of New England, especially by his willingness to accept a fugitive slave act. On account of his support of the compromise proposals a storm of abuse and vituperation broke over his head in New England. He was compared by his contemporaries to Benedict Arnold, and Whittier condemned him in his poem "Ichabod" as a statesman who had sacrificed his honor. Actually, he deliberately sacrificed his presidential ambitions to save the Union.

President Zachary Taylor proved a bitter disappointment to Southerners, who had hoped that he would support their sectional interests. His long service in the army had desectionalized him, and he came under the influence of the antislavery Senator Seward. As long as Taylor lived, he blocked the settlement of a compromise along the lines proposed by Clay, against whom he had developed a strong prejudice. When the Southern Whig statesmen, Alexander H. Stephens, Robert Toombs, and Thomas L. Clingman called on Taylor to ascertain his attitude toward the admission of California and the Wilmot Proviso, they found that he favored admission of California as a free state without any compensation to the South and that he would sign the Wilmot Proviso if it passed Congress. They threatened a withdrawal of the section from the Union if this obnoxious measure was forced on the South. Angered by this threat, the old general informed them that if the South resisted the federal government, he would place himself at the head of an army to suppress rebellion and would hang secession leaders with as little compunction as he had hanged deserters and spies in Mexico.[12] Fortunately for the success of compromise, Taylor died early in July. Vice-President Millard Fillmore, who succeeded to the presidency, was sympathetic to Southern demands and facilitated the adoption of compromise measures.

In the adoption of the settlement of 1850 the work of Stephen A. Douglas, Senator from the Northern border state of Illinois, was perhaps more decisive than the influence of Henry Clay. Clay insisted upon passing the compromise proposals in one great comprehensive bill, an "omnibus bill," but such a measure could not command a majority vote. Finally, the Compromise was enacted in separate laws during August and September under the leadership of Douglas while Clay was absent from Congress in Newport, Rhode Island. Furthermore, the solution of the slavery question in the territories was based on Douglas's proposals rather than on Clay's plan that the question of slavery be decided by the Mexican law prohibiting slavery.

A sectional truce, the Compromise of 1850, was drawn up, which provided for the admission of California with its free-state constitution and the

---

[11] *The Writings and Speeches of Daniel Webster* (Boston, 1903), X, 84.
[12] Brainerd Dyer, *Zachary Taylor* (New York, 1946), 381; see also Holman Hamilton, *Zachary Taylor; Soldier in the White House* (Indianapolis, 1951).

creation of two new territories, New Mexico and Utah, the thirty-seventh parallel being the dividing line between them. No mention of slavery was made in these territorial bills. Thus, the principle of nonintervention by Congress in the slavery question within the territories was adopted, permitting the principle of popular sovereignty to operate. The question whether these two territories should establish slavery was left to the territorial legislature, with an appeal to the Supreme Court.[13] The slave trade, but not slavery itself, was abolished in the District of Columbia. A large area of land claimed by Texas was added to the territory of New Mexico but Texas was compensated by the payment of $10,000,000—with which the state could pay the Texas bondholders and speculators living mainly in the Eastern states, headed by William W. Corcoran of the Washington banking house of Corcoran and Riggs.[14] The Texas bondholders lobby exerted a sinister influence in accomplishing the golden deed of saving the Union.

A vital part of the Compromise of 1850 was the enactment of a new and stringent Fugitive Slave Act, drafted by Senator James M. Mason of Virginia, whose grandfather George Mason, of *Gunston Hall,* had strongly condemned the institution of slavery. It was the part of the Compromise that led to its undoing, for it offended the moral conscience of many Northern people. The fugitive slave law of 1793 had depended upon state authorities for its enforcement. The Supreme Court in *Prigg* v. *Pennsylvania* (1842) had decided that the federal government could not compel a state to enforce federal laws. The new fugitive slave act, therefore, created federal commissioners to try fugitive slave cases by a summary process. The slave master, or the slave catcher employed by him, could arrest a Negro and take him before a commissioner and swear an affidavit that the captive belonged to him. If the commissioner decided in favor of the master, his fee was $10, but only $5 if his verdict liberated the captive. The marshal, or other federal officer, was given the authority to call on bystanders to act as a *posse comitatus* to aid in arresting a fugitive or to prevent a rescue by a mob. If a marshal allowed a slave to escape from his custody he was liable to the master for the full value of the slave. This law did not permit the fugitive to testify in his behalf or have a jury trial nor did it safeguard free Negroes from being kidnapped.

Before the compromise measures had passed Congress, the Southern Convention promoted by Calhoun met at Nashville to concert measures to protect the vital interests of the South. Yet only 9 of the 15 slave states sent delegates, and of the 175 delegates, 102 came from Tennessee. The Southern Whigs opposed the convention partly because they did not wish to injure the Taylor administration. The meetings were held in the largest church in the city, and the delegates were surrounded by Southern belles and matrons,

[13] R. R. Russell "What Was the Compromise of 1850?" *Journal of Southern History,* XXII (August, 1956), 295–308.
[14] Holman Hamilton, *Prologue to Conflict: the Crisis and Compromise of 1850* (Lexington, Ky., 1964).

"like borders of flowers." The delegates were inspired by the occasion and audience to unfurl their most elegant figures of speech, their most graceful gestures, and their richest tones of forensic eloquence; "at one moment, the audience would be startled with the thunders of rock-beating surges; and at another, soothed by the soft zephyrs of a summer sea." One of the most violent of the delegates, Beverley Tucker of Virginia, imitated the vituperative style of John Randolph of Roanoke, and was sometimes "forgetful that ladies were present." [15]

Despite the most vehement oratory, the convention had a lame conclusion. Although the delegates passed one resolution demanding that all the federal territories be open to slavery, they consented, for the sake of preserving the Union, to accept the extension of the Missouri Compromise line of 36° 30' to the Pacific, "as an extreme concession." The convention then adjourned until November, but the second session at that time was attended by only 59 delegates, mostly radical secessionists, who passed resolutions urging an economic and social boycott of the North. In the meanwhile, the compromise measures had been adopted, which took the wind out of the sails of the fire-eaters. The fiasco of this resistance movement revealed to the Southern nationalists the extreme difficulty of getting the Southern states to cooperate in the defense of Southern Rights, and from now on, fire-eaters eschewed "cooperation" as a means of secession and advocated single state secession.

The Southern movement of 1849–1851, initiated by Calhoun and the bantam-sized Henry S. Foote of Mississippi, was now followed by a reaction. The Whig leaders of the South started a Union movement that soon became nonpartisan. The old labels of Whig and Democrat were temporarily laid aside, and campaigns were waged on the question of the acceptance of the Compromise of 1850 by the Constitutional Union party and the opposing Southern Rights group. The first Southern state to make a decision on the acceptance of the compromise measures was Georgia at the close of 1850. The Constitutional Union party in Georgia was led by Toombs and Stephens, Whigs, and Howell Cobb, who had recently been elected the Democratic Speaker of the National House of Representatives. The Constitutional Union party won control of the state convention by a large margin, but this body gave warning to the North that Georgia would secede if the Compromise were violated. The "Georgia Platform," adopted by the convention, listed a series of encroachments on Southern rights that would justify the recourse to secession: abolition of slavery in the District of Columbia, suppression of the internal slave trade by an act of Congress, any law prohibiting the introduction of slaves into the territories of Utah or New Mexico, refusal to admit a slave state into the Union, and serious modification of the Fugitive Slave Law.[16] Georgia's example of the acceptance of the Compromise was followed by the states of the upper South and by Louisiana and Alabama. In Alabama the

[15] J. H. Ingraham, *The Sunny South, or the Southerner at Home* (Philadelphia, 1860).
[16] See R. H. Shryock, *Georgia and the Union in 1850* (Durham, 1926).

contest over secession was fought between the Southern Rights group, led by William L. Yancey, and the Unionists, led by the eloquent Whig Congressman, Henry W. Hilliard, who advocated adoption of the Compromise of 1850 as a finality. In the August elections of 1851 the Unionists elected a majority of the legislature and also of the delegation to Congress.

The only Southern states in which the fire-eaters remained powerful were Mississippi and South Carolina, yet even in these states they were narrowly defeated by the Unionists in 1851 over the question of the acceptance of the Compromise. In Mississippi Governor Quitman tried to lead a disunion movement, but a state convention called by the legislature voted in favor of accepting the Compromise. In the gubernatorial election of 1851, both of Mississippi's senators resigned to become candidates for governor, Jefferson Davis for the Southern Rights group, which contemplated secession as a last resort, and Henry S. Foote for the Union party. Foote had been one of the originators of the Southern movement, but as soon as the Compromise was adopted he changed his position to advocate its acceptance, thus securing the Whig vote. Jefferson Davis was defeated and retired from political life until recalled by Franklin Pierce to be his secretary of war. In accepting the Compromise, the Mississippi Convention issued a solemn warning to the North, in a resolution, "Resolved, that it is our deliberate opinion, that upon the faithful execution of the Fugitive Slave law, by the proper authorities, depends the preservation of our much-loved Union." [17]

In South Carolina, the Compromise of 1850 was not acceptable to the people, but they were unwilling to follow Robert Barnwell Rhett's leadership in seceding. Instead, the "co-operationists" under the leadership of Senator Andrew P. Butler, Robert W. Barnwell, and James L. Orr, controlled the state convention called to consider immediate secession. The cause of the Union was ably championed by Benjamin F. Perry, editor of *The Southern Patriot* of Greenville, and by the most prominent Whig leader in South Carolina, William C. Preston. The Tidewater parishes were for secession, but the up-country favored cooperation. The convention asserted the right of secession, but favored such a movement only in cooperation with other Southern states.

The Southern movement and the Compromise of 1850 have been variously interpreted by American historians. Some modern historians have regarded the Southern movement of 1849–1850 as mainly a bluff, using the threat of secession to secure concessions from the North. It worked, they point out, for the Compromise of 1850 prevented the application of the Wilmot Proviso or the abolition of slavery in the District of Columbia, objectives of the North. On the other hand, the North was the real gainer by the terms of the settlement. The admission of California as a free state destroyed the sectional balance of power in the Senate, depriving the South of its veto over legislation in Congress. The South won the dubious right to take slaves into the

---

[17] Allan Nevins, *Ordeal of the Union* (New York, 1947), I, 379.

territories of New Mexico and Utah, subject to the final approval of the Supreme Court, but this was a hollow victory, for both sides admitted that this territory would never be settled by slaves on account of its climate and soil. The North secured the abolition of the slave trade in the District of Columbia, and the South was placated with the new Fugitive Slave Act, which was quickly scrapped in the Northern states. The greatest advantage derived by the North from the Compromise was that it checked a dangerous secession movement and thus saved the Union for a decade, during which foreign immigration expanded the population of the North and railroads were built between the Eastern and the Ohio Valley states, so that when secession did come in 1860 the Northwest joined the Union cause. The fire-eaters were right: the Compromise of 1850 was a bad bargain for the slave interests of the South. It was only "a sectional truce" that permitted the Northern adversary to grow stronger.

The Compromise of 1850 was accepted generally in the North and the South as a great tranquilizing settlement of the differences that had divided the nation. The country was entering upon a cycle of economic prosperity, with cotton selling at 13 cents a pound and the business interests in the North expanding. The conservatives of both sections sighed with relief at the passage of the Compromise measures, which have rightly been called "the Businessman's Peace." The Compromise was regarded as "a final settlement," and it was hoped that slavery agitation would end.

Nevertheless, the Compromise was soon overthrown by the failure of the North to observe its terms, especially in regard to the enforcement of the Fugitive Slave Act. The leaders of the older generation who had a love for the Union had died or disappeared from public life—Calhoun and Zachary Taylor died in 1850, Clay and Webster died in 1852, and Thomas Hart Benton, who after thirty years of service in the Senate, was defeated for re-election in 1851. The leaders of the new generation were less restrained and more inclined to violent sectional courses. Furthermore, by 1854 large numbers of Northern people had been converted to a belief that the abolition of slavery was a high moral issue that concerned the nation as a whole. After the passage of the drastic Fugitive Slave Act of 1850, many Northern states in which antislavery feeling predominated passed Personal Liberty Acts, which made the recovery of fugitive slaves extremely difficult. These laws stipulated a heavy penalty against kidnapping; extended the rights of jury trial and the writ of habeas corpus to fugitive slaves and free Negroes; denied the use of state and county jails to confine fugitive slaves; prohibited state officials or citizens from aiding in the arrest or return of fugitive slaves; required state attorneys to defend fugitive slaves at state expense; and two states, Connecticut and Vermont, granted freedom to all slaves brought within the state. Some of these laws were clear violations of a federal statute and constituted a real grievance of the South. The Supreme Court of Wisconsin in the Booth Case (1854) declared the Fugitive Slave Act unconstitutional and released Sherman Booth, a member of a mob that had rescued a fugitive slave from jail, from the legal consequences of his act. The Supreme Court of the United States, however, reversed this decision and lectured the Supreme Court of Wisconsin for thus nullifying a federal law (*Ableman* v. *Booth*, 1859).

The federal government tried vigorously to enforce the Fugitive Slave Act (only twenty-three fugitives were rescued or lost in federal custody between 1850 and 1860), but Southerners were discouraged by the danger of mobs and costly, long-drawn-out suits seeking to recover their fugitive slaves.[18] Public sentiment in the North was inflamed against the return of fugitive slaves by the publication of *Uncle Tom's Cabin* and by the storm aroused two years later over the Kansas-Nebraska Act, which annulled the long-standing Missouri Compromise. The depth of this feeling was demonstrated in Boston in 1854 by the dramatic return of Anthony Burns to his master in Virginia. It took twenty-two companies of militia, a large police force, and troops of U.S. cavalry and marines to guard Burns's passage to the Boston harbor along streets draped in crepe. When Commissioner Loring, a Harvard law professor who had tried the case, returned to his class he was booed and hissed by the students.

The presidents from the death of Taylor to the election of Lincoln were "doughfaces"—Northern men with Southern principles. Thus, during the last decade before the Civil War the South controlled the executive branch of the federal government. This was especially true during the administration of Franklin Pierce from 1853 to 1857. This handsome, charming man, who became an alcoholic after the death of his son in an accident, was dominated by Jefferson Davis, whom he had appointed secretary of war.[19] The pro-Southern influence over Pierce was strikingly illustrated in the passage of the fateful Kansas-Nebraska Act.

Prior to 1854 Southern Congressmen had vigorously opposed the creation of a Nebraska Territory, because it lay north of the Missouri Compromise line and therefore would be a free territory. On the other hand, the settlers in that region were eager to have it organized into a territorial government. The Wyandot Indians and the white immigrants of Nebraska had actually sent two delegates to Washington for that purpose. Moreover, ex-Senator Thomas Hart Benton, of the neighboring state of Missouri, had begun a campaign for reelection to the Senate on a platform calling for the organization of the Nebraska territory in order that a transcontinental railroad might be built through this region with its eastern terminal at St. Louis. Senator David R. Atchison, leader of the proslavery forces in Missouri, determined to defeat Benton by advocating the organization of the territory with the repeal of the Missouri Compromise line. Thus, he would kill three birds with one stone: defeat his rival Benton, organize the territory so that a transconti-

---

[18] See S. W. Campbell, *The Slave Catchers: Enforcement of the Fugitive Slave Law, 1850–1860* (Chapel Hill, 1970).
[19] See R. F. Nichols, *Franklin Pierce* (Philadelphia, 1931).

nental railroad could be built to St. Louis, and open up the territory to slavery, thereby protecting Missouri's proslavery interests. Atchison was a friend of Douglas, and he put strong pressure on him to report a bill organizing this Western territory with a clause repealing the Missouri Compromise restriction.

The question of building a railroad through this relatively unoccupied country was an important factor in promoting legislation relating to the Kansas-Nebraska territory. It was believed that only one railroad connecting the Pacific coast with the East would be built for a long span of time. Consequently, there was great rivalry between the cities of the Mississippi Valley to be chosen the eastern terminal of such a railroad. Government aid in the form of land grants was needed to finance this huge project, but the government survey of land and the establishment of a stable territorial government must precede such grants. The most dynamic railroad statesman in the Senate was Stephen A. Douglas of Illinois, who had secured federal land grants for the Illinois Central Railroad and the Mobile and Ohio. Douglas held a strategic position as chairman of the Senate Committee on Territories. To his committee was reported in December, 1853, a bill for organizing the Nebraska Territory, which Senator Augustus C. Dodge of Iowa had introduced.[20] In the following January Douglas brought forward a bill for the creation of a single territory of Nebraska. In his report on this measure he said that the Compromise of 1850 had introduced the principle of nonintervention by Congress in determining the status of slavery within the territories, or in other words leaving the question of whether a territory should exclude slavery to the inhabitants.

Senator Archibald Dixon of Kentucky now proposed an amendment to the bill definitely repealing the slavery restriction clause of the Missouri Compromise. Douglas finally accepted this amendment in order to gain Southern votes for the passage of his territorial bill. Furthermore, his amended bill also provided for the creation of two territories out of the vast region to the west of Iowa and Missouri—Kansas and Nebraska. The division of the territory was not for the design of permitting a new slave state to be created, but such a division was desired by the people of this region and was expedient in obtaining votes in Congress for the bill. The act as finally passed declared that when the two territories applied for admission as states they should enter the Union with or without slavery according to their constitutions. This momentous bill was passed after Douglas had secured the support of President Pierce during a visit to the latter in company with Jefferson Davis on a Sunday, when Pierce's scruples against doing worldly work on the Sabbath had to be overcome. Pierce used his patronage to force the bill through Congress.

[20] See P. O. Ray, *Repeal of the Missouri Compromise, Its Origin and Authorship* (Cleveland, 1909); F. H. Hodder, "Railroad Background of the Kansas–Nebraska Act," *Mississippi Valley Historical Review, XII* (June 1925), 3–22.

The Southern congressmen, regardless of party, voted almost solidly for the Kansas–Nebraska Act. The Whig senator, Robert Toombs of Georgia, declared that the repeal of the Missouri Compromise restriction restored to the South "the principle unwisely surrendered in 1820." [21] Southerners maintained that the Missouri Compromise had already been violated by admitting California as a free state when a large portion of its territory lay below the line of 36° 30'. Only a few Southern members of Congress, Senators Sam Houston and John Bell, and nine representatives, all but one from the upper South, dared to vote against the bill. Bell believed that the enactment of this bill would not lead to the advance of slavery into this region which was unsuited to it but instead would reopen a violent agitation of the slavery question. Theodore G. Hunt, a Whig congressman from Louisiana, made a noble speech against the Kansas–Nebraska Bill, observing that the South would gain only a point of honor but no practical advantage from the bill, which would gravely impair fraternal relations between the North and South.[22]

The effects of the Kansas–Nebraska Act were the opposite from what Douglas had anticipated. Contrary to the hopes of its sponsors, the bill did not result in the passage of a Pacific railroad act, because sectional rivalry prevented it until Southern congressmen were removed by the secession movement. Instead of settling the irritating question of slavery in the territories by the establishment of the principle of popular sovereignty, the Kansas–Nebraska Act revived more intensely the wrangling over slavery. Although the Missouri Compromise was merely a law of Congress and could have been repealed by a subsequent Congress at any time, the North had come to regard it is a sacred compact. Its annulment aroused the antislavery men in the North to found the Republican party, whose main program was to secure the repeal of the Kansas–Nebraska Act. This controversial bill also shattered the Whig party, which had been a great brake against the momentum of sectionalism in politics. One of the most important consequences of the enactment of the Kansas-Nebraska bill was that it aroused the moral indignation of Abraham Lincoln and brought him out of retirement again into politics. Finally, the doctrine of popular sovereignty it embodied proved unworkable and provoked civil war in Kansas.

The Kansas–Nebraska Act not only led directly to the formation of the Republican party but also to the growth of the Know-Nothing movement (secret in organization, its members would reply to questions that they knew nothing) into a national party. Their platform advocated that an immigrant must have resided twenty-one years in the United States before he could be naturalized, that only native-born Americans and non-Catholics should hold office, and that foreigners should be discriminated against in land legislation. In the South the Know-Nothing party was strongest in the border states. The

---

[21] U. B. Phillips, *The Life of Robert Toombs* (New York, 1913), 119. See also W. Y. Thompson, *Robert Toombs of Georgia* (Baton Rouge, 1966).
[22] *Congressional Globe,* 33rd Congress, 1st Session, Appendix, pp. 434–439.

party controlled the city of Baltimore, the center of the Catholic Church in America, from 1855 to 1860. Know-Nothing mobs, called "Rip Raps," "Plug Uglies," and "Bloody Tubs," who used awls to mutilate their opponents, terrorized the Democratic voters and drove many of them away from the polls. In 1855 the Maryland legislature was captured by the Know-Nothings. The party was also strong in Kentucky, where George D. Prentice, editor of the *Louisville Journal*, Garrett Davis, and Robert J. Breckinridge waged a bitter anti-Catholic campaign. In the August 1855 election, mobs in Louisville killed Catholics and foreigners, and the Know-Nothings won the state. In Missouri Edward Bates, candidate in 1860 for the Republican nomination for president, was a prominent leader. The party was more anti-foreign than anti-Catholic in the Southern states, which explains why some Creole Catholics, such as the historian Charles Gayarré, joined it.[23]

The growth of the Know-Nothings into a national political organization, the American party, was accelerated by the break-up of the Whig party. This great party had followers both north and south of the Mason-Dixon line, and was one of the elastic bands holding the Union together. But the Whigs began to decline after the Compromise of 1850 and the Kansas–Nebraska Act gave their organization a fatal blow. Many of the Whigs in the North entered the Republican ranks, but in the South they either joined the Democratic party, like Robert Toombs and Alexander H. Stephens, or became Americans, like John Bell. The American party's ritual contained an oath to preserve the Union. Southerners who wished to find a safer issue than the slavery question turned to this party, which sought to divert attention to the nativist issue.

The Know-Nothings received a severe check in Virginia, however, when their candidate for governor, Thomas S. Flournoy, was defeated by the eloquent Henry A. Wise. Wise condemned the party in 1855 for its secrecy, its intolerance toward Catholics, and its alliance in the North with the abolition cause. He made a strenuous campaign, concentrating on the western part of the state, where he had a large following as a result of his advocacy of the white basis of representation in the Constitutional Convention of 1850. After this reverse, and a defeat in Tennessee by the Democratic candidate for governor, Andrew Johnson, the Know-Nothings could make little headway below the Potomac in winning state elections.

The attempt to carry out the popular sovereignty principle in Kansas turned into a power struggle between the North and South. Shortly after the Kansas–Nebraska Act was passed, a movement arose in New England to stimulate the emigration of free-state settlers to make Kansas a free territory. It was recognized that Nebraska, on account of climate and soil, would inevitably be a free state, but there was a question about Kansas. In April, 1854, the New England Emigrant Aid Company, with Eli Thayer as president, was chartered to assist free-state settlers to go to Kansas. This attempt

---

[23] W. D. Overdyke, *The Know-Nothing Party in the South* (Baton Rouge, 1950).

on the part of New England to decide the question of slavery in the territory by artificially stimulated emigration seemed unfair to the South and explains partly the bloody struggle that followed. Efforts were made by Southern communities to retaliate in kind, especially the expedition of Colonel Jefferson Buford of Alabama into the debatable land. However, the North had decided advantages over the South in any contest over settling Kansas, such as an easy river route down the Ohio and Mississippi, a surplus population, and more capital. Furthermore, the South was handicapped by the great risk of taking slaves into a debatable territory, where they would be enticed to flee by abolitionists. Of the 107,000 people living in Kansas in 1860, only 27,440 had been born in slaveholding states. This region was not suited to the staple crops that made slavery profitable; in other words, it was outside the natural limits of slavery expansion. After all the hullabaloo concerning the spread of slavery, Kansas had only two slaves in 1860.

In the Kansas imbroglio, partisan politics and land speculation played a significant role. The proslavery element of Missouri, led by Senator David R. Atchison and Benjamin F. Stringfellow, regarded Kansas as a natural sphere of influence, the expansion of which the New England element was trying to rob them. Accordingly, in the first election for the territorial legislature, March, 1855, 3,000 Missourians, called "Border Ruffians" by Horace Greeley, crossed the boundary line and voted. A proslavery legislature was elected, which adopted the slave code of Missouri for Kansas Territory and, in addition, limited officeholding to proslavery men and made it a crime to deny that slavery existed legally in the territory.[24] Had there been no illegal voting on either side, the proslavery group would nonetheless have carried this election. The illegal voting of the Missourians was a serious blunder, injuring the Southern cause.

As a result of the struggle between the pro- and antislavery factions two rival governments were set up in Kansas. A savage internecine war arose. During its violent course the free-state town of Lawrence was sacked, and John Brown and his sons in retaliation murdered five proslavery men. Exploited by politicians and the Republican press, the Kansas question was making new votes every day for the Republican party. Finally in 1858 President Buchanan and the administration Democrats used all the power of patronage and influence to push through Congress the acceptance of the Lecompton Constitution drawn up by the proslavery forces Kansas. The compromise English bill that Congress passed provided for the submission of the notorious constitution to the voters of Kansas along with a normal instead of the huge grant of federal land demanded by the proslavery party, but the people of Kansas overwhelmingly rejected it. The significance of the struggle in Congress over the admission of Kansas with a proslavery consti-

[24] Excellent modern accounts of the Kansas–Nebraska Bill and its consequences are found in Avery Craven, *The Coming of the Civil War* (Chicago, 1957); Allan Nevins, *Ordeal of the Union* (New York, 1947), 2 vol., and Roy F. Nichols, *The Disruption of American Democracy* (New York, 1948).

tution was that it split the Democratic party into the followers of Douglas, who voted against the English bill, and the adherents of Buchanan, thus making the election of a Republican president in 1860 highly likely.

Senator Charles Sumner used the Kansas imbroglio for his terrible indictment of the South in his speech in the Senate of May 19, 1856, entitled "The Crime against Kansas." Sumner was a Harvard man, who prided himself on his culture, his classic language, and his New England breeding. Yet this speech, although couched in elegant language, was a disgraceful exhibition. In it he arraigned Southern civilization and brutally attacked the white-haired senator from South Carolina, Andrew Pickens Butler. He had the bad taste to refer to an unfortunate habit of the old Carolinian senator of expectorating while he spoke. Butler's relative, Congressman Preston Brooks, determined to punish this insult. He approached Sumner in the Senate chamber while the latter was working at his desk and beat him over the head with a gutta-percha cane. Sumner was a powerful man, six feet in height, and in struggling to rise from his desk, he tore it from its moorings on the floor. Brooks's attack was undoubtedly a mistake, and probably was not approved by the majority of Southerners. In South Carolina, however, he was a hero, and when he resigned from his seat in Congress he was triumphantly reelected. Many canes were sent to him by his Southern admirers, but in the North he was called "Bully" Brooks. Charles Sumner was so injured that he did not resume his place in the Senate for three years. His seat was kept vacant by Massachusetts during this period, a mute but eloquent reminder of "the barbarity" of slaveholders. Southerners maintained that his wounds were light and that he was only shamming, to which they adduced some suspicious circumstances. To "Bleeding Kansas" the Republicans added the slogan, "Bleeding Sumner." [25]

The election of 1856 revealed how deeply sectionalism had cut across the political life of the nation. The Democrats in their convention at Cincinnati nominated James Buchanan of Pennsylvania, who had been out of the country as minister to England during the exciting contest over the Kansas–Nebraska Bill. He was a doughface, whose record on slavery was without a blemish in Southern eyes. The American party nominated the vice-president Millard Fillmore. The Republicans in convention at Philadelphia passed over the well-known and able leaders of the party, Salmon P. Chase, Justice John McLean, and William H. Seward, and selected a candidate of availability, John C. Fremont. Fremont had been born in a Southern state, but he had spent most of his life in the West, and he was popularly known as "the Pathfinder" because of his explorations along the Oregon Trail. The chief planks in the Republican platform were the repeal of the Kansas–Nebraska Act and opposition to the extension of slavery into the territories.

The campaign was one of the bitterest in American history. The Republicans were called "Black Republicans" in the South because of their stand on

[25] David H. Donald, *Charles Sumner and the Coming of the Civil War* (New York, 1970).

the slavery question. The Southerners freely threatened that they would secede from the Union if the "Black Republican" candidate was chosen.[26] The crucial state in this contest was Pennsylvania, where the slogan "The Union Is in Danger," plus a liberal use of money, probably carried the state for Buchanan. The Republicans appealed to the workingmen of the North to fight against the aggression of the aristocratic slave power, and they used as propaganda the violent struggle in Kansas between the pro-slavery and free-state groups, "Bleeding Kansas." Although Buchanan won, he did not receive a majority of the popular vote. Moreover, the Republican party, which drew all of its votes from north of the Mason-Dixon line, polled such a surprising vote that it was an ominous sign for the future of the proslavery interests.

While the Kansas question was raging, another slavery episode exacerbated the bitter sectional feeling between the North and the South. Two days after Buchanan was inaugurated, on March 6, 1857, the Supreme Court rendered a decision on slavery in the case of *Dred Scott* v. *Sanford* that was a great technical victory for the South. Dred Scott was the slave of an army surgeon who took him into the free state of Illinois and then into the unorganized territory of Minnesota and after some years of residence there brought him back to Missouri. Scott brought suit in a Missouri court for his freedom on the contention that he was liberated by residing in free territory. He won a favorable verdict, but the case was appealed to the Supreme Court of the state, which in 1852 reversed the decision of the lower court, holding that Scott by returning to Missouri had reverted to his former status of a slave. The widow of the army surgeon transferred the ownership of the slave to her brother John F. A. Sanford of New York, and Scott now appealed to the federal courts for his freedom, alleging that he was a citizen of Missouri bringing suit against a citizen of New York. The case finally was argued before the Supreme Court of the United States, with Montgomery Blair of Maryland as the leading counsel for Dred Scott.

The first question for the court to decide was whether it had jurisdiction over the case. If Dred Scott was not a citizen of Missouri but a slave, he was not entitled to sue in the Supreme Court. The Missouri Supreme Court, which was the proper authority to determine Dred Scott's status, had decided that he was not a citizen of that state. It would have been logical for the Supreme Court to have accepted this ruling and refuse to grant the plea of Scott with a statement of lack of jurisdiction. Such a course of action would have been in line with a previous ruling in the case of *Strader* v. *Graham* (1851), involving some Kentucky slaves who crossed into Ohio where they entertained as minstrels and returned to their native state, later suing for freedom. The court had held that the status of slaves who resided temporarily in a free state and returned to their original home was governed by the laws of the state to which they returned.

---

[26] Clement Eaton, "Henry A. Wise and the Virginia Fire Eaters of 1856," *Mississippi Valley Historical Review*, XXI (March 1935), 495–512.

The majority of the Court had decided to follow the precedent in the *Strader* v. *Graham* case and rule that Dred Scott was not a citizen of Missouri and therefore the Court had no jurisdiction over the case. Justice Nelson had been assigned the task of writing an opinion to that effect. But the majority learned that two members of the Court, Justice McLean of Ohio and Justice Curtis of Massachusetts, planned to write dissenting opinions in which they would uphold the constitutionality of the Missouri Compromise. Five of the justices came from slave states, and they were much disturbed by this news. McLean was an ambitious man, eager to become the Republican candidate for president, and Curtis had been severely criticized in his native state for his vote sustaining the constitutionality of the Fugitive Slave Act, and he may have wished to regain his popularity in the North. Justice James M. Wayne of Georgia was influential in persuading the majority of the Court to reply to McLean and Curtis in an opinion declaring the Missouri Compromise unconstitutional.

While a decision was pending Justice Catron of Tennessee wrote to the President-elect suggesting that he write to Justice Grier of Pennsylvania to the effect that the Court should avoid even the appearance of a sectional vote. Buchanan followed this advice and in reply Grier agreed with this point of view and informed the president-elect that a majority opinion would declare the famous compromise law of 1820 of "non-effect." Grier voted with the Southern justices, and his concurrence was important; otherwise, they might have hesitated to take the bold step. With this inside information, Buchanan in his inaugural address announced that the Supreme Court would shortly render an important decision in the Dred Scott case and that it was the duty of all good citizens cheerfully to accept their decision.[27]

Chief Justice Taney, nearly eighty years of age, wrote the opinion of the Court, but its force was greatly weakened by the fact that the six concurring judges also wrote opinions reaching the same conclusion by several different processes of reasoning. Taney held that Dred Scott was not a citizen of Missouri and had no right to sue in a federal Court. It would have been wisdom for him to have stopped at this point and to have dismissed the case for lack of jurisdiction. But he proceeded to discuss the broader question of whether Negroes could be citizens of the United States. He declared that Negroes had never been citizens of the United States, that the Constitution was made exclusively for the white people, and that the Negroes had no rights under the Constitution. Furthermore, he declared that slaves were recognized as property by the Constitution and that neither Congress nor a territorial legislature had any right to interfere with a master carrying his slave property into the common territories of the United States. Then came his momentous decision

[27] F. H. Hodder, "Some Phases of the Dred Scott Case," *Mississippi Valley Historical Review*, XVI (June 1929), 3–22; and Will D. Gilliam, Jr., "Some Textbooks on the Dred Scott Case," *The Negro History Bulletin*, XIV (February 1951), 106–108; and Broadus and Louise Mitchell, *Biography of the Constitution*, "Wanderings of Dred Scott, Geographical and Judicial" (New York, 1964).

that the Missouri Compromise line of 1820 had always been unconstitutional and therefore null and void.

The announcement of the decision aroused a storm of wrath among the Republicans and antislavery men in the North. The ruling of the Court denied the main plank in the Republican platform that advocated the exclusion of slavery from the territories of the United States by act of Congress. It also made the doctrine of popular sovereignty held by Douglas and the Northern Democrats untenable. The Republicans found in the dissenting opinion of Justice Curtis a statement that Taney's opinions on the unconstitutionality of the Missouri Compromise and the incapacity of Negroes to hold federal citizenship were *obiter dicta,* or opinions outside of the legitimate limits of the case, and therefore not binding. Accordingly, the Republicans took the position that such unwarranted decisions should not be obeyed and that the personnel of the Court should be changed so as to reverse the Dred Scott decision. Actually, Taney's opinions were not *obiter dicta* any more than many of John Marshall's opinions or the opinions of later judges.

But the Republicans and antislavery men launched a campaign to undermine the authority of the court and bring it into disrepute. Taney's unfortunate statement that at the time the Constitution was drawn up the "Negroes had no rights which the white man was bound to respect" was torn from its context and the venerable judge was misrepresented as expressing this sentiment as his own opinion. The New York *Tribune* declared that the decision was "entitled to just so much moral weight as would be the judgment of a majority of those congregated in any Washington bar-room." [28] Instead of the Dred Scott case settling forever the vexing question of the status of slavery in the territories and removing that sore problem from discussion in Congress it immensely stimulated sectional wrangling and bitterness. The South felt that the North had first nullified the Fugitive Slave Act and now it refused to accept a decision of the Supreme Court which went counter to the antislavery cause.

To the growing estrangement of the North and South John Brown gave a mighty impulse by his raid on Harpers Ferry. This Connecticut Yankee had spent most of his life (he was born in 1800) in a shiftless change from one job to another, such as the trade of a tanner, farming, and selling wool. He had failed in everything except in producing a bumper crop of 20 children. Deeply religious, although more in the spirit of the Old Testament than in the gentle spirit of Christ, he was an advocate of the doctrine of violence— direct action in the antislavery crusade rather than the use of methods of persuasion and constitutional change. Slavery was so dark a sin, he believed, that it should be wiped out by the blood of the masters. By brooding over this crime of Southern slaveholders, he became a monomaniac on the subject. With his long white beard, stately form, and intensity of gaze, John Brown looked as though he were a patriarch of Biblical times.

---

[28] Charles Warren, *The Supreme Court in United States History* (Boston, 1924), III, 27.

After his escapade in Kansas and his activities in Missouri of rescuing slaves and taking them to Canada, Brown conceived of a far more ambitious project of striking a blow at slavery. In 1858 he drew up a constitution for a Negro republic to be founded in the mountains of Virginia, which was adopted by a convention of Negroes and whites at Chatham, Canada. The proposed Negro state should engage in guerrilla warfare against the white slaveholders and start a vast slave insurrection over the South. A Negro was chosen as president of the black Utopia, and Brown was elected secretary of war. Oswald Garrison Villard, a distinguished biographer of Brown, says that this project was so fantastic that it is a serious indictment of his sanity.[29] Yet Brown was so persuasive that he succeeded in getting the financial support of Gerrit Smith of Peterboro, New York, a millionaire abolitionist, and of New England businessmen and ministers, although he did not reveal to them the full extent of his plans.

Brown rented a farm on the Maryland side of the Potomac River near Harpers Ferry, Virginia, where he gathered his little army of sons, free Negroes, and desperate white abolitionists, twenty-one in number. On October 16 he marched with his followers against the federal arsenal at Harpers Ferry. This act of attacking an agency of the federal government seems crazy, but Brown, who had a keen sense of the dramatic, planned thus to attract worldwide attention to his cause as well as gain ammunition and supplies. Brown's invasion was based on the theory that the slaves would rise in insurrection and join his little army.[30] In fact, he had one thousand iron pike heads made by a blacksmith to distribute to the slaves for arms against their masters —pike heads to be used in an age of guns and cannon. The arsenal at Harpers Ferry was easily captured, and Brown sent out a detachment into the countryside to arouse the slaves and to capture Colonel Lewis Washington, a planter related to George Washington who owned the sword that Frederick the Great had presented to Washington. John Brown girded himself with this historic sword as he stood a siege and an attack in the fire engine house of the arsenal grounds by United States marines under Colonel Robert E. Lee. Lee sent Captain "Jeb" Stuart, later to become the famous cavalry leader of the Confederacy, to demand that Brown and his followers surrender. When this demand was refused, a small attacking party led by Lieutenant Israel Green battered down the door of the arsenal, and Green wounded Brown with his sword. This officer wore only a light dress sword, which broke in his hands as he struck the fanatical leader, and consequently Brown survived to become a martyr.

Brown could have been tried for treason by the federal courts, because he had attacked a United States arsenal. Nevertheless, because he had also invaded the soil of the sovereign state of Virginia, he was turned over to the

---

[29] O. G. Villard, *John Brown, 1800–1859* (Boston, 1910), 334–336.
[30] See C. V. Woodward, *The Burden of Southern History* (Baton Rouge, 1960), chap. 3, John Brown's Private War.

Virginia authorities for trial. Governor Wise visited him in jail in Charlestown, Virginia, and concluded that he was sane and should be tried for his life. It would have been much wiser if the governor had followed his original impulse and had ordered the fanatical leader to be examined by the superintendent of the State Insane Hospital. Instead, the fanatical leader was assigned counsel and given a fair trial. To save him from the gallows, Brown's relatives and acquaintances gave affidavits that there was a strain of insanity in his family, but Brown himself rejected a plea of insanity and his latest biographer has cast doubt on the validity of the statements in the affidavits.[31] Meanwhile, the people of Virginia were deeply excited over this invasion, and Governor Wise, according to his enemies, magnified the danger of a rescue by Northern abolitionists in order to militarize the state. When Brown was hanged on December 2, 1859, more than fifteen hundred troops surrounded the gallows, including cadets of the Virginia Military Institute. Among the cadets enrolled for the occasion was the venerable fire-eater Edmund Ruffin. While Brown was in prison he wrote noble letters to relatives and friends, and displayed a heroic attitude toward death, making him a martyr in the eyes of the North.

Nonetheless, John Brown's violent act did tremendous damage toward attaining a peaceful and rational settlement of the slavery question. The sympathy shown for Brown in the North after his capture led to the belief in the South that Northerners hated the South. It was revealed that money to finance Brown's harebrained attempt was furnished by Northern abolitionists and businessmen. The South blamed the Republican party for this outrage, but conservative members of that party, such as Abraham Lincoln, condemned the abolition revolutionists. The great New England literary leader Ralph Waldo Emerson, however, declared that John Brown had made the gallows as glorious as the Cross. In the South a wave of mob violence against suspected Northerners followed the John Brown invasion. This episode of violence, which should have been interpreted as the misguided act of a fanatic, was an important factor in destroying the fraternal feelings and bonds of sentiment that held the Union together.

The state of bitter feelings that formed a prelude to the Civil War was revealed in the contest for Speaker of the House of Representatives, 1859–1860. The voting was held in an atmosphere surcharged with passion, for John Brown had recently been hanged. The Republicans offered John Sherman of Ohio as their candidate for Speaker. Although they were the largest group in the House of Representatives, 119 members, the Republicans could not command a majority, for there were 88 administration Democrats, 13 anti-Lecompton Democrats, and 27 Americans and Know-Nothings. Sherman could not be elected Speaker largely because he had been one of the 50 leading Republicans who had endorsed Hinton Rowan Helper's *Impending*

---

[31] S. B. Oates, *To Purge This Land with Blood: A Biography of John Brown* (New York, 1970), 329–333.

Crisis, which had been published in 1859 as a campaign document by Horace Greeley. The debates were violent and unworthy of Congress. A pistol dropped to the floor from the pocket of one vehement member, and many representatives were reported to be armed with pistols. For two months the nation's legislative business was suspended while the House of Representatives continued in a deadlock over the selection of a presiding officer. Finally, on February 1, 1860, William Pennington of New Jersey, a conservative Republican, was chosen. This struggle over the election of the Speaker foreboded a physical conflict between the two sections of the nation that came the following year.

Establishing a Southern Republic

PRIOR to the fateful campaign year of 1860, many of the elastic bands holding the United States together had been broken. As early as 1844–1845 the national Baptist and Methodist churches had divided into hostile Northern and Southern organizations. The Whig party, which had been a powerful cohesive national force in 1850, had been shattered by the Kansas–Nebraska Act. The John Brown Raid had rudely torn the fraternal bonds between the two sections, which in the last analysis were the only enduring basis of a union. After this event there was an exodus of Southern students attending Northern colleges, who returned home. As an eminent authority on the Civil War has observed, "the Democratic Party, the Roman Catholic Church, the Episcopal Church, the American Medical Association, and the Constitution were among the few ties that had not snapped." [1]

The Democrats met in convention on April 23 at Charleston, South Carolina, an unfortunate location for moderate decisions. The magnolia gardens and the azaleas in bloom at this season made the city the most wistful and alluring place in America, but it was also the citadel of the fire-eaters. The control of the convention was obtained by the followers of Stephen Douglas, partly as a result of the seating of the New York delegation headed by Dean Richmond, instead of a contesting group led by Mayor Fernando Wood of New York City, who were favorable to Southern rights.[2] The Douglas men made a mistake in insisting that the platform of the party be adopted before the election of a candidate, hoping by this maneuver to drive out of the convention a few ultra-Southerners and ensure the election of their candidate. The scheme succeeded too well, leading to the disruption of the party.

The platform the Northern Democrats advocated left the question of the extension of slavery in the territories to the federal courts, but, in effect sanctioned the popular sovereignty ideas of Douglas. Such a solution of the slavery issue, accompanied as it was by Douglas' interpretation in the Freeport Doctrine, enunciated in his debates with Lincoln in 1858, was unacceptable to the lower South, whose ultimatum was presented by William L. Yancey of Alabama.[3] As this fire-eater advanced to the rostrum his compatriots arose to their feet in tribute, and the ladies in the galleries waved

[1] Carl R. Fish, *The American Civil War* (London, 1937); see also Avery Craven, *Civil War in the Making, 1815–1860* (Baton Rouge, 1959).
[2] Allan Nevins, *The Emergence of Lincoln* (New York, 1950), II.
[3] See W. B. Hesseltine (ed.), *Three Against Lincoln: Murat Halsted Reports the Caucuses of 1860* (Baton Rouge, 1960).

their handkerchiefs. In an impassioned speech he tried to persuade the Northern Democrats to accept the Alabama platform, which stated the minimum demands of the lower South—a Congressional slave code for the protection of slavery in the territories and the nomination of a candidate who accepted the proslavery creed. The delegates from the Northern states, however, realizing that such an extreme proslavery platform would not carry a single Northern state, rejected Yancey's ultimatum. Accordingly, the Douglas platform was adopted by the convention by a vote of 165 to 138.

When the Douglas platform was adopted, the Alabama delegates, following instructions of their convention, led a bolt of cotton states from the convention hall. The rump convention was unable to nominate a candidate, for after the withdrawal of the Yancey group, largely from the lower South, there did not remain the two-thirds majority of the whole convention requisite for the choice of a nominee. Accordingly, the delegates adjourned, to meet at Baltimore on June 18 and the seceders at Richmond. There was still a chance that the Democratic party might be reunited, but this hope was dashed after the Baltimore convention voted to readmit some of the old bolting delegations at Charleston but refused to accept the original Alabama and Louisiana delegations headed by Yancey and Slidell, who had applied for admission. Douglas offered to withdraw his candidacy in the interest of party harmony and throw his support to Alexander H. Stephens, but his floor manager, William A. Richardson, and his followers from the Northwest and New York refused to yield.[4] After the decision to seat new delegations from Alabama and Louisiana headed by John Forsyth and Pierre Soulé, a second bolt occurred, this one taking most of the delegates of the upper South from the convention. Then the Douglas adherents nominated their hero for president and Senator Benjamin Fitzpatrick of Alabama for vice-president, who declined and was replaced by Herschel V. Johnson of Georgia. The bolters in Baltimore, joined by some delegates from Richmond, formed the Constitutional Democratic party, as distinguished from the National Democratic party, and nominated John C. Breckinridge of Kentucky and Senator Joseph Lane of Oregon as their candidates. Breckinridge, a handsome and eloquent gentleman, who had been vice-president in the Buchanan administration, was a staunch supporter of slavery and believed in the theoretical right of secession, but at the same time he was a sincere Union man.[5]

Still another Southern group, who distrusted both Douglas and Breckinridge, formed the Constitutional Union party. There was only one plank in their platform, the preservation of the Union, the Constitution, and the enforcement of the laws. Meeting also at Baltimore, they chose John Bell of Tennessee as their presidential candidate, and Edward Everett, a former president of Harvard University, for vice-president. This peace-loving party

---

[4] Roy F. Nichols, *The Disruption of American Democracy* (New York, 1948), 317–318.

[5] See W. C. Davis, *Breckinridge; Statesman, Soldier, Symbol* (Baton Rouge, 1974).

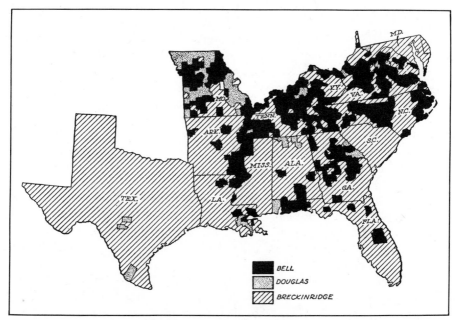

The Vote for President, 1860

was composed chiefly of former Whigs, the conservative, older men of the country. Its platform and nominees appealed especially to the border states of the South. Bell would have a good chance of election, if the electoral college failed to return a majority for any one of the candidates and the election were thrown into the House of Representatives.

As a result of the division of the Democrats, a golden opportunity was presented to the Republican party to win the election of 1860. Passing over the outstanding leaders of the party, the Republican convention chose a candidate of availability, the Illinois lawyer and publicized rail-splitter, Abraham Lincoln. The platform they adopted was a masterpiece of strategy, appealing to the material interests of the East, especially the crucial state of Pennsylvania, by its advocacy of a protective tariff, to the workingmen of the North and the German immigrants by a homestead plank, and to the moral fervor aroused by the antislavery crusade.[6] Lincoln was elected by a majority of 180 electoral votes to 123 for his opponents, although he received only 39.9 per cent of the popular vote of the country. Douglas carried the electoral vote of only one state, Missouri, and shared the electoral vote of New Jersey with Lincoln. Nevertheless he received 1,376,957 popular votes as compared with 1,866,542 popular votes for Lincoln. John Bell won the electoral vote of a tier of states in the upper South, Kentucky, Tennessee, and

[6] H. C. Perkins (ed.), *Northern Editorials on Secession* (New York, 1942), 2 vols.; see also R. H. Luthin, *The First Lincoln Campaign* (New York, 1944).

Virginia (by a close vote) and nearly won North Carolina from Breckinridge. In addition to North Carolina and Maryland, Breckinridge carried the states of the lower South. He received, however, only 44.7 per cent of the popular vote of the slave states. Although he himself was opposed to secession, he was the candidate of the Southern extremists, and his lack of support below the Mason-Dixon line presents the strong probability that the Southern people as a whole were not then in favor of disunion. Furthermore, the election revealed that the city electorates were opposed to the extremists, whereas the rural vote was in favor of taking a more radical stand on the slavery issue. There was also an interesting distribution by age and wealth of votes in the election. The younger, more dynamic, and adventurous element along with the non-slaveholders voted for Breckinridge; the older men and those who had accumulated property voted for Douglas and Bell.[7] Lincoln won the election of 1860 because he carried every Northern state as well as the Pacific coast by narrow majorities. Even if his opponents had united in these states, modern studies of the election have shown strong probability that Lincoln would still have won.

The election of Lincoln elevated into the presidential office a leader who was disposed to follow a moderate course, but unfortunately Southerners had a distorted view of his personality.[8] The president-elect was regarded as an uncouth countryman who would be a figurehead in an administration controlled by Seward and the radical antislavery wing of the party. It was widely rumored among the ignorant classes of the South that Hannibal Hamlin, the Republican vice-president, was a mulatto. Southerners believed that Lincoln's real intention was to use his political power to destroy slavery within the Southern states, as indicated by his "House Divided Speech" of 1858, in which he had declared that the nation could not remain half slave and half free. It is true that the Republican platform had denied any such purpose, but political platforms are often forgotten after the campaign, and Southerners feared that slavery within the states would not be safe under Republican rule. It was the fear of future developments rather than present danger that eventually caused the South to secede.

For the moment, however, the South had little to fear from the election of Lincoln. Some of the old Whig leaders pointed out that Lincoln would be powerless to destroy slavery in the Southern states even if he had such a design. The Supreme Court, under the lead of Taney, would shield Southern interests. In the Thirty-seventh Congress, elected in November, 1860, the Republicans would have 29 Senators, and the opposition would have 37; in the House of Representatives the opposition could defeat the Republicans by a vote of 120 to 108. Yet there was no guarantee that Northern Democrats would vote for the preservation of slave interests, and the victorious Republi-

[7] Ollinger Crenshaw, "Urban and Rural Voting in the Election of 1860," E. F. Goldman (ed.), *Historiography and Urbanization* (Baltimore, 1941), 58–66; and *The Slave States in the Presidential Election of 1860* (Baltimore, 1945); and W. L. Barney, *The Secessionist Impulse: Alabama and Mississippi in 1860* (Princeton, 1974).
[8] See Benjamin P. Thomas, *Abraham Lincoln, a Biography* (New York, 1952).

can party would necessarily exclude the South from all share in the administration of the national government, for no representative Southerners would accept office from a "Black Republican." Thus the South had come to the end of a long period of control over the federal government, which had been maintained by the mastery of the Democratic party, by the domination of the Supreme Court, and by the election of doughfaces such as Pierce and Buchanan to the presidency.

The supreme question of 1860–1861 was whether the country would demonstrate the ability that had previously distinguished Anglo-Saxons of governing by the art of fair compromise. President Buchanan advocated this method of settling the serious controversy before the country in his message of December 3 to Congress. Although he denied the right of secession, nevertheless, following the legal advice of his attorney general, Jeremiah Black, he declared that the federal government had no authority to coerce a sovereign state. Upon Congress he placed the responsibility of deciding what was to be done in case South Carolina seceded. At the same time he proposed that Congress should submit to the states certain "explanatory amendments" to the Constitution that would guarantee explicitly the right of holding slaves in the states and protect slave property in the federal territories during the territorial stage. Moreover, he urged the Northern states to repeal their Personal Liberty Acts. In a noble passage he declared, "Our Union rests upon public opinion, and can never be cemented by the blood of its citizens shed in civil war. If it cannot live in the affections of the people it must one day perish. Congress possesses many means of preserving it by conciliation; but the sword was not placed in their hands to preserve it by force." [9]

Buchanan's policy in this crisis has been severely criticized by the older historians of the nationalist and antislavery school as well as by some recent scholars. They have condemned him for vacillation and weakness during this crisis and have unfavorably contrasted his conduct with the firmness of Andrew Jackson in the nullification movement. Actually, Buchanan tried to create a political atmosphere favorable to compromise and adjustment. He believed that the rights of a minority should be protected and that the decision of the Supreme Court on the question of slavery in the territories should be respected. A strong believer in constitutionalism, he held to the doctrine of divided sovereignty, and therefore did not favor the coercion of a state. The sensible course, he thought, was to refrain from drastic action against a seceding state, that would precipitate a civil war. His policy was to gain time for reflection, for he believed that thus the good sense of the people would assert itself.[10]

---

[9] Richardson (ed.), *Messages and Papers of the Presidents* (Washington, 1907), V, 636.
[10] See F. W. Klingberg, "James Buchanan and the Crisis of the Nation," *Journal of Southern History,* IX (November 1943), 455–474; and Philip Klein, *President James Buchanan, a Biography* (New York, 1962); actually Buchanan's policy, after the reorganization of his cabinet in January, 1861, was essentially the same as that pursued by Lincoln. He was firm in his resolution not to surrender Fort Sumter. See Kenneth M. Stampp, *And the War Came* (Baton Rouge, 1950).

When the news of Lincoln's election reached South Carolina, the legislature without a dissenting vote called a convention to consider the question of secession. So strong was the emotionalism of the hour in this state that thousands wore the blue cockade in their hats and formed companies of "minute men." Congressman John D. Ashmore, who had formerly opposed the fire-eaters, expressed this emotionalism when he declared that Southerners would never permit Abe Lincoln's banner inscribed with such slogans as "the higher law," "negro equality," irrepressible conflict," and "final emancipation" to wave over them nor submit to "the logical results" of this victory, "amalgamation." [11] In the election of delegates to the convention the secessionists won an overwhelming victory. Even in the extreme western part of the state, where Unionism had been strongest, the opponents of secession, led by Benjamin F. Perry, were badly defeated. The old cooperationists, or Unionists of 1850–1851, now voted for secessionist delegates. Nevertheless, it is interesting to note that a majority of the eligible voters of the state did not vote in this critical election for delegates, and it is reasonable to conclude that some of them stayed away from the polls because they were afraid to vote in the negative and thus be branded as "Submissionists." The convention, composed predominantly of elderly men, met first at the capital, Columbia, but adjourned on account of smallpox to Charleston, where on December 20, 1860, they passed an ordinance of secession by a unanimous vote.

Thus the method of precipitating a secession movement by the action of a single state was carried out. By recent experience South Carolina had learned that it was impossible to get the Southern states to cooperate in a resistance movement through an All-Southern Convention. In the previous December, after the John Brown Raid, she had issued a call for a Southern convention to meet at Atlanta and had sent Christopher Memminger, a Charleston lawyer and banker, as a commissioner to persuade Virginia to send delegates, but the leader of the upper South had turned a cold shoulder to this proposal, and it had failed. But now South Carolina received assurances from commissioners sent by Mississippi and Alabama that those states would follow her lead in a secession movement.

After taking the momentous step of dissolving the Union, the Convention appointed Memminger to draw up a Declaration of the Causes of Secession. His statement explained the secession of South Carolina as necessary to assure the safety of slavery and as thoroughly justified by the numerous violations of the Constitution, such as the Personal Liberty Acts, by Northern states. Robert Barnwell Rhett was chosen at the same time by the Convention to compose an address to the people of the slaveholding states. In this document Rhett emphasized the fact that the secession movement was motivated by a desire for self-government and for Southern nationality, comparable to the

[11] Roy F. Nichols, *Disruption of American Democracy*, 372–373; Clement Eaton, *A History of the Southern Confederacy* (New York, 1954), chap. 1, points out that the secession movement in this state was essentially "a conservative revolt."

motives that had produced the American Revolution of 1776. He and his compatriots were irrevocably opposed to any reconstruction of the Union.

South Carolina had taken the initiative in the secession movement, partly because of economic reasons, especially her large stake in the preservation of slavery. Nearly 57 per cent of her population consisted of black slaves, a greater percentage than any other state, and they were held in large blocks. In 1860 eight South Carolinians owned five hundred or more slaves, whereas in the rest of the slave states only seven individuals held as many. Seventy-two South Carolina planters owned between three hundred and five hundred slaves, as compared to only twenty such slaveholding magnates in Louisiana, the state having the next highest percentage of great planters. Furthermore, South Carolina was the most aristocratic state in the Union, whose boundaries contained a smaller area of land occupied by mountains and unsuited to slavery than most Southern states. Led by Calhoun, Rhett, and Hammond, the Palmetto State had nourished a tradition of independence that had flared forth in the nullification controversy, the Bluffton movement, the Nashville Convention, and finally in 1860. Consequently, South Carolina welcomed an occasion, such as the election of Lincoln, to go out of the Union.[12]

The section of the country that most ardently desired to bring about a fair adjustment between the free states and the slave states was the upper South. This part of the South was deeply attached to the Union and did not regard the election of the Republican candidate as a sufficient justification to secede. Slavery in this region was not so strong a vested interest nor was it quite so needed as a means of racial control as in the deep South, for less than one third of the population consisted of slaves. Furthermore, if war should come as the result of secession, the upper South would be the battleground. In this crisis, therefore, the upper South was anxious to find a compromise solution, and it was fitting that the leader in this movement was Senator John J. Crittenden, the successor of Henry Clay, "the Great Pacificator."

Crittenden, a venerable gentleman seventy-three years of age, presented his plan of compromise to the Senate on December 18, two days before South Carolina seceded. He proposed the restoration of the Missouri Compromise line of 36°30′ in the federal territories, the guarantee of slavery within the states and in the District of Columbia, and the preservation of the interstate slave trade. These provisions were to be adopted as irrepealable constitutional amendments. In regard to the problem of fugitive slaves he advocated the repeal of the Personal Liberty Acts and the compensation by the United States government of slaveowners for fugitive slaves lost as a result of the intimidation of federal officers by mobs, equivalent damages to be assessed on counties in which such outrages occurred. The North was offered concessions in the strict enforcement of the laws suppressing the African slave trade, in a

---

[12] See Steven A. Channing, *Crisis of Fear: Secession in South Carolina* (New York, 1970), and Harold Schultz, *Nationalism and Sectionalism in South Carolina, 1852–1860* (Durham, 1950).

modification of the Fugitive Slave Act, freeing Northerners from the duty of serving in posses for the arrest of fugitive slaves, unless there was an attempt to rescue the slave from officers, and in equalizing the fee of the judge in fugitive slave cases regardless of his decision. The most important provision of the Crittenden Compromise was the restoration of the Missouri Compromise line. It was doubtful if any territory would be open to the expansion of slavery under this provision, as both prominent Southerners and Republicans recognized, for New Mexico was unsuited to slavery. Crittenden immediately accepted an amendment, however, which provided that territory hereafter acquired south of that line should be open to slavery. Although the Crittenden Compromise may seem one-sided and primarily an appeasement of the South, it must be remembered that the Southern states threatened to leave the Union, and it seemed imperative in order to save the Union to reassure them that Southern rights would not be violated by the Republican victory.[13]

In this crisis the Republicans, with the exception of the business interests in the party, were in no mood for compromise. Too often they had heard the threat of secession made by Southerners to be alarmed for the safety of the Union. The evidence indicates that Lincoln and the Republican party leaders entertained serious misconceptions about the strength and nature of the Union sentiment below the Potomac. They were therefore not disposed to a policy of appeasement of the South.[14] The only practicable compromise would involve a concession in regard to the main plank of the Republican platform, no further extension of slavery in the territories. The prestige and the political interests of the victorious party would be lowered by any compromise on this issue. More important than this consideration, the Republican party had succeeded in making a moral issue of excluding slavery from territory that was naturally and economically unsuited to its expansion. In such an issue many Northern antislavery men had come to believe that a high moral principle was involved, from which there should be no retreat or surrender to expediency.

Faced by the grave prospect of the dissolution of the Union, Congress tried to formulate a plan of compromise. The Republican Speaker of the House appointed a committee of thirty-three members, one from each state, to deal with the problem, but no Douglas Democrats were on this committee. Also Vice-President Breckinridge on December 20 appointed a Committee of Thirteen in the Senate, which was representative of the various sections. It included Jefferson Davis and Robert Toombs from the lower South, John J. Crittenden from the upper South, Stephen Douglas, leader of the Northern Democrats, and William H. Seward and Ben Wade, two of the most powerful figures in the Republican party. This committee proved to be the decisive body to determine the fate of the compromise efforts.

[13] See Albert D. Kirwan, *John J. Crittenden: The Struggle for the Union* (Lexington, Ky., 1962).
[14] D. M. Potter, *Lincoln and His Party in the Secession Crisis* (New Haven, 1942).

When the Senate Committee of Thirteen met, they accepted a motion of Jefferson Davis (December 22) that no report should be adopted unless it received the assent both of a majority of the Republican members and a majority of the other members of the committee. The reason for this procedure was that no measure unacceptable to the Republicans would be likely to pass Congress. The key man on the committee, therefore, was William H. Seward, the most prominent Republican leader.[15] This New Yorker was so strongly influenced by the astute politician Thurlow Weed, editor of the Albany, New York, *Evening Journal* that the connection was recognized in the epigram "Weed is Seward and Seward is Weed." Before Seward made his decision as to how he would vote on compromise proposals and also whether he should accept a position in Lincoln's Cabinet as secretary of state he consulted Weed. This powerful Republican politician had just returned from Springfield, Illinois, where he had had an interview with Lincoln. Shortly before his pilgrimage to Springfield, Weed, who represented the business interests, had publicly supported compromise on the territorial question in his newspaper. However, in his memorable interview with the president-elect he learned that Lincoln was opposed to the restoration of the Missouri Compromise line. Weed reported this information to Seward, and the latter, accordingly, followed the leader of his party in rejecting compromise on the territorial issue contained in the Crittenden proposals.

The Republican members voted unanimously against this plan of adjustment. The representatives of the lower South on the committee also voted in the negative. This unwise action of the Southerners was taken only because the Republicans had voted against the Crittenden Compromise, although Toombs, Davis, and other prominent Southern leaders were willing to accept it. Consequently the Senate Committee of Thirteen reported on December 31, nine days after meeting, that they were unable to agree on any plan of adjustment. Crittenden on January 3, 1861, urged Congress to allow the people of the whole country to vote on his proposals in a solemn referendum, but his plea was rejected by a majority of the Republicans. Delaying tactics by the Republicans prevented a vote in the Senate on the Crittenden Compromise until March 3, when it was rejected by a vote of twenty to nineteen, after many of the Southern senators had departed. From the vantage point of the hindsight of today it seems that it would have been wise for the Southern Senators, instead of leaving their seats after the secession of their states, to have remained in Congress and to have voted for the Compromise.

The committee appointed by the House of Representatives also made a final report recommending the adoption of some measures that would appease the South. These proposals were the repeal of the Personal Liberty Acts, the enforcement of the Fugitive Slave Act, a Constitutional amendment protecting slavery within the states, and the admission of New Mexico as a state, "with or without slavery" as determined by its constitution. These mild proposals

[15] See G. G. Van Deusen, *Thurlow Weed: Wizard of the Lobby* (Boston, 1947), and *William H. Seward* (New York, 1969).

were rejected by the House of Representatives in the last days of February, as well as the Crittenden Compromise, which for over two months had been held back by parliamentary obstruction from a vote. Representative John C. Burch of California and Senators George E. Pugh of Ohio, a Douglas follower, and Joseph Lane of Oregon urged the summoning of a national convention to consider a plan of adjustment, but their plea was brushed aside.

The Virginia legislature called the Washington Peace Conference to meet on February 4 in the national capitol.[16] Twenty-one states sent delegates, but the seven seceded states refused to participate in the conference. Since the number of delegates from each state varied greatly, it was necessary to vote by states. The venerable ex-President John Tyler was chosen presiding officer. The convention adopted a plan of conciliation consisting of six amendments to the Constitution quite similar to the Crittenden proposals. The chief innovation was an amendment that no new territory could be added to the United States (except by discovery and for naval stations), unless a majority of all the Senators from the free states and a majority of all the Senators from the slave states concurred. With the exception of Rhode Island, the New England states voted against every important amendment proposed in the conference. Michigan, Wisconsin, and Minnesota, the children of New England, failed even to send delegates to the conference, and the leaders of the Republican party in those states were opposed to compromise. The final proposals of the Peace Conference were not acceptable to the Southern border states, Virginia, North Carolina, Tennessee, and Arkansas. Nevertheless, the Washington conference, which sat until February 27, probably delayed the secession movement in the upper South.

The efforts of Kentucky to avert the disruption of the Union were notable. The legislature of this state urged the calling of a national convention, a proposal that President Buchanan submitted to Congress with his approval. In the latter part of April, Governor Beriah Magoffin appealed to Governor Oliver P. Morton of Indiana and to Governor William Dennison of Ohio to unite with him in a plea for a political truce between the hostile sections and the summoning of an extraordinary session of Congress to bring about a peaceful settlement. These partisan Republican governors rejected this constructive proposal, and as a matter of record Congress was not called into extra session by Lincoln until July 4, 83 days after war had started. The Kentucky legislature on April 3 also issued a call for a border-state conference to meet at Frankfort on May 27, but this convention was attended only by representatives from Kentucky, Missouri, and a single delegate from Tennessee.

The responsibility for the failure of compromise must be shared by Congress, the Southern extremists, and President-elect Lincoln. The real chance for adjustment of the sectional controversy was lost by the failure of quick

---

[16] See R. G. Gunderson, *Old Gentleman's Convention: the Washington Peace Conference of 1861* (Madison, Wis., 1961).

action in December, 1860, while the cotton states were still in the Union. The blundering and partisanship of Congress during this crisis is one of the great examples of destructive partisanship displayed by Congress, comparable to its action in defeating the League of Nations in 1919. Yet the temper of the majority of Northern people also seems to have been uncompromising on the slavery question at this period. One evidence of a conciliatory spirit would have been the repeal of the Personal Liberty Acts, but those of the Northern states that had such laws refused to repeal or significantly modify them after the election of November, 1860, with the exception of New Jersey and Rhode Island.[17]

The Southern extremists also did not wish to facilitate the compromise movement by showing a willingness to make concessions. On December 13 a group of Southern Congressmen met in the room of Reuben Davis of Mississippi and telegraphed a manifesto "To our Constituents" in which they declared that there was no hope of obtaining justice to the South within the Union and advised secession by separate state action and the creation of a Southern Confederacy. Unfavorable to the spirit of compromise was the suspicion entertained by Southerners of Northern politicians, such as Lincoln and Seward, or as "Bull Run" Russell observed: "Disbelief of anything a Northern man—that is, a Republican—can say, is a fixed principle in their minds." [18]

The action of President-elect Lincoln must be counted as a very powerful factor in defeating compromise. As previously described, he exerted his influence to defeat compromise on the territorial question in the Senate Committee of Thirteen. Although it is debatable whether the Republican members of the committee would have voted for compromise regardless of his attitude, Lincoln's influence undoubtedly stiffened the backbone of Republican Senators to vote against the consideration of the Crittenden Compromise by the Senate. Lincoln believed that the restoration of the Missouri Compromise line would lead to an expansionist movement in order to acquire new slave territory. He wrote on December 11 to Congressman William Kellogg of Illinois: "Entertain no proposition for a compromise in regard to the extension of slavery. The instant you do they have us under again; all our labor is lost, and sooner or later must be done over. . . . The tug has to come, and better now than later." [19]

As to Lincoln's fears that the restoration of the Missouri Compromise line would lead to filibustering and a drive to acquire Cuba and Mexico, such apprehension was a questionable basis on which to run the risk of a bloody civil war. There was a practical way of preventing this contingency, namely the proposal of Congressman Emerson Etheridge of Tennessee, spokesman

---

[17] Carl R. Fish, *The American Civil War* (London, 1937), 89–97.
[18] W. H. Russell, *My Diary, North and South* (Boston, 1863), 64.
[19] J. G. Nicolay and J. Hay (eds.), *Complete Works of Abraham Lincoln* (Lincoln Memorial University, 1894), VI, 77–78.

for a caucus of border-state congressmen, who on January 7 tried to present a plan providing that any annexation of territory to the United States must receive a two-thirds vote of Congress. This provision would have met the main objection of Lincoln to the Crittenden Compromise, but it was opposed both by Republicans and the secessionists. If we criticize Lincoln and the Republicans for taking an uncompromising and unrealistic stand on the expansion of slavery into the federal territories, we must also condemn those Southerners who were unwilling to surrender the empty right of taking slaves into a region unsuited to the expansion of the "peculiar institution." Both sides were struggling for the advantage in the game of power politics.[20]

During this critical period President-elect Lincoln exercised the silver virtue of being noncommittal. The people of the South had genuine fears for the safety of their way of life when the Republicans should assume control of the government, but Lincoln maintained a "perilous silence," probably because he was afraid of the radicals in his own party. In the Lincoln papers in the Library of Congress is a letter from Maximilian Schele de Vere of the University of Virginia (March 13, 1861) expressing "the intense anxiety with which the loyal and Union loving men of Virginia look for some evidence of the conciliatory spirit of the administration." [21] Actually, Lincoln was a decided moderate in regard to the slavery question, being opposed to disturbing slavery in the states, and he tried to appoint a Southerner, Congressman John A. Gilmer of North Carolina, to his Cabinet. But he refused appeals from moderate Southerners, such as Alexander H. Stephens, John A. Gilmer, and George D. Prentice, to make public statements of his conservative views on the grounds that these sentiments had already been recorded in his speeches. This decision seems to have been a mistake.

After the rejection of the Crittenden Compromise by the Senate committee at the end of December, 1860, the Gulf states acted hastily in calling conventions and passing ordinances of secession. Mississippi was the second state to leave the Union, on January 9, 1861; Florida seceded the following day, Alabama on January 11, Georgia on January 19, Louisiana on January 26, and Texas on February 1, 1861. The secessionists were in favor of quick measures in precipitating a revolution, and wished to take advantage of the emotional reaction of the people toward the election of Lincoln. Consequently, they were more active and better organized than their opponents, whom they branded as "Submissionists." They promised that secession would be peaceful and that it would bring prosperity to the South. The secession movement, moreover, was accelerated by interstate commissioners, who acted as ambassadors to urge sister states to secede.[22]

[20] J. G. Randall, *Lincoln the President* (New York, 1945), I, 240–241.
[21] Maximilian Schele de Vere to William H. Seward, March 13, 1861. Lincoln papers, MSS in Library of Congress.
[22] Basic in the study of the secession movement are Dwight L. Dumond (ed.), *Southern Editorials on Secession* (New York, 1931); and *The Secession Movement, 1860–1861* (New York, 1931); and Ralph A. Wooster, *The Secession Conventions of the South* (Princeton, 1962).

In every state there was a group known as cooperationists, who were opposed to immediate secession. They wished to called a Southern convention to discuss the grievances of their section, and, if secession became necessary, they proposed cooperation in seceding and forming a new nation instead of separate state action. Some of the cooperationists hoped by these tactics to produce delay so that compromise and sober second thought would prevent the dissolution of the Union. Most of these moderates admitted the legal right of secession, but questioned its expediency. They were strong in the Piedmont and mountainous sections of the South, where slavery was relatively weak.[23]

In Mississippi the secession feeling was more powerful than in any other state except South Carolina. Like South Carolina, the population of the state was over half Negro, and in certain areas along the Mississippi River, 93 per cent black. The poorer whites followed the leadership of Senator Albert Gallatin Brown, who for a long period had never been defeated at the polls. This politician, who had arisen from the common people, made frequent use of the race issue, portraying the danger and the degradation of the poor whites if the black slaves should be emancipated. In December, 1860, the people of the lower South were alarmed by rumors of Negro insurrection. Furthermore, South Carolina influence had always been strong in the state. Not only had native sons of the Palmetto State emigrated to the rich black lands of Mississippi but many wealthy Carolinians, including the millionaire Wade Hampton, drew much of their income from their faraway Mississippi plantations. It was this state that at the instigation of Calhoun had taken the lead in calling the Nashville Convention. To the pride of the planter was joined a frontier spirit of violence and direct action, for the state of Mississippi was less than fifty years old.

In November, 1860, a conference of the political leaders of the state was held in Jackson to determine whether Mississippi should encourage South Carolina to precipitate a secession movement. Jefferson Davis and L. Q. C. Lamar voted for a moderate policy, but they were overruled by the deciding vote of Governor J. J. Pettus, a man with a frontier background. South Carolina was accordingly assured of Mississippi's support in her design of secession, and commissioners to the other Gulf states brought back reports that these states would secede if Mississippi did. The convention that met at the capital, Jackson, was composed of one hundred members, of whom at least sixty were professional men, lawyers chiefly, and the others were mostly small slaveowners, or "planters on the make." The vote in the election of delegates to this convention was less than two thirds of the vote in the recent presidential election.[24] A resolution to submit the ordinance of secession to popular decision was overwhelmingly defeated.

[23] See Clement Eaton, *The Freedom-of-Thought Struggle in the Old South* (New York, 1964), chap. 14, Men of Independence, 1860–1861.
[24] Percy Rainwater, *Mississippi, Storm Center of Secession, 1856–1861* (Baton Rouge, 1938), 203–204.

In Florida the secessionists had practically no difficulty in sweeping the state into secession. Senator David Levy Yulee was one of the leading fire-eaters of the South, and the governor, Madison S. Perry, a former native of South Carolina, was also an ardent secessionist. Without a dissenting vote the legislature called a convention to meet at Tallahassee, that passed a secession ordinance by a majority of 62 to 7. This vote is surprising in view of the fact that there were only 5,152 slaveholders in the state, with a white population of nearly 78,000. A resolution to submit the ordinance to popular ratification was defeated.

A free debate over the secession issue took place in the Alabama convention, in which those opposed to immediate secession were given a fair hearing. The cooperationists, who came principally from the hill country in the northern part of the state, were very strong. Their able leader, Jeremiah Clemens of Huntsville in the Tennessee Valley, made a minority report from a Committee of Thirteen on Federal Relations, that gave a good summary of the point of view of the cooperationists. He proposed a Southern Conference, including the border states, to meet at Nashville, Tennessee, on February 22. He advocated the settlement of the difficulties between the North and the South on the basis of the Crittenden Compromise. Secession should be the last resort of the South, only to be accepted after thorough investigation and discussion, and then, if an ordinance should be adopted, it should be submitted to the vote of the people.

At any time from the beginning of the convention, the secessionists had the power to pass a secession ordinance, but they allowed four days for debate. This tolerance was the policy of wisdom, for a strong intrastate sectional feeling existed between the Union-loving people of north Alabama and the inhabitants of the black belt, who were for immediate secession. The strength of the Unionist feeling in the state was registered by the vote for the ordinance of secession of sixty-one to thirty-nine. Thirty-three delegates refused to sign the ordinance and published a broadside giving their reasons for this nonconformity. They maintained that all the Southern states should be consulted before taking such drastic action as separating from the Union, and they demanded that the secession ordinance be submitted to a popular vote.[25]

The most brilliant and the most significant debate in all the Southern states on the question of secession was held in Georgia. Georgia was a strategic state, for if she voted to remain in the Union, any league of seceded states would be split into two segments. Georgia had always been truculent in defending states' rights, and there was hardly a Georgian who would deny the right of secession. It was a question of expediency with them in 1861, an occasion for the exercise of cool judgment instead of passion. Before the members of the legislature passed a bill for the calling of a convention, they

[25] W. R. Smith, *History and Debates of the Convention of the People of Alabama* (Montgomery, 1861), 445–447.

invited the two most illustrious men of the state to speak before them. The frank statesman, Alexander H. Stephens, upheld the negative side of the secession debate, whereas the robust, flamboyant Robert Toombs urged his native state to secede. Stephens declared that the election of Lincoln was not sufficient cause for secession. He pointed out that Lincoln was relatively powerless without the control of Congress and of the Supreme Court, which his party did not possess. Also he reminded his audience that the grievance of the tariff had been redressed by the act of 1857, which had been voted for by both South Carolina and Massachusetts. The chief grievance of the South that remained was the existence of the Personal Liberty Acts, but before seceding, an appeal should be made by the South to the Northern states to repeal these unconstitutional laws. He urged delay and the calling of a Southern convention.

Robert Toombs, on the other hand, told the legislature that now was the time to strike for independence. His speech was a tirade against the Northern people who had oppressed and exploited the Southern people. On December 10, however, he wrote to a group in Georgia proposing that an ultimatum be offered to the North in the form of constitutional amendments that would secure the rights of the South. If a majority of the Republicans in Congress should vote for them the South should postpone final action until the legislatures of the Northern states had acted. Ten days later Toombs sent a telegram from Washington to the people of Georgia in which he declared that it was useless to hope that the North would grant to the South her constitutional rights in the Union and that "Secession by the fourth of March next should be thundered from the ballot-box by the unanimous vote of Georgia on the second day of January next" [26] (the date of the election of delegates to the convention).

The secessionist party in the state was led by a group of unusually dynamic men. The governor, Joseph E. Brown, who had started life as a poor farmer boy in the mountains of north Georgia, was an ardent secessionist. The two senators from Georgia, Robert Toombs and Alfred Iverson, were determined to take the state out of the Union. The wealthy Howell Cobb, the leading Democrat of the state, who had recently resigned from Buchanan's Cabinet, wrote an address to the people of Georgia declaring that the purpose of the victorious Republican party was the ultimate extinction of slavery, and urging secession before March 4; "each hour that Georgia remains thereafter a member of the Union will be an hour of degradation, to be followed by certain and speedy ruin." [27] His half-brother, T. R. R. Cobb, was an apostle of secession, who was called by Stephens "the Peter the Hermit of the secession movement in Georgia."

[26] U. B. Phillips (ed.), "The Correspondence of Robert Toombs, Alexander H. Stephens, and Howell Cobb," *Annual Report of the American Historical Association of the Year 1911* (Washington, D.C., 1913), 521, 525.
[27] Ibid., 516.

The cooperationists, or "Unionists," in Georgia had abler leaders than in any other state of the lower South. The dominant figure among them in the convention was Herschel V. Johnson, who had been the candidate for Vice-President in 1860 on the Douglas ticket. Supporting him were such forceful men as Benjamin H. Hill and Alexander H. Stephens. Outside of the convention the Union cause was advocated by the powerful Methodist divine, Lovick Pierce, and by Judge Garnett Andrews, who remained a Union man through the war. Johnson proposed that a conference of the slaveholding states should be held at Atlanta and that an appeal should be made to the North with a statement of the minimum terms of the South.

The secessionists did most of the campaigning, in which they maintained that secession would not lead to war. For some strange reason Stephens, according to Herschel Johnson, "failed to make a zealous fight against sesession [sic] in the convention." [28] Perhaps the deep melancholy and pessimism of his nature paralyzed his efforts, for he believed resistance to the strong flowing current of secession would be in vain. The Breckinridge men in the convention were arrogant and intolerant toward the moderate delegates and were "rampant for secession." Moreover, fervid appeals for Georgia to secede were made by interstate commissioners from the Gulf states. Nevertheless, the cooperationists made a surprisingly good fight, as shown by the fact that a motion to substitute "cooperation" for immediate secession failed to carry by only 16 votes in a total vote of 297 members. After this close defeat, the secession ordinance was passed by a vote of 208 to 89.

Louisiana and Texas were the last states in the lower South to secede. In Louisiana there was much Union sentiment, especially among the commercial classes, the sugar planters, and the hill and piney woods areas of the northern section of the state. The port of New Orleans was enjoying great prosperity, one half of the total exports of the United States passing through that port. Furthermore, New Orleans had extensive economic connections with the Northwest, which floated its products down to this port of the Mississippi River. The sugar planters of Louisiana, moreover, had no relish to give up the tariff protection they enjoyed to enter a Confederacy predisposed to free trade. After the election of Lincoln, three of the influential newspapers of the city, the *Picayune,* the *Bee* (the chief Creole paper), and the *True Delta,* were for compromise instead of secession. In December, however, there was a shift of sentiment from opposition to support of secession, caused in part by the failure of the Republicans to reassure the South by guarantees or to accept a reasonable compromise. The most prominent minister of New Orleans, Benjamin M. Palmer, advocated secession in his sermons, which were printed and widely circulated. In the election of January 7 for delegates to a convention, the popular vote for secessionist delegates was 20,214 and for cooperationist delegates 18,451, yet the total vote was 12,766 less than

---

[28] "From the Autobiography of Herschel V. Johnson, 1856–1867," *American Historical Review,* XXX (January 1925), 325–326.

that cast in the presidential election of the preceding autumn.[29] This decided falling off of the vote may be explained by the failure of Union men to go to the polls. Despite the fact that it was decidedly against the economic interest of Louisiana to withdraw from the Union, the convention, influenced by the contagious example of neighboring states and by a feeling that Southern honor was at stake, passed a secession ordinance on January 26 by a vote of 113 to 17.[30]

In Texas there were complications of geography and race that affected the action of the state in regard to secession. The frontier section was bitterly resentful against the federal government for its failure to protect the frontier from Indian attacks. However, a group of antislavery Germans had settled near San Antonio who were in favor of the Union. The plantation areas of east Texas and along the Colorado and Red River valleys were secessionist in sentiment. The leader of this group was Senator Louis T. Wigfall, a fire-eater who had emigrated from South Carolina after killing a man in a duel. Also the state had recently been thrown into a panic over rumors of servile insurrection, which was believed to be plotted by white abolitionists.

Governor Sam Houston, however, was a strong Unionist and refused to summon the legislature into extra session because he feared it would call a secession convention. The powerful opposition of Houston, nevertheless, did not prevent the popular will from expressing itself.[31] On December 3, 1860, a group of secessionists at Austin issued an address advocating the election of delegates to a convention to be held at the capital on January 28, 1861. The popular pressure on Houston became so insistent that he finally called the legislature in session one week before the meeting of the Austin assembly, and it validated the extralegal convention. Not all the counties sent delegates to this convention, for some counties were so strongly Unionist that they refused to take part in a movement to withdraw the state from the Union. On February 1 the Austin convention by a vote of 166 to 7 passed an ordinance of secession. Because of the irregularity of the elections to the convention, this body provided that the secession ordinance should be submitted to popular vote. Texas was the only state of the lower South to allow the people to vote directly on this issue. The popular vote on the secession ordinance, which was held in February 23, resulted in 46,129 votes for and 14,697 votes against secession.

In surveying the secession movement, the evidence points to the conclusion that it was not a conspiracy of a few leaders but a genuinely popular

[29] Charles B. Dew, in an article entitled "Who Won the Secession Election in Louisiana?", *Journal of Southern History*, XXXVI (February 1970), 18–32, has shown from the official returns, which were suppressed, that the secessionists polled 52.3 per cent of the popular vote and the cooperationists polled almost 48 per cent.
[30] See J. D. Bragg, *Louisiana in the Confederacy* (Baton Rouge, 1941), chap. 1, and William M. Caskey, *Secession and Restoration of Louisiana* (University, La., 1938).
[31] Houston refused to accept the secession ordinance and was deposed from office. See M. K. Wisehart, *Sam Houston, American Giant* (Washington, D.C., 1962).

movement in the *lower* South.[32] It was true that strong minorities in Alabama, Georgia, Louisiana, and Texas were opposed to immediate secession. Moreover, the secession movement seems to have been rushed through in its last stages without a thorough canvass. Yet the Southern people had contemplated the probability of dissolving the Union for ten years, and had debated the pros and cons of secession in countless debates. The wave of rejoicing throughout the lower South that followed the passage of the secession ordinances indicated a deep popular approval. The common people of the lower South, except in the mountain and hilly area that jutted into the South from Pennsylvania, agreed with the aristocrats that the victory of the Republican party was a danger to Southern society that had to be met by secession. Rejecting the sagacious advice of the little statesman, Alexander H. Stephens, "Let us not anticipate a threatened evil," six states of the lower South (later to be joined by the delegates from Texas) sent delegates to a convention at Montgomery, Alabama, February 4, 1861, which created the Southern Confederacy.[33]

The rise of this new nation was a part of that romantic nationalism of the mid-nineteenth century that was agitating Europe. At last the dream of Southern nationality that the fire-eaters had cherished seemed to be realized —the romantic vision expressed by Langdon Cheves ten years earlier at the Nashville Convention: "Unite and you shall form one of the most splendid empires on which the sun ever shone." [34] It was a vision, however, that did not appeal to the common people—only to men like William Gilmore Simms and Sidney Lanier, who were romantics, or extremists and Yankee-haters such as Edmund Ruffin and Robert Barnwell Rhett.

Far more important among the emotional forces propelling the Southern people to seek independence, a motivation that has been grossly underestimated by historians, was the call to uphold Southern honor (today, in contrast to 1860 in the South, honor seems to be in disrepute). Shortly before the South seceded L. Q. C. Lamar of Mississippi boldly expressed this sentiment in Congress when he declared: "Others may boast of their . . . comprehensive love of this union. With me, I confess that the promotion of Southern interests is second in importance only to the preservation of Southern honor." [35] Also, Governor Beriah Magoffin of Kentucky in replying sympathetically to the fervid plea of Alabama's inter-state commissioner for Kentucky to secede, mentioned chivalry once and honor four times—these were

---

[32] The conflicting interpretation of the forces that led to secession and civil war are admirably presented in Howard K. Beale, "What Historians Have Said about the Causes of the Civil War," *Theory and Practice in Historical Study* (New York, 1946) and Thomas I. Pressly, *Americans Interpret their Civil War* (Princeton, 1954).

[33] R. M. Johnston and W. H. Browne, *Life of Alexander H. Stephens* (Philadelphia, 1878), 566; see also Rudolph Von Abele *Alexander H. Stephens, a Biography* (New York, 1946).

[34] R. G. Osterweis, *Romanticism and Nationalism in the Old South* (New Haven, 1949), 7.

[35] J. B. Murphy, *L. Q. C. Lamar, Pragmatic Patriot* (Baton Rouge, 1973), 38.

terms that were used so often by Southerners of this period.[36] Honor and chivalry, Southerners believed, were based on a high feeling of self-respect inherent in a gentleman that prohibited the South from accepting less than equality in the territories or from submitting to the sectional victory of a party pledged ultimately to destroy the vital institution of slavery in the Southern states.

The Montgomery Convention was completely dominated by slaveholders—there were 33 planters and 43 trained as lawyers in the body and only one of the members owned no slaves,[37] the largest slaveholder being Duncan Kenner of Louisiana, master of 473 slaves. The youngest member was the brilliant, talkative Lawrence Keith, former congressman from South Carolina whose wife told him when he left for the Convention to keep his mouth shut and his hair brushed. As a whole, the delegates were men of large political experience and were animated by a spirit of moderation—neither Rhett nor Yancey had been elected to the convention. In the drafting of a Constitution, the delegates took the Constitution of the United States as their model, modifying it chiefly in respect to strengthening the states' rights character of the document and firmly protecting slavery. The little statesman, Alexander H. Stephens, of *Liberty Hall,* was the guiding spirit of conservatism in retaining the old Constitution of 1787. Nevertheless, the convention made some very progressive improvements over the old Constitution. They adopted, for instance, a budget system that in essentials was taken over by the government of the United States years later (1921); the right of the executive to veto separate items of appropriation bills in the Confederate Constitution was an improvement that forty states have now accepted; the method of amending the Constitution was liberalized and made more flexible; and the president was limited to a single term of six years—in the 22nd Amendment (1951) the United States adopted a limitation of eight years of office for the president.[38]

After making a provisional constitution the convention, voting by states, elected a provisional president and vice-president. In both cases they chose men who had been conservative in their attitude toward secession, Jefferson Davis and Alexander H. Stephens. At the time these statesmen seemed the best that South had to offer, but they proved to be unfit and unhappy choices to lead a revolutionary movement. On February 18, 1861, they were inaugurated in the state capitol at Montgomery, and at the ceremonies a band played the new song "Dixie," with its pervading nostalgia. Like the cradles, coffins, patent medicines, tall silk hats, plows—indeed, most manufactured articles used in the South—the song that was destined to become the unofficial anthem of the Confederacy was also an import from the Yankees, first

[36] Lowell H. Harrison, "Governor Magoffin and the Secession Crisis," *Register of the Kentucky Historical Society,* Vol. 72 (April 1974), 91–110.
[37] Charles R. Lee, Jr., *The Confederate Constitutions* (Chapel Hill, 1963).
[38] E. Merton Coulter, *The Confederate States of America, 1861–1865* (Baton Rouge, 1950).

The First White House of the Confederacy at Montgomery, Alabama. (Courtesy of Library of Congress)

sung by a blackface minstrel, Dan Emmett of Mount Vernon, Ohio, on a New York stage in 1859.

The ladies in crinoline skirts, waving their handkerchiefs and parasols, the planters with their tall hats, the red-necked yeomen, even the Negroes were joyous, the mood of which was caught by the young Carolinian Henry Timrod in his poem "Ethnogenesis." But the answer to an ominous question that the gay and irresponsible crowd hardly considered lay in the future. Would the government of the United States under Abraham Lincoln allow the Southern people the right of self-determination—a right that the United States was to champion so zealously in the twentieth century? The answer came on April 12, 1861, when a federal expedition tried to relieve Fort Sumter, and the first shot of the Civil War awakened the citizens of Charleston.

Modern scholarship has doubted that President Lincoln cleverly maneuvered the situation at Fort Sumter in Machiavellian fashion so that the South would fire the first shot in a civil war that most Southerners believed would not come as the result of secession.[39] Lincoln's call for seventy-five thousand

[39] See the excellent article by Ludwell H. Johnson, "Fort Sumter and Confederate Diplomacy," *Journal of Southern History*, XXVI (November 1960), 441–477 and D. M. Potter, *Lincoln and His Party in the Secession Crisis* (New Haven, 1942), and R. N. Current, *Lincoln and the First Shot* (Philadelphia, 1963).

militia to suppress the rebellion and his blockade of the Southern coasts forced the border states, who were unwilling to secede because of Lincoln's election, to decide whether they would join the Confederacy or remain in the Union. Virginia, the leader of the upper South, decided to secede in a convention on April 17, 1861. Mrs. Chesnut, who was in Montgomery when the Virginia commissioners arrived, wrote on May 9th: "They say Virginia has no grievance; she comes out on a point of honor. Could she stand by and see her sovereign sister states invaded?" [40] A similar sentiment animated the other border states that now seceded, Tennessee and Arkansas on May 6, and North Carolina on May 20, although other motives contributed to their decision. Kentucky declared its neutrality, until a Confederate army under Leonidas Polk violated that neutrality by seizing the strategic city of Columbus at the junction of the Ohio and Mississippi rivers; Maryland was prevented from possible secession by the federal government's strong-arm methods to forestall a free choice, whereas Missouri, torn by factional strife, did not secede. Since both Kentucky and Missouri had governments-in-exile representing the pro-Confederate elements in those states, the Confederacy claimed them as integral parts of the "Confederate States of America," and its flag carried thirteen stars instead of eleven.[41]

There can be little doubt that the upper South very reluctantly joined the new nation created at Montgomery. As to the seven states of the lower South, it is probable that a majority, after Lincoln's election on November 6, 1860, favored secession and the creation of an independent nation. Before that event, however, at least in the spring of 1860, Southern newspapers as a whole, according to a recent in-depth study of approximately two hundred Southern newspapers, were opposed to secession.[42] If opinion in all the fifteen slave states and not simply the lower South is considered, the evidence indicates that the majority of Southerners in 1860–61 were opposed to the breakup of the Union.

Why then was the decision made to do so? Since 1846, the date of the introduction of the Wilmot Proviso in Congress, a sense of alienation from the Northern people grew stronger and deeper in the Southern consciousness. Each section created pejorative stereotypes of the other. When William H. Russell, the London *Times* correspondent, interviewed Seward, the Republican leader, in New York, Seward told him that the Southern people were very different from the Northern people. The Northern politician said that the society of the South (about which he knew very little, although he had spent a brief period in his young manhood as a teacher in Virginia) was

[40] B. A. Williams (ed.), *A Diary from Dixie by Mary Boykin Chesnut* (New York, 1949), 147–148.

[41] See Clement Eaton, *A History of the Southern Confederacy* (New York, 1954), chap. 2, The Decision for War.

[42] See D. E. Reynolds, *Editors Make War: Southern Newspapers in the Secession Crisis* (Nashville, 1970), and J. C. Andrews, *The South Reports the Civil War* (Princeton, 1970).

based on black labor and idle extravagance. He described tumbled-down old hackney coaches such as had not been seen north of the Potomac for half a century, harnesses that were never cleaned, ungroomed horses, badly furnished houses, bad cookery, and imperfect education. The North, on the other hand, he described as a section of the country where "all was life, enterprise, industry and mechanical skill." [43] The Southern people, who also knew little of the North from experience, had equally distorted images of society above the Mason-Dixon line.[44] In 1858, the Tennessee planter and historian Dr. James G. M. Ramsay wrote of the alienation of the South from the North: "We are essentially two people [s]—we are not only not homogeneous, but we have become radically heterogeneous—our passions, our tastes, our character, even our vices are different and dissimilar. Our interests conflict." [45] Henry S. Commager has remarked in his conversation on "American Nationalism," in Garraty (ed.), *Interpreting American History,* that "on the whole, the South had more of the ingredients of nationalism in 1860 than the United States had in 1776." [46]

Although pronounced cultural and economic differences divided the two sections, these alone were not sufficient to lead to the formation of a Southern republic. The old idea advanced so brilliantly by Charles A. and Mary Beard in *The Rise of American Civilization* that the clash between the economic interests of the agrarian society of the South and the predominantly industrial society of the North, rather than the issue of slavery expansion, brought on the Civil War is now discarded by most historians. Strong cultural as well as economic differences can exist within a nation without necessarily impairing the unity.[47] In the United States the likenesses between North and South were far more fundamental than were the dissimilarities. Yet it was a combination of strong, not superficial, cultural differences *and* vital interests (mainly the issue of preserving slavery) that produced the confrontation between North and South in the crisis of 1860–61.

Today the reasoning and especially the emotions of Southerners in what seems the far-distant crisis of 1860–61 are almost incomprehensible. What was so dreadful about the election of Lincoln as president in a lawful manner to impel Southerners to secede? Certainly there was no immediate threat to slavery as long as both the Supreme Court and the majority of Congress

---

[43] Cited by Clement Eaton in "The Confederacy," John A. Garraty (ed.), *Interpreting American History: Conversations with Historians* (New York, 1970), I, 319.

[44] The plain people got a false impression of the Northerners from the ubiquitous Yankee peddlers, who often took advantage of their ignorance and outrageously cheated them. See Schwaab (ed.), *Travels in the Old South, Selected from Periodicals of the Times,* II, 330.

[45] W. B. Hesseltine (ed.), *Dr. J. G. M. Ramsey: Autobiography and Letters* (Nashville, 1954).

[46] Garraty (ed.), *Interpreting American History: Conversations with Historians,* I, 108.

[47] D. M. Potter, *The South and the Sectional Conflict* (Baton Rouge, 1968). Chap. 2 de-emphasizes the importance of cultural differences between the two sections as a cause for secession.

stood as a bar to radical action against the South. It is true that Lincoln could open the postal system to a flood of abolition literature; he might have the unlikely opportunity to change the composition of the Supreme Court; he could refuse to enforce the Fugitive Slave Act; and he and his party could prevent any further expansion of slavery into federal territory. But were these contingencies grave enough to justify secession? The crucial question in 1860 undoubtedly turned upon the right of the South to expand the slave system. Many Southerners believed that slavery had to expand into new territory to survive and some modern writers, notably Eugene D. Genovese, have taken that position. But from a practical, economic point of view, were they right? The convincing conclusion of the cliometric historians, Fogel and Engerman, that slavery was in fact a very profitable institution, leads to the corollary that it did not need to expand to survive. In addition, the land available to Southerners in the Southwest was not suited to the expansion of agriculture, especially cotton, although slaves could be used in mining. Ramsdell's thesis of the natural limits of slavery expansion remain valid despite its faults and the recent attacks on it.[48] Many intelligent Southerners realized that it was futile artificially to foist the slave system where it would not naturally go, and they knew furthermore that property, particularly slave property was timid, and would not venture into a debatable land. Nevertheless, probably the mass of ignorant provincial farmers did not realize the conditions hostile to farming with slaves in the semiarid lands between Texas and California (which had already excluded slavery). It is significant that in 1860 although New Mexico had been open to slavery expansion for some years, it did not have a single slave.

Some recent writers, notably Steven Channing and William L. Barney, have emphasized racial fears as well as the need to provide room for the alarming growth of the slave population. The loss of good arable land from exhaustion and erosion, very noticeable in Alabama and Mississippi, pointed to the need of obtaining reserve land for the future.[49] These considerations did influence Southerners in the secession crisis. But the fight against the containment of slavery demanded by the Republican program, aroused the deepest feelings. The drive to prevent this "unjust" prohibition was motivated primarily not by economic need, but by political advantage, namely to obtain new (at least technically) slave states whose Senators would restore the lost equilibrium in the Senate and thereby giving the South a sense of greater security. Southerners *believed* that the institution of slavery was imperilled and that the honor of the section was at stake. Furthermore, relatively few Southerners questioned the legal right of secession, though a great number of them doubted the expediency of exercising this right.

[48] Eugene D. Genovese, *The Political Economy of Slavery* . . . (New York, 1965), 251–256.
[49] Steven Channing, *Crisis of Fear: Secession in South Carolina* (New York, 1972), and William L. Barney, *The Secessionist Impulse: Alabama and Mississippi in 1860* (Princeton, 1974).

Despite the thoughtless rejoicing over secession in a few states of the lower South, the Southern people as a whole left the Union reluctantly. To sum up the evidence for this conclusion, (1) a majority of the Southern voters in the presidential election of November 1860 did not cast their ballots for the candidate of the Southern nationalists, (2) until the election of Lincoln was announced the newspapers of the region as a whole opposed secession, (3) in the largest states of the lower South—Georgia, Alabama, and Louisiana— the vote of the Unionists, including the cooperationists, was so formidable (and many of them stayed away from the polls out of expediency) that it is debatable what the real sentiment of the people was, (4) the secession conventions, except in Texas and in Virginia (after it already had seceded) refused to submit the secession ordinances to a vote of the people, suggesting that they feared the people might reject them, (5) the two most prominent political leaders in the South, Jefferson Davis and Alexander H. Stephens, were strongly averse to precipitating a secession movement, and finally (6) the states of the upper South resisted almost to the last moment the movement to break up the Union. Illusions upon illusions, notably a belief that secession would not be followed by war and if perchance war came, "Cotton is King," and that the *élan* of the Southern people would prevail against technology and numbers, played a decisive role in the disastrous decision.

Selected Bibliography

Travel Accounts

Since the observations and reports of travelers in the South prior to 1860 have been used extensively in this volume to illuminate various aspects of Southern life, such as slavery, agriculture and industry, education, religion, manners and customs, and the structure of the unique society of the South, it is a valuable aid to the student to list the more important accounts that have been used. A much fuller list is included in the bibliography of Clement Eaton, *The Growth of Southern Civilization, 1790–1860* (New York, 1961). Indispensable as a guide to Southern travel accounts is T. D. Clark (ed.) *Travels in the Old South, A Bibliography* (Norman, Okla., 1956–1959), 3 vols., and Laura W. Roper, *F.L.O.: a Biography of Frederick Law Olmsted* (Baltimore, 1974), gives a recent analysis of the observations of the most informative traveler that visited the South in the decade, 1850–1860. A selected list of travel accounts includes:

Abdy, E. S., *Journal of a Residence and Tour in the United States, 1833–1834* (London, 1835).

Anburey, Thomas, *Travels Through the Interior Parts of America* (Boston. 1923), 2 vols.

Arfwedson, C. D., *The United States and Canada* (London, 1834), 2 vols.

Bremer, Fredrika, *The Homes of the New World, Impressions of America* (New York, 1853), 2 vols.

Buckingham, J. S., *The Slave States of America* (London, 1842), 2 vols.

Burnaby, Andrew, *Burnaby's Travels through North America* (New York, 1904).

Chastellux, F. J. Marquis de, *Travels in North America in the Years 1780, 1781, 1782,* ed. by W. H. Price, Jr. (Chapel Hill, 1963), 2 vols.

Durand of Dauphiné, *A Frenchman in Virginia* (Privately printed, 1923).

Featherstonhaugh, G. W., *Excursion through the Slave States* (London, 1844), 2 vols.

Grund, F. J., *Aristocracy in America* (New York, 1959).

Hall, Basil, Captain, *Travels in North America in the Years 1827–28* (Edinburgh, 1929), 3 vols.

Hamilton, Alexander, *Gentleman's Progress: The Itinerarium of Dr. Alexander Hamilton, 1744,* ed. by Carl Bridenbaugh (Chapel Hill, 1948).

Lyell, Sir Charles, *A Second Visit to the United States* (New York, 1849), 2 vols.

Martineau, Harriet, *Society in America* (London, 1837), 3 vols.

Olmsted, Frederick Law, *A Journey in the Seaboard Slave States* (New York, 1856).

———, *A Journey in the Back Country,* with an Introduction by Clement Eaton (New York, 1970).

————, *A Journey through Texas, or a Saddle Trip on the Southwestern Frontier* (New York, 1857).

Power, Tyrone, *Impressions of America* (Philadelphia, 1836).

Robinson, Solon, *Solon Robinson, Pioneer and Agriculturist*, ed. by A. A. Kellar (Indianapolis, 1936), 2 vols.

Rochefoucauld-Liancourt, F., *Travels through the United States of America* (London, 1799), 2 vols.

Russell, Robert, *North America, Its Agriculture and Its Climate* (Edinburgh, 1857).

Russell, W. H., *My Diary North and South* (Boston, 1863).

Schoepf, J. D., *Travels in the Confederation* [1782–1783], ed. by A. J. Morrison (Philadelphia, 1911), 2 vols.

Sterling, James, *Letters from the Slave States* (London, 1857).

Schulz, Christian, Jr., *Travels on an Inland Voyage* (New York, 1810).

Schwaab, E. L. (ed.), *Travels in the Old South, Selected from Periodicals of the Time* (Lexington, Ky., 1973), 2 vols.

Tocqueville, Alexis de, *Democracy in America* (New York, 1946).

Toulmin, Harry, *The Western Country in 1793* (San Marino, Calif., 1948).

Woodmason, Charles, *The Carolina Backcountry on the Eve of the Revolution: the Journal and Other Writings of Charles Woodmason, Anglican Itinerant*, ed. by R. J. Hooker (Chapel Hill, 1953).

Agriculture

The best account of Southern agriculture is:

L. C. Gray, *History of Agriculture in the Southern United States to 1860* (Washington, 1933), 2 vols.

Other valuable general works are:

H. H. Bennett, *The Soils and Agriculture of the Southern States* (New York, 1921).

Avery Craven, *Soil Exhaustion As a Factor in the Agricultural History of Virginia and Maryland, 1606–1860* (Urbana, 1922).

U. B. Phillips, *Life and Labor in the Old South* (Boston, 1929).

J. C. Bonner, *A History of Georgia Agriculture, 1732–1860* (Athens, Ga., 1964).

C. O. Cathey, *Agricultural Developments in North Carolina 1783–1860* (Chapel Hill, 1956).

J. H. Moore, *Agriculture in Ante-Bellum Mississippi* (New York, 1958).

Herbert Weaver, *Mississippi Farmers, 1850–1860* (Nashville, 1945).

Particular crops are discussed in the following works:

Cotton
C. S. Davis, *The Cotton Kingdom in Alabama* (Montgomery, 1939).

E. A. Davis (ed.), *Plantation Life in the Florida Parishes of Louisiana, 1836–1846, As Reflected in the Diary of Bennett H. Barrow* (New York, 1943).

W. T. Jordan, *Hugh Davis and His Alabama Plantation* (Univ. of Alabama, 1948).

A. G. Smith, *Economic Adjustment of an Old Cotton State: South Carolina 1820–1860* (Columbia, S. C., 1958).
Fletcher Green (ed.), *The Lides Go South and West* (Columbia, S. C., 1950).
E. M. Coulter, *Thomas Spalding of Sapelo* (Univ. of Louisiana, 1940).

Hemp
J. H. Hopkins, *A History of the Hemp Industry in Kentucky* (Lexington, Ky., 1957).

Rice
D. C. Heyward, *Seed from Madegascar* (Chapel Hill, 1937).
J. H. Easterby (ed.), *The South Carolina Rice Plantation As Revealed in the Papers of Robert F. W. Allston* (Chicago, 1945).
A. R. Childs (ed.), *Rice Planter and Sportsman: The Recollections of J. Motte Alston, 1821–1909* (Columbia, S. C., 1953).
A. V. House, *Plantation Management and Capitalism in Ante-Bellum Georgia: the Journal of Hugh Frazer Grant, Rice Grower* (New York, 1954).

Sugar
J. K. Menn, *The Large Slaveholders of Louisiana, 1860* (New Orleans, 1964).
J. C. Sitterson, *Sugar Country: The Cane Sugar Industry in the South, 1753–1950* (Lexington, Ky., 1953).
C. P. Roland, *Louisiana Sugar Plantations During the American Civil War* (Baton Rouge, 1957).

Tobacco
Louis Morton, *Robert Carter of Nomini Hall: A Virginia Tobacco Planter of the Eighteenth Century* (Princeton, 1940).
R. D. Davis (ed.), *William Fitzhugh and His Chesapeake World: The Fitzhugh Letters and Other Documents* (Chapel Hill, 1963).
W. K. Scarborough (ed.), *The Diary of Edmund Ruffin* (Baton Rouge, 1972). 2 vols.
Avery Craven, *Edmund Ruffin, Southerner* (New York, 1932).
Betsy Fleet and Clement Eaton (eds.), *Green Mount: A Virginia Plantation Family during the Civil War* (Lexington, Ky., 1962).
William Tatham, *An Historical and Practical Essay on the Culture and Commerce of Tobacco* (London, 1800).
G. M. Herndon, *William Tatham and the Culture of Tobacco* (Coral Gables, Fla., 1969).

Wheat, Corn, and Cattle
Fletcher Green (ed.), *Ferry Hill Plantation Journal, 1838–1839* (Chapel Hill, 1961).
P. C. Henlein, *Cattle Kingdom in the Ohio Valley, 1785–1860* (Lexington, Ky., 1959).
B. L. Henry, *The Tennessee Yeomen, 1840–1860*.
J. S. Bassett (ed.), *The Westover Journal of John A. Selden* (Northhampton, Mass., 1921).
S. B. Hilliard, *Hogmeat and Hoecake: Food Supply in the Old South* (Carbondale, Ill., 1972).

Travel accounts that are especially useful for observations on agriculture are:

H. A. Kellar (ed.), *Solon Robinson Pioneer, and Agriculturist, 1825–1848* (Indianapolis, 1936), 2 vols.
and the accounts of Sir Charles Lyell and Frederick Law Olmsted.

Agricultural publications are considered in:

A. L. Demaree, *The American Agricultural Press, 1819–1860* (New York, 1941).
E. M. Coulter, *Daniel Lee, Agriculturist: His Life, North and South* (Athens, Ga., 1972).

Plantation management is realistically described in:

W. K. Scarborough, *The Overseer: Plantation Management in the Old South* (Baton Rouge, 1966).
J. S. Bassett, *The Southern Plantation Overseer As Revealed in His Letters* (Northampton, Mass., 1925).
C. S. Sydnor, *A Gentleman of the Old Natchez Region: Benjamin L. C. Wailes* (Durham, 1938).

Architecture, Painting, and Music

Adams, A. B., *John James Audubon, A Biography* (New York, 1966).

Christ-Janer, A., *George Caleb Bingham of Missouri* (New York, 1941).

Fisher, M. M., *Negro Slave Songs in the United States* (Ithaca, 1953).

Ford, A., *John James Audubon* (Norman, Okla., 1964).

Forman, H. C., *The Architecture of the Old South: the Medieval Style, 1585–1850* (Cambridge, Mass., 1948).

Flexner, J. T., *The Light of Distant Skies, 1700–1835* [painting] (New York, 1954).

Hamlin, T. F., *Greek Revival Architecture in America* (New York, 1944).

———, *Benjamin Henry Latrobe* (New York, 1955).

Jackson, G. P., *White Spirituals in the Southern Uplands* (New York, 1913).

Kimball, S. Fiske, *Domestic Architecture of the American Colonies and of the Early Republic* (New York, 1927).

Lancaster, Clay, *Back Streets and Pine Forests: The Work of John McMurtry* (Lexington, Ky., 1956).

Latrobe, B. H., *The Journal of Latrobe* (New York, 1905).

Lomax, J. A. and Allan, *American Ballads and Folk Songs* (New York, 1934).

McDermott, J. F., *George Caleb Bingham: River Portraitist* (Norman, Okla., 1959).

Mumford, Lewis, *The South in Architecture* (New York, 1941).

Newcomb, Rexford, *Architecture in Old Kentucky* (Urbana, 1953).

Scully, A., Jr., *James Dakin, Architect: His Career in New York and the South* (Baton Rouge, 1974).

Sellers, C. C., *Charles Willson Peale* (Philadelphia, 1947), 2 vols.

Smith, J. F., *White Pillars: Early Life and Architecture of the Lower Mississippi Valley Country* (New York, 1941).

Waterman, T. T. and J. H. Barrows, *Domestic Colonial Architecture of Tidewater Virginia* (Chapel Hill, 1947).

Wertenbaker, T. J., *The Golden Age of Colonial Culture* (New York, 1942).

White, John, *The American Drawings of John White, 1577–1590*, ed. by F. Hutton and D. B. Quinn (Chapel Hill, 1964).

Wittke, Carl, *Tambo and Bones, a History of the American Minstrel Stage* (Durham, 1930).

Education

The history of education in the South prior to 1860, strangely, has not been very well developed; the most scholarly works are on higher education:

Battle, Kemp, *History of the University of North Carolina* (Raleigh, 1907–1912), 2 vols.

Bruce, P. A., *History of the University of Virginia, 1819–1919* (New York, 1920–1922).

Chafin, Nora, *Trinity College 1839–1892: Beginnings of Duke University* (Durham, 1950).

Connor, R. D. W., *A Documentary History of the University of North Carolina, 1776–1799* (Chapel Hill, 1935), 2 vols.

Coulter, E. M., *College Life in the Old South* (New York, 1928).

Easterby, J. H., *A History of the College of Charleston* (Charleston, 1935).

Fleming, W. L., *Louisiana State University, 1860–1896* (Baton Rouge, 1936).

Freidel, Frank, *Francis Lieber, Nineteenth Century Liberal* (Baton Rouge, 1948).

Godbold, A., *The Church College of the Old South* (Durham, 1944).

Hollis, D. V., *University of South Carolina* (Columbia, S. C., 1951–56), 2 vols.

Jennings, W. W., *Transylvania, Pioneer University of the West* (New York, 1955).

Johnson, T. C., Jr., *Scientific Interests in the Old South* (New York, 1936).

Malone, Dumas, *The Public Life of Thomas Cooper 1783–1839* (Columbia, S. C., 1961).

Paschal, G. W., *History of Wake Forest College* (Wake Forest, 1935–1943), 3 vols.

Public Schools

Coon, C. L. (ed.), *The Beginnings of Public Education in North Carolina: A Documentary History* (Raleigh, 1908), 3 vols.

Dabney, C. W., *Universal Education in the South* (Chapel Hill, 1936), 2 vols.

Eaton, Clement, *Freedom of Thought in the Old South* (Durham, 1940).

Farish, H. D. (ed.), *Journal and Letters of Philip Vickers Fithian, 1773–1774: A Plantation Tutor of the Old Dominion* (Williamsburg, 1957).

Knight, E. W., *A Documentary History of Education in the South Before 1860* (Chapel Hill, 1949–1953), 4 vols.

———, *Public Education in the South* (New York, 1922).

McVey, F. L., *The Gates Open Slowly: A History of Education in Kentucky* (Lexington, Ky., 1949).
Wright, L. B., *The Cultural Life of the American Colonies, 1607–1763* (New York, 1957).

Government, Politics, and Military Affairs to 1800

Abbott, W. W., *The Royal Governors of Georgia, 1754–1775* (Chapel Hill, 1959).
Abernethy, T. P., *Three Virginia Frontiers* (Baton Rouge, 1940).
———, *Western Lands and the American Revolution* (New York, 1937).
———, *From Frontier to Plantation in Tennessee: A Study in Frontier Democracy* (Chapel Hill, 1932).
Alden, J. R., *The First South* (Baton Rouge, 1961).
———, *John Stuart and the Southern Colonial Frontier* (Ann Arbor, 1944).
———, *The South in the Revolution, 1763–1789* (Baton Rouge, 1957).
Andrews, C. M., *The Colonial Period of American History* (New Haven, 1934–38), 4 vols.
Bailyn, Bernard, *Ideological Origins of the American Revolution* (New York, 1967).
———, *Pamphlets on the American Revolution* (New York, 1965–7), 4 vols.
Barbour, P. L., *The Three Worlds of Captain John Smith* (Boston, 1964).
Barker, C. A., *The Background of the Revolution in Maryland* (New Haven, 1940).
Beard, C. A., *An Economic Interpretation of the Constitution of the United States* (New York, 1936, originally published, 1913).
———, *Economic Origins of Jeffersonian Democracy* (New York, 1915).
Beer, G. L., *Origins of the British Colonial System, 1578–1660* (New York, 1908).
———, *The Old Colonial System, 1660–1754* (New York, 1912).
Beverley, Robert, *The History and Present State of Virginia*, edit. by L. B. Wright (Chapel Hill, 1944).
Brant, Irving, *James Madison* (Indianapolis, 1941–61), 6 vols.
Bridenbaugh, Carl, *Cities in the Wilderness: the First Century of Urban Life in America, 1625–1742* (New York, 1938).
———, *Cities in Revolt, Urban Life in America, 1743–1776* (New York, 1955).
———, *Seat of Empire: The Political Role of Eighteenth Century Williamsburg* (Charlottesville, 1958).
Brown, R. E., *Charles Beard and the Constitution: A Critical Analysis* (New York, 1956).
———, and B.K., *Virginia, 1705–1786: Democracy or Aristocracy?* (East Lansing, Mich., 1964).
Brown, R. M., *The South Carolina Regulators* (Cambridge, 1963).
Bruce, P. A., *Institutional History of Virginia in the Seventeenth Century* (New York, 1895), 2 vols.
Burnett, E. C., *The Continental Congress* (New York, 1941).
———, *Letters of Members of the Continental Congress* (Washington, D.C., 1921).

Byrd, William II, *The Secret Diary of William Byrd, 1709–1712*, ed. by M. H. Woodfin (Richmond, 1941).

———, *Another Secret Diary of William Byrd of Westover* (Richmond, 1942).

———, *William Byrd's Histories of the Dividing Line Betwixt Virginia and North Carolina*, ed. by W. K. Boyd (Raleigh, 1929).

Carter, Landon, *The Diary of Colonel Landon Carter of Sabine Hall, 1752–1778*, ed. by J. P. Greene (Charlottesville, 1965), 2 vols.

Caughey, J. W., *Bernardo de Gálvez in Louisiana, 1776–1783* (Gretna, La., 1972 reprint).

———, *McGillivray of the Creeks* (Norman, Okla., 1938).

Cooke, Jacob (ed.), *The Federalist* (Middletown, Conn., 1961).

Crane, V. M., *The Southern Frontier, 1676–1732* (Philadelphia, 1929).

Craven, W. F., *The Dissolution of the Virginia Company* (New York, 1932).

———, *The Southern Colonies in the Seventeenth Century, 1607–1689* (Baton Rouge, 1949).

Crowl, P. A., *Maryland During and After the Revolution.*

Dickinson, O. M., *American Colonial Government, 1696–1765: A Study of the British Board of Trade in Its Relation to the American Colonies* (Cleveland, 1912).

Dodson, Leonidas, *Alexander Spotswood* (Philadelphia, 1932).

Douglas, E. P., *Rebels and Democrats: The Struggle for Equal Political Rights and Majority Rule during the American Revolution* (Chapel Hill, 1955).

Driver, C. W., *John Sevier* (Chapel Hill, 1932).

Eddis, William, *Letters from America* (London, 1792).

Elliott, J. (ed.), *The Debates in the Several State Conventions on the Adoption of the Federal Constitution* (Philadelphia, 1891), 5 vols.

Ettinger, A. A., *James Edward Oglethorpe, Imperial Idealist* (Oxford, 1936).

Freeman, D. S., *George Washington, a Biography* (New York, 1948–54), 7 vols.

Fries, A. L., *The Road to Salem* (Chapel Hill, 1944).

———, and K. G. Hamilton (eds.), *Records of the Moravians in North Carolina* (Raleigh, 1922–1969), 11 vols.

Gayarré, C. E. A., *History of Louisiana* (New Orleans, 1885), 4 vols.

Gibson, C., *Spain in America* (New York, 1966).

Gipson, L. H., *The British Empire before the American Revolution* (New York, 1946), 6 vols.

———, *The Coming of the Revolution, 1763–1775* (New York, 1954).

Giraud, Marcel, *History of French Louisiana* (Baton Rouge, 1973), I.

Greene, J. P., *The Quest for Power: the Lower House of Assembly in the Southern Royal Colonies, 1689–1776* (Chapel Hill, 1964).

Grigsby, H. B., *The History of the Virginia Federal Convention of 1788* (Richmond, 1890–91), 2 vols.

Hart, F. H., *The Valley of Virginia in the American Revolution, 1763–1789* (Chapel Hill, 1942).

Henderson, Archibald, *The Conquest of the Old Southwest* (New York, 1920).

Hendrick, B. J., *The Lees of Virginia: Biography of a Family* (Boston, 1935).

Hill, Helen, *George Mason, Constitutionalist* (Cambridge, Mass., 1938).

Hofstadter, Richard, *The American Political Tradition and the Men Who Made It* (New York, 1948).

James, J. A., *The Life of George Rogers Clark* (Chicago, 1928).

Jameson, J. F., *The American Revolution Considered As a Social Movement* (Princeton, 1926).

Jefferson, Thomas, *Notes on the State of Virginia*, ed. by T. P. Abernethy (New York, 1963).

———, *The Papers of Thomas Jefferson*, ed. by Julian P. Boyd (Princeton, 1950—), 19 vols. to date—to 1791.

Jensen, Merrill, *The Articles of Confederation* (Madison, Wis., 1948).

———, *The New Nation: A History of the United States during the Confederation, 1781–1789* (New York, 1950).

Jones, H., *The Present State of Virginia*, ed. by R. L. Morton (Chapel Hill, 1956).

Ketcham, Ralph, *James Madison, A Biography* (New York, 1971).

Kincaid, R. L., *The Wilderness Road* (Indianapolis, 1947).

Koontz, L. K., *Robert Dinwiddie: His Career in American Colonial Government and Westward Expansion* (Glendale, Calif., 1949).

Labaree, L. W., *Conservatism in Early American History* (New York, 1948).

McDonald, Forest, *We the People: The Economic Origins of the Constitution* (Chicago, 1958).

McRee, G. J., *James Iredell* (New York, 1857), 2 vols.

Malone, Dumas, *Jefferson and His Time* (Boston, 1948–1974), 5 vols.

Madison, James, *Notes on the Federal Convention of 1787* (Athens, Ohio, 1966).

———, *The Papers of James Madison*, ed. by M. E. Rachal and R. A. Rutland (Chicago, 1962—), 8 vols., to 1786 to date.

Main, J. T., *The Antifederalists: Critics of the Constitution, 1781–1788* (Chapel Hill, 1961).

Mayo, Bernard, *Myths and Men* (Athens, Ga., 1959).

Mays, D. J., *Edmund Pendleton, 1721–1803, A Biography* (Cambridge, Mass., 1952), 2 vols.

Meade, R. D., *Patrick Henry* . . . (Philadelphia, 1969), 2 vols.

Morgan, E. S., *The Stamp Act Congress: Prologue to the Revolution* (Chapel Hill, 1953).

Morton, R., *Colonial Virginia* (Chapel Hill, 1960), 2 vols.

Mowat, C. L., *East Florida As a British Province, 1763–1784* (Berkeley, 1943).

Mitchell, Broadus and Louise, *A Biography of the Constitution of the United States* (New York, 1964).

Pendleton, Edmund, *The Papers of Edmund Pendleton, 1734–1803*, ed. by D. A. Mays (Charlottesville, 1967).

Peterson, M. D., *Thomas Jefferson and the New Nation* (New York, 1970).

———, *The Jefferson Image in the American Mind* (New York, 1960).

Rogers, G. C., Jr., *Evolution of a Federalist: William Loughton Smith of Charleston, 1758–1812* (Columbia, S.C., 1962).

Rutland, R. A., *The Birth of the Bill of Rights* (Chapel Hill, 1955).

———, *George Mason, Reluctant Statesman* (Williamsburg, 1961).

Rutman, D. B. (ed.), *The Old Dominion: Essays for Thomas Perkins Abernethy* (Charlottesville, 1964).

Smith, J. M. (ed.), *Seventeenth Century America* (Chapel Hill, 1959).

Sydnor, C. S., *Gentlemen Freeholders: Political Practices in Washington's Virginia* (Chapel Hill, 1952).

Turner, F. J., *The Frontier in American History* (New York, 1921).

Wallace, D. D., *Life of Henry Laurens* (New York, 1915).

Wallace, W. M., *Appeal to Arms: A Military History of the Revolution* (New York, 1951).

Walsh, R., *Charleston's Sons of Liberty: A Study of the Artisans, 1763–1789* (Columbia, 1959).

Ward, C., *The War of the Revolution* (New York, 1952), 2 vols.

Washburne, W. E., *The Governor and the Rebel: A History of Bacon's Rebellion in Virginia* (Chapel Hill, 1957).

Washington, George, *The Diaries of George Washington, 1748–1799*, ed., by J. C. Fitzpatrick (Boston, 1925), 4 vols.

Watlington, Patricia, *The Partisan Spirit: Kentucky Politics 1779–1792* (New York, 1972).

Wertenbaker, T. J., *The Old South: The Founding of American Civilization* (New York, 1942).

———, *Patrician and Plebeian in Virginia* (Charlottesville, 1940).

———, *Planters of Colonial Virginia* (Princeton, 1922).

———, *Torchbearer of the Revolution: The Story of Bacon's Rebellion and Its Leader* (Princeton, 1940).

Zahniser, M. R., *Charles Cotesworth Pinckney* (Chapel Hill, 1967).

Government, Politics, and Military Affairs, 1800–1861

Abernethy, T. P., *The Burr Conspiracy* (New York, 1954).

Alexander, T. B., *Sectional Stress and Party Strength: A Study of Roll-Call Voting Patterns in the United States House of Representatives, 1836–1860* (Nashville, 1967).

———, *Thomas A. R. Nelson of East Tennessee* (Nashville, 1967).

Ambler, C. H., *Thomas Ritchie, a Study in Virginia Politics* (Chicago, 1913).

Ammon, H. *James Monroe: The Quest for Nationality* (New York, 1971).

Barney, William L., *The Road to Secession: A New Perspective on the Old South* (New York, 1972).

———, *The Secessionist Impulse: Alabama and Mississippi in 1860* (Princeton, 1974).

Bassett, J. S., *Correspondence of Andrew Jackson* (Washington, 1926–31), 7 vols.

———, *Life of Andrew Jackson* (New York, 1911), 2 vols.

Benton, T. H., *Thirty Years' View . . .* (New York, 1854–56), 2 vols.

Boney, F. N., *John Letcher of Virginia: The Story of Virginia's Civil War Governor* (Univ. of Alabama, 1966).

Boyd, Julian P., *The Papers of Thomas Jefferson* (1950—), 19 vols. to date.

Brodie, Fawn M., *Thomas Jefferson: An Intimate History* (New York, 1974).

Brownlow, W. G., *Sketches of the Rise, Progress and Decline of Secession* (Philadelphia, 1862).

Beveridge, A. J., *Life of John Marshall* (New York, 1916–19), 4 vols.

Binkley, W. C., *The Expansionist Movement in Texas, 1836–1850* (Berkeley, 1925).

———, *The Texas Revolution* (New York, 1932).

Birney, James G., *The Letters of James Gillespie Birney, 1831–1857*, ed. by D. L. Dumond (Ann Arbor, 1928), 2 vols.

Bruce, W. C., *John Randolph of Roanoke, 1773–1833* (New York, 1922), 2 vols.

Calhoun, J. C. *The Papers of John C. Calhoun*, ed. by R. L. Meriwether and W. E. Hemphill (Columbia, S.C., 1959), 4 vols to date–through 1823.

———, "Correspondence of John C. Calhoun," ed. by J. F. Jameson, *American Historical Association Report, 1899* (Washington, 1900), II.

Capers, G. M., Jr., *John C. Calhoun, Opportunist: A Reappraisal* (Gainesville, 1960).

Carson, J. P., *Life, Letters and Speeches of James Louis Petigru* (Washington, 1920).

Castaneda, C. E., *The Mexican Side of the Texas Revolution* (Dallas, 1928).

Cate, W. A., *Lucius Q. C. Lamar, Statesman of Secession and Reunion* (Chapel Hill, 1938).

Channing, Steven, *Crisis of Fear: Secession in South Carolina* (New York, 1972).

Clay, Henry, *The Papers of Henry Clay*, ed. by J. F. Hopkins and M. W. M. Hargreaves (Lexington, Ky., 1972), 5 vols. to date, through 1826.

Coles, H. L., *The War of 1812* (Chicago, 1965).

Coulter, E. M., *William G. Brownlow, Fighting Parson of the Southern Highlands* (Chapel Hill, 1937).

Cox, I. J., *The West Florida Controversy, 1798–1813* (Baltimore, 1918).

Craven, Avery, *An Historian and the Civil War* (Baton Rouge, 1971).

———, *Civil War in the Making, 1815–1860* (Baton Rouge, 1959).

———, *The Coming of the Civil War* (Chicago, 1957).

———, *Edmund Ruffin, Southerner: A Study in Secession* (New York, 1932).

———, *The Repressible Conflict, 1830–1861* (University, La., 1939).

———, *The Growth of Southern Nationalism, 1848–1861* (Baton Rouge, 1953).

Cresson, W. P., *James Monroe* (Chapel Hill, 1946).

Current, R. N., *Lincoln and the First Shot* (New York, 1963).

———, *John C. Calhoun* (New York, 1963).

Davis, Jefferson, *Jefferson Davis, Constitutionalist: His Letters, Papers and Speeches*, ed. by Dunbar Rowland (Jackson, Miss., 1923), 10 vols.

———, *Private Letters, 1883–1889*, ed. by Hudson Strode (New York, 1966).

Davis, Varina Howell (Mrs.), *Jefferson Davis, Ex-President of the Confederate States of America, A Memoir by His Wife* (New York, 1890), 2 vols.

Davis, W. C., *Breckinridge: Statesman, Soldier, Symbol* (Baton Rouge, 1974).

Denman, C. P., *The Secession Movement in Alabama* (Montgomery, 1933).

Dickey, D. C., *Sergeant S. Prentiss, Whig Orator of the Old South* (Baton Rouge, 1945).

Doherty, H. J., *Richard Keith Call, Southern Unionist* (Gainesville, Fla., 1961).

Dodd, Dorothy (ed.), *Florida Becomes a State* (Tallahassee, Fla., 1945).

Dodd, W. E., *Jefferson Davis, Statesman of the Old South* (Philadelphia 1907).

———, *Life of Nathaniel Macon* (Raleigh, 1908).

———, *Statesmen of the Old South* (New York, 1911).

DuBose, J. W., *The Life and Times of William Lowndes Yancey* (Birmingham, 1892), 2 vols.

Dumond, D. L., *The Secession Movement, 1860–61* (New York, 1931).

———, *Southern Editorials on Secession* (New York, 1931).

Dyer, Brainerd, *Zachary Taylor* (New York, 1946).

Eaton, Clement, *Freedom of Thought in the Old South* (Durham, 1940).

———, *The Freedom-of-Thought Struggle in the Old South* (New York, 1964).

———, *The Growth of Southern Civilization, 1790–1860* (New York, 1961).

———, *Henry Clay and the Art of American Politics* (Boston, 1956).

———, *A History of the Southern Confederacy* (New York, 1954), chapters on secession and the Fort Sumter crisis, I and II.

———, *A History of the Southern Confederacy* (New York, 1954).

———, *The Leaven of Democracy: The Growth of the Democratic Spirit in the Time of Jackson* (New York, 1963).

———, *The Mind of the Old South* (Baton Rouge, 1964. Enlarged ed., 1967).

——— (ed.), with Betsy Fleet, *Green Mount: A Virginia Plantation Family During the Civil War* (Lexington, 1962).

———, *The Waning of the Old South Civilization* (New York, 1969).

Ettinger, A. A., *Mission to Spain of Pierre Soulé* (New York, 1932).

Fielder, H., *Sketch of the Life and Times of Joseph E. Brown* (Springfield, 1883).

Flippin, P. S., *Herschel V. Johnson of Georgia* (Richmond, 1931).

Foreman, Grant, *Indian Removal: Emigration of the Five Civilized Tribes* (Norman, Okla., 1932).

Freehling, W. W., *Prelude to Civil War: The Nullification Controversy in South Carolina, 1816–1836* (New York, 1965).

Friend, Llerina, *Sam Houston, the Great Designer* (Austin, 1954).

Fuller, J. D. P., *The Movement for the Acquisition of All Mexico, 1846–1848* (Baltimore, 1936).

Gambrell, H. P., *Amson Jones: The Last President of Texas* (Garden City, N.Y., 1948).

Graham, W. A., *The Papers of William Alexander Graham*, ed. by J. G. D. Hamilton (Raleigh, 1961), 4 vols.

Green, E. L., *George McDuffie* (Columbia, S.C., 1936).

Green, F. M., *Constitutional Development in the South Atlantic States 1776–1860* (Chapel Hill, 1930).

———, *The Role of the Yankee in the Old South* (Athens, Ga., 1972).

Gunderson, R. G., *The Log-Cabin Campaign* (Lexington, Ky., 1957).

———, *Old Gentleman's Convention: the Washington Peace Conference of 1861* (Madison, Wis., 1961).

Hall, C. H., *Abel Parker Upshur, Conservative Virginian, 1790–1844* (Madison, Wis., 1963).

Hamilton, Holman, *Zachary Taylor . . .* (Indianapolis, 1941, 1951), 2 vols.

———, *Prologue to Conflict: The Crisis and the Compromise of 1850* (Lexington, Ky., 1964).

Hampton, Wade, *Family Letters of the Three Wade Hamptons, 1782–1901*, ed. by C. E. Cauthen (Columbia, S.C., 1953).

Harrison, Lowell, *John Breckinridge, Jeffersonian Democrat* (Louisville, 1969).

Hatcher, W. B., *Edward Livingston—Jeffersonian Republican and Jacksonian Democrat* (University, La., 1940).

Hay, T. R. and Werner, M. R., *The Admirable Trumpeter: A Biography of General James Wilkinson* (New York, 1941).

Heath, M. S., *The Role of the State in Constructive Liberalism: Economic Developments in Georgia to 1860* (Cambridge, Mass., 1954).

Henry, R. S., *The Story of the Mexican War* (Indianapolis, 1950).

Hesseltine, W. B. (ed.), *Dr. J. G. M. Ramsey: Autobiography and Letters* (Nashville, 1954).

Hill, J. D., *The Texas Navy* (Chicago, 1937).

Hogan, W. R., *The Texas Republic, a Social and Economic History* (Norman, Okla., 1946).

Hunter, R. M. T., *Correspondence of R. M. T. Hunter, 1826–1876,* ed. by C. H. Ambler (Washington, 1918).

Ireland, R. M. *The County Courts in Antebellum Kentucky* (Lexington, Ky., 1972).

James, Marquis, *Andrew Jackson . . .* (Indianapolis, 1933, 1937), 2 vols.

———, *The Raven: A Biography of Sam Houston* (Indianapolis, 1929).

Jefferson, Thomas, *The Papers of Thomas Jefferson,* ed. by J. P. Boyd (Princeton, 1950—), 19 vols. to date, extending to 1791.

Jervey, T. D., *Robert Y. Hayne and His Times* (New York, 1909).

Johannsen, R. W., *Stephen A. Douglas* (New York, 1973).

Johnson, Andrew, *The Papers of Andrew Johnson, 1822–1856,* ed. by L. P. Graf and R. W. Haskins (Knoxville, 1967—) 2 vols. to date.

Johnson, R. M. and Browne, W. H., *Life of Alexander H. Stephens* (Philadelphia, 1878).

Kibler, L. A., *Benjamin F. Perry, South Carolina Unionist* (Durham, 1946).

King, Alvy L., *Louis T. Wigfall: Southern Fire-eater* (Baton Rouge, 1970).

Kirk, Russell, *John Randolph of Roanoke* (Chicago, 1964).

Kirwan, A. D., *John J. Crittenden: The Struggle for the Union* (Lexington, 1962).

Klein, Philip, *President James Buchanan, a Biography* (New York, 1962).

Lathrop, Barnes, *Migration into East Texas, 1835–1860* (Austin, 1949).

Lemmon, Sarah M., *Frustrated Patriots: North Carolina and the War of 1812* (Chapel Hill, 1974).

Levy, L. W., *Jefferson and Civil Liberties: The Darker Side* (Cambridge, Mass., 1963).

McCaleb, W. F., *The Aaron Burr Conspiracy* (New York, 1903).

Malone, Dumas, *Jefferson and His Time* (New York, 1948–1974), 5 vols. to date.

Malone, H. T., *Cherokees of the Old South* (Norman, Okla., 1956).

Mangum, Willie P., *The Papers of Willie P. Mangum,* ed. by H. T. Shanks (Raleigh, 1950–55), 4 vols.

Mayo, Bernard, *Henry Clay, Spokesman of the New West* (Boston, 1937).

Meade, R. D., *Judah P. Benjamin, Confederate Statesman* (New York, 1943).

Merk, Frederick, *Slavery and the Annexation of Texas* (New York, 1972).

———, *Manifest Destiny and Mission in American History* (New York, 1963).

Merritt, Elizabeth, *James Henry Hammond* (1807–1864) (Baltimore, 1973).

Meyer, L. W., *The Life and Times of Colonel Richard M. Johnson of Kentucky* (New York, 1932).

Mitchell, Broadus, *Frederick Law Olmsted, A Critic of the Old South* (Baltimore, 1924).

Mooney, C. C., *William H. Crawford, 1772–1834* (Lexington, Ky., 1974).

Murphy, J. B., *L. Q. C. Lamar, Pragmatic Patriot* (Baton Rouge, 1973).

Murray, Paul, *The Whig Party in Georgia, 1825–1853* (Chapel Hill, 1948).

Myers, Marvin, *The Jacksonian Persuasion* (Chicago, 1957).

Nevins, Allan, *Ordeal of the Union* (New York, 1947), 2 vols.

————, *The Emergence of Lincoln* (New York, 1950), 2 vols.

Newsome, A. R., *The Presidential Election of 1824 in North Carolina* (Chapel Hill, 1939).

Nichols, R. F., *The Disruption of American Democracy* (New York, 1948).

Nuermberger, R. K., *The Clays of Alabama* . . . (Lexington, Ky., 1958).

Osterweis, R. G., *Romanticism and Nationalism in the Old South* (New Haven, 1949).

Overdyke, W. D., *The Know-Nothing Party in the South* (Baton Rouge, 1950).

Parks, J. H., *John Bell of Tennessee* (Baton Rouge, 1950).

————, *Felix Grundy, Champion of Democracy* (University, La., 1940).

Perkins, B., *The Causes of the War of 1812: National Honor or National Interest?* (New York, 1962).

Philbrick, F. S., *The Rise of the West 1754–1830* (New York, 1965).

Phillips, U. B., *The Course of the South to Secession: An Interpretation by Ulrich Bonnell Phillips,* ed. by E. M. Coulter (New York, 1939).

————, *Georgia and State Rights* (Washington, D.C., 1902).

————, *The Life of Robert Toombs* (New York, 1913).

———— (ed.), "Correspondence of Robert Toombs, Alexander H. Stephens, and Howell Cobb," *American Historical Association Annual Report,* 1901, vol. II (Washington, 1912).

Pletcher, D. M., *The Politics of Annexation: Texas, Oregon, and the Mexican War* (Columbia, Mo., 1973).

Poage, G. R., *Henry Clay and the Whig Party* (Chapel Hill, 1936).

Polk, James K., *Diary of James K. Polk During His Presidency, 1845–1849,* ed. by M. M. Quaife (Chicago, 1910), 4 vols.

————, *Correspondence of James K. Polk,* ed. by H. Weaver and P. H. Bergeson (1969—), 2 vols. to 1834.

Potter, D. M., *Lincoln and His Party in the Secession Crisis* (New Haven, 1942).

————, *The South and the Concurrent Majority* (Baton Rouge, 1972).

————, *The South and the Sectional Conflict* (Baton Rouge, 1969).

Rainwater, P. L., *Mississippi, Storm Center of Secession, 1856–1861* (Baton Rouge, 1938).

Ranck, J. B., *Albert Gallatin Brown, Radical Southern Nationalist* (New York, 1937).

Remini, R. V., *The Election of Andrew Jackson* (Philadelphia, 1963).

Rice, Otis, *The Allegheny Frontier: West Virginia Beginnings, 1730–1830* (Lexington, Ky., 1970).

Richardson, R. N., *Texas, the Lone Star State* (New York, 1943).

Rippy, I. F., *Joel R. Poinsett* (Durham, 1935).

Risjord, N. K., *The Old Republicans: Southern Conservatism in the Age of Jefferson* (New York, 1965).

Roemer, Ferdinand, *Texas, with Particular Reference to German Immigrations* (San Antonio, 1935).

Roland, Charles, *Albert Sidney Johnston: Soldier of Three Republics* (Austin, 1946).

Ruffin, Edmund, *The Diary of Edmund Ruffin,* ed. by W. K. Scarborough (Baton Rouge, 1972), vol. I, 1856–1861.

Schauinger, I. H., *William Gaston, Carolinian* (Milwaukee, 1949).

Schlesinger, A. M., Jr., *The Age of Jackson* (Boston, 1945).

Schultz, Harold, *Nationalism and Sectionalism in South Carolina, 1852–1860* (Durham, 1950).

Seager, Robert III, *And Tyler Too: A Biography of John Tyler and Julia Gardner Tyler* (New York, 1963).

Sears, L. M., *John Slidell* (Durham, 1925).

Sellers, C. C., Jr., *James K. Polk* . . . (Princeton, 1957, 1966), 2 vols.

Shanks, H. T., *The Secession Movement in Virginia, 1847–1861* (Richmond, 1934).

Shenton, J. P., *Robert John Walker, a Politician from Jackson to Lincoln* (New York, 1961).

Simms, H. H., *Life of John Taylor* (Richmond, 1932).

———, *Life of Robert M. T. Hunter* . . . (Richmond, 1935).

Singletary, O. A., *The Mexican War* (Chicago, 1960).

Sitterson, J. C., *The Secession Movement in North Carolina* (Chapel Hill, 1939).

Smith, J. H., *The War With Mexico* (New York, 1919), 2 vols.

Smith, W. E., *The Francis Preston Blair Family in Politics* (New York, 1933), 2 vols.

Stampp, K. M., *And the War Came* (Baton Rouge, 1950).

Starkey, M. L., *The Cherokee Nation* (New York, 1946).

Stephenson, W. H., *Alexander Porter, Whig Planter of Old Louisiana* (Baton Rouge, 1934).

Strode, Hudson, *Jefferson Davis, American Patriot, 1808–1861* (New York, 1955), vol. I.

Swearingen, Mark, *The Early Life of George Poindexter: A Story of the First Southwest* (New Orleans, 1934).

Swisher, C. B., *Roger B. Taney* (New York, 1935).

Sydnor, C. S., *The Development of Southern Sectionalism, 1819–1848* (Baton Rouge, 1948).

Thomas, B. P., *Abraham Lincoln, A Biography* (New York, 1952).

Thompson, W. Y., *Robert Toombs of Georgia* (Baton Rouge, 1966).

Turner, F. J., *The United States, 1830–1850: The Nations and Its Sections* (New York, 1935).

Tyler, L. G. (ed.), *Letters and Times of the Tylers* (Richmond, 1884–86), 3 vols.

Van Deusen, G. G., *Life of Henry Clay* (Boston, 1937).

———, *The Jacksonian Era, 1828–1845* (New York, 1959).

Von Abele, R., *Alexander H. Stephens: A Biography* (New York, 1946).

Ward, J. W., *Andrew Jackson, Symbol for an Age* (New York, 1962).

White, Laura, *Robert Barnwell Rhett: Father of Secession* (New York, 1931).

White, Leonard, *The Jacksonians: A Study in Administrative History, 1829–1861* (New York, 1954).

Williamson, Chilton, *American Suffrage from Property to Democracy, 1760–1860* (Princeton, 1960).

Wiltse, C. M., *John C. Calhoun* . . . (Indianapolis, 1944—), 3 vols.

Wise, B. H., *Henry A. Wise of Virginia, 1806–1876* (New York, 1899).

Wise, J. S., *The End of an Era* (Boston, 1902).

Wisehart, *Sam Houston, American Giant* (Washington, D.C., 1962).

Wooster, R. A., *The Secession Conventions of the South* (Princeton, 1962).

———, *The People in Power: Courthouse and Statehouse in the Lower South* (Knoxville, 1969).

Zuber, R. L., *Johnathan Worth: A Biography of a Southern Unionist* (Chapel Hill, 1965).

Industry and Commerce

Albion, R. G., *The Rise of the Port of New York, 1815–1860* (New York, 1939).
Atherton, L. E., *The Pioneer Merchant in Mid-America* (Columbia, 1943).
———, *The Southern Country Store* (New York, 1949).
Black, R. C. III, *The Railroads of the Confederacy* (Chapel Hill, 1932).
Bruce, Kathleen, *Virginia Iron Manufacture in the Slave Era* (New York, 1932).
Bruchey, Stuart, *Cotton and the Growth of the American Economy* (New York, 1967) and *Robert Oliver: Merchant of Baltimore, 1783–1819* (Baltimore, 1956).
Childs, A. R. (ed.), *Planters and Businessmen: the Guignard Family of South Carolina, 1795–1930* (Columbia, 1951).
Childs, W. T., *John McDonogh, His Life and Work* (Baltimore, 1939).
Clark, T. D., *A Pioneer Southern Railroad from New Orleans to Cairo* (Chapel Hill, 1936).
———, *The Beginnings of the L and N . . .* (Louisville, Ky., 1933).
———, *Pills, Petticoats, and Plows: The Southern Country Store* (Indianapolis, 1944).
Coulter, E. M., *Auraria: The Story of a Georgia Gold-Mining Town* (Athens, Ga., 1956).
Crittenden, C. C., *The Commerce of North Carolina, 1763–1789* (New Haven, 1936).
Crowgey, H. G., *Kentucky Bourbon: The Early Years of Whiskey-Making* (Lexington, Ky., 1971).
DeBow, J. D. B., *The Industrial Resources, etc. of the Southern and Western States* (New Orleans, 1853), 3 vols.
Dew, C. B., *Ironmaker to the Confederacy: Joseph R. Anderson and the Tredegar Iron Works* (New Haven, 1966).
Dunaway, F., *History of the James River and Kanawha Company* (New York, 1922).
Folmsbee, S. J., *Sectionalism and Internal Improvements in Tennessee, 1796–1845* (Knoxville, 1939).
Hammond, Bray, *Banks and Politics in America from the Revolution to the Civil War* (Princeton, 1957).
Harper, L. A., *The Navigation Laws* (New York, 1939).
Hopkins, James F., *A History of the Hemp Industry in Kentucky* (Lexington, Ky., 1951).
Hunter, L. C., *Steamboats on the Western Waters* (Cambridge, Mass., 1949).
Hutchinson, W. T., *Cyrus Hall McCormick* (New York, 1930–35), 2 vols.
Jordan, W. T., *Rebels in the Making, Planters' Conventions and Southern Propaganda* (Tuscaloosa, 1958).
Kettell, T. P., *Southern Wealth and Northern Profits* (New York, 1860).
Laurens, Henry, *The Papers of Henry Laurens,* ed. by P. M. Hamer and G. C. Rogers, Jr. (Columbia, S.C., 1972), 2 vols. to 1763.

Lesesne, J. J., *The Bank of the State of South Carolina: A General and Political History* (Columbia, S.C., 1970).

Mason, F. N. (ed.), *John Norton and Sons, Merchants of London and Virginia* (Richmond, 1937).

Mitchell, Broadus, *William Gregg, Factory Master of the Old South* (Chapel Hill, 1928).

Moore, J. H., *Andrew Brown and Cypress Lumbering in the Old Southwest* (Baton Rouge, 1967).

Nettles, C. P., *The Money Supply of the Colonies before 1720* (Madison, Wis., 1934).

Phillips, U. B., *A History of Transportation in the Eastern Cotton Belt to 1860* (New York, 1908).

Robert, J. C., *The Story of Tobacco in America* (New York, 1949).

Russell, R. R., *Economic Aspects of Southern Sectionalism, 1840–1861* (Urbana, 1924).

Sanderlin, W. S., *The Great National Project* [*Chesapeake and Ohio Canal*] (Baltimore, 1946).

Sellers, Leila, *Charleston Business on the Eve of the American Revolution* (Chapel Hill, 1934).

Sinclair, Harold, *The Port of New Orleans* (Garden City, N.Y., 1942).

Skipper, O. T., *J. D. B. DeBow, Magazinist of the Old South* (Athens, Ga., 1958).

Summersell, C. D., *Mobile, History of a Seaport Town* (University, Ala., 1949).

Weaver, C. C., *Internal Improvements in North Carolina Previous to 1860* (Baltimore, 1903).

Wendes, Herbert, *Southern Commercial Conventions, 1837–1859* (Baltimore, 1930.

Wertenbaker, T. J., *Norfolk, Historic Southern Port* (Durham, 1937).

Woodman, H. D., *King Cotton and His Retainers: Financing and Marketing the Cotton Crop of the South, 1800–1925* (Lexington, Ky., 1968).

Literature, Theater, and Science

In Hubbell, J. B., *The South in American Literature, 1607–1900* (Durham, 1954) and Parrington, Vernon L., *Main Currents in American Thought* (New York, 1927), 3 vols., and Brooks, V. W., *The World of Washington Irving* (New York, 1944) are presented good surveys of Southern literature of the antebellum period.

Allen, J. D., *Philip Pendleton Cooke* (Chapel Hill, 1942).

Braden, W. W., *Oratory in the Old South, 1808–1860* (Baton Rouge, 1970).

Davis, C. C., *Chronicler of the Cavaliers: A Life of William A. Caruthers* (Richmond, 1953).

Dormon, J. H., Jr., *Theater in the Ante-Bellum South, 1815–1861* (Chapel Hill, 1967).

Duffy, John (ed.), *The Rudolph Matas History of Medicine in Louisiana* (Baton Rouge, 1958), 2 vols.

Dupré, Huntley, *Rafinesque in Lexington, 1819–1826* (Lexington, Ky., 1945).

Eaton, Clement, *The Mind of the Old South*, enlarged ed. (Baton Rouge, 1967), chapter on William Gilmore Simms.

Hoole, W. S., *The Ante-Bellum Charleston Theater* (Tuscaloosa, 1946).

——, *Alias Simon Suggs: The Life and Times of Johnson Jones Hooper* (University, Ala., 1952).

Johnson, T. C., *Scientific Interests in the Old South* (New York, 1936).

LeConte, Joseph, *The Autobiography of Joseph Le Conte,* ed. by W. D. Armes (New York, 1903).

Meine, F. J. (ed.), *Tall Tales of the Southwest: An Anthology of Southern and Southwestern Humor, 1830–1860* (New York, 1937).

Minor, B. B., *The Southern Literary Messenger, 1834–1864* (New York, 1905).

Mott, F. L. A., *A History of American Magazines* (Cambridge, Mass., 1930), 2 vols.

Quinn, A. H., *Edgar Allan Poe, A Critical Biography* (New York, 1942).

Rankin, H. F., *The Theater in Colonial America* (Chapel Hill, 1965).

Ravenel, H. W., *The Private Journal of Henry William Ravenel, 1859–1887,* ed. by A. R. Childs (Columbia, S.C., 1947).

Rhea, Linda, *Hugh Swinton Legaré: A Charleston Intellectual* (Chapel Hill, 1934).

Ridgely, J. V., *John Pendleton Kennedy* (New York, 1966).

Rogers, W. B., *Life and Letters of William Barton Rogers,* ed. by Emma S. Rogers (Boston, 1896), 2 vols.

Simms, William Gilmore, *The Letters of William Gilmore Simms,* ed. by M. C. S. Oliphant et al. (Columbia, S.C., 1953–54), 5 vols.

Smith, Sol, *Theatrical Management in the South and West for Thirty Years* (New York, 1868).

Starke, Aubrey, *Sidney Lanier* (Chapel Hill, 1933).

Trent, W. P., *William Gilmore Simms* (Boston, 1892).

Wade, J. D., *August Baldwin Longstreet . . .* (New York, 1924).

Watts, C. H., *Thomas Holley Chivers: His Literary Career and His Poetry* (Athens, Ga., 1956).

Williams, F. L., *Matthew Fontaine Maury, Scientist of the Sea* (New Brunswick, N.J., 1963).

Religion

For studies of religion in the South, see:

Asbury, Francis, *The Journal and Letters of Francis Asbury,* ed. by E. T. Clark (Nashville, 1958).

Billington, R. A., *The Protestant Crusade, 1800–1860: A Study of the Origins of Nativism* (New York, 1938).

Boles, J. B., *The Great Revival, 1787–1805: The Origins of the Southern Evangelical Mind* (Lexington, Ky., 1972).

Brydon, G. M., *Virginia's Mother Church . . .* (Philadelphia, 1952).

Duffy, John (ed.), *Parson Clapp of the Stranger's Church* (Baton Rouge, 1957).

Eaton, Clement, *The Freedom-of-Thought Struggle in the Old South* (New York, 1964).

——, *The Mind of the Old South* (Baton Rouge, 1967), chapter on Leonidas Polk.

Gewehr, W. M., *The Great Awakening in Virginia, 1740–1790* (Durham, 1930).

Gohdes, Clarence, "Some Notes on the Unitarian Church in the Ante-Bellum South," in D. K. Jackson (ed.), *American Studies in Honor of William Kenneth Boyd* (Durham, 1940).

Guilday, Peter, *The Life and Times of John England, First Bishop of Charleston, 1786–1842* (New York, 1927), 2 vols.

Johnson, C. A., *The Frontier Camp Meeting* (Dallas, 1955).

Johnson, T. C., *The Life and Times of Robert L. Dabney* (Richmond, 1903).

———, *The Life and Letters of Benjamin M. Palmer* (Richmond, 1906).

Morais, R. B., *Deism in Eighteenth Century America* (New York, 1946).

Polk, W. M., *Leonidas Polk, Bishop and General* (New York, 1893), 2 vols.

Posey, Walter, *The Development of Methodism in the Old Southwest, 1783–1824* (Tuscaloosa, 1933).

———, *The Baptist Church in the Lower Mississippi Valley, 1776–1845* (Lexington, Ky., 1957).

———, *The Presbyterian Church in the Old Southwest, 1778–1838* (Richmond, 1952).

Shea, J. G., *History of the Catholic Church in the United States* (New York, 1886–1892), 4 vols.

Sonne, N. H., *Liberal Kentucky, 1780–1829* (Lexington, Ky., 1939).

Sweet, W. W., *Revivalism in America* (New York, 1944).

Thompson, E. T., *Presbyterians in the South, 1617–1860* (Richmond, 1967).

Slavery

Within recent years an astonishing number of books and articles have been published on slavery and the blacks in the United States, stimulated by the Civil Rights struggle and the rise of the blacks to a new status. The three most comprehensive studies of Southern slavery are:

U. B. Phillips, *American Negro Slavery,* ed. by Eugene Genovese (Baton Rouge, 1968), a genial view of the institution.

Kenneth Stampp, *The Peculiar Institution: Slavery in the Ante-Bellum South* (New York, 1956), a harsh view of the institution.

R. W. Fogel and S. M. Engerman, *Time on the Cross: The Economics of American Negro Slavery* (Boston, 1974), 2 vols. have advanced revolutionary conclusions.

John Hope Franklin, a prominent black historian, has presented a balanced account in his updated volume, *From Slavery to Freedom: History of American Negroes* (New York, 1972).

John W. Blassingame, a younger black historian, has explored the psychology of slaves from black sources in *The Slave Community: Plantation Life in the Antebellum South* (New York, 1972), as has Eugene Genovese in a manuscript to be published entitled, "Roll, Jordan, Roll! Afro-American Slaves in the Making of the Modern World."

David B. Davis, *The Problem of Slavery in Western Culture* (New York, 1966) and Stanley Elkins, *Slavery: A Problem in American Institutional Intellectual Life* (Chicago, 1959) have presented slavery in a new light.

The statistics of slave population are conveniently to be found in D. B. and W. S. Dodd, *Historical Statistics of the South, 1790–1970* (University, Ala., 1973).

Other modern studies of various aspects of Southern slavery are:

Curtin, Philip D., *The Atlantic Slave Trade: A Census* (Madison, Wis., 1969).

Degler, Carl, *Neither Black Nor White: Slavery and Race Relations in Brazil and the United States* (New York, 1971).

Frederickson, G. M., *The Black Image in the White Mind* (New York, 1971).

Klein, H. E., *Slavery in the Americas: A Comparative Study of Virginia and Cuba* (Chicago, 1967).

Litwak, Leon, *North of Slavery: The Negro in the Free States, 1790–1860* (Chicago, 1961).

Starobin, R. S., *Industrial Slavery in the Old South,* (New York, 1970).

Wade, R. C., *Slavery in the Cities: The South, 1820–1860* (New York, 1970).

Woodward, C. V., *American Counterpoint: Slavery and Racism in the North-South Dialogue* (Boston, 1971).

The older historians discussed Southern slavery largely in state studies, Mississippi by C. S. Sydnor, Alabama by J. B. Sellers, Georgia by R. B. Flanders, Louisiana by J. G. Taylor (1963), Arkansas by O. W. Taylor, North Carolina by J. S. Bassett and R. H. Taylor, Kentucky by J. W. Coleman, Jr., Missouri by H. A. Trexler, Tennessee by C. C. Mooney and Texas by Abigail Curlee; and in general they were pro-Southern in their interpretations. The latest study is J. F. Smith, *Slavery and Plantation Growth in Antebellum Florida, 1821–1860* (Gainesville, Fla., 1973). Recently historians have begun to examine slavery from the Negro's point of view and for this purpose there is a vast amount of source material, scarcely untouched, in the Slave Narratives collected by the W.P.A., 1936–1938. A selection of these interviews has been published by:

Botkin, B. A. (ed.), *Lay My Burden Down: A Folk History of Slavery* (Chicago, 1945).

Rawick, G. P. (ed.), *The American Slave: A Composite Autobiography* (Westport, Conn., 1972), who is publishing the collection in 19 vols.

Yetman, N. R. (ed.), *Life Under the "Peculiar Institution": Selections from the Slave Narrative Collection* (New York, 1970).

There are also many narratives published by fugitive slaves, of unequal value, and too numerous to list, the most important being Frederick Douglass, *Narrative of the Life . . . of an American Slave* (Boston, 1845). John Blassingame of Yale University is editing the Douglass Papers. See also Louis Harlan, *Booker T. Washington: The Making of a Black Leader, 1856–1901* (New York, 1972). The most solid evidence of slavery is contained in the documents and laws:

Donnan, Elizabeth (ed.), *Documents Illustrative of the Slave Trade to American* (Washington, 1930–35), 4 vols.

Catterall, Helen T. (ed.), *Judicial Cases Concerning American Slavery and the Negro* (Washington, D.C., 1926–36), 4 vols.

Hurd, J. C., *The Law of Freedom and Bondage in the United States* (Boston, 1858–1862), 2 vols.

Mangum, C. S., *The Legal Status of the Negro* (Chapel Hill, 1940).
Phillips, U. B. and J. D. Glunt (eds.), *Florida Plantation Records* (St. Louis, 1927).

Southern slavery had many facets, such as:

The health of slaves:
Postell, W. D., *The Health of Slaves on Southern Plantations* (Baton Rouge, 1951).

Slave revolts:
Carroll, J. C., *Slave Insurrections in the United States, 1800–1865* (Boston, 1938).
Drewry, W. S., *The Southampton Insurrection* (Washington, D.C., 1900).
Starobin, R. S., *Denmark Vesey: The Slave Conspiracy of 1822* (Englewood Cliffs, N.J., 1970).

The slave trade:
Bancroft, Frederic, *Slave-Trading in the Old South* (Baltimore, 1931), prejudiced and inaccurate—see Foley and Engerman, *Time on the Cross.*
DuBois, W. E. B., *The Suppression of the African Slave Trade to the United States of America, 1638–1870* (New York, 1896).
Mannix, D. P., *Black Cargoes, a History of the Atlantic Slave Trade, 1518–1865* (New York, 1962).
Stephenson, W. H., *Isaac Franklin, Slave Trader and Planter of the Old South* (Baton Rouge, 1938).

Slave smuggling:
Howard, W. S., *American Slavers and the Federal Law* (Berkeley, 1963).

The profitability of slavery:
See Foley and Engerman, *Time on the Cross.*
Genovese, Eugene, *The Political Economy of Slavery* . . . (New York, 1965).

Race relations:
Craven, W. F., *White, Red, Black: the Seventeenth Century Virginian* (Charlottesville, 1971).
Jordan, W. D., *White Over Black: American Attitudes toward the Negro, 1550–1812* (Chapel Hill, 1968).
Johnston, J. H., *Race Relations in Virginia and Miscegenation in the South, 1776–1860* (Boston, 1970).

The escape of slaves:
Buckmaster, H., *Let My People Go: The Story of the Underground Railroad and the Growth of the Abolition Movement* (New York, 1941).
Campbell, S. W., *The Slave Catchers: Enforcement of the Fugitive Slave Law, 1850–1860* (Chapel Hill, 1970).
Gara, Larry, *The Liberty Line: The Legend of the Underground Railroad* (Lexington, Ky., 1961).

Slave life:
Crum, M., *Gullah, Negro Life in the Carolina Sea Islands* (Durham, 1940).
Turner, Lorenzo, *Africanisms in the Gullah Dialect* (New York, 1947).

Especially notable are slaves who overcame the handicaps of slavery and developed their minds and personalities:

Blassingame, J. H., *Black New Orleans, 1860–1880* (Chicago, 1973).

Desdunes, R. L. (a Creole black), *Our People and Our History* (Baton Rouge, 1973).

Eaton, Clement, *The Mind of the Old South* (enlarged ed., 1967), chap. IX, The Mind of the Southern Negro: The Remarkable Individuals.

Franklin, J. H., *The Free Negro in North Carolina, 1790–1860* (Chapel Hill, 1943).

Hogan, W. D. and Edwin Davis (eds.), *William Johnson's Natchez: The Ante-Bellum Diary of a Free Negro* (Baton Rouge, 1951).

Jackson, L. P., *Free Negro Labor and Property-Holding in Virginia, 1830–1860* (New York, 1942).

Sterx, H. E., *The Free Negro in Ante-Bellum Louisiana* (Madison, Wis., 1972).

Woodson, C. G., *The Education of the Negro Prior to 1861* (Washington, 1919).

The Debate over Slavery—the Attack From Without

The best general study of the antislavery movement is:

Filler, Louis, *The Crusade against Slavery, 1830–1860* (New York, 1960).

Other valuable studies are:

Duberman, Martin (ed.), *The Antislavery Vanguard: New Essays on the Abolitionists* (Princeton, 1965).

McPherson, J. M., *The Struggle for Equality: Abolitionists and the Negro in the Civil War and Reconstruction* (Princeton, 1964).

Adams, A. D., *The Neglected Period of Anti-Slavery in America, 1808–1831* (Cambridge, Mass., 1908).

Barnes, G. H., *The Antislavery Impulse, 1830–1844* (New York, 1933).

Barnes, G. H. and D. L. Dumond (eds.), *Letters of Theodore Dwight Weld, Angelina Grimké, and Sarah Grimké, 1822–1848* (New York, 1934), 2 vols.

Curry, R. O. and J. D. Cowden (eds.), *Slavery in America, Theodore Weld's American Slavery As It Is* (Itasca, Ill., 1972).

Donald, David, *Charles Sumner and the Coming of the Civil War* (New York, 1970).

Dumond, D. L., *Antislavery: The Crusade for Freedom in America* (Ann Arbor, N.J., 1961).

Merrill, W. N., *Against Wind and Tide: A Biography of William Lloyd Garrison* (Cambridge, Mass., 1963).

Oates, S. B., *To Purge This Land of Blood, a Biography of John Brown* (New York, 1970).

Pease, W. H. and J. H. Pease (eds.), *The Antislavery Argument* (Indianapolis, 1965).

Ruchames, Louis, *The Abolitionists: a Collection of Their Writings* (New York, 1963.

Thomas, Benjamin P., *Theodore Weld, Crusader for Freedom* (New Brunswick, N.J., 1950).
Thomas, J. L., *The Liberator, William Lloyd Garrison, a Biography* (Boston, 1963).
Villard, O. G., *John Brown, 1800–1859* (Boston, 1910).
Wyatt-Brown, B., *Lewis Tappan and the Evangelical War Against Slavery* (Cleveland, 1969).

The Debate over Slavery—the Attack From Within

Bailey, Hugh, *Hinton Rowan Helper, Abolitionist-Racist* (University, Ala., 1965).
Blackford, L. M., *Mine Eyes Have Seen the Glory . . .* (Cambridge, Mass., 1954).
Crallé, R. (ed.), *Works of John C. Calhoun* (New York 1851–56), 6 vols.
Degler, Carl N., *The Other South: Southern Dissenters in the Nineteenth Century* (New York, 1974).
Dumond, D. L., *Letters of James Gillespie Birney, 1831–1857,* (New York, 1938), 2 vols.
Eaton, Clement, *The Freedom-of-Thought Struggle in the Old South* (New York, 1964).
Eaton, Clement, *The Mind of the Old South,* chaps. 1, 2, and 8.
Fladeland, Betty L., *James Gillespie Birney: Slaveholder to Abolitionist* (Ithaca, 1955).
Helper, Hinton Rowan, *The Impending Crisis of the South: How to Meet It* (New York, 1957).
Martin, Asa, *The Anti-Slavery Movement in Kentucky* (Louisville, Ky., 1918).
Matthews, D. G., *Slavery and Methodism: a Chapter in American Morality* (Princeton, 1965).
McColley, R., *Slavery and Jeffersonian Virginia* (Urbana, 1973).
Robert, J. C., *The Road from Monticello: A Study of the Virginia Slavery Debate of 1832* (Durham, 1941).
Smiley, D. L., *Lion of White Hall: The Life of Cassius M. Clay* (Madison, Wis., 1962).
Staudenraus, P. J., *The African Colonization Movement, 1815–1865* (New York, 1961).
Weeks, S. B., *Southern Quakers and Slavery* (Baltimore, 1896).

Slavery: The Defense

The first important defenses of slavery were:

Dew, Thomas R., *Review of the Debates in the Virginia Legislature of 1831 and 1832,* a pamphlet published in Richmond in 1832, which was followed in 1852 by *The Pro-Slavery Argument* published in Charleston.
John C. Calhoun, *The Works of John C. Calhoun,* ed. by Richard Crallé (New York, 1853–55), 6 vols.

Other defenses have been presented by:

Fitzhugh, George, *Cannibals All; or Slaves Without Masters,* ed. by C. V. Woodward (Cambridge, Mass., 1960), and *Sociology for the South* (New York, 1953).

Jenkins, W. S., *Pro-Slavery Thought in the Old South* (Chapel Hill, 1935).

McKitrick, E. L., *Slavery Defended: The Views of the Old South* (Englewood Cliffs, N.J., 1963).

Stanton, W. R., *The Leopard's Spots: Scientific Attitudes toward Race in America, 1815–1859* (Chicago, 1960).

Wish, Harvey, *George Fitzhugh, Propagandist of the Old South* (Baton Rouge, 1943).

The Southern Way of Life

The Southern way of life can be studied in a great variety of sources listed elsewhere in the bibliography under different categories such as "Agriculture," "Slavery," etc. The works dealing with Southern society as it differed from the general American pattern, in regard to social structure, regional characteristics and customs, the national groups that formed the Southern population, and the realities behind the glamorous legend of the plantation, are listed as follows:

Baldwin, J. G., *The Flush Times of Alabama and Mississippi* (New York, 1853).

Beatty, R. C., *William Byrd of Westover* (Boston, 1932).

Boorstin, Daniel, *The Americans: The Colonial Experience* (New York, 1958).

Bridenbaugh, Carl, *Myths and Realities: Societies of the Colonial South* (Baton Rouge, 1952).

Brodie, Fawn M., *Thomas Jefferson: An Intimate History* (New York, 1974).

Capers, G. M., Jr., *Biography of a River Town: Memphis, Its Heroic Age* (Chapel Hill, 1939).

Cash, W. J., *The Mind of the South* (New York, 1941).

Chesnut, Mary Boykin, *A Diary from Dixie,* ed. by B. A. Williams (New York, 1949).

Clay-Clopton, Virginia [Mrs. Clement C. Clay, Jr.], *A Belle of the Fifties* ed. by Ada Sterling (New York, 1905).

Coleman, J. W., Jr., *Famous Kentucky Duels* (Frankfort, Ky., 1953).

Cunz, Dieter, *The Maryland Germans, a History* (Princeton, 1948).

Davenport, F. G., *Ante-Bellum Kentucky: a Social History, 1800–1860* (Oxford, Ohio, 1943).

Davis, R. B., *Intellectual Life in Jefferson's Virginia, 1790–1830* (Chapel Hill, 1964).

Dick, Everett, *The Dixie Frontier: a Social History* (New York, 1948).

Dodd, W. E., *The Cotton Kingdom* (New Haven, 1919).

Eaton, Clement, *The Waning of the Old South Civilization* (Paperback ed., New York, 1969).

———, *The Civilization of the Old South: Writings of Clement Eaton,* ed. with an Introduction by Albert D. Kirwan (Lexington, Ky., 1968).

Felton, Rebecca L., *Country Life in Georgia in the Days of My Youth* (Atlanta, 1914).

Fitzhugh, William, *William Fitzhugh and His Chesapeake World: The Fitzhugh Letters and Other Documents,* ed. by R. B. Davis (Chapel Hill, 1963).

Franklin, J. H., *The Militant South, 1800–1860* (Cambridge, Mass., 1956).

Fleet, Betsy, and Eaton, Clement (eds.) *Green Mount: A Virginia Plantation Family during the Civil War* (Lexington, Ky., 1962).

Gaines, F. P., *The Southern Plantation: A Study in the Development and Accuracy of a Tradition* (New York, 1924).

Glen, James, *A Description of South Carolina* (London, 1761).

Hall, Margaret (Mrs. Basil), *The Aristocratic Journey . . . ,* ed. by Una Pope-Hennessy (New York, 1931).

Harrower, John, *The Journal of John Harrower, an Indentured Servant in the Colony of Virginia, 1773–1776,* ed. by E. W. Riley (New York, 1963).

Hirsch, A. H., *The Huguenots of Colonial South Carolina* (Durham, 1928).

Hogan, W. R., *The Texas Republic: A Social and Economic History* (Norman, Okla., 1946).

Hopley, C. C., *Life in the South; from the Commencement of the War By a Blockaded British Subject* (London 1863), 2 vols.

Hume, Ivor, *Here Lies Virginia: An Archeologist's View of Colonial Life and History* (New York, 1965).

Hundley, D. R., *Social Relations in Our Southern States* (New York, 1860).

Johnson, G. G., *Ante-Bellum North Carolina, A Social History* (Chapel Hill, 1937).

Jordan, W. T., *Ante-Bellum Alabama, Town and Country* (Tallahassee, 1957).

Kephart, Horace, *Our Southern Highlanders* (New York, 1913).

King, Grace E., *Creole Families of New Orleans* (New York, 1921).

Leyburn, J. C., *The Scotch-Irish, A Social History* (Chapel Hill, 1963).

Lonn, Ella, *Foreigners in the Confederacy* (Chapel Hill, 1940).

Longstreet, A. B., *Georgia Scenes* (Augusta, 1840).

McWhiney, Grady, *The Southerners and Other Americans* (New York, 1973).

Morgan, E. S., *Virginians at Home: Family Life in the Eighteenth Century* (Williamsburg, 1952).

Meyers, R. M. ed., *The Children of Pride: A True Story of Georgia and the Civil War* (New Haven, 1972). [The Charles Colcock Jones family letters].

Notestein, Wallace, *The English People on the Eve of Colonization, 1603–1630* (New York, 1954).

Owsley, F. L., *Plain Folk of the Old South* (Baton Rouge, 1948).

Phillips, U. B., *Life and Labor in the Old South* (Boston, 1929).

Pinckney, Eliza Lucas, *The Letterbook of Eliza Lucas Pinckney,* ed. by Eliza Pinckney (Chapel Hill, 1972).

Randolph, Sarah N., *The Domestic Life of Thomas Jefferson* (Cambridge, Mass., 1939).

Reniers, Percival, *The Springs of Virginia* (Chapel Hill, 1941).

Rogers, G. C., Jr., *Charleston in the Age of the Pinckneys* (Norman, Okla., 1968).

Schuricht, Hermann, *History of the German Element in Virginia* (Baltimore, 1900).

Scott, A. F., *The Southern Lady: From Pedestal to Politics, 1830–1930* (Chicago, 1970).

Sellers, C. G., *The Southerner as American* (Chapel Hill, 1960).

Shugg, R. W., *Origins of the Class Struggle in Louisiana: A Social History of White Farmers and Laborers during Slavery and After, 1840–1875* (University, La., 1939).

Smedes, Susan D., *Memorials of a Southern Planter,* ed. by F. M. Green (New York, 1965).

Smith, A. E., *Colonists in Bondage, White Servitude and Convict Labor in America, 1607–1776* (Chapel Hill, 1947).

Spruill, J. C., *Women's Life and Work in the Southern Colonies* (Chapel Hill, 1938).

Stone, Kate, *Brokenburn: the Journal of Kate Stone,* ed. by J. Q. Anderson (Baton Rouge, 1955).

Taylor, R. H., *Ante-Bellum South Carolina* (Chapel Hill, 1942).

Taylor, W. R., *Cavalier and Yankee: the Old South and the American National Character* (New York, 1961).

Toulmin, Harry, *The Western Country in 1793* (San Marino, Calif., 1948).

Wayland, J. W., *The German Element of the Shenandoah Valley* (Charlottesville, 1907).

Wiley, B. I., *The Plain People of the Confederacy* (Baton Rouge, 1943).

Williams, J. K., *Vogues in Villainy: Crime and Retribution in Ante-Bellum South Carolina* (Columbia, S.C., 1959).

Wilson, John Lyde, *The Code of Honor: Or Rules for the Government of Principals and Seconds in Duelling* (Charleston, 1858).

Wise, J. S., *The End of an Era* (Boston, 1902).

Wright, L. B., *The First Gentlemen of Virginia: Intellectual Qualities of the Early Colonial Ruling Class* (San Marino, Calif., 1940).

———— ed., *Prose Works of William Byrd; Narratives of a Colonial Virginian* (Cambridge, Mass., 1966).

Index

Slater, Samuel, 211
Slave traders, 236
Slaveholders, number, 390
Slavery, colonial, 10, 31–35; effects of American Revolution, 109–10; effect on Negro personality, 267; effects on whites, 383; guilt over, 5, 381–82; patrols, 261; profitability, 243–48, 394; social effects, 247–48; Southern, compared with Brazilian and Cuban, 261–62; testimony of ex-slaves, 249–50; urban and industrial, 240–42, 267
Slaves, African origins, 33; auctions, 221; Indian, 19, 35; efficiency of, 240, 245–47; emancipation, 110, 387–88; fugitive, 1, 3, 135, 203, 251, 257–58; health, 213, 255; hiring, 240–43; education of 239–40, 252, 257; legal code after 1830, 260–61; psychology of, 250, 253; treatment of, 113, 122–23, 251n, 250–55; separation of families, 87, 235–37; songs, 252, smuggling of, 234; insurrection of, 17, 40, 107; punishment of, 34, 59, 63–64, 239, 256–57; number in 1808 and 1860, 148; prices, 237; percentage on large plantations, 252–53; rewards and privileges, 241–42, 254; skilled, 240–42, 268–69; colonization of, 318, 388; household, 398; industrial, 240–42, 267, 431; instruction of, 388; light hours of labor, 399; mild punishment, 383, 392, 400; religious instruction, 398; religion, 459–60; see also Negroes, remarkable
Slidell, John, 361, 367, 488
Slocumb, Benjamin, 235
Smith, Gerrit, 373, 484
Smith, Captain John, 9, 13
Smith, Sol, 403
Smith, William A., 378
Smuggling, 91, 100
Social mobility, 288–89
Social stratification, colonial, 54–56; antebellum, 273
Society for the Propagation of the Gospel, 75
Soil exhaustion, erosion, and conservation, 21–22, 39, 44, 272, 285, 368; checked, 218
Soulé, Pierre, 465, 488
South, romantic stereotype of, 389, 446
South Carolina social structure in 1860, 493
Southern bloc, 466–67
Southern characteristics, 507–508; see also Planters
Southern Commercial Conventions, 434–35
Southern identity, 1–8; sense of superiority, 5
Southern Manifesto, 1860, 497
Southern Rights, 463, 471–72
Spaight, Richard Dobbs, 133
Spalding, Thomas, 46, 220
Spanish Conspiracy, 126, 127

Spanish rule in Louisiana, 176–78
Sparks, Jared, 455
Special Circular, 198, 309
Spoils system, 311
Spotswood, Alexander, 22–23, 38–39, 82, 427
Spratt, Leonidas, 238
Springs, Virginia, 392, 465
Squatters, 46; see also McCulloh
Stamp Act, 101, 103, 107–108
State rights, 144–45, 166, 321–22
Steamboats, 128, 231, 413, 416, 420–21
Steel, Ferdinand, Jr., 275
Stephens, Alexander H., 278–79, 323, 363, 470, 478, 498, 501–505, 410
Stone, Barton W., 459
Stone, Kate, 399
Stringfellow, Benjamin, 479
Stringfellow, Thornton, 378, 382
Sugar and Molasses Acts, 91, 100
Sugar cane, introduced 174, 222–27; cultivation of, 223–24; extent of cultivation, 224; profits, 227
Sumner, Charles, 480
Sumter, Thomas, 27, 107
Stiles, Charles W., 282
Strikes, white workers, 242, 425
Sub-Treasury Bill, 322
Suffrage Manhood, lack of, 112; see also Kentucky
Swiss settlers, 11, 41

Taliaferro, Harden E., 276
Tallmadge, James Jr., 199
Taney, Roger B., 27, 307–308, 482–83, 490
Tappan brothers, Lewis and Arthur, 373
Tariff, protective, Compromise Tariff bill of 1833, 194, 322, 336; of 1846, 361, 432, 501–502
Tarleton, Gen. Banastre, 108
Tatham, William, 57–58
Taxation of colonies, 8, 52, 64, 67, 92, 99, 103; of slaves, 50; antebellum, 328–29, 392
Taylor, John, 155, 195, 218
Taylor, Zachary, 363–66, 468, 470
Tecumseh, 188
Temperance Movement, 401, 460, 493
Test Oath in South Carolina, 337
Texas Revolution, 348–49; annexation, 354–60; bonds, 353, 355; Rangers, 353
Textbooks, censorship of, 439–40
Thayer, Eli, 478
Theater, colonial, 78; antebellum, 403
Theus, Jeremiah, 49
Thomas, Mrs. Gertrude, 402
Thomas, James Jr., 427
Thomas, Jesse B., 199
Thomas, Philemon, 202

Thompson, Jacob, 235
Thompson, Waddy, 382
Thompson, William Tappan, 276, 450
Thomson, William, 2–3
Thornwell, Rev. J. H., 378
Thorpe, Thomas Bangs, 276, 450
Ticknor, Francis O., 449
Timrod, Henry, 449
Tippecanoe, battle, 320
Tipton, John, 125
Tobacco, cultivation, 16–19, 21, 36, 56, 63; exports, 93, 94; transportation, 40; decline in Tidewater, 29, 142; antebellum period, 214–16
Tobacco factories, 426–28
Toombs, Robert, 323, 466, 478, 494, 501
Tories, 47, 106–107, 108; estates confiscated, 109
Toulmin, Harry, 62, 454
Tournaments, 3, 445–46
Touro, Judah, 416, 455
Trade Acts, 20; enforcement, 100; effect on colonies, 92–93
Trade, direct with Europe, 434; with North, 418–19
Transcontinental Railroad, 476–77
Transportation, 231, 420; see also Steamboats; Railroads
Transylvania University, 118–19
Travis, Lt. Col. W. B., 349
Treat, James, 353
Treaties, Ghent, 193; Jay, 142, 144; Jay-Gardoqui, 126; Paris (1763), 97; Paris (1783), 109; Pinckney, 126; Guadeloupe Hidalgo, 365
Tredegar Iron Works, 242, 428
Trist, Nicholas P., 365
Troup, George M., 188, 304, 312
Tryon, Gov. William, 50, 72
Tucker, Beverley, 465–66, 472
Tucker, St. George, 369
Turner, Frederick Jackson, 7, 114, 308
Turner, Joseph, 261
Turner, Nat, 258–60
Tutors and teachers, 29, 84–85, 116, 292, 394, 398, 403, 404, 432, 449, 507
Tyler, John, 138, 199, 320–23, 326, 355–60

Ulloa, Don Antonio de, 176
Uncle Tom's Cabin, 475
Underground Railroad, 257
Unionists, 51, 274–75, 496, 499, 500–504
Unions, trade, 329
Unitarianism, 455; decline of, 457
Universities and colleges, 393, 398, 433, 440–43; Bethany College, 459; College of Charleston, 441, 462; Jefferson, 129; North Carolina, 387, 441, 443; South Carolina, 2; Transylvania, 128, 221, 441–42; universities in lower South, 442–43; Virginia, 406–407, 441, 456;